Progress in IS

For further volumes:
http://www.springer.com/series/10440

Jan Devos · Hendrik van Landeghem
Dirk Deschoolmeester
Editors

Information Systems for Small and Medium-Sized Enterprises

State of Art of IS Research in SMEs

Springer

Editors
Jan Devos
ELIT-Lab
University College West-Flanders
Kortrijk
Belgium

and

Ghent University
Ghent
Belgium

Hendrik van Landeghem
Industrial Management
Ghent University
Ghent
Belgium

Dirk Deschoolmeester
Department of Management, Innovation and Entrepreneurship
Faculty of Economics and Business Administration
Ghent University
Ghent
Belgium

ISSN 2196-8705 ISSN 2196-8713 (electronic)
ISBN 978-3-642-38243-7 ISBN 978-3-642-38244-4 (eBook)
DOI 10.1007/978-3-642-38244-4
Springer Heidelberg New York Dordrecht London

Library of Congress Control Number: 2013948746

Printed on acid-free paper

Springer is part of Springer Science+Business Media (www.springer.com)

Foreword

This book presenting articles of diverse and varied nature is of utmost importance to help scholars and practitioners having also academic interests to analyse, interpret and support discussions about the real world of ICT and SMEs.

In the seventies and eighties I saw major large-sized companies and organisations being confronted with a gradual penetration of computerisation efforts to support, with hopefully relevant data being of proper quality (information), and their administrative tasks occurring in a variety of functional domains. The concerns that most often large-sized institutions, but to some extent also companies or organisations of medium-size then have was to be focused on questions like how to organise—centralise or decentralise—their planning, control and execution with a steadily growing IT/IS infrastructure. And thus supporting management and employees with timely, effective and efficient managerial and operational decision-making and execution capabilities. From early research on, then emerging with bits and pieces, I learned that the volume of investments and recurrent costs made in IT/IS, were most often related to the sheer size of the organisation. More specifically, own research taught me that the size in employment, more specifically the number of white collar employees, was a measure for the volume and complexity of organisation's administrative tasks (Debrabander et al. 1972). Thus the statistical relationship between IT-investments and costs seen over time and the number of white collar employees was found very relevant and the highest significance was found between all relationships hypothesised as potentially relevant. In other words, the size variable expressed in numbers of white collar employment, representing the volume, complexity and variability of the administrative tasks of an organisation was a major driver for investing in IT. So in this 1970–1980s period it was understandable that SMEs logically were more laggards than early IT adopters.

Once these more quantitative observations were made, the research agenda changed with new questions on quality, value and impact on organisational performance of IT/IS efforts. Most of these efforts had to be realised by very engaged personnel having either a very technical IT education or a higher level education excluding on IS-aspects. So personnel lacking proper education for IT/IS in a business context, having also no sufficient experience in connecting and integrating IT with business domains, were asked to develop IT applications for senior management. IT/IS-Capabilities for organisations were being developed from scratch with personnel not really having been properly educated for IT/IS.

Of course assigned professionals were doing their very best, but the upside and downside risks were so high that many efforts for new IS systems failed to a large extent. A steady and fast introduction of newer information technologies were adding a constant risk to yield IT/IS-investments failures and thus organisational pain, misery and often annoying chaos. More automation was continuously breeding a excessive need for more and more automation while efforts continued all too often to result in illusions and promises for obtaining stable results from IT/IS at some distant future. This good enough culture around IT/IS efforts, especially when external service providers were involved, all too often created serious clashes due to misaligned or badly executed agreements about IT/IS products and services. Coping with angriness about failure and idle promises occasionally needed involvement of legal court, lawyers and experts given a role for mediating and brokering the litigate case. These cases of IT failures usually showed that proper planning, evaluation ex-ante and more,especially trust between partners, was missing despite great expectations of managers to improve performance of their organisation. It is therefore unfortunate to recognise that more recent research shows that similar struggling to improve integration and impact of IT/IS for better performance of organisations might still be too frequently a lasting and troublesome concern (Poels 2012). And this situation is clearly worse when observing and studying computerisation in SMEs. Indeed, SMEs do experience a series of more adverse conditions when selecting and implementing IT applications and infrastructure. They generally lack sufficient resources and often are hampered in their efforts for attracting the internal and external high-skilled personnel or service providers with proper knowledge and experience in both the IT and business domains. While outsourcing became a choice for larger companies , for SMEs this is the major option. They have to bring in external service providers, hopefully also knowledgeable in their business domain and models of operating. SME management being often seduced for sourcing on less stable products, also designed and introduced in a style of 'bricolage'. Luckily also exceptions on this rather negative state exist. Indeed, there exists also a minority of visionary and knowledgeable SME-directors who succeed to bring their IT-efforts under adequate control. And who understand how to succeed at reasonable costs and efforts, with engagement of their collaborators, to gradually work out IT-investments that help them to perform well.

The set of articles in this book on "ICT and SMEs" is of course coming too late for helping to avoid the many IT-failures of the past. But today in a context of social media and penetration of ubiquitous and omnipresent computing I would gladly say this book is published in due time. I was honoured for the invitation to assist and help as a co-editor and I congratulate my co-editors and especially the initiator of this contributed volume, Dr. Jan Devos, together with all the authors he could reassemble on the subject, because they created a step-stone for scholars and practitioners who coach and advise SMEs to improve their capabilities to realise better conditions than earlier IT systems needed for quality decision-making and operations.

Gent Belgium

Prof emer Dr. ir Dirk Deschoolmeester
Vlerick Business School
Ghent University
Gent, Belgium

References

Debrabander, B., Deschoolmeester, D., Leyder, R., & Vanlomme, E. (1972). Effect of task volume and complexity upon computer use. *Journal of Business 45*(1), pp 56–84.

Poels, G. (2012). International Conference on Research and Practical Issues of Enterprise Information, Enterprise information systems of the future 6th IFIP WG 8.9 Working Conference, CONFENIS, Ghent, Belgium, September 19–21, 2012, revised selected papers, Berlin, New York: Springer.

Preface

Small and Medium-Sized Enterprises (SMEs) constitute nowadays a major business sector all over the world, covering a wide spectrum of industries. The number of SMEs far exceeds the number of large and very large organisations. SMEs contribute strongly to the GDP and even more to the growth in employment of most countries. In Europe, two-thirds of all new jobs are created by SMEs and more than 99 % of all enterprises are SMEs (Commission 2011a; Commission 2011b). Even today, the U.S. economy is by no means dominated by giant corporations. More than 99 % of all independent enterprises employ fewer than 500 employees (SBA 2011). These SMES account for 52 % of all U.S. workers. Similar numbers can be found for other developed as well as for developing countries all over the globe. SMEs contribute disproportionately to innovation, generating 13 times as many patents per employee as large companies do (Horn et al. 2012).

Contradictorily, many SMEs struggle to survive and grow and they display limited productivity. In spite of being a key economic contributor in many countries, SMEs suffer from various challenges, often inherent, often induced by social, economic, geographical or cultural grounds or other reasons beyond their control. Although there are quite some factors contributing to low SME survival rates, one crucial factor that has been singled out is the (lack of) successful adoption and use of Information Technologies (IT). IT can be seen as an enabler for business growth, effective competition, and innovation in SMEs (Higon 2012; Levy et al. 2005). However, when it comes to IT adoption and use, SMEs are not the best pupils in class as many studies have shown (Antlova 2009; Arbore et al. 2006; Sharma 2009; Wielicki et al. 2010). SMEs often express a reluctant vision to IT adoption which is mainly based on a lack of managerial IT capabilities. This is due to organisational immaturity and results in an asymmetric relationship with IT suppliers dominating the arena (Devos et al. 2012). SMEs are vulnerable organisations with a shortage of expertise, resources and managerial maturity (Welsh et al. 1981).

On the other hand we see that in the field of IS research most empirical work is conducted in large organisations and SMEs are often left on their own (Devos 2011). The reasons for this are manifold. Some scholars do not always believe that SMEs constitute a different unit of analysis for IS research. There is still much debate going on in that domain. Research has revealed that the success of bringing

IT into organisations is positively related to organisation size (Eindor et al. 1978). Although it is very cumbersome to clearly define what constitutes IT success, it was shown that success of bringing, for instance, ERP into organisations supports the size hypothesis (Ifinedo 2007; Mabert et al. 2003). There is also the problem of defining what constitutes an SME. In Europe SMEs are defined as companies with less than 250 employees, but in the U.S. SMEs are defined as companies with up to 500 employees (Commission 2003).

However in view of the current economic turbulence, it has never been more important to focus on the collection of scientific knowledge on SMEs in relation to IT/IS, since it is on the back of these organisations that innovation, growth and potential recovery will be realised. To stimulate the IS research in SMEs we decided to bring various works of scholars and practitioners together in a contributed volume. There are two dimensions in every contributed chapter: an IT/IS phenomenon and an SME environment. Both dimensions are intertwined, but in their concerted action a unique subfield of IS research is created.

This volume is divided into six part, which cover various aspects of IS research in SMEs. In all chapters the unit of analysis is the SME. The first part, "IT Governance", contains three chapters presenting various aspects of governance and management in SMEs. The first chapter, "Governance of IT in Small and Medium-Sized Enterprises" by Erik Guldentops addresses the enterprise governance of IT as the responsibility of the top layer of an entity to ensure IT is effective and efficient and provides value to the enterprise while keeping risks to an acceptable level. Enterprise governance of IT focuses on IT Value and IT Risk and consists of practices, organisational structures and relationships between executive and management. In SMEs however, these structures and relationships very often rest in one person, the owner/entrepreneur. The biggest value and risk challenge for SMEs is the acquisition of automated solutions because they often do not have sufficient capabilities to deal with it, they do not occur often and represent a relatively large risk. To address this, a set of acquisition guidelines is proposed. Finally, four management practices that resulted from recent pragmatic research are proposed for SME leadership to consider. This exertion is of high relevance since it is based on a long and intense work on IT Governance within the COBIT framework. The COBIT framework helps managers deal with enterprise governance of IT.

The second chapter, "Business Process Management in Small Business: A Case Study", by Ian Dallas and Moe T. Wynn brings a case study of a BPM initiative to develop process infrastructure in an establishing small business. It explores whether mainstream BPM tools, techniques and technologies can be applied in a small business setting. The chapter provides a background to the case organisation, outlines the activities undertaken in the BPM initiative and distils key observations drawn from participation in the initiative and consultation with stakeholders. Based on case study experiences, a number of implications are identified for further consideration by the BPM community as it continues to address the question of how it can become more widely adopted amongst SMEs.

In the third chapter, "Information Technology (IT) Security in Small and Medium Enterprises", Michael W. Kimwele addresses the issue of IT security in SMEs. SMEs should embrace IT security in order to realise the benefits of IT without compromising the IT security status. Much like any other business asset, information is an asset that needs to be strategically managed and protected. It is therefore imperative that SMEs understand the value of information contained within their business systems and have a framework for assessing and implementing IT security. To address challenges faced by SMEs, this research establishes an Information Technology (IT) framework that can allow SMEs implement cost effective security measures. The framework is likely to assist SME stakeholders measure the effectiveness of their security enhancing mechanisms.

The second part, "Adoption and Use" consists of five chapters. In the fourth chapter, "Enterprise Architecture for Small and Medium-Sized Enterprises: A Starting Point for Bridging EA to SMEs, Based on Adoption Models", by Maxime Bernaert, Geert Poels, Monique Snoeck and Manu De Backer investigate why Enterprise Architecture (EA) is not yet adopted by SMEs, despite the benefits EA can offer. This chapter offers a starting point for EA technique developers to really adapt EA techniques to an SME context. Research steps are given to start developing EA techniques, as well as a starting point for a metamodel based on only four concepts, because the characteristics of SMEs emphasise the need for simple EA techniques. These concepts refer to four dimensions that are present in a broad spectrum of EA techniques.

The fifth chapter entitled, "Assessment of Information Technology Use in Small and Medium-Sized Enterprises: Empirical Investigation in Five Cases", by Emre Sezgin and Sevgi Özkan presents an exploratory study with the practice of a new model for assessment of IT use in SMEs, which is called ITMEM: Information Technology Management Enhancement Model. This model aims to enhance IT management and processes within five domains (Identification, Selection, Acquisition, Exploitation and Protection) which brings together the organisational use of IT in a coherent whole. The results presented that practicing assessment in companies is encouraging in terms of IT use by employees and increasing quality of business processes. The reported findings would be a valuable asset for researchers who are developing a model, and for practitioners who are developing managerial implications on IT management and IT use in SMEs.

The sixth chapter, "ICT Policy to Foster Interorganisational ICT Adoption by SMEs: The Netherlands Goes Digital Case", by Marijn G. A. Plomp, Ronald S. Batenburg and Pim den Hertog deals with a policy programme that a government set in place to improve SMEs on their adoption of ICT, particularly interorganisational ICT. Previous research provides unclear evidence on the effectiveness of these programmes. With this study the authors aim to provide new insight into the impact of such policy choices on ICT adoption. They assess a policy programme that ran in the Netherlands from 2002–2007. Participants are found to use significantly more interorganisational ICT and also more often find that ICT has enhanced their firm's performance compared to the control group. However, preselection effects cannot be ruled out. Based on these results, the authors suggest basic, awareness-focused policy programmes, as opposed to complex, government supported implementation processes.

In the seventh chapter of this part, "Main factors for ICT Adoption in the Czech SMEs", Klara Antlova outlines the findings of a long-term survey among 30 small and medium enterprises (SMEs) in the Czech Republic and describe the important factors related to barriers to adoption of information technology and information systems. This qualitative survey of the examined companies was made by using multiple interviews, monitoring the attitudes of the management to the information and communication technology (ICT), using ICT as a competitive advantage, use of various types of applications and their impact on the organisation's performance. It can be seen that managers or owners of SMEs are, however, often afraid of the organisational and financial demands of implementation of ICT. From the successfully growing companies the author analysed the importance of establishing business, information and knowledge strategy. Without the articulation of these strategies companies will, with difficulty, find their way in the current business environment. These three strategies have to be followed by other supporting strategies, i.e. marketing, finance and human resources.

The eighth and last chapter of this part, "Adoption of Free/Open Source ERP Software by SMEs", by Constantinos J. Stefanou provides an insight into the adoption decision made by SMEs regarding FOS-ERP software. To remain competitive, SMEs find that they need to invest in information and communication technologies and especially in modern integrated business software. However, state-of-the-art propriety Enterprise Resource Planning (ERP) systems are not only too expensive but also too complex to install for the majority of SMEs. Viable alternative options, such as Free and Open Source ERP (FOS/ERP) software, are increasingly gaining attention by SMEs worldwide. The chapter aims at informing scholars, students, researcher managers of the issues and the risks involved and the factors influencing the decision of SMEs to adopt FOS-ERP software.

The third part, "Enterprise Applications" contains four chapters. The ninth chapter, "Customer Relationship Management System. A Case Study on Small- and Medium-Sized Companies in North Germany", by Malte Menzel and Torsten Reiners focuses on Customer Relationship Management (CRM). CRM is a common tool in large enterprises; yet it seems not to be successful with small- and medium-sized enterprises (SME). The authors conducted a survey to analyse the state-of-the-art customer relationship management systems and the degree of pervasion in SME. The survey covers 253 SMEs from North Germany and evaluates the available systems, desired and actually delivered functionality, integration in the Information Technology landscape, client satisfaction, and arguments about benefits and drawbacks of current CRM-systems. The main contribution of the chapter is improving the awareness of the importance that CRM has specifically for SMEs and benefits which SMEs can gain using CRM.

The tenth chapter of this part, "Empirical Study on Differences and Similarities in ERP Usage Among European SMEs", by Pedro Ruivo, Tiago Oliveira, Björn Johansson and Miguel Neto presents a cross-country European empirical study. This chapter evaluates the determinants of enterprise resource planning (ERP) usage among SMEs. The authors empirically test six determinants (compatibility, complexity, efficiency, best-practices, training and competitive pressure) based on the diffusion of innovation (DOI) model to explain ERP actual usage across four European countries. They explore the differences and similarities in usage across Denmark, Portugal, Sweden and Spain. The cross-country analysis reveals that while for Portuguese and Swedish firms, SMEs system compatibility is an important facilitator for ERP usage, it is an inhibitor for Danish firms. Moreover, whereas system complexity is an important inhibitor for ERP usage in Portuguese and Danish firms, it is a facilitator for Spanish firms. Additionally, while for Portuguese, Danish and Swedish firms, transactional efficiency is significant, it is not so for Spanish firms. In addition, best-practices and competitive pressure are important determinants of ERP usage for all SMEs across all countries. Training is an important facilitator for Portuguese and Spanish SMEs. The main finding is that Portuguese and Spanish SMEs show different results despite the fact that they seem to be so similar and the same prevails among Danish and Swedish SMEs. The fact that this research is based on a large-scale survey across countries makes it important to understand the actual ERP usage among SMEs, alongside its value in adding an international dimension to the DOI literature.

The eleventh chapter of this part, "ERP Implementation in an SME: A Failure Case", by Eli Hustad and Dag H. Olsen examines a failed ERP implementation in an SME. The improper handling of critical success factors (CSFs), particularly those relating to support from top management, project management and the use of consultants, led to severe problems. This placed stress on the organisation, caused employees to leave the company, workarounds and led to serious errors in the systems and a significant cost overrun. This chapter contributes to the literature on ERP implementation in SMEs. In particular, it contributes to our understanding of the socio-technical dynamics of ERP implementation projects. Failed ERP cases are little documented in the IS research literature and can yield insight into the complexity of ERP implementation projects and further our understanding of what may take place if CSFs are not handled properly.

The twelfth chapter of the part, "Understand Marketing Information Systems from the Perspective of SMEs: Reviewing the Literature", by Canan Eryigit examines the existing literature on marketing information systems in SMEs for the period 2002–2012 in order to identify active research area, emerging topics and gaps in the literature. The author has encountered 48 empirical studies conducted on SMEs and investigated applications of information systems to marketing. The studies are categorised on the bases of journal, research area, publication year, country and research design. The categorisation leads to six main research areas namely adaption, competitive strategy, e-marketing, performance outcomes, customer relationship management and distribution strategy. Then, patterns in past research are identified and future research areas are provided.

Part 4 of this volume, "Capabilities and Knowledge" contains three chapters. The thirteenth chapter, "The Ability of SMEs to Use Trust in Managing Offshore Activities", by Franz Josef Gellert and Hugo Velthuijsen focuses on how

SMEs have found their way into multi-cultural relations to outsource or offshore their business processes. Relationships are built either from an economic or emotional point of view. Their study particularly focused on how SMEs owner/managers build, maintain and—when necessary—exit their relationships with other SMEs by using trust as a core element. The authors have chosen for a qualitative research strategy by conducting semi-structured interviews in The Netherlands, Germany, UK, Denmark and Sweden. The countries selected are representatives of the application of Northern-European and Anglo-Saxon business models. The results suggest that trust is of essence in the relationship building process and that the perception of trust needs to be understood and managed in multi-cultural relations by all parties involved. The can also conclude from their results that SMEs are intrinsically inclined to base their offshore activities on trust. For practical reasons, partners in relationships need to be educated and trained how to build trust in multi-cultural relations.

The fourteenth chapter, "Exploring Knowledge Capabilities in SMEs: Cases in Five Irish Software SMEs", by Ciara Heavin and Frederic Adam explores how a knowledge management (KM) approach for SMEs differs from that implemented by a larger organisation. Unquestionably, KM has established considerable focus in multinational enterprises (MNEs) during the past decade, it is therefore imperative that policy makers engage SMEs in order to better comprehend the role of SMEs in the global economy. This chapter examines the knowledge capabilities in five Irish software SMEs with the objective of developing a greater understanding of an SMEs approach to KM and therefore developing an actionable way of assessing how important knowledge is managed, in this type of organisation. The transcripts derived from 28 interviews conducted were coded in order to identify the types of knowledge activities (KA) and modes of knowledge processing used to serve the knowledge needs of these organisations. While the total number of KAs varied from firm to firm, it was discovered that software SMEs are good at knowledge transfer activity. This finding is largely attributed to the size and the focused business objectives of these firms.

The fifteenth and last chapter of this part, "Business Agility and Flexibility in Enterprise Service-based Information Systems: Application to PLM Systems", by Safa Hachani, Hervé Verjus and Lilia Gzara investigate how small industrial companies collaborating to develop new products need to implement the effective management of their product design processes (PDPs) and product information. PDPs are known for their changing, emergent and non-deterministic characteristics due to the business environment within which they are executed. Unfortunately, Product Lifecycle Management (PLM) systems, which are dedicated to support product design activities, are not as efficient as might be expected. PLM systems are based on workflow technology, which does not support PDPs agility. Process support flexibility requirements are necessary in order to facilitate coupling with the business reality. Furthermore, systems based on Service Oriented Architectures (SOA) have the inherent ability to evolve. The authors believe that SOA can promote the support of flexible PDPs. The aim of the work presented in this chapter is to propose an alternative approach for flexible product design process support within PLM systems, by making profiles from SOA. The objective is to specify, design and implement PDPs in a flexible manner, in order to ensure that business changes can be rapidly made in PLM solutions. A generic services identification approach is proposed for architecting agile process-centred service-based information systems.

The fifth part of the book, "Innovation" consists of two chapters. The sixteenth chapter, "Open Innovation in SMEs: Prospects and Challenges", by Hakikur Rahman and Isabel Ramos, describes how newly evolved technologies and multi-faceted researches along the setting of entrepreneurship development, philosophy, framework and business handling have been transformed from being traditional to innovative. Depending on the demand, diversity and nature of the transformation, innovation has been shifted from closed to open paradigm. Ranging from micro to small or, medium to corporate houses are being immensely benefited by the innovation techniques, especially utilising information and communication technologies (ICTs). However, the road to innovation, despite being seen or taken as a paradigm shift is not quite smooth and not even ready for many, particularly the SMEs who mainly deal with the clients at the outer peripheries of the social circle. This study synthesises issues of prospects and challenges in adopting open innovation for SMEs by carrying out a longitudinal literature review. Furthermore, the chapter provides a few research hints for researchers and research institutions.

The seventeenth chapter, "Government Support to Information Systems Innovation in Small and Medium Enterprises", by Vega Arturo and Mike Chiasson investigates how SMEs need external assistance to accomplish their information systems initiatives. Governments have been addressing this by funding numerous programmes. The aim of the chapter is to understand these programmes. The findings indicate that programme workers tend to exert considerable discretion. This discretion appears to be the result of inadequate evaluation and auditing mechanisms, a probable collaboration of policy administrators, as well as broad and ambiguous policies. Apart from this, programmes tend to operate within problematic contexts. These contexts are composed of poor evaluation mechanisms, power of programmes over SMEs, scarcity of resources, low demand for programme services and alienation of workers. A relevant implication is that the improvement of contexts could also reduce discretion. However, the actors that could do this are located at diverse parts of the system. Therefore, the reform of programmes is a difficult task given the priorities and power of the participants. Finally, the chapter suggests that SME associations may represent a counteractive force to these policy influences in order to materialise policy reforms.

The last part of the book, "Internet and Internet-Related Technologies", contains two chapters. The eighteenth chapter, "Forums and Blogs and Wikis, Oh My!: An analysis of On-line Sources of Support for End-User Development", by Henri Korvela presents and argues a framework of four key factors: context, cooperation, interactivity, and immediacy that, it is argued, influence end-user developers' ability to obtain/use development support. These four factors which were derived from an extensive literature review are used to analyse and compare the effectiveness of several existing support sources (mainly focusing on the online versions) for end-user developers: personal contacts; help desks; trial and error several different knowledge repositories; virtual communities and Internet searches. Based on this analysis, tempered with the perceived needs of (mainly novice) developers from real-life situations, the chapter concludes that virtual communities is the most suitable support source (in the sense that it fulfils needs that developers may or may not beware of), especially for this category of end-user developers.

The last chapter of the book, "Internet Technologies to Support SMEs' Growth in New Markets", by Cerquitelli Tania, Chianese Stefano, Ferrero Merlino Chiara, Raimondi Francesca, Scapeccia Giuseppe, Spagnuolo Michele and Zolotukhina Irina analyses the existing Internet technologies that can support SMEs in their internationalisation process, emphasising the study of web-based platforms. The authors propose two classifications to categorise portals and websites based on the services provided. The aim of this study was to gather a list of current services offered online to ease SMEs' internationalisation.

All 19 chapters of this book present a novel and innovative collection of work from various scholars presenting their recent research on IT and SMEs. The editors hope that this contributed volume will benefit both academics and practitioners. It is hoped by the editors that through this book, "Information Systems and Small and Medium-Sized Enterprises: State of art of IS research in SMEs", both communities will find each other.

Jan Devos
Hendrik van Landeghem
Dirk Deschoolmeester

References

Antlova, K. (2009). Motivation and barriers of ict adoption in small and medium-sized enterprises. *E &M Ekonomie a Management*, *12*(2), pp 140–155.

Arbore, A., & Ordanini, A. (2006). Broadband divide among SMEs: The role of size, location and outsourcing strategies. *International Small Business Journal*, *24*(1) February, pp 83–99.

Commission, E. (2003). Commission Recommendation 2003/361/EC. *Official Journal of the European Union*, *46*(L 124), p 6.

Commission, E. (2011a). EU Trade Policy and SME. Fact sheet. p 2.

Commission, E. (2011b). Fact and Figures about the EU's Small and Medium Enterprise (SME), in *Small and medium-sized enterprises*.

Devos, J. (2011). *IT Governance for SMEs*. Ghent University, Ghent.

Devos, J., Van Landeghem, H., & Deschoolmeester, D. (2012). Rethinking IT governance for SMEs. *Industrial Management & Data Systems*, *112*(1–2), pp 206–223.

Eindor, P., & Segev, E. (1978). Organizational context and success of management information-systems. *Management Science*, *24*(10), pp 1064–1077.

Higon, D. A. (2012). The impact of ICT on innovation activities: Evidence for UK SMEs. *International Small Business Journal*, *30*(6) September, pp 684–699.

Horn, J., & Pleasance, D. (2012). Restarting the US small-business growth engine. *McKinsey Quarterly* (November 2012), p 8.

Ifinedo, P. (2007). Interactions between organizational size, culture, and structure and some it factors in the context of ERP success assessment: An exploratory investigation. *Journal of Computer Information Systems*, *47*(4) Sum, pp 28–44.
Levy, M., & Powell, P. (2005). *Strategies for Growth in SMEs: The Role of Information and Information Systems*. Oxford: Elsevier.
Mabert, V. A., Soni, A., & Venkataramanan, M. A. (2003). The impact of organization size on enterprise resource planning (ERP) implementations in the US manufacturing sector. *Omega-International Journal of Management Science*, *31*(3) June, pp 235–246.
SBA (2011). U.S. Small Business Administration.
Sharma, M. K. (2009). Receptivity of India's small and medium-sized enterprises to information system adoption. *Enterprise Information Systems*, *3*(1), pp 95–115.
Welsh, J. A., & White, J. F. (1981). A small business is not a little big business. *Harvard Business Review*, *59*(4), pp 18–32.
Wielicki, T., & Arendt, L. (2010). A knowledge-driven shift in perception of ICT implementation barriers: Comparative study of US and European SMEs. *Journal of Information Science*, *36*(2) April, pp 162–174.

Acknowledgments

Editing a book requires a lot of goodwill, support and collaboration of many people who have been involved in the making of this book.

First, we would like to thank all of the contributing authors who were willing to send in a contribution. Their work and patience is finally rewarded. They devoted a lot of effort into the writing of their chapter and to the various comments and suggestions made by the reviewers.

We are also indebted to the large number of reviewers who were so kind and willing to review one or more chapters of this book. Each chapter of the book was blind reviewed by two reviewers who did a splendid job.

We also wish to express our gratitude to our publisher Springer for the willingness to accept the production of this volume and the great support and assistance in the process of making it a final publication.

Jan Devos
Hendrik van Landeghem
Dirk Deschoolmeester

Contents

Part III Enterprise Applications

Part IV Capabilities and Knowledge

Part V Innovation

Reviewers

Richard Baskerville, Georgia State University, USA
Nargiza Bekmamedova, University of Melbourne, Australia
Maxime Bernaert, Ghent University, Belgium
Filipe Caldeira, IPV-Escola Superior de Tecnologia de Viseu, Portugal
Walter Castelnovo, University of Insubria, Italy
Cristina Chuva, ISEC, Portugal
Jan Claes, Ghent University, Belgium
Johannes Cottyn, Ghent University, Belgium
Filip De Pauw, Ghent University, Belgium
Brecht Deconinck, Ghent University, Belgium
Wim Dejonghe, Ghent University, Belgium
Drik Deschoolmeester, Ghent University, Belgium
Yogesh Dwivedi, Swansea University, UK
Willie Golden, NUI Galway, Ireland
Johan Jacobs, Flemish Government, Belgium
Pirkko Lahdelma, Aalto University, Aalto Service Factory, Finland
Tadhg Nagle, University College Cork, Ireland
Tiago Oliveira, ISEGI, Universidade Nova de Lisboa, Portugal
Dag H. Olsen, University of Agder, Norway
Jonathan Owens, The Priory City of Lincoln Academy, UK
Cristiane Pedron, ISEG, Portugal
Jo Pierson, Vrije Universiteit Brussel, Belgium
Geert Poels, Ghent University, Belgium
Vitor Prisca, Novabase IMS, Portugal
Ben Ramdani, Bristol Business School, UK
Isabel Ramos, University of Minho, Portugal
Dave Sammon, University College Cork, Ireland
Vitor Santos, Universidade de Tras os Montes e Alto Douro, Portugal
Michael Schermann, Technical University Munchen, Germany

Theo Thiadens, Fontys Hogeschool, The Netherlands
Hans van der Heijden, Royal Holloway University London, UK
Gert Van Der Pijl, Erasmus University Rotterdam, The Netherlands
Wim Van Grembergen, University of Antwerp, Belgium
Hendrik Van Landeghem, Ghent University, Belgium

Part I
IT Governance

Governance of IT in Small and Medium Sized Enterprises

Erik Guldentops

1 Introduction

At a recent power lunch with several CIO's, one of them threw this issue on the table while looking at me knowing I have been a strong advocate of enterprise governance IT for years: "What do you do if the CEO tells you to get it done and to hell with the governance? Well you probably go away and just do it no?"

Even though it is the CEO's prerogative to accept risk and also choose expedience over cost-efficiency (especially if he is also the owner of the SME), that was not necessarily the best response. The reason is that in such situations:

- Liability and compliance risks will more easily arise and consequences[1] are rarely properly being considered.
- Effectiveness is not guaranteed by the sole actions of the CIO despite the fact that leadership is an important governance mechanism.
- The position on risk and cost-efficiency is rarely clear to all up front and will result in fierce debates after the fact if risk or cost become intolerable.

The enterprise in this case is active in the food industry and is relatively small on an international scale with an IT infrastructure that is neither too strategic nor representing a large percentage of total expenditure. This may explain the CEO's reaction which nevertheless illustrates the attitude often shown by owning boards: risk-taking, quick decisions, profit-first and short-term view.

[1] An effective way to address consequences is to consider what is **acceptable** when a liability issue arises relative to IT: What are the possible damages, what do others do, what do international standards prescribe? For product liability, the concept of **reasonable** is important to assign accountability: Do users know there is a risk? Do they know what to do about it? Do they have a choice as to what needs to be done?

E. Guldentops (✉)
Antwerp Management School, Sint Jacobsmarkt 9-13 B-2000 Antwerp, Belgium
e-mail: erik.guldentops@telenet.be

J. Devos et al. (eds.), *Information Systems for Small and Medium-sized Enterprises*, Progress in IS, DOI: 10.1007/978-3-642-38244-4_1,

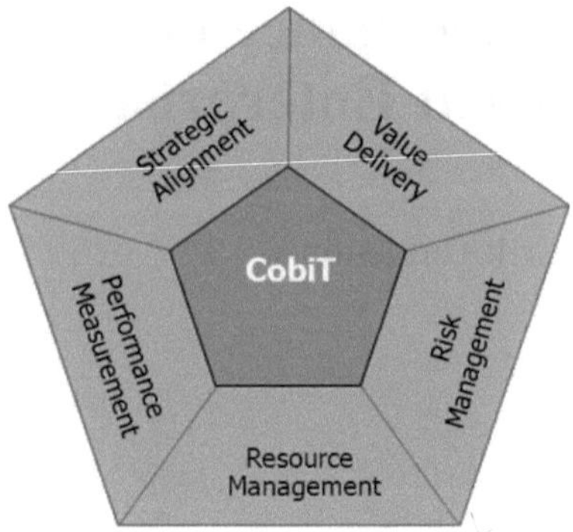

Fig. 1 The 5 domains of IT governance

So, to hell with the governance? Yes, but only if more than one of these conditions are true: you're small, IT is not important and the CEO is the owner (Guldentops 2012b).

2 Enterprise Governance of IT

Hence most SME's will need some governance to ensure IT is effective and efficient, providing value to the enterprise while keeping risks to an acceptable level (ITGI 2003a, b). IT governance[2] is an integral part of enterprise governance and consists of the leadership and organizational structures and processes that ensure that the organization's IT sustains and extends the organization's strategies and objectives. It is the responsibility of the board of directors and executive management and describes the relationship with the management layer providing direction and supervision over the value of IT, where value is Benefits minus Cost adjusted for Risk. Adjusted for risk means that the higher the risk in an IT enabled business initiative, the larger the benefits should be (ITGI 2007b).

As such, enterprise governance of IT is really about IT Value. The IT Governance Institute defined however 5 domains that need to be considered when thinking about what Boards and Executives need to do for proper governance (ITGI 2003a, b):

- *Value and Risk* inherently intertwined as already mentioned.
- *Strategic alignment* to stress that IT needs to deliver what the business needs and consequently that IT and the business need to work closely together.

[2] It is only during the development of CobiT5 starting in 2007 that the IT Governance Institute started replacing 'IT Governance' with the more appropriate term of 'Enterprise Governance of IT'. Hence the old terminology will be used when refering to IT Governance Institute's publications from before that period.

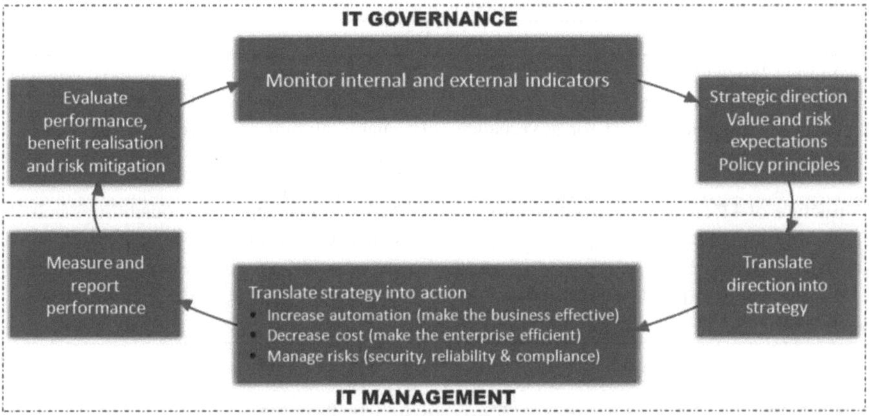

Fig. 2 The relationship of IT governance and IT management

- *Resource management* which represents the cost of IT but also needs attention for efficiency such as making the right technology choices and leveraging the potential of re-use.
- *Performance measurement* as an essential element in governance and management to get assurance that objectives are achieved and as a basis for improvement (Fig. 1).

ISO 38500, the international standard to which CobiT has recently been aligned, also provides a succinct definition and overview of IT Governance (ISO/IEC 38500 2008). Figure 2 describes the relationship between the governance and management layers and is build based on the original ideas of the IT Governance Institute and the concepts of ISO 38500.

IT Governance consists of practices, organisational structures and relationships between executive and management (Van Grembergen et al. 2004). A framework is needed to efficiently implement this. During the last 15 years, CobiT has become the framework "par excellence" to implement IT governance.

It helps management to achieve objectives and manage risks by (a) linking to the most common measurable business and IT goals, and (b) by breaking IT's complexity into manageable processes and by providing for each of these processes a set of possible management practices.

CobiT is a management control framework aligned to the most important IT governance related standards and provides a common language, business focus and process orientation for IT management and governance. Table 1 provides an overview of the objectives and drivers of the CobiT framework.

Table 1 The objectives and drivers of CobiT

What	Why
A common language for IT activities and key management practices	To avoid misunderstandings, to have efficient dialogues and to enable synergy
A business focus and support for governance expectations	To enable alignment between business and IT and engage executives in the governance of IT
A structure of IT tasks and activities into discrete processes	To better define scope, responsibilities and extent of coverage
Consistency with generally accepted IT good practices and corporate governance standards	To be generally acceptable and to have a provably complete basis to select from

3 CobiT: A Management Framework for IT

CobiT starts from a relatively simple premise: The business needs reliable information to support their goals and is willing to invest in resources so that IT processes deliver the information the business needs to be successful (ITGI 2007c) (Fig. 3).

The requirements are driven by financial soundness, customer perception, operational excellence and capability to grow which are the 4 dimensions of the Balanced Scorecard (Kaplan and Norton 2000). The resources that need to be leveraged are infrastructure, information, applications and people (skills, knowledge and behaviour). The processes leveraging these resources need to deliver information services the business needs to be successful in their turn.

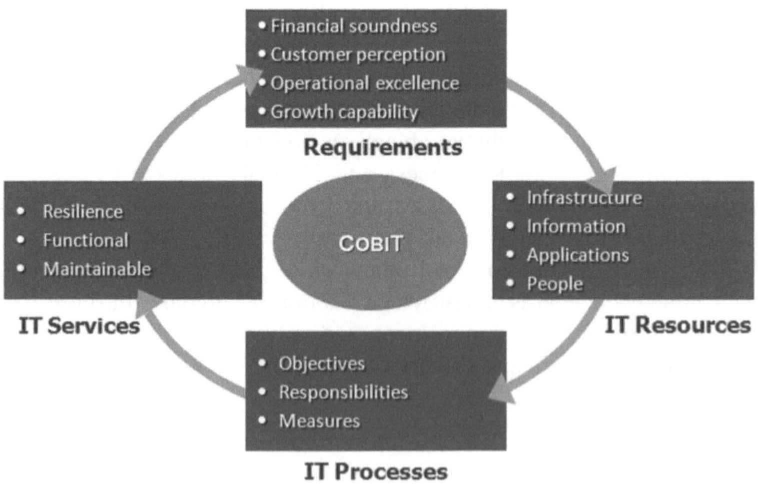

Fig. 3 The basic premise of CobiT

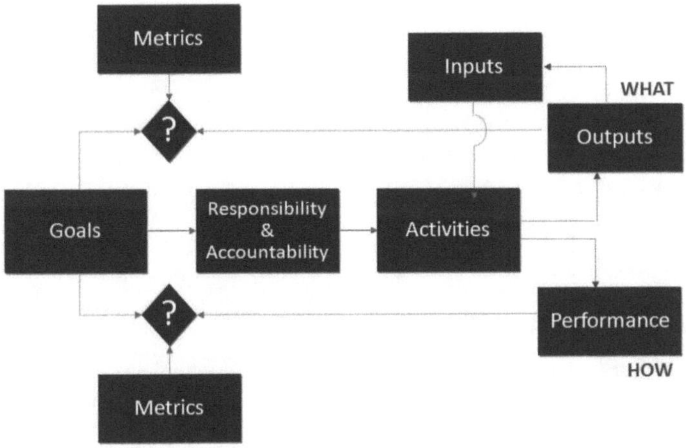

Fig. 4 The elements IT processes need to be governed successfully

These services need to be functional; resilient and maintainable. As shown Fig. 4, the processes—whether they are formal or not, need clear responsibilities and accountabilities that lead to activities in order to achieve the goals of the process. The deliverables, but also the manner in which the processes operate, need to be verified so that they respond to the business and the governance requirements.

To this end, CobiT provides—in addition to a process structure for IT, the following for each process:

- A process goal.
- The IT goals supported.
- Management practices.
- A RACI[3] chart.
- Process Inputs and outputs.
- Process and activity metrics.
- A maturity model.

The IT process domains of CobiT follow the generally accepted pattern of Plan, Build and Run, with the additional process domain of Monitor. It presents a total of 34 processes in CobiT4.1 as well as in the recent CobiT5. The latter version reduced the number of original processes on the one hand but has on the other added the necessary layer to deal with the governance of value and risk.

The process orientation makes CobiT into an IT accountability framework for the IT organisation. Furthermore, the business and IT goal structure it provides makes it business focused. CobiT4 originally provided a set of 18 enterprise goals

[3] RACI stands for who is Responsible and Accountable and who needs to be Consulted or Informed for each of the process activities.

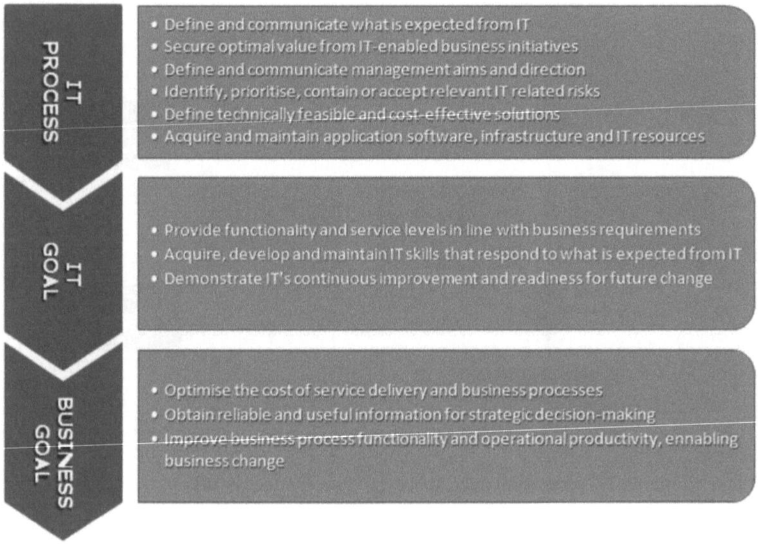

Fig. 5 How a set of processes drive a set of IT goals which in turn drive a set of business goals

that linked to 28 IT goals that supported them which in turn linked to processes that particularly supported that goal. This cascade was somewhat reduced by CobiT4.1 and further in CobiT5. The cascade now has 17 enterprise goals and 17 IT goals. Some 500 enterprises were surveyed in an ISACA sponsored research an analysed to find correlations between the goals and the practices as represented by the processes (Van Grembergen et al. 2009).

Some cluster correlations were the result and are here adapted in line with the simplified IT framework as described in Sect. 1.4 and provided in Appendix 2 (Fig. 5).

The CobiT material has been developed with the help of hundreds of expert practitioners and hence is complete while not being prescriptive, i.e., it is a reference framework and not a standard. Furthermore, enterprises with an organised IT department already do much of what is described in CobiT, maybe not all the time or as consistently or efficiently as could be.

Nevertheless, the whole can be somewhat overwhelming with more than 30 processes, more than 300 management practices and several hundreds of metrics. Because CobiT is not a standard but a reference framework it comes with the warning that enterprises should analyse it and take from it what they need. The many testimonials, cases and conference presentations on CobiT indicate that implementation usually considers between 10 and 30 % of the material after analysis of what the key objective, pain point and/or improvement strategy is.

Even though CobiT comes with this advice that while complete, enterprises should be selective in what they adopt, there has been early on a strong demand for a version for SME's which became CobiT QuickStart.

4 QuickStart: A Management Framework for IT in SME's

The objective was to customise the CobiT material so it would be more suitable for small and medium-sized enterprises, while realising they take more risk and are strongly profit orientated. Therefor the focus should be on practices with high effectiveness, low cost and expedient implementation.

It was decided early on that the material should be presented in a simple form, applying an 80/20 rule (identifying 20 % of the material that provides 80 % of the result), i.e., considering the "smart things to do". As such it becomes a sort of minimum baseline for governance and control of IT in SME's.

But what is an SME? It was quickly realised that econometric measures like staff size or financial ratios did not work for the purpose of developing an IT governance framework. The reason is that it was always easy to find counter examples, i.e. "small" enterprises where IT governance was important or "larger" ones where it was not. Given the objective, it was decided to use the characteristics of governance, control and IT of an enterprise, to define it as an SME and suitable for CobiT QuickStart.

This characteristics where close supervision by management supported by an effective span of control and a simple command structure. Also management's familiarity with resources, staff and processes was an aspect including its ability to leverage a short communications path. Staff in these SME's would often have multiple responsibilities and hence there would be less segregation between important control fucntions. The SME's as considered would also have less than average IT capabilities, i.e., less build and more buy, less complex IT infrastructure and would generally be less 'savvy' about IT. This places the target enterprises more towards the lower left-hand quarter of the IT-strategic grid (McFarlan et al. 1983) where new IT applications provide local improvements but do not affect business strategy and where it needs a significant disturbance in IT operations over an extended period to have a major impact.

Nevertheless, even with these definitions there are circumstances where a simplified approach to governing IT may not be sufficient. For example, in smaller enterprises that:

- have open as opposed to closed systems, i.e., are extensively connected to the outside world;
- are subject to IT related regulations or IT related contractual obligations;
- have had IT problems that has management worried;
- have identified a need for formal training relative to IT and/or have begun defining some IT practices and procedures in a formal manner;
- have realized that common tools make some IT processes more effective and efficient; and
- need IT 'expert(s)' for developing/improving business processes.

Consequently, tools were developed to verify the applicability of CobiT QuickStart, looking at the objectives for the target audience and verifying the exceptions. These tools have been supplied together with the framework and can be downloaded without charge at www.isaca.org.

The first tool "Stay in the Blue Zone" checks the objectives by using a maturity scale for the seven dimensions identified above:

- Command structure.
- Communications path.
- Span of Control.
- IT Leadership.
- IT's Strategic Importance.
- IT Expenditure.
- Segregation of duties.

The scale was developed and preset by the group of SME experts who helped develop CobiT QuickStart and is illustrated in Table 2.

The presets are also defined by the "Blue Zone"-tool as shown in Fig. 6. Should the responses for the SME in question go out of this zone for 2 or more dimensions, then the tool suggests to consider a larger framework than QuickStart. That is the case in the example in Fig. 6 for Communications Path and IT Strategic Importance.

A second tool was provided in Fig. 7 is called "Watch the Heat" and tests with a heat-chart the degree of applicability against 8 IT governance related statements: Degree of connectivity with customers, suppliers etc.; IT related regulations or contractual requirements; The need to provide outside assurance; Management awareness of IT issues; Identification of the need for formal IT training; Formal definition of IT practices and procedures; The need for common automated tools and IT expertise requirements.

As for the other tool de experts developing CobiT QuickStart defined the scales as shown in Table 3.

The more management agrees with the statement the more the result turns to red (black in Table 3). The darker the response the more the enterprise should consider a broader framework than QuickStart.

The first version of QuickStart, based on CobiT3, presented some 60 management practices organised by process as shown in the example in Fig. 8, together with a reference to the full CobiT material, some critical success factors and metrics. It also suggested an maturity scale for tracking implementation.

The second version of QuickStart leveraged the new developments of CobiT4 and added a RACI chart as developed for CobiT4. It also provided two sets of metrics, one for the process which are more like outcome measures and one set for the practices which are more performance indicators. An example for the same process as shown for QuickStart version 1, is provided in Fig. 9.

CobiT version 2 also "raised he bar" by adding practices and stating many of them at a more demanding level so that the framework was more applicable to a larger set of the SME's.

ISACA has released CobiT5 and its most important feature is the extension of the model for the governance processes operating largely outside of the traditional

Table 2 Definition of SME based on IT related attributes and presets (*darker area*)

	1	2	3	4	
Command structure	is strictly informal and verbal, short-term & tactical	is primarily informal and verbal, somewhat short-term but largely medium-term oriented, and analytical	is primarily formal and documented, somewhat long-term but more medium-term oriented, and tactical	is strictly formal and documented, long-term & strategic	l,
Comunications path	HOE (Head of the entity) knows everyone's IT related tasks	HOE knows most people's IT related tasks	HOE only knows about IT tasks for key personnel	HOE does not know all IT related tasks of key personnel	asks
Span of Control	HOE directs and monitors everyone's IT related responsibilities	HOE directs and monitors most people's IT related responsibilities	HOE only directs and monitors IT responsibilities of key personnel	HOE does not direct nor monitors all IT related responsibilities of key personnel	all
IT Sophistication	Laggard, i.e. well behind in technology adoption	Follower, i.e. adopting technology after peers have done so	Leader, i.e. adopting technology before peers have done so	Pioneer, i.e. early adopter of new emerging technology well ahead of the industry	f the
IT Strategic Importance	Reliable IT is not critical to the functioning of the enterprise and is not likely to become strategically important	Reliable IT is critical to current operations, but application development is not fundamental to the firm's ability to compete	Uninterrupted functioning of IT is not absolutely vital to current objectives but developments will be critical to future competitive success	Reliable IT support is critical to the enterprise's current operation, and development are critical to future competitive success	ie d
IT Expenditure	is not more than profits and not much different from peers	is different from peers and only marginally increasing every year	is more that profits or significantly different from peers and is showing an annual increasing trend	is significantly more than the entity's profits	ty's
Segregation of Duties	Those who monitor have at least two other functions (build, operate, or influence).	Those who monitor have at most 'building' or 'operating' as other functions. Those who influence can also have 'building' and 'operating' functions.	Monitoring is totally segregated, but 'building' and 'operating' can be executed by the same person. Those who influence have at most 'operating' or 'building' as	At most 'influencing' and 'monitoring' is executed by one person	ing'

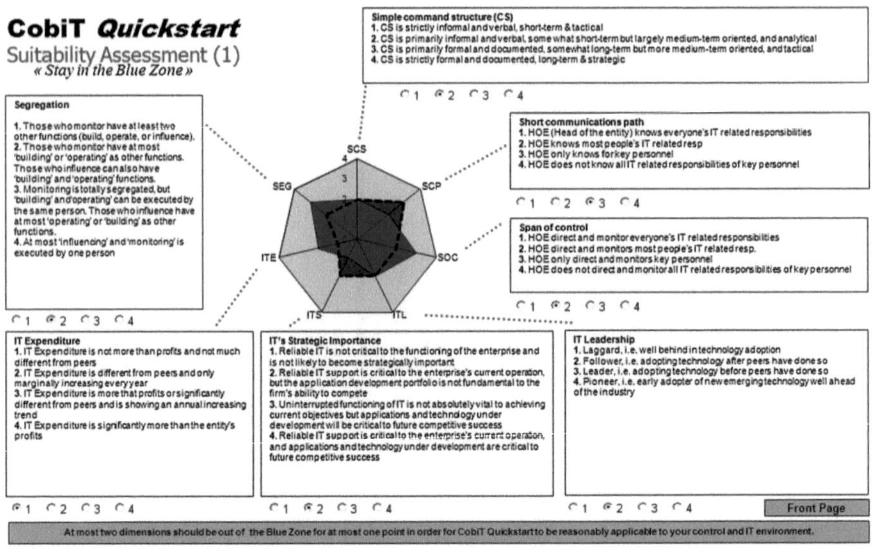

Fig. 6 QuickStart tool to check applicability of the framework

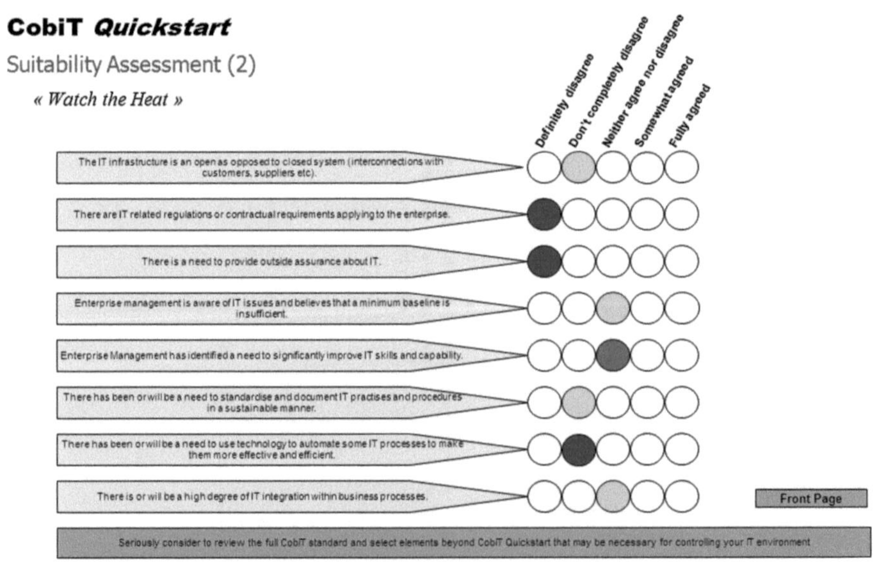

Fig. 7 QuickStart tool to check exceptions to its applicability

IT environment and focussing primarily on value and risk. Taking this into consideration and to provide a framework also usable for the smaller segment of SME's as defined above, a concise framework is provided in appendix 1 and is introduced in the next section.

Table 3 IT Governance situations that imply a stronger dependence on IT

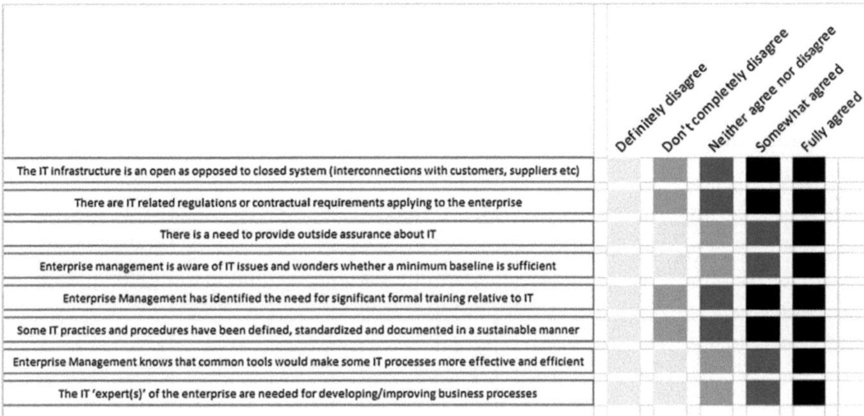

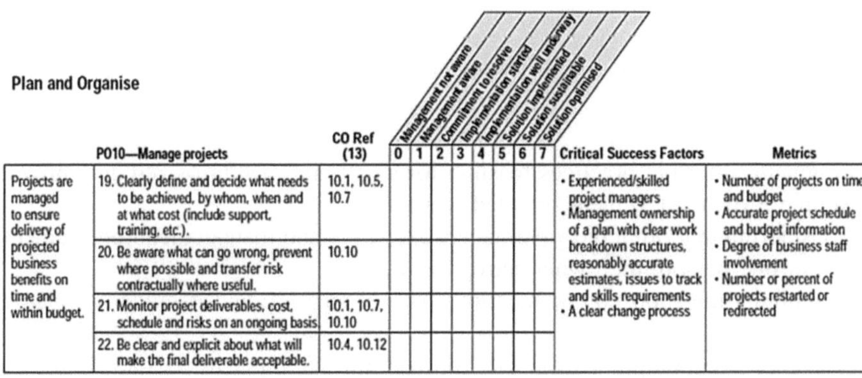

Fig. 8 CobiT QuickStart version1 for managing projects

5 A Pragmatic Set of Management Practices to Govern IT in SME's

In appendix 1 you will find a succinct set of management practices for the head of an SME to oversee IT and make sure it delivers value to the enterprise while keeping risks to a tolerable level. This set was developed extending the QuickStart applicability principles to the smaller segment of SME's where all IT governance and executive practices are the responsibility of the person at the head of the SME. The set was developed as follows:

1. Start from QuickStart version 2, which was based on CobiT4, and then condensed and reworded with the following objectives:

Processes and Good Practices			Self-assessment								Responsibilities					Key Metrics	
			Management is not aware.	Management is aware.	There is commitment to resolve.	Implementation has started.	Implementation is well under way.	Solution is implemented.	Solution is sustainable.	Solution has been optimised.							
PO10 Manage projects.																	
CobiT Quickstart Process	*CobiT Quickstart* Management Practices	CO Ref	0	1	2	3	4	5	6	7	Exec Committee	Head of IT	IT Development Manager	IT Operations Manager	Business Managers	Control Objective Metric	IT Process Metrics
Define a programme and project management approach that is applied to all IT projects, enables stakeholder participation and monitors project risks and progress.	18. Ensure the correct prioritisation and co-ordination of all projects, by clearly defining what needs to be achieved, by whom, when, at what cost and with which benefits.	PO10.1 PO10.2 PO10.6 PO10.7									I	A/R			C	• Percent of stakeholders participating in projects (involvement index)	• Percent of projects on time and on budget
	19. Define and communicate project management guidelines for all project managers. Describe explicitly the project scope and the final deliverable acceptance criteria. Support the business changes linked to the project with a proper training plan.	PO10.9										A/R	I	I	I	• Percent of projects following project management standards and practices	
	20. Implement a project quality plan to monitor project deliverables, cost, schedule and risks on an ongoing basis.	PO10.2 PO10.7 PO10.9									C	A	R	R		• Percent of projects receiving implementation reviews	

Fig. 9 CobiT QuickStart version2 for managing projects

- Pragmatic informal practices feasible for small and medium-sized enterprises.
- Simple SME management oriented wording.
- Considering that often the governance, executive and management requirements rest in one person, the owner/entrepreneur.
- Leveraging the short communications path of an SME and its effective span of control.
- Assuming that compliance or other forms of outside reporting do rarely apply to an SME (see the QuickStart applicability tools in the previous section.

2. Validated against the first QuickStart version which was based on CobiT), and more in line with the above objectives.
3. Aligned with CobiT5 for completeness and references.
4. Structured along Plan, Build and Run themes.
5. Distributing any remaining applicable governance practices across these three domains.

The end result is a table with 7 Planning processes which has 18 management practices, 7 Build Processes with 16 management practices and 7 Run processes with 20 management practices. For each of the processes an objective statement and management practices are provided, and a set of metrics is suggested. The processes are also mapped to the CobiT5 process indicators should one wish for more detailed information generally applicable to larger organisations.

An example is follows in Table 4. The left column has the process number, the process objective and the reference to CobiT5. The middle column the

Table 4 Example of pragmatic IT management practices

Plan process	Practice	Measure
1. Define and communicate what is expected from IT *(EDM02, APO02, APO11)*	1.1. Communicate the goals of the enterprise and state what you expect from IT in support of that. Be clear on the balance needed between cost, speed, quality and risk	• Percent of joint (business/IT) presentations of challenges and solutions • Clarity of solutions
	1.2. Require that IT and business people always address problems and solutions together while thinking in terms of value for the enterprise	• Number of major deviations in IT solutions and services • Number of critical business processes supported by obsolete (or soon-to-be obsolete) infrastructure
	1.3. Consider the current state of the infrastructure and the potential of new but proven technology	

management practices to govern that process, and the right column has a number of outcome measures and performance indicators.

6 Implementing an IT Governance Framework for IT in SME's

To get the IT governance initiatives headed in the right direction, the enterprise needs an effective action plan that suits its particular needs and circumstances.

First, it is important for the head of the SME to take ownership of IT governance and set the direction to be followed. This implies:

- Challenging the entity's activities with regard to IT, to make sure IT issues and potential are uncovered.
- Guiding those responsible to make sure IT initiatives have a real business need, create value for the enterprise (i.e. new or better business capabilities, reduction of risk and/or optimization of resources) and do not negatively impact the business.
- Insisting that IT performance be measured and reported.
- Establishing regular meetings with key staff to discuss IT's performance, value and risks.
- Identifying pragmatic practices to manage IT.

The simplified and condensed framework as provided is a place to start on these pragmatic practices.

A simple method for identifying the goal and current status of implementation for each ofthe practices can then be established. One point on a scale of 1 to 7 identifies the current state and a second the goal. The scale is as folows:

1. Management is not aware of the need to implement this practice.
2. Management is aware of the need.
3. Management is committed to resolve the underlying issues.
4. Implementation has started.
5. Implementation is well under way.
6. The solution is sustainable.
7. The solution is optimised.

Some analysis is needed as not all practices may need to be implemented, or need not be implemented as thoroughly as others. The analysis needs to be based on the value and risk drivers of the entity, on what is being done now and on what should be done in the future. This can then be turned into an action plan that needs to be measured and monitored. Objectives, current status and very important, a vision of the end goal of the implementation effort, needs to be continuously shared with all involved.

While Fig. 10 provides a skeleton implementation plan, there are also some obvious but pragmatic rules that management ought to follow for such an implementation plan (ITGI 2003a, b):

- Treat the IT governance initiative as a project with a series of phases rather than a "one-off" step.
- Remember that IT governance involves most probably a different way of doing things and therefore a key success factor is people's motivation for these changes.
- Make sure there is a clear understanding of the objectives.
- Consider old and new responsibilities and engage those involved early on.
- Manage expectations. In most enterprises, achieving successful oversight of IT will take some time and is a continuous improvement process.
- Focus first on where it is easiest to make changes and deliver improvements. Build from there one step at a time.
- Do not underestimate the challenge of making changes sustainable over time.

7 Sourcing Guidelines for SME's

Probably the biggest challenge relative to governing IT in small or medium-sized enterprises is the fact that they rarely have the resources to build the automated solutions they need and are therefore dependent on outsourcers. What aggravates the problem is that these projects are usually very big given the size of the SME, and that the enterprise is very dependent on their success.

When looking at a break-down of a traditional acquisition process it is clear that several of these steps may well be performed informally in many SME's. Nevertheless, SME's need to formally address the three most important steps of this

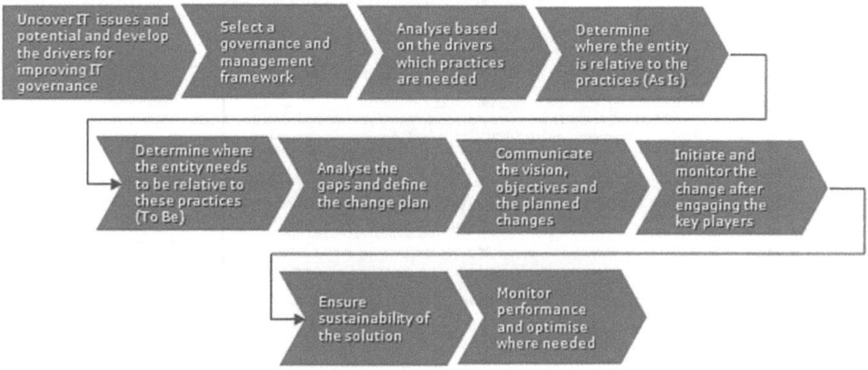

Fig. 10 A 10 step IT governance implementation plan for SME's

process and often could use a set of guidelines to assist them in making proposals, in evaluating them and in making subsequent contracts. Because the risk of failure to an SME is so large, good guidance can be obtained from a set of checklists I produced in the 90'ties at SWIFT, an institution where reliability and security are very high and hence have a similar kind of risk-aversion an SME should have when committing to a major IT related project. These guidelines can be found in Appendix 2.

It is not my intention to suggest these guidelines should be used completely and to the letter, but much of it can be of help for an SME who would like to control the risk of a major outsourcing project (Fig. 11).

The general objective of the guidelines for making an Request For Proposal (RFP) is to create an efficient and fair process, such that:

- the company obtains the product with the best fit
  - economically
  - technically and
  - organisationally.
- all risks are analysed and mitigated
- decisions are made in line with the company's mission and guiding principles
- the issuer can prove to the company's stakeholders that due diligence was applied.

The objective for evaluating the response to an RFP is to clarify for the project members and for the potential suppliers, what responses are expected, how they should be presented and how the responses to the RFP will be evaluated.

The objective of the contract guidelines is to define mutually manageable commitments to the RFP and the subsequent acquisition process, to obtain the quality service expected and to manage risks relative to premature contract termination and other liabilities. These contractual standards should be communicated during the RFP process.

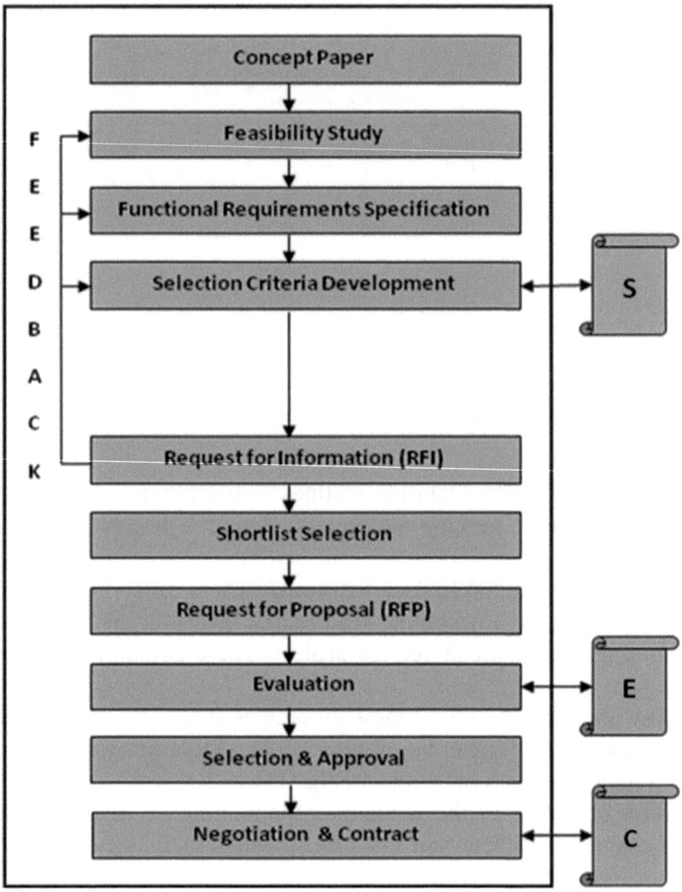

Fig. 11 Acquisition process steps

8 Research Guidance also Applicable to SME's

Following is some guidance from IT governance research from different sources that also applies to the governance of small enterprises:

- Investing in management practices has a high return on investment.
- Informal exchanges between enterprise management and key IT staff is very important.
- Getting things done on time and on budget is more important than being aligned.
- Focus on those management practices that have proven to work.

8.1 *Invest in Management Practices as they have a Better ROI that Investing in IT*

In October 2004 Mc Kinsey and the London School of Economics measured the increase in productivity from investments in IT vs. investments in management practices in 100 enterprises (McKinsey 2004).

When looking at the 4 extreme percentiles, it is clear that the return on investment in management practices is significantly higher[4] than in IT itself. Not that an SME should invest less in IT, on the contrary, there are many indications that investments in IT have a high return…if they are managed well!

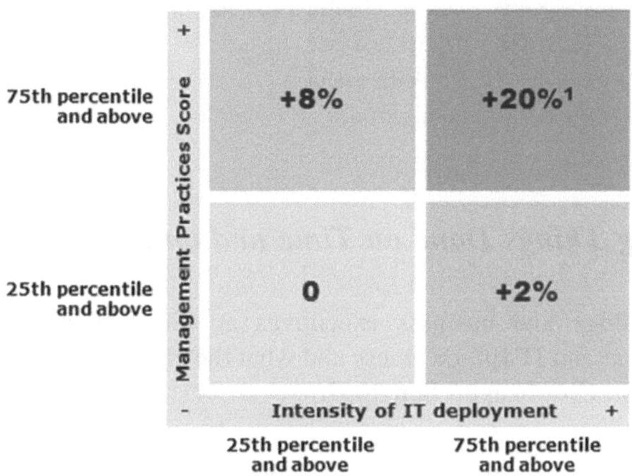

8.2 *Make Time for Informal Exchanges*

In the summer of 2012 I worked on a survey of some 90 CIO's (CIONET 2012) on Communication between CIO and CEO. In parallel I developed together with a lot of support from 4 students from the Solvay Business School in Brussels, a literature study to have a reference base for the survey results. Two somewhat related findings are of interest to SME's. First the literature study found research claiming that the reporting line of the CIO is not as important as the CIO having access to CEO and Board. Second, the web survey as well as the face to face surveys indicated that for many CIO's the informal information exchanges with CEO and Board were more useful than the formal channels. My conclusion for SME's is that their CEO's should make themselves available as much as necessary for informal exchanges with key people relative to IT. That is a governance model that really suits the type of enterprises that SME's are.

[4] Up to 20 % productivity improvement in 9 out of 10 enterprises in that quartile.

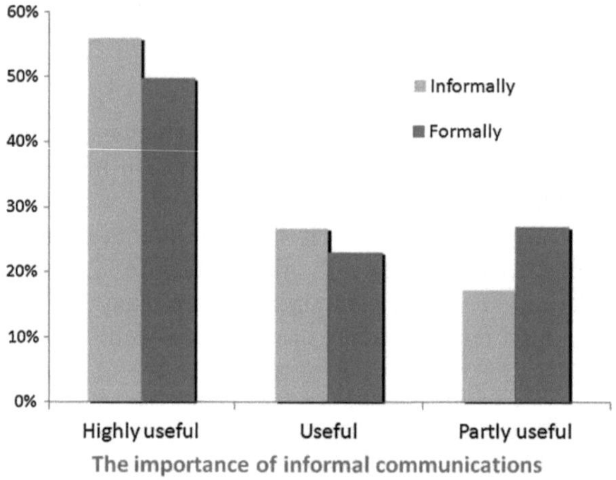

8.3 Focus on Getting Things Done on Time and on Budget

Bain &C° polled technology and business executives at 450 publicly-traded companies on IT Alignment and IT Effectiveness and what the effect is on Growth and IT Spend, published in CIO Insight, Sep 2007.

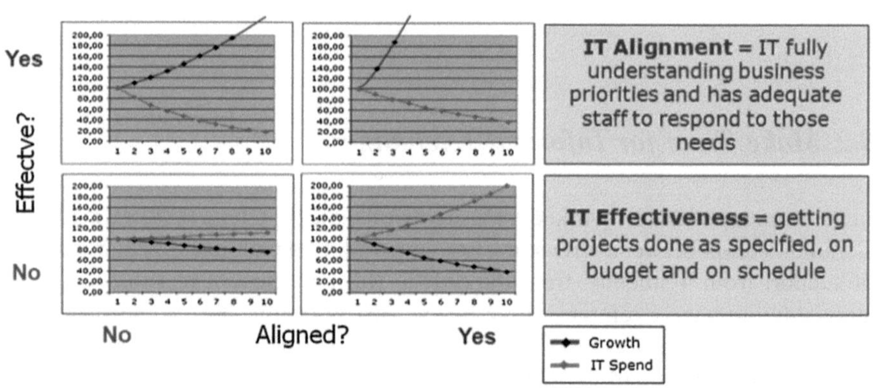

What they found was that getting things done on time and budget is so much more important to contain future IT spend and to increase the capacity to grow than being aligned with the business (Bain 2008).

8.4 Consider Management Practices that Work

What makes companies perform well? To find this holy grail of management studies, a McKinsey team analyzed upward of 100,000 questionnaires to uncover the practices of 400 business units in 230 companies around the world (McKinsey 2007).

The team eventually arrived at one winning combination:

- clear roles for employees (accountability)
- a compelling vision of change (direction), and
- an environment that encourages openness, trust, and challenge (culture).

Nothing else came close in improving organisational performance and provides clear guidance for the governance of IT in an SME: State clearly what you expect of your staff, communicate clearly and repeatedly what you want IT to achieve and that in an environment that allows for open and informal exchanges.

9 Conclusions

Enterprise governance of IT is the responsibility of the top layer of an entity to ensure IT is effective and efficient and provides value to the enterprise while keeping risks to an acceptable level. Enterprise governance of IT focuses on IT Value and IT Risk and consists of practices, organisational structures and relationships between executive and management. In Small and Medium-sized Enterprises (SME's) however, these structures and relationships very often rest in one person, the owner/entrepreneur.

As the importance of IT grows for SME's, I am reminded of a statement by Richard Nolan and F. Warren McFarlan in 'Information Technology and the Board of Directors', in Harvard Business Review of October 2005: "A lack of Board oversight for IT activities is dangerous; it puts the firm at risk in the same way that failing to audit its books would."

What does that mean for an SME which usually does not have a board or an audit function? Keeping tight control and oversight over its finances is the first priority of the entrepreneur of an SME. Therefore, oversight of IT should get a similar priority.

Furthermore, Nolan and McFarlan in the same article proclaim: "Board practices for monitoring technology investments vary widely and often wildly. As technology's cost, complexity, and consequences grow, directors need a framework to develop IT policies that fit the companies they oversee."

Like Boards of larger enterprises, the SME entrepreneur needs help and that is where frameworks can assist but they have to be concise and pragmatic, for an SME more so than for larger enterprises. CobiT is too large and complex for application in SME's and hence a simpler version called QuickStart was developed. An updated and more compact version has been provided in of Appendix 1.

The biggest value and risk challenge for SME's is the acquisition of automated solutions because they often do not have sufficient capabilities to deal with it; they do not occur often and represent a relatively large risk. Therefore a set of acquisition guidelines for assisting in often high risk IT sourcing initiatives in an SME has been provided in of Appendix 2.

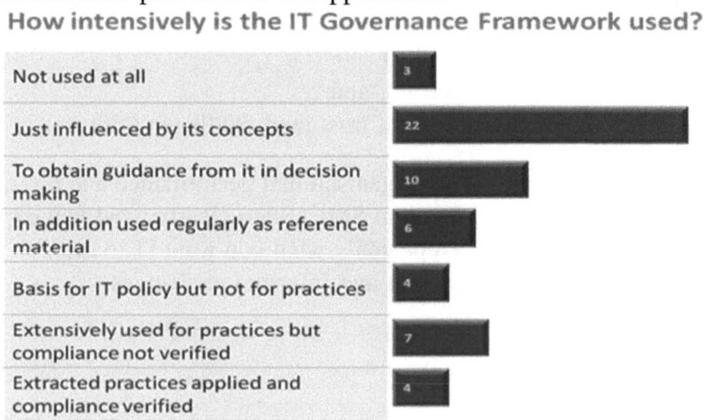

Hopefully the condensed frameworks supplied will be used more extensively than the full fledged frameworks for IT Governance by CIO's of larger companies as was shown in this CIONET survey in 2011 where 56 CIO's identified to what extent they were using CobiT for IT Governance. Nearly 70 % used it at most as a reference.

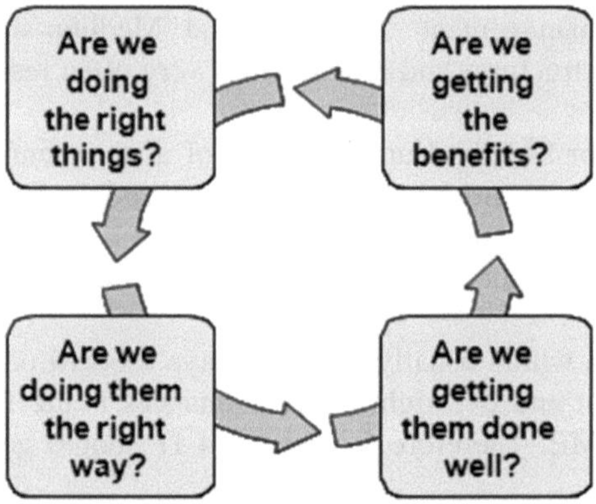

With the help of a framework the head of an SME should seek answers to these 4 questions about IT as proposed in ValIT (ITGI 2007b):

Are we doing the right things? : The strategy question. Are we doing them well? : The architecture question. Are we getting them done well? : The service quality question. And the ultimate and most important question: ARE WE GETTING THE BENEFITS?

$$Value = (Benefits - Cost)_{adjusted\ for\ Risk}$$

Benefits are expressed in terms of value and risk, the true drivers of enterprise governance of IT as I stated in the introduction. Both value and risk have something in common though: *Uncertainty*! But uncertainty can and needs to be managed. Major risks are unpredictable as the concept of Black Swans has made clear (Taleb 2007). Rather than with big contingency plans, uncertainty in *managing IT risk* needs to be dealt with by creating a flexible organisation and training people so they are aware and able to deal with the unexpected. We also have to accept that the outcome of a business case—the ideal and necessary tool for *managing IT value*, is uncertain and that we need to track the cost, time and risk variables continuously, stopping projects when they are out of bounds. Hopefully the sourcing guidelines supplied will help SME managers deal with that too.

References

Bain, C., Puryear, R., Berez, S., & Sachin, S. (2008). Is your company caught in an IT alignment trap? published in The Financial Times, June 12, 2008. http://www.bain.com/publications/articles/is-your-company-caught-in-an-it-alignment-trap.aspx.

CIONET (2011). The value of IT frameworks. CIONET 2012 publication of the Results of the CIONET survey of European CIO's on the business value of IT Frameworks, June–September 2011.

CIONET (2012). Results of the CIONET survey of European CIO's on the business value of IT Frameworks, June-September 2012.

Guldentops, E. (2004). Governing information technology through CobiT. In W. Van Grembergen (Ed.), *Strategies for information technology governance*. USA: Idea Group Publishing, ISBN 1-59140-284-0.

Guldentops, E, (2012a). Between fear and greed, IT value is losing out! *COBIT Focus*, Volume 2, ISACA, USA, April 2012, www.isaca.org.

Guldentops, E. (2012b). What do you do if the CEO tells you to get it done?. *CIONET Newsletter*, Belgium, June 2012.

ISACA (2012). CobiT5: Enabling processes. USA: Information Systems Audit and Control Association, ISBN 978-1-60420-239-7, www.isaca.org.

ISO/IEC 38500 (2008). Corporate governance of information technology. ISO/IEC JTC1 subcommittee SC7, Software and systems engineering, International Standards Organisation, Geneva, Switzerland.

ITGI (2003a). IT Governance Briefing 2nd Edition, IT Governance Institute, USA, ISBN 1-8932209-4, www.itgi.org.

ITGI (2003b). CobiT QuickStart, IT Governance Institute, ISBN 1-8932209-59-8, www.itgi.org.

ITGI (2007a). CobiT QuickStart 2nd Edition, IT Governance Institute, ISBN 1-8932209-54-1, www.itgi.org.

ITGI (2007b). Enterprise value: Governance of IT investments—The ValIT framework. IT Governance Institute, ISBN 1-933284-32-3, www.itgi.org.

ITGI (2007c). CobiT4.1, IT Governance Institute, ISBN 1-933284-72-2, www.itgi.org.

Kaplan, R. S., & Norton, D. P. (2000). *The strategy focused organization*. USA: HBS Press.

McFarlan, F. W., McKenney, J. L., & Pyburn, P. (1983). *The information archipelago: Plotting a course*. USA: Harvard Business Review Press.

McKinsey (2004). "When IT Lifts Productivity", Stephen J. Dorgan and John Dowdy, *The McKinsey Quarterly*, November 2004, http://mkqpreview1.qdweb.net/When_IT_lifts_productivity_1477.

McKinsey (2007). Management practices that work. The McKinsey Quarterly Chart Focus Newsletter, September 2007. http://www.mckinseyquarterly.com/newsletters/chartfocus/2007_09.htm.

Taleb, N. N. (2007). *The black swan: The impact of the highly improbable*. US: Random House, UK: Allen Lane, ISBN 978-1-4000-6351-2.

Van Grembergen, W., De Haes, S., & Guldentops, E. (2004). Structures, processes and relational mechanisms for IT governance. In W. Van Grembergen (Ed.), *Strategies for information technology governance*. Idea Group Publishing, USA, ISBN 1-59140-284-0.

Van Grembergen, W., De Haes, S., & Van den Brempt, H. (2009). *Building a business case for CobiT and ValIT: An executive briefing*. USA: Information Systems Audit and Control Association, www.isaca.org.

Author Biography

E. Guldentops is Lecturer and past Executive Professor at the Management School of the University of Antwerp in Belgium. He was a member and advisor of the Boards of ISACA and the IT Governance Institute from 1993 till 2007. He invented the concepts of CobiT as a business and process oriented IT framework in 1991 and was instrumental in its developments. He was active in the banking industry more notably at SWIFT where he held positions of Inspector-General and Director of Security, dealing since the late seventies with its board on matters of governance, risk, liability, compliance and security.

Business Process Management in Small Business: A Case Study

Ian Dallas and Moe Thandar Wynn

1 Introduction and Background

Business Process Management (BPM) is a management discipline concerned with lifting an organisation's performance through improvement, management and control of business processes (Jeston and Nelis 2006). It encapsulates methods, techniques and software involved throughout all stages of the process lifecycle including analysis, design, enactment and control (Ter Hofstede et al. 2003). BPM consistently rates highly on the management agendas of information professionals as a means of improving enterprise productivity (Gartner 2010). Some of the performance benefits typically targeted by BPM include greater flexibility, increased accuracy, faster execution, cost savings and reduced investment (Hammer 2010).

BPM has gained prevalence during the last decade. It evolved from a series of approaches to improving business performance including Total Quality Management, Business Process Reengineering and Six Sigma (Harmon 2010). The proliferation of Enterprise Resource Planning systems has been one major reason for BPM's increasing prominence (Al-Mudimigh 2007). While it has inherited many of the principles of the above predecessor approaches, BPM represents a more holistic discipline as opposed to a single structured methodology, toolset or software type (De Bruin and Rosemann 2005).

Although BPM is a broad discipline, there are a small number of concepts at its core. BPM recognises the capacity to separate the definition, design, analysis and refinement of processes from their execution. In this regard it is distinguished from

I. Dallas
Queensland University of Technology, Brisbane, QLD, Australia
e-mail: ian.dallas@dallasbarends.com.au

M. T. Wynn (✉)
NICTA Queensland Research Lab, Queensland University of Technology, Brisbane, QLD, Australia
e-mail: m.wynn@qut.edu.au

J. Devos et al. (eds.), *Information Systems for Small and Medium-sized Enterprises*, Progress in IS, DOI: 10.1007/978-3-642-38244-4_2,

minor, unconscious or undirected improvement of operational practices. BPM also takes an end-to-end view of processes across an organisation, in particular across functional boundaries. This differs from management approaches that are interested only in activities within functional silos (Hammer 2010).

There is an extensive body of research on BPM adoption, both of approaches and organisational conditions necessary for BPM success (see for example De Bruin and Rosemann 2005; Bucher and Winter 2010; Rummler and Ramias 2010). Within established organisations, the adoption process typically starts with fostering a general awareness of BPM and conducting isolated improvement projects on a number of processes. Over time, assuming the outcomes of such projects are seen as beneficial, activities can be corralled into a formal program and supported with a more rounded focus on strategy, governance, methods, technology, people and culture (Rosemann and vom Brocke 2010).

While much of the available research provides good guidance to larger, established organisations, there is less commentary addressing the challenges of and approaches to adoption of BPM within Small Businesses in the early stages of their establishment. Small businesses often operate under considerable cost and time pressure, with constrained human resources and have limited access to skills (Fogarty and Armstong 2009). These characteristics can negatively impact the adoption of BPM within Small Businesses. On the other hand, Small Businesses often have tight integration of activities, a strong work ethic and rapid decision-making; factors that can positively impact BPM adoption and effectiveness (Kirchmer 2011b). Recently, a number of authors attempted to address this topic with case studies conducted in a number of small and medium businesses (SMEs). Chong (2007) conducted an exploratory study on barriers to adopt BPM techniques within SMEs in the wine industry in Australia. Imanipour et al. (2012a, b) looked into inhibiting factors for BPM adoption within the Iranian E-Retail industry. While Bazhenova et al. (2012) explored the use of BPM and adaptive technologies in SMEs in emerging economies.

This chapter discusses a case study BPM initiative (the "BPM Initiative") within an Australian Small Business. It considers the significance of the Small Business sector and the potential, through its application to the sector, for BPM to contribute to addressing widespread productivity issues. After outlining the background of the case organisation, the chapter details the BPM Initiative, its activities, findings and recommendations. Based on the case study experiences, a number of potential implications have been identified for the BPM discipline in approaching the Small Business sector.

1.1 Small Business and Productivity

Small Businesses account for a significant proportion of business activity in Australia. While there is no universally accepted definition, for statistical purposes the Australian Bureau of Statistics defines businesses with 0–19 employees as

Small Businesses (Australian Bureau of Statistics 2008). As at June 2010 there were more than 1.9 million Small Businesses in Australia, accounting for over 47 % of employment in major business sectors (Key Statistics Australian Small Business 2011).

Over the past decade, Australia has experienced a slump in productivity (Parham 2012). Productivity growth is critical in addressing major issues such as coping with an ageing population and meeting the fiscal challenges of the Global Financial Crisis (Banks 2011). Respected economists have noted that improvements in productivity depend on decisions taken and implemented within businesses (Eslake 2011). Arguably, BPM has a significant role to play in achieving productivity growth within businesses. With Small Businesses comprising a large proportion of Australian business, successful, widespread adoption of BPM within this sector could help achieve meaningful inroads into productivity improvement.

1.2 Research Approach

This case study was developed to explore the research question:

Can mainstream BPM tools, techniques and technologies be successfully applied in a Small Business environment? What are the advantages of applying BPM in a Small Business?

A case study approach has been adopted due to the method's effectiveness in examining application in real-world scenarios, particularly in emerging research domains (Yin 2003). From a practical perspective, it also provided an opportunity to contribute a further example of the application of BPM within a Small Business. Such examples are important if the discipline is to gain momentum within the Small Business sector. While it is recognised that observations from a single case study cannot accurately represent the diverse nature of small businesses and that the requirements and the findings cannot be generalised without conducting multiple case-studies (Yin 2003), it is hoped that insights gained from this case study may serve to stimulate further research into this important area.

The case study involved participation in a BPM Initiative to develop and test key elements of process infrastructure for a Small Business. The main tasks were:

1. Preparing a Process Governance Framework;
2. Preparing a Process Architecture;
3. Modelling the core service delivery processes;
4. Developing a pilot Process and Procedures Library; and
5. Developing a demonstration Resource Allocation System.

A detailed scoping exercise was conducted to gain an understanding of the case organisation's plans, strategy, method of client engagement and organisational structures.

The organisational stakeholders ("Stakeholders") in the BPM Initiative were:

- *Management*—The owner and director of the organisation who currently holds executive management responsibility;
- *Staff*—Personnel involved in day-to-day service delivery processes; and
- *Consultants*—Specialist Management Accounting consultants currently providing domain expertise to the organisation.

Observations were made during participation in each of the tasks. Stakeholders were also consulted after each task to seek their feedback on the benefits and issues arising from the application of the approaches, techniques and technologies both within the case organisation and within Small Businesses generally.

2 The Case Organisation

The case organisation ("The Business") was established to develop a suite of outsourced Management Accounting services designed to meet the needs of small and medium sized, professional services businesses. It is currently in pilot phase, testing its service model and developing underlying business processes and systems while providing a full suite of services to a number of pilot clients. The Business' long-term viability and competitiveness will heavily rely on the efficient and effective delivery of business processes. Strategically, the adoption of Business Process Management is targeted to support:

- Consistent quality and timeliness of outputs versus competitors who fail to reliably meet standards and deadlines;
- Better labour management ensuring that tasks can be performed by the cheapest resource versus competitors who tend to utilise single, more highly qualified resources to complete entire processes; and
- The capacity to implement technologies (such as workflow systems, document management systems, scanning and business intelligence) the use of which is currently limited amongst competitors.

Importantly, the evolution of The Business' structure and culture as a process-aware organisation is seen as a strategic imperative. There is minimal culture or practice currently embedded within the organisation, meaning there is more focus on establishing healthy attitudes and modes-of-operation rather than the need to change the status quo. Management wishes to ensure that The Business evolves with a strong focus on process in order to avoid the need to change dysfunctional systems and behaviours in the future.

3 Development of Process Infrastructure

The first author worked with Management to determine the activities that would be involved in the Initiative, as outlined in Sect. 2 above. It was identified that The Business would require the documentation of processes for the following purposes:

- To support alignment of different Stakeholder perspectives of processes (e.g., management, staff and client understanding of how processes are undertaken);
- As a training guide and reference source for staff;
- To assist in process design and improvement efforts; and
- To help inform the development of information systems.

A Process Governance Framework and Process Architecture were needed to guide and control the development of processes and documentation (Braganza and Lambert 2000; Davis and Brabänder 2007). Core service delivery processes were modelled and documented and a Process and Procedures Library was developed as a means of deploying process documentation to business users. Finally, a demonstration resource allocation system was developed to showcase how technology could be employed to automate aspects of the core service delivery processes.

3.1 Process Governance Framework

A Process Governance Framework provides a high-level layer of BPM definition and a frame of reference to guide activities and ensure consistency of approach (Kirchmer 2011a). A Process Governance Framework was developed that addressed the following:

- *Decision-making*—Key categories of process decisions were identified and responsibilities for each category were assigned to organisational roles.
- *Process Roles and Responsibilities*—Guidelines were developed to assist in determining who should be appointed as the Process Owner of each process. Responsibilities were also outlined for process approval, feedback and analysis support.
- *Process Standards*—Standards were detailed for process referencing, storage, modelling notation and tools.
- *Measurement and Compliance*—A set of performance measures and compliance activities were identified. Due to the relative infancy of The Business, these were focussed on near-term BPM activities.

The following **findings** were identified during preparation of the Process Governance Framework and subsequent Stakeholder consultations:

- *Perceptions of Relevance*—During scoping and early development, Stakeholders found it difficult to fully appreciate the relevance of a Process Governance

Framework. It was only after the application of the completed framework in the development of the process models and other process infrastructure that Stakeholders more fully appreciated the need for the framework.

- *Limited Availability of Practical Guidance and References*—The Initiative encountered a lack of readily available examples of Process Governance Frameworks. There was also limited practical guidance available on how to develop such a framework. This made the process far more time consuming than could be the case if best-practise guides, templates and examples were readily available.
- *Industry Standards*—Where industry standards were available, for example Business Process Model and Notation (BPMN), they enabled considerable rigour to be easily incorporated into the framework. There was also a wealth of tools and resources available in the public domain to assist with education and training of users.
- *Measurement and Compliance*—Developing measurement and compliance elements of the Process Governance Framework was made difficult by the infancy of BPM within the organisation. There was a risk that measures and controls would either yield meaningless results or consume considerable resources. The Stakeholders contemplated excluding measurement and compliance from the framework altogether, but settled on a set of measures which principally focused on establishment and adoption of BPM and fairly simple, review-based controls.

Based on the case study experiences and findings related to the Process Governance Framework, the following **observations** can be made:

- *Use of Industry Standards*—Industry BPM standards, such as BPMN, are likely to be readily applicable within many Small Business environments. Practitioners undertaking Small Businesses BPM initiatives should consider adopting industry standards to minimise the effort required in developing, communicating and using the process infrastructure.
- *Small Business, BPM Reference Base*—A reference base of Small Business BPM resources including practical guides and examples would assist Small Businesses to articulate BPM practice and benefits as well as enabling such businesses to more efficiently establish important BPM foundations. Such a resource would be most effective if it is broad-based (that is, not only focussed on notations and technical standards) and readily available at low or no cost.
- *BPM Measurement and Compliance*—When working with establishing businesses, BPM practitioners may prefer to focus measurement and compliance targets on process infrastructure development milestones rather than measures of adoption, utilisation and maturity, as may be the case in later stages of the business' lifecycle.

3.2 Process Architecture

A Process Architecture sets out at a high level how business processes are co-ordinated to support the achievement of organisational strategy and objectives. The structure and principles set out in the Process Architecture provides an overall roadmap for the development of business processes (Jeston and Nelis 2006).

A six-level Process Architecture was developed, as outlined in Fig. 1, and documented. Model numbering guidelines were developed in a cascading order for each level.

The Process Architecture involves a reasonably typical cascading hierarchy of process levels, with each lower level representing processes in greater detail. Three types of Process Variants (Reference, Industry and Client) are recognised for processes in levels 3–6.

The Level 1 Strategic Activities were developed using the Strategy, Operations and Support categories, as outlined in Fig. 2.

The following **findings** were identified from observations during preparation of the Process Architecture and subsequent Stakeholder consultations:

- *Limited Availability of Practical Guidance and References*—While examples of process architectures were more readily available than was the case for process

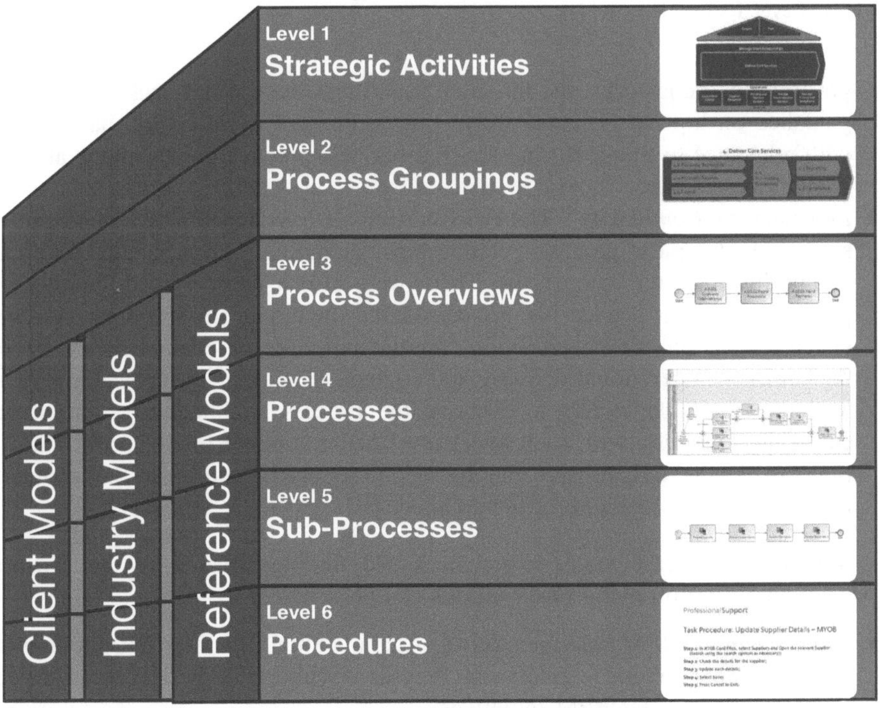

Fig. 1 Business process architecture

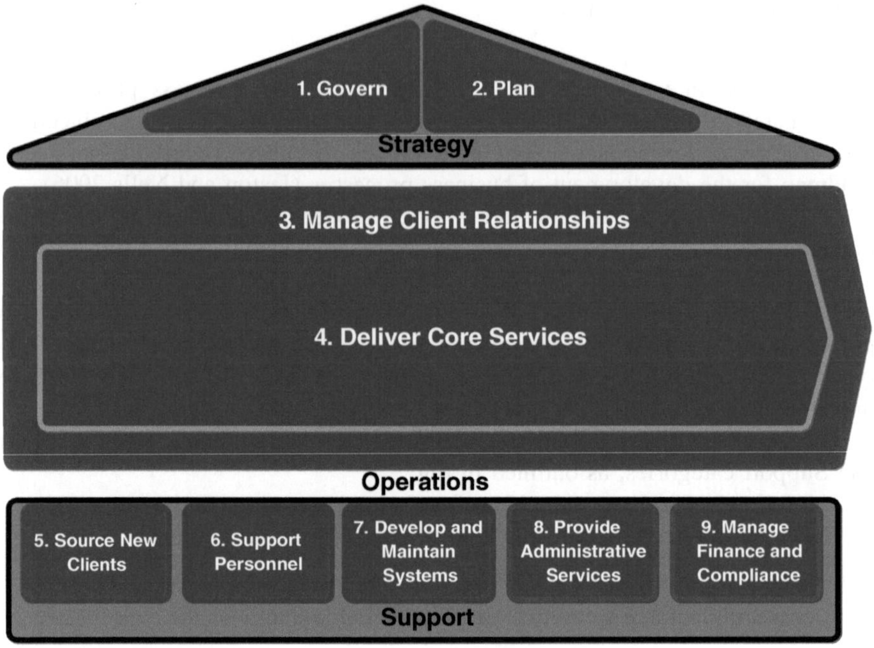

Fig. 2 Level 1 strategic activities

governance frameworks, the initiative found that there was a lack of practical guidance on how to go about developing a Process Architecture, particularly with relevance to Small Businesses. Further best-practice guides and examples would have assisted.

- *Representing Complexity*—The Process Architecture needed to accommodate a series of complex process relationships including variants and different compositions of the same tasks. There were also a number of different user perspectives that needed to be considered including information systems development, service specification (for the purposes of client Service Level Agreements), operational delivery and strategic planning. There was a natural tendency for Stakeholders to perceive the Process Architecture as a simple cascading hierarchy with each lower level being a subset of its parent. Unfortunately, this led to confusion and the need to regularly reiterate to Stakeholders the purposes and structure of the architecture.

Based on the case study experiences and findings related to the Process Architecture, the following **observations** can been made:

- *Small Business, BPM Reference Base*—Again, a Small Business BPM reference base including practical guides on Process Architecture development would assist Small Business BPM initiatives.

- *Stakeholder Perceptions*—When developing Process Architectures with "Business" stakeholders as well as "Technical" stakeholders, it may be beneficial for BPM practitioners to reinforce the degree of abstraction involved. This may help to reduce confusion that can arise from trying to rigidly represent and reconcile different perspectives of complex process relationships.

3.3 Process Modelling

Process models were prepared for 22 processes which comprise core service delivery, using Business Process Model and Notation (BPMN) Version 2.0 2011). Figure 3 lists the processes which were modelled under each core service delivery heading.

The modelling process involved documentation review, process observation, model drafting, Stakeholder review and revision. The following findings were identified during process modelling and subsequent Stakeholder consultations:

- *Modelling Tools and Standards*—Mainstream tools and standards were adopted in the modelling process. These were generally easy to use and readily applicable within the Small Business context.
- *Modelling Effort*—The modelling effort was significantly less difficult and resource-consuming than was anticipated. While process modelling within an

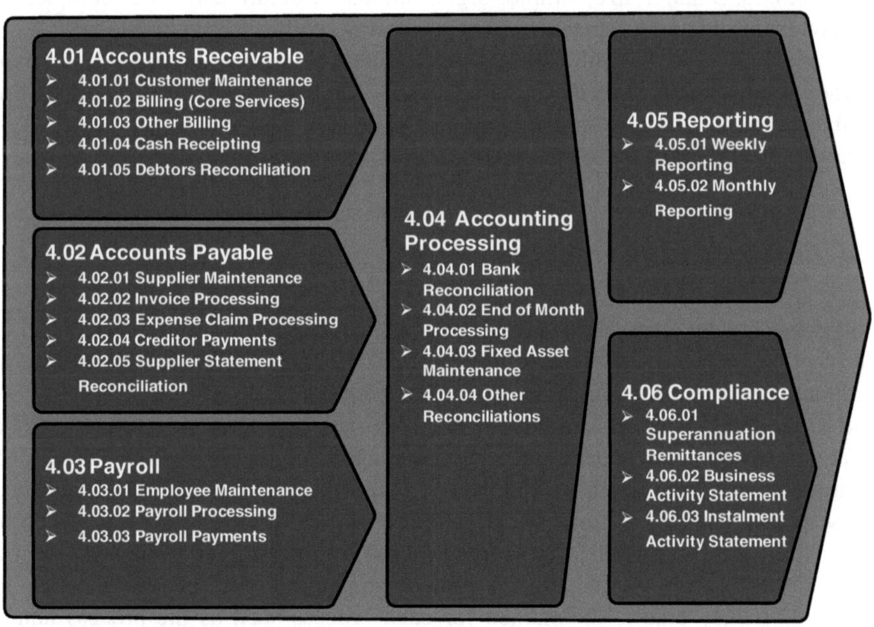

Fig. 3 Processes by core service delivery area

organisation in its infancy has some challenges, the small number of Stakeholders and the absence of highly-embedded work practices, meant that the modelling process did not require as much consultation or dialog about change as can be the case in more developed organisations.

- *BPM Skills*—Another factor that influenced the modelling effort was the first author's combination of BPM, domain and organisational expertise. The process modelling could have taken much longer to complete if it demanded collaboration between separate BPM, domain and organisational professionals.
- *Elicitation Methodology*—It was found that preparing draft models which could be adjusted in consultation with Stakeholders resulted in a much more efficient process than attempting to develop models from scratch in a workshop context. The BPM practitioners' domain expertise and the small organisation size were important factors that enabled this methodology.

Based on the case study experiences and findings from process modelling, the following **observations** can be made:

- *Modelling Tools and Standards*—Practitioners undertaking process modelling in Small Businesses should consider adopting mainstream modelling tools. This will enable stakeholders to leverage the extensive base of supporting resources available, maximise modelling efficiency and ensure usability of process models.
- *Small Business BPM Methodologies*—Small Business BPM initiatives may benefit from adopting different methodologies to those typically used in larger businesses. Smaller size, simpler organisational structure and lower complexity may enable methodologies that are not feasible within larger businesses.
- *BPM Skills*—The breadth of BPM practitioners' expertise, particularly domain and organisational experience, will influence the efficiency with which they are able to conduct initiatives within Small Businesses. This will be an important, if not essential, influence on the feasibility of Small Business BPM initiatives.

3.4 Process and Procedures Library

Following the development of process models, Stakeholders identified the need to deploy these process assets to business users to support training and up-skilling of staff and as a reference source during service delivery. A proof-of-concept Process and Procedures Library was developed to provide an example of how such a reference source may operate. It was developed on the Microsoft Office 365 SharePoint platform which was adopted by The Business for other document and knowledge management functions. Example pages from the Library are shown in Fig. 4. The Library enables the entire Process Architecture to be navigated (via click-through) from Strategic Activities to detailed Processes and through to Procedures. Key data is maintained for each process such as the process name, reference, owner and designer.

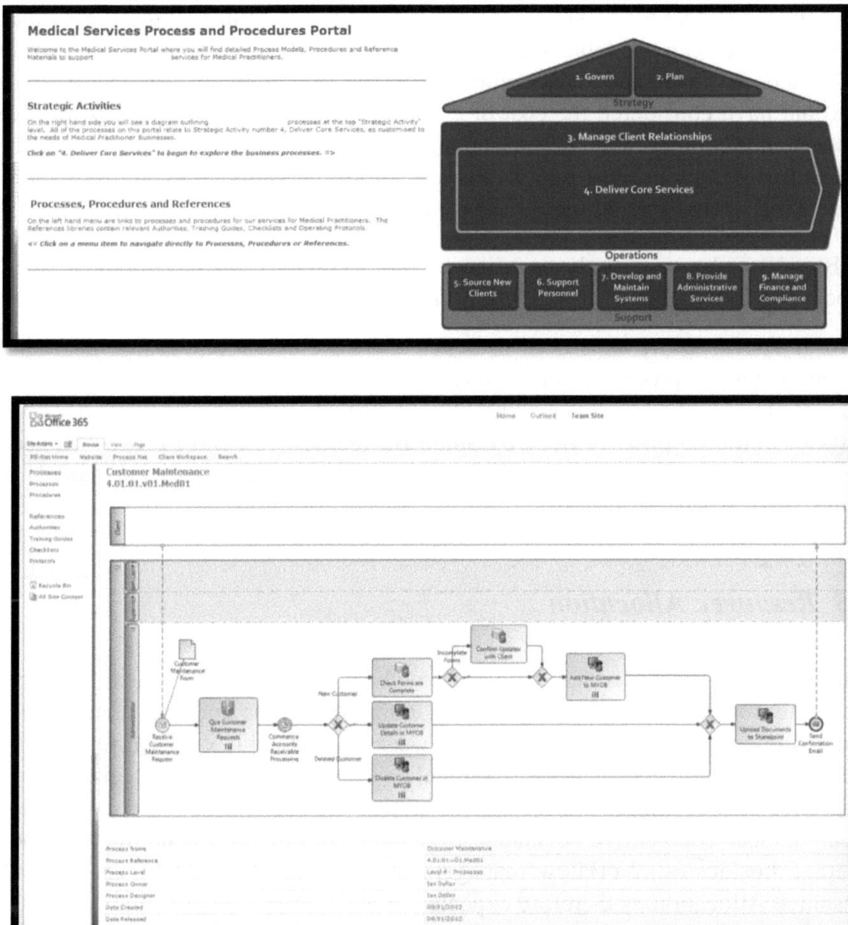

Fig. 4 Example pages—process and procedures library. Example screenshot showing strategic activities. Example screenshot showing a process model

The following **findings** were identified during the development of the Process and Procedures Library and subsequent Stakeholder consultations:

- *BPM Tools*—Deployment of the processes to business users to support training and as a reference source during service delivery was one of the key uses for the documented business processes. Stakeholders believed that this could be the case in many Small Businesses. Despite this the initiative was not able to identify any low or no-cost BPM software tool that enabled adequate deployment of process models and documentation to business users. Hence the Process and Procedures Library needed to be developed as a bespoke solution.
- *Development Skills*—A significant effort was required to develop the Process and Procedures Library. The skills were made available as part of the research

effort at no charge. Stakeholders noted that it was unlikely that the skillsets would have been available amongst typical Small Business information systems advisers. Even if such skills could be sourced, it is unlikely that The Business would have considered the cost of employing the skills as financially feasible.
- *Maintenance*—As with development, an outstanding issue will be whether The Business will be able to access and afford the skills necessary to maintain the Process and Procedures Library on an ongoing basis.

Based on the case study experiences and findings from development of the Process and Procedures Library, the following **observations** can be made:

- *BPM Tools*—BPM tools need to better address efficient and easily maintained deployment of process assets to business users.
- *BPM Skills*—The cost and availability of BPM expertise will likely be a limiting factor in the adoption of BPM by Small Businesses. The BPM Profession needs to further consider the type of skills required and the best delivery models for the Small Business sector.

3.5 Resource Allocation

The Business' core service delivery involves a series of cyclical processes requiring co-ordination of human tasks, communications and data transmission. The majority of processes conform to a weekly or monthly cycle. Effective allocation and supervision of work is critical to achieving the level of management efficiency and leverage (maximum delegation to junior resources) required to create a clear competitive advantage over more traditional accounting and bookkeeping businesses. Workflow management (Ouyang et al. 2010), in particular Resource Allocation, is therefore expected to be an important strategic component of The Business' process infrastructure, particularly as it grows in number of clients and number of personnel.

In order to provide Management with a clearer understanding of how a Resource Allocation system, as part of process automation efforts, may be implemented within The Business and its potential benefits, a demonstration pilot Resource Allocation system was developed. The YAWL workflow language and workflow system were used as the platform for development of the pilot (van der Aalst and Ter Hofstede 2005). Two YAWL workflows were developed to represent examples of workflow processes within The Business. Figure 5 outlines the organisational hierarchy based on the expected medium-term team structure and Table 1 lists the attributes which were assumed for the purpose of the demonstration.

A number of core delivery processes of the Businesses which were part of the Weekly Processing cycle was modelled as a YAWL workflow (see Fig. 6).

In addition to regular processing requirements, the Business also handles ad-hoc queries from the clients. It is a relatively simple process whereby a query is

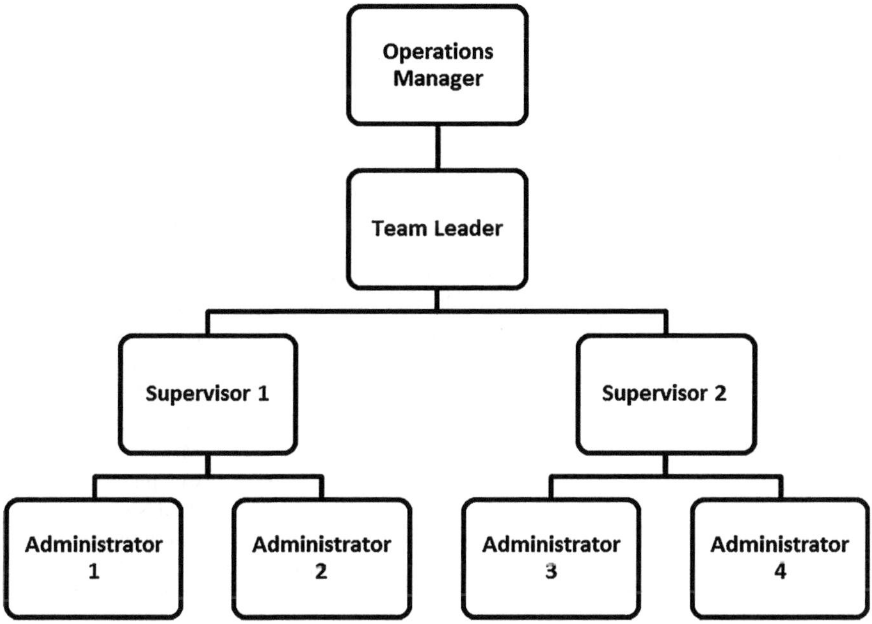

Fig. 5 Organisational hierarchy

received, investigated, reviewed if necessary and then a response is the output. The YAWL model for this query process is detailed in Fig. 7.

A series of ten demonstration cases were specified; six cases of weekly process and four cases of ad-hoc query process. To demonstrate the Resource Allocation system, the ten cases were executed concurrently to show how the system handles work allocation in real-time. Stakeholders were able to view participant work lists and see how tasks are allocated, completed and re-assigned. They could also see how data is captured and handled by the system including how it can control the flow and allocation of work.

The following **findings** were identified during the development of the Resource Allocation system and subsequent Stakeholder consultations:

- *Automation Benefits*—Stakeholder feedback strongly recognised the benefits of a Resource Allocation system to The Business. The benefits are expected to be similar in nature to those expected within a larger business including reduced labour costs, more consistent service delivery and better activity monitoring capabilities.
- *Workflow System*—The workflow system supported most of the resource allocation capabilities required by The Business. Further development work would be required to address user interface and data integration issues.
- *BPM Skills*—The availability of BPM expertise to support the development and maintenance of the Resource Allocation system was raised as a major consideration in its adoption within this Small Business environment.

Table 1 Organisational model attributes

Organisational attribute	YAWL category	Description	Options
Delivery unit	Role	A particular service unit under a supervisor	Team blue Team red
Position	Position	The position within the organisational hierarchy	Operations manager Team leader Supervisor Administrator
Service line	Role	Indicates competence to perform services for the given service line	Legal Medical
Competency	Capability	Indicates competence to undertake service	Accounts receivable Accounts payable Payroll Accounting Management reporting Compliance Analysis Consulting
Client	Role	Indicates familiarity/assignment to client	Clients A–F

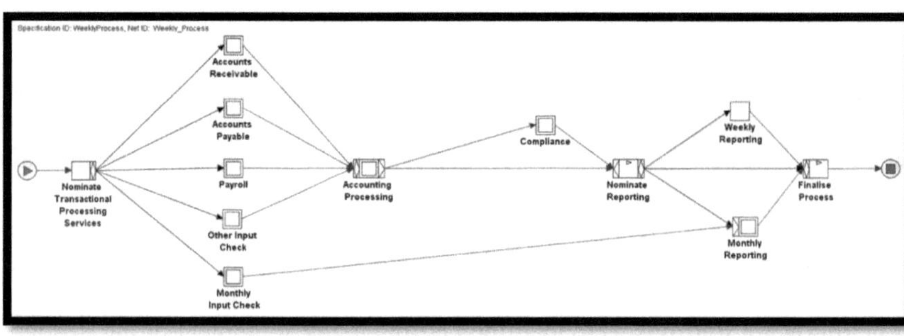

Fig. 6 A YAWL workflow model of (weekly) processing activities

Based on the case study experiences and findings from development of the resource allocation system, the following **observations** can be made:

- *Workflow Systems*—While capable and flexible workflow systems are available at low or no cost, the expense of adapting these tools for use may make their adoption prohibitive for Small Businesses. Further development of these products into packages incorporating more capable, user-friendly interfaces, would improve the feasibility of adopting such systems within Small Businesses.

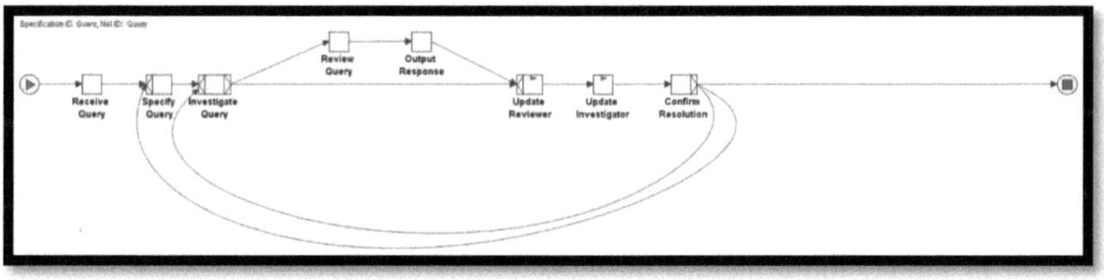

Fig. 7 A YAWL workflow modelling depicting handling of ad-hoc queries

- *BPM Skills*—The BPM profession will need to consider how to make workflow skills more available and affordable if process automation is to be brought within the reach of Small Businesses.

4 Key Observations

4.1 BPM Benefits

The case study has demonstrated that there is considerable scope for The Business to leverage benefits through BPM. The process models and documentation on the Process and Procedures Library have proved to be useful training and reference tools, improving the efficiency of client service implementation and ongoing delivery. They have also assisted in gaining a consistent, shared understanding of how work is undertaken and provided a means of capturing procedural information that would otherwise be retained by individuals as tacit knowledge.

Demonstrating the capabilities of the Resource Allocation system has raised awareness of the potential for such systems within The Business. Stakeholders have indicated that prior to the demonstration, would have likely resorted to manual checklists, task lists or spread sheet-based allocation schedules. The Business will proceed with further development and a live pilot of the system. Consideration is also being given to how the workflow system can be leveraged to support other capabilities including automation of manual tasks, status/progress reporting to clients, workforce decentralisation and improvements to worker interfaces (such as process context awareness).

BPM awareness is actively shaping Management's medium and long-term plans. For example, Management are using processes documentation to develop a Service Level Agreement with performance measures for each core service area. This could lead to The Business becoming one of the first in its market to offer service level guarantees; a significant strategic differentiator. Management is also using this newfound understanding of the business processes to identify critical communication points. This enables them with protocols and technologies that will allow services to be delivered over large geographical distances. This will support a better offering to more isolated, regional markets which often have had trouble accessing quality service providers.

Many of the potential benefits are similar in nature to those that would be targeted in larger, more mature businesses. Interestingly, while the quantum of operational benefits may be smaller than in higher-volume businesses, substantial strategic benefits have been identified that are arguably easier to leverage due to The Business' agility and flat decision-making structure.

4.2 Efficiency

The efficiency of BPM was a significant focus for Management who were concerned about the potential financial cost and drain on resources. As with many Small Businesses, particularly in the establishment phase, there was a host of competing priorities for a constrained investment pool. The Initiative tasks could be divided into two categories: those that Stakeholders perceived as "value-adding"; and those that were perceived as "non-value-adding".

Perceived non-value-adding tasks such as the development of the Process Governance Framework and Process Architecture, consumed a significant amount of time. Unfortunately, there were few templates or best-practice examples available in the public domain to assist with these tasks. If these materials were readily available, the efficiency of perceived non-value-adding tasks could have been vastly improved.

Process modelling was perceived as value-adding because the outputs were practical, tangible and able to be immediately put to use by Stakeholders. Interestingly, the modelling effort did not take as long as expected. This was attributed to the flat decision-making structure, the combined BPM and domain expertise available and the elicitation methodology adopted. The Process and Procedures Library and Resource Allocation tasks, which were also perceived as value-adding, could have been made more efficient if tools and systems were better tailored to the needs of business users in a Small Business environment.

Overall, with better templates and best-practices, particularly those that might enable perceived non-value-adding tasks to be completed more quickly, and some further tailoring of tools towards Small Business users, Stakeholders felt that the exercise could have been readily conducted within The Business' normal investment limitations.

4.3 Compatibility of BPM Tools and Standards

Where they were available, mainstream BPM tools, standards and systems were adopted. These included BPMN, process modelling tools and workflow systems. In general these were found to be as useful in the Small Business environment as would be expected in a larger business environment. The availability of BPM standards and tools on a low or no-cost basis made it particularly easy to adopt mainstream methods, as opposed to developing approaches and tools from the ground up. This is potentially more important in a Small Business context than in larger businesses that may be better able to invest in development of tools and standards.

The process modelling tools that were investigated and ultimately adopted were found to be capable model design tools, but lacked the ability to deploy process models to business users in a user-friendly and controlled format. No doubt, enterprise-level systems are available with better business user interfaces, but many Small Businesses would have trouble justifying an investment is such a system, particularly in the early stages of BPM maturity.

The workflow system (YAWL) was found to have functionality and pattern support that was more than adequate for the near-term needs of The Business. It has been developed as a highly customisable platform which provides significant flexibility to organisations to adapt it to their particular needs. Despite its capabilities, some of the interfaces would need to be enriched for adoption by The Business in a live environment. A more "packaged" version with improved interfaces may be more attractive to Small Businesses as it would reduce or eliminate customisation effort, even if this came at the expense of flexibility.

4.4 Resources and Skills

It was noted that, without the close involvement of the authors, The Business would have had difficulty accessing appropriately skilled BPM resources. Management indicated that the skills would not have been available in-house and would have been difficult to source amongst consultants typically servicing the sector.

Accessing skills to maintain the process infrastructure (both content and technical structure) may also prove difficult. It is anticipated that a standardised and documented maintenance regime together with appropriate training of in-house personnel could address many of these concerns.

4.5 Culture

The Initiative did not specifically address the cultural enablers or barriers to BPM. However, it should be noted that Stakeholders generally exhibited a very positive and proactive attitude to BPM and process improvement. Within The Business, innovation through BPM is seen as an imperative and is driving a commitment to explore the area.

The Director, who has considerable experience in consulting to Small Businesses, indicated that it was his belief that in many Small Businesses the cultural setting could create resistance to BPM and to change more generally. Although the issue was not fully explored, the cultural setting was almost certainly a critical precondition to the mandate for, and ultimately the achievements of, the Initiative within The Business.

5 Implications

The case study points to a range of potential implications for the BPM discipline. An overarching question is whether there is a need for a more defined stream of BPM research and practice focussing specifically on Small Business. This stream would potentially be less concerned with ground-breaking discoveries, instead focusing on how to distil the large body of existing BPM knowledge into a set of tools, techniques, best-practices, software and approaches which are more practical and relevant to Small Businesses.

Some key implications identified from the case study are outlined below. These could be focus areas for a more defined Small Business BPM stream.

5.1 BPM Awareness Within Small Businesses

With BPM traditionally being perceived as the domain of larger businesses, Small Businesses could benefit from a greater awareness of the possible application and benefits of BPM within the sector (Imanipour et al. 2012a, b). Further examples and case studies would assist practitioners working with Small Businesses to articulate the processes and likely benefits of BPM. Creating greater awareness of key Small Business BPM barriers and enablers may help organisations to identify whether they are appropriate candidates for BPM adoption. It may also be beneficial to identify the characteristics of Small Businesses that may indicate a strategic disposition to BPM; for example a desire to pursue rapid growth and commercialisation.

Consideration may also be given to whether BPM maturity models and implementation roadmaps need to be tailored or simplified for Small Businesses.

In particular, what BPM initiatives should developing businesses be targeting at different stages in their lifecycle. For example, does it make sense to set the process landscape and begin capturing process models early in a business' development; when is a good time to tackle process automation?

5.2 BPM Approach in Small Businesses

Traditionally, many BPM efforts have been initiated as part of information systems projects where there is a well-trodden regime typically involving a number of BPM participants including vendors, implementation consultants and change managers (Al-Mudimigh 2007). In more recent times attention has turned to how BPM capabilities can be established and managed independently from information systems projects (Rosemann 2010). The experiences of this case study indicate that for some, potentially many, Small Businesses neither approach will work. In light of resource and investment constraints that many Small Businesses face, engaging teams of external consultants or building dedicated in-house capabilities will not be feasible.

There is scope to further investigate the adaptation of delivery models to achieve the maximum BPM impact for Small Businesses. This includes consideration of resourcing models and decision-making processes for BPM projects that take advantage of organisational agility and flatter management structures. Techniques, toolsets (further discussed in Sect. 0 below) and expertise (further discussed in Sect. 0 below) will likely require some shaping alongside new delivery models.

5.3 BPM Tools and Techniques for Small Businesses

The Initiative found that many mainstream BPM tools and techniques could be applied in a Small Business environment. However, there is a need to better adapt some tools and to provide a more complete resource set to make the adoption and ongoing management of BPM by the sector as efficient and cost-effective as possible. Some key considerations in this process are:

- Enabling streamlined adoption through practical guides and templates (for example of Process Architectures and Process Governance Frameworks), even if these came at the expense of exhaustiveness;
- Ensuring tools are developed with sufficient focus on potential deployment to business users as opposed to process analysts and software developers;
- Providing low-cost, business-ready systems even if they are less flexible or customisable than existing products;
- Supporting low-cost, self-managed BPM maintenance regimes, both for systems and content.

5.4 BPM Practitioners

The pursuit of more efficient BPM approaches and the adaptation of BPM delivery models, tools and technologies will potentially create demand for a different profile of Small Business BPM practitioner compared with their larger business counterparts. As well as possessing a good knowledge of Small Business BPM benefits, delivery models, tools and techniques, the often resource-constrained environment is likely to require practitioners to have a greater breadth of experience. This may include industry/domain and software expertise as practitioners may not be afforded the luxury of engaging supplementary domain or vendor expertise.

These demands may mean that Small Business BPM practitioners should consider different career pathways to other BPM practitioners. For example, Small Business BPM practitioners may be better grown from experienced workers, managers or consultants within Small Business domains who have undertaken supplementary BPM training, as opposed to "born and bred" BPM practitioners.

6 Conclusions

This chapter presented a case study of the development of process infrastructure within an establishing Small Business. The case study has shown that mainstream BPM tools and techniques can be applied in a Small Business environment to yield benefits similar in nature to those that would be targeted in larger businesses. Limited availability of a comprehensive reference source of Small Business BPM tools, templates, examples and expertise was a major issue encountered during the initiative. The environment presented constraints on financial and human resources, but the flat organisational and decision-making structure, limited number of stakeholders and the proactive culture enabled many tasks to progress more rapidly than anticipated.

A number of potential implications have been identified for further consideration by the BPM discipline including whether there is a need for a more defined Small Business BPM stream. Such a stream could better focus on raising BPM awareness in the sector and tailoring standards, tools, techniques and templates to enable more efficient application of BPM within Small Businesses. It was also identified that further consideration needs to be given to the development of Small Business specific implementation and delivery methodologies as well as supporting practitioner skillsets in order for the discipline to better meet the demands of the sector.

The case study presented here has a number of limitations. It has involved observations made within a single business services organisation based in Australia. The organisation is in a very specific stage in its business lifecycle; establishment. The study has not explored whether the observations and findings would be equally applicable to organisations of different sizes or those operating in different industries, cultures or jurisdictions. Nor has it investigated whether the experiences would have been different within businesses that are in a more developed stage of their life-cycle. It should also be mentioned that the case organisation possessed a distinct culture which, if not present in other organisations, could lead to different experiences and outcomes in relation to BPM initiatives. It is therefore difficult to discern the degree to which the observations can be generalised to the wider Small Business sector.

Acknowledgments We wish to thank The Business and the Stakeholders for allowing the case study to be conducted within the organisation and for their valuable contributions. This research has received ethical clearance by the Queensland University of Technology University Human Research Ethics Committee (Approval number: 1100001155). It has been confirmed as meeting the requirements of the National Statement on Ethical Conduct in Human Research.

References

Al-Mudimigh, A. S. (2007). The role and impact of business process management in enterprise systems implementation. *Business Process Management Journal, 13*(6), 866–874.

Australian Bureau of Statistics, (2008). Australian small business operators: Findings from the 2005 and 2006 characteristics of small business surveys, volume cat no 8127.0, Canberra: Australian Bureau of Statistics.

Banks, G. (2011). *Successful reform: Past lessons, future challenges*. Paper presented at the productivity commission, Sydney. 8 December 2010.

Bazhenova, E., Taratukhin, V., & Becker, J. (2012). *Towards on business process management on small-to medium enterprises in the emerging economies*. 7th International Forum on Strategic Strategic Technology (IFOST), pp 1–5.

Braganza, A., & Lambert, R. (2000). Strategic integration: Developing a process–governance framework. *Knowledge and Process Management, 7*(3), 177–186.

Bucher, T., & Winter, R. (2010). Taxonomy of business process management approaches. In J. vom Brocke & M. Rosemann (Eds.), *Handbook on business process management 2. International handbooks on information systems* (pp. 93–114). Berlin Heidelberg: Springer, doi:10.1007/978-3-642-01982-1_5.

Business Process Model and Notation (BPMN) Version 2.0. (2011). The object management group. http://www.omg.org/spec/BPMN/2.0. Accessed 29 July 2012.

Chong, S. (2007). Business process management for SMEs: An exploratory study of implementation factors for the Australian wine industry. *Journal of Information Systems and Small Business, 1*(1–2), 41–58.

Davis, R., & Brabänder, E. (2007). *Business process architecture with ARIS Design Platform*. London: Springer. doi:10.1007/978-1-84628-613-1_4.

De Bruin, T., & Rosemann, M. (2005). *Towards a business process management maturity model*. Paper presented at the ECIS 2005 Proceedings of the 13th European Conference on Information Systems, CD Rom.

Eslake, S. (2011). *Productivity: The lost decade*. Paper presented at the Annual Policy Conference of the Reserve Bank of Australia, Sydney, 15 August 2011.

Gartner (2010) Leading in times of transition: The 2010 CIO Agenda.

Gerard Fogarty, & Douglas Bruce Armstrong (2009). Modelling the interactions among factors that influence successful computerisation of small business. *Australasian Journal of Information Systems* 15(2)

Hammer, M. (2010). What is business process management? In J. vom Brocke & M Rosemann (Eds.), *Handbook on business process management 1. International handbooks on information systems* (pp. 3–16). Berlin Heidelberg: Springer. doi:10.1007/978-3-642-00416-2_1.

Harmon, P. (2010). The scope and evolution of business process management. In J. vom Brocke & M Rosemann (Eds.), *Handbook on business process management 1. International handbooks on information systems* (pp. 37–81). Berlin Heidelberg: Springer. doi:10.1007/978-3-642-00416-2_3.

Imanipour, N., Talebi, K., & Rezazadeh, S. (2012a). Business process management (BPM) implementation and adoption in SMEs: Inhibiting factors for Iranian e-retail industry. *Journal of Knowledge and Process Management, Forthcoming.*

Imanipour, N., Talebi, K., Rezazadeh, S. (2012b). Obstacles in business process management (BPM) implementation and adoption in SMEs. Available at SSRN: http://ssrn.com/abstract=1990609. Accessed 29 July 2012.

Jeston, J., & Nelis, J. (2006). *Business process management*. Oxford: Butterworth-Heinemann.

Key Statistics Australian Small Business (2011). Department of innovation, industry, science and research, Canberra.

Kirchmer, M. (2011a). Business process Governance for MPE. In M. Kirchmer (Ed.) *High performance through process excellence* (pp 69–85). Berlin Heidelberg: Springer, doi:10.1007/978-3-642-21165-2_5.

Kirchmer, M. (2011b). Small and medium enterprises also benefit from MPE. In M. Kirchmer (Ed.) *High performance through process excellence* (pp. 147–157). Berlin Heidelberg: Springer, doi:10.1007/978-3-642-21165-2_10.

Ouyang, C., Adams, M., Wynn, M., & ter Hofstede, AHM. (2010). Workflow management: An overview. In J. vom Brocke & M. Rosemann (Eds.), *The international handbook on business process management*, Berlin: Springer.

Parham, D. (2012). *Australia's productivity growth slump: Signs of crisis, adjustment or both? Visiting research paper*. Canberra: Productivity Commission.

Rosemann, M. (2010). The service portfolio of a BPM center of excellence. In J. vom Brocke & M. Rosemann (Eds.), *Handbook on business process management 2. International handbooks on information systems* (pp 267–284). Berlin Heidelberg: Springer, doi:10.1007/978-3-642-01982-1_13.

Rosemann, M., & vom Brocke, J. (2010). The six core elements of business process management. In J. vom Brocke & M. Rosemann (Eds.), *Handbook on Business Process Management 1. International Handbooks on Information Systems* (pp. 107–122). Berlin Heidelberg: Springer, doi:10.1007/978-3-642-00416-2_5.

Rummler, G. A., Ramias, A. J. (2010). A framework for defining and designing the structure of work. In J. vom Brocke, M. Rosemann (Eds.), *Handbook on business process management 1. International handbooks on information systems* (pp. 83–106). Berlin Heidelberg: Springer, doi:10.1007/978-3-642-00416-2_4.

ter Hofstede, A., van der Aalst, W., & Weske, M. (2003). Business process management: A survey. In M. Weske (Ed.), Business *process management*, volume 2678 (pp. 1019–1019). Lecture Notes in Computer Science. Berlin Heidelberg: Springer, doi:10.1007/3-540-44895-0_1.

van der Aalst, W. M. P., & ter Hofstede, A. H. M. (2005). YAWL: Yet another workflow language. *Information Systems, 30*(4), 245–275.

Yin, R. K. (2003). *Case study research: Design and methods* (3rd ed.). London: Sage Publications.

Information Technology (IT) Security in Small and Medium Enterprises (SMEs)

Michael W. Kimwele

1 Introduction

With the rapid advances in networked computer technology during the past decade and the unprecedented growth of the Internet, the public has become increasingly aware of the threats to personal privacy through computer crime (Merkow and Breithaupt 2007).

According to Whitman and Mattord, "Information security is the protection of information within a business, and the systems and hardware used to store, process and transmit this information".

Small and Medium Enterprises (SMEs) are usually born out of entrepreneurial passion and limited funding, with business systems that lack any degree of integration and sophistication (Upfold and Sewry 2005). Policies and frameworks for information security planning and disaster recovery are usually non-existent. Inadvertent threats pose some of the highest information security risk to SMEs and yet personnel training and awareness programmes are often neglected.

1.1 Background

Companies are not spending millions of dollars in information security just for the sake of security. IT security is needed to protect the business both from itself and from outsiders who would cause it harm (Merkow and Breithaupt 2007).

We can no longer rely entirely on our traditional security controls- e.g. physical access controls, security guards –to ensure the security of an organization's assets, processes and communications (Tarimo 2006). The multiplicity of new technical

M. W. Kimwele (✉)
Institute of Computer Science and Information Technology, Jomo Kenyatta University of Agriculture and Technology, 62000- 00200 Nairobi, Kenya
e-mail: mikekimwele@yahoo.com

J. Devos et al. (eds.), *Information Systems for Small and Medium-sized Enterprises*, Progress in IS, DOI: 10.1007/978-3-642-38244-4_3,

possibilities gives rise not only to new products, services and more efficient and effective of doing things, but also the possibility of misuse of the technology. However, research findings show that, in many cases, security issues come as an-after-thought in the ongoing transformation to ICT-enabled organizational or governmental context.

Numerous internationally approved security frameworks and schemes may be implemented to safeguard an organization against information loss and potential liability (Upfold and Sewry 2005). Most of the frameworks are complex and expensive to implement and most of the times are adopted by large organizations.

A survey done by PricewaterhouseCoopers (2002) highlight some of the many concerns surrounding information security in SMEs

- Between 19 and 25 % of small and medium businesses do not have any formal data back up and storage facilities.
- Twenty six percentage of small and medium businesses are not confident they could restore files after an e-mail virus.
- Two thirds of businesses surveyed had a premeditated or malicious incident during 2004 compared with just under half in the previous 2 years.
- A quarter of businesses surveyed had a significant incident involving accidental systems failure and data corruption.
- Virus infections and inappropriate use of systems by staff were the cause of most of the incidents. Viruses also caused the greatest number of serious incidents.

According to Upfold and Sewry (2005), lack of adequate information security policies and procedures in SMEs is prevalent when business connectivity to public networks is increasing, and E-Business is enabling SMEs to leverage markets that were previously the reserve of enterprise business. SME management must be aware that information security risk extends to legal, regulatory, and to a lesser extent, government liability.

Digital security is achievable- theoretically- but in practice the human factor plays a major role subverting the best-laid plans of system administrators and security experts. The user is often referred to as the "weak link" in computer security. Renaud (2003) points out people generally don't understand risks, and they sometimes don't understand computers. E-mail-attachment viruses prove this admirably: even though users know that they ought not to open unexpected attachments they still do; and viruses spread because of a lack of security consciousness. The Internet has exposed millions of computer-illiterate people to substantial risks that they are completely unaware of.

Users' naivety with respect to security issues is exacerbated by a mismatch of goals (Renaud 2003). The goal of the authentication mechanism is to ensure that the current user is not masquerading as another user, whilst the goal of the user is to gain access to the website to carry out a task. Unfortunately, the stronger the authentication mechanism, the more time-consuming and potentially difficult it will be for legitimate user to gain access to the system to achieve his/her goals. If the system makes authentication time-consuming the user will probably find a way around it- especially in an uncontrolled environment such as the web.

Security of data is critical to the operations of firms. Without the ability to store, process and transmit data securely, operations may be compromised, with the potential for serious consequences to trading integrity (Clear 2007). Thus, data security is important especially in the light of the fact that much of the communication is based on the use of open networks (i.e. the Internet). Clear (2007) noted that data security requires three aspects to be maintained: integrity (i.e. providing an accurate representation of the physical reality that data represents); availability (i.e. allowing those authorized to have access to data); and confidentiality (i.e. the protection of data and information from disclosure to unauthorized persons). Without the ability to store, process and transmit data securely, operations may be compromised for which there can be detrimental consequences to trading. Thus, the role that electronic communications play in business today and its dependency on data security is of critical interest.

According to Clear (2007), there are a number of guides offering advice on "good practice" in relation to data security when working in a distributed and electronically-mediated manner and three are noted here:

- Workers should be trained to protect data security through anti-virus software, password use and taking back ups of work in progress; if such training were not forthcoming, then workers should be held responsible for losses of data.
- Safe data handling is dependent not just on technical measures and procedures but also on having reliable and vetted staff.
- Staff should be given guidance on selecting appropriate technology, software packages and tools for best practice in data security to be followed.

Given that smaller firms are less likely to have a formal security policy than larger equivalents, then it is possible to speculate that smaller firms are more likely to have unsafe handling practices than larger firms.

If technology providers fail to meet the needs of firms then there is a role for government agencies to step into the market gap to help ensure firms handle data securely (Clear 2007). However, there is an acute lack of engagement on behalf of small business owners/managers who are largely suspicious of government interference in industry.

1.2 Strategic Importance of SMEs

Parallel with ownership reform and privatization, the number of SMEs is increasing. According to Sunje the strategic importance of SMEs is today acknowledged around the world for the following reasons:

- Small and medium-sized enterprises are contributing to employment growth at a higher rate than larger firms. In the European Union economy about 99.9 % of the enterprises are SMEs
- The private sector and in particular SMEs form the backbone of a market economy and for the transition economies in the long-term might provide most of the employment (as is the case in the European Union countries)
- They curb the monopoly of the large enterprises and offer them complimentary services and absorb the fluctuation of a modern economy
- Through inter-enterprise corporation, they raise the level of skills with their flexible and innovative nature
- A characteristic of small industrial enterprises is that they produce predominantly for the domestic market, drawing in on natural resources
- The structural shift from the former large state-owned enterprises to small and private SMEs will increase the number of owners, a group that represents greater responsibility and commitment than in the former centrally planned economies
- An increased number of SMEs will bring more flexibility to society and the economy and might facilitate technological innovation, as well as provide significant opportunities for the development of new ideas and skills
- SMEs use and develop predominantly domestic technologies and skills.

1.3 Motivation for the Research

Certainly there are very strong motivations for this research. While large companies often invest a large amount of resources in the organizational aspect of IT security, the management of SMEs usually ignore these areas (Park et al. 2008). A corporate security culture would be an important strategic guideline for the day-to-day operational security-related decisions of IT administration personnel, who otherwise have to make decisions in an ad-hoc manner and without a coherent strategy. In contrast to large companies, SMEs rarely develop strategic policies; written IT security policies and even system documentation are often non-existent (Park et al. 2008).

Upfold and Sewry (2005) suggest that SME leadership need to engage, understand and implement formal information security processes, failing which their organizations may be severely impacted by inadvertent threats/deliberate attacks on their information systems which could ultimately lead to business failure.

2 A Socio-Technical Approach to Information Technology Security

Recent research has recognized that technological factors are not the only key to the effectiveness of information security controls; there is also a need to understand the impact of human and organizational factors (Beznosov and Beznosova

2007). As Schneier pointed out technical security measures are often breached through social means, but little research has tackled the problem of system security in the context of the entire socio-technical system, with the interactions between the social and technical parts being integrated into one model.

There has been research on specific challenges of managing IT security; but none seems to provide an integrated approach to tackling the challenges faced by organizations. As a result, security practitioners need a better understanding of how different technological, human, and organizational factors lead to security problems in organizations and specifically SMEs because of their economic importance to developing countries.

Werlinger et al. (2009) noted that security processes should consider that IT security practitioners have to effectively communicate security issues to other stakeholders who have different perceptions of risks and do not have security as the first priority within the organization.

Human factors can be defined as those related to cognition at the individual level, as well as culture and interaction with other people (Beznosov and Beznosova 2007). Organizational aspects are those related to the structure of the organization, including size and managerial decisions about IT security. Technological aspects involve technical solutions such as applications and protocols.

2.1 Human Factors

From the human perspective, embracing security practices can present numerous challenges. For instance, how well and effective security risks are communicated to stakeholders can determine how they are understood. Different people may use different strategies to communicate their perceptions on risks to other stakeholders. Human judgement is very important in interpreting reports.

2.2 Organizational Factors

Security efforts in our own opinion should be sanctioned or at least supported by the management of the organization. Bigger companies and particularly financial organizations invest more resources in bad security practices deterrent controls than smaller companies.

IT security management in terms of organizational factors can be affected by:

- Competitors' behaviors
- Customers' security requirements
- Change in legislation
- Rapid change of technology.

Top management should be in a position of predicting the enforcement of policy and assess the IT security culture in the organization.

It is important for organizations to prioritize resources to be well prepared to tackle security incidents. As a result, a method should be found for assessing vulnerabilities as a means of assisting practitioners to deal with them.

2.3 Need for a Different Approach to IT Security

We might be tempted to think that the field of Information Security is primarily about technology. As Stewart (2005) noted it is a multidisciplinary field that draws from economics, sociology, technology, business, and law. Much as technology plays a critical role, we feel that users should not be over expectant to what technology can accomplish. In the literature, we do not seem to find any relationship between how much an organization spends on security technologies and the subsequent reduction in computer abuse incidents.

It is commonly acknowledged that security requirements cannot be addressed by technical means alone, and that a significant aspect of protection comes down to attitudes, awareness, behaviour, and capabilities of the people involved (Pattinson and Anderson 2007). Considerable literature asserts that "there is more to managing information security than focusing on software and hardware vulnerabilities".

Beznosov and Beznosova (2007) state, that over 94 % of the public research in computer security has been concentrated on technological advances. Yet attackers seem to employ more and more human and social factors in their attacks. This realization by attackers has enabled them to continue achieving their results. Which ever side- either the attackers or security practitioners which capitalizes on the social factors is likely to gain advantage over the other. We believe that researchers on their part should broaden their computer security research to include social factors and this will call for the modeling of IT security systems in the socio-technical context. The computer security community can better understand and design effective solutions by studying among other things- the social dimensions of the information security problem space.

Lee and Lee (2002) noted that social theories can add to the explanation of computer abuse. Social theories state that the greatest threats to computer abuse are employees and their social relationships with their referents. Some computer abuse studies based on social criminology theories have been found to confirm this view. For instance, people can be motivated to commit computer abuses by their social bonds.

3 IT Security Requirements and Metrics

A survey of published literature shows that most reports on IT security (Upfold and Sewry 2005; Tarimo 2006; Pattinson and Anderson 2007; Werlinger et al. 2009) cite the following requirements:

- The need for risk assessments. Risks must be understood and acknowledged and the IT security measures that are taken must be commensurate with these risks.
- The need for an IT security organizational culture.
- The need to create, communicate, implement, endorse, monitor, and enforce security policies across an organization.
- The need to make every member of the organization aware of the importance of IT security and to train them in good IT security practices.
- The need for access controls to make certain only identified and authorized users with a legitimate need access information and system resources.
- The need to monitor, audit, and review IT security measures regularly.
- The need for business continuity plans that are tested regularly.

We propose a framework that considers the above requirements in defining a coherent way of dealing with IT security in SMEs. In an endeavor to address IT security challenges in SMEs, there is need to resolve the following:

- Who is responsible for ensuring security?
- Who authorizes decisions that have to be made in regard to IT security?
- Who has to be consulted to ensure that every aspect of IT security is covered?
- Who has to be kept informed to ensure that the organization copes with resulting changes resulting from putting in place IT security measures?

To be able to measure the effectiveness of IT security measures in SMEs, our recommended framework requires that there should be some "IT security metrics". IT security metrics are quantifiable measurements or any identifiable attributes that collectively characterize changes in security awareness/behavior of employees. It is against those metrics that the effectiveness of the proposed IT security measures in place can be evaluated.

IT security metrics should be designed to yield quantifiable information (Swanson et al. 2003; Ammann and Black 2001). The quantifiable information is useful for the following purposes:

- Comparison of security maturity
- Cost justification when insecurities occur can be clearly shown in metrics
- Indication and determination of critical and non-critical security parameters
- Redirect assets and set proper priorities for most critical security needs
- Security problem isolation
- Determine the effectiveness of security testing efforts.

IT security metrics can be created to guide each aspect of security program including systems evaluation, internal security processes such as training and systems testing and risk assessment. The use of IT security metrics will allow organizations to determine effectiveness of implemented IT security processes, and control by relating results of IT security activities measurements (Chaula 2006).

IT security metrics may vary from one organization to another depending on the business environment of the organization in question among other factors. Some of the IT security metrics we propose include but not limited to the following:

- Decreased number of reported security incidents
- Reduced number of viruses or other malicious code outbreak
- Increased comments on the IT security measures in place
- Reduced number of cases for use of pirated software
- Reduced traffic to unethical websites
- Decreased number of virus problems resulting from opening unexpected email attachments
- Decreased number of malicious codes resulting downloading contents from untrusted websites
- Increased adherence to back up routines and procedures
- Reduced IT equipment failure
- Increased reported compliance to IT security standards.

IT security metrics should be reviewed on a regular basis. During the review, new metrics should be developed and those found obsolete discarded. Each organization should develop its own set of IT security metrics.

4 Research Methodology

The different categories of primary data collection methods include laboratory measurements, field observations, archives/collections, questionnaires and interviews (Sharp and Howard 1998). However, only questionnaires and interviews are suitable for the data required, as the opinions of a large and diverse group of people are needed. Questionnaires provide a more structured way of gathering and recording data. The research entailed a survey of SMEs in Kenya, were primary data was collected by means of a questionnaire. Most of the questions were adopted from previous studies but modified to capture data relevant to the current SME study. These were measured on a five-point likert scale whereby 1 represented "strongly agree" and 5 "strongly disagree". A preliminary version of the questionnaire was discussed with scholars and managers. Some questions were reworded and the original structure of the questionnaire was amended.

This research is based on collected data which is then analyzed and organized to unveil some problems regarding IT security in Kenyan SMEs. We believe that to be able to address IT security issues effectively in SMEs, it is important to properly understand how IT security is currently being practiced in Kenyan SMEs. SMEs targeted in the survey included those in the consulting, recruitment, vehicles, cleaning, legal, estate agent, medical, equipment leasing/rental, equipment repairs, and any others so long as the organization has got not more than 100 full time employees.

The sample consisted of:

- Formally registered businesses, the informal sector was not considered.
- The telephone directory was used to get regional distribution of SMEs.

Table 1 What is the nature of your business?

Valid	Frequency	Percent	Valid percent	Cumulative percent
Consulting	5	23.8	23.8	23.8
Computers	3	14.3	14.3	38.1
Equipment repairs	2	9.5	9.5	47.6
Other professional service	6	28.6	28.6	76.2
Recruitment	1	4.8	4.8	81.0
Vehicle services	1	4.8	4.8	85.7
Estate agent	3	14.3	14.3	100.0
Total	21	100.0	100.0	

- Sectoral distribution of SMEs was based on national data from the Central Bureau of Statistics.

The researchers administered the questionnaire over a period of 4 months between October 2009 and January 2010 to SMEs selected from all over Kenya. One hundred and twelve (112) SMEs were randomly identified to participate in the survey. The researchers then contacted the SMEs requesting them to participate in the survey. Those who responded positively were then e-mailed the questionnaire which they were free to fill and e-mail back or they could fill and inform the researchers when to pick. In some cases, the questionnaire was delivered physically by the researchers and picked. The respondents were assured that all personal respondents would remain strictly confidential. Finally, twenty one (21) completed questionnaires were collected.

The respondents included business decision makers, IT managers, or people who take care of computers systems in SMEs. Out of the 21 SMEs that participated in the questionnaire survey, thirteen agreed to post-survey interviews to obtain "richer" information about IT security issues affecting them. As a consequence, in addition to responses to the questionnaire, other useful insights were also gathered. The exact of respondents in terms of nature of business, length of time the business has been in operation, current number of employees, number of computers used in the businesses and how long they have used computers are represented in Table 1 through to Table 5.

Table 1 shows the nature of the surveyed firms in terms of their operations. Majority of the enterprises are in Consulting and Professional Services.

Table 2 shows the length of time (years) the surveyed SMEs have been in operation. More than 90 % of firms surveyed were less than 14 years old.

From Table 3, we note that majority of the SMEs surveyed had 11–25 employees (28.6 %), followed by 6–10 employees (23.8 %) and 51-upwards (23.8 %).

From Table 4, it is evident that more than 50 % of the surveyed SMEs were using not more than 15 computers in their operations.

Nineteen percentage of the respondents have been using computers in their operations for 1 year or less while 4.8 % have been using computers for 19 years as shown in Table 5.

Table 2 How long has the business in operation?

Valid	Frequency	Percent	Valid percent	Cumulative percent
1	2	9.5	9.5	9.5
2	2	9.5	9.5	19.0
3	1	4.8	4.8	23.8
4	2	9.5	9.5	33.3
5	3	14.3	14.3	47.6
6	1	4.8	4.8	52.4
7	2	9.5	9.5	61.9
8	2	9.5	9.5	71.4
10	2	9.5	9.5	81.0
12	1	4.8	4.8	85.7
14	1	4.8	4.8	90.5
37	1	4.8	4.8	95.2
89	1	4.8	4.8	100.0
Total	21	100.0	100.0	

Table 3 What is your current number of employees?

Valid	Frequency	Percent	Valid percent	Cumulative percent
0–5	4	19.0	19.0	19.0
11–25	6	28.6	28.6	47.6
36–50	1	4.8	4.8	52.4
51–	5	23.8	23.8	76.2
6–10	5	23.8	23.8	100.0
Total	21	100.0	100.0	

Table 4 How many computers do you use in your business?

Valid	Frequency	Percent	Valid percent	Cumulative percent
1	2	9.5	9.5	9.5
2	1	4.8	4.8	14.3
3	2	9.5	9.5	23.8
5	2	9.5	9.5	33.3
6	1	4.8	4.8	38.1
7	1	4.8	4.8	42.9
9	2	9.5	9.5	52.4
11	1	4.8	4.8	57.1
14	2	9.5	9.5	66.7
15	1	4.8	4.8	71.4
25	1	4.8	4.8	76.2
35	1	4.8	4.8	81.0
40	1	4.8	4.8	85.7
50	1	4.8	4.8	90.5
60	1	4.8	4.8	95.2
80	1	4.8	4.8	100.0
Total	21	100.0	100.0	

Table 5 How long have you been using computers in your business?

Valid	Frequency	Percent	Valid percent	Cumulative percent
1	4	19.0	19.0	19.0
3	2	9.5	9.5	28.6
4	3	14.3	14.3	42.9
5	2	9.5	9.5	52.4
7	3	14.3	14.3	66.7
8	1	4.8	4.8	71.4
10	3	14.3	14.3	85.7
14	1	4.8	4.8	90.5
15	1	4.8	4.8	95.2
19	1	4.8	4.8	100.0
Total	21	100.0	100.0	

5 Results and Analysis

The survey was conducted to establish the nature of IT infrastructure particularly its organization, employees and state of security measures. Considering the proportion and scope of SMEs in Kenya, poor information technology security of SMEs can yield catastrophic results both socially and economically. Among the issues considered in the survey, the following were found to be SME problem areas:

- Security Policy: 47.6 % of respondents strongly agreed and agreed that their organizations have a well documented information security policy. 33.3 % of staff are aware of the organizations IT security policy. Only 28.6 % reported being given adequate and appropriate information security education and training.
- Organizational Security: 38.1 % of respondents reported having a director (or equivalent) member of staff being responsible for IT security. 47.6 % reported that the access to their information systems by outsiders requires approval by a senior manager.
- Personnel Security: Only 42.9 % of employees have been trained to secure their computers at all times, especially when moving away from their workstations. 33.3 % have a formal disciplinary process for employees who have violated the organization's IT security policies and processes.
- Communications and Operations Management: 47.6 % of respondents reported that they are confident, that in the event of equipment failure, theft or a site disaster, their back ups and storage would enable them to retrieve their information systems with minimal business interruption. 38.1 % reported that their systems are updated/upgraded according to a structured plan and not in an ad-hoc fashion. 42.9 % reported that, in the event of a security incident, procedures define what to do and who to call for assistance.

- Business Continuity Management: 28.6 % have a business continuity plan which specifies who must take action and what has to be done to ensure that the organization can continue functioning in the event of a disaster such as a fire/flood. 33.3 % of respondents reported that they have a nominated person in the organization who is responsible for managing the business continuity process. 33.3 % reported having had their security measures having been reviewed with the last year.
- IT Security Standards: Despite the fact that there are some standards which organizations can adopt, 61.9 % of the SMEs surveyed reported that they were not aware of any standards they could adopt.

In view of the above problem areas, we recommend that SMEs should adopt the following in their quest to realize enhanced IT security:

- Development of IT security policies
- Identification of roles and responsibilities of each individual regarding IT security
- Make all employees aware of IT security issues
- Select and implement appropriate security measures
- Put in place data recovery measures in case of accidents
- Identify and protect all organizational assets that need to be protected
- Adopt appropriate IT security standards.

We aim at synthesizing from the discussions, analysis, and interpretations made so far in an attempt to establish a means that can help in evaluation, formation, and implementation of a possible IT security controls to address the security situation observed and described in the previous section. Based on empirical analysis of security practices in organizations, this work proposes a framework that can be used to address SME IT security issues.

Schneier (2000), and Mitnick and Simon (2002) refer to human as the weakest link in a security chain. Mitnick and Simon (2002) specifically say that as security technologies improve and systems become more difficult to exploit, attackers will turn more and more to exploiting the human element. It is against this background that we are proposing an approach in our framework that puts into consideration the human element in addition to technological issues in addressing IT security issues in SMEs.

The resulting framework brings together numerous concepts into a coherent explanation that should be useful for SMEs or any other individual seeking to understand the underlying principles of IT security. It contains organizational, cultural and technical issues that should be looked at when considering and applying IT security. Because of limited IT budgets for SMEs, the framework is necessary to enable SMEs implement IT security measures at low costs.

6 IT Security Framework for SMEs

Our recommended framework consists of the following:

- A mapping of identified IT security metrics and the IT security issues/activities/aspects the metrics can measure (Table 6).
- An approach for tackling IT security issues which deals with continual improvement and establishment of new measures should the implemented ones at any one particular time appear ineffective (Fig. 1).
- An illustration of how the approach can be utilized in an IT security enhancing mechanism for SMEs. This illustration is done using data that was collected during the survey (Table 7).

Table 6 demonstrates various IT security control issues/activities/aspects and the metrics which can be used to measure such issues. Although metrics have been proposed over a long period of time, an ideal metrics is one which is easy to understand, effective and efficient (Khurana 2007). In order to develop an ideal metric, metrics should be validated and characterized effectively.

Our framework recommends the following approach to tackling IT security issues in SMEs

In our subsequent section, we provide a summary of selected SMEs in terms of the security controls they have in place and then evaluate them in light of the security breaches the organizations have suffered within the past year. Through this it is possible to examine and show that some measures are effective than other based on experience of the surveyed SMEs.

The above checklist (Table 7) is an illustration of the use of the recommended approach in Fig. 1 above. The illustration is based on four SMEs surveyed. It shows that despite SMEs having implemented various security controls, they still suffered various security breaches within the past 1 year. This is essential in determining whether the current state of affairs (security controls in place and resulting reduction/increase in security breaches) is satisfactory. In the event that the security breaches increase in number and the organization considers them significant, then as per our approach, new controls should be established and the process as shown in Fig. 1 iterated/repeated. This process should continue until the organization is satisfied that the security measures/controls in place yield the desired results/state in terms of IT security.

It is worth appreciating the fact that in our checklist (Table 2) time is essential since the security breaches have to be observed and reported over a determined time (say, 1 year). This helps in measuring the effectiveness of implemented security controls is also consistent with the way other metrics are established/defined. For instance, Reliability can be defined as the ability of the software product to perform its required functions under stated conditions for a specified period of time, or a specified number of operations. Reliability can be measured using 'mean time between failure' (MTBF), which is the average time between successive failures (Khurana 2007). A similar measure to MTBF is 'mean time to

Table 6 Mapping of IT security metrics and the IT security issues/activities/aspects they can measure

		IT security metrics									
		Decreased number of reported security incidents	Reduced number of viruses or other malicious code outbreak	Increased comments on the IT security measures in place	Reduced number of cases for use of pirated software	Reduced traffic to unethical websites	Decreased number of virus problems resulting from opening unexpected email attachments	Decreased number of malicious codes resulting downloading contents from untrusted websites	Increased adherence to back up routines and procedures	Reduced IT equipment failure	Increased reported compliance to IT security standards
IT control issues/ activities/ aspects	**Security policy** (Is our IT security policy effective?)	✔	✔	✔	✔	✔	✔	✔	✔	✔	✔
	Organizational security (Is there a Director or equivalent member of staff responsible for IT security?)			✔						✔	✔
	Asset control (Can all assets including hardware and software used for information security handling be identified and located?)								✔		
	Personnel security (Are Staff aware that security incidents should be reported to management immediately?)	✔	✔	✔							
	Physical and environmental security (Is there appropriate physical and environmental security procedures in place to prevent interference with business premises and IT systems?)			✔						✔	

(continued)

Table 6 (continued)

	IT security metrics									
	Decreased number of reported security incidents	Reduced number of viruses or other malicious code outbreak	Increased comments on the IT security measures in place	Reduced number of cases for use of pirated software	Reduced traffic to unethical websites	Decreased number of virus problems resulting from opening unexpected email attachments	Decreased number of malicious codes resulting downloading contents from untrusted websites	Increased adherence to back up routines and procedures	Reduced IT equipment failure	Increased reported compliance to IT security standards
Communications and operations management (Are we confident that our anti-virus systems are up to date, and in the event of a virus outbreak, we should be able to protect our systems?)	✔	✔				✔	✔			✔
Access control (Can users logon/gain access to our systems without being formally registered with their own user account?)			✔							✔
System development and maintenance (Can our systems provide audit trails so that usage of the system and data input/changes can be audited?)		✔			✔		✔			✔
Business continuity management (Have our security measures been reviewed within the last year?)								✔		✔
Compliance (Is our organization aware that there are established, international IT security standards available for adoption?)	✔									✔

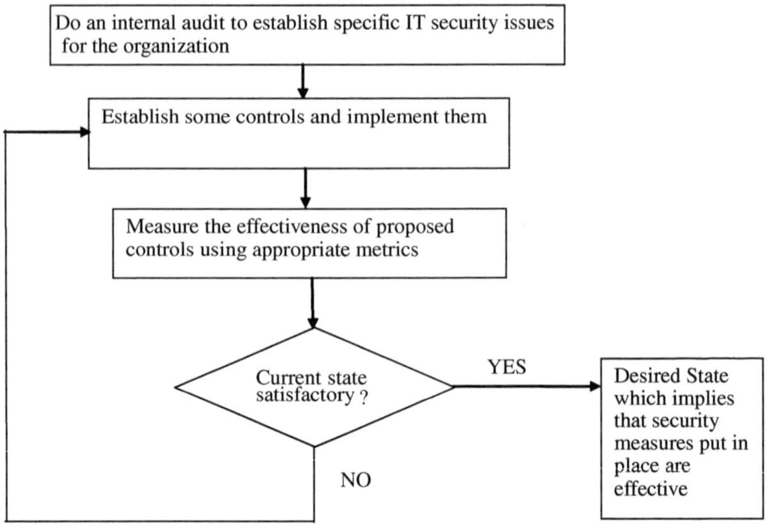

Fig. 1 Approach for evaluating the effectiveness of IT security measures in SMEs

Table 7 Implemented security controls and security breaches suffered within the last year

Implemented security controls	SME 1	SME 2	SME 3	SME 4
Have a security policy	YES	YES	YES	YES
A director (or equivalent) member of staff has responsibility for IT security	NO	YES	YES	YES
All assets can be identified	NO	YES	YES	YES
Security incidents are reported to management immediately	NO	NO	YES	YES
Have appropriate physical and environmental procedures	YES	YES	YES	YES
Up to date antivirus systems	YES	YES	YES	YES
Proper system access control mechanisms like user accounts	YES	YES	YES	YES
System usage audit trails	NO	NO	NO	NO
Security measures have been reviewed within past year	YES	NO	YES	YES
Adopted/complied with IT security standards	NO	NO	NO	NO
Security breaches suffered within past year				
No information security breeches				
Inadvertent breech (e.g. user accidentally deleted files or changed computer configuration)	✔	✔		
Deliberate attack (e.g. hacker/disgruntled staff gained access, deleting or stealing data)			✔	✔
Asset theft (e.g. software application misplaced causing re-installation delay/costs)	✔	✔		
Equipment failure (e.g. hard drive crashed causing loss of data and business disruption)	✔		✔	✔

(continued)

Table 7 (continued)

Implemented security controls	SME 1	SME 2	SME 3	SME 4
Back up failure (e.g. system restore failure due to corrupt/ inadequate back ups)			✔	
Data theft (e.g. espionage which resulted in data loss and possible legal exposure)				
Site disaster (e.g. fire or flood causing damage to systems and business disruption)	✔			
Copyright infringement (e.g. staff loading pirated software, legally exposing the organization)	✔			✔
Compliance (e.g. passing on confidential information, legally exposing the organization)	✔			

repair' (MTTR) which is the average time taken to repair the software after a failure occurs.

7 Conclusion

To address current difficulties of organizations reluctant to invest in IT security due to cost, this work proposes an IT security implementation framework that will allow SMEs adopt cost effective security measures whose effectiveness can be evaluated using appropriate metrics.

This framework is significant in that it allows SMEs to take necessary security measures and to realize what actions they can take in case they are faced with IT security issues. This will help SMEs protect their information assets. It is also significant in that it is a new approach presenting an IT security framework for SMEs that considers human, technical, and organizational factors.

Since the framework has not been tested in a real working environment of SMEs, further analysis on the effectiveness of the framework is required, and the results should be reflected in future frameworks.

References

Ammann, P. E., & Black, P. E. (2001). A specification-based coverage metric to evaluate test sets. *International Journal of Reliability, Quality, and Safety Engineering*, *8*(4), 275–300; Singapore, World Scientific Publishing.

Beznosov, K., & Beznosova, O. (2007). On the imbalance of the security problem space and its expected consequences. *Information Management and Computer Security, 15*(5), 420–431.

Chaula, J. A. (2006). *A socio-technical analysis of information systems security assurance: A case study for effective assurance* (pp. 1101–8526). Stockholm: Stockholm University, Department of Computer and Systems Sciences, Report Series/DSV No. 06-016, ISSN.

Clear, F. (2007). SMEs, electronically-mediated working and data security: Cause for concern? *International Journal of Business Science and Applied Management, 2*(2), 2007.
Khurana, R. (2007). *Software engineering: Principles and practices*. New Delhi, India: ITL Education Solutions Ltd.
Lee, J., & Lee, Y. (2002). A holistic model of computer abuse within organizations. *Information Management and Computer Security, 10*(2), 57–63.
Merkow, M., & Breithaupt, J. (2007). *Information security-principles and practices*. India: Pearson Prentice Hall.
Mitnick, K. D., & Simon, W. L. (2002). *The art of deception: Controlling the human element of security*. New York: Wiley.
Park, J et al. (2008). IT Security Strategies for SMEs. *International Journal of Software Engineering and its Applications*, *2*(3), 91–98.
Pattinson, M. R., & Anderson, G. (2007). How well are information risks being communicated to your computer end-users? *Information Management and Computer Security, 15*(5), 362–371.
PricewaterhouseCoopers (2002), *Interdepartmental committee on network and information security*: *Information security awareness campaign*, SME Section, October 2002.
Renaud, K. (2003). Quantifying the quality of web authentication mechanisms: A usability perspective. *Journal of Web Engineering*, *3*, 95–123.
Schneier, B. (2000). *Secrets and lies: Digital security in a networked world.* New York: Wiley Computer Publishing.
Sharp, J. A., & Howard, K. (1998). The management of a student research project, (2nd ed.) http://www.hlss.mmu.ac.uk/infocomms/people/staffpub/rjh.doc (12/2/2010).
Stewart, A. (2005). Information security technologies as a commodity input. *Information Management and Computer Security, 13*(1), 5–15.
Swanson, M., Bartol, N., Sabato, J., Hash, J., & Graffo, L. (2003). Security metrics guide for information technology systems. http://csrc.nist.gov/csspab/june13-15/sec-metrics.html (16/8/2010).
Tarimo, C. N. (2006). *ICT security readiness checklist for developing countries: A social-technical approach.* Stockholm: Stockholm University, Department of Computer and Systems Sciences, December 2006.
Upfold, C. T. & Sewry, D. A. (2005). An investigation of information security in small and medium enterprises (SME's) in the Eastern Cape.
Werlinger, R et al. (2009). An integrated view of human, organizational, and technological challenges of IT security. *Information Management and Computer Security, 17*(1), 4–19.

Part II
Adoption and Use

Enterprise Architecture for Small and Medium-Sized Enterprises: A Starting Point for Bringing EA to SMEs, Based on Adoption Models

Maxime Bernaert, Geert Poels, Monique Snoeck and Manu De Backer

1 Introduction

To explain the proposed approach to bridge the gap between small and medium-sized enterprises (SMEs) and enterprise architecture (EA), this chapter is divided in four main parts: SMEs, EA, EA for SMEs, and recommendations for EA technique developers. The first two parts on SMEs and EA are descriptive, the third part is analytical and the fourth part is rather prescriptive.

In the first part, the definition of SMEs in Europe and the U.S. is explained. Then, SME characteristics related to IT adoption are given, out of which six well-documented characteristics can be derived. These characteristics lead to the development of six criteria that can be of guidance for developing IS techniques that have a higher fit with SMEs. The first part ends with a discussion of problems that SMEs are facing, due to a lack of structure and overview of the company.

The second part starts with an introduction of what the definition of EA is, what it really means, and why it is used. Then, a broad spectrum of EA techniques are being discussed. The key concepts of these techniques, which structure and dimensions they really have in common, are discussed in a subsequent section.

M. Bernaert (✉) · G. Poels
Department of Management Information Systems and Operations Management, Ghent University, Tweekerkenstraat 2 B-9000 Ghent, Belgium
e-mail: Maxime.Bernaert@UGent.be

G. Poels
e-mail: Geert.Poels@UGent.be

M. Snoeck
Department of Decision Sciences and Information Management, K.U. Leuven, Naamsestraat 69 B-3000 Leuven, Belgium
e-mail: Monique.Snoeck@KULeuven.be

M. De Backer
Department of Management Information Systems, University of Antwerp, Prinsstraat 13 B-2000 Antwerp, Belgium
e-mail: Manu.DeBacker@ua.ac.be

J. Devos et al. (eds.), *Information Systems for Small and Medium-sized Enterprises*, Progress in IS, DOI: 10.1007/978-3-642-38244-4_4,

Afterwards, similar to the part on SMEs, five criteria for EA techniques are derived from the definition of EA. These criteria can be a guide for developing EA techniques. The second part ends with a discussion of benefits EA can offer to companies, and more specifically a discussion of benefits EA can offer to the previously mentioned problems that SMEs are dealing with.

After discussing both SMEs and EA, it seems obvious that EA can really offer benefits to SMEs. However, neither academia nor practice demonstrate the existence and use of EA in SMEs. This advocates for a third part on bridging the gap between EA and SMEs.

The third part begins with discussing adoption models, starting with the technology acceptance model (TAM). This model has been extended by Moody to be used for IS method adoption, and is known as the method evaluation model (MEM). Thereafter, adoption models of IT in an SME context are being discussed. The adoption of EA in SMEs is about adoption of an IS method in an SME context. Therefore, the MEM is further used to get insight in bridging the gap between EA and SMEs.

The third part continues with analyzing which actions are necessary to bring EA to SMEs, based on the adoption models. The perceived efficacy (perceived usefulness and perceived ease of use) has to be increased, and the actual efficacy has to influence this perceived efficacy. This can only be done by stimulating implementation and research of EA in SMEs.

Finally, the fourth part gives recommendations for developing EA techniques that are specifically adapted to an SME context. First, a plan with research steps is given to develop three artifacts: a metamodel explaining the syntax and semantics of EA models for SMEs, a method with detailed guidelines explaining the process of using this metamodel for building an EA model of an SME, and software tool support to facilitate the input and adjustment, and enhance the output of the EA models. Second, a design science approach is applied to these research steps. Third and finally, a basis and starting point for the dimensions of an EA metamodel for SMEs is proposed.

2 Small and Medium-Sized Enterprises

2.1 *What is a Small and Medium-Sized Enterprise?*

An enterprise can be interpreted in a very wide sense. It could mean the whole enterprise, a smaller part of it (e.g., a business unit), or an area of activity of the enterprise (e.g., the purchasing). This research limits itself to small and medium-sized enterprises (SMEs), although the problems addressed and proposed solutions could be similar in larger organizations as well.

In the U.S., the Office of Advocacy defines a small business as an independent business having fewer than 500 employees (Small Business Administration 2012).

SMEs are important to the U.S. economy. Small firms represent 99.7 % of all employer firms, employ about half of all private-sector employees, pay 43 % of total U.S. private payroll, and have generated 65 % of net new jobs over the past 17 years from 1993 till 2009 (Small Business Administration 2011). Further, SMEs play a critical role in nurturing industrial innovation, constituting 40 % of highly innovative firms in 2002 (CHI Research Inc. 2004). SMEs also play a significant role in enhancing the competitiveness of an economy through the process of economic renewal by creation, elimination, and restructuring of economic sectors.

In Europe, micro, small and medium-sized enterprises are often referred to as the backbone of the European economy. There were close to 20.8 million SMEs in Europe, which accounts for 99.8 % of all companies. Furthermore the lion's share of those SMEs are micro enterprises with a total of 19.2 million. Around 70 % of European jobs are provided by the SMEs in the private sector and they account for 58.4 % of total gross-value added production (European Commission 2010). The European Commission defines SMEs as companies that employ less than 250 employees and of which the annual turnover is less than 50 million euros or of which the total assets are less than 43 million euros (European Commission 2003).

This article uses the term SME. However, SMEs are not a homogeneous group. Therefore, it is important to focus on a clearly defined type of SMEs in research and development efforts. Distinctions can be made based on regional differences (e.g., U.S. versus Europe), on size (based on the number of employees or based on the definition), on industry (e.g., production, trade, services, and government), on growth, on family owned or not, on influence of the CEO, on education of the CEO, on number of years in business, and even based on workforce age (Meyer 2011).

2.2 *Relevant Literature of SME Characteristics Influencing IT Adoption*

In academia and practice, a lot of discussion arises on whether SMEs are different from large companies and whether a different IT approach is required for SMEs. In the next paragraphs, relevant literature is discussed and summarized in a set of six characteristics.

Literature regarding IT application in SMEs shows a substantial lack of empirically grounded explanatory models and emphasizes SMEs' technological lag with regard to IT tools adoption and implementation, disregarding the role played by contingencies (Mariano et al. 2003). This literature weakness has been ascribed to the use of unsuitable research methods, mostly conceived for large firms, and wrong assumptions concerning SMEs (Thorpe et al. 2005). As a matter of fact, the small size is interpreted as synonymous of the inability to commit financial and human resources, to rely on relevant external technical skills, to assign IT tools to something different from shortly-ranged operating issues, and to understand IT benefits.

Welsh and White (1981) identified important differences in the financial management of small and large businesses while Ballantine et al. (1998) identified unique characteristics of SMEs as lack of business and IT strategy, limited access to capital resources, greater emphasis on using IT and IS to automate rather than informate, influence of major customers, and limited information skills. Similar assertions and findings are given in other papers (Metaxiotis 2009; Grandon and Pearson 2004; Street and Meister 2004; Chen et al. 2003; Mariano et al. 2003; Poon and Swatman 1999; Cragg and King 1993; Raymond 1985).

The SME characteristics influencing the IT adoption can be grouped into six main characteristics. The low level IT adoption in SMEs is first ascribed to a lack of expertise and time on the management side (Malhotra and Temponi 2010; Yap et al. 1992; Berryman 1983; Welsh and White 1981) and second to a lack of financial resources and skilled manpower within SMEs (Malhotra and Temponi 2010; Lefebvre et al. 1996; Yap et al. 1992; Noori 1990; Montazemi 1988; Welsh and White 1981). Third, if management is not directly involved in the IT implementation process and if SMEs are not endowed with technical expertise, then the role played by external actors becomes of crucial importance. The problem then lies on the lack of good external technical skills, as SMEs only occasionally seek advice from IT vendors or external consultants (Sels et al. 2006; Fuller 1996). SMEs are more likely than large companies to suffer from resource poverty such as financial constraints, lack of professional expertise, and susceptibility to external forces (Kroon et al. 2012; Montazemi 2006; Thong et al. 1996). Furthermore, when relied upon, external consultants not only have to adapt to firm's way of thinking and working, but also see activities fading out when leaving the firm (Alstrup 2000). Furthermore, it frequently happens that an outsourced IT project becomes a failure (Devos 2011).

Fourth, most papers consider IT as a set of tools used to a large degree for solving short-term operating problems, rather than long-term strategic plans (Harvey et al. 1992; Khan and Khan 1992; Lincoln and Warberg 1987; Malone 1985; Deeks 1976), because of the unpredictability of SMEs strategic future. Fuller (1996) mentioned that strategic planning is described as an "emerging vision" or "strategic awareness", "neither of which lend themselves easily to the explicit definitions required for systematic investment in information technology".

Fifth, SMEs tend to have simple and highly centralized structures with the executive officers making most of the critical decisions (Montazemi 2006; Thong et al. 1996).

Sixth, top-management support has been found to be a key critical factor in IS effectiveness in SMEs (Montazemi 2006; Caldeira and Ward 2003; Yap et al. 1992).

Last, but less documented, some researchers link the delay in IT usage to presumed SMEs cultural delay (Rullani and Micelli 1998).

2.3 Six Well-Documented Characteristics

From the relevant literature on characteristics influencing IT adoption in SMEs, six characteristics can be distilled, some of which are different from larger companies:

1. Employees and management are typically overwhelmed with day-to-day business, leaving little time for themselves to look at strategic matters such as process management, not to mention quality and process improvement (Malhotra and Temponi 2010; Kamsties et al. 1998; Berryman 1983; Welsh and White 1981).
2. SMEs have limited IT knowledge and technical skills (Haug et al. 2010; Levy et al. 2001; Lefebvre et al. 1996; Thong et al. 1996; Thong and Yap 1995; Blili and Raymond 1993; Gable 1991; Noori 1990; DeLone 1981, 1988; Montazemi 1988; Welsh and White 1981). The main reason why European SMEs fail in utilizing IT is their lack of IT knowledge (Neidleman 1979).
3. Smaller companies have significantly fewer resources than larger companies, due to the highly competitive environment, financial constraints, lack of expertise, and sensitivity to external influences (Kroon et al. 2012; Ballantine et al. 1998; Thong et al. 1996; Thong and Yap 1995; Welsh and White 1981). The smaller the company, the fewer resources it has to hire experts, for example, employees with IT skills (Montazemi 2006; Levy et al. 2001; Ballantine et al. 1998; Fuller 1996; Lefebvre et al. 1996; Thong and Yap 1995; Blili and Raymond 1993; Alpar and Reeves 1990; Noori 1990; Montazemi 1988; DeLone 1981).
4. There is a big demand in these companies for knowledge regarding the performance of tasks and how things are done (Kamsties et al. 1998; Harvey et al. 1992; Khan and Khan 1992; Lincoln and Warberg 1987; Malone 1985; Deeks 1976).
5. By definition, SMEs are organizations with fewer employees than large companies. The manager or CEO, who is often the company's owner, is commonly the single person who decides on strategic issues. The CEO is the central figure who determines the direction of an SME (Levy and Powell 2008; Bharati and Chaudhury 2006; Montazemi 2006; Thong et al. 1996; Thong and Yap 1995; Blili and Raymond 1993; Rizzoni 1991). His/her skills and preferences have a major impact on the extent to which the SME changes (Thong and Yap 1995; Birley 1982).
6. In SMEs, the CEO takes the decision whether or not to adopt a new approach (Levy and Powell 2008; Bharati and Chaudhury 2006; Levy and Powell 2005; Southern and Tilley 2000; Thong and Yap 1995). With every decision there is a degree of uncertainty. The expected returns must exceed the expected risks and costs (time, money, effort) in order to accept a new approach (Levy et al. 2001; Rogers 1983). Adoption will be covered in more detail later in this chapter.

2.4 Six Criteria for SMEs

From these characteristics it is possible to derive criteria that can be a guidance for developing IS techniques that have a higher fit with SMEs:

1. The approach should enable SMEs to work in a time efficient manner on strategic issues.
2. A person with limited IT skills should be able to apply the approach.
3. It should be possible to apply the approach with little assistance of external experts.
4. The approach should enable making descriptions of how things are done in the company.
5. The CEO must be involved in the approach (Caldeira and Ward 2003; Yap et al. 1992).
6. The expected revenues of the approach must exceed the expected costs and risks. Later on in this chapter, the terminology perceived usefulness and perceived ease of use will be introduced.

2.5 Problems Faced by SMEs

SMEs are very important for economy, however, not all new SMEs make it through the first years. 70 % survive at least 2 years, 50 % at least 5 years, a third at least 10 years, and only a quarter stay in business 15 years or more (Bureau of Labor Statistics 2011; Census Bureau 2011). Although there are many reasons for these numbers, some problems can be related to a lack of structure and overview in the company to pursue a superior competitive strategy (O'Gorman 2001).

In an SME, the entrepreneur (CEO) controls the enterprise. However, while most entrepreneurs have a good knowledge about their company, the overview tends to stay unspoken. This can cause some problems to occur:

- For ERP adoption, the most important criterion used by European SMEs in selecting an information system is the best fit with current business procedures (van Everdingen et al. 2000). This is also confirmed in the case studies of De Nil et al. (2012). However, in nearly all SMEs they visited, a clear overview of the business was lacking.
- In an enterprise, employees tend to know less about the structure of the company and why things are done. Although the entrepreneur knows the overview of the company, it is difficult for him/her to communicate with its employees about strategic issues without having an explicit overview (Kamsties et al. 1998).
- A concrete job description and overview of tasks and responsibilities of employees is difficult to keep track of, especially in a changing environment and enterprise (Kamsties et al. 1998). In (Chan and Chao 2008) it is said that the majority of the employees (88 %) stated that they are required to spend a lot of time doing additional work that is not specified in their job description.

- A strategy is not static, neither are processes. Keeping processes at all time in line with the strategy is difficult to achieve (Dougherty 1992).
- In an ever-changing environment, assessing the impact of changes can help to prevent problems to occur. What if the economy changes? What if the strategy has to be adapted? What if an employee leaves the company? (Porter 1998)
- An SME has different stakeholders with different desires and goals. Balancing these goals as good as possible is not a simple assignment (Heyse et al. 2012).
- If the CEO leaves the company for some reason (e.g., he/she sells the company or a child takes over), the knowledge about the overview of the company has to be transferred to the new CEO (Yong et al. 2004; Bjuggren and Sund 2001).

Furthermore, knowledge and more specifically entrepreneurial knowledge is important for SMEs. Knowledge cannot be reduced to its purely technical sense, as a collection of patentable inventions. Knowledge is fundamentally linked to an individual with an idea that is being realized (Devos 2011). This entrepreneurial knowledge gives SMEs a competitive advantage over larger companies. Larger companies are using capital and labor as resources and are trying to control their transaction and management costs (Jensen and Meckling 1976; Coase 1937).

Knowledge is very important for an SME, however, this knowledge is linked to a person with his idea (Audretsch et al. 2004). Next to capital and labor, this extra production factor, entrepreneurial capital, is important for SMEs to maintain and communicate, especially when the company is growing and the CEO tends to loose grip (Carree and Thurik 2005; Weick et al. 2005; Audretsch and Thurik 2000).

3 Enterprise Architecture

3.1 Enterprise Architecture Introduction

Enterprise architecture (EA) is used as a holistic approach to keep things aligned in a company. Some emphasize the use of EA to align IT with the business, others see it broader and use it to also keep the processes aligned with the strategy. EA is a key instrument in controlling the complexity of the enterprise and its processes and systems. Lankhorst defines EA as "a coherent whole of principles, methods, and models that are used in the design and realization of an enterprise's organizational structure, business processes, information systems, and infrastructure" (Lankhorst 2009, p. 3). As such, EA has to capture the essentials of the enterprise, because they are more stable than the specific solutions found for the problems currently at hand. The most important characteristic of an EA is that it provides a holistic overview of the enterprise. This enables optimization of the company as a whole instead of doing local optimization within individual domains. EA facilitates the translation from corporate strategy to daily operations. To achieve this quality, it is necessary to use an approach that is understood by all those involved from these different domains (Lankhorst 2009).

3.2 Existing Techniques

Research on EA has primarily focused on integrating business with IT, often referred to as business-IT alignment (Henderson and Venkatraman 1993). An overview of some well-known EA frameworks, methods, metamodels, ontologies, and languages is given in the next paragraphs. However not exhaustive, this overview covers a broad spectrum of EA techniques: the initial EA framework (Zachman's Framework), the Open Group standards (TOGAF and ArchiMate), the U.S. Department of Defense Architecture Framework (DoDAF), a technique developed by a consulting firm based on best practices (Capgemini's IAF), and two techniques developed in an academic context (REA and EKD).

Zachman's Framework (Zachman 1987) (see Fig. 1) is probably the first and most famous EA framework. This framework is a structured way, based on two dimensions (focus and view), to classify and organize the representations of an organization. Each dimension consists of six parts, resulting in a matrix with 36 cells. Zachman's Framework is only a classification framework and offers no method to develop EAs. Therefore, it is often used in conjunction with TOGAF.

The Open Group Architecture Framework (TOGAF) (The Open Group 2009) (see Fig. 2) is a framework and method to develop and manage EAs. TOGAF consists of four major components, of which the Architecture Development Method (ADM) is considered the core. It describes an iterative method for EA development. The ADM states that the business architecture is first developed, followed by the information system architectures (applications and data) and the technology architecture. TOGAF is frequently used with ArchiMate.

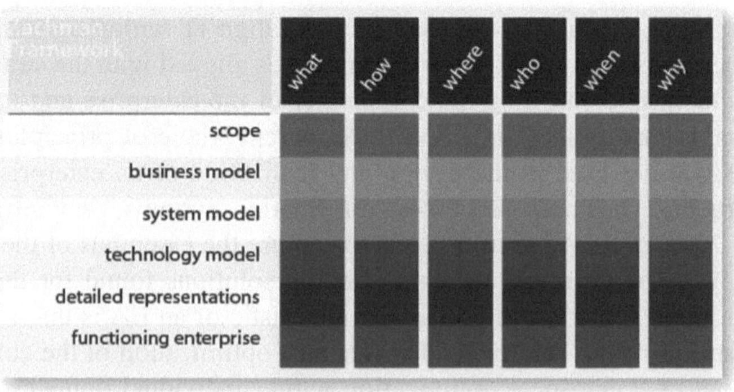

Fig. 1 Zachman's framework

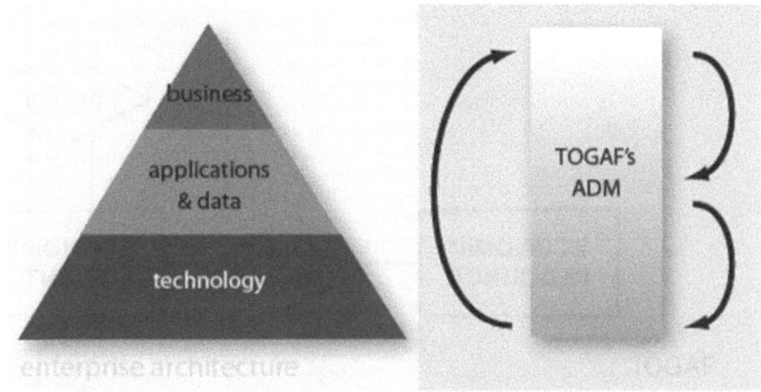

Fig. 2 A simplification of TOGAF's ADM

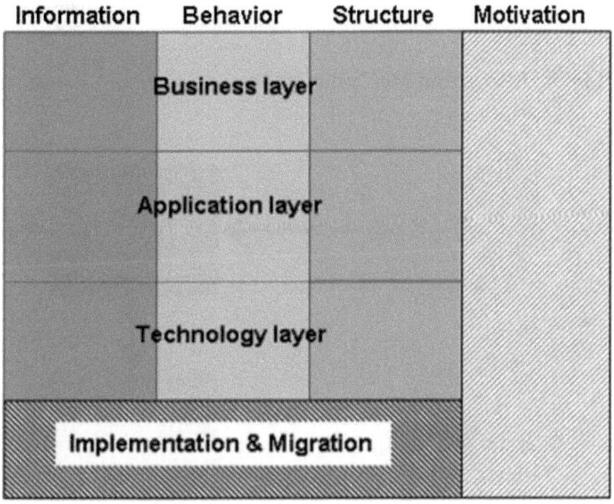

Fig. 3 ArchiMate 2.0 (from The Open Group 2012)

ArchiMate (The Open Group 2012; Lankhorst 2009) (see Fig. 3) proposes a standard language and metamodel for describing EAs and is widely supported by tools and consulting companies. The metamodel shows that ArchiMate works with three layers of architectural models, namely a business architecture layer, an application architecture layer (includes applications and data), and a technology architecture layer. Within each layer there is a section that reflects behavioral or dynamic aspects and two sections representing structural or static aspects. The static aspects can be active (structure) or passive (information). The new version of ArchiMate (ArchiMate 2.0) provides a tighter alignment with TOGAF and also includes a strategic dimension (motivation) (The Open Group 2012).

While being intensively elaborated to be as complete as possible, the previous approaches are becoming more difficult to implement. Extensive training and certification are needed to be able to start using these approaches.

The resource-event-agent (REA) ontology (McCarthy 1982) (see Fig. 4) was developed as a basis for accounting information systems and has been extended to form a basis for enterprise information systems architectures. The core concepts in

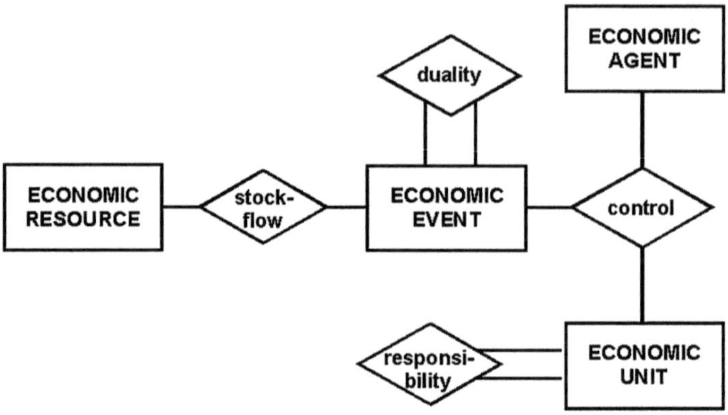

Fig. 4 REA (from McCarthy 1999)

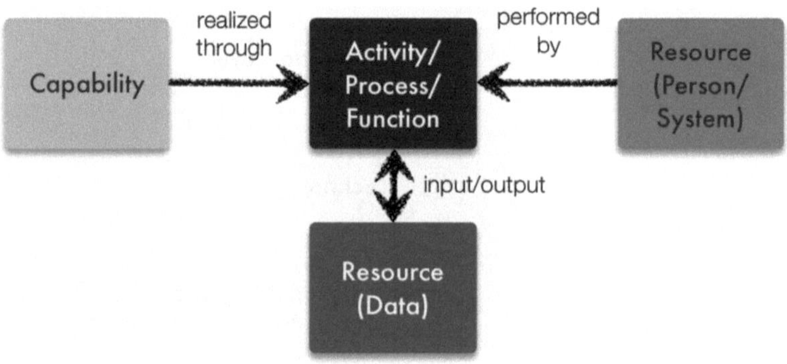

Fig. 5 CARP (from zur Muehlen 2011)

this ontology are Resource, Event, and Agent. In Andersson et al. (2009), the REA ontology has been extended with goal modeling.

In his keynote on the Confenis 2011 conference (zur Muehlen 2011), zur Muehlen talked about his vision on semantic EA. He introduced CARP (capability, activity, resource, and performer) (see Fig. 5) as a domain ontology for EA, based on the dimensions of DoDAF (DoD 2010).

Capgemini's Integrated Architecture Framework (IAF) (see Fig. 6) has been developed by Capgemini since the 1990s (van 't Wout et al. 2010). This framework is the result of the experience of practicing architects on projects for clients across the group, so it has really evolved based on real-world experience. The framework includes four questions (why?, what?, how?, with what?) across the different layers of EA (business, information, information systems, and technology layer).

Enterprise modeling (Bubenko 1993) has put a lot of effort in developing the enterprise model, in which different submodels are interrelated and describe four dimensions. More recent work on the Enterprise Knowledge Development (EKD)

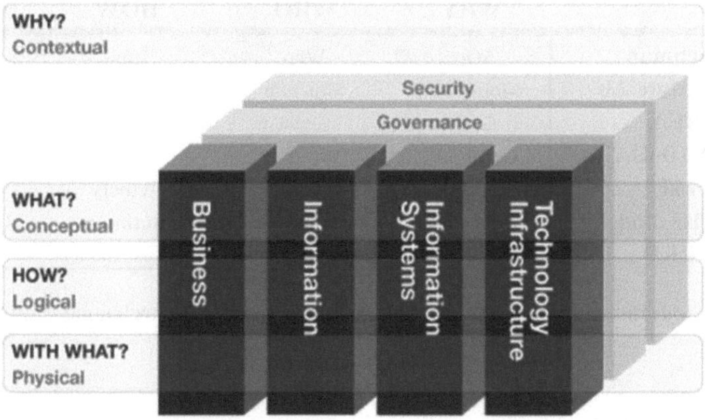

Fig. 6 Capgemini's IAF

Fig. 7 The three layers of a traditional enterprise architecture technique

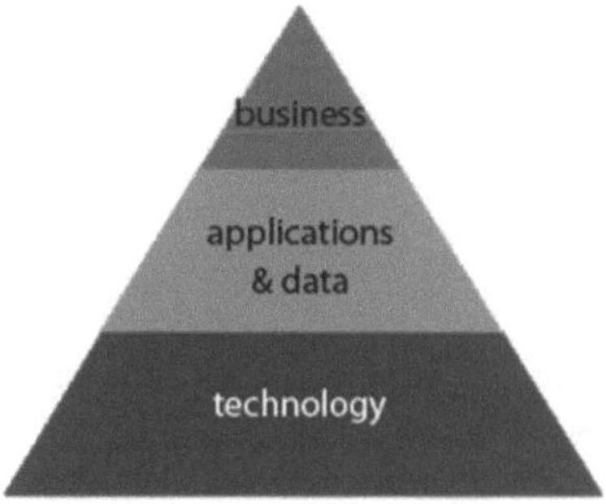

method for enterprise modeling (Stirna and Persson 2007) defines six submodels, but agrees that its Goals Model, Business Process Model, Concepts Model, and Actors and Resources Model tend to dominate EKD usage.

3.3 The Key Concepts of Enterprise Architecture Techniques

Most EA techniques work with three layers of architectural models, namely a business architecture layer, an application architecture layer (includes applications and data), and a technology architecture layer. As EA is primarily developed by IT researchers, it focuses primarily on IT and its alignment with the business [business-IT alignment (Henderson and Venkatraman 1993)] (see Fig. 7). However, nowadays, the business architecture part gets more and more attention, because it is the basis where everything starts (Lankhorst 2009; Ross et al. 2006).

In the business architecture layer we can distinguish four dimensions that are shared by all EA techniques. Either Zachman, ArchiMate 2.0, REA with goal modeling, CARP, Capgemini's IAF, enterprise modeling, and EKD include a

	WHY	WHO	HOW	WHAT
Zachman	Why	Who	How	What
ArchiMate 2.0	Motivation	Structure	Behavior	Information
REA	Goals	Agent	Event	Resource
CARP (DoDAF)	Capability	Performer	Activity	Resource
IAF	Goal	Actor	Activity	Object
Enterprise modeling / EKD	Goals model	Actors and recources model	Business process model	Concepts model

Fig. 8 The four dimensions of a traditional enterprise architecture technique

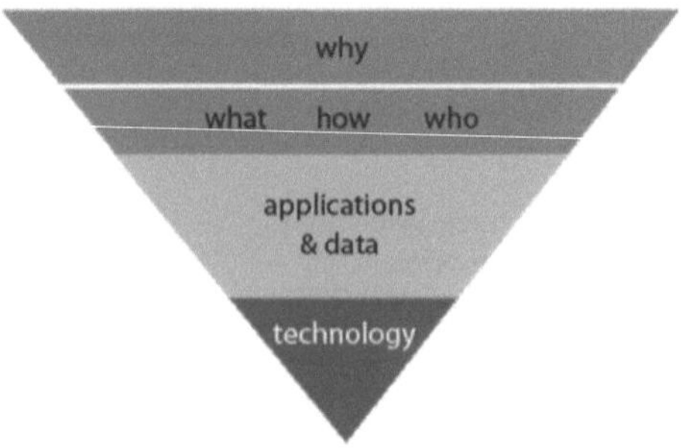

Fig. 9 Enterprise architecture with more focus on the four core dimensions of the business architecture

strategic dimension, an active actor, an operation, and an object (input or output) (see Fig. 8).

These four dimensions (why, who, how, what) can be used as a basis of an approach for EA in SMEs. Zachman's Framework also includes two additional dimensions: when and where. These dimensions can be seen as attributes of an operation (how).

Figure 9 is an inverted pyramid, unlike Fig. 7, to emphasize that nowadays, it is assumed that the business architecture is the foundation of a good EA, and an EA technique has to start with a strategic question (why). Strategy is the most important part (Porter 1985), especially because different stakeholders have different goals. Most techniques for EA first made abstraction of this part, while this is the most important step. ArchiMate for instance now also incorporates this dimension in its new 2.0 standard (The Open Group 2012).

3.4 Five Criteria for EA Techniques

From Lankhorst's definition and description of EA (Lankhorst 2009, p. 3), five criteria for an EA approach are derived:

1. Control: "EA is a key instrument in controlling the complexity of the enterprise and its processes and systems."

2. Holistic Overview: "The most important characteristic of an EA is that it provides a holistic overview of the enterprise.", "EA has to capture the essentials of the enterprise, because they are more stable than the specific solutions found for the problems currently at hand."
3. Objectives: "EA facilitates the translation from corporate strategy to daily operations."
4. Suitable for its target audience (here: SMEs): "It is necessary to use an approach that is understood by all those involved from these different domains."
5. Enterprise: "This enables optimization of the company as a whole instead of doing local optimization within individual domains."

Currently there are few EA approaches specifically adapted to be used in an SME context, which does not conform to criterion four. In the previous part on SMEs, it has however been shown that SMEs have some specific characteristics.

3.5 Benefits of Enterprise and Business Architecture

EA provides several benefits to companies, including the following: (Lankhorst 2009; Ross et al. 2006)

- Creating a common architecture means that the architect takes into account the needs of all stakeholders of the company, allowing the architecture to become an acceptable design for these stakeholders.
- The architecture provides an overview of the main areas of the company and it is possible to see only a part of this overview, without irrelevant details, using different viewpoints. For example, a marketeer can ask to just see the products of the company, its customers (groups), and the value proposition.
- The viewpoints can be used as documentation of the building blocks of the company. Changes in the company can for example first be tested on the EA model of the company, before implementing them in reality.
- The representation of and relationships between the elements of the EA can be used for analysis and optimization purposes. It is for example possible for a bank to calculate the network capacity required to process all transactions timely and accurately, based on the number of daily transactions.
- The representation of and relationships between the elements can also enable change impact analysis. If, for example, it is decided to fully automate the payment process through formatted numbers on invoices, it could be examined to what extent these changes affect the other elements of the EA. For example, an application will have to be developed or purchased to be able to identify these formatted numbers and be able to link the payment automatically to the correct invoice. This analysis will make it also possible to draw up a good budget.

- The survey of (van Everdingen et al. 2000) revealed that for ERP adoption, the most important criterion used by European SMEs in selecting an information system (ERP adoption) is the best fit with current business procedures. By developing a business architecture, a clear overview of the business can help selecting the most appropriate ERP system for the company.

Besides these general advantages, EA could help reducing the previously mentioned problems from SMEs. First of all, EA makes it possible to clearly define a competitive strategy (Porter 1985) as part of the business architecture and to align the company with this strategy to achieve a competitive advantage. Second, a clearly defined EA model could make it easier to find an ERP system that best fits the current business. Third, an explicit business architecture model can show the links between operations and strategy and enables an entrepreneur to communicate with the employees. Fourth, a job description can be queried from the relationships of employees with operations. Fifth, by explicitly linking strategic and operational items, it becomes easier to achieve and maintain alignment of the processes with the strategy. Sixth, these links make it possible to perform change impact analysis. Seventh, linking goals in a goal tree and including goals from different stakeholders makes it possible to develop a global goal tree and see which goals are conflicting. These conflicts can be resolved by balancing the different desires and goals (Heyse et al. 2012). Eighth, relevant knowledge of the company and the entrepreneurial knowledge can be made explicit in the EA model by modeling these concepts in the business layer, making it easier for employees and successors to gain insight in this knowledge.

EA could help to reduce the previously mentioned problems from SMEs, however, EA is generally an unknown and unused concept in SMEs. In literature, articles about EA for SMEs are very scarce. In fact, in a literature study of Devos (2011, pp. 41–87) of A1 papers found from 1979 to 2008 about SMEs and IT, no single paper discussed EA for SMEs. Furthermore, an exploratory case study research in 27 SMEs in Belgium (De Nil et al. 2012) delivered interesting insight in which factors determine whether an SME documents its processes, its strategy, and whether there is a link between both. While some companies have a link between their processes and strategy, none of them uses an EA or business architecture method.

4 Enterprise Architecture for SMEs

In the next part, we will discuss the most important adoption models for IS and IS methods. These models will help us to propose guidelines for EA technique developers in order to be able to develop EA techniques that are easier adapted by SMEs. User acceptance of information systems has become an important issue in the IS field (Hu et al. 1999; Brancheau et al. 1996; Gaynor 1996; Hartwick and Barki 1994; Markus and Keil 1994; Alavi and Carlson 1992; Keen 1991; Cooper and Zmud 1990; Davis et al. 1989). Regardless of the technical superiority or potential benefits of a particular information system, if it is not used or is underutilized, the benefits cannot be realized (Chau 1996).

4.1 Adoption Models

4.1.1 Technology Acceptance Model

Of all the models that have been proposed for user technology acceptance, the Technology Acceptance Model (TAM) has been the most influential (Altaf and Schuff 2010; Lederer et al. 2000; Hu et al. 1999; Chau 1996; Szajna 1996; Venkatesh and Davis 1996; Taylor and Todd 1995; Subramanian 1994; Szajna 1994; Hendrickson et al. 1993; Adams et al. 1992; Mathieson 1991; Davis 1989; Davis et al. 1989; Igbaria et al. 1997).

Davis (1989) introduced the TAM, a well-known and widely referred model regarding the adoption of technology. He developed and validated a measurement scale for predicting user acceptance of technology, based on two variables, perceived usefulness and perceived ease of use, which are hypothesized to be fundamental determinants of user acceptance.

People tend to use or not use an application to the extent they believe it will help them to perform their job better. This first variable is called perceived usefulness. However, even if potential users believe that a given application is useful, they may, at the same time, believe that the system is too hard to use and that the performance benefits of usage are outweighed by the effort of using the application. This second variable is called perceived ease of use. Both variables have an impact on the intention to use (see Fig. 10).

Perceived usefulness is "the degree to which a person believes that using a particular system would enhance his or her job performance". Perceived ease of use, in contrast, refers to "the degree to which a person believes that using a particular system would be free of effort". The intention to use is "the extent to which a person intends to use a particular system".

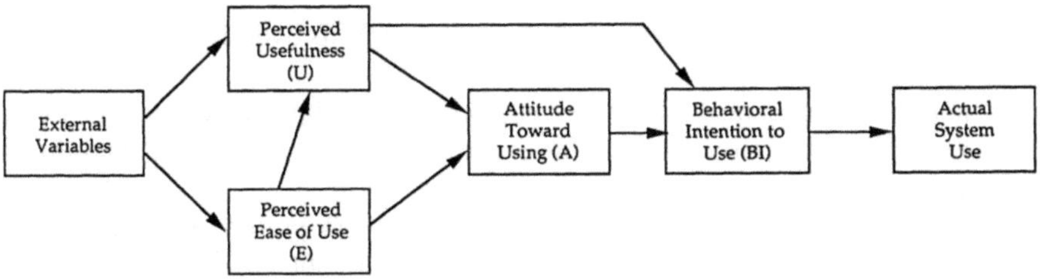

Fig. 10 Technology acceptance model (from Davis et al. 1989)

Davis (1989) refined the measures and streamlined them, which resulted in two six-item scales for perceived usefulness and perceived ease of use.

Perceived usefulness:

1. Work more quickly
2. Improve job performance
3. Increase productivity
4. Enhance effectiveness
5. Make job easier
6. It is useful

For perceived usefulness, notice that the items fall into three main clusters. The first cluster relates to job effectiveness (2,4), the second to productivity and time savings (1,3), and the third to the importance of the system to one's job (5,6).

Perceived ease of use:

1. Easy to learn
2. Controllable (get it to do what I want it to do)
3. Clear and understandable
4. Flexible to interact with
5. Easy to become skillful
6. Easy to use

These items also fall into three main clusters. The first relates to physical effort (2,4), while the second relates to mental effort (3,6). The third cluster is somewhat more difficult to interpret but appears to be tapping perceptions of how easy a system is to learn (1,5).

In both studies performed by Davis, perceived usefulness was significantly more strongly linked to usage than was perceived ease of use. Users are driven to adopt an application primarily because of the functions it performs for them, and secondarily for how easy or hard it is to get the system to perform those functions. For instance, users are often willing to cope with some difficulty of use in a system that provides critically needed functionality. Although difficulty of use can discourage adoption of an otherwise useful system, no amount of ease of use can compensate for a system that does not perform a useful function. Ease of use may in this way be an antecedent to usefulness, rather than a parallel, direct determinant of usage (see Fig. 10). All else being equal, the easier a system is to interact with, the less effort needed to operate it, and the more effort one can allocate to other activities (Radner and Rothschild 1975), contributing to overall job performance and perceived usefulness.

It should be emphasized that perceived usefulness and perceived ease of use are people's subjective appraisal of performance and effort, respectively, and do not necessarily reflect objective reality.

Practitioners generally evaluate systems not only to predict acceptability but also to diagnose the reasons underlying lack of acceptance and to formulate interventions to improve user acceptance. In this sense, research on how usefulness and ease of use of EA techniques can be influenced by various controllable factors (e.g., design, user interface, functional characteristics, training and education, case study testing and user involvement in design,...) is important.

4.1.2 Method Evaluation Model

Moody (2003) noticed that IS design research emphasized the development of new methods, while the evaluation of methods was only addressed in a limited fashion (Westrup 1993; Fitzgerald 1991; Bubenko 1986; Curtis 1986). Wynekoop and Russo (1997) conducted a review of IS design research published in the leading IS journals and concluded that there was a "lack of serious empirical research into the efficacy of methods in practice" and a "need for validation of methods in organizational contexts using real practitioners". *Regardless of the potential benefits of IS design methods published, unless they are used in practice, these benefits cannot be realized.* The issue of practitioner acceptance of methods is something which has been largely ignored in IS design research and could help improving the acceptance of EA techniques in SMEs. However, usage is an important pragmatic measure of the "success" of a method and also of the impact of research on practice (Fitzgerald 1991).

Moody proposed a theoretical model and associated measurement instrument for evaluating IS design methods, like EA methods. The method is based on the previously mentioned TAM (Davis 1989) and Methodological Pragmatism (Rescher 1977).

4.1.3 Methodological Pragmatism

Methodological Pragmatism (Rescher 1977) assumes that methods have no truth value, only pragmatic value. A method does not describe any external reality, so it cannot be true or false, only effective or ineffective. Unlike theses, methods cannot be established deductively from known facts or inductively from observations. *The validity of a method can only be established by applicative success in practice.* The objective of validation should not be to demonstrate that the method is "correct", but that it is rational practice to adopt the method based on its pragmatic success. Pragmatic success is defined as "the efficiency and effectiveness with which a method achieves its objectives". All methods are designed to improve performance of a task (see Fig. 11). Task performance can be improved in two ways:

- Efficiency improvement: reducing the effort required to complete the task, i.e. reducing the inputs.
- Effectiveness improvement: improving the quality of the result, i.e. improving the outputs.

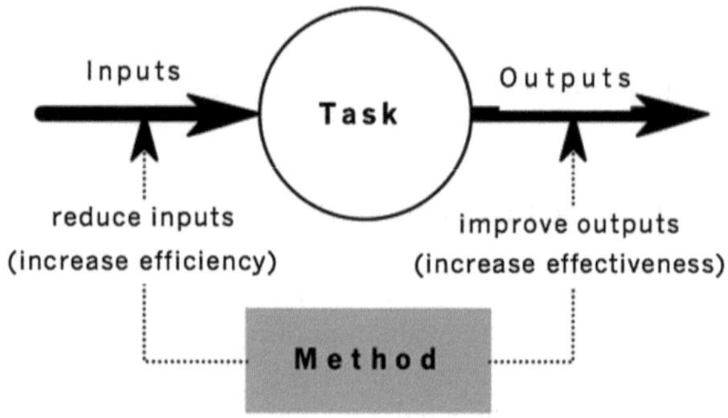

Fig. 11 Efficiency vs. effectiveness (from Moody 2003)

4.1.4 Combining Methodological Pragmatism and the Technology Acceptance Model

Moody (2003) argued that there are clear parallels between user acceptance of information systems and practitioner adoption of methods. Both are subject to individual choice: users make decisions about what systems they will use and practitioners make decisions about what methods they will use. Both are therefore the result of reasoned action. For this reason, Moody argued that theoretical models used to explain and predict user acceptance of information technology may be adapted to explain and predict the adoption of methods.

Actual efficacy and adoption in practice are two dimensions of success. On their own, neither actual efficacy nor adoption in practice will lead to improved practices. A method that improves performance but that is not used will have no effect on practices. Similarly, a method that people use but which reduces performance of the task will have a negative effect on practices. Nowadays, as already mentioned, EA is hardly used in SMEs, although it could improve performance.

Both TAM and Methodological Pragmatism are combined in the Method Evaluation Model, a theoretical model for evaluating methods. Figure 12 shows the primary constructs of the model and causal relationships.

The definitions of the constructs of the model are:

- Actual efficiency: the effort required to apply a method.
- Actual effectiveness: the degree to which a method achieves its objectives.
- Perceived ease of use: the degree to which a person *believes* that using a particular method would be free of effort.
- Perceived usefulness: the degree to which a person *believes* that a particular method will be effective in achieving its intended objectives.
- Intention to use: the extent to which a person intends to use a particular method.
- Actual usage: the extent to which a method is used in practice.

Actual efficiency and actual effectiveness are constructs from Methodological Pragmatism. Perceived ease of use, perceived usefulness and intention to use are the constructs of TAM.

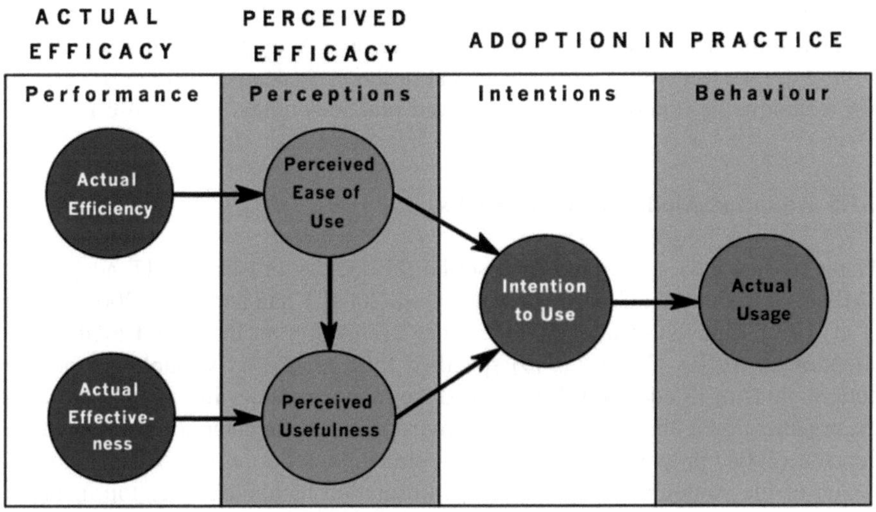

Fig. 12 The Method Evaluation Model (from Moody 2003)

The causal relationships between the constructs of the model are:

- Perceived ease of use is determined by actual efficiency: actual efficiency measures the effort required to apply the method, which should determine perceptions of effort required.
- Perceived usefulness is determined by actual effectiveness: actual effectiveness measures how well the method achieves its objectives, which should determine perceptions of its effectiveness.
- Perceived usefulness is determined by its perceived ease of use. This follows from TAM.
- Intention to use a method is jointly determined by its perceived ease of use and perceived usefulness. This follows from TAM.
- Actual usage of a method is determined by intention to use. This also follows from TAM and the Theory of Planned Behavior (Ajzen 1991), which establishes that perceptions influence intentions which in turn influence the actual behavior of the individual.

The main difference with TAM is that in the Method Evaluation Model actual efficiency and effectiveness determine intentions to use a method only via perceptions of ease of use and usefulness. This is a subtle difference, but an important one: in human behavior, subjective reality is more important than objective reality. The perceptions will also be influenced by other factors (e.g., prior knowledge, experience with particular methods, normative influences).

Moody also concluded that the relative importance of perceived ease of use in making decisions about method adoption is much higher for practitioners than it is for undergraduate students. This asks for EA techniques that are easily applicable by practitioners in SMEs. As well as trying to develop EA techniques that produce better results, it is equally important to develop EA techniques that people are willing to use. Regardless of the technical or theoretical superiority of a particular EA technique, it cannot result in improved practices unless people use it.

4.1.5 Adoption Models of IT in SMEs

Many studies have attempted to describe the factors influencing IT adoption in SMEs (Altaf and Schuff 2010; Chwelos et al. 2001; Kuan and Chau 2001; Igbaria et al. 1997; Iacovou et al. 1995). In order to develop an integrated model of IS adoption in SMEs, Thong (1999) specified four contextual variables as primary determinants of IS adoption. He grouped the many variables in four groups: CEO, IS, organizational characteristics, and environmental characteristics. Grandon and Pearson (2004) proposed a model for e-commerce adoption in SMEs based on a fusion of the strategic value of certain information technologies to top managers (Subramanian and Nosek 2001; Chan 2000; Barua et al. 1995) and factors that influence the adoption of IT [TAM (Davis 1989)]. The results confirmed TAM in the sense that perceived usefulness and perceived ease of use turned out to be the most influential factors of e-commerce adoption as perceived by top managers of SMEs.

Although these models discuss the adoption of information technology and not methods in SMEs, they confirm the factors of TAM as being the most influential for adoption in SMEs. The Method Evaluation Model of Moody (2003), although not specifically developed for evaluation of methods in SMEs, is based on the factors of TAM and will be further used as an evaluation model for EA methods in SMEs.

4.2 Bringing EA to SMEs

From the TAM (Davis 1989) and the Method Evaluation Model (Moody 2003), three actions can be defined in order to enhance the adoption of EA techniques in SMEs.

First, the perceived usefulness has to be increased. Second, the perceived ease of use has to be increased. Third, the actual efficacy has to influence the perceived efficacy.

4.2.1 Increase the Perceived Usefulness

Usefulness can be related to the advantages of EA techniques for SMEs. However, perceived usefulness is influenced by actual effectiveness. To increase the actual effectiveness of EA techniques for SMEs, the techniques have to be implemented in practice (e.g., case studies, testing companies,…) and feedback from the SMEs has to help developing EA techniques that bring more advantages for SMEs. The six-item scale of TAM can be used to assess the perceived usefulness.

4.2.2 Increase the Perceived Ease of Use

Ease of use is related to the effort that has to be spent to implement an EA technique. Complexity, defined by Rogers and Shoemaker (1971, p. 154) as "the degree to which an innovation is perceived as relatively difficult to understand and use", parallels perceived ease of use quite closely. As SMEs have rather limited free time to work on strategic issues, limited IT knowledge, and limited resources to spend (see the previously mentioned characteristics of SMEs), a special effort has to be made to adapt EA techniques to an SME context. As Lankhorst (2009) mentioned, it is necessary to use an approach that is understood by all those involved from the different domains (see the fourth criterion for EA techniques). Perceived ease of use is influenced by the actual efficiency, so these techniques have to be implemented and tested in practice. The six-item scale of TAM can be used to assess the perceived ease of use.

4.2.3 From Actual to Perceived Efficacy

To get a positive influence of the actual on the perceived efficacy, EA techniques have to be implemented in SMEs. The advantage is twofold. First, feedback can be used to adapt the EA techniques and enhance the perceived ease of use and usefulness. Second, by implementing EA techniques in practice, EA can get better known in SMEs and especially the advantages can get widespread. Positive testimonials and word of mouth can generate a higher perceived efficacy.

5 Recommendations for EA Technique Developers

5.1 Research Steps

Figure 13 summarizes different research steps that can be taken to develop EA techniques that have a higher likelihood of acceptance in SMEs.

First, both SMEs and EA have to be analyzed and relevant characteristics should be examined. From these characteristics, criteria could be extracted. This step is already done for SMEs (see the criteria for SMEs) and EA (see the criteria for EA techniques). The criteria should enable a good fit of EA with SMEs, which enhances both the actual efficiency and effectiveness.

Second, an initial metamodel can be developed, based on these criteria.

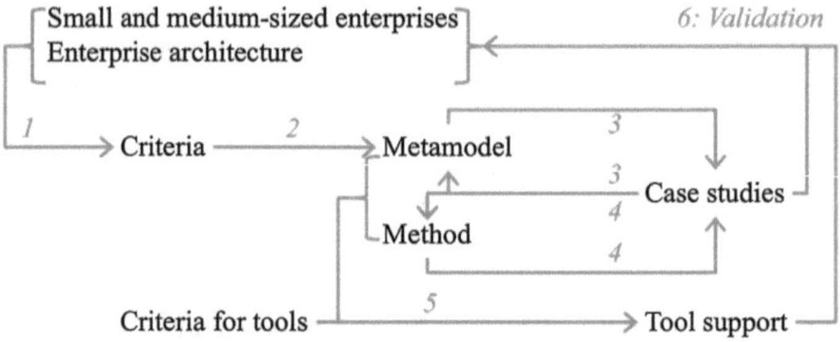

Fig. 13 Research steps

Third, during case studies in SMEs, the initial metamodel can be refined.

Fourth, the case studies will also help to develop and refine a method including step-by-step guidelines to develop an EA model of the SME. The criteria are not directly linked with the method, because it is developed from scratch during the case studies. As Moody (2003) and Rescher (1977) emphasized, the validity of a method can only be established by applicative success in practice.

Fifth, software tool support has to be developed. Tool support can help automating certain tasks, but cannot help if we do not understand the development process (Lindland et al. 1994). Tool support can have several advantages. It can facilitate the input (actual efficiency) and enhance the output (actual effectiveness). However, tool support can have disadvantages as well, especially with respect to the actual efficiency (e.g., it can be costly, there is a learning curve, users need to be able to work on a computer,…). Perceived ease of use refers to user friendliness of the system, the ease in learning the system, and the help features provided by the system. Therefore, we can infer that a user-friendly business architecture method and tool is more likely to be adopted by small businesses. This user-friendliness could be operationalized as context-sensitive help or an intuitive user interface. We argue that tool support, if properly developed, can have substantial benefits for EA techniques. The metamodel and method, in combination with criteria for developing effective and efficient tool support, can be used to develop this tool support.

Sixth, this tool support enables both the validation in the case studies, as the validation by SMEs themselves that can use the tools. This validation step is crucial in getting from actual to perceived efficacy.

5.2 Design Science

Design science (Hevner et al. 2004) is a well-known methodology to develop an artifact (construct, model, method, or instantiation). The different steps of design science can be applied to the research steps for the development of EA techniques for SMEs (see Fig. 14). The development and refinement of the metamodel and method are part of the build step. The validation by the case studies is part of the

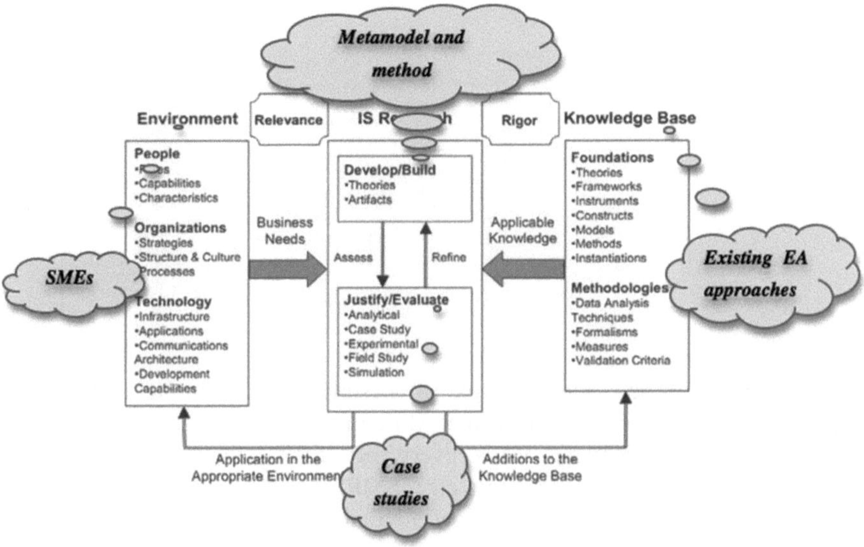

Fig. 14 Information systems research framework (from Hevner et al. 2004)

evaluate step, while the tool support enables the evaluate step. The goal of design science is not the truth, but utility. Utility is found in the search for a higher perceived ease of use and usefulness of EA in SMEs. The link to existing EA approaches has to enhance the rigor of the research, while the link to and case studies in SMEs enhances the relevance of the research.

The seven guidelines presented in (Hevner et al. 2004) can be applied to the research steps. A metamodel and method are created (guideline 1: creation of an artifact) for SMEs (guideline 2: for a specified problem domain). The approach is evaluated in case studies (guideline 3: thorough evaluation of the artifact). No specific EA approach for SMEs exists (guideline 4: innovative, novelty). The metamodel and method have to be formalized (guideline 5: the artifact must be rigorously defined, formally represented, coherent, and internally consistent). The case studies are used to refine the metamodel and develop and refine the method (guideline 6: search process). Finally, articles have to be written about the approach, both in academic journals as in journals for practitioners. Even more important, the approach has to be implemented and tested in practice (guideline 7: communication both to a technical and managerial audience).

5.3 A Starting Point for EA for SMEs

Bharati and Chaudhury (2006) noticed that simpler technologies and software packages have a much wider application in SMEs than more complex ones. It could be a good idea to make an initial approach according to Einstein's principle:

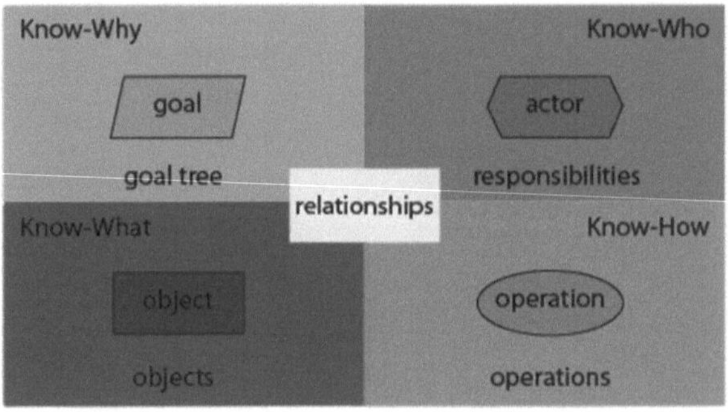

Fig. 15 An example of a starting point for the business architecture layer (from Bernaert and Poels 2011a)

"Everything should be made as simple as possible, but not simpler". In order to keep the approach as simple as possible, while mitigating the risk of making it too simple and loosing advantages of EA, every part of the metamodel later on has to be carefully discussed with experts (e.g., SME experts, practitioners, and academics) and tested in case studies to get a balanced result. A good starting point could be to make an EA approach, based on the core elements of existing EA techniques (see the key concepts of enterprise architecture techniques), to make the approach as simple as possible, but not simpler (see Fig. 9). A strategic dimension (why), an active actor dimension (who), an operation dimension (how), and an object dimension (what) can form the highest and most important layer, the business architecture layer, of the EA model. To get a holistic overview, these four dimensions should be interrelated. An example of this proposed business architecture layer (Bernaert and Poels 2011b) is given in Fig. 15.

This business architecture layer has to be supported by an application layer, which has to be supported by a technology layer.

The initial metamodel should be developed according to the criteria of both SMEs and EA techniques (see the previously mentioned criteria), and more important, it should be tested extensively in real SMEs. Regardless of the potential benefits of EA approaches published, unless they are used in practice, these benefits cannot be realized.

References

Adams, D. A., Nelson, R. R., & Todd, P. A. (1992). Perceived usefulness, ease of use, and usage of information technology: A replication. *MIS Q, 16*(2), 227–247.

Ajzen, I. (1991). The theory of planned behavior. *Organizational Behavior and Human Decision Processes, 50*(2), 179–211.

Alavi, M., & Carlson, P. (1992). A review of MIS research and disciplinary development. *Journal of Management Information Systems, 8*(4), 45–62.

Alpar, P., & Reeves, S. (1990). Predictors of MS/OR application in small businesses. *Interfaces, 20*(2), 2–11.

Alstrup, L. (2000). Coaching continuous improvement in small enterprises. *Integrated Manufacturing Systems, 11*(3), 165–170.

Altaf, F., & Schuff, D. (2010). Taking a flexible approach to ASPs. *Communications of the ACM, 53*(2), 139–143.

Andersson, B., Johannesson, P., & Zdravkovic, J. (2009). Aligning goals and services through goal and business modelling. *Information Systems and E-Business Management, 7*(2), 143–169.

Audretsch, D. B., & Thurik, A. R. (2000). Capitalism and democracy in the 21st century: From the managed to the entrepreneurial economy. *Journal of Evolutionary Economics, 10*(1), 17–34.

Audretsch, D. B., Thurik, A. R., Kwaak, T., & Bosma, N. (2004). *SMEs in Europe 2003*. Luxembourg: European Communities.

Ballantine, J., Levy, M., & Powell, P. (1998). Evaluating information systems in small and medium-sized enterprises: Issues and evidence. *European Journal of Information Systems, 7*(4), 241–251.

Barua, A., Kriebel, C. H., & Mukhopadhyay, T. (1995). Information technologies and business value: An analytic and empirical investigation. *Information Systems Research, 6*(1), 3–23.

Bernaert, M., & Poels, G. (2011a). De zoektocht naar know-how, know-why, know-what en know-who: architectuur voor kleinere bedrijven in vier dimensies. *Informatie (Amsterdam), 53*(9), 34–41.

Bernaert, M., Poels, G. (2011b). The quest for know-how, know-why, know-what and know-who: Using KAOS for enterprise modelling. In C. Salinesi & O. Pastor (Eds.), *CAiSE Workshops, London. Lecture Notes in Business Information Processing* (pp. 29–40). Springer Berlin Heidelberg.

Berryman, J. (1983). Small business failure and survey of the literature. *International Small Business Journal, 1*(4), 47–59.

Bharati, P., & Chaudhury, A. (2006). Studying the current status of technology adoption. *Communications of the ACM, 49*(10), 88–93.

Birley, S. J. (1982). Corporate strategy and the small firm. *Journal of General Management, 8*(2), 82–86.

Bjuggren, P.-O., & Sund, L.-G. (2001). Strategic decision making in intergenerational successions of small- and medium-size family-owned businesses. *Family Business Review, 14*(1), 11–24.

Blili, S., & Raymond, L. (1993). Information technology: Threats and opportunities for small and medium-sized enterprises. *International Journal of Information Management, 13*(6), 439–448.

Brancheau, J. C., Janz, B. D., & Wetherbe, J. C. (1996). Key issues in information systems management: 1994–95 SIM Delphi Results. *MIS Q, 20*(2), 225–242.

Bubenko, J. (1986). Information system methodologies—A research view. In: T. W. Olle, H. G. Sol, & A. A. Verrijn-Stuart (Eds.), Information systems design methodologies: Improving the practice (pp. 289–318). North-Holland.

Bubenko, J. (1993). Extending the scope of information modelling. In *International Workshop on the Deductive Approach to Information Systems and Databases*. Lloret: Costa Brava.

Bureau of Labor Statistics US. (2011). Business employment dynamics. U.S. Department of Labor. http://www.bls.gov/bdm/. Accessed July 2012.

Caldeira, M. M., & Ward, J. M. (2003). Using resource-based theory to interpret the successful adoption and use of information systems and technology in manufacturing small and medium sized enterprises. *European Journal of Information Systems, 12*(2), 127–141.

Carree, M. A., & Thurik, A. R. (2005). The impact of entrepreneurship on economic growth. In Z. J. Acs & D. B. Audretsch (Eds.), *Handbook of entrepreneurship research* (Vol. 1, pp. 437–471). Springer US: International Handbook Series on Entrepreneurship.

Census Bureau US. (2011). Business dynamics statistics. U.S. Department of Commerce. http://www.census.gov/. Accessed July 2012.

Chan, I., & Chao, C.-K. (2008). Knowledge management in small and medium-sized enterprises. *Communications of the ACM, 51*(4), 83–88.

Chan, Y. E. (2000). IT value: The great divide between qualitative and quantitative and individual and organizational measures. *Journal of Management Information Systems, 16*(4), 225–261.

Chau, P. Y. K. (1996). An empirical assessment of a modified technology acceptance model. *Journal of Management Information Systems, 13*(2), 185–204.

Chen, L.-D., Haney, S., Pandzik, A., Spigarelli, J., & Jesseman, C. (2003). Small business internet commerce: A case study. *Journal of Information Resource Management, 16*(3), 17–41.

CHI Research Inc. (2004). *Small firms and technology: Acquisitions, inventor movement, and technology transfer*. New Jersey: Haddon Heights.

Chwelos, P., Benbasat, I., & Dexter, A. S. (2001). Research report: Empirical test of an EDI adoption model. *Information Systems Research, 12*(3), 304–321.

Coase, R. H. (1937). The nature of the firm. *Economica, 4*(16), 386–405.

Cooper, R. B., & Zmud, R. W. (1990). Information technology implementation research: A technological diffusion approach. *Management Science, 36*(2), 123–139.

Cragg, P. B., & King, M. (1993). Small-firm computing: Motivators and inhibitors. *MIS Q, 17*(1), 47–60.

Curtis, B. (1986). By the way, did anyone study any real programmers? In E. Soloway, & S. Iyengar (Eds.), Empirical studies of programmers (pp. 256–262). Ablex Publication: Norward, NJ.

Davis, F. D. (1989). Perceived usefulness, perceived ease of use, and user acceptance of information technology. *MIS Q, 13*(3), 319–340.

Davis, F. D., Bagozzi, R. P., & Warshaw, P. R. (1989). User acceptance of computer technology: A comparison of two theoretical models. *Management Science, 35*(8), 982–1003.

De Nil, S., Deprost, E., Bernaert, M., & Poels, G. (2012). *Van Strategie tot Procesmodellering in Kleine en Middelgrote Organisaties: Een Exploratief Onderzoek*. Ghent: University of Ghent.

Deeks, J. (1976). *The small firm owner-manager-entrepreneurial behavior and management practice*. New York: Praeger Publishers.

DeLone, W. H. (1981). Firm size and the characteristics of computer use. *MIS Q, 5*(4), 65–77.

DeLone, W. H. (1988). Determinants of success for computer usage in small business. *MIS Q, 12*(1), 51–61.

Devos, J. (2011). *IT governance for SMEs*. Ghent: University of Ghent.

DoD, D. (2010). Department of defense architecture framework (DoDAF) version 2.2. http://dodcio.defense.gov/dodaf20.aspx.

Dougherty, D. (1992). A practice-centered model of organizational renewal through product innovation. *Journal of Strategic Management, 13*(S1), 77–92.

European Commission. (2003). Recommendation 2003/361/EC: SME Definition. *Official Journal of the European Union, 46*(L124), 6.

European Commission. (2010). Are EU SMEs recovering from the crisis? In *Annual Report on EU Small and Medium Sized Enterprises 2011*.

Fitzgerald, G. (1991). Validating new information systems techniques: A retrospective analysis. In: H. E. Nissen, H. K. Klein, & R. Hirscheim (Eds.), Information systems research: Contemporary approaches and emergent traditions (pp. 657–672). North-Holland, Amsterdam.

Fuller, T. (1996). Fulfilling IT needs in small businesses: A recursive learning model. *International Small Business Journal, 14*(4), 25–44.

Gable, G. G. (1991). Consultant engagement for computer system selection: A pro-active client role in small businesses. *Information Management, 20*(2), 83–93.

Gaynor, G. H. (1996). *Handbook of technology management*. New York: McGraw-Hill.

Grandon, E. E., & Pearson, J. M. (2004). Electronic commerce adoption: An empirical study of small and medium US businesses. *Information Management, 42*(1), 197–216.

Hartwick, J., & Barki, H. (1994). Explaining the role of user participation in information system use. *Management Science, 40*(4), 440–465.

Harvey, J., Lefebvre, L. A., & Lefebvre, E. (1992). Exploring the relationship between productivity problems and technology adoption in small manufacturing firms. *IEEE Transactions on Engineering Management, 39*(4), 352–358.

Haug, A., Pedersen, S. G. , Arlbjørn, J. S. (2010). Identifying the IT readiness of small and medium sized enterprises. In *Proceedings of the Sixteenth Americas Conference on Information Systems (AMCIS)*. Lima, Peru.

Henderson, J. C., & Venkatraman, N. (1993). Strategic alignment: leveraging information technology for transforming organizations. *IBM Systems Journal, 32*(1), 4–16.

Hendrickson, A. R., Massey, P. D., & Cronan, T. P. (1993). On the test-retest reliability of perceived usefulness and perceived ease of use scales. *MIS Q, 17*(2), 227–230.

Hevner, A. R., March, S. T., Park, J., & Ram, S. (2004). Design science in information systems research. *MIS Q, 28*(1), 75–105.

Heyse, M., Bernaert, M., & Poels, G. (2012). *Keuzes Maken binnen Processen: Het Vermijden van een Russische Roulette voor de Organisaties*. Ghent: University of Ghent.

Hu, P. J., Chau, P. Y. K., Sheng, O. R. L., & Tam, K. Y. (1999). Examining the technology acceptance model using physician acceptance of telemedicine technology. *Journal of Management Information Systems, 16*(2), 91–112.

Iacovou, C. L., Benbasat, I., & Dexter, A. S. (1995). Electronic data interchange and small organizations: adoption and impact of technology. *MIS Q, 19*(4), 465–485.

Igbaria, M., Zinatelli, N., Cragg, P., & Cavaye, A. L. M. (1997). Personal computing acceptance factors in small firms: A structural equation model. *MIS Q, 21*(3), 279–305.

Jensen, M. C., & Meckling, W. H. (1976). Theory of the firm: Managerial behavior, agency costs and ownership structure. *Journal of Financial Economics, 3*(4), 305–360.

Kamsties, E., Hörmann, K., & Schlich, M. (1998). Requirements engineering in small and medium enterprises. *Requirements Engineering, 3*(2), 84–90.

Keen, P. G. W. (1991). *Shaping the future: Business design through information technology*. Boston: Harvard Business School Press.

Khan, E. H., & Khan, G. M. (1992). Microcomputers and small businesses in Bahrain. *Industrial Management & Data Systems, 92*(6), 24–28.

Kroon, B., Voorde, K., & Timmers, J. (2012). High performance work practices in small firms: a resource-poverty and strategic decision-making perspective. *Small Business Economics, 1*, 1–21.

Kuan, K. K. Y., & Chau, P. Y. K. (2001). A perception-based model for EDI adoption in small businesses using a technology-organization-environment framework. *Information Management, 38*(8), 507–521.

Lankhorst, M. (2009). *Enterprise architecture at work: Modelling communication and analysis*. New York: Springer-Verlag.

Lederer, A. L., Maupin, D. J., Sena, M. P., & Zhuang, Y. (2000). The technology acceptance model and the World Wide Web. *Decision Support Systems, 29*(3), 269–282.

Lefebvre, L. A., Lefebvre, E., & Harvey, J. (1996). Intangible assets as determinants of advanced manufacturing technology adoption in SME's: Toward an evolutionary model. *IEEE Transactions on Engineering Management, 43*(3), 307–322.

Levy, M., & Powell, P. (2005). *Strategies for growth in SMEs: The role of information and information systems*. Butterworth-Heinemann: Elsevier.

Levy, M., & Powell, P. (2008). Small firm transformation through IS. *International Journal of Technology Management, 43*(1–3), 123–141.

Levy, M., Powell, P., & Yetton, P. (2001). SMEs: Aligning IS and the strategic context. *Journal of Information Technology, 16*(3), 133–144.

Lincoln, D. J., & Warberg, W. B. (1987). The role of microcomputers in small business marketing. *Journal of Small Business Management, 25*(2), 8–17.

Lindland, O. I., Sindre, G., & Solvberg, A. (1994). Understanding quality in conceptual modeling. *IEEE Software, 11*(2), 42–49.

Malhotra, R., & Temponi, C. (2010). Critical decisions for ERP integration: Small business issues. *International Journal of Information Management, 30*(1), 28–37.

Malone, S. C. (1985). Computerizing small business information systems. *Journal of Small Business Management, 23*(2), 10–16.

Mariano, C., Antonella, M., Emilio, P., & Luisa, P. (2003). Knowledge management configurations in Italian small-to-medium enterprises. *Integrated Manufacturing Systems, 14*(1), 46–56.
Markus, M. L., & Keil, M. (1994). If we build it, they will come: designing information systems that people want to use. *MIT Sloan Management Review, 35*(4), 11–25.
Mathieson, K. (1991). Predicting user intentions: Comparing the technology acceptance model with the theory of planned behavior. *Information systems research, 2*(3), 173–191.
McCarthy, W. (1999). Semantic modeling in accounting education, practice, and research: Some progress and impediments. In G. Goos, J. Hartmanis, & J. van Leeuwen et al. (Eds.), *Conceptual modeling. Lecture Notes in Computer Science* (pp. 144–153). Berlin/Heidelberg: Springer.
McCarthy, W. E. (1982). The REA accounting model: A generalized framework for accounting systems in a shared data environment. *Accounting Review, 57*(3), 554–578.
Metaxiotis, K. (2009). Exploring the rationales for ERP and knowledge management integration in SMEs. *Journal of Enterprise Information Management, 22*(1/2), 51–62.
Meyer, J. (2011). Workforce age and technology adoption in small and medium-sized service firms. *Small Business Economics, 37*(3), 305–324.
Montazemi, A. R. (1988). Factors affecting information satisfaction in the context of the small business environment. *MIS Q, 12*(2), 239–256.
Montazemi, A. R. (2006). How they manage IT: SMEs in Canada and the U.S. *Communications of the ACM, 49*(12), 109–112.
Moody, D. L. (2003). The method evaluation model: A theoretical model for validating information systems design methods. In *Proceedings of the 11th European Conference on Information Systems*, Naples, Italy.
Neidleman, L. D. (1979). Computer usage by small and medium sized European firms: An empirical study. *Information & Management, 2*(2), 67–77.
Noori, H. (1990). *Managing the dynamics of new technology: Issues in manufacturing management*. Englewood Cliffs, NJ: Prentice Hall.
O'Gorman, C. (2001). The sustainability of growth in small- and medium-sized enterprises. *International Journal of Entrepreneurial Behaviour & Research, 7*(2), 60–75.
Poon, S., & Swatman, P. M. C. (1999). An exploratory study of small business internet commerce issues. *Information & Management, 35*(1), 9–18.
Porter, M. E. (1985). *Competitive advantage: creating and sustaining superior performance*. New York: The Free Press.
Porter, M. E. (1998). *Competitive strategy: Techniques for analyzing industries and competitors*. New York: The Free Press.
Radner, R., & Rothschild, M. (1975). On the allocation of effort. *Journal of Economic Theory, 10*(3), 358–376.
Raymond, L. (1985). Organizational characteristics and MIS success in the context of small business. *MIS Q, 9*(1), 37–52.
Rescher, N. (1977). *Methodological pragmatism: A systems-theoretic approach to the theory of knowledge*. Oxford: Basil Blackwell.
Rizzoni, A. (1991). Technological innovation and small firms: A taxonomy. *International Small Business Journal, 9*(3), 31–42.
Rogers, E. M. (1983). *Diffusion of innovations*. New York: The Free Press.
Rogers, E. M., & Shoemaker, F. F. (1971). *Communication of innovations: A cross-cultural approach*. New York: The Free Press.
Ross, J. W., Weill, P., & Robertson, D. (2006). *Enterprise architecture as strategy: Creating a foundation for business execution*. Boston: Harvard Business School Press.
Rullani, E., Micelli, S. (1998). Networks without technology: The future of italian districts in the age of the net. In *SMEs and Districts: Hybrid Governance Forms, Knowledge Creation & Technology Transfer*, Castellanza, Italy, 5–7 Nov.

Sels, L., De Winne, S., Maes, J., Delmotte, J., Faems, D., & Forrier, A. (2006). Unravelling the HRM–performance link: Value-creating and cost-increasing effects of small business HRM*. *Journal of Management Studies, 43*(2), 319–342.

Small Business Administration US. (2011). How important are small businesses to the U.S. economy? Office of advocacy. http://www.sba.gov/advo. Accessed July 2012.

Small Business Administration US. (2012). What is a small business? Office of advocacy. http://www.sba.gov/size. Accessed July 2012.

Southern, A., & Tilley, F. (2000). Small firms and information and communication technologies (ICTs): Toward a typology of ICTs usage. *New Technology, Work and Employment, 15*(2), 138–154.

Stirna, J., & Persson, A. (2007). Ten years plus with EKD: Reflections from using an enterprise modeling method in practice. In B. Pernici & J. A. Gulla (Eds.), *EMMSAD* (pp. 99–108). Norway: Trondheim.

Street, C. T., & Meister, D. B. (2004). Small business growth and internal transparency: The role of information systems. *MIS Q, 28*(3), 473–506.

Subramanian, G. H. (1994). A Replication of perceived usefulness and perceived ease of use measurement. *Decision Sciences, 25*(5–6), 863–874.

Subramanian, G. H., & Nosek, J. T. (2001). An empirical study of the measurement and instrument validation of perceived strategy value of information systems. *Journal of Computer Information Systems, 41*(3), 64–69.

Szajna, B. (1994). Software evaluation and choice: Predictive validation of the technology acceptance instrument. *MIS Q, 18*(3), 319–324.

Szajna, B. (1996). Empirical evaluation of the revised technology acceptance model. *Management Science, 42*(1), 85–92.

Taylor, S., & Todd, P. A. (1995). Understanding information technology usage: A test of competing models. *Information Systems Research, 6*(2), 144–176.

The Open Group. (2009). TOGAF Version 9. Van Haren Publishing. http://www.opengroup.org/togaf. Accessed July 2012.

The Open Group. (2012). ArchiMate 2.0. http://www3.opengroup.org/subjectareas/enterprise/archimate. Accessed July 2012.

Thong, J. Y. L. (1999). An integrated model of information systems adoption in small businesses. *Journal of Management Information Systems, 15*(4), 187–214.

Thong, J. Y. L., & Yap, C. S. (1995). CEO characteristics, organizational characteristics and information technology adoption in small businesses. *Omega, International Journal of Management Science, 23*(4), 429–442.

Thong, J. Y. L., Yap, C. S., & Raman, K. S. (1996). Top management support, external expertise and information systems implementation in small businesses. *Information Systems Research, 7*(2), 248–267.

Thorpe, R., Holt, R., Macpherson, A., & Pittaway, L. (2005). Using knowledge within small and medium-sized firms: A systematic review of the evidence. *International Journal of Management Reviews, 7*(4), 257–281.

Van't Wout, J., Waage, M., Hartman, H., Stahlecker, M., & Hofman, A. (2010). *The integrated architecture framework explained.* Heidelberg: Springer.

van Everdingen, Y., van Hillegersberg, J., & Waarts, E. (2000). Enterprise resource planning: ERP adoption by European midsize companies. *Communications of the ACM, 43*(4), 27–31.

Venkatesh, V., & Davis, F. D. (1996). A model of the antecedents of perceived ease of use: Development and test. *Decision Sciences, 27*(3), 451–481.

Weick, K. E., Sutcliffe, K. M., & Obstfeld, D. (2005). Organizing and the process of sense making. *Organization Science, 16*(4), 409–421.

Welsh, J. A., & White, J. F. (1981). A small business is not a little big business. *Harvard Business Review, 59*(4), 18–32.

Westrup, C. (1993). Information systems methodologies in use. *Journal of Information Technology, 8*(4), 267–275.

Wynekoop, J. L., & Russo, N. L. (1997). Studying system development methodologies: An examination of research methods. *Information Systems Journal, 7*(1), 47–65.

Yap, C. S., Soh, C. P. P., & Raman, K. S. (1992). Information systems success factors in small business. *OMEGA International Journal of Management Sciences, 20*(5/6), 597–609.

Yong, W., David, W., Neil, H., & Keith, S. (2004). The relationship between succession issues and business performance: Evidence from UK family SMEs. *International Journal of Entrepreneurial Behaviour & Research, 10*(1–2), 59–84.

Zachman, J. A. (1987). A framework for information systems architecture. *IBM Systems Journal, 26*(3), 276–292.

zur Muehlen, M. (2011). Keynote: Semantic enterprise architecture. In *CONFENIS*, Aalborg, Denmark.

Assessment of Information Technology Use in Small and Medium-Sized Enterprises: Empirical Investigation in Five Cases

Emre Sezgin and Sevgi Özkan

1 Introduction

Information technology (IT) has brought a new era for society as well as the industry. Today, organizations are required to use IT in order to maintain the business operations and keep the competitive advantage in the market (Martin et al. 2011). The roots of IT are based on the need of information. However, it is still a challenge to reach valuable information and use IT effectively in business operations. Since the information became a major asset by organizations, IT has been needed to be diffused into organizational processes in order to achieve business goals. Oyelaran-Oyeyinka and Lal (2006) emphasized on importance of IT with stating that IT had an important role for success of a company under uncertain economic conditions and unstable market environments. It is a fact that IT is not a silver bullet that saves a business and increases the profit. However, by the effective usage, it can assist to increase the business performance (Powell and Dent-Micallef 1997; Ruiz-Mercader et al. 2006). Thus, it is required to concentrate on controlling IT and involving it into business processes by effective management techniques (Boynton et al. 1994; Carr 2003).

Management of information technology, conceptually, has the same measures considering the basics of management (Applegate et al. 2003). However, it has major upgrades because business processes which involved IT would require extensive knowledge covering business side, social side and technical side (Laudon and Laudon 2012). Badawy (1998) defined IT management as following: "Information Technology Management is concerned with exploring and understanding Information Technology as a corporate resource that determines both the strategic and operational capabilities of the firm in designing and developing

E. Sezgin (✉) · S. Özkan
Middle East Technical University, Ankara, Turkey
e-mail: esezgin@metu.edu.tr; esezgin@ii.metu.edu.tr

S. Özkan
e-mail: sevgiozk@metu.edu.tr

J. Devos et al. (eds.), *Information Systems for Small and Medium-sized Enterprises*, Progress in IS, DOI: 10.1007/978-3-642-38244-4_5,

products and services for maximum customer satisfaction, corporate productivity, profitability and competitiveness". Henceforth, IT management is crucial as much as IT itself that is used in an organization. However, implementing IT in business processes and its management are challenging topics in an organization. Within this context, adopting IT as a coherent concept requires a major change (Kling and Lamb 1999; Legris and Ingham 2003) which all together bring the need of control and guidance. Those needs constituted the basis for assessment of IT and emergence of best practices.

Here, the question is that if an organization faces usage and management challenges in IT, what would be the impact for Small or Medium-sized Enterprises? The aim of the research in this chapter is to evaluate of IT use considering the multifaceted nature of information technologies and to provide a holistic model to unveil latent facts about Small or Medium-Sized Enterprises (SMEs). The scope of the study includes companies classified as SMEs and using IT as a tool or approach to assist their business processes or to manage decision making.

The contribution of this research was primarily to bring new aspects to IT assessment for SMEs which would be applicable with limited time and budget organizations. The findings provided that the model enables SMEs to assess their IT use, and by this way, enhance IT management practices and approaches. Its contribution to the literature was outlined by identifying SMEs need in Turkey and providing assessment tool of IT use. The next section presents information about the status of small and medium-sized enterprises in Europe and Turkey.

1.1 Small or Medium-Sized Enterprises and Information Technology

According to European commission, SMEs should have employees under 250 and 43 million Euro balance sheets in total or 50 million Euro turnovers. They are classified as micro enterprises (1–9 occupied persons), small (10–49) and medium-sized enterprises (50–249). In addition to that, report of European Commission in 2011 declared that there are around 23 million SMEs and 43,000 large companies in the European Union (EU). SMEs constitute 99.8 % of all enterprises. Financially, 57.9 % of EU-27's non-financial business economy value added was generated and 67 % of the jobs in the private sector provided by SMEs (European Commission 2011). In international market it was reported that 25 % of SMEs in Europe are actively operating (European Commission 2010). In terms of information technology, internet constitutes the major part of information and communication technology of an organization. According to European Commission report, 93 % of SMEs in EU have internet access; 20 % have secure server technology and Customer Relationship Management system which enable for e-business operations; average of 12 % has Enterprise Resource Planning and Document Management Systems, which are classified as major communication mediums (European Commission 2008). However, barriers for information technologies exist due to company size, budget and technology complexity (Kartiwi and MacGregor 2007).

On the other side, Turkey has demonstrated an increasing trend in the number of SMEs for ten years. In Turkey, SME was defined by Ministry of Industry as companies which have employees less than 250 and balance sheet of 25 million TL (KOSGEB 2011). In this context, 99.9 % of enterprises in Turkey were classified as SMEs. According to the report of SME Development Organization of Turkey in 2009, 96 % of enterprises were micro-sized, 4 % were small-sized, 0.5 % were medium-sized and 0.1 % were large enterprises, which had more than 250 employees. Industry based classification presented that 82 % of SMEs are active in the service and trading industry, 13 % were active in manufacturing industry. In addition to that, SMEs in Turkey constitutes 78 % of total employment, 65 % of total sales and more than 50 % of total value added, total investments and total exports (KOSGEB 2011).

Considerably, these numbers represent a majority of economy as much as SMEs in EU. On the other hand, in terms of information technology, SMEs in Turkey have similarities with EU. It was reported by Ministry of Development that SMEs were insufficient in terms of technology and technology management in Turkey (SME Strategy and Action Plan 2004). Technological improvements were occurred by 49 % for large enterprises; however, it remained at 28 % for SMEs between 2007 and 2010 (KOSGEB 2011). Similarly, financial support by government remained around 25 %. Thus, 86 % of SMEs in manufacturing industry were operated in low technological conditions. In addition to that, IT outsourcing were remained at 4.2 % for consultancy and 6.8 % for training (KOSGEB 2011; OECD 2004). The SWOT analysis of SMEs of Turkey revealed that management skills were main strengths of SMEs in terms of IT. Weaknesses were listed as lack of knowledge in existing and new technologies and lack of capital for technological investments. Opportunities were identified as government incentives and increasing support by low interest rate credit loans. Threats were presented as market domination by large enterprises, low cost production in Asian countries (KOSGEB 2011).

In this chapter, SMEs of software industry were under the investigation in terms of IT use, which covered the usage of information processing tools and techniques in business operations. Even though software companies have inevitably used in IT as a part of the business processes, it was observed that the success depends on the effective use of IT in operations. It was reported that number of companies was not able to survive in software industry of Turkey due to lack of adapting and using tools and techniques in IT, insufficient support and lack of capital and knowledge (9th Nationwide Development Plan 2006). Many more were reported for inefficiently use of IT in business operations (OECD 2004). Thus, in this research, SMEs in software industry of Turkey was subject to assessment in terms of IT use. A new model of IT assessment, Information Technology Management Enhancement Model (ITMEM), was employed in order to reveal facts about SMEs in terms of IT use in organizations. The following sections will present insight about IT assessment and the new IT assessment model.

1.2 IT Assessment

After the emergence of IT and its management practices, the quality and the control of the IT in business processes became an important issue (Marquis 2006). In order to meet the IT service quality and to keep the control of IT at a standard level, supportive tools and techniques were needed for IT management. For this purpose, standardized procedures, such as best practices and standards, were developed to help managers to control IT processes and to measure its quality (Tranchard 2008). Today, there are number of best practices and standards which were developed for assessment of IT ant processes. However, they may vary considering their applicability, generic use and benefits. After an extensive review of the literature, and with the experts' opinion from the software industry, the most applicable best practices and standards in IT assessment were identified as:

(1) **The Control Objectives for Information and related Technology–COBIT**. COBIT brought a set of measure and processes to managers, auditors and IT users for assisting the use of information technology and appropriately developing company's IT management and its control (COBIT Framework for IT Governance and Control 2011).
(2) **The Information Technology Infrastructure Library–ITIL**. ITIL is the guide for quality IT services and required facilities for supporting IT (ITIL 2007).
(3) **Capability Maturity Model Integration–CMMI**. CMMI is an approach to improve performance of a company by its processes. Purpose of CMMI is gathering separate organizational functions, setting objectives for process improvement, presenting guidance for quality processes and for evaluating current processes and providing reference point (Forrester et al. 2011).

The most applicable standards used in IT management were identified as:

(4) **ISO 38500** provided government measures in terms of information for organizations (ISO 2008),
(5) **ISO 27002** presented security guidelines for the IT users in an organization (ISO 2005).

In this study, COBIT, ITIL, CMMI and ISO standards 38500 & 27002 were categorized and labeled as "best practices ad standards".

Even though there are mostly used best practices and standards available in the market, it was reported that they had drawbacks in practical implementation (COBIT Framework for IT Governance and Control 2011). The most important and the most common problem with their implementation was the lack of know-how. It was observed that the organization which needed to implement the best practices or standards would require expertise for implementation and for training. This issue reduced availability and applicability of the practices. In addition to that, their aggregate cost, including time, training, purchasing license of use and expert payments, can be beyond affordable boundaries for most of the companies, especially for the SMEs which had limited budget to be allocated for assessment. For instance, COBIT requires in-depth knowledge for practicing, and its context may lead to problems in practice due to being too generic (Morimoto 2009). In addition to that, it was observed that COBIT addresses "what must be done" instead of "how" that leads to problems in defining paths and processes of implementation (Von Solms 2005). In the literature, varieties of limitations were observed in practices of models from different disciplines (Karabacak and Sogukpinar 2005; Rush et al. 2007). Table 1 presented strength and weaknesses of these best practices and standards.

It is a fact that demonstrated practices and standards serve to particular IT domains which slightly intersect with the purpose of ITMEM. But they were all classified under the hood of "IT and its management". Hence, they should be investigated, and their strength and weaknesses should be assessed in order to maintain applicable assessment model. According to the report of European Commission, cases of SMEs presented that following the best practices, using IT and software in operations and continuously improving the system are important part of the success (European Commission 2009). Thus, considering the status of current best practices and standards, a new model was developed to provide affordable and practical model in terms of applicability to assess IT use. It was believed it would be in benefit of SMEs to use a model collectively providing an assessment of IT use with the light of best practices and standards.

1.3 The New IT Assessment Model: Information Technology Management Enhancement Model

In this chapter, a new assessment model was practiced in order to assess IT use in small and medium sized enterprises. The model is called ITMEM: Information Technology Management Enhancement Model, which was designed to assess IT use in the companies and assist the IT managers in decision making (Sezgin and Özkan 2010). The model was developed upon a three-fold structure including academic studies, best practices and IT standards. The best practices fundamentally consisted of COBIT, ITIL and CMMI; standards were ISO38500 and ISO27002, and academic studies constituted the framework of the model. ITMEM's conceptual framework and domains of IT use were essentially based on the study of Phaal, Farrukh and Probert (Rush et al. 2007) which was developed upon Gregory's (1995) technology assessment management procedure framework. In addition to that, the framework based on the number of studies about technology management and assessment in the literature (Cetindamar et al. 2009; Phaal et al. 1998, 2004). Five elements of IT use were identified by the literature research, and they were determined as domains of ITMEM. These domains were explained as follows:

Table 1 Strengths and limitations of best practices and standards (COBIT Framework for IT Governance and Control 2011; Forrester et al. 2011; ITIL 2007; Yoo et al. 2006; Özkan et al. 2008)

	COBIT	ITIL	CMMI	ISO Standards
Strengths	Good checklists for IT	Well established, mature, detailed, and focused on IT production and operational quality issues	Most comprehensive process improvement models available for product and service development and maintenance	Contribute more to a company's economic sustainability
	Enables IT to address risks not explicitly addressed by other frameworks and to pass audits	Can combine with CMMI to cover all of IT	Strong in organizational practices and provide a roadmap for continuous process improvement	Provides more efficient and cost-effective production processes
	Can work well with other quality frameworks, especially ITIL	In compliance with ISO standards	Build on and extend the best practices of CMMIs and other process improvement models	Brings reliability and trust in international business relationships
			Can be used for self-assessment	Enhance image and reputation of a company
			Detailed engineering practices	
			Comprehensive program management practices	
Limitations	Says what to do but not how to do it	Does not address the development of quality management systems	Does not address IT operations issues, such as security, change and configuration management, capacity planning, troubleshooting and help desk functions	Requires rigorous and time-intensive process
	Does not deal directly with software development or IT services	Not geared to software development processes	Focused exclusively on software development processes	Can be expensive to adapt and implement
	Does not provide road map for continuous process improvement	Use is highly dependent on interpretation	Sets goals, but no guidance	Heavy emphasis on documentation
		Limited in security and system development		Length of the process
				Does not guarantee better quality

- Identification: Identification points out the issues of awareness about information technologies that are significant for business operations. It contains research subjects targeting existing and emerging information technologies.
- Selection: Selection involves preferences of information technologies that should be encouraged and promoted within the company.
- Acquisition: The acquisition is related with decisions about suitable ways of selected information technologies' acquisition and embedding them effectively. Selected information technologies may be acquired internally or externally.
- Exploitation: Exploitation is concerned with realization of information technologies' value or systematic conversion of information technologies into marketable products. The link among market, technologies and platforms is important. It involves contribution of IT in the final product and to the market share.
- Protection: It is concerned with preservation of the expertise and knowledge that are related in products and systems. It also includes legal issues, such as patenting and licensing. Protection is matters for the operations about all other constructs.

2 Methodology: ITMEM and Case Selection

2.1 IT Assessment Procedure Using ITMEM

ITMEM has been developed as a coherent model to assess IT use in organizations. The model has been practically approved by a prior study, and it has been also statistically approved for reliability and consistency (Sezgin and Özkan 2010, 2011). In this chapter, ITMEM has been practiced on five SMEs following 3-step implementation process as depicted in Fig. 1.

Practice phase was conducted systematically by employing case study methodology which enabled to conduct in-depth study by utilizing multiple sources of evidence (Yin 2009). In this phase, ITMEM was practiced by conducting questionnaire with employees, maintaining interview and retrieving evidential documents. The questionnaire had 64 questions which were grouped under five domains of ITMEM. A sample set of questions were given in Appendix A. As given in Fig. 2, practice phase was in accordance with triangulation approach in order to reach reliable information during the implementation. Triangulation consisted of (1) semi-structured interview (Lindlof and Taylor 2002), (2) questionnaire and (3) collection of documentations, which enable the surveyor to retrieve reliable proof of given information, emerging data and latent insight of the companies (Denzin 2006).

Due to the fact that the study involved qualitative and quantitative methods in the implementation process, it was needed to transform findings into interpretable levels. Step 2 was initialized after the data was collected by quantitative and qualitative approaches which included questionnaire and-semi structured interview

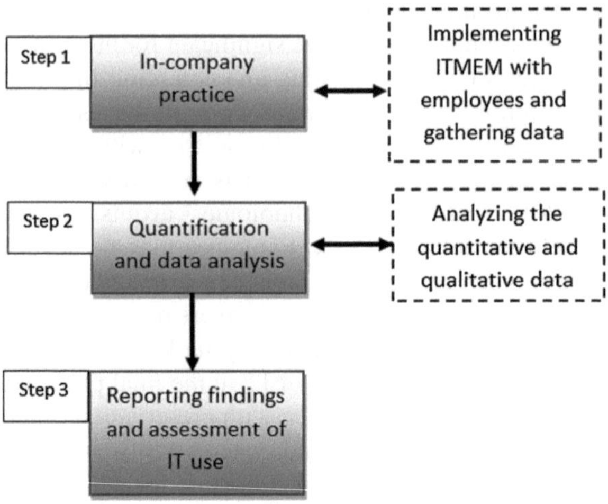

Fig. 1 Process of implementation of the ITMEM

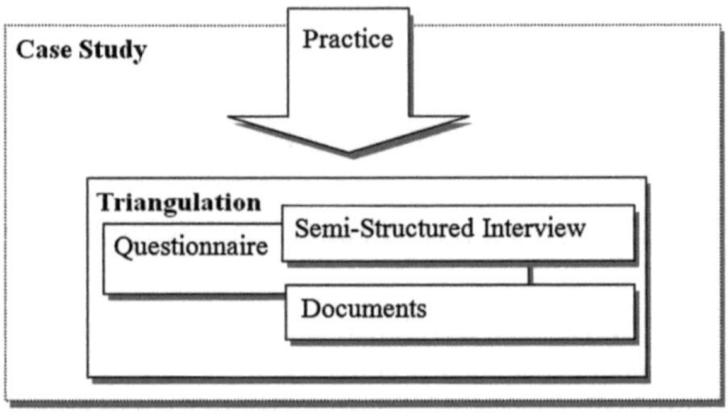

Fig. 2 In-company practice phase

methods. Descriptive statistical analysis was employed to measure reliability, consistency and correlation of the items. Qualitative data that was collected by interview were recorded and transcribed in order to maintain analysis. Coding method was employed for qualitative analysis (Corbin and Strauss 2008). After analysis of qualitative and quantitative data, quantitative degrees were assigned to organizations in order to conceptualize the level of IT use. Table 2 presented the quantitative levels.

At the final step, reporting was conducted by transforming the data into interpretable results. In this context, the quantitative levels were presented into a form of interpretable guide in order to be useful for decision makers. Since quantitative levels present the degree to which a company achieved in terms of IT use, it was renamed as "maturity level". Table 3 presents the interpretation guide of maturity levels of a company at 5 levels: 1-Initial, 2-Rising, 3-Promising, 4-Manageable, 5-Improved. The table was prepared to help authorities to understand the missing points and achievements in IT use. In other words, purpose of maturity level interpretation table was to provide a profile to companies which describe their current status with regards to their quantitative levels.

Table 2 Quantitative levels

Intervals of success level	Qualitative level	Quantitative level
0–30	Very low/none use of IT	1
31–55	Low use of IT	2
56–75	Medium use of IT	3
76–90	High use of IT	4
91–100	Very high use of IT	5

Table 3 Maturity level interpretation guide

Levels	Explanations of maturity levels
1 Initial	There is no evidence or little evidence that the company is aware of IT issues which are required to be addressed. Standardized processes do not exist in IT; instead, there are demand-base methods in which IT is partially applied to satisfy specific needs on demands. The overall methods and processes in IT management are inapplicable. No compliance is observed in IT and related approaches
2 Rising	IT has been developed to the level where employees are responsible of IT tasks which operates similar procedures. The IT awareness is low. Awareness of standardized processes of IT exists but not implemented. There is not communication or formal training of IT; instead, responsibility of IT training is at individual basis. There is confidence about IT knowledge of employees at a significant level which may cause problems in operations including IT. Low compliance is observed in IT and related fields
3 Promising	IT procedures and processes are mostly communicated, documented and standardized. But updating processes and tools may not be applicable. Company accepted IT as a part of the culture but small problems are possible in its applications. IT mostly takes place in long term and short term plans. Continuous improvement is not applied but promising. Compliance is observed in IT and related fields in a rising trend
4 Manageable	IT awareness is high. IT Management includes monitoring and measuring IT use and procedures compliance, and brings precautions in problems. IT applications and processes are continuously improving and help for effective and efficient business operations. IT automation is quite used in routine operations. High compliance is observed in IT and related fields. Continuous improvement started to becomes a part of company culture in IT
5 Improved	IT becomes an inevitable part of company culture and operations. IT processes and IT use has been reached to an effective level through continuous improvement and effective use of IT in every division. IT is integrated to business processes, and used to automate and control the workflow. IT applications are used to increase quality and effectiveness and increase flexibility of the company for adapting market changes. Compliance and continuous improvement are important part of the business

2.2 Case Selection

The cases were selected from a set of companies considering the following criteria. It was ensured that (1) the companies were classified as SMEs by their size and balance sheet, (2) the companies are conscious about the their potential and need for business process improvement, (3) cases are from a number of diverse sectors of software industry. On the other hand, as the common characteristics, all the companies were appraised or ready to be appraised in CMMI level 3 and above (Published Appraisal Results 2011). CMMI appraisal brought the ability for comparing companies on particular platform and collecting standardized information about organizational processes. These criteria also enabled to make comparison of practical results in the common ground with ITMEM. Characteristics of companies were derived from the examination of company profiles and official declarations (Forrester et al. 2011; Published Appraisal Results 2011). Due to the bilateral confidentiality agreement with companies, the names of the companies were not shared in the study. Table 4 presented the list of SMEs which were assessed for IT use by employing ITMEM. In the table, size of companies, number of IT personnel, the sector of software industry and foundation year were given. In addition to that, CMMI appraisal levels were given, however, only one company was officially appraised but others were preparing to be appraised. These companies were unofficially assessed and graded for the expected appraisal level by independent consultants. Last three columns demonstrated degree of the of IT standards, overall use of IT utilities and internet, self-developed standards and software in order to present the status of companies in the following terms: (1) to what degree they are following the standards in IT-based procedures, (2) to what degree companies are using information and communication technologies (ICT) in business operations (including internet based communication utilities), and (3) if the companies are using self-developed standards and software in order to meet particular IT needs in operations.

3 Results and Discussion of Cases

3.1 Results of Cases

ITMEM was practiced on five SMEs in software industry. In each company, at least 2 IT employees, who had in-depth knowledge about IT related operations of their organizations were involved in the survey, such as IT experts and IT directors. They were also participated to the interview. In the questionnaire, 64 questions were answered. In order to maintain reliable data collection process by triangulation method, questionnaire was supported by reports and documents from the companies and interview records. The responses for questionnaire were found in accordance with the evidential documents. Inconsistencies were detected

Table 4 Information about companies

Company name	Size (# of employees)	# of IT employees	Sector	Foundation year	Capability maturity model integration appraisal level[a]	Degree of the use of IT standards (low–average–high)	Degree of the overall use of ICT utilities (low–average–high)	Self-developed standards and software
Company A	240	200	System integration and software quality, simulation and modeling for defense industry	1998	CMMI level 5	Average	High	Yes
Company B	80	70	Health informatics, software	1989	Preparing (expected level 3)	Low	Average	No
Company C	30	28	Software, modeling and simulation	2006	Preparing (expected level 2)	Low	Average	No
Company D	200	160	Educational software and information technologies, networking	1988	Preparing (expected level 3)	Low	High	No
Company E	40	35	Health informatics, software, project development and consultancy	2002	Preparing (expected level 2)	Low	Average	No

[a] A company can be appraised from 1 to 5 maturity levels in CMMI

Table 5 Maturity levels of the companies

	Company A—maturity level	Company B—maturity level	Company C—maturity level	Company D—maturity level	Company E—maturity level
Identification	5	4	4	4	4
Selection	5	4	3	5	3
Acquisition	4	3	3	3	3
Exploitation	5	4	4	4	3
Protection	4	2	3	4	3
Total	5	3	3	4	3

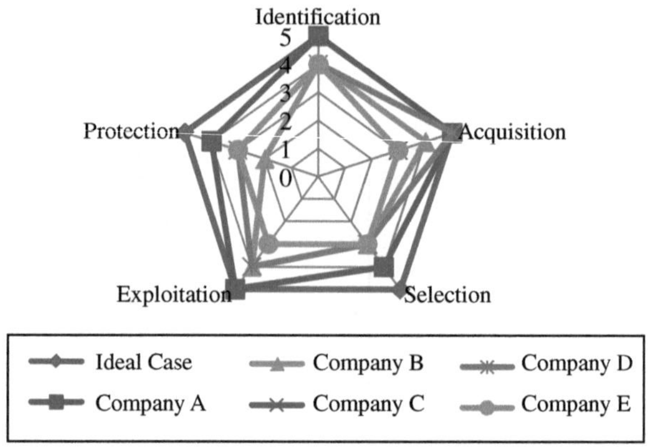

Fig. 3 Web graph of maturity levels

by cross-checking of documents including company reports, operation processes, procedures, certificates and standards, and they eliminated considering documented facts and interview reports. Interviews were recorded and transcribed for analysis. Interview reports were prepared as written documents based on coding analysis (Glaser and Strauss 2009) which was supported by observational notes and ad-hoc questions Descriptive statistics were applied for five cases including reliability, consistency and correlation tests. It was found that each item under the domains was correlated and consistent within each domain, and the model was reported as reliable in terms of measuring items.

The final scores and maturity levels were calculated accordingly to the ITMEM quantification processes (Sezgin and Özkan 2010). The survey results were demonstrated in Table 5. Web graph of maturity levels were also given Fig. 3. The differences among the ideal profile and companies' profile were demonstrated explicitly the strengths and weaknesses in terms of five domains of ITMEM. It was found that Company A achieved the highest scores and the Company E got the lowest score considering summation of maturity levels of five domains. In other terms, companies were mostly ranked at "promising" and "manageable" levels (Please see Table 3). The ranking of companies was as following: Company A, D, B, C and E respectively.

3.2 Discussion

In this section, the results of the ITMEM practice on five SMEs in software industry were discussed. The major source of the results were composed of questionnaire responses, interview reports and the documents including reports, certificates, standards, policies and procedures. During the practice of ITMEM, triangulation method helped to reach reliable insight about each company and assist to collect data. In this section, these insights about cases in terms of IT use of SMEs in software industry were summarized.

ITMEM practices demonstrated that companies require periodic assessment. ITMEM practice revealed that the revision of operations and procedures through practices demonstrates strength and weaknesses of the company. In addition to that, ITMEM met at the common ground with COBIT about assessment by revealing that IT assessment helps to conduct effective control, maximize the utilization of resources and increase the savings. IT director of Company A confirmed that: "Control and assessment tools like CMMI, COBIT or ITMEM help to revise procedures of company operations, and provide insight about the state of company, especially in terms of budget and resources…" From the operational perspective, it was found that assessment by best practices and standards are constitutively influential in using IT, involving IT in strategic and tactical plans and controlling over ITs in business processes. IT director of Company A stated that "…even though we have missing links in terms of using IT into the business, this assessment enlightened us regarding to the aimed value and the real value of IT in the company's current state and in the long term plans…" It was observed that the adaptive and flexible structure of SMEs suits to use IT in all processes. However, without assessment, improvement in IT processes would be unlikely to occur.

Importance of domains. The domains of ITMEM presented a concept about IT and its practice in business operations. During the practice of ITMEM, it was observed that there was a common perception about identification, selection, acquisition and exploitation domains. Considering the small size and ability to adapt changing conditions, for SMEs, it is normal to be aware of particular technologies. It was also found that the more personnel were aware of the issues about IT, the better implementations about IT use were applied in the business operations. In this term, the top score company, Company A is a good example. IT expert of Company A stated that "…self-improvement in information technologies was highly motivated…" The results of questionnaire, as well as interview reports, presented the positive relation of the awareness of IT and its adoption in business processes. On the other side, the protection domain was found ambiguous and problematic. Due to lacks of knowledge and limited budgets of companies, it was observed that intangible assets were not securely stored. The scope of protection is not covering enough to include external links, including social, systematic and environmental factors. As Solms (1998) stated, there was a common understanding that protection of information and technologies was the major concern to preserve the products and other outcomes, however, the implementations were mostly resulted as failures.

Relationship between organizational processes and IT use. The major outcome of the ITMEM was revealing the relation between IT use and organizational processes including business operations and process quality. In this context, CMMI provided a measure to identify organizational processes with the appraisal levels, and maturity levels of ITMEM helped to investigate relationship between those two concepts. Conceptually, CMMI aimed to assist improving processes and performance, and ITMEM aimed to assess IT use in companies. However, it was reported that in order to fulfill the requirements of effectively performing organization processes, involvement of IT was inevitable that led to increase the use of IT in the company. Report of appraisal requirements of CMMI supported by outlining that planning, preparing, data collection and verification require certain amount of IT involvement (Carnegie Mellon University Software Engineering Institute 2006). In addition to that, organizational progress reports of Company A and D presented that improvements in organizational processes triggered improvements in IT, which allowed the companies to reach a more dynamic level under the principle of 'continuous improvement'. An IT expert of Company A supported as: "…improving processes increases credibility of the company. In this term, IT developments are absolutely required. These requirements carried our company into a more effective track in the market…" IT expert in Company D demonstrated the need of effective organizational processes and IT by: "…implementing CMMI has carried the production processes to an upper level. It is very helpful in challenging projects, and should be supported by proper use of IT. It became part of our culture by the time…" It can be concluded that acts for continuous improvement in processes enhances the use of IT, which eventually affects the performance of companies. Thus, SMEs' use of best practices or assessment tools in organizational processes, as CMMI and ITMEM, would be helpful to improve IT use in companies. Company A was demonstrated the most explicit example in this manner.

On the other hand, ITMEM also unveiled insights about IT by domain-specific findings as awareness of IT, IT preferences and promotion, acquiring IT, converting IT value into marketable products and preservation of IT. Those were discussed in the following paragraphs by domain basis.

Identification: Awareness of IT. Identification aimed to measure awareness about IT. The results showed that it was successfully fulfilled by the Company A. But the awareness of IT was at "manageable" levels for other companies. Considering the facts about the awareness in each company, it was found that company culture and awareness in IT has a subtle relationship. Investigations presented that the culture of Company A was well-established, and it encouraged employees to use IT tools and to involve in IT developments. The observation notes of company A about operations and communication channels demonstrated that IT awareness was at a high level. The periodic IT meetings, regular software and system trainings, periodic IT process reports, interactive meetings and efficiently working communication infrastructure were supportive instances that presented identification domain was effectively fulfilled in the company. Interview results supported that other companies had relatively inefficient communication channels within the organization. Company E had problems with encouraging employees for using particular IT tools. The IT director of Company E supported as "…We routinely deliver the IT reports but that are not encouraging employees to stay aware of the advancements in IT…" It also appeared on the reports and documents that identification did not get the expected attention by the authorities of company C and D. Company B had IT procedures and effective communication channels to fulfill the needs. But it was observed that the culture was partially adapted the awareness needs of IT. It was reported that in SMEs the awareness of IT can be diffused rapidly, however, challenge laid under the organizational resistance to those technologies by employees, especially top and mid-level managers.

Selection: IT preferences and their promotion. Selection domain aimed to identify preferences of information technologies that should be encouraged and promoted within the company. Selection was resulted similarly to identification for each company. Company A and D had periodic schedule for processes and programs, operation methods and ad-hoc procedures for IT operations. In addition to that, Company D had schedule for routine control and update of IT processes. The IT director of Company D stated that: "We have prepared all the procedures and policies required for operations, which included IT. They are all in compliance with the standards and regulations…" Company C and E also had procedures for IT operations but it was found that they were not applicable enough to cover all required IT operations and were prepared in order to fulfill paperwork. On the other side, problems in IT use were also exploited. Company E particularly had problems in IT investments and developments. They were characterized themselves as laggards in developments. IT director of Company E agreed as "…we need improvements to fulfill 'selection' issues…" Company C's main problem was about supporting business with IT. But it was reported that they took measures to make amends. IT expert of Company C supported as: "There are undeniable issues and problems in procedures for IT but we are currently working on it as one of our primary concerns…" From the bright side, it was acknowledged that small size of company is a positive side in problem solving phase. A IT expert of Company B stated that "…the SMEs had quick steps in intervention to problems but complications were required to pin rapidly…". It was supported by Company A as "…it is not costly to solve an IT problem in this kind of a small company in terms of monetary expenses and human resources…".

Acquisition: Acquiring information technologies and their use. The acquisition domain was designed to investigate the decisions in information technologies' acquisition and embedding them effectively. Acquisition was identified by the company authorities of B, C, D and E as a new, developing concept. They stated that the requirements of acquisition had not been fulfilled yet. The reports, interview statements and questionnaire responses supported their view by exploiting their deficiencies in this term. The IT director of Company B approved that "Acquisition issues requires detailed procedures and effectively processing decision making systems. For now, these issues are on trial and preparation phases. Considering the needs, it will proceed to the next level…" IT expert from Company E supported as: "Acquisition involves risky issues which is hard to measure especially in IT business. We cannot claim that we successfully manage risky processes but we did not face great problems in this context either…" In the bottom line, procedures for selecting IT, embedding IT into business operations and measuring its risks were not mature for all of the companies. They have taken particular measures but the assessment resulted that they still had problems. More specifically, the reports showed that Company B and D had problems in risk measurement, Company C and E frequently faced problems in preparing and implementing procedures. Company A was less problematic than others, but it had issues in effective involvement of IT and to prepare procedures of new technologies. The IT director of Company A stated that "SMEs like us have limited budget to allocate IT resources. We mostly prefer to deal with IT sources inside the company in order to keep the budget reserves…" So, as much as the processes, acquisition of IT constituted major problems for companies. On the other side, since the incentives were low, it was inevitable to get low maturity levels. IT director of Company E stated that it would be fruitful to have government support funding to acquire IT in specific fields.

Exploitation: Conversion of IT value into marketable products. Exploitation domain was concerned with realization of information technologies' value or systematic conversion of information technologies into marketable products. Results showed that exploitation was successfully fulfilled by Company A and followed by companies D, E and F respectively. In addition to survey, interview reports and documentation of procedures showed that Company A's IT utilities contributed value to the products and effectively used in every process of production. The IT director stated that "…IT is the inevitable part of the production process. We mostly produce software products. Thus IT provides major advantage in the market…" Company A has procedures and standards for the processes about value added by IT. Self-developed IT quality control systems helped to get assistance of IT tools in the operations without possible problems. Company E had required systems and infrastructure to utilize IT in production which was basically working effectively. But the problem occurrence rate was above average, which is 12.2 % according to the annual report. It was observed that it was interfered even small routine operations. Identified problems were system crashes, work overloads, network bottlenecks and unstable communication channels. IT expert in Company E stated that "…we try to reduce problem occurrence rate below 6 % in order to use IT in the processes effectively". Company D had the similar problems with Company E but they faced more severe consequences for market operations. The quality director of Company D stated that "IT is vital for final product but the problems that are occurred during the production cause to lose customers and eventually loss in market share…" The results showed that the problem was mainly lack of knowledge in IT use and the utilities. Considering the current market for SMEs, this problem can be generalized for all SMEs in variety of industries in Turkey. The bias caused by lack of IT knowledge had damage with the increasing need to IT use in business operations.

Protection: Preservation of information and technologies. Protection domain aimed the preservation of the expertise and knowledge about products and systems. It was considered as priority for software industry due to ease of fraudulence in the market. Thus, satisfaction of protection needs was considered as a "must", but in fact, it was hard to accomplish. In the case, Company A used variety of security tools and procedures in essential fields, such as IT infrastructure and system security, planning and preparing IT procedures. IT expert of Company A stated as "…we employed the word 'secure' as the rule of thumb…" Even though Company A considered protection priority in the business processes, security software which were off-the-shelf security systems created problems by limiting the control over unexpected circumstances. "Protection is taken as a high priority issue. Thus, in this study, getting high scores in protection construct of ITMEM was our major purpose. But we could not have managed to purely accomplish…" stated by an IT expert of Company A. Different from Company A, Company D cooperates with the competent companies for protection. Company D had a skeptic characteristic in security, thus they did not fully outsource third parties especially in protection issues. The IT quality director of Company D stated as: "We protect our assets, products and projects in high level of security tools and systems. But overtime, it is inevitable to confront some protection problems by forthcoming developments. It is very challenging to purely take all protection measures at once…" Company C, similar to Company A, had been using off-the-shelf security tools and systems. The procedures and standards considered as prior objectives to fulfill protection requirements. The IT director explained as "…I ensure you that we have enough protection measures to secure our assets and products. But that is not a promise for tomorrow…" After all, each company had taken measures for protection but interview reports showed that the measures were not sufficient in rapidly changing demands and IT developments. Unlike others, Company B had lowest score in protection. The reason behind was determined by interviews as the lack in infrastructure and policies in protective status. Overall, for SMEs in software industry, protection can be labeled as the "prior" measure to be taken. However, the concept was identified as not standardized but adaptable based on conception of authorities. This can be pinned as a major drawback in the industry.

The ITMEM study demonstrated the strength and weaknesses of five companies in five domains of IT use. The results presented the current position of SMEs in terms of IT use in software industry. Several issues were identified through the analysis. Majority can be labeled as the result of lack of knowledge and insufficient management measures in IT involved business processes. For the companies that highly suffer from unexpected problems of IT operations, it was recommended to adopt proactive behavior which requires well-defined IT plans, policies and trainings of IT personnel. Long term IT investment plan was recommended for the companies which had costly IT investments. On the other side, the awareness was also an issue. The effective use of IT systems and IT awareness of employees as well as management were highly depending on divisional trainings and clearly identified communication channels. The problems were identified as a part of deficiencies in company culture. To shape the culture to create IT aligned structure, regulatory policies and procedures were needed (Von Solms and Von Solms

2004). The effective use of IT systems was offered by outsourcing system services or transferring the knowledge from experienced companies. Even though outsourcing the IT services can be one solution, it also has fundamental drawbacks regarding to impractical use and trust issues (Devos et al. 2008).

4 Conclusion

IT use has an important role in operations of any organization to stay competitive in the market and to effectively maintain business processes. SMEs constitute the majority of the market since they had a significant place in economy. The current position of IT in the market had raised importance of IT use as well as IT management itself. On divisional basis, it was reported that almost every SME had IT in their operations. However, the control of IT in organizations was also important in order to maintaining business operations (Applegate et al. 2003; Benamati e al. 1997; Nieto and Fernández 2005). Thus, effective use of IT was the major concern. The emergence of best practices and standards demonstrated a solution for the need of assessment and control over operations. However, implementing these best practices and standards has particular drawbacks. These were mainly: (1) high cost of implementation, (2) focusing on only limited area of IT involved operations, (3) need for training, (4) lacking in guiding for solutions. ITMEM framework was developed and practiced considering those major needs in assessment practices.

The results of the research provided insights which have potential knowledge for assisting to IT management in decision making and for guiding improvement of IT structure by exploring strengths and weaknesses of the SMEs about IT use. The results were promising since ITMEM unveiled latent facts about IT use in each companies and provided insight from the perspective of IT use. Considering the findings of the study and the feedbacks from the cases, it was found that ITMEM had substantially fulfilled its purposes for SMEs in software industry by providing leverage to the awareness of IT use and needs. The case studies enlightened that SMEs were able to apply best practices in IT use as well as corporations. However, there were issues that were mainly ignored by SMEs in terms of utilizing best practices and standards. ITMEM practice demonstrated that the following issues are important when implementing IT assessment practices in a SME:

- **Cost saving**. The cost of implementing assessment practices needed to be relatively low. It provides considerable deduction from control expenses. In this context, time and budget constitute main cost inputs.
  - **Training time**. Training should be simple and clear which enable company to act quickly and less costly.
  - **Practical**. Implementation should not require any additional tool, procedure or preparation in order to save from time and budget.
  - **Duration**. The practice should be applied in a short time which does not interfere the company operations for long term.

- **Flexible**. Implementation should be customizable according to user needs. Modularity of practice phases and identification of company needs are essentials to be addressed.
- **Reliability of assessment**. The source of information is important for acting in business. The findings of an assessment should be reliable in order to take measures in organizational operations.
- **Interpretable results**. The results should be easily interpretable and understandable by top management in order to convey them into the actions. Guidelines would be helpful in this manner.
- **Broader perspective**. Instead of focusing on specific field of IT, a practice should have broader sense which comprehensively includes IT. A socio-technical approach would be essential to involve all parameters influencing IT use.

In this research, it was tried to assess IT use in SMEs by employing ITMEM. Findings were interpreted by five domains of the model and requirements for an assessment were outlined. Future studies should involve SMEs in different industries in order to identify industry specific needs and differences among industries. Furthermore, a longitudinal study would be beneficial in terms of observing the change before and after the assessment.

Appendix A. Sample List[1] of Survey Questions of ITMEM

Survey questions	References For each question, the first row of references represents the primary reference as the source, and the following rows are supportive references	Related section of the references
Identification		
To what degree does IT take place in main strategic business goals?	Rush, H. Bessant, J. Hobday, M. Assessing the technological capabilities of firms: developing a policy tool, R&D Management, 2007, vol. 37, pp. 221–36	Awareness
	COBIT 4.1, IT governance Institute, 2007	Plan and organize 1.4.
	ISO 38500—Cooperate Governance of Information Technology, ISO/IEC, 2008	Strategy
	CMMI, Software Engineering Institute, 2008	Strategic service management

(continued)

[1] The actual survey consisted of 64 questions. The following 16 questions are presented to give the idea of how survey questions have been developed.

(continued)

Survey questions	References For each question, the first row of references represents the primary reference as the source, and the following rows are supportive references	Related section of the references
Please degree the importance of certificate and standards about IT for your company	AIA0109—Technology capability survey, Enterprise Europe Network, 2009	"What are the certifications that are aimed to acquire by the company?"
	COBIT 4.1, IT governance Institute, 2007	Plan and organize 3.4.
	ISO 38500—Cooperate Governance of Information Technology, ISO/IEC, 2008	Conformance
To what degree IT performance and efficiency are measured in the company?	ISO 38500—Cooperate Governance of Information Technology, ISO/IEC, 2008	Performance: "Does IT support business processes with the required capability and capacity?"
	COBIT 4.1, IT governance Institute, 2007	Plan and organize 1.3; deliver and support 3.3; monitor and evaluate 1.1–1.6
	CMMI, Software Engineering Institute, 2008	Organizational process performance
Selection		
To what degree are businesses goals in accordance with IT structure?	ISO 38500—Cooperate Governance of Information Technology, ISO/IEC, 2008	Strategy: "Does IT align with organizations objectives?"
	COBIT 4.1, IT governance Institute, 2007	Acquire and implement 1.2
	ISO 38500—Cooperate Governance of Information Technology, ISO/IEC, 2008	Conformance
What is the importance of IT outsourcing for your company?	Rush, H. Bessant, J. Hobday, M. Assessing the technological capabilities of firms: developing a policy tool, R&D Management, 2007, vol. 37, pp. 221–36	Technology acquisition
	ISO 17799, Information Security Management BS 7799.2:2002 -Audit Check List, Sans Institute, 2002	12.5 Security in development and support processes
	COBIT 4.1, IT governance Institute, 2007	Deliver and support 2

(continued)

(continued)

Survey questions	References For each question, the first row of references represents the primary reference as the source, and the following rows are supportive references	Related section of the references
To what extent does IT investments take place in your long term plans?	"AIA0109 Technology Capability Survey 2009"	
	COBIT 4.1, IT governance Institute, 2007	Plan and organize 5
	ISO 38500—Cooperate Governance of Information Technology, ISO/IEC, 2008	Acquisition
	ITIL, Office Of Government Commerce, 2007	Financial management
Acquisition		
To what extent is IT used in project management?	COBIT 4.1, IT governance Institute, 2007	Plan and organize 10.2, 10.5
	CMMI, Software Engineering Institute, 2008	Project management
To what extent is IT used to determine risks and alternatives in investments?	ISO 38500—Cooperate Governance of Information Technology, ISO/IEC, 2008	Acquisition: "Does the organization have IT investment system to assess the risk, alternatives by documentation"
	COBIT 4.1, IT governance Institute, 2007	Plan and organize 10
Does your company use service level agreement for provided IT services? Degree	COBIT 4.1, IT governance Institute, 2007	Plan and organize 1.1, 10.1; deliver and support 2.2
	CMMI, Software Engineering Institute, 2008	Supplier agreement management
	ITIL, Office Of Government Commerce, 2007	Service design -service level management
Exploitation		
To what extent does IT used to create new advantages in your future businesses?	Rush, H. Bessant, J. Hobday, M. Assessing the technological capabilities of firms: developing a policy tool, R&D Management, 2007, vol. 37, pp. 221–36	Building core competence
	COBIT 4.1, IT governance Institute, 2007	Plan and organize 3.3

(continued)

(continued)

Survey questions	References For each question, the first row of references represents the primary reference as the source, and the following rows are supportive references	Related section of the references
Does the IT responsibilities allocated in the company which is resulted effectively? Degree.	ISO 38500—Cooperate Governance of Information Technology, ISO/IEC, 2008	Responsibility: "Does the IT responsibilities allocated in the company which is resulted effectively?"
	COBIT 4.1, IT governance Institute, 2007	Plan and organize 4
	ISO 38500—Cooperate Governance of Information Technology, ISO/IEC, 2008	Responsibility
To what extend does your company use IT capabilities to create strategic advantage in the market?	Rush, H. Bessant, J. Hobday, M. Assessing the technological capabilities of firms: developing a policy tool, R&D Management, 2007, vol. 37, pp. 221–36	Building core competence
	ITIL, Office Of Government Commerce, 2007	Continual service improvement
	ISO 38500—Cooperate Governance of Information Technology, ISO/IEC, 2008	Performance
Protection		
To what extent IT security management and its concept are placed in your company's corporate culture?	COBIT 4.1, IT governance Institute, 2007	Deliver and support 5
	ISO 17799, Information Security Management BS 7799.2:2002 -Audit Check List, Sans Institute, 2002	5.1 Information security policy
	ITIL, Office Of Government Commerce, 2007	Service design -security management
	ISO 38500—Cooperate Governance of Information Technology, ISO/IEC, 2008	Conformance

(continued)

(continued)

Survey questions	References For each question, the first row of references represents the primary reference as the source, and the following rows are supportive references	Related section of the references
Does your company maintain copyright protection policies and plans for intellectual properties? Degree the importance.	Rush, H. Bessant, J. Hobday, M. Assessing the technological capabilities of firms: developing a policy tool, R&D Management, 2007, vol. 37, pp. 221–36	Building external linkages
	ISO 17799, Information Security Management BS 7799.2:2002 -Audit Check List, Sans Institute, 2002	Compliance with legal requirements
To what extent does your company use IT-based monitoring in production?	ISO 38500—Cooperate Governance of Information Technology, ISO/IEC, 2008	Performance
	COBIT 4.1, IT governance Institute, 2007	Deliver and support 3.1
	ITIL, Office Of Government Commerce, 2007	Capacity management
	ISO 17799, Information Security Management BS 7799.2:2002 -Audit Check List, Sans Institute, 2002	8.2.1 Capacity planning

References

Applegate, L., Austin, R., & Soule, D. (2003). *Corporate information strategy and management: Text and Cases* (6th ed., pp. 114–151). OH: McGraw-Hill.

Badawy, M. K. (1998). Technology management education: Alternative models. *California Management Review, 40*(4), 94–116.

Benamati, J., Lederer, A. L., & Singh, M. (1997). Changing information technology and information technology management. *Information & Management, 31*(5), 275–288.

Boynton, A. C., Zmud, R. W., & Jacobs, G. C. (1994). The influence of IT management practice on IT use in large organizations. *MIS Quarterly, 18*(3), 299–318.

Carnegie Mellon University Software Engineering Institute. (2006). Appraisal requirements for CMMI (V 1.2). *Integration the Vlsi Journal, 2*. http://www.sei.cmu.edu/library/abstracts/reports/06tr011.cfm. Accessed 19 Sept 2011.

Carr, N. G. (2003). IT doesn't matter. *Harvard Business Review, 5*, 5–12.

Cetindamar, D., Phaal, R., & Probert, D. (2009). Understanding technology management as a dynamic capability: A framework for technology management activities. *Technovation, 29*(4), 237–246.

Corbin, J., & Strauss, A. (2008). *Basics of qualitative research. Basics of qualitative research grounded theory procedures and techniques*. London: Sage.

Denzin, N. K. (2006). *Sociological methods: A sourcebook* (6th ed.). NJ: Transaction Publishers.
Devos, J., Landeghem, H. V., & Deschoolmeester, D. (2008). Outsourced information systems failures in SMEs: A multiple case study. *Electronic Journal Information Systems Evaluation, 11*(2), 73–82.
European Commission. (2008). eBusiness guide for SMEs. http://ec.europa.eu/enterprise/e-bsn/ebusiness-solutions-guide/docs/eBusiness_Guide_for_SMEs.pdf. Accessed 9 April 2012.
European Commission. (2009). Learning from peers: Best practices among European SMEs. http://ec.europa.eu/enterprise/sectors/ict/files/e-bsn/learning_from_peers_en.pdf. Accessed 2 April 2012.
European Commission. (2010). Internationalisation of European SMEs. http://ec.europa.eu/enterprise/policies/sme/market-access/files/internationalisation_of_european_smes_final_en.pdf. Accessed 20 April 2012.
European Commission. (2011). EU trade policy and SMEs. http://trade.ec.europa.eu/doclib/html/147637.htm. Accessed 27 May 2012.
Forrester, E. C., Buteau, B. L., & Shrum, S. (2011). *CMMI for services: Guidelines for superior service* (2nd ed.). Pennsylvania: SEI.
Glaser, B. G., & Strauss, A. L. (2009). *The discovery of grounded theory: Strategies for qualitative research* (4th ed.). Germany: Aldine de Gruyter.
Gregory, M. J. (1995). Technology management: a process approach. *Proceedings of the Institution of Mechanical Engineers—Part B Journal of Engineering Manufacture, 209*(52), 347–356. doi:10.1243/PIME_PROC_1995_209_094_02.
ISACA. (2011). COBIT-framework for IT Governance and control. http://www.isaca.org/Knowledge-Center/COBIT/Pages/Overview.aspx. Accessed 19 Sept 2011.
ISO. (2005). ISO/IEC 27002: Code of practice for information security management. http://www.iso.org/iso/catalogue_detail?csnumber=50297. Accessed 20 January 2011.
ISO. (2008). ISO/IEC 38500: Corporate governance of information technology. http://www.iso.org/iso/catalogue_detail?csnumber=51639. Accessed 2 January 2011.
ITIL. (2007). *ITIL Version 3 Service Improvement*. London: The stationery Office.
Karabacak, B., & Sogukpinar, I. (2005). ISRAM: Information security risk analysis method. *Computers Security, 24*(2), 147–159.
Kartiwi, M., & MacGregor, R. C. (2007). Electronic commerce adoption barriers in small to medium-sized enterprises (SMEs) in developed and developing countries. *Journal of Electronic Commerce in Organizations, 5*(3), 35–51.
Kling, R., & Lamb, R. (1999). IT and organizational change in digital economies. *ACM SIGCAS Computers and Society, 29*(3), 17.
KOSGEB. (2011). 2011–2013 KOBİ Stratejisi ve Eylem Planı (2011–13 SME strategies and action plans). http://www.sanayi.gov.tr/Files/Documents/KOSGEB_Katalog.pdf. Accessed 7 June 2012.
Laudon, J. P., & Laudon, K. C. (2012). Essentials of management information systems. Networks (10th ed., pp. 561–571). Prentice Hall.
Legris, P., & Ingham, J. (2003). Why do people use information technology? A critical review of the technology acceptance model. *Information and Management, 40*(3), 191–204.
Lindlof, T. R., & Taylor, B. C. (2002). *Qualitative communication research methods*. London: Sage.
Marquis, H. (2006). ITIL: What it is and what it isn't? *Business Communications Review, 36*(12), 49–52.
Martin, E. W., Brown, C. V., Hoffer, J. A., Perkins, W. C., & DeHayes, D. W. (2011). *Managing information technology: What managers need to know* (7th ed.). NJ: Prentice Hall.
Ministry of Development. (2004). *SME Strategy and action plan*. http://www.dpt.gov.tr/DocObjects/Download/2297/strateji.pdf. Accessed 21 June 2012.
Ministry of Development. (2006). *9th Nationwide development plan*. http://ekutup.dpt.gov.tr/plan/plan9.pdf. Accessed 21 June 2012.

Morimoto, S. (2009). Application of COBIT to security management in information systems development. In *Proceedings of Fourth International Conference on Frontier of Computer Science and Technology*, pp. 625–630.
Nieto, M. J., & Fernández, Z. (2005). The role of information technology in corporate strategy of small and medium enterprises. *Journal of International Entrepreneurship, 3*(4), 251–262.
OECD (2004).Türkiye'deki Küçük ve Orta Ölçekli Isletmeler-Mevcut Durum ve Politikalar (SMEs in Turkey-current status and policies). http://www.oecd.org/dataoecd/37/37/33705673.pdf. Accessed 3 May 2012.
Oyelaran-Oyeyinka, B., & Lal, K. (2006). Learning new technologies by small and medium enterprises in developing countries. *Technovation, 26*(2), 220–231.
Özkan, S., Hackney, R. A., & Bilgen, S. (2008). Process based information systems evaluation: towards the attributes of "PRISE". *Journal of Enterprise Information Management, 20*(6), 700–725.
Phaal, R., Paterson, C. J., & Probert, D. R. (1998). Technology management in manufacturing business: process and practical assessment. *Technovation, 18*(8–9), 541–553.
Phaal, R., Farrukh, C. J. P., & Probert, D. R. (2004). A framework for supporting the management of technological knowledge. *International Journal of Technology Management, 27*(1), 1–15.
Powell, T. C., & Dent-Micallef, A. (1997). Information technology as competitive advantage: the role of human, business, and technology resources. *Strategic Management Journal, 18*(5), 375–405.
Ruiz-Mercader, J., Meroño-Cerdan, A. L., & Sabater-Sánchez, R. (2006). Information technology and learning: Their relationship and impact on organisational performance in small businesses. *International Journal of Information Management, 26*(1), 16–29.
Rush, H., Bessant, J., & Hobday, M. (2007). Assessing the technological capabilities of firms: Developing a policy tool. *R&D Management, 37*(3), 221–236.
SEI. (2011). Published appraisal results. https://sas.sei.cmu.edu/pars/pars.aspx. Accessed 21 June 2011.
Sezgin, E., & Özkan, S. (2010). ITMEM-information technology management enhancement model: Assessment of information technology use in organizations. Msc. thesis, Middle East Technical University (http://etd.lib.metu.edu.tr/upload/12612353/index.pdf).
Sezgin, E., & Özkan, S. (2011). Assessing information technology use in organizations: Developing a framework. *Communications in Computer and Information Science, 220*(4), 388–397.
Solms, R. V. (1998). Information security management (2): guidelines to the management of information technology security (GMITS). *Information Management Computer Security, 6*(5), 221–223.
Tranchard, S. (2008). ISO standard for corporate governance of information technology, ISO management systems, September–October 2008, p. 29 (www.iso.org/ims).
Von Solms, B. (2005). Information security governance: COBIT or ISO 17799 or both? *Computers Security, 24*(2), 99–104.
Von Solms, R., & Von Solms, S. (2004). From policies to culture. *Computers Security, 23*(4), 275–279.
Yin, R. K. (2009). *Case study research: Design and methods* (4th ed.). London: Sage.
Yoo, C., Yoon, J., Lee, B., Lee, C., Lee, J., Hyun, S., et al. (2006). A unified model for the implementation of both ISO 9001:2000 and CMMI by ISO-certified organizations. *Journal of Systems and Software, 79*(7), 954–961.

ICT Policy to Foster Interorganisational ICT Adoption by SMEs: The Netherlands Goes Digital Case

Marijn G. A. Plomp, Ronald S. Batenburg and Pim den Hertog

1 Introduction

It is widely acknowledged that SMEs are of vital importance for economy and society. The vast majority (99.8 %) of all enterprises in the European Union are small or medium (i.e. employ less than 250), and 92 % of the companies even employ less than 10 persons. SMEs provide over two thirds (67.4 %) of all jobs in Europe and are estimated to be responsible for 58 % of the total turnover in 2008 (EIM 2010).

In any value chain, collaboration between its actors has become critical and so has the linkage of ICT of its partners (cf. Barrett and Konsynski 1982; Meier and Sprague 1991; Daft 2001; Morrell and Ezingeard 2002; Shapiro 2009). ICT potentially improves the effectiveness and efficiency of value chains through cost reduction and increasing possibilities for interorganisational communication, coordination and information exchange (Williams 1997). As Papazoglou and Ribbers (2006, p. 280) put it: "Interorganisational information systems (IOSs) are a specific class of information systems that automate the flow of information

M. G. A. Plomp (✉)
Department of Information, Logistics and Innovation, VU University Amsterdam,
De Boelelaan 1105 1081 HV Amsterdam, The Netherlands
e-mail: m.g.a.plomp@vu.nl

R. S. Batenburg
Department of Information and Computing Sciences, Utrecht University,
P.O. Box 80.089 3508 TB Utrecht, The Netherlands
e-mail: r.s.batenburg@uu.nl

R. S. Batenburg
Netherlands Institute for Health Services Research,
P.O. Box 1568 3500 BN Utrecht, The Netherlands

P. den Hertog
Dialogic Innovation and Interaction, Hooghiemstraplein 33-36,
3514 AX Utrecht, The Netherlands
e-mail: denhertog@dialogic.nl

J. Devos et al. (eds.), *Information Systems for Small and Medium-sized Enterprises*,
Progress in IS, DOI: 10.1007/978-3-642-38244-4_6,

across organizational boundaries and enterprise information systems, and link an organization to suppliers, customers and possibly other organizations". On both organisational and chain level, the adoption, implementation and usage of inter-organisational information systems and ICT is intensively studied (Zhu and Kraemer 2002; Nelson 2003). Within this ICT domain, SMEs are traditionally less mature and innovative than their larger counterparts (cf. Premkumar et al. 1992; Damanpour 1992) as they lag behind in the uptake of these systems (European Commission 2008, 2010).

To address this backlog, various policy instruments are being applied in different countries (European Commission 2008, 2010). Internationally there is (and has been) a wide mix of policy instruments and programmes on SME-oriented ICT adoption. It has been identified that in almost thirty OECD countries such policy is currently developed or deployed. The OECD Information Technology Outlook 2010 presents a typology of 24 types of ICT policies that they divide in five main categories: 'fostering ICT innovation' (including government procurement policy), 'increasing diffusion/use', 'maintaining a healthy ICT business environment', 'enhancing the infrastructure' and 'promoting trust online' (OECD 2010).

A prominent example for the Netherlands is the policy programme 'the Netherlands Goes Digital' (*Nederland Gaat Digitaal*, abbreviated to NGD) that was in place between 2002 and 2007. With this programme, a budget of € 33.5 million was spent to promote and support the adoption and use of ICT by SMEs; including interorganisational ICT such as e-business applications. SMEs could participate in the programme and receive free or sponsored workshops, seminars, consultancy advice and information materials. Initially in 2002, SMEs that are 'technology followers' were the target group of the NGD programme, but since 2004 the focus was on SMEs that are 'technology leading'. The NGD programme was, for the Netherlands, a comprehensive and ambitious programme. It is estimated that some 27,000 SMEs (about 8 %) have been reached by the various components of the programme. In addition, the programme has reached 85 industry organisations in the SME sector that actively contributed to its activities and events.

In this chapter we present the results of an evaluation study of the NGD programme, which was initiated by its sponsor (the Dutch Ministry of Economic Affairs) near the end of the programme in 2006. At that time, the first notion was that the programme as such was successful in terms of its reach and publicity. It was unknown however, if the targeted SMEs actually set the next step in their ICT maturity and additionally became more aware about the added value of ICT. As argued above, ICT for interorganisational exchange can be considered as the most lacking, and yet most promising area for SMEs to innovate and boost their performance. The main question is therefore whether the NGD policy programme reached this far reaching goal and supported SMEs to become what is often called an 'extended enterprise' (cf. Bovet and Martha 2000; Davis and Spekman 2004). The related question is about situationality of the potential effect of the programme, i.e. did it differ between types of SMEs and/or types of interorganisational ICT?

This chapter is driven by these two questions and structured as follows. In the next section we review related work on SMEs, policy and interorganisational ICT, which feed our conceptual model. We then discuss the data collection, being the surveys that were done after the policy programme was finished among participating and non-participating Dutch SMEs. Section 4 contains the results of comparative analyses and in the concluding section we reflect on the implications of the results, including some critical reflection.

2 Theory and Conceptual Model

2.1 *Related work*

Chau and Turner (2002) find through 34 case studies of Australian SMEs that government support only played a minor role in the adoption and utilisation of web-based electronic commerce. They state that: "[e]ducation and awareness programs for breaking down the barriers of misinformation and EC adoption fears [...] helped a number of the small and micro enterprises". Using the technology–organisation–environment framework, Kuan and Chau (2001) look at the adoption of EDI in SMEs. They identify government policy as one of the relevant factors, however only as a 'stick' (government pressure), whereas we are interested in the effects of a 'carrot' here, namely an innovation programme. Earlier, Iacovou et al. (1995) performed similar work on EDI adoption, through seven case studies. They also include the government in their analysis, but then look at the concept of dependency, as all seven organisations were trading partners of the government. Another example of a study in which the government is only viewed from a 'push'-factor perspective, is the work of Salleh et al. (2006) on the adoption of a government e-procurement system by Malaysian SMEs. They take this mainly as a given, as they focus primarily on other factors in their study.

Prananto et al. (2004) do include policy/initiatives as one of the possible drivers in their model of e-business progression among SMEs. They mention that this is considered the least influential driver by their sample of 104 survey respondents, but unfortunately do not elaborate on this. Through analysing 50 cases in the UK using network actor theory, Beckinsale et al. (2006) also find that the government has no influence on the adoption of internet by SMEs. This could be related to the fact that none of the SMEs is aware of government schemes to support e-business adoption. In their survey among 378 UK-based SMEs, Harindranath et al. (2008) also find ignorance of policy initiatives. Their results clearly show that this ignorance is significant, although it is unclear whether this is due to a lack of awareness or a lack of use of these initiatives.

In an extensive analysis of 54 Pakistani cases, Seyal et al. (2004) find that government support is a significant factor in determining the adoption of e-commerce by SMEs. Wymer and Regan (2005) also conclude that government rules and regulations are a significant factor in the adoption decision of e-commerce/e-business internet technologies, based on a survey of 102 USA SMEs. In addition, they state that this factor has not received much attention in prior studies, possibly unjustified.

Although perhaps not complete, the above review gives an impression of the *status quo*. Overall, we can say that 'government' is not regularly included as a factor in adoption studies. If so, it often is in the form of a push (external pressure) instead of a pull factor, like NGD is. The general outcome of the studies we found that *did* analyse government policy is unclear. Some scholars say it is highly relevant, others indicate minor or no relevance at all. Already in 1994, in their European Journal of Information Systems paper on the effect of government incentives on computerisation of small businesses, Yap et al. (1994) report on this apparent duality: "[…] participation in a government computerisation programme does not result in more effective information systems. However, […] government incentives, in the form of subsidies, low-interest loans, seminars and technical expertise, lower the barriers to computerisation and make it more attractive". It is this second type of effect (not more effective information systems per se, just a higher degree of interorganisational ICT) that we will discuss in the remainder of this chapter. We believe that our study into the *effect* (i.e. not just the awareness) of a major government policy programme, using a large sample and control group, forms a valuable contribution to this field.

2.2 SME-focused ICT Policy and the Productivity Paradox

In general, ICT solutions for most SMEs are not ready-made packages. The successful realisation of ICT applications and the actual utilisation of ICT, involves lengthy and expensive learning and it is not possible to determine in advance that entrepreneurs will obtain all benefits of ICT. For many SMEs markets lack transparency. Combined with the fact that there are insufficient knowledgeable demanders (asymmetric information), this forms a relevant theoretical argument for promoting ICT application and use in SMEs. Especially considering the economy-wide positive impact of the application of ICT, this provides an argument to support the implementation of ICT, provoke ICT investments and improve the utilisation of ICT for SMEs.

However, a government intervention in industry is always accompanied by questions about its efficiency and effectiveness, as well as more fundamental questions about the rationale and legitimacy. In fact, this concerns the type of governance role a government should take in the economy. There are divergent views about this, which are partly ideologically determined. When a government plans to 'repair' market failures through policy interventions, there is the possible risk that these market failures get *replaced* by government failure. Policy also involves costs and the (sometimes limited) market could be hindered by government intervention. For that reason, one should prevent too far-reaching and too specific ICT policy. In the Netherlands, Raes et al. (2004, pp. 317–318) advocate generic policies for ICT and policies that stimulate co-operation between firms and knowledge institutions, but also warn: "However, the risk of government failure in such volatile markets is more than imaginary. Again, a careful approach by governments in designing and implementing such schemes is necessary". It should be noted that this mainly seems to refer to promoting technological progress in ICT and less to policy focused on ICT diffusion.

Still, there are many arguments to initiate and execute an ICT policy that focuses upon SMEs. These arguments have been collected in a series of OECD-reports in 2004 ("ICT diffusion to business: peer review"; OECD 2004) which included country studies on Denmark, Finland, Italy, Korea, Norway, and Switzerland. It appeared that in most countries, similar arguments are at stake for stimulating SMEs in their ICT uptake by the specific development of ICT policy. Examples of such arguments in those countries are:

- *Contribution of ICT to productivity growth and economic performances in combination with the dominant presence of SMEs.* Almost all countries point to recent OECD studies on the significant contribution of ICT to productivity and economic performances. This is often confirmed by national studies that sometimes are even specifically aimed at SMEs. The Danish ministry of Science, Technology and Innovation has for example calculated that there exists a positive correlation between ICT usage and added value per employee for companies in the range of 10–49 employees. In addition, it is determined that SMEs play a very large role in the national economy and that there is much space to improve the utilisation of ICT.
- *ICT backlog of SMEs.* It is found for many countries of the peer review that SMEs have a significant backlog compared to large enterprises with regard to use and actual utilisation of ICT. Most countries view this as an argument for having ICT policy aimed at SMEs. In doing so however, boundaries are encountered. With some ICT applications that backlog of SMEs will never change, because not all ICT applications are relevant for all organisations (this is for instance one of the conclusions in the Danish peer review). In addition, the large differences between sectors and regions are often pointed out (e.g. Italy).
- *Market failure.* There are examples of countries (e.g. Denmark and Finland) where taking out market failures and realising attractive conditions for companies to use ICT are indicated as argument in favour of governmental intervention. SMEs would suffer most from market failures in the ICT domain. An example of a market failure is the lack of transparency of the ICT services and applications that are on offer in the market.
- *Connection between SMEs and the knowledge infrastructure is insufficient.* In most countries, SMEs collaborate less with knowledge institutions on ICT R&D compared to large organisations (e.g. Denmark and Italy). On average SMEs are less innovative than large companies, while according to policy makers it is of great importance to have competitive and knowledge intensive SMEs that stimulate future economic development. Overall, countries differ in the degree to which the themes of ICT and innovation are being coupled.

- *Alleviating a number of concrete problems of SMEs in the application of ICT*. In the peer review several SME-specific problems are presented that are used as arguments for an SME-specific ICT policy. Examples of these problems are:
  - SME management is insufficiently aware of the potential advantages of usage of ICT (Denmark, Korea).
  - Opportunities are not being pursued because SMEs lack sufficient ICT skills (Denmark, Korea, Switzerland).
  - SMEs are insufficiently able to determine their ICT needs and find suitable ICT solutions (Denmark).
  - SME customers have different demands for ICT applications and that problem is aggravated by a lack of standardisation (Denmark, Finland, Norway).
  - SMEs are uncertain about protection of privacy and consumer interests in the ICT era (Finland, Switzerland).

From the OECD study, it was also argued that international rankings (e.g. the e-readiness index of The Economist) constitute a trigger for the development of ICT policy by countries. If a country holds low scores in these rankings, this is used as an argument to use ICT policies to catch up (Italy). Likewise, leader countries use these rankings as an argument to (continue to) invest in ICT policy (Finland).

Although there is strong policy interest in the usage of ICT by SMEs, the question remains if ICT is indeed the performance driver for these organisations. This goes back to the 'productivity paradox': "we see the computer age everywhere but in the productivity statistics" (Solow 1987, p. 36). Solow observed that ICT investment levels were not positively related to productivity levels of countries and sectors. Currently, the consensus is that this phenomenon was indeed a paradox at that time and supported by that type of analysis, but now this has changed. Van Ark and De Jong (2004, pp. 42–43) show that on a macro level, in the Netherlands, a quarter of the growth of labour productivity between 1979 and 2001 was caused by an increase in computers (and other ICT assets). For 1995–2001 this was more than 50 % of the productivity growth. In addition, it has been shown that on organisational and individual levels ICT *does* increase productivity (e.g. Brynjolfsson and Hitt 2000; Donselaar et al. 2004; European Commission 2010). For interorganisational ICT, this relationship is less certain and more research is needed.

2.3 A Conceptual Model to Investigate Policy Effects

In this study we design a conceptual model to investigate the effect of the Dutch NGD policy programme to improve the uptake of interorganisational ICT by SMEs. The model, which is depicted in Fig. 1, consists of two parts that are assumed to be dependent upon participation in the NGD programme. The first part entails the question if participation by SMEs in the NGD programme has led to higher usage of interorganisational ICT systems and applications. The second part

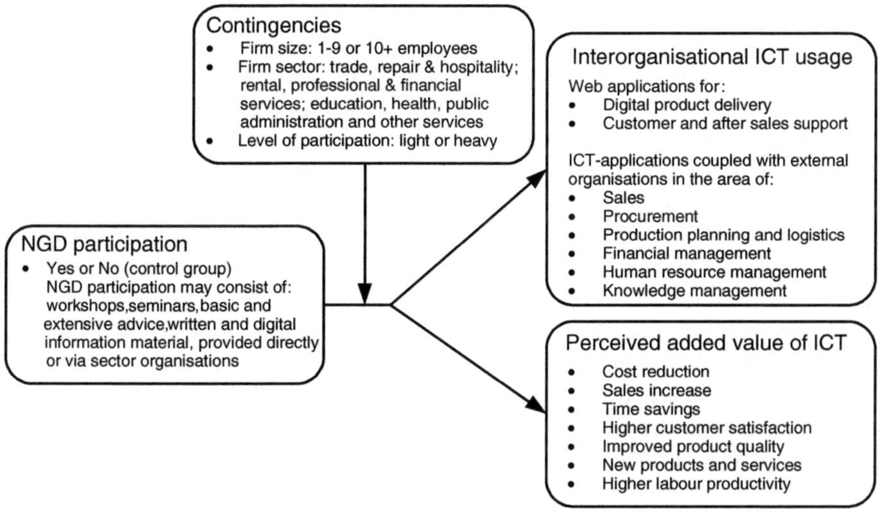

Fig. 1 The conceptual model for this study

of the conceptual model is about the question if the participating SMEs, through the NGD programme, experienced a higher added value from ICT. Also listed in Fig. 1 are specifications of the programme's activities, of the indicators of use of interorganisational ICT systems, and of the indicators of the perceived added value of ICT. Finally, the conceptual model illustrates that the potential effect of the policy programme is also investigated by controlling for contingencies, being the firm size, sector and level of participation of SMEs. In the next section, it is described how in practice these measurements were conducted in an extensive field study among participants and non-participants of the NGD policy programme.

3 Data and Methods

Initiated by the Dutch Ministry of Economic Affairs a field research was executed in 2006, which resulted in a number of evaluation activities, including two extended surveys conducted by telephone and the internet. The advantage of employing the survey method here is that we were able to query a substantial amount of participants of the programme, and do so in exactly the same way. Two target groups were approached to complete a tailor-made survey: a sample of the SME participants of the NGD programme (n = 516), and a control group consisting of SME organisations comparable to the NGD participants, but who did not took part in the NGD programme (n = 124).

The first group was selected by a (stratified) sample from the database of the NGD programme organisation. An e-mail with a request to complete a web survey was sent to 2,482 participants. This e-mail was preceded by an explanatory letter from the Ministry of Economic Affairs. The questionnaire includes—among other things—components on ICT usage and ICT impact on business. After about 1 week, and again after another 2 weeks, a reminder was sent via e-mail to those that did not respond (yet). After 3 weeks, 516 respondents completed the questionnaire in its entirety. This is a gross response rate of 21 %. Excluding the e-mail addresses that appeared to be outdated (n = 434, 17.5 %) results in a net response rate of 25.2 %. Comparative survey studies among SMEs (e.g. the E-Busines W@tch survey; European Commission 2008) reach similar or lower response rates.

The second group can be considered a control group of SMEs (n = 124). This group was selected from an address database that was available for surveying through a Dutch market research company. The composition of this control group was matched with the response group of the web survey among the NGD SME participants. For each SME respondent to the web survey, a 'counterpart' SME (according to size and industry) was selected, to ensure a 'fair' and unbiased comparison as good as possible. The control group of SMEs was surveyed by telephone, immediately after the completed web surveys of the SME participants were received. Within 2 weeks, 124 telephone interviews were realised according to a stratified sampling matrix. An abridged version of the web survey was used, including similar questions about interorganisational ICT use and perceived added value of ICT to the SME. In achieving the response of 124, refusals (do not want to participate, too busy to participate, not available) were obviously encountered; through 464 calls, a net response rate of 26.7 % was achieved.

Due to this sampling design, it is possible to compare NGD participants with non-participating SMEs, on the different aspects of interorganisational ICT usage and the perceived added value of ICT. Although selection bias cannot be excluded, it is at least reduced, which improves the measurement of the contribution of the policy programme to the use of interorganisational ICT and to the perceived added value of ICT by Dutch SMEs.

4 Results

4.1 Usage of Interorganisational ICT

In this section we analyse the differences (and their statistical significance) in use of interorganisational ICT between participants and non-participants of the NGD programme. We deliberately consider the differences on a number of indicators for interorganisational ICT, as it is a broad concept that covers several distinct business domains. In addition, the NGD programme was set up to improve adoption of ICT in general, so we can expect effects on all types. Also, this gives

Table 1 Differences in ICT usage between participants and non-participants

SME uses:	Non-participants (n = 124) Mean %	Participants (n = 516) Mean %	t-value	p
A web application for:				
Digital product delivery	7.3	25.6	−5.98	0.00*
Customer and after sales support	16.9	42.1	−6.19	0.00*
ICT applications coupled with external organisations in the area of:				
Sales	4.9	41.1	−12.42	0.00*
Procurement	6.8	31.8	−8.15	0.00*
Production planning and logistics	4.6	29.8	−9.13	0.00*
Financial management	10.3	42.1	−9.05	0.00*
Human resource management	12.8	23.5	−2.90	0.00*
Knowledge management	9.7	23.8	−4.26	0.00*

* Difference between the groups is significant (two-tailed t-test, $p < 0.01$)

us the opportunity to see whether participants in the NGD programme favoured specific types of interorganisational ICT above others.

Table 1 shows that the participants in the NGD programme scored higher than non-participants on all interorganisational ICT indicators. The differences between participants and non-participants are the largest for interorganisational ICT applications in the sales domain (36 %), followed by those for financial management (32 %). For digital product delivery (18 %), knowledge management (14 %) and human resource management (11 %) the differences are smaller, compared to the other indicators. However, all differences are statistically significant.

An important question is whether the observed differences still exist when we take into account company size and industry, two characteristics that have a 'proven' effect on the level of ICT development of organisations. Table 2 provides an overview of some analyses performed for this purpose. We determined whether the above significant differences between participants and non-participants are still statistically significant when we isolate the following groups:

- Organisations with 1–9 employees (column '10−' in the tables);
- Organisations with 10–250 employees ('10+');
- Organisations in Trade, Repair and Hospitality ('TRH');
- Organisations in Rental, Professional and Financial services ('RPF');
- Organisations in Education, Health, Public administration and other services ('EHP').

We need to define these fairly coarse subcategories, because of the number of observations. When defining too specific subclasses, the number of respondents may become so small that no reliable averages can be calculated. Here we use the

Table 2 Differences between participants and non-participants by subgroups of size and sector

	Firm size		Sector		
SME uses:	10–	10+	TRH	RPF	EHP
A web application for:					
Digital product delivery	*	*		*	
Customer and after sales support	*		*	*	*
ICT applications coupled with external organisations in the area of:					
Sales	*	*	*	*	*
Procurement	*	*	*	*	
Production planning and logistics	*	*			
Financial management	*	*	*		
Human resource management		*			
Knowledge management	*	*			

* Difference within the subgroup is significant (two-tailed t-test, $p < 0.01$)

rule of thumb that analyses should be performed on categories with 15 or more respondents. We combined organisational sectors based on similarity of industry. An '*' in Table 2 indicates that the difference between participants and non-participants is statistically significant, based on a *t* test (significance level is 0.01 or less, two-tailed testing).

These results partly support the idea that all participants within the NGD programme use more interorganisational ICT. Both the relatively small and relatively large organisations score higher on almost all different interorganisational ICT applications when compared to their non-participating peers. For the three sectors that we distinguished, the results are more mixed: the differences are only significant for four (TRH, RPF) or two (EHP) out of eight indicators. A possible explanation for this result is that some of the interorganisational ICT application domains are not very relevant for the sector (e.g. digital product delivery for trade, repair and hospitality organisations, and production planning and logistics for all three sectors).

Finally, we analyse the impact of the programme by comparing differences *between* participants. To do so, we make a distinction between light and heavy users, based on a major dividing aspect within the programme: whether or not use has been made of the 'extensive advice'. This activity can be considered the most complex and far-reaching for the organisation based on its contents. It is also distinctive because SMEs had to invest themselves, while other programme activities were provided at little or no cost. The expectation here is that heavy users of the programme have developed further in their use of interorganisational ICT compared to light users. The results are listed in Table 3.

On all indicators, heavy users score higher than light users. Obviously, the absolute differences are smaller than those between participants and the control group, but still five out of eight are statistically significant.

Table 3 Differences between light and heavy users

SME uses	Light users (n = 286) (%)	Heavy users (n = 230) (%)
A web application for:		
Digital product delivery*	16	29
Customer and after sales support	23	29
ICT applications coupled with external organisations in the area of:		
Sales*	34	50
Procurement*	27	38
Production planning and logistics*	22	40
Financial management	38	47
Human resource management	21	27
Knowledge management*	19	30

*Difference between the groups is significant (two-tailed t-test, $p < 0.01$)

4.2 Perceived Added Value of (Interorganisational) ICT

We now move to the second part of our analysis: whether SMEs that participate in the NGD programme perceive higher added value of ICT for their organisations. Here we need to make the important reservation that assessing the direct economic impact of instruments such as NGD is not easy. There are indeed many non-policy factors that determine the state of corporate performance (in conjunction with the use of ICT). We measure the *perceived* added value of ICT on several indicators, as a proxy to the real added value. This entails a subjective evaluation of the respondent, but is therefore not of less value. This method of measuring ICT revenues has been used more often in IS research (cf. Tallon et al. 2000). It should also be noted that these measurements cover both *intra-* and *inter*organisational ICT, so we cannot completely attribute the experienced benefits to the latter category. However, in selecting these types of added value, we chose items that are generally considered to be benefits of interorganisational ICT.

Table 4 shows the results of this measurement, compared between participants and non-participants. Respondents could score the indicators on a scale from 1 = almost nil, 2 = little, 3 = neither small/great, 4 = fairly high, 5 = high.

All differences are in favour of the participating organisations, and are statistically significant. On the economic-related performance indicators (such as cost reduction, time savings and labour productivity) the NGD participants hold significantly higher scores compared to the non-participants. This is in favour of the expectation that for SMEs in general, time and money are prerequisites for entrepreneurship, and ICT can improve these key conditions.

The next step in the analysis again aims to determine whether the above conclusion is robust when the data are broken down with regard to industry and size of the SMEs. The results of this step are listed in Table 5.

Compared with the earlier analysis on ICT usage, Table 5 quite clearly shows that the participants significantly differ from the non-participants in a consistent

Table 4 Differences in perceived added value of ICT (5-point scale) between participants and non-participants

SME has experienced added value of ICT through:	Non-participants (n = 124)		Participants (n = 516)		t-value	p (2-tailed)
	Mean	SD	Mean	SD		
Cost reduction	2.0	1.2	2.8	1.4	−5.85	0.00*
Sales increase	1.9	1.2	2.9	1.3	−7.02	0.00*
Time savings	2.8	1.5	3.5	1.3	−4.97	0.00*
Higher customer satisfaction	2.2	1.4	3.2	1.3	−6.81	0.00*
Improved product quality	2.0	1.4	2.8	1.5	−5.55	0.00*
New products and services	1.9	1.3	2.9	1.5	−7.80	0.00*
Higher labour productivity	2.1	1.4	3.0	1.4	−6.36	0.00*

* Difference between the groups is significant (two-tailed t-test, $p < 0.01$)

Table 5 Differences between participants and non-participants by subgroups of size and sector

SME has experienced added value of ICT through:	Firm size		Sector		
	10−	10+	TRH	RPF	EHP
Cost reduction	*	*	*	*	*
Sales increase	*	*	*	*	*
Time savings	*	*	*		
Higher customer satisfaction	*	*	*	*	*
Improved product quality	*	*	*	*	
New products and services	*	*	*	*	*
Higher labour productivity	*	*	*	*	*

* Difference within the subgroup is significant (two-tailed t-test, $p < 0.01$)

way (i.e. for almost all industries and sizes). We therefore conclude that a robust difference can be found in comparing both datasets.

Finally, we examine whether these clear differences remain when we distinguish between light and heavy users. Table 6 contains the results of this comparison.

On almost all indicators, the differences in added value are in favour of the heavy users. These differences are statistically significant for two types of added value, however. While in the previous analysis participants scored systematically above the non-participants, within the group of participants there is only a significant difference in terms of increasing turnover and customer satisfaction. These results show that the programme participants are fairly consistently positive about the contribution of ICT to their business performance. The contribution they experience of ICT does not differ between different degrees of programme usage. Apparently light users are also already in a relatively ‘satisfied’ situation.

Table 6 Differences in perceived added value of ICT (5-point scale) between light and heavy users

SME has experienced added value of ICT through:	Light users (n = 286) Mean	Heavy users (n = 230) Mean
Cost reduction	2.9	2.7
Sales increase*	2.7	3.1
Time savings	3.5	3.6
Higher customer satisfaction*	3.0	3.4
Improved product quality	2.7	2.9
New products and services	2.8	3.0
Higher labour productivity	3.0	3.0

* Difference between the groups is significant (two-tailed t-test, $p < 0.01$)

5 Conclusion and Discussion

In this chapter, we discussed the importance of SMEs for economy and society, and the backlog they generally have in terms of their (interorganisational) ICT uptake. A review of existing research into this subject was presented, revealing little insight into the effect of governmental ICT policy. We then listed the theoretical and practical arguments for an ICT policy that focuses upon SMEs, like the bewildering array of ICT solutions available on the market, combined with SMEs that are insufficiently informed (asymmetrical information). In addition, the shortcomings in a variety of other systems can serve to substantiate an ICT policy that is directed towards SMEs. This does perhaps not justify any far-reaching measures, but does justify promoting awareness-raising and transparency in the marketplace.

Next, we set out to evaluate NGD, a substantial ICT policy programme in the Netherlands, aimed at increasing adoption and use of (interorganisational) ICT by SMEs. Based upon our results, we arrive at the following conclusions. NGD participants are SMEs that, in comparison to the control group:

- Use significantly more interorganisational ICT, and
- State considerably more frequently that ICT has enhanced their company's performance.

These outcomes fit with the aims of the programme. When subgroups are defined, these results are consistent for firm size (employees). The results are less clear when a division is made into sectors, but this could be related to the irrelevance of certain types of interorganisational ICT for certain sectors. Within the group of NGD participants, heavy users do not differ from light users on all indicators, especially regarding the perceived added value of ICT.

Participants in NGD are relatively high performing SMEs. This could be the effect of taking part in the programme, (self-)selection or a combination of both. Two possible selection effects could play a role. First of all, not all SMEs have ever been invited—directly and individually—to take part in the NGD programme. We can therefore expect that SMEs that did participate already possessed a certain awareness of and familiarity with interorganisational ICT. Secondly, self-selection may take place, with the result that better-achieving organisations are more likely to take part in web surveys such as those used in this study.

It should be clear that the above results are very favourable for the NGD programme. They support the conclusion that it gave these SMEs a major incentive to become 'ICT mature' sooner, and to reap the benefits of these ICT investments sooner and better. However, forms of self-selection that could weaken this conclusion should thus seriously be considered. The selection effect relies on a number of phenomena that are hard to operationalise:

- Programmes like NGD typically attract those organisations that are already (pro-)actively engaged with ICT and internet, if not professionally then out of personal interest of the company's employees;
- Programmes like NGD typically attract those organisations that are already (pro-)actively engaged with their environment, including campaigns and schemes from industry associations and governments.
- Organisations that are already in a favourable stage of development are typically better able to make use of programmes such as NGD and reap additional benefits from it.

The basis of these phenomena is in principle supported by the research of Van der Veen (2004) among NGD participants. In her conclusion, she stressed that government should aim to encourage conventional ICT as much as 'renewed entrepreneurship'. The intended effect is that entrepreneurial SMEs receive the right incentives this way, the unintended effect is that the position of less attentive SMEs becomes harder and harder to improve.

In our study, it appears from the comparative analyses that taking part in the programme plays a more decisive role in the use of interorganisational ICT and perceived added value than the nature/intensity of participation. In terms of policy recommendations, this could be interpreted as a plea for basic, awareness-focused programmes, instead of complex, government supported implementation processes. Based on our results, reach seems to be more important and cost-effective than very intensive measures. Taking this into account, it would be important for government bodies to design policy programmes that are as undemanding and simple to understand for SMEs as possible, as Harindranath et al. (2008, p. 95) found that these programmes are often perceived as "bureaucratic and cumbersome".

An important limitation of this study is that we analysed the added value of ICT in general. Although we investigated factors of which it can reasonably be expected that they are influenced by *interorganisational* ICT, future research should explicitly focus on these effects. It would be interesting if we could then also surpass the level of *perceived* benefits and assess the *real* added value of interorganisational ICT. This is no easy task, and perhaps longitudinal, in-depth case studies are better suited to this kind of research.

As our data collection took place a few years ago, more recent types of interorganisational ICT were not included. Examples of this would be service-oriented architectures (SOA) and web services, which are known to be insufficiently considered in IOS research (Löhe and Legner 2010). It would be good if future studies included these more novel applications as well.

A final shortcoming of our current work is that it focuses only on the Dutch situation. Although the OECD (2004) peer reviews present results from some other countries, it would be valuable to replicate our current study in other countries with a specific focus on interorganisational systems. However, if the exact same study were to be replicated, that would require a similar policy instrument to be in place in the countries to be studied. But, the conceptual model could also be broadened. Here, we only looked at the influence of ICT policy (i.e. NGD participation) on adoption and the added value of (interorganisational) ICT, moderated by several contingencies. If we would also take other factors in consideration, e.g. technological and organisational characteristics, we could create a more general framework of the determinants influencing adoption of interorganisational ICT by SMEs. This is important, as Ramdani et al. (2009) found that the adoption factors for enterprise systems (e.g. SCM and e-procurement) differ from those of other information systems.

Acknowledgments A preliminary version of this chapter has been presented at the Bled eConference in 2011: Plomp, M. G. A., Batenburg, R. S., & Den Hertog, P. (2011). Does ICT policy improve interorganisational ICT for SMEs? A Dutch policy evaluation study. In *Proceedings of the 24th Bled eConference "eFuture: Creating Solutions for the Individual, Organisations and Society"* (pp. 558–571). Bled, Slovenia.

References

Barrett, S., & Konsynski, B. (1982). Inter-organization information sharing systems. *MIS Quarterly, 6*, 93–105.

Beckinsale, M., Levy, M., & Powell, P. (2006). Exploring internet adoption drivers in SMEs. *Electronic Markets, 16*(4), 361–370.

Bovet, D., & Martha, J. (2000). *Value nets: Breaking the supply chain to unlock hidden profits*. New York: Wiley.

Brynjolfsson, E., & Hitt, L. M. (2000). Beyond computation: Information technology, organizational transformation and business performance. *Journal of Economic Perspectives, 14*(4), 23–48.

Chau, S. B., & Turner, P. (2002). *A framework for analysing factors influencing small to medium sized enterprises (SMEs) ability to derive benefit from the conduct of web-based electronic commerce (EC)—34 Australian case studies*. Paper presented at the Tenth European Conference on Information Systems.

Daft, R. L. (2001). *Organizational theory and design* (7th ed.). Cincinnati, Ohio: South-Western Educational Publishing.

Damanpour, F. (1992). Organizational size and innovation. *Organization Studies, 13*(3), 375–402.

Davis, E. W., & Spekman, R. E. (2004). *The extended enterprise: Gaining competitive advantage through collaborative supply chains*. Upper Saddle River, NJ: Prentice Hall.

Donselaar, P., Erken, H., & Klomp, L. (2004). R&D and innovation: Drivers of productivity growth. In G. Gelauff, L. Klomp, S. Raes, & T. Roelandt (Eds.), *Fostering productivity. Patterns, determinants and policy implications* (Vol. 263, pp. 75–91). Amsterdam: Elsevier.

EIM. (2010). *European SMEs under pressure: Annual report on EU small and medium-sized enterprises 2009*. Zoetermeer, The Netherlands: EIM Business and Policy Research.

European Commission. (2008). *The European e-business report 2008: The impact of ICT and e-business on firms, sectors and the economy*. Luxembourg: Office for Official Publications of the European Communities.

European Commission. (2010). *Europe's digital competitiveness report 2010* (Vol. 1). Luxembourg: Publications Office of the European Union.

Harindranath, G., Dyerson, R., & Barnes, D. (2008). ICT adoption and use in UK SMEs: A failure of initiatives? *Electronic Journal of Information Systems Evaluation, 11*(2), 91–96.

Iacovou, C. L., Benbasat, I., & Dexter, A. S. (1995). Electronic data interchange and small organizations: Adoption and impact of technology. *MIS Quarterly, 19*(4), 465–485.

Kuan, K. K. Y., & Chau, P. Y. K. (2001). A perception-based model for EDI adoption in small businesses using a technology-organization-environment framework. *Information and Management, 38*(8), 507–521.

Löhe, J., & Legner, C. (2010). SOA adoption in business networks: Do service-oriented architectures really advance inter-organizational integration? *Electronic Markets, 20*(3–4), 181–196.

Meier, J., & Sprague, R. (1991). The evolution of interorganizational systems. *Journal of Information Technology, 6*(3), 184–191.

Morrell, M., & Ezingeard, J.-N. (2002). Revisiting adoption factors of inter-organisational information systems in SMEs. *Logistics Information Management, 15*(1), 46–57.

Nelson, M. L. (2003). *The adoption and diffusion of interorganizational system standards and process innovations*. Champaign, Illinois: University of Illinois.

OECD. (2004). *ICT diffusion to business: Peer review. Country reports Denmark, Finland, Italy, Korea, Norway, and Switzerland*. Paris: OECD Publishing.

OECD. (2010). *OECD information technology outlook 2010*. Paris: OECD Publishing.

Papazoglou, M. P., & Ribbers, P. M. A. (2006). *E-business: Organizational and technical foundations*. Chichester: Wiley.

Prananto, A., McKay, J., & Marshall, P. (2004). *Exploring the perceptions of inhibitors and drivers of e-business progression among SMEs at different stages of e-business maturity*. Paper presented at the 12th European Conference on Information Systems.

Premkumar, G. P., Ramamurthy, K., & Nilakanta, S. (1992). *An empirical assessment of the impact of interorganizational relationships on the adoption and diffusion of interorganizational systems*. Paper presented at the Thirteenth Annual International Conference on Information Systems (ICIS)

Raes, S., Gelauff, G., Klomp, L., & Roelandt, T. (2004). A policy agenda for higher productivity growth. In G. Gelauff, L. Klomp, S. Raes, & T. Roelandt (Eds.), *Fostering productivity. Patterns, determinants and policy implications* (Vol. 263, pp. 305–321). Amsterdam: Elsevier.

Ramdani, B., Kawalek, P., & Lorenzo, O. (2009). Predicting SMEs' adoption of enterprise systems. *Journal of Enterprise Information Management, 22*(1/2), 10–24.

Salleh, N. A. M., Rohde, F., & Green, P. (2006). The effect of enacted capabilities on adoption of a government electronic procurement system by Malaysian SMEs. *Electronic Markets, 16*(4), 292–311.

Seyal, A. H., Awais, M. M., Shamail, S., & Abbas, A. (2004). Determinants of electronic commerce in Pakistan: Preliminary evidence from small and medium enterprises. *Electronic Markets, 14*(4), 372–387.

Shapiro, J. F. (2009). *Modeling the supply chain* (2nd ed.). Pacific Grove, CL: Duxbury.

Solow, R. (1987). We'd better watch out. *New York Times Book Review, July 12*, 36.

Tallon, P., Kraemer, K. L., & Gurbaxani, V. (2000). Executives' perceptions of the business value of information technology: A process-oriented approach. *Journal of Management Information Systems, 16*(4), 137–165.

Van Ark, B., & De Jong, G. (2004). *Productiviteit en Dienstverlenende Ondernemingen [Productivity and service firms].* Koninklijke van Gorcum/Stichting Management Studies (SMS): Assen.

Van der Veen, M. (2004). *Explaining e-business adoption: Innovation & entrepreneurship in Dutch SMEs.* Enschede: University of Twente.

Williams, T. (1997). Interorganisational information systems: Issues affecting interorganisational cooperation. *The Journal of Strategic Information Systems, 6*(3), 231–250.

Wymer, S. A., & Regan, E. A. (2005). Factors influencing e-commerce adoption and use by small and medium businesses. *Electronic Markets, 15*(4), 438–453.

Yap, C. S., Thong, J. Y. L., & Raman, K. S. (1994). Effect of government incentives on computerisation in small business. *European Journal of Information Systems, 3*(3), 191–206.

Zhu, K., & Kraemer, K. L. (2002). E-commerce metrics for net-enhanced organizations: Assessing the value of e-commerce to firm performance in the manufacturing sector. *Information Systems Research, 13*(3), 275–295.

Main Factors for ICT Adoption in the Czech SMEs

Klara Antlova

1 Introduction

SMEs play an important role in the economy. They employ an increasing proportion of the total working population; bring new products and new services. They contribute to exports, national wealth, and competitiveness. The constant and rapid changes occurring in the markets, force the SMEs to look for new ways of how to survive and be competitive. The customers make higher demands on the products or services they buy. Products have to be introduced on the market faster and have to meet individual demands. Therefore the knowledge of customers' demands is regarded as one the most important source of innovation (Rivard et al. 2005).

When compared to large enterprises, SMEs have a simpler organisational structure with less specialised tasks, poor human, financial and material resources. Also most SMEs are very dependent on their daily environment (suppliers, competitors, and customers). The owners or managers have not many people with whom they can discuss or consult about their decisions. But when they want to survive they have to respond to longer term changes in the environment. SMEs also have more limited use of ICT and the employees have less ICT capabilities (Parker and Custleman 2007). This low level of organisational readiness, insufficient skills and knowledge are the reasons for slow adoption of ICT. When the ICT is successfully implemented and used, the companies improve the following areas of business: reduced costs, less errors, reduced inventories, creation of new market opportunities, better communication and co-operation with customers and suppliers (Tetteh and Burn 2001; E-Business Indicators 2007).

The structure of this chapter is as follows; the second part brings literature review, the third part explains the data collection and methodology and the fourth

K. Antlova (✉)
Technical University of Liberec, Economic School,
Voronezska 13, 46117 Liberec, Czech Republic
e-mail: Klara.antlova@tul.cz

J. Devos et al. (eds.), *Information Systems for Small and Medium-sized Enterprises*, Progress in IS, DOI: 10.1007/978-3-642-38244-4_7,

part contains ICT drivers in SMEs. The barriers and reasons for ICT adoption are in Sect. 5. The last part consists of discussion and conclusion.

2 Literature Review

The current business environment is characterised as highly turbulent, influenced by modern ICT, globalisation, short innovation and production cycles and employees' mobility. It is not easy to compete in such an environment; organisations have to utilise their corporate resources to the greatest possible extent. Such resources include finance, employees, tangible assets, technologies and also knowledge (Powell et al. 2001).

SMEs also have particular problems in adopting and using ICT. They usually do not have the appropriate skills available in-house and thus have to train existing staff or purchase those skills in the marketplace (Valkokari and Helander 2007). But ICT must be associated with a systematic approach to management and decision making and its introduction requires careful planning (Kerney and Abul-Nour 2004). Although the technology is much cheaper than before, it still represents a considerable investment for SMEs that traditionally lack such funds (Levy et al. 2002). The introduction of ICT, which may lead to dramatic changes in the business's fundamental activities, requires an awareness and basic knowledge of the management function, but many owners of SMEs appear to be to busy "surviving" to invest time in such projects (Oh and Pinsonneault 2007; Cocrill and Lewis 2002). Therefore, there is a significant risk that such efforts to implement ICT will be unsuccessful, and the cost of such failure may be fatal for the small firm lacking adequate financial and productive cushioning (Craig and Annear 2003). It is not surprising that many SMEs have avoided such risks by ignoring ICT (Gemino et al. 2006).
Existing literature review proposes major differences between SMEs and large organisations (Levy and Powell 2005a, b):

- SMEs tend to use computers more as tools and less as a communications medium (Heikkila 1991; Chau and Turner 2002; Antlova and Popelinsky 2012).
- SMEs have much fewer resources available to implement ICT solutions (Covin and Slevin 1990; Peppard and Ward 2004).

Planning in a small firm has the following characteristics:

- Often done on an ad hoc basis (Kerste et al. 2002; Jeffocate 2002).
- Frequently done as a mental activity of the owner or manager (Martin and Matlay 2010; Sudzina 2010).
- Is informal, sporadic, and closed (Choi and Lee 2003; Antlova et al. 2011).
- Often relying on advice from random acquaintances with less skill and/or less experience than the owner himself (Antlova 2007; Vicente and Lopez 2009).

3 Data Collection and Methodology

The thirty SMEs (all from Czech Republic) have been analysed during qualitative research for 17 years. The data has been collected through interviews with the managers or the owners. The interviews (the structure of interview is described detailed in Sect. 4.1) have been realized with the same managers or the persons on the same positions every year. In these companies the students of bachelor studying course Business Computing practised their one year trainee. During their stay they had to report every month their projects and activities. Every semester they also had to prepare the company analysis and once a year the results of the interviews. This long term network of cooperation companies consists of three companies from the automotive sector, six companies do business in ICT area, two are logistic partners, eleven companies are in services, four are from the building industry and the last four are manufacturers). The student's reports are stored in database (http//:informaticke-praxe.tul.cz).

4 ICT Drivers

The analysed organisations were divided into five groups according to the level of their development during their business existence. Each group has its specific way of managing the organisation, its organisational structure, presence or absence of the corporate strategy, level of utilisation of ICT, internal and external integration of ICT supporting processes in the organisation and way of utilisation of knowledge of the employees. The objective of this division is to emphasise changes of the management, information needs and better understanding of their approach to ICT. For the purpose of division the following parameters have been used, as they significantly contribute to acceptance (or not) of using ICT:

- Defining corporate strategy (long-term financial situation of the organisation, competitive environment and position in the market, parameters of the planning process and assumed development of the organisation, ways of managing and general culture in the organisation).
- Defining the information strategy: the status and expected development of utilisation of ICT (internal communication of employees, using an internal computer network or internet, access from home, support of the management process).
- Management of knowledge (focused on knowledge and skills of employees, way of sharing their knowledge).
- Innovation (investment into research and design, searching for new ways and possibilities of services and marketing).
- Communication with customers and suppliers including management of the supply chain and online ordering.

4.1 Five Stages of SMEs Development

During this long period, the researched SMEs developed and passed through the different levels of changes that impact their size, style of management and ICT adoption. This development of SMEs is also discussed in the literature (Greiner 1972; Nolan 1979; Matlay 2004). Above mentioned division of examined companies corresponds with five stages model from Levy and Powell (2000, 2005a, b). Therefore this research has used this model and the companies were divided to five groups according five stages of development:

- Commencement (focus on profit, necessity of transparency and acceleration of administration).
- Survival (increasing the number of customers, greater need for data share inside the company).
- Successful position in the market (competitive pressure, implementation of quality certificates, etc.).
- Expansion (financial issues, electronic communication with customers and suppliers).
- Maturity (necessity of innovation, changes in the management, training and education of employees).

The above mentioned stages are influenced by competitive pressure, changes to the company's environment, necessity of managerial changes and also by a number of other internal and external factors. Therefore the questions for interview with the managers or owners were focused on the development of organisations and the identification of stages such as:

- Market opportunities and managerial experience.
- Surrounding environment of the company.
- New technologies and new products of competitors on the market.
- Legal environment etc.
- Cultural internal environment in the company.
- Approach to learning of employees.
- Formulation of business strategy, the potential of new technologies, defining of ICT management.
- Formulation of information strategy, the portfolio of investment, relevant R&D into how ICT can be used.
- Information, application and technology architectures, organisation structures and processes to manage the resources.
- Identifying and planning the benefits from ICT investment, monitoring, measuring and evaluating the benefits derived from ICT investment.

- Implementing of information, systems and technology solutions that satisfy business needs, business continuity and security.
- Recruiting, training and deploying appropriate staff and ensuring technical, business and personal skills meet the needs of the organisation.

From results of interviews it is possible to characterize the common factors of each stage of development in searched companies. Next part detailed describes these factors.

4.2 First Stage of Growth: Commencement

At the beginning of a company's development the owners are able to manage it on their own and are familiar with details. Taking a more detailed look at this initial stage, we can observe very simple organisation structure in this first period, employees and the owner have close relations together, strategic decisions are short-term and long-term strategic plans are missing. Investment into ICT is minimal, usually for the purpose of administration. The objective of the organisation is mainly to generate profit and to maintain its position in the market. Gradual growth of the company is connected with transmission into the second stage that can be described as "survival".

In research this lowest level is represented by a group of small companies (till 10 employees) where strategic objectives exist only in the minds of the owners or managers and can be often summed up as an effort to survive. It is common that a corporate strategy is not written and companies in this examined group run their business mainly in the area of services. Also the development in skills and knowledge of employees is neglected; employees are not motivated to improve their skills and knowledge.

Analysed organisations have the following characteristics:

- Lack of financial resources for purchase of ICT, training, etc.
- The corporate strategy can be described as "survival" and maintaining its position in the competitive environment of the market.
- Limited number of employees.
- Insufficient knowledge of ICT.
- Communication with customers and suppliers only by e-mail, phone or in writing.
- Information support is by an office software package.
- Failure of the customers to comply with financial obligations.
- Often little specialisation of individual associates with everybody doing what is presently needed.

4.3 Second Stage of Growth: Survival

In this next level the majority of effort is devoted to maintaining a stable group of customers with the emphasis on maintaining its position in the market. These examined companies are bigger then in previous stage. The strategic plan is still missing and information systems in the organisation are usually simple (often a standard office software package). The owner, however, begins to have issues with maintaining his detailed insight into all orders and with the increasing number of employees. Gradually, as the number of orders increases together with the number of customers, employees, suppliers and partners, the owner has to delegate a number of tasks to others employees. Despite this the owner still remains a key person for strategic decision-making. Simultaneously, the need for management changes is emerging. These circumstances lead the company into the third stage when it becomes established in the market.

The survival stage is represented by a group of organisations with slight growth where the increasing number of customers drives the need to speed up administrative processes. Also the need for employees to share growing amount of data and the managers need a better overview of customers' orders. The owners in this group are already trying to search for and formulate their own corporate strategy. The organisation typically tries to establish itself in the areas with lower competition, such as in newly developing areas focused on specialised services requiring, for instance, environment-related certificates. Information strategy in such organisations is still not defined. Parameters of these organisations can be summed up as follows:

- The organisation aims to survive successfully in the competitive environment and possibly improve its position in the market. The corporate strategy is formulated with the objective to decrease cost and increase effectiveness, but some strategies are based on innovated special services responding to (e.g.) environmental requirements utilising the benefit of a less competitive environment.
- The owners respond to increasing number of customers by efforts to multiply economic administrative activities and striving for maintaining better overview of the financial situation and individual orders.
- Customers of this group are usually small and middle-sized organisations. Some organisations have already tried to utilise some applications of electronic business, e.g. electronic e-shop, or at least started to consider it.
- The organisations typically have software applications for accounting and warehouse management.
- These organisations are very often owned by families and their relationships play key roles in decision making, innovation and growth.

4.4 Third Stage of Growth: Successful Position in the Market

In the third stage of growth the examined company is successfully growing and the manager begins to undertake mid-term planning. In this phase of development, the further growth of the company significantly depends on the approach of the manager or owner. The companies are forced to respond to market demands, wishes of the customers and have to be competitive in order to avoid declining to an earlier stage. Consequently the managers need to have a vision for the organisation and to share it with the employees. The need for strategic management is growing and simultaneously the necessity of possessing sufficient information about the company is increasing. This stage is connected to requirements for better utilisation of ICT. Typically the companies utilize a database of customers, accounting systems and warehouse systems. In this examined group there are organisations trying to increase the number of customers and to respond flexibly to their needs and wishes. In this group of organisations are small manufacturing companies focused on quite special products, e.g. machines for crushing and processing of metal waste, special glass furnaces. These organisations have the following common characteristics:

- Using ICT is based on applications such as CAD (Computer Aided Design—software design application), in addition to accounting and other administrative applications.
- These organisations are aware of the importance of ICT and often have an information strategy, within which they consider future integration of electronic shopping into their business model.
- The organisations have certain organisational structures, i.e. the owner has got co-workers participating in managing areas of the organisation, e.g. commercial, marketing and manufacturing.

4.5 Fourth Stage of Growth: Expansion

This fourth stage of growth or expansion is very hard for the SME, as the company is trying to be an important player in its business area. That is why this stage requires the owner or the manager to have experience of planning and management, as well as sufficient finance to realize these plans. There is also a requirement for increased internal and external communication.

These examined organisations are aiming to become important market players. The owners or managers have defined visions they wish to achieve and share them with their employees. With increasing number of employees there is a need for the owner to formalise the organisation structure and to delegate responsibility. This is connected with the need to share visions and business strategies of the organisation with a greater number of employees. This means taking into account more opinions, experience and knowledge, which is important for success and growth. This examined group already contains organisations, usually manufacturing facilities that are often a part of a supply chain with the following characteristics:

- Standard ERP (Enterprise Resource Planning), systems for communication with their partners, so they utilise electronic exchange of data.
- The organisations have defined corporate and information strategy, they have a hierarchic organisational structure and aim to optimise their processes and information support.
- This group differs from the previous groups of organisations by higher utilisation of knowledge of the employees.

4.6 Fifth Stage of Growth: Maturity

To achieve further growth the examined organisations have an increasing need for data and information to support planning, managing and strategic decision-making. Information is a strategic source determining the business success and providing data about customers, financial results, capabilities and opportunities for evaluating changes to business objectives. That is the only way the organisation may ensure its development and growth. Consequently it needs effective tools, i.e. information system enabling the company to maintain, sort, analyse and search for data for the purpose of supporting internal processes. The information system may now yield a competitive advantage compared to other companies.

Investment in ICT requires a long-term strategic plan for the organisation based on detailed analysis of the current status. The manager or the owner has to have a clear vision of the expected outcome and benefit of ICT, this is demanding on the knowledge of the managers or owners. The purchase of information technology creates a lasting obligation, as financial resources of SMEs are limited. Owners of the companies should recognise that information systems may strongly impact on capacity, strength and chances for survival of the company. Speed of technological innovation together with the demanding implementation in the company environment support the serious need for planning the use of information technology. To be successful here it implies that each decision regarding information systems will conform to the wider business strategy of the company.

This level of growth is represented by examined organisations that are significant market players. These organisations typically have higher number of employees (80–250), are managed by a team of managers and have a hierarchic structure of leadership. The group differs from the previous groups especially with its focus on management of knowledge within the workforce. These organisations show effort to optimise internal and external processes. Two organisations run their business in the area of ICT and three remaining organisations are manufacturing companies in the building industry. Companies in this last group, with their approach to using ICT and emphasis on sharing of employees knowledge, can be good role models for others companies. They have the following common characteristics:

- Existence of written corporate and information strategy.
- Matured level of ICT processes is typical.
- Awarding of the importance of knowledge of their employees.
- Access to the information system by employees from home.
- Willingness to support training of employees.
- A culture of innovation in the organisation.
- Application of different management methods (Balanced Scorecard, ABC analysis, etc.).
- On-line communication with customers and suppliers.
- Using e-commerce (buying and selling on internet).

Contribution of the above mentioned categorisation of examined organisations is in the identification of different approaches that managers or owners have to adopt ICT as strategic tool. The companies from the fourth and fifth groups are successfully developing and growing in the long term. The research also investigated the drivers for the purchase of ICT. It was typical in these companies that the adoption of ICT was not a given reason to achieve strategic advantages but the most frequent reasons cited were:

- Pressure from suppliers, customers and competitors.
- Influence of the specific area of business.
- Size of the organisation.
- Implementation of different quality certificates.
- Knowledge of the employees or owners.

Also the majority of the specified factors contributing to decision-making about acceptance of ICT are:

- Technological factors (image of company, relative advantage, need of compatibility).
- Factors arising from the environment of the organisation (competitive pressure of customers and suppliers, changes in the market place).
- Organisational factors (management, size of company, specialisation of company, costs).
- Individual factors (knowledge of the manager, enthusiasm for ICT, innovation).

It is obvious that the factors mentioned are not all-inclusive and it is recognised that certain simplifications and judgments were applied. These analysed factors can help to better understand the issues connected to ICT adoption. The next part of the chapter explains the barriers in more details.

5 Barriers to ICT Adoption in SMEs

In examined organisations the most significant barriers to ICT purchase are mainly internal issues of the organisations, such as shortage of associates with appropriate knowledge, financial and often family reasons.

Similarly the division of individual factors contributing to acceptance of ICT in the following section indicates the cited barriers to ICT adoption in SMEs. They are:

- Technological barriers (problems of security, insufficient infrastructure).
- Organisational barriers (management style, shortage of financial sources).
- Barriers arising from the surrounding environment (insufficient knowledge of the market, present economic crises).
- Individual barriers (Insufficient knowledge, personal relations in organisations).

5.1 Technological Barriers

The biggest barrier to utilisation of new trends in ICT is, apart from insufficient infrastructure in the organisation, the fear regarding security of internal data. This fear is sometimes a reason for non purchase of ICT from a well-established provider. Some organisations consequently try to design such applications internally although this solution is not always successful. The employees working on this task often lack sufficient knowledge and experience and are also unable to document their solution, which can bring some problems in the future. Another barrier may be caused by fear from financial demand but this can be resolved by the purchase of application information services using an external supplier.

5.2 Decision-Making in SMEs

One of the significant barriers to ICT acceptance in SMEs is resistance to organisational changes, especially in connection with older managers or owners. Another barrier may be missing long-term corporate strategies often omitted due to shortage of long-term orders and stable customers. Companies frequently have to respond quickly to individual demands of random customers and do not consider any long-term corporate strategy. That is why planning in such organisations is focused on "sole survival" and on short-term activities. The managers or owners of SMEs make their decisions on the basis of current needs and the current situations. Consequently management processes are very sensitive to market behaviour, changing external conditions and market trends.

Time horizons of decision-making in SMEs are typically short-term, usually in a form of response to specific events rather than targeted assumptions. Low level of detailed planning often causes issues during implementation and utilisation of information systems. Moreover, only a small percentage of leaders of small companies utilise different methods of forecast, financial analysis, and project management. These results are also supported by a study (Ghobadian and Oregon 2006) analysing 276 small and medium-sized companies in England. Decision-making process of the managers is rather intuitive, based on instinctive decisions and less dependant on formal models of decision-making. They tend not to pass on information and not to delegate decision-making authority to their inferiors. They are often the only people in the company who have the authority, responsibility and access to the information necessary for identifying business opportunities including utilisation of information technology for strategic and competitive purposes.

5.3 Surrounding Environment

Barrier preventing wider acceptance of ICT in SMEs is furthermore influenced by an inability to apply ICT in relations with customers and suppliers. The important issue is the fact that SMEs do not influence their business-specific surrounding environment, but the SMEs are influenced by it and particularly by their customers. Especially the present economic crises bring many restrictions and a decrease in orders.

5.4 Individual Factors

One of the main barriers preventing acceptance of ICT, especially by small organisations, is knowledge and skills regarding information technology. Small companies do not have ICT departments (except for organisations with higher number of employees in the analysed sample) and rely on either external consultants or friends. A role of such a consultant is not always fully understood which leads to a number of mutual misunderstandings during specification, purchase and implementation of ICT applications. This problem is connected to a missing information strategy and as previously mentioned an insufficient knowledge of ICT on the part of the owner or manager of the organisation. According to this research where the analysed samples were often from using employing less experienced students, owners typically searched for simple and cheap solutions using their own resources, relatives or friends. Based on such solutions different problems connected with lack of experience and specific knowledge arise. These solutions do not bring the expected benefits. It is often only a "quick fix" and unfortunately a short-term solution of a given issue forgetting about further possibilities of the utilisation of ICT. This is connected to short-term planning of the organisations. ICT consequently cannot contribute to increased competitiveness and becomes only a tool for cost decrease and minimisation of the administrative burden.

In order to remove this barrier, universities may contribute high-quality knowledge to managers and owners of SMEs by providing education and training in the area of management and ICT. Other options would be the utilisation of specific ICT knowledge and skills in co-operation with other organisations or business networks.

6 Discussion

ICT as a strategic tool is one of the most significant impacts on enterprise in the near future and it does not matter whether they are big or small. Companies have to think about the using this strategic factor in their corporate strategies if they want to be competitive. These factors will have to integrate the communication with the customers and their data with product information as a part of an information strategy. Also the communication and sharing of knowledge inside the company is more and more important and plays a key role in competitive strategies.

Organisations need to quickly respond to consistently changing conditions, innovation of products and services, which requires employees observing new trends, technologies to be able to improve their knowledge. Such organisations are classified as learning or intelligent organisations. These learning organisations (Schwaninger 2006; Mulej and Potocan 2007):

- Are able to adapt to changing conditions.
- Are able to change their environment.
- Contribute to development of the whole organisation.

It does not mean only learning new things, but also to be able to learn from mistakes, in order to prevent re-occurrence of the mistakes. That is why the experience and knowledge needs to be shared across the organisation and readily available to all employees. Again appropriate use of ICT is important.

SMEs are exposed to highly competitive pressure. When they wish to survive the current business competition, they have to search for new business opportunities. This effort has to be significantly supported by information and communication technology. But the implementation of ICT can cause a number of issues for SMEs, such as insufficient financial resources, lack of experience with ICT and insufficient knowledge and skills in the area of computer literacy of employees. That is why the most frequent purpose of implementation of ICT in SMEs is, as supported by this research, on survival of the organisation in its competitive environment. Apart from that, adoption of ICT in the organisations is strongly influenced by the managerial style of the owner or manager. That is why

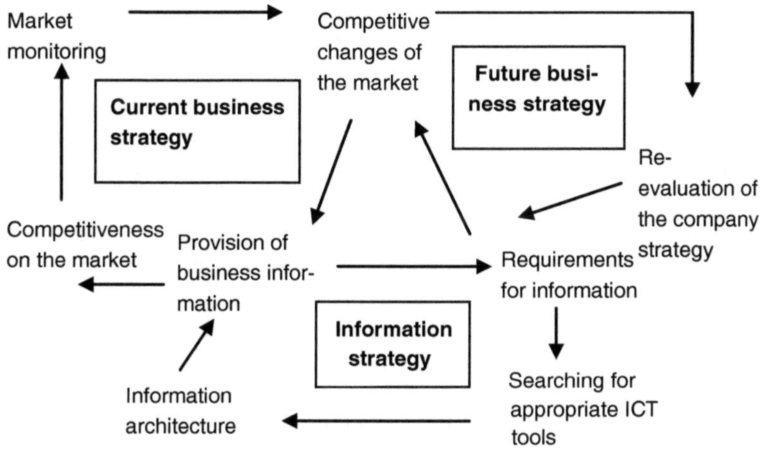

Fig. 1 Relation between business and information strategy

motivation to the purchase and implementation of ICT is also connected to clarification of ownership relations and the authority of individual owners.

Successful performance of SMEs in the business environment and their consequent development is influenced by the ability of the organisation to respond flexibly to customer's demands and by the ability to innovate in products or services. That is why the owner or manager should, from all of the researched groups of companies, consistently re-evaluate and search for appropriate corporate strategy, to keep developing himself and his employees, monitor the competitive environment of the market and be familiar with demands and wishes of customers. This consistently repeated process is illustrated by the following Fig. 1. All specified activities require the support of adequate tools and are currently available within the domain of ICT.

For ICT to become one of the tools of competitive advantage, organisations will have to have a clear vision of the future goals and how to reach them. Current ICT enables a whole range of new business opportunities and is consistently upgraded but especially for the owners of SMEs it is not easy to keep abreast. Adoption of ICT is connected to higher investment demands that often create barriers to wider acceptance of ICT in small and middle-sized enterprises. Another issue may also be the fact that financial benefit and payback of ICT is not easily quantifiable without specific knowledge.

7 Conclusion

Current business entities are forced to consistently improve their products and services. They have to utilise ICT and modern management methods. This is the only way they can succeed in such competitive environments. Companies have to search for appropriate business strategies using an approach that reflects its own characteristics and to use as many benefits of ICT in the proposed business strategy as possible. Organisations are more and more connected with their suppliers and customers but yet need not lose their legal identity. They have their own culture and managerial style; they search for their own business strategies and should seek to share management decisions with their co-operating partners and customers.

Technology availability has increased dramatically during the past 10 years as a part of the internet phenomenon, mobile applications and the consumer electronics movement. The simplicity of technology solutions has provided users with the ability to make their own choices rather than rely on ICT staff. Now, personal e-mail packages, instant messaging, laptop computers, mobile devices, smart phones, personal IP (internet protocol) based telephony (Skype) and even personal networking and storage preferences are becoming commonplace.

Software as a service or cloud computing (from an external supplier) is becoming a viable option which supports wider ICT adoption in SMEs. This option removes the need for trained specialists and brings cost-saving. Its benefit is a comparably quick implementation, professional technical support and certainty of high-quality backup of the data. Wide implementation of this option now is prevented especially by SMEs not fully trusting external data storage and low levels of trust in outsource providers and suspicions regarding risk of their bankruptcy.

The growing presence of **open source software** cannot be ignored, so the use of open-source technology will become a common place strategy in more and more organisations. A big advantage of this solution is the minimal level of investment. But on the other hand it requires good ICT knowledge and experience to be had by employees.

The long term research of 30 SMEs proved that managers or owners of SMEs are, however, often afraid of organisational and financial demands of the implementation of ICT. This fear can be prevented by adequate strategic planning and preparation. From the successfully growing companies we can see the importance of business information and knowledge strategy. Without articulation of these strategies, companies will find it difficult to search their way in the current business environment. These strategies have to be followed by other supporting strategies, i.e. marketing, finance and human resources. It is highly important that even these supporting strategies are in mutual harmony and support the defined global business strategy.

As futures work the author plan to extend the document collection with the information from the web (web presentations, news that concerns a company). It is also intended to employ natural language processing tools—morphological disambiguation and shallow syntax analysis.

References

Antlová, K. (2007). Strategic use of ICT in small businesses. In *Conference on E-activity and leading technologies* (pp. 414–418), Porto.

Antlova, K., & Popelinsky, L. (2012). Text mining from students report in Czech enterprises. In *Innovation and Sustainable Economic Competitive Advantage, IBIMA 2012*, Istanbul.

Antlova, K., Popelinsky, L. & Tandler, J. (2011). Long term growth of SME from the view of ICT competencies and web presentations. *E+M Ekonomie a management. 1. vyd. Liberec: Technická univerzita v Liberci, 14*, 125–138.

Cocrill, A., & Lewis, R. (2002). Going global—remaining local. *International Journal of Information Management, 22*, 195–209.

Covin, J. G., & Slevin, D. P. (1990). Juggling entrepreneurial style and organisational structure. *Sloan Management Review, 31*, 43–53.

Craig, A., & Annear, J. (2003). A framework for the adoption of ICT and security technologies by SMEs. In *16th Conference Small Entrerprise Association of Australia*, Ballarat.

E-Business Indicators. (2007). A pocket- book, ISBN 92-79-02037-4. http://www.ebusiness-watch.org. Accessed 26 June 2007

Chau, S. B., & Turner, P. (2002). A Four phase model of EC business transformation amongst SME. In *Proceedings of the 12th Australasian Conference on Information Systems*, Australia.

Choi, B., & Lee, H. (2003). An empirical investigation of KM styles and their effect on corporate performance. *Information and Management, 40*, 403–417.

Gemino, A., Mackay, N., & Reich, B. H. (2006). Executive decision about ICT adoption in SME. *Journal of Information Technology Management, 17*(1), 34–49.

Ghobadian, A., & Oregan, N. (2006). The impact of ownership on small firm behavior performance. *International Small Business Journal, 24*(6), 555–586.

Greiner, L. E. (1972). Evolution and revolution as organisations grow. *Harvard Business Review, 50*(4), 37–46.

Heikkila, J. (1991). Success of software packages in small businesses. *European Journal of Information Systems, 1*(1), 159–169.

Jeffocate, J. (2002). Best practice in SME adoption of E-commerce. *Benchmarking an International Journal, 9*(2), 122–132.

Kerney, S., & Abdul-Nour, G. (2004). SME and quality performance in networking environment. *Computers and Industrial Engineering, 46*, 905–909.

Kerste, R., Muizer, A., & Zoetermeer, A. (2002). Effective knowledge transfer to SMEs. In *Strategic Study B200202*.

Levy, M., & Powell, P. (2000). Information strategy for SMEs: An organizational perspective. *Journal of Strategic Information Systems, 9*, 63–84.

Levy, M., & Powell, P. (2005a). *Strategies for growth in SMEs*. Oxford, England: Butterworth Heinemann.

Levy, M., & Powell, P. (2005b). Strategic intent and E-business in SMEs: enablers and inhibitors. *Information Resources Management Journal, 18*(4), 1–20. (IGI Global).

Levy, M., Powell, P., & Yetton, P. (2002). The dynamics of SME information systems. *Small Business Economics, 19*, 341–354.

Martin, L. M., & Matlay, H. (2010). Approaches to promoting ICT in SMEs. *Internet Research: Electronic Network Applications and Policy, 11*(5), 399–410.

Matlay, H. (2004). E-entrepreneurship and small e-business development. Towards a comparative research agenda. *Journal of Small Business and Enterprise Development, 11*(3), 408–414.

Mulej, M., & Potocan, V. (2007). *Transition into an innovative enterprise*. Slovenian: University of Maribor.

Nolan, R. L. (1979). Managing the crises in data processing. *Harvard Business Review, 57*(2), 115–126.

Oh, W., & Pinsonneault, A. (2007). On the assessment of the strategic value of information technologies. *MIS Quarterly, 31*(2), 239–265.

Parker, C. M., & Castleman, T. (2007). New directions for research on SME e-business. *Journal of Information Systems and Small Business, 1*(2–2), 21–40.
Peppard, J., & Ward, J. (2004). Beyond strategic information systems: Towards an IS capability. *Journal of Strategic Information Systems, 13*, 167–194.
Powell, P., Levy, M., & Duhan, S. (2001). Infornation system strategies in knowledge-based SMEs. *European Journal of Information Systems, 10*, 25–40.
Rivard, S., Raymond, L., & Verreault, D. (2005). Resource-based view and competitive strategy. *Journal of Strategic Information Systems, 20*, 1–22.
Schwaninger, M. (2006). *Intelligent organisations*. Berlin: Springer.
Sudzina, F. (2010). Impact of ERP systems implementation. In *IDIMT 2010, Information technology—human, Values, Innovation and Economy*, Trauner Verlag, Linz.
Tetteh, E., & Burn, J. (2001). Global strategies for SME. *Logistic Information Management, 14*(1), 171–180.
Valkokari, K., & Helander, N. (2007). Knowledge management in different types of strategic SME network. *Management Research News, 30*(7), 597–608.
Vicente, M. R., & López, A. J. (2009). Patterns of e-commerce adoption and intensity evidence for the European Union-27. Documento de Trabajo, n.47/2009.

Adoption of Free/Open Source ERP Software by SMEs

Constantinos J. Stefanou

1 Introduction

Although there is a huge literature on both Small and Medium-sized Enterprises (SMEs) and Free and Open Software (FOSS), there is surprisingly little academic research concerning the interaction of Information Technology (IT) issues in general and SMEs. This happens despite the fact that SMEs, firstly, are the backbone not only of European but also of the world economy, and secondly, are distinctly different from large enterprises in a number of ways. In the context of IT, for example, the IT acceptance models and information systems (IS) acquisition practices differ significantly between SMEs and large enterprises (Ramdani et al. 2009; Buonanno et al. 2005).

Relatively recently, competitive pressures have forced SMEs to invest in Enterprise Resource Planning (ERP) systems. ERP systems are enterprise-wide software packages that provide fully integrated business processes using a common database and offering data visibility and information from various viewpoints (Stefanou 2012). ERP systems, by tightly and seamlessly integrating business processes have the potential to enhance business performance and achieving competitive advantage. Enterprises find more often than not that they have to adapt their processes to the software rather than the other way round, if they are to take advantage of ERP software embedded best practices (Davenport 1998; Stefanou 2001). Thus, the ERP software implementation is an expensive activity, time consuming and prone to failure, which can be hardly afforded by SMEs. Taking into account the initial capital investment for the purchase of the licenses, user training expenses, consulting fees and maintenance costs, we can safely conclude that the acquisition of standard state-of-the-art ERP systems offered by vendors such as SAP or Oracle is out of question due to the extremely high Total Cost of

C. J. Stefanou (✉)
Adoption of Free/Open Source ERP Software by SMEs, Thessaloniki, Greece
e-mail: stefanou@acc.teithe.gr

J. Devos et al. (eds.), *Information Systems for Small and Medium-sized Enterprises*, Progress in IS, DOI: 10.1007/978-3-642-38244-4_8,

Ownership (TCO) in relation to SMEs' financial resources. The extended functionality of these systems is also unused by SMEs and vendors have tried to fill this mid-market gap by specifically developing low cost but low functionality alternative solutions for SMEs.

SMEs, in their effort to reduce IT costs, investigate this option of acquiring and running on premise downscaled and pre-configurable ERP software or operating propriety ERP software though the Software as a Service (SaaS) model [see e.g. Juell-Skielse and Enquist (2012)]. Another available option is the acquisition of Free and Open Source ERP software (FOS/ERP) either downloaded and operated on premise or as a SaaS, which will be discussed in more detail in the next section. FOS-ERP systems, such as Adempiere, Compiere, Openbravo, Postbooks, WebERP and ERP5, to name but a few, have gained a high rate of acceptance by companies having limited IT budgets but wishing to implement an enterprise-wide integrated business information system. However, the way SMEs are adopting ERP systems is still debatable (Carvalho and Johansson 2012). Despite the fact that open source software is now a part of the IT infrastructure of organizations (Madsen 2009), as for example, the widespread use of the Linux operating system proves, FOS-ERP is still considered an immature solution by the majority of at least the large enterprises (Jutras 2009). Nevertheless, it seems to suit best SMEs for a number of reasons, notably reduced costs and access to the source code of the software (Carvalho 2006; Carvalho and de Campos 2006).

Considering the scarcity of research on non-commercial ERP systems (Light and Sawyer 2007) the objective of this chapter is to provide an insight regarding the adoption decision made by SMEs focusing especially on FOS-ERP software. Understanding of the mechanics of the ERP software acquisition is important as it could reduce costs, improve administrative procedures and reduce risks associated with ERP systems acquisition (Verville et al. 2005). It should be noted that the terms adoption, acquisition and even implementation of ERP software have extensively been used interchangeably in the ERP literature. In this chapter, the adoption decision refers to the decision made by companies before the actual selection/acquisition and the subsequent implementation of the FOS-ERP software. This chapter, based on a literature review in the intersection of FOS-ERP and SMEs, aims at informing scholars, students, researchers and managers of the issues and the risks involved and the factors influencing the decision of SMEs to adopt FOS-ERP software.

The remainder of the chapter is organized as follows: Next section discusses SMEs and Free and Open Source ERP software characteristics. The following section presents the factors that seem to affect significantly the decision of SMEs to adopt FOS-ERP software. The final section offer suggestions for future research related to adoption of FOS-ERP systems by SMEs and final conclusions.

2 SMEs Characteristics and Free Open Source ERP Software

As noted in the previous section, research regarding non-commercial ERP systems such as FOS-ERP is limited especially in the context of SMEs. In addition, findings from research conducted on large firms cannot be generalized and applied to SMEs due to inherent differences between large and small enterprises (Buonanno et al. 2005; Rohde 2004; Mabert et al. 2003). Another issue affecting the generalization of research findings is that there is not a unanimous definition of what constitutes a small or a medium-sized enterprise. For example, enterprises considered large in Europe are usually categorized as medium in the US and care should be exercised when interpreting research findings.

In any case, the impact of organizational size on ERP outcomes and productivity in SMEs or on the availability of resources, such as IT skills, and the outsourcing of non-core IT functions, has been documented in the literature (Devos et al. 2012; Zach 2011; Bohórquez and Esteves 2008; Sedera et al. 2003; Mabert et al. 2003; Gable et al. 2003). SMEs are also very sensitive to external market forces, competition, government regulations, macroeconomic environment, and fiscal and tax policy (Malhotra and Temponi 2010). On the other hand, communication between employees, managers, owners and the implementation team, which can be a hard problem to tackle in large scale ERP projectss, could be managed more effectively in small business environments, where more intimate relationships exist.

Today, SMEs certainly need user friendly and light but substantial and flexible business information system which can be rapidly adapt to changing information needs ensuring continuity of operations and providing at the same time the necessary information to take business decisions.

The adoption decision let al.one the selection of the appropriate ERP software solution or package is a difficult task for the majority of SMEs. Shortage of financial resources, limited IT personnel expertise, inadequate number of IT personnel, lack of capabilities and lack of available time have been cited as some of the factors that make this task difficult and risky [see e.g. Devos et al. (2012), Malhotra and Temponi (2010). Devos et al. (2012) point out an additional problem as far as the ERP system selection is concerned, that of the information asymmetry that exists between SMEs and independent software vendors (ISVs) on which SMEs usually depend upon for the management and development of their IT projects; SMEs due to limited IT/IS expertise are not fully aware about the possible inadequacy of the IT/IS capabilities of the ISVs and on the functionalities of the ERP software packages, which may lead to opportunistic market behavior from the side of ISVs and moral hazard.

Relatively recently, FOS-ERP systems seem to be of an increasing interest to SMEs as the number of FOS/ERP projects in the Sourceforge.net website, which provides free hosting to open source ERP development projects, reveals. According to Johansson and Sudzina (2008) FOS-ERP software was developed as a result of dissatisfaction with proprietary ERP systems and took advantage of the maturity level of the open source phenomenon. It should be noted at the outset that FOS-ERP is not a risk free option and the decision to adopt, acquire and install a FOS-ERP system is neither an easy nor a free one. It is acknowledged, however, that SMEs are among the organizations that are to be benefited by FOS-ERP systems [see e.g. Bueno and Callego (2010), Carvalho (2006)].

Users having free access to the code of the open source software can modify the software according to their specific business needs and develop new versions of the software. At the same time they contribute along a worldwide community of users to software quality and provide solutions which can be used by anyone. It has been argued that a cost effective ERP implementation can be achieved (Wu and Cao 2007; Carvalho 2006). This virtual collaboration enriches ERP software development as synthesizes the experiences of developers working in diverse situations and trying to implement unique business processes (Wu and Cao 2007). Web-based knowledge repository systems and emerging Web 2.0 technologies such as wiki and social networking can further assist developers of FOS-ERP systems.

However, this collaborative procedure of FOS/ERP development may not have the expected positive outcome outlined above. The lack of leadership of the ERP development project and generally the lack of a structured process may lead even to the abandonment of a certain project jeopardizing company resources put into that project and disrupting smooth execution of its daily operations. On the other hand, companies adopting FOS-ERP are not making long term commitments with software vendors, although it would be difficult for them to abandon a project they had invested in a considerable amount of resources.

FOS-ERP has created a new market of supporting services. Vendors are not interested in selling the software per se but providing services associated with the software, such as implementation, maintenance, and user training and support. Thus, FOS-ERP implementation is not without costs neither without risks. Nevertheless, in an environment of reduced IT budgets and worldwide economic recession, FOS-ERP software seems especially appropriate for SMEs. SMEs show an increasing interest in FOS-ERP software at they perceive it provides an acceptable, stable, flexible and efficient alternative solution to proprietary integrated enterprise software and certainly a more affordable one.

3 Factors Affecting the Decision to Adopt FOS-ERP Software

The majority of SMEs, as it was documented in the previous section, is characterized by limited resources and capabilities and IS competence as well as by structural, ownership and cultural elements which may affect their attitude not only towards ERP system implementation and evaluation (Zach 2011) but also towards the decision making process of adopting an ERP system in the first place.

SMEs decide to adopt an ERP solution either due to competitive pressures or due to their willingness to achieve product and customer service excellence. Usually an internal (e.g. need for cost-efficiency) or an external factor (e.g. supply chain partners pressure) triggers the decision (Seethamraju and Seethamraju 2008). Based on findings proposed in the literature [see e.g. Poba-Nzaou et al. (2012), Haddara and Zach (2011), Hung et al. (2004), Ramdani et al. (2009), Winkelmann and Klose (2008), Seethamraju and Seethamraju (2008), Raymond and Uwi-zeyemungu (2007), Buonanno et al. (2005), Verville et al. (2005)] a taxonomy of the motivation factors of SMEs to adopt an ERP solution is presented in Table 1. Industry specific motivations have been also identified in the literature [see e.g. Poba-Nzaou et al. (2012)].

Irrespectively of what initiates SMEs to investigate the option of adopting ERP software, the process of making this decision should depend initially on the business vision of the company, which in turn determines the strategic and tactical activities necessary to achieve the pre-defined goals. This defines current and future information needs which have to be judged against available and future resources necessary to finance the provision of the required information. Other resources apart the financial ones, such as people capabilities, and fundamental characteristics of the company play also a crucial role. Organizational readiness, IT capabilities, culture, user acceptance of new technology, educated personnel, relationships between employees, are some basic parameters that have to be considered carefully. It is crucial that the solution selected should be in alignment with the company's core business processes as this is a prerequisite for the success

Table 1 Motivation factors for adopting ERP software by SMEs

Operational	Dysfunctional areas of business or company functions
Financial	Need to improve financial ratios such as ROI or ROA and to strengthen the financial position of the company
Managerial	Better coordination of functional areas, integration of business processes, web-based monitoring of company's activities
Strategic	Expansion to new markets may require business software that can handle simultaneously different currencies, languages or accounting standards
Environmental	External pressures by partners to adopt an ERP solution compatible with the ERP systems operating in the supply chain competitors
	Pressure to keep up with competitors
	Compliance to regulations affecting SMEs
Competitive	Desire and need to improve quality of customer service thus retaining satisfied customers and providing an attractive environment to acquire new ones
Technological	Change or replacement of IT infrastructure or systems due to various reasons (e.g. situation analogous to Y2K problem, new innovative technology, migration to e-business, etc.) can be seen as providing an opportunity to move forward in implementing a more sophisticated business computing platform covering current and future needs. Especially this is true when current software cannot be enhanced to include extended functionality due to its aged technology
Entrepreneurial	To reach product or customer service excellence, to advance innovation, to lead the (niche) market in which SME operates

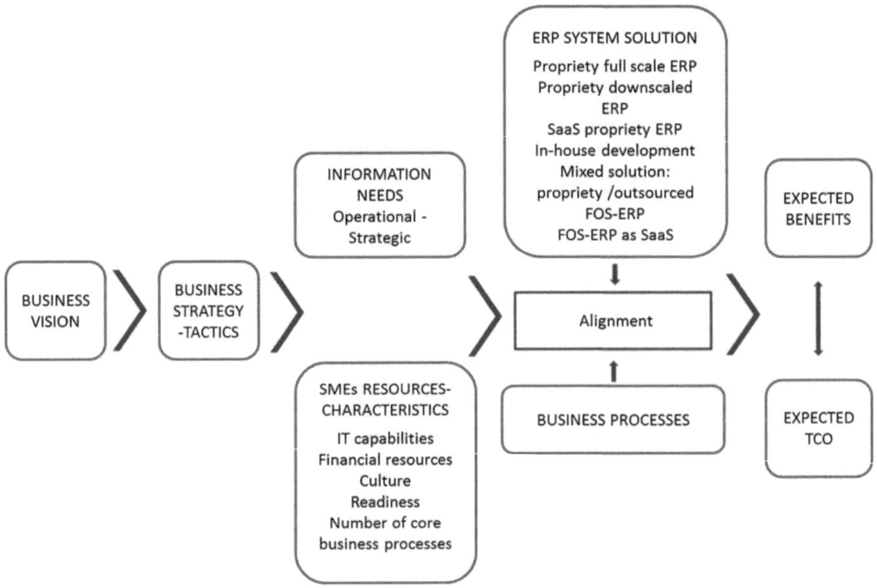

Fig. 1 The making decision process to adopt ERP software by SMEs

of the delivered system. In several studies [see e.g. Huq et al. (2012)], best fit with current business processes gets a high ranking of importance in users' answers. Finally, the TCO should be estimated and evaluated against expected benefits of the chosen solution. The above described process, based on a general model of ERP selection proposed by Stefanou (2000) and modified to include SMEs characteristics, is depicted in Fig. 1.

It is true that the majority of SMEs cannot afford to acquire and implement a standard ERP solution, although other solutions (downscaled systems, on-demand ERPs etc.) are available to them. FOS-ERP is a viable option for companies exhibiting certain characteristics. SMEs with limited financial resources which cannot afford an initial capital investment to buy propriety software licenses are the first candidates. Also knowledgeable companies that choose to save the initial amount required to buy software licenses and invest it in rightly implementing the software and aligning it to company's core business processes. As mentioned above, apart from lower costs, access to the source code of the software is another main reason that companies are attracted to FOS-ERP systems. This is a very strong incentive for companies in need of a flexible ERP system which can be easily adapted to changing conditions and user information needs. However, and although adaptability of FOS-ERP is considered an adopting criterion (Serrano and Sarriegi 2006) scalability of FOS-ERP software is rather low. Therefore, FOS-ERP may not be a good choice for SMEs wishing or expecting to expand considerably in the near future, to acquire or merge with other companies or to be tightly connected with other partners in a supply chain.

Decreased reliance on a single supplier is also a basic motive why SMEs choose FOS-ERP (Serrano and Sarriegi 2006). Many SMEs have had very bad experiences with business software vendors and independent software distributors and they would prefer the relative independence offered by FOS-ERP software.

Implementation and maintenance costs will certainly occur in FOS-ERP systems installations. Although the extent of the customization effort will vary considerably among SMEs due to their inhomogeneity, it is rather certain that SMEs will need in many cases to customize their ERP systems similarly to larger firms (Malhotra and Temponi 2010). Considering the scarcity of IT resources inside SMEs, the availability of external FOS-ERP software consultants is of the utmost importance. However, the cost to employ external consultants is usually high. The consulting fees may overweight the zero cost of the license considering the Total Cost of Ownership (Johansson and Sudzina 2008).

Table 2 summarizes SME's characteristics which are compatible with taking the final decision to adopt FOS-ERP software.

Besides company characteristics discussed above, software related characteristics are also important in influencing the FOS-ERP adoption decision. For example, an active developers' community and a large number of FOS-ERP systems installations will certainly influence positively the decision of a company to, firstly, adopt FOS-ERP software and, secondly to choose the right package. Low cost upgrades are common in FOS-ERP (King 2010) as well as low user training costs. The availability of specific development and support tools or compatible packaged tools offered by FOS-ERP software projects are also positively considered (Carvalho and Monnerat 2008). Documentation of several FOS-ERP projects maybe incomplete and not regularly updated but active user communities compensate for the lack of formal documentation.

FOS-ERP software stability and reliability is rather uncertain and customization is inevitable to a certain extent. Thus, it seems that FOS-ERP is suited to 'larger' of the SMEs which have rather limited but existing IT resources needed to run and manage the installation and cutting external consultants costs. If FOS-ERP is

Table 2 SME's characteristics compatible with adopting FOS-ERP software

Limited capital resources for initial capital spending on licenses
Limited financial resources and restricted IT budget
Limited product lines
Limited geographical sales area
National rather than multinational company
Organizational culture of openness and sharing of information
Open-minded entrepreneurship
Informed personnel about open source software philosophy
New company without established rigid processes requiring reengineering
"Small to medium" rather "medium to large" sized company
Outsourced functions, such as e.g. payroll, not critical for company integration
Extensive customization needed to support (few in number) core business processes

appealing, small companies with no IT personnel and capabilities maybe better off in selecting a FOS-ERP system offered through the SaaS model.

It should be finally noted that SMEs choosing FOS-ERP avoid vendor lock-in but the exit cost is not insignificant as the investment put into the project cannot be easily abandoned by SMEs.

4 Conclusions and Future Research Directions

FOS-ERP software provides an important opportunity for SMEs to become competitive by operating a type of software they could not even think of before its flourishing. Companies keep low their initial capital spending aiming at acquiring a flexible and robust piece of software which can be adapted at a fraction of time and cost to their core business processes. This is a basic motive for SMEs to adopt a FOS-ERP solution as the funds they save for user licenses can be used to extensively customize the software in their effort to gain a competitive advantage over competitors.

It should be noted however that the decision to adopt a FOS-ERP solution may be appealing but risks and uncertainties are present and implementation failures may occur. Certain characteristics of SMEs, such as open organizational culture, intimate relationships between personnel, and limited number of core business functions, seem to positively affect the decision to adopt FOS-ERP software and minimize related risks. As far as the software related factors are concerned, it seems that the general activity level of the FOS-ERP community is a decisive factor. Large and active FOS-ERP software developer communities constitute a factor influencing positively the decision to adopt FOS-ERP software, as well as the availability of a comprehensive set of tools facilitating configuration and implementation of FOS-ERP software.

On the other hand, considering the scarcity of IT resources inside SMEs and the usually high cost required to employ external consultants, SMEs need to balance very carefully the expected benefits and the total cost of ownership of an FOS ERP solution. This is certainly not an easy task and due to limited internal expertise external services might be acquired for the evaluation of the proposed ERP solution.

Despite the importance of the FOS–ERP phenomenon, research especially concerning the all-important mid-market segment is quite limited. The growing penetration of FOS-ERP especially in the SMEs, calls for further empirical research to validate anecdotal and secondary data analysis findings. FOS-ERP implementation is a collaborative approach quite different from the traditional collaboration software development. Both the development and deployment models of this kind of software are calling for further research in order to evaluate their virtues and disadvantages and assess their potential customer value.

References

Bohórquez, V., & Esteves, J. (2008). Analyzing SMEs Size as a Moderator of ERP Impact in SMEs Productivity. *Communications of the IIMA, 8*, 67–80.

Bueno, S., & Gallego, M. D. (2010). Evaluating acceptance of OSS-ERP based on user perceptions. In T. Sobh (Ed.), *Innovations and advances in computer sciences and engineering*. Netherland: Springer Science+Business Media B.V.

Buonanno, G., Faverio, P., Pigni, F., Ravarini, A., Sciuto, D., & Tagliavini, M. (2005). Factors affecting ERP system adoption. *Journal of Enterprise Information Management, 18*(4), 384–426.

Carvalho, R.A., (2006). Research and practical issues of enterprise information systems. International federation for information processing, 205.

Carvalho, R. A., & de Campos, R. (2006). *Development process proposal for the ERP5 system. IEEE international conference on Systems, man, and cybernetics* (pp. 4703–4708). Taiwan: Taipei. 8–11 Oct.

Carvalho, R. A., & Monneratm, R. M. (2008). Development support tools for enterprise resource planning. IEEE, Computer.org/ITPro.

Carvalho, R. A., & Johansson, B. (2012). Key aspects of free and open source enterprise resource planning systems. In Carvalho RA and Johansson B (Eds.): *Free and open source enterprise resource planning- systems and strategy*. Business Science Reference. IGI Global, USA, 1–17.

Davenport, T. H. (1998). Putting the enterprise into the enterprise system. *Harvard Business Review, 76*(4), 121–131.

Devos, J., Van Landeghem, H., & Deschoolmeester, D. (2012). SMEs and IT: Evidence for a market for "Lemons". *The Electronic Journal Information Systems Evaluation, 15*(1), 25–35. http://www.ejise.com.

Gable, G., Sedera, D., & Chan, T. (2003). Enterprise systems success: a measurement model. In: T. Salvatore and Massey, Anne & DeGross, I. Janice I (Eds.), *Proceedings 24th International Conference on Information Systems*, (pp. 576–591), Seattle, USA.

Gruman, G. (2007). More midmarket firms choose open-source ERP. Computer World.

Haddara, M., & Zach, O. (2011). ERP Systems in SMEs: A literature review. *Proceedings of the 44th Hawaii International Conference on System Sciences.*

Hung, S. Y., Chang, S. I., & Lee, P. J. (2004). *Critical factors of ERP adoption for small- and medium-sized enterprises: An empirical study.* : Pacific Asia conference on information systems (PACIS).

Huq, N., Shah Ali, S. M., & Mihailescu, M. (2012). Why select an open source ERP over propriety ERP? A focus on SMEs and supplier's perspective. In: Carvalho RA and Johansson B (Eds): *Free and open source enterprise resource planning- systems and strategy*. 33–56. Business Science Reference, IGI Global, USA.

Johansson, B., & Sudzina, F. (2008). ERP systems and open source: An initial review and some implications for SMEs. *Journal of Enterprise Information Management, 21*(6), 649–658.

Juell-Skielse, G., & Enquist, H. (2012). *Implications of ERP as service. In: Re-conceptualizing enterprise information systems. Lecture notes in business information systems* (Vol. 105, pp. 129–151). UK: Springer.

Jutras, C. (2009). "SaaS ERP: trends and observations". An Aberdeen Report.

King, S. (2010). Implementing open source software. In Simon F (Ed.), The next wave of technologies opportunities from Chaos. Wiley New Jersey: USA.

Light, B., & Sawyer, S. (2007). Locating packaged software in information systems research. *European Journal of Information Systems, 16*, 527–530.

Mabert, V. A., Soni, A., & Venkataramanan, M. A. (2003). The impact of organizationsize onen terprise resource planning (ERP) implementations in the US manufacturing sector. *Omega, 31*(2003), 235–246.

Madsen, M. (2009). The role of open source in data integration. Third nature Technology Report.

Poba-Nzaou, P., Uwizeyemungu, S., Raymond, L., & Pare, G. (2012). Motivations underlying the adoption of ERP systems in healthcare organizations: Insights from online stories. *Information Systems Frontiers,*. doi:10.1007/s10796-012-9361-1.

Malhotra, R., & Temponi, C. (2010). Critical decisions for ERP integration: Small business issues. *International Journal of Information Management, 30*(1), 28–37

Ramdani, B., Kawalek, P., & Lorenzo, O. (2009). Predicting SME's adoption of enterprise systems. *Journal of Enterprise Information Management, 22*(1/2), 10–24.

Raymond, L., & Uwizeyemungu, S. (2007). A profile of ERP adoption in manufacturing SMEs. *Journal of Enterprise Information Management, 20*, 487–502.

Rohde, F. H. (2004). IS/IT outsourcing practices of small- and medium-sized manufacturers. *International Journal of Accounting Information Systems, 5*(2004), 429–451.

Sedera, D., Gable, G., & Chan, T. (2003). *ERP success: Does organisation size matter? Pacific Asia conference on information systems (PACIS)*. South Australia: Adelaide.

Seethamraju, R., & Seethamraju, J. (2008). Adoption of ERPs in a medium-sized enterprise: A case study. *19th Australasian Conference on Information Systems (ACIS)*, 887–896, Christchurch.

Serrano, N. S., & Sarriegi, J. M. (2006). Open source software ERPs: A new alternative for an old need. *IEEE Software, 23*(3), 94–97.

Stefanou, C. J. (2000). The selection process of enterprise resource planning (ERP) systems. In H. M. Chung (Ed.), *Proceedings of the Sixth Americas Conference on Information Systems*. Long Beach, CA: CD-ROM.

Stefanou, C. J. (2001). A framework for the evaluation and selection of ERP systems. *European Journal of Information Systems, 10*, 204–215.

Stefanou, C. J. (2012). SMEs and FOS-ERP systems: Risks and opportunities. In R. A. Carvalho & B. Johansson (Eds.), *Free and open source enterprise resource planning- systems and strategy* (pp. 134–143). USA: Business Science Reference, IGI Global.

Verville, J., Bernadas, C., & Halingten, A. (2005). A three-dimensional approach in evaluating ERP software within the acquisition process. *International Journal of Enterprise Information Systems, 1*(3), 1–16.

Winkelmann, A., & Klose, K. (2008). Experiences while selecting, adapting and implementing ERP systems in SMEs: A case study. In: *Proceedings: Americas Conference on Information Systems (AMCIS)*.

Wu, H., & Cao, L. (2007). Community Collaboration for ERP Implementation, *Software IEEE, 26*(6), 48–56.

Zach, O. (2011). Exploring ERP system outcomes in SMEs: A multiple case study. In: *Proceedings ECIS 2011*. http://aisel.aisnet.org/ecis2011/7.

Part III
Enterprise Applications

Customer Relationship Management System a Case Study on Small-Medium-Sized Companies in North Germany

C. Malte Menzel and Torsten Reiners

1 Introduction

Globalisation and in particular the fast growth of Internet caused a decrease in local and closed markets. Transparency of markets is further increased by services to compare products and prices on-the-fly; allowing the best overall acquisition for purchase (Stengl et al. 2001). This increased competitive pressure (Müller 2004), in especially the convergence of product quality and their prices (Hippner and Wilde 2005), affected the companies' opportunity to identify themselves through their core products alone. A differentiation towards the competition could be achieved by offering extended services beyond the product; a high-quality customised liaison and support for the customer (Brendel 2003). Rather than focusing on transactions and products, the importance of the customers and especially the nurturing relations with them was emphasised (Hippner and Wilde 2005). The competiveness increased the high cost for customer acquisition (Rapp 2000) such that the long-term binding of customers and maintenance of the relationship became a new business field (Sexauer 2002). The gain in effectiveness and efficiency of supply chains resulted from aggregating, managing, and analysing customer information and actively integrating these in the operational process (Buck-Emden and Saddei 2003).

The objective of long-term customer satisfaction is not necessarily related to the products and service anymore, as this could be equally delivered by competitors, but on targeting future sales and other opportunities to interact with customers. Studies repeatedly demonstrated that a strongly bound customer positively affects the success of enterprises. Depending on the sector, reducing the churn by as little as 5 % can result in a significant increase in revenue (Diller 2006; Stengl et al. 2001).

C. M. Menzel
Industry Projects & Solutions GmbH, Hamburg, Germany
e-mail: mmenzel@c1-ips.com

T. Reiners (✉)
School of Information Systems, Curtin University, Bentley, WA 6102, Australia
e-mail: t.reiners@curtin.edu.au

J. Devos et al. (eds.), *Information Systems for Small and Medium-sized Enterprises*, Progress in IS, DOI: 10.1007/978-3-642-38244-4_9,

Support for customer loyalty and relationship management can be achieved through sophisticated customer relationship management (CRM) systems, which have become increasingly important with the advances in information technology over the last decades (Helmke et al. 2001). Successfully applied CRM-philosophy and CRM-systems generally contribute to the success of enterprises; see e.g., study by Terlutter and Kricsfalussym (2006). Nevertheless, small- and medium-sized enterprises (SME) still have a historically evolved Information Technology (IT) system landscape with numerous independent systems for marketing, sales, or services (Loh et al. 2011; Schulze 2002). The diversity and generally decentralised structure often contradicts attempts to maintain a correct, consistent, complete, and up-to-date database with customer information; not enabling the before mentioned customer support and satisfaction (Schumacher and Meyerm 2004). Hence, system integration in all business units is core function of CRM.

The main contribution of the chapter is about creating awareness for the importance and benefits of CRM-systems for SMEs. The following section presents a short overview about what functionality is supported and how SMEs can benefit from the system integration. After describing the outline of our research, we discuss the survey on the state-of-the-art of customer relationship management systems and the degree of pervasion in SMEs, and the data analysis. The results are crosschecked via expert interviews; i.e., to verify that the results from the survey are valid and to gain further insight in CRM systems beyond the questions on the questionnaire. The experts were invited from 4 different SME; all being in charge of the CRM systems and the CRM integration. The organisations are active on international markets, 3 of 4 do Business-to-Business, and all are market leader in their area of expertise.

2 Small- and Medium-Sized Enterprises

In this chapter, we restricted the scope on small- and medium-sized enterprises as the pervasion of sophisticated CRM-systems is still considered to be at an early stage (Horn 2007; Kemper et al. 2005; Loh et al. 2011); even though the market development and increased global competition dictates a stronger reflection and integration of customer relations (Koelwel 2006). A further observation during our study revealed that even with CRM-system availability, most enterprises do not take advantage of the full potential of the systems as they either lack a full integration in other systems or business units, or are not trained to use the functionality efficiently or at all, respectively. In our study, we set the scope as following:

- **North Germany**: Lower Saxony, Hamburg, North Rhine-Westphalia
- **Small- and medium-sized enterprises**: SMEs represent 99 % of German enterprises; even though the criteria for SMEs vary with respect to, e.g., number of employees or annual revenue, [quantitative criteria, (Horn 2007)], ownership or type of management [qualitative criteria, (Wolter and Hauser 2001)].

The criteria vary from country, industry sector, and organisation; thus the EU is having other criteria (e.g., number of employees, revenue) than those would be used in Germany. Due to the focus of the paper, we are not further exploring this; see the applied criteria in the Section "Survey". Note that we did not consider criteria as revenue, profit, or market position.

- **Industry/manufacturing**: In Germany, the proportion with respect to the overall production is relatively high with strong dependencies on customers (in general in a business-to-business context) and suppliers. We focused further on the following industrial sectors: metal processing and manufacturing, mechanical engineering, industrial plants, and electro technique. This focus is due to the generally low affinity towards CRM-systems (Gohr 2007) in these sectors as they tend to have a higher stability customer retention, particularly in comparison to telecommunication providers or financial service providers.
- **Focus on functionality**: The undertaken study was not about specific systems [see, e.g., studies by Horn (2007), Kemper et al. (2005), Torggler (2007)] but the general pervasion of systems and the kind of applied functionality and integration.

3 Customer Relationship Management

The focus of the chapter is on the survey about the perception of CRM in SME. Therefore, we are limiting ourselves on a short introduction and do not elaborate every CRM definition and approach. In general, CRM is a customer-centric strategy, where the enterprise utilises people, processes, and technology to support a holistic long-term customer retention and relationship development; including marketing, sales, and service concepts (Chen and Popovich 2003; Hippner and Wilde 2003). CRM represents characteristic principles about customer orientation, economic feasibility, systemisation, individualisation, and IT-systems (Homburg and Sieben 2005); the latter one being the focus of our survey. In general, IT-systems do not guarantee an improved customer relationship; yet are essential to realise CRM-strategies in the first place (Schwetz 2006). Here, we define a CRM-system as a holistic approach to merge functionality and information in an IT-system to administrate customers and their relationship with other organisations. A CRM-system must be considered as the core of any CRM-concept.

3.1 Background to CRM

CRM originates from the continuous progress in IT and networking; where the formerly large number of isolated systems (e.g., marketing databases, computer aided selling, or online marketing) is integrated to create a holistic system

(Stengl et al. 2001). The alignment and replication of enterprise-wide customer information allowed a more efficient and effective handling of customer related activities (Helmke et al. 2001). CRM can be tracked back to relationship marketing, an operative instrument to create, administrate, and maintain customer relations (Berry 1983; Grönroos 1990); with inclusion of relationship management for suppliers. CRM-systems distinguish themselves from former customer-retention-systems by comprising customer acquisition and customer win-back (Hippner 2006). The rush for CRM-systems was started by a report about the trend to gain advantage by analysing and forecasting customer information (Stengl et al. 2001) and hyped in the early years of the millennium (Hippner and Wilde 2005). The high expectations in integrated systems was contrasted by the circumstances that projects were managed by the IT departments; missing crucial considerations about strategic and organisational aspects (Stengl et al. 2001). Projects mainly failed due to missing acceptance by the stakeholders (Diller 2006), the technical focus (Andersen and Andreasen 1999), and missing cost-benefits-considerations (Stengl et al. 2001).

Over the last years, the IT-focused approach was redefined after some years of stagnation by a more comprehensively perspective on all requirements to administrate customer relations (Zähres 2007). Larger companies realised that beneficial systems need to go beyond a pure CRM-system and need to be an enterprise-wide strategy about objectives, processes, culture, and employees (Bauer and Oswald 2007). Only smoothly integrated processes concerning the customer allow taking advantage of the potential inherited by CRM-systems (Stengl et al. 2001).

The permeation of CRM-systems started with large enterprises, while SMEs still relied on other solutions like office software and mail applications. A noticeable change occurred with the strengthening of supply chain integration, where mandatory systems were dictated by large enterprises, and stronger competition on relevant markets. In addition, the customer received enhanced tools to search and analyse markets for best offers, causing a shift in enterprises from pure goods and service providers to actually focus the core business on the customers' needs (Schmid et al. 2000).

According to functionality and main purpose of application, we can distinguish three main categories of CRM (Kemper et al. 2005).

- **Operative CRM**: Support for day-to-day business in CRM-relevant areas like sales, marketing, or services. Here, most information and data about customers is collected, processed and stored in enterprise resource planning (ERP) systems.
- **Communicative CRM**: Control and synchronisation of all customer-oriented communication in sale, marketing, and services. The idea is, that enterprises have "one face to the customer" (Horn 2007). Furthermore, inter- and intra-organisational collaboration is supported; providing opportunities for e-marketing, e-selling, and e-services (Buck-Emden and Saddei 2005; Gerdes 2005; Neckel and Knobloch 2005; Schnauffer and Jung 2004).

- **Analytic CRM**: Establishing one source of rich data and information to analyse customer interactions and create forecasts with different horizons. Data mining and knowledge discovery tools are used to predict customer requirements and adjust customisation processes (Hippner and Wilde 2008).

In our anticipated target group (SME), we expect—if CRM-systems are used at all—to see mainly operative CRM-systems as a comprehensive integration is mandatory before extensions like communicative or analytic CRM can be applied or even considered. With limited resources for advanced IT departments and overhead to train and use CRM-systems, the main focus of SMEs is set on keeping the operative data-to-day business alive (Kemper et al. 2005).

The main objective of CRM is to build and maintain a long-term, profitable customer-relationship (Diller 2001; Hippner and Wilde 2002). The importance of (voluntary) customer retention is given as it generally results in higher customer satisfaction (Herrmann and Johnson 1999), opportunities for up- and cross-selling and often a disposition to sell further products for higher prices and (Homburg and Bruhn 2005; Schumacher and Meyerm 2004). The economical perspective covers the customer value, the sustainability, and intensity of customer services (Günter and Helm 2006), and the effect on monetary and non-monetary targets (Cornelsen 2000; Gelbrich 2001; Schemuth 1996). The complexity often limited the integration of enterprise-wide needs and resulted in maximizing the profit/customer value, but did not consider the advantages for customers or business partners (Buck-Emden and Saddei 2005). Integrated CRM-systems allow a systematic exploitation and distribution of information and, therefore, holistic customer evaluation for whole supply chains (Hippner 2006; Homburg and Sieben 2005).

Systems are supportive tools and an essential requirement to achieve objectives; yet, their success depends on further factors; i.e., humans, processes, and management. Case studies by Gartner Group showed that 70 % of the problems during the implementation of new systems is not caused by the software itself (Nelson and Eisenfeld 2002). Acceptance and application is a critical success factor and often forgotten if decisions are made without inclusion of all affected departments (Jensen 2005); e.g., if the initiative is coming from the IT department with focus on the storage and administration of customer information. These systems often end up as a control and monitoring system and provide limited value for customer liaison; sometimes even reducing productivity (Buck-Emden and Saddei 2005).

3.2 CRM-Systems in SME

The market for CRM-systems is still expected to be growing, with over US $6.6b in revenue and US $3.6 b in maintenance (forecast for 2012, n.n. 2006). An analysis by Gohr (2006) showed that the proportion of CRM-systems in SMEs was increasing and forecasts a growing trend. With a large proportion of SMEs considering office and mail-systems to be an appropriate tool for managing customer relations, the CRM-potential is significantly underexploited; i.e., regarding changing market structures, stronger competition and higher expectations in service (Koelwel 2006; Schwetz 2006). The selection of a CRM-system for SMEs often involves various difficulties and challenges not being given for larger enterprises. Main arguments to support this are (1) traditionally grown systems emphasise the storage of customer data (Kemper et al. 2005); (2) lack of transparencies for most CRM-systems addressing CRM issues; i.e., regarding 4 cost, depth of integration, benefits; (3) high number of solutions and software providers with large variety in functionality; (4) insufficient experience regarding large IT-integration and priority on core operational day-to-day-business (Kemper et al. 2005); and (5) limited resources for an integrated IT (Brehm et al. 2008). Brendel (2003) analysed how CRM-implementation projects differ depending on the size of an enterprise. In SME, the implementation is done iteratively by installing single functionality in each step to increase acceptance with stakeholders and to keep the complexity on manageable levels; e.g., installing support for management of contacts, tasks, sales, offers, and orders in separated steps (Brendel 2003). This bottom-up approach is often neglected by larger enterprises as they consider CRM as a vision that requires complete commitment rather than single functionalities (Stengl et al. 2001).

The tendency to restrict the usage of CRM to basic functionality can be observed in most SMEs; often they just use address and contact management as well as basic sales controlling (Brendel 2003). Brendel (2003) differentiates between elemental and advanced components of CRM-systems: elemental components like address-, contact-, and appointment-management, offer and order administration, and opportunity management; advanced components like Internet integration, workflow management with all business units. In general, operative CRM is of greater interest to SMEs; i.e., sales controlling and complaint management (Hippner 2006; Kemper et al. 2005). Using only part of the CRM-systems limits the outcome and often only sub-optimal results are achieved (Kemper et al. 2005). Brendel (2003) depicts that even centralised address management could contribute over 50 % to the success of CRM. Brendel (2003) also shows that projects introducing CRM often ignore customer-oriented processes and strategies but focus on the pure system installation and integration.

4 Survey

We used a mixed approach with an anonymous online questionnaire and aligned expert interview to verify and intensify the survey results (Schnell et al. 1999). The main objective of the survey was about the *where* and *how* CRM-systems were used, *what* the companies aimed for, *how* well the CRM-system was integrated, and *which* problems occurred. We did not ask for specifics about the software brand (Horn 2007), IT security, or any organisational questions (Kemper et al. 2005); as this was done in previous surveys. Due to these restrictions, the transfer feasibility of outcomes to other industrial areas might be limited and has to be evaluated on future test samples. The survey was done in cooperation with the Institute of Information Systems, University of Hamburg, and C: 1 Industry Projects & Solutions. We used' ABC der Deutschen Wirtschaft' (database for enterprises in Germany; program name: ABC Quellenwerk CD-Buch 2007.3) to access over 230,000 profiles and addresses. The database accuracy for revenue was below our threshold; therefore we limited the selection on number of employees as well as industrial area and regions. We used an online survey to simplify distribution, improve acceptance by participants, increase the turnover rate, decrease the cost, integrate dynamic question selection, and gain access to a broader number of enterprises (Broda 2006). We did not expect a media objection as we expected familiarity with IT for their daily business activities among the target group. We used the software' umfragecenter 5.1—Surveycenter' by n.n. (2008).

The selection process was designed as follows: (1) select all enterprises with 50-1, 200 employees; (2) deselect enterprises which are subsidiaries for larger enterprises; (3) deselect all not in one of the following industry sectors: electrotechnique, metal industry (iron, steel, further metal), mechanical engineering; (4) deselect if not located in North Germany with zip code areas 2, 3, and 4; (5) deselect if they have no identifiable contact address; (6) randomly verify previously not selected enterprises for inclusion/exclusion. Regarding SMEs, we anticipated that the sales manager or the sales group is most knowledgeable about their CRM-system, and most likely observed or participate in the launch of the system itself. Where possible, we investigated the name and email-address of sales managers; otherwise the document was sent to the main office or front desk with a request to forward the survey to an appropriate manager (we verified the validity of the information by calling a small random sample; the result of 60 % was low but still valid with respect to our targeted return rate). Finally, we processed the data for the mailing procedure; i.e., improving the formatting and the choice of appropriate form of address. In total, we had **1,422** records with sales manager names and **931** data sets with just the name of the enterprise requiring the involvement of the front desk. Of these 2,353 emails, 212 had non-working addresses. After the initial distribution, reminders were sent after 10 days; an additional distribution of the survey in online networks like the German version of LinkedIn (Xing) did not result a considerable increase in response rate; for return rate see the result section.

5 Questionnaire

Online questionnaires often lack a high response rate; especially in our case with no direct contact and addressing employees in higher positions. The initial selection of the sample using the not necessarily representative address database inherits already drawbacks regarding generalizability; a low return rate decreases this even further (Mayer 2006). Our benefit is that objective of the survey is about tendencies and trends and not as much about precise predictions over all areas. The questionnaire has 20 questions of which a respondent would be required to respond to a maximum of 16 and a minimum of 8; five questions are about the enterprise to help the classification of results (see Fig. 1). The average time for answering all questions is between 6 and 10 min. The questionnaire followed general and agreed construction rules; see (Kirschhofer-Bozenhardt and Kaplitza 1986; Schnell et al. 1999).

The survey targets electronic CRM-systems in general and does not encompass any associated CRM-processes, differentiate CRM-systems, or their operationalisation; i.e., as most SMEs often (parts of) use lean systems or even software like Outlook for purposes other than intended. Figure 1 shows the three different paths through the questions; depending on the answer for Q1. We distinguish between SMEs that already have CRM, plan on integrating CRM, or do not intend to use CRM. The SMEs with existing CRM-systems are divided in two further groups: (1) stand-alone CRM-systems; (2) integrated CRM-systems; and (3) office

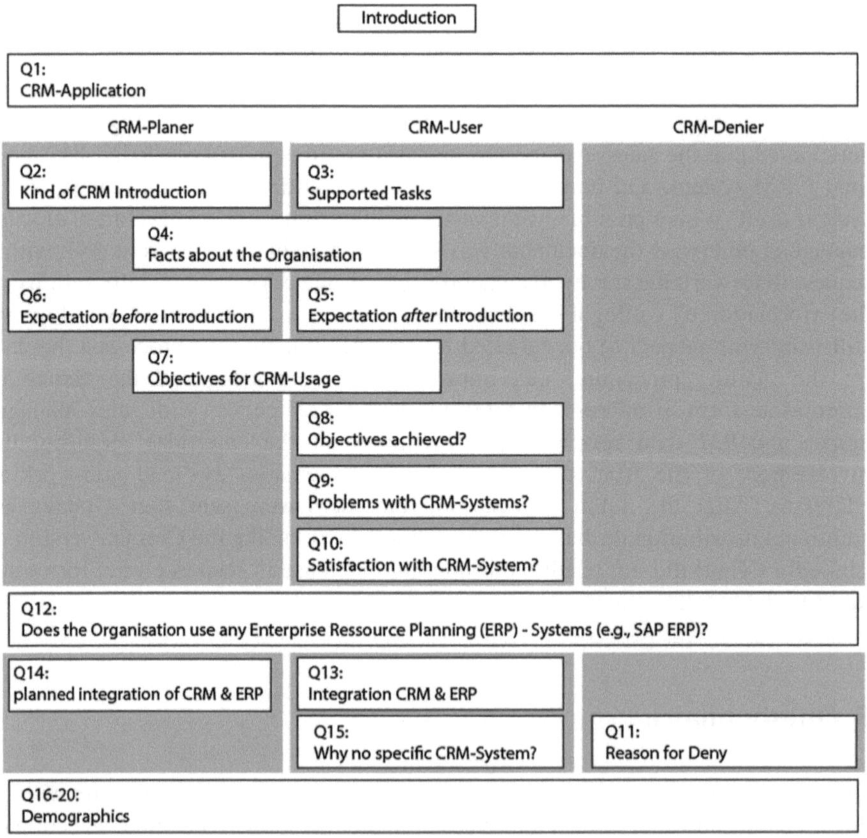

Fig. 1 Structure of the survey. The columns structure the survey with respect to the target groups: CRM-Planer, CRM-User, CRM-Denier. Questions across multiple columns were used for more than one group; whereas the question was modified to match the group

application used for CRM. **CRM-deniers** have the shortest survey as we are only interested in their reasons and demographics data, yet Q11 (and Q15 for the CRM-user) are crucial as they reveal weaknesses of existing CRM-systems. The survey examines if sales manager have awareness of the kind of potential that CRM-systems can have and if the topic is already under investigation; or not. **CRM-planers** are asked about intended and required functionality (Q4) and their expectation on this. Q5 and Q6 are used to verify the main question in this survey (Q7); difference is in how the target group is addressed. **CRM-users** are asked about their implemented and required CRM functionality to verify the degree of coverage. Q8 examines the difference between targeted and actual CRM-system (only items being selected in Q7 are shown). Here, we are interested in targets like customer acquisition, customer loyalty, customer win-back, common information database, cost reduction, and improved effectiveness of processes. We also asked about their impression about competiveness to verify how sale managers see CRM-systems as a tool to improve their opportunities. Q9 is about uncovering problem areas with CRM-systems to suggest solutions. Q12-Q15 are about ERP-systems in general and how well and in which way CRM-systems are already integrated or connected in SME. We expected that either CRM-systems are stand-alone-systems without integration or part of an ERP solution. The survey ends with questions about demographics and the registration via email for the results.

The design of the questionnaire emphasises quantitative results. The main reason for excluding free/open answer fields was to enhance simplicity and make it faster for the sales manager to answer the survey, in an attempt to increase the return rate. Strengthening and verification of discovered information in the quantitative data was achieved by multiple (guided) expert interviews selected from the given sample of enterprises. The interviews were based on the questionnaire, but allowed exploration of other problem areas that we did not foresee. Subjects of the interviews were: (1) information about the enterprise; (2) CRM usage; (3) CRM functions; (4) CRM targets and CRM successes; (5) CRM problems; (6) integration with ERP systems; (7) reasons for not using large stand-alone CRM-systems; (8) general questions.

6 Results

This section summarises the analysis of the answers and their interdependencies. We used a level of significance α of 5 % in case of normal significance and 1 % in case of high significance. Most of the variables in the survey are nominally scaled (non-value categories), the answers *not sure* and *no answer* were not included. The marginal frequency in the contingency table was ≥ 5; in other cases the variable characteristics were combined for the calculation. Furthermore, we analysed subsets on one attribute by taking two characteristics for a comparison with this attribute. Finally, we used in some cases the contingency coefficient Yule's Q for 2×2 cross-classified tables.

6.1 Demographics

We contacted 2,147 enterprises and got a respond from 402 (18.7 %); of which 149 did not proceed further than 20 % into the questionnaire. In total, we had 253 valid replies of which most completed the questionnaire. The question about their customer group had the lowest number of replies with 181 answers (B2B: 55.7 %; B2B/B2C: 28.1 %; no reply: 16.2 %). The geographic distribution in North Germany and their business area is shown in Fig. 2; the sum is larger than 100 as we allowed multiple answers. Figure 3 shows the distribution of employees in the enterprises. With 85.4 % having fewer than 500 employees, we were able to address our intended target group. Despite having more than 500 employees, we still classified the other 14.6 % as SMEs based on other quantitative measures such as appropriate revenue or other qualitative (market reach) criteria.

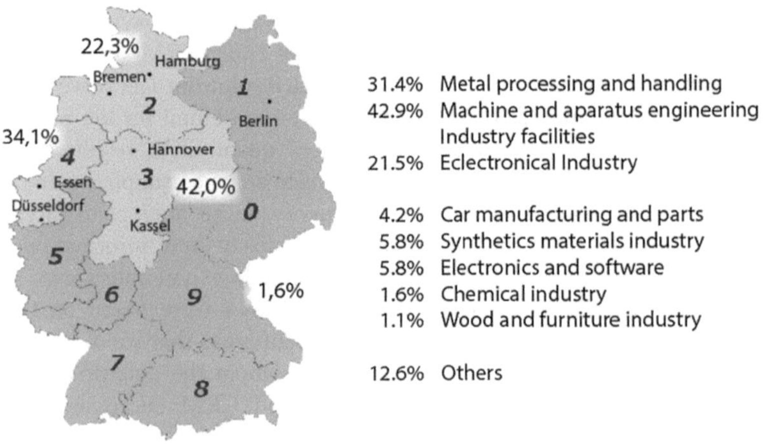

Fig. 2 Geographic distribution of participating SMEs (191 answers, multiple answers)

Fig. 3 Distribution of employees (191 answers)

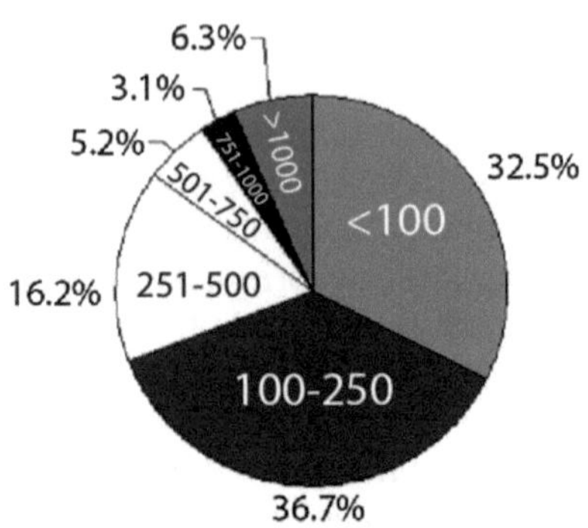

6.2 CRM Usage

Despite the selected target group of SMEs from an industrial area not known to have a strong affinity for CRM-systems, we could observe a relatively high distribution of specialised (25.3 %) and integrated (18.6 %) CRM-systems (Fig. 4). The results also verify our expectation that generic office application functionality is often matched with the CRM requirements (37.6 %). The large number of SMEs not having and not planning on a CRM-system argue that the low distribution is caused by the different needs compared to large enterprise as the number of relations is either to low or not requiring an intensive relation management. CRM-systems would exceed the need; thus a justification for investment in software and training is not given.

The application of CRM-systems in our focus group showed an equal distribution with respect to required functionality and objectives, and does not be affected by the industry area or enterprise attributes like size or revenue.

6.3 CRM Functions

Contact (79.23 %) and master data (63 %) management was, as expected, identified as the core functionality for CRM-systems; however, we would have expected an even higher percentage for the latter one. An explanation might be that a CRM-system-providers origins is CAS (computer aided selling) and not from IT, marketing, or management. In addition, we have to take under consideration, that the participants either did not assume that master data are essential for CRM or that the functionality is implemented in other (ERP) systems and therefore not associated with the CRM-systems. Other functionalities are supported as listed below (Fig. 5):

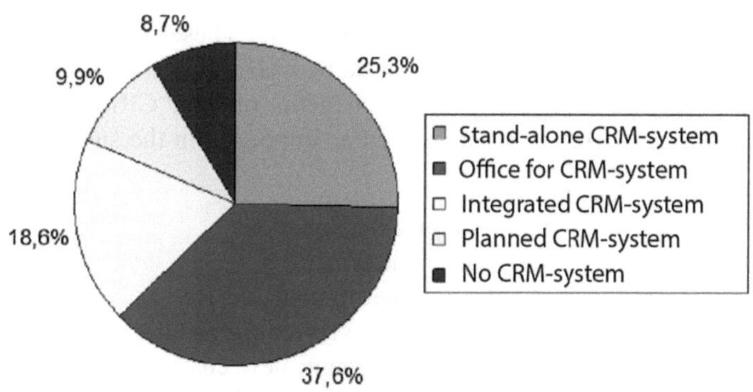

Fig. 4 Distribution of CRM-systems (253 answers)

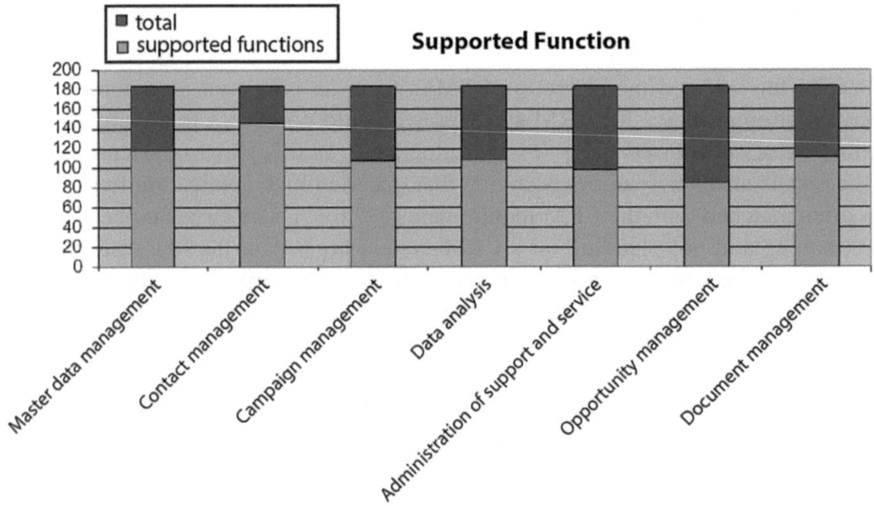

Fig. 5 Supported function (189 answers, 6 do not known)

- **77.3 %**: Collection and management of customer contacts; including visits, telephone calls, correspondence
- **58.3 %**: Collection and systematic storage of documents linked to customers and activities; including sales, marketing, or service
- **44.8 %**: Administration of potential customers and business opportunities
- **51.9 %**: Documentation of customer complain a well as service and support requests
- **58.2 %**: Data analysis of sales, marketing, and service
- **63.0 %**: Collection and management of customer information and contact details
- **57.1 %** Preparation and submission of circular mail and newsletters

In accordance with other studies (e.g., Torggler 2007), we also found functions like the administration and analysis of master data, contact information, and documents to be most relevant for effective CRM use. These functions are not well-supported by traditional office products used by SME; thus, SMEs using only office products are not achieving the potential benefits of their CRM efforts. The following functionality for CRM was named as important in the survey (see Fig. 6):

- **92.0 %**: Master data management
- **82.1 %**: Contact documentation and management
- **43.3 %**: Campaign mailing and management
- **78.1 %**: Data analysis of sales, marketing and service
- **48.3 %**: Administration of support and service procedures
- **43.3 %**: Lead and opportunity management, new customer management
- **64.7 %**: Document management in sales, marketing and service

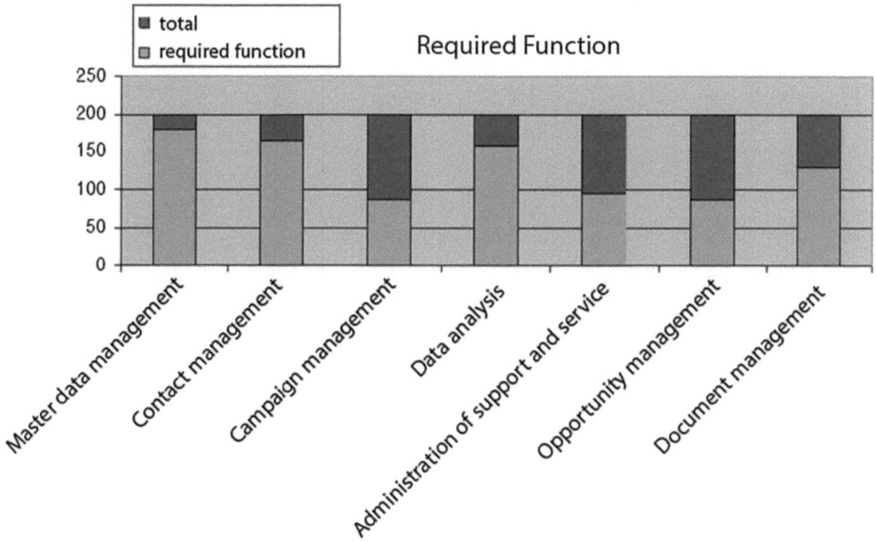

Fig. 6 Required functions (201 answers, 1 do not now; multiple selection)

Using the contingency coefficient Yule's Q, we analysed the overlap between support activities and required functionality to estimate the suitability of used CRM-systems in the SMEs. A third of the participants claimed that besides the administration of contacts they were not sufficiently supported in their activities. One reason might be the implementation of non-market-leading or inapplicable CRM-systems. On the other hand, new CRM-systems are generally future-oriented with functions not currently required or even anticipated by the CRM users.

6.4 CRM-Objectives and Target Achievement

Objectives like cost reduction (72.3 %), creating a central information source (92.0 %), and increasing competitiveness (50.5 %) were often mentioned; even though two answers are not generally associated with CRM-systems as core functionality; see Fig. 7. One reason could be the understanding that, at first, any system is primarily used to support the strategic aims (e.g., survival and growth) and then specialised operational needs in business units; that is customer retention (54.3 %), acquisition (54.3 %), and effective recovery (19.7).

Figure 8 shows that achievement of objectives using CRM is overall assessed positively (Q8); yet SMEs could only achieve minor success in terms of their objectives. The only real exception is the creation of a standardised information source (92.1 %). Noticeable is that all targets were mentioned, on average not statistically significantly more by SMEs with specialised CRM-systems including the achievement of these targets; i.e., cost reduction and improved availability of

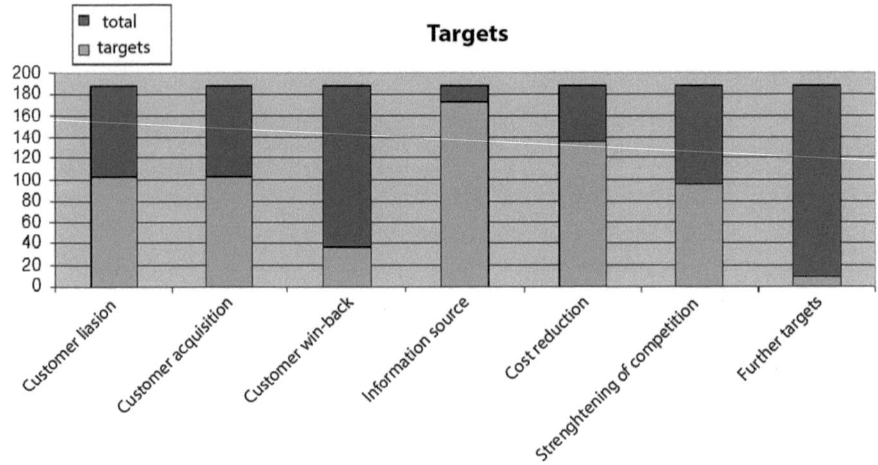

Fig. 7 Targets (188 answers; multiple selections)

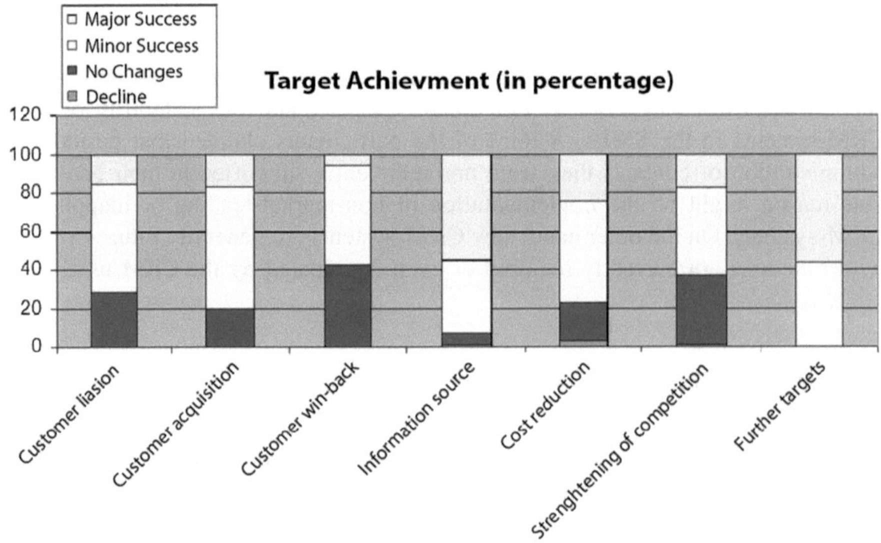

Fig. 8 Target achievement (168 answers, percentage)

information. SMEs using Office-systems for CRM-activities mentioned some objectives less frequent and noticed some disadvantages in realising anticipated targets like creating a global information source. SMEs with integrated CRM-systems position themselves in between the specialised systems on the use of office products. The majority of CRM-users are, according to Q10, satisfied or very satisfied (51.5 %); 37.7 % are neutral, 10.8 % are unsatisfied, and no one very unsatisfied (150 valid answers; including 20 abstention from voting); see Fig. 9.

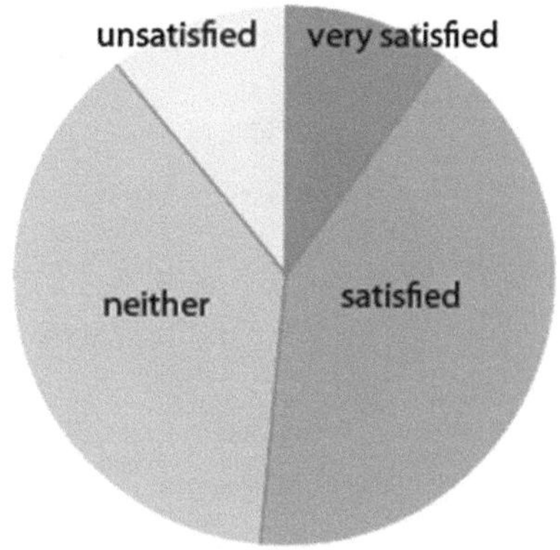

Fig. 9 CRM satisfaction (150 answers, 20 did not answer)

Employee satisfaction positively correlates with the availability of specialised CRM-systems (with office products having the lowest value) and the achievement of set targets.

6.5 Problems with CRM-Systems

80.6 % of all sales managers using CRM approaches (systems, integrated, office) mention in Q9, the existence of still unsolved problems. The most often mentioned problem is about the missing system-wide integration of CRM; in especially regarding up-to-date data (40.0 %); followed by employees' acceptance (23.8 %), understanding of CRM and customer focus (22.5 %), missing of features (17.5 %), wasted potential (25.6 %), and no satisfactory metric to evaluate achievement of targets (18.1 %). Again, in SMEs with specialised (26.3 %) or integrated (25.0 %) CRM-systems, users are significantly more satisfied than with office as an alternative (9.7 %). The observation of less integration problems with specialised than integrated CRM-systems contradicts our expectation. Users report that the specialised CRM-systems have a higher homogeneity rate in the enterprise-wide data than integrated systems. This result is important to follow-up in further investigations as it raises concerns either about the systems itself or the awareness of the users using the specialised systems regarding the quality of the data.

6.6 CRM Integration in ERP-Systems

Figure 10 visualises how SME integrate their CRM functionality with existing ERP systems; if available (58.9 %). As expected, the use of CRM-systems correlates with the availability of ERP-systems.

Here, the ERP-system usage correlates significantly with the CRM-system deployment. Companies with ERP-systems have more frequent, integrated,

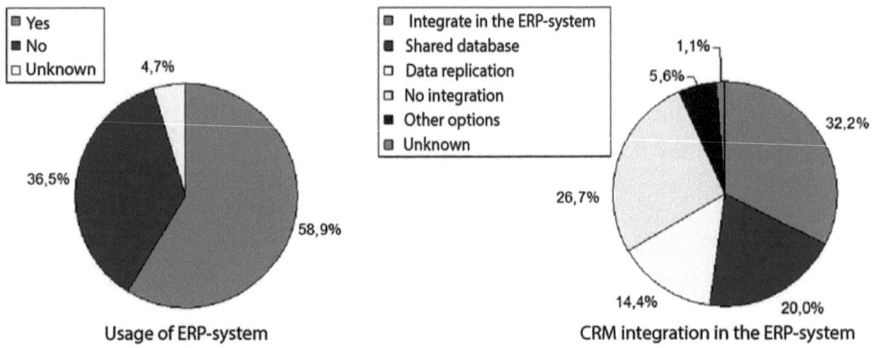

Fig. 10 ERP usage (192 answers) and CRM-integration in ERP-system (90 answers)

CRM-systems in use. Our assumption, that larger SMEs are more likely to have ERP-systems implemented, could not be confirmed within this study. The proportion of ERP-systems is similar both in SME with less than 100 employees and with more than 250 employees. This phenomena was further investigated in the expert interviews where all agreed on the same two arguments that make ERP-systems absolute essential: (1) the complexity of processes is unrelated to the size of an enterprise; and, (2) enterprises are 'forced' into certain data and process standards by larger companies and corporations to allow and secure contracts and collaboration.

Despite the usage of ERP-systems, it is remarkable that over 30 % still do not integrate their CRM approach (26.7 % no integration; 5.6 % other exchange like printed documents). Only 34.4 % integrate their CRM-system by either having a shared master database (20.0 %) or replicate the data in defined time intervals (14.4 %). 32.2 % do not use a stand-alone CRM-system but use the integrated ERP-functionality for this purpose; this could be most often observed with smaller SME who try to minimise their IT overhead. In case of shared master data, the storage and administration is generally associated with the ERP-system to reduce the complexity of distributed databases. Table 1 matches integration method with anticipated results. Similar to the observation reported in Section "Problems with CRM-systems", it is surprising that a full integration of both systems is regarded less effective than replication or shared data bases (1.38 vs. 1.25/1.33 [persistent database]; 1.95 vs. 1.67/1.75 [cost reduction, efficient work]; lower value better). The expert interviews indicate that this is most likely related to the users' failure to fully understand the technology and require specialised training.

Table 1 Matching integration method with anticipated results, lower values are better)

Integration method/targets	Full integration	Shared database	Replication	No integration
Persistent database	1.38	1.33	1.25	1.81
Cost reduction/efficient work	1.95	1.75	1.67	2.31

6.7 Future Integration of CRM-Systems

The small group of SME without and not planned CRM-systems indicate that they do not require these systems (38.9 %), is not yet considered (38.9 %), or found different approaches to compensate the functionality. Only one SME argued with the low cost-benefit-ratio (5.6 %), overall cost was not used as an argument at all (0.0 %). Further reasons for not having CRM are political (5.6 %) or strategic reasons (11.2 %), or expected problems of integrating the CRM into the given IT landscape (22.4 %). In our study, the number of SME without CRM was with 19 participants (and one not answering this question) relatively low; such further studies are required to investigate reasons for missing CRM support and how to approach technical and political problems (Figs. 11, 12).

If we look at the SME group using office products for their CRM, we can observe different tendencies for the future. 29.3 % are satisfied with their current solution, while 32.8 % intend to migrate to a full CRM-system (integrated in ERP and stand-alone). The other SME currently do not consider other systems (18.0 %) as the use alternative methods for customer retention (9.8 %), fear the cost (11.5 %), expect an unsatisfying cost-benefit-ratio (9.8 %), or expect problems during the IT-integration (19.7 %).

6.8 Integration of CRM/Expert Interviews

All three groups from the survey share one common problem: integration. Integration prevents over 20 % of non CRM-users initiating projects and over 25 % of

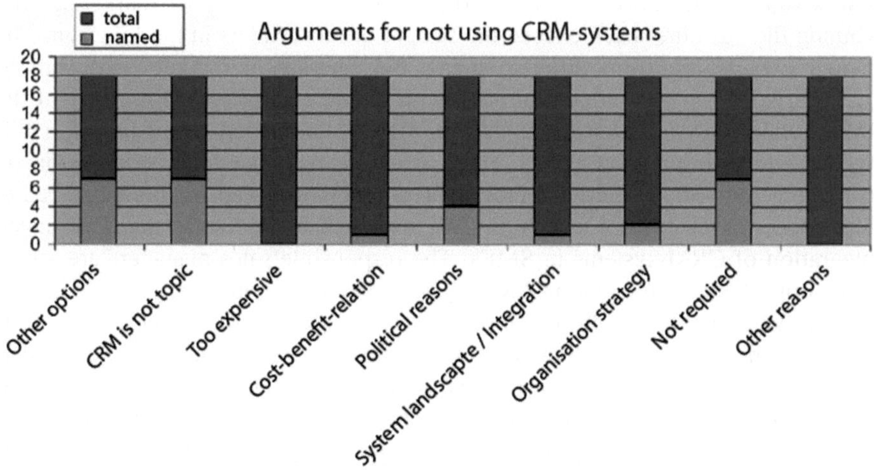

Fig. 11 Arguments for not using CRM (19 answers, 1 do not know)

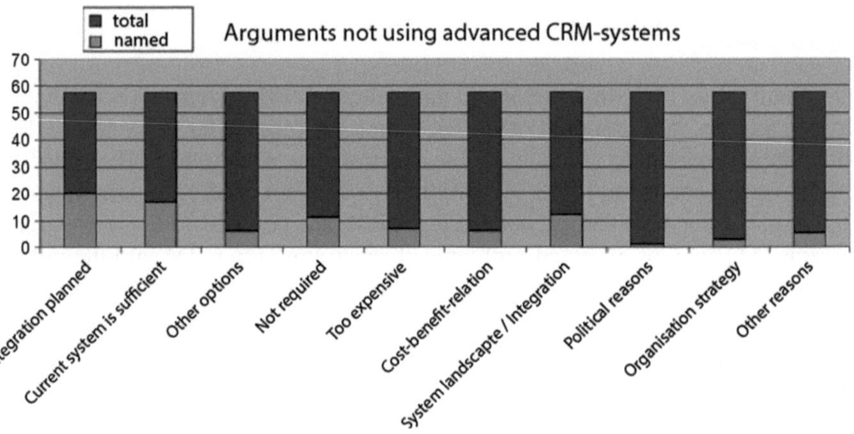

Fig. 12 Argument for not using advanced CRM-systems (61 answers, 3 do not know)

CRM-system owners, either special or integrated in ERP, mention problems or need for improvements. One of the major reasons stated during the expert interview is about the complexity of these systems. In comparison to larger enterprise, SMEs often do not have the capacity, knowledge, or financial opportunities for consultants. In addition, most CRM-systems offer a functionality that goes far beyond the need of most SMEs; CRM-Lite systems are often sufficient but lack the acceptance of SMEs and larger enterprises.

The experts stated without doubt that the relationships with customers are essential for enterprises, independent of factors such as industrial area, size, revenue, integration in supply chains, or location. The changes in communication technology, the success of social networks, and the immediate availability of information allows customers to be informed about the market and the competition. Customer retention becomes crucial as costs relating to marketing and winning the customer back exceed the budget of most SMEs in the long run. The invited experts are from different areas, but operate in markets with similar characteristics: strong competition; i.e., with global enterprises. Still, many of the SMEs retain global market leadership through technological innovation, flexibility, and addressing market niches. Their success is the close relation to customers to explore individual solutions and adapt products to given requirements rather than expecting customers to change. We expected to find a far more advanced integration of CRM-systems in SMEs. The responsible sales managers are aware of the importance of integrating CRM-systems in their companies, yet have to deal with grown structures, traditional methods to keep records and manage customers, as well as the focus on the core business. Compared to large enterprise, the SMEs do not have the resources, financial and human, to initiate large IT projects and have to find solutions that are simple to implement and use, do not interfere with the operational business, and match with the needs of their business (purpose not functionality decides about success). The experts emphasised that it is important to add functionality in an iterative step-by-step process rather than a complex system at once. The acceptance and willingness of employees towards changes in the software and the processes is crucial and easier to achieve if the complexity and the amount of redundant training is kept low.

The use of office systems seems to be an adequate tool to manage customer relations in a first cost-effective step to a more profound solation. Employees do not require basic training, the structures in SMEs often allow data management on local systems, and it can be adapted to a certain extent. Nevertheless, the survey showed that SME are aware of future changes and that they have to define a path to integrate CRM. Up-to-date, specific CRM-systems, still dominate integrated systems, but according to the survey SME intend to migrate to integrated systems; especially smaller enterprises as they need to keep the administrative overhead down.

The survey revealed some unexpected results. Integration problems were mentioned more often with integrated CRM-systems; same is said about the satisfaction with the systems and achieving the defined targets. Even the homogeneity of data and reduction in cost, two factors we would have expected the benefit with the integrated systems, were more often selected of specific CRM-systems. One expert pointed out that the success of the stand-alone CRM-systems result from their specialisation. Fully integrated systems often have weaknesses like acceptance, flexibility, functionality and connectivity to in-house systems and, therefore, do not allow 100 % integration in the enterprise.

The experts place a higher importance on customer retention than the survey suggested. The results in the survey reflect the current status-quo of opportunities to actively provide a successful management and retention of customers; as most SME do not have the required availability of information and an enterprise-wide database to synchronise actions. Customer retention is the long-term objective, the creation of a centralised database the path to achieve this.

The expert interviews covered further technical-organisational problems; e.g., the sensible quantity of data employees can collect, difficulties in objectives regarding CRM-projects, missing support from executives, limited resources, and definition of expected features for the CRM-system. Besides integrated systems (e.g., offered by SAP), all agreed that so-called CRM-light or CRM-lite solutions are an interesting alternative as they provide core functionalities without disadvantages like overhead, costs, and extensive training needs; see also (Sulewski and Höliner 2004).

7 Conclusion

The survey took a snapshot of small- and medium-sized enterprise in the Northwest region of Germany, focusing on how they are currently integrating CRM functionality in their IT landscape. The outcome of the survey was analysed and the validity was increased by discussing unexpected outcomes with four experts from different industrial sectors than those surveyed. For example, the survey showed a favour for stand-alone systems with respect to features that are more common with fully integrated systems. We agree with the experts that this results from the organisational structure, the immediate requirements for a CRM-system, the lack of resources for IT experts, acceptance, and integrated systems not matching the needs. Based on the survey, only small enterprises with limited needs for CRM functionality use integrated CRM-systems as the functionality comes with the ERP-system and can generally implemented with basic customisation.

The specification of a CRM-system for SME is substantially different from CRM-systems for large enterprises. Employees in SME often have a higher workload; any extra time-consuming workload like entering additional data into systems, operating complex systems, or integrating new technology into their processes has to be balanced with substantial benefits. In addition, SME operate differently in highly competitive markets as they use their flexibility to find market niches. The day-to-day business in SME has priority over any other project; thus the implementation of CRM-systems has to follow different rules than it would be in larger enterprises. One of the experts mentioned that CRM-systems "are not allowed to become our biggest project; our biggest project is always the customer".

8 Questionnaire

Welcome to the survey about Customer Relationship Management Systems in small- and medium-sized businesses![1]

Customer Relationship Management (CRM) systems are electronic systems, which are used systematically by organisations during the process of customer retention as well as creating sustainable customer relationships. CRM-systems administrate different types of information, which can be used to address customer needs much more precisely and therefore reach a higher level of customer satisfaction. Examples for typical CRM functions are the administration of contacts, lead- and opportunity management, servicing, sales management and customer analysis.

Question 1: Which electronic system is your first choice regarding administration of customer relations and sale opportunities (CRM)?
[only single choice][mandatory question]
(CRM-usage)

- We use a special CRM-system (electronic system for administration of customer relations)
- We just use office and mailing applications (e.g., Microsoft Outlook and Office) for managing typical CRM tasks

[1] The given brackets specify type of question [] and variables for controlling the path through the survey ().

- We use CRM-functions, which are part of an extensive system; e.g., Enterprise Resource Planning (ERP) System
- We do not use an electronic system for managing typical CRM-tasks, but have plans about an implementation
- We do not use an electronic system for managing typical CRM-tasks and do not plan the implementation of these systems

Question 2: In case you are planning an implementation: What kind of CRM-system will be presumably implemented in your company?
[only single choice]
(CRM-planning)

- A specific CRM-system
- We are planning on extending the use of office and mailing programs or an extension for CRM-usage
- We will be implementing or extending a system (e.g., ERP-system) which will be used for CRM-tasks
- Not yet decided

Question 3: In which tasks do you benefit from your current CRM-system?
[multiple choices possible]
(only for CRM-users)

- Collection and administration of customer contacts (e.g., visits, communication) *(supports: contact administration)* [1]
- Collection and systematic organisation of customer and customer process documents regarding sales management, marketing and service *(supports: document management)* [2]
- Administration of business opportunities or leads as well as potential customers *(supports: opportunity-management)* [3]
- Documentation of customer complaints, service and support *(supports: service functions)* [4]
- Evaluation of sales, marketing and service data regarding different aspects *(supports: evaluation)* [5]
- Collection and administration of versatile information regarding customers and contact persons *(supports: master data)* [6]
- Preparation, dissemination and analysis of circular letters/mailings *(supports: campaign management)* [7]
- Not sure about it

Question 4: Which are the essential functions for your company (regardless of your currently used or planned system)?
[multiple choices possible]
(only for CRM-users or CRM-planners)

- Customer base and address administration to extract detailed customer and contact information *(requires: base data)* [6]

- Contact administration and history (e.g., regarding visits, phone calls) *(requires: contact administration)* [1]
- Campaign management and mailings *(requires: campaign management)* [7]
- Evaluation and analysis within sales management, marketing and service *(requires: analysis)* [5]
- Administration of information within support and servicing *(requires: service functions)* [4]
- Lead and opportunity management, interested parties *(requires: opportunity management)* [3]
- Document management within sale management, marketing and servicing *(requires: document management)* [2]
- Not sure about it

Question 5: Which benefit did you expect for your company from the implementation of your CRM-system?
[multiple choices possible]
(only for CRM-users)

- To improve customer loyalty and tie them stronger to your company/strengthening the bond between customer and company *(control: customer loyalty)* [A]
- To prevent scattering of information or expert with intrinsic knowledge *(control: information source)* [D]
- Advanced administration of leads/interested parties; to win them easier as customer *(control: customer acquisition)* [B]
- To strengthen or extend our market position by the improvement of customer relations administration *(control: competition)* [F]
- Improved opportunities of regaining lost customers/customer win-back *(control: customer win-back)* [C]
- Our CRM-system simplifies work and therefore leads to time and cost reduction *(control: cost reduction)* [E]
- Not sure about it

Question 6: Which benefit do you expect from the future implementation of a planned CRM-system for your company?
[multiple choices possible]
(only for CRM-planners)

- To improve customer loyalty and tie them stronger to your company *(control: customer loyalty)* [A]
- To prevent scattering of information or expert with intrinsic knowledge *(control: information source)* [D]
- Advanced administration of leads/interested parties; to win them easier as customer (control: customer acquisition) [B]
- To strengthen or extend our market position by the improvement of customer relations administration *(control: competition)* [F]

- Our CRM-system simplifies work and therefore leads to time and cost reduction *(control: cost reduction)* [E]
- Not sure about it

Question 7: What are the most important business objectives and strategies of customer retention, which you pursue by using a CRM-system?
[multiple choices possible][mandatory question]
(only for CRM-user and CRM-planers)

- strengthening customer loyalty *(customer loyalty)* [A]
- improving customer acquisition *(customer acquisition)* [B]
- improving customer win-back *(customer win-back)* [C]
- centralised source of information *(source of information)* [D]
- cost reduction and more efficient work *(cost reduction)* [E]
- improve competitive advantage *(competitive advantage)* [F]
- others

Question 8: To what extent did you achieve your aims?
[matrix-question– per aim no multiple choice]
(only for CRM-users, only before mentioned items are shown)

- considerable success
- light success
- no changes
- degradation
- no information about this

Question 9: In which areas did you observe difficulties using your CRM-system?
[multiple choices possible]
(only for CRM-users)

- We did not experience any problems with our CRM-system (problem: no problems)
- low acceptance by users *(problem: acceptance)*
- lack of essential functionalities *(problem: missing functions)*
- many unused functions waste potential *(problem: unused functions)*
- different data sources or systems are not sufficiently connected within our company *(problem: integration)*
- low comprehension of CRM and customer centrification within the company degrade the benefit *(problem: low comprehension)*
- no satisfactory solution how to measure CRM achievements *(problem: measuring)*
- others: [+ text field]
- not sure about it

Question 10: How satisfied are you with your CRM-system?
[single choice only]
(only CRM-users, CRM-satisfaction):

- very satisfied—the concept of customer centrification is full success within our company
- satisfied—with our CRM-system we were able to achieve our essential goals
- neither very satisfied nor unsatisfied
- unsatisfied—many things did not work out as expected
- very unsatisfied—investing in this system was a failure
- no opinion

Question 11: What are the reasons that keep you from implementing an electronic CRM-system in your company?
[multiple choices possible]
(only CRM-deniers)

- so far CRM was not under consideration for us *(denial: no consideration)*
- CRM-systems are too expensive for us
- We currently use other means to enhance customer satisfaction and loyalty [+ text field] *(denial: other means)*
- *(denial: too expensive)*
- CRM-systems do not give us a satisfying cost-benefit ratio *(denial: cost-benefit ratio)*
- reasons are based on our system e.g., difficulties to integrate within existing IT *(denial: integration)*
- political reasons *(denial: politics)*
- reasons are based on our enterprise strategies *(denial: strategy)*
- we do not need such a system, because .....[+ text field] *(denial: no need)*
- other reasons: [+ text field]
- not sure about it

Question 12: Is your company currently using an Enterprise Resource Planning (ERP) - System (e.g., SAP, ERP)?
[only single choice]

- Yes
- No
- Not sure about it

Question 13 (ERP-CRM-integration): How did manage to share data between ERP- and CRM-system?
[only single choice]
(only for CRM-users, who use ERP-system (question12))

- we use a shared database for both systems

- Our CRM-system is part of the ERP-system, therefore no need to integrate anything
- we use data replication/redundant data management and frequent data synchronisation
- Both systems are not linked
- Other options of integration: [+ Textfeld]
- Not sure about it

Question 14: How do you plan to manage the integration of data between ERP- and CRM-system?
[only single choice]
(only CRM-planners and users of ERP-systems (question 12))

- The CRM-system will be part of the ERP-system, therefore no need of integration
- we will use a shared database for both systems
- we will use data replication/redundant data management and frequent data synchronisation
- Both systems are not linked
- Other options of integration: [+ Textfeld]
- Not yet decided on

Question 15: What are the reasons for your company not to use an advanced/ specialised CRM-system?
[multiple choice possible]
(only CRM-users, who currently use office and other mailing systems (question 1))

- We plan to implement an advanced system (Office: system is planned)
- Currently used system fulfils our needs (Office: needs fulfilled)
- Not necessary, because we have other means to improve customer loyalty and satisfaction [+ text field] (Office: other means)
- Such systems are not yet under consideration *(Office: no consideration)*
- Advanced CRM-systems are too expensive for us (Office: too expensive)
- Advanced CRM-systems do not offer a satisfying cost-benefit ratio *(Office: cost-benefit ratio)*
- Reasons are based on our system e.g., difficulties to integrate within existing it *(Office: integration)*
- political reasons *(Office: politics)*
- reasons are based on our enterprise strategies *(Office: strategy)*
- we do not need such a system, because… [+ text field] *(Office: no need)*
- other reasons: [+ text field]
- not sure about it

Question 16: **In which field is your company operating?**
[only single choice]

- Business-to-Business (B2B)
- Business-to-Customer (B2C)
- both—B2B as well as B2C

Question 17 [mandatory question]: In which of the following fields is your company operating?
[multiple choice possible]

- Metal working and processing (Metal)
- Machine- and apparatus engineering, industrial facilities (Machines)
- Electronics, electro-technical industry
- (Electronics)
- Vehicles e.g., vehicles construction, vehicles parts (Vehicles)
- Synthetic material or goods, (Synthetic)
- Electronic engineering, software (Electronic)
- Chemical industry (Chemistry)
- Wood- and furniture industry
- (wood/furniture)
- others: [+ text field]

Question 18: How many employees work in your company?
[only single choice][mandatory question]

- less than 100
- 100–250
- 251–500
- 501–750
- 751–1,000
- over 1,000
- not sure about it

Question 19 (total revenue): How was the total revenue of your company within the last business year?
[only single choice]

- less than 10 Million
- 10–25 Million
- 26–50 Million
- 51–75 Million
- 76–100 Million
- more than 100 Million
- no information
- not sure about it

Question 20 (zip-code): Where is your company/main office located? (pick the first number of your zip-code.)
[only single choice]

- zip-code area 2
- zip-code area 3
- zip-code area 4
- in a different zip-code area : [+ text field]

References

Andersen, H., & Andreasen, M. D. (1999). *The CRM handbook: From group to multi-individual.* Norhaven: PricewaterhouseCoopers.

Bauer, T., & Oswald, C. (2007). Weiterentwicklung von Systemen und Anwendungen im CRM: Ziele, Prioritäten und Herausforderungen Retrieved 144.

Berry, L. L. (1983). Relationship marketing. In L. L. Berry, G. L. Shostack, & G. D. Upah (Eds.), *Emerging perspectives on services marketing* (pp. 25–28). Chicago: American Marketing Association.

Brehm, N., Heyer, N., Marx Gómez, J., & Richter, B. (2008). *Das ERP-KMU-Dilemma und Anforderungen an Service-orientierte Architekturen zur Nutzung von Verbesserungspotentialen.* Paper presented at the Multikonferenz Wirtschaftsinformatik, 2008, Berlin.

Brendel, M. (2003). *CRM für den Mittelstand: Voraussetzungen und Ideen für die erfolgreiche Implementierung* (2nd ed.). Wiesbaden: Gabler.

Broda, S. (2006). *Marktforschungs-Praxis: Konzepte, Methoden, Erfahrungen.* Wiesbaden: Gabler.

Buck-Emden, R., & Saddei, D. (2003). Informationstechnologische Perspektiven von CRM. In M. Bruhn & C. Homburg (Eds.), *Handbuch Kundenbindungsmanagement: Strategien und Instrumente für ein erfolgreiches CRM* (pp. 483–504). Wiesbaden: Gabler.

Buck-Emden, R., & Saddei, D. (2005). Informationstechnologische Perspektiven von CRM. In M. Bruhn & C. Homburg (Eds.), *Handbuch Kundenbindungsmanagement: Strategien und Instrumente für ein erfolgreiches CRM* (pp. 503–525). Wiesbaden: Gabler.

Chen, I. J., & Popovich, K. (2003). Understanding customer relationship management (CRM): People, process and technology. *Business Process Management Journal, 9*(5), 672–688.

Cornelsen, J. (2000). Kundenwertanalysen im Beziehungsmarketing: Theoretische Grundlegung und Ergebnisse einer empirischen Studie im Automobilbereich *Schriften zum innovativen Marketing* (Vol. 3). GIM.

Diller, H. (2001). Geschäftsbeziehung *Vahlens Großes Marketinglexikon* (2nd ed., pp. 529–530). Vahlen.

Diller, H. (2006). Die Bedeutung des Beziehungsmarketing für den Unternehmenserfolg. In H. Hippner & K. D. Wilde (Eds.), *Grundlagen des CRM: Konzepte und Gestaltung* (pp. 98–120). Wiesbaden: Gabler.

Gelbrich, K. (2001). Kundenwert : Wertorientierte Akquisition von Kunden im Automobilbereich. Cuvillier.

Gerdes, J. (2005). Kundenbindung durch Dialogmarketing. In M. Bruhn & C. Homburg (Eds.), *Handbuch Kundenbindungsmanagement: Strategien und Instrumente für ein erfolgreiches CRM* (pp. 379–397). Wiesbaden: Gabler.

Gohr, S. (2006). Augen auf und durch: Von der Theorie zur CRM-Praxis. *Database Marketing, 4*, 4–11.

Gohr, S. (2007). Branchen unterschiedlich weit im CRM. *Database Marketing, 1*, 6–7.

Grönroos, C. (1990). *Service Management und Marketing: Managing Moments of Truth in Service Competition*. Lexington.
Günter, B., & Helm, S. (2006). Kundenbewertung im Rahmen des CRM. In H. Hippner & K. D. Wilde (Eds.), *Grundlagen des CRM: Konzepte und Gestaltung* (pp. 358–378). Wiesbaden: Gabler.
Helmke, S., Uebel, M. F., & Dangelmaier, W. (2001). *Effektives customer relationship management: instrumente, einführungskonzepte, organisation* (1st ed.). Wiesbaden: Gabler.
Herrmann, A., & Johnson, M. D. (1999). Die Kundenzufriedenheit als Bestimmungsfaktor der Kundenbindung. *Zeitschrift für betriebswirtschaftliche Forschung, 6*, 579–599.
Hippner, H. (2006). CRM: Grundlagen, Ziele und Konzepte. In H. Hippner & K. D. Wilde (Eds.), *Grundlagen des CRM: Konzepte und Gestaltung* (pp. 16–44). Wiesbaden: Gabler.
Hippner, H., & Wilde, K. D. (2002). CRM: Ein Überblick. In S. Helmke, M. Uebel, & W. Dangelmaier (Eds.), *Effektives customer relationship management* (pp. 3–38). Wiesbaden: Gabler.
Hippner, H., & Wilde, K. D. (2003). CRM: Ein Überblick. In S. Helmke, M. Uebel, & W. Dangelmaier (Eds.), *Effektives customer relationship management* (pp. 3–37). Wiesbaden: Gabler.
Hippner, H., & Wilde, K. D. (2005). Informationstechnologische Grundlagen der Kundenbindung. In M. Bruhn & C. Homburg (Eds.), *Handbuch Kundenbindungsmanagement: Strategien und Instrumente für ein erfolgreiches CRM* (pp. 463–499). Wiesbaden: Gabler.
Hippner, H., & Wilde, K. D. (2008). Customer relationship management: Grundlagen und aktuelle Entwicklungen. *Das Wirtschaftsstudium, 1*, 105–111.
Homburg, C., & Bruhn, M. (2005). Kundenbindungsmanagement: Eine Einführung in die theoretischen und praktischen Problemstellungen. In M. Bruhn & C. Homburg (Eds.),Kundenbindungsmanagement: Strategien und Instrumente für ein erfolgreiches CRM (pp. 3–37). Wiesbaden: Gabler.
Homburg, C., & Sieben, F. G. (2005). Customer relationship management (CRM): Strategische Ausrichtung statt IT-getriebenem Aktivismus. In M. Bruhn & C. Homburg (Eds.), *Handbuch Kundenbindungsmanagement: Strategien und Instrumente für ein erfolgreiches CRM* (pp. 435–462). Wiesbaden: Gabler.
Horn, M. (2007). *Markt- und Anforderungsanalyse für CRM-Systeme im Mittelstand: Ein Anbieter- und Softwareüberblick*. Saarbrücken: VDM.
Jensen, O. (2005). Key account management (KAM) als Implementierungsform des Kundenbindungsmanagement. In M. Bruhn & C. Homburg (Eds.), *Handbuch Kundenbindungsmanagement: Strategien und Instrumente für ein erfolgreiches CRM* (pp. 527–551). Wiesbaden: Gabler.
Kemper, H.-G., Eggensperger, J., Lasi, H., & Miricanac, A. (2005). Customer Relationship Management im industriellen Mittelstand: Ergebnisse einer empirischen Befragung: Industrie—und Handelskammer Region Stuttgart.
Kirschhofer-Bozenhardt, A., & Kaplitza, G. (1986). Der Fragebogen. In K. Holm (Ed.), *Die Befragung 1: der Fragebogen—Die Stichprobe* (pp. 92–126). Tübingen: Francke.
Koelwel, D. (2006). Souveränität macht gelassen. *e-commerce Magazin, 7*, 12–13.
Loh, B. K., Koo, K. L., Ho, K. F., & Idrus, R. (2011). *A review of customer relationship management system benefits and implementation in small and medium enterprises*. Paper presented at the Mathematics and Computers in Biology, Business and Acoustics, 12th WSEAS International Congference on Mathematics and Computers in Biology and Chemistry, Transilvania, University of Brasov, Romania.
Mayer, H. O. (2006). *Interview und schriftliche Befragung: Entwicklung, Durchführung und Auswertung* (3rd ed.). München: Oldenbourg Wissenschaftsverlag.
Müller, H. (2004). *Einsatz von customer relationship management systemen*. Wiesbaden: Deutscher Universitäts-Verlag.
Neckel, P., & Knobloch, B. (2005). *Customer relationship analytics*. Heidelberg: Dpunkt.
Nelson, S., & Eisenfeld, B. (2002). Salvaging a failed CRM initiative. Research Note SPA-15-4007: Gartner Group.

MarketingCharts. (2006). CRM applications revenue set to double in value Retrieved 15/8/2012, from http://www.marketingcharts.com/direct/crm-applications-revenue-set-to-double-in-value-2225/datamonitor-crm-market-growth-revenues-2006-20012jpg/.

GlobalPark. (2008). globalpark.de Retrieved 10/8/2012, from http://www.globalpark.de.

Rapp, R. (2000). *Customer Relationship Management: Das neue Konzept zur Revolutionierung der Kundenbeziehungen*. Frankfurt A.M.: Campus-Verlag.

Schemuth, J. (1996). Möglichkeiten und Grenzen der Bestimmung des Wertes eines Kunden für ein Unternehmen der Automobilindustrie : Darstellung am Beispiel eines Käufers der C-Klasse von Mercedes-Benz. *Arbeitspapiere zur Schriftenreihe Schwerpunkt Marketing* (Vol. 74). FGM-Verlag.

Schmid, R., Bach, V., & Österle, H. (2000). Mit Customer Relationship zum Prozessportal. In V. Bach & H. Österle (Eds.), *Customer Relationship Management in der Praxis* (pp. 3–56). Berlin: Springer.

Schnauffer, R., & Jung, H.-H. (2004). *CRM-Entscheidungen richtig treffen*. Berlin: Springer.

Schnell, R., Hill, P. B., & Esser, E. (1999). *Methoden der empirischen Sozialforschung* (6th ed.). München: Oldenbourg.

Schulze, J. (2002). *CRM erfolgreich einführen*. Berlin: Springer.

Schumacher, J., & Meyerm, M. (2004). *Customer relationship management strukturiert dargestellt: Prozesse, Systeme, Technologien*. Berlin: Springer.

Schwetz, W. (2006). *Marktspiegel CRM 2007* (15 ed.). Schwetz Consulting.

Sexauer, H. J. (2002). Entwicklungslinien des Customer Relationship Management (CRM). *Wirtschaftswissenschaftliches Studium (WiSt): Zeitschrift für Ausbildung und Hochschulkontakt, 4*, 218–222.

Stengl, B., Sommer, R., & Ematinger, R. (2001). *CRM mit Methode: Intelligente Kundenbindung in Projekt und Praxis mit iCRM*. Bonn: Galileo Press.

Sulewski, G., & Höliner, R. G. (2004). CRM Light: Lösung für den Mittelstand: SAP Systems Integration (Schweiz) AG.

Terlutter, R., & Kricsfalussym, A. (2006). Der Einsatz von Instrumenten im Rahmen des Relationship Marketing: Ergebnisse einer empirischen Erhebung. In H. Hippner & K. D. Wilde (Eds.), *Grundlagen des CRM: Konzepte und Gestaltung* (pp. 634–649). Wiesbaden: Gabler.

Torggler, M. (2007). Einsatz von CRM-Systemen 2007: Eine empirische Studie zum praktischen Einsatz von CRM-Systemen in Österreich.: Fachhochschule Wiener Neustadtfür Wirtschaft und Technik GmbH.

Wolter, H.-J., & Hauser, H.-E. (2001). Die Bedeutung des Eigentümerunternehmens in Deutschland: Eine Auseinandersetzung mit der qualitativen und quantitativen Definition des Mittelstands *Jahrbuch zur Mittelstandsforschung: Schriften zur Mittelstandsforschung* (Vol. 1, pp. 25–77). Wiesbaden: Institut für Mittelstandsforschung Bonn.

Zähres, M. (2007). Trends und Entwicklungen im CRM-Markt. In H. Hippner, O. Hoffmann, & K. D. Wilde (Eds.), *CRM-Studie 2007* (pp. 37–43). Weßling: Weßling.

Empirical Study on Differences and Similarities in ERP Usage Amongst European SMEs

Pedro Ruivo, Tiago Oliveira, Björn Johansson and Miguel Neto

1 Introduction

The importance of small and medium-sized enterprises (SMEs) businesses has been recognised in recent decades due to their roles in creating jobs and enhancing local and global economic activity. To increase their productivity and efficiency, firms often adopt information technology (IT). Business applications such as enterprise resource planning (ERP) systems could provide a better way to execute business operations in an effective, organized, and sophisticated way. The adoption of ERP applications as been described as being one of the most innovative developments associated with the enterprise use of IT (Davenport 1998). The main purpose of ERP systems is to integrate as many enterprise functions as possible into a commercial off-the-shelf (COTS) product. Such systems manage both information and resources by supporting execution of operational transactions and advanced planning, alongside with real–time data access (Klaus et al. 2000). SMEs have been recognized as being fundamentally different environments compared to large enterprises and in relation to ERP usage, organizational size plays an important role (Buonanno et al. 2005; Carvalho and Johansson 2012; Mabert et al. 2003). The literature argues that little attention has been given to research on ERP in SMEs, as the majority of the ERP studies are based on findings from large enterprises (Devaraj and Kohli 2003) and less on cross-national studies. Moreover,

P. Ruivo (✉) · T. Oliveira · M. Neto
ISEGI, Universidade Nova de Lisboa, Campus de Campolide 1070-312 Lisbon, Portugal
e-mail: pruivo@isegi.unl.pt

T. Oliveira
e-mail: toliveira@isegi.unl.pt

M. Neto
e-mail: mneto@isegi.unl.pt

B. Johansson
School of Economics and Management, Lund University, SE-223 63 Lund, Sweden
e-mail: bjorn.johansson@ics.lu.se

J. Devos et al. (eds.), *Information Systems for Small and Medium-sized Enterprises*, Progress in IS, DOI: 10.1007/978-3-642-38244-4_10,

according to the European Commission report of Commission (2011), 99 % of all European firms have fewer than 250 employees, and although culturally disparate, Denmark, Portugal, Spain, and Sweden adhere to this profile, and with the same percentage. Because SMEs are the backbone of Europe's economy, are important for increasing productivity, and are important drivers of innovation and transformation, studying ERP at the SME level across countries is of great interest (Maguire et al. 2010).

The aim of this chapter is to explore similarities and differences in ERP usage among SMEs across Sweden, Denmark, Portugal and Spain, and from that to increase the knowledge base on usage of ERPs among SMEs. We test a model based on the diffusion of innovation (DOI) to explain ERP usage. The theoretical perspective is outlined in the next section. We use a dataset of 883 web survey SMEs that all use an ERP in their business. The rest of the chapter is organized as follows: research model and hypotheses; research method and characteristics of the sample; data analysis and results; discussion of the results focusing especially on similarities and differences between SMEs; and conclusions and future research.

2 Theoretical Perspective and Hypotheses

The globalisation of the economy is forcing many enterprises to change in order to survive. A better understanding of the ways in which SMEs use IT is necessary because previous research in the area is limited and mostly out-of-date due to the rapidly changing costs of using IT, and as a result of the increasing adoption of IT by SMEs increased (Chang et al. 2011). Because of weak of bargaining power, scarce resources, and low management skills, European SMEs have been deeply affected by the increasing globalisation of the world economy (Ruivo et al. 2012a, b, c). The current research seeks to provide an in-depth understanding and explanation of the relative levels of success in ERP usage, and understanding of causes of the relative levels of adoption and success with reference to appropriate theory. Information system (IS) research is often criticised for lacking theoretical foundations or for insufficient reference to theory in explanations of findings (Oliveira and Martins 2011). This paper describes how the findings from the study can be understood with reference to the diffusion of innovation model.

As suggested in literature, the impact of ERP systems on a firm's performance is mostly long-term and indirect, and linked primarily to system usage (Devaraj and Kohli 2003; Nicolaou 2004a, b; Ruivo et al. 2012a, b, c; Zhu and Kraemer 2005). ERP usage refers to the experience of managing the operation of the system software throughout the system's post-implementation stages (Nicolaou 2004a, b; Nah et al. 2004). Through greater use and diffusion, ERP systems not only extend basic business and streamline integration with suppliers and customers, but also direct system use to the firm's performance (Zhu and Kraemer 2005; Nicolaou and Bhattacharya 2006; Ruivo et al. 2012a, b, c). As described in the Oliveira and

Fig. 1 Research Model

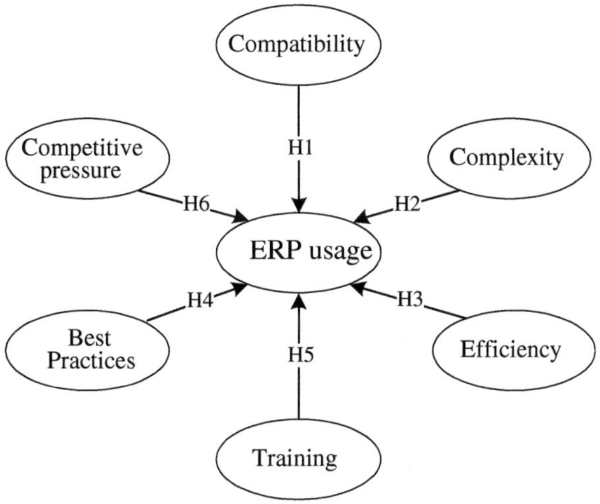

Martins study (2011), Rogers (1995) DOI model and Tornatsky and Fleischer (1990) Technology-Organization-Environment (TOE) framework both explain adoption at the firm level. While the TOE dependent construct is based on the likelihood to adopt IT, the DOI is based on the implementation success for IT use. Studies conducted by Bradford and Florin (2003) verify some DOI determinants regarding successful ERP usage, including, compatibility, complexity, training, and competitive pressure. Light and Papazafeiropoulou (2004) and Waarts et al. (2002) assess best-practices and transactional efficiency variable, as important dimensions for ERP usage. With this in mind, it can be suggested that DOI has the potential to provide a more favourable framework to explain ERP usage with regards to performance at the firm level. In this study we suggest that six factors are embedded in the DOI context: Compatibility, Complexity, Efficiency, Best-practices, Training, and, Competitive pressure explaining ERP usage (Fig. 1).

Based on DOI literature and the six factors we postulate six hypotheses to explain ERP usage (Hypothesis 1—Hypothesis 6):

Hypothesis 1 ERP systems with high compatibility positively influence ERP usage

Hypothesis 2 ERP systems with high complexity negatively influence ERP usage

Hypothesis 3 ERP systems with high transactional efficiency positively influence ERP usage

Hypothesis 4 ERP systems implemented best-practices positively influence ERP usage

Hypothesis 5 User training of ERP systems positively influences ERP usage

Hypothesis 6 Competitive pressure positively influences ERP usage

Compatibility is measured by the degree to which the ERP system matches IT features, such as compatibility with hardware and other software. Bradford and

Florin (2003) and Elbertsen et al. (2006) concluded that the degree of compatibility of ERP systems with existing software and hardware have a positive relationship with implementation success (system adoption and use).

Complexity is measured by how intuitive the application is; how quickly users can become proficient with the application, and how comfortable they are using it. Cooper and Zmud's (1990) research indicates that system use enhances job performance. Studies conducted by Kositanurit et al. (2006) and Chang et al. (2011) conclude that ERP complexity is a major factor affecting user performance. Bradford and Florin (2003) concluded that ERP complexity is a critical factor for successful implementation.

Efficiency is measured by how easy it is for users to execute common and repetitive tasks, the effectiveness of the user interface and the speed and reliability of the software. Bendoly and Kaefer (2004) assessed transactional efficiency and found that its communication over the ERP improves the firm's overall performance. Rajagopal (2002) found that transactional efficiency has a direct influence on ERP usage. Business process benefits of ERP investment include transactional efficiency, where reliability effectiveness on the application improves user confidence. Along the same lines, Gattiker and Goodhue (2005) found that efficiency greatly benefits ERP usage.

Best-practices is measured by how easy it is for users to set up the application and map workflows based on local requirements, and the system's adaptability to business needs. From the perspective of business process reengineering, there are two main options in implementing ERP systems: modify/customise the system to suit the firm's requirements, or implement the system with minimum deviation from the standard settings (adopting best-practices) (Davenport 1998). According to Chou and Chang (2008) and Maguire et al. (2010) the reason for adopting "best-practices" is the belief that ERP design does things in the right way. In line with Quattrone and Hopper (2005) and Wenrich and Ahmad (2009), firms that implement industry best-practices dramatically reduce risk and time consuming project tasks such as configuration, documentation, testing, and training.

Training is the measure of how easy it is for users to be trained on the system, to understand the content material, and to navigate through topics applied to daily tasks. Several researchers, including O'Leary (2000), Bradford and Florin (2003), and Maguire et al. (2010) state that one of the main determinants for the successful use of ERPs is training of users. The state of preparedness of users to carry out a planned sequence of actions without upstream errors has a positive impact on business. Providing knowledge and skills to employees on how to use the system improves familiarity and boosts its usage.

Competitive pressure is a measure of the degree of pressure that firms feel from competitors in the industry to use ERP. Competitive pressure has long been recognised in the innovation diffusion literature as an important driver of technology diffusion (Zhu and Kraemer 2005; Bradford and Florin 2003; Oliveira and Martins 2010). These studies have shown that innovation diffusion is accelerated by the competitive pressure in the environment. Thus, we postulate that competitive pressure plays an important role in pushing firms toward using ERP systems.

The ERP usage construct is measured by how many employees use the system daily, how much time per day, and how many reports it generates per day. A study conducted by Shahin and Ainin (2011) found that user fit on ERP is critical in explaining the ERP usage, and a successful adaptation of new functionalities with firms' processes and data flow makes ERP worthwhile. Through the integration capability of ERP systems firms can form a specific resource that guides performance. As a result, it is only when firms are actually using ERP systems to conduct business that ERP can have an impact on firm performance. Several authors demonstrate that system usage is an important dimension in the post-adoption phase (Devaraj and Kohli 2003; Zhu and Kraemer 2005; Nicolaou and Bhattacharya 2006).

3 Research Methodology

A web-survey was used for data collection and each item-question was reviewed for content validity by ERP experts. The initial questionnaires were pilot tested on 10 firms and some items were revised for clarity with assistance from the IDC. To ensure the generalisation of the survey results, the sampling was stratified by country (Sweden, Denmark, Portugal and Spain), by firm size (fewer than 250 employees), and by industry (finance, distribution, manufacturing, and professional-services) (Dillman 2000). Questionnaires were translated into the four languages with the aid of local market research professionals and sent in September and October 2011. In total, 2000 SMEs received the web-survey, and 883 valid responses were returned. Table 1 shows characteristics of the sample regarding the industry type and position of respondent. In general there are more similarities between Sweden, Denmark, Portugal and Spain than there are differences in the sample.

Table 1 The characteristics of the samples

Characteristics	Portugal (N = 134) (%)	Denmark (N = 107) (%)	Spain (N = 424) (%)	Sweden (N = 218) (%)
Industry type				
Distribution	28.4	27.1	30.0	27.5
Manufacturing	23.9	21.5	33.0	18.3
Finance	24.6	23.4	17.5	33.1
Professional Services	23.1	28.0	19.6	21.1
Respondent type				
CEO, owner	20.9	22.4	17.7	30.2
IT/IS manager	27.6	24.3	27.4	18.8
Finance manager	20.1	14.9	19.8	10.2
Sales manager	23.1	8.5	22.9	12.4
Manufacturing manager	8.2	29.9	12.3	28.4

4 Data Analysis

The survey instrument was based on well-established scales as adapted to the context of ERP (see Appendix A). We examined all of our model variables and believes that they are reflective in nature. We performed the Kolmogorov–Smirnov test and confirmed that none of the items measured are distributed normally ($p < 0.001$). For this reason we used partial least squares (PLS), since this statistical technique does not require normal distribution. We used the SmartPLS software to estimate the model. In accordance with Chin et al. (2003), factor loadings should be at least 0.6 and preferably greater than 0.7. For this reason (low loading) CB3, CX1, TN1, CP2, and ERPU1 question-items of Appendix A were excluded from our research model following the PLS model estimation. We retain the items presented in Table 2, except for CX2 (0.698) and BP2 (0.691), all other items have loadings above 0.7 and are significant at ($p < 0.001$). Furthermore, Table 2 shows that composite reliability (CR) and average variance extracted (AVE) for each construct are above the cut-off of 0.7 and 0.5, respectively (Hair et al. 1998).

In short, our measurement model satisfies convergent validity criteria. Consequently, the variables developed can be used to test the conceptual model and its hypotheses.

We tested the conceptual model by using the Denmark, Portugal, Spain, and Sweden samples. Table 3 shows the path coefficients and t-statistics derived from bootstrapping (300 resamples), as well as the R^2 values for dependent variables.

The analysis of hypotheses was based on the examination of the standardised paths, and the variability of the dependent variable (ERP usage) through the examination of R^2 value, shown in Table 3.

In the Portuguese sample, for ERP usage complexity has a negative path (as expected) while the other five factors have positive paths and all six DOI determinants are statistically significant. Thus, H1 to H6 regarding ERP usage are supported. That is, our study finds that for Portuguese SMEs, the ERP usage variability was explained in 52.9 % through all six variables of the model, more precisely; compatibility, complexity, efficiency, best-practices, training, and competitive pressure.

In the Danish sample, five out of six DOI determinants are found to be significant for ERP usage, while training is insignificant. Compatibility was expected to be positive, but it is negative. Complexity was expected to be negative and, so it is. Therefore, H2, H3, H4, and H6 are supported, while H1 and H5 are not supported. That is, our study finds that for Danish SMEs the ERP usage variability was explained in 33.3 % through four variables of the model, more precisely; complexity, efficiency, best-practices, and competitive pressure.

In the Spanish sample, for ERP usage, although all six DOI determinants are positive, only four are found to be significant; compatibility and efficiency are non-significant. Complexity was expected to be negative but it is not, and therefore

Table 2 PLS factor loading, composite reliability and average variance extracted

Item	Portugal (N = 134)		Denmark (N = 107)		Spain (N = 424)		Sweden (N = 218)	
	Loading	t-Stat	Loading	t-Stat	Loading	t-Stat	Loading	t-Stat
CB1	0.925	7.360	0.967	219.978	0.953	178.696	0.954	190.622
CB2	0.991	12.141	0.982	454.356	0.963	231.001	0.953	200.172
CX2	0.936	97.797	0.698	13.032	0.813	10.621	0.943	13.524
CX3	0.919	93.032	0.945	62.111	0.923	24.525	0.821	7.843
EF1	0.764	32.003	0.851	31.579	0.823	36.359	0.788	8.120
EF2	0.768	26.920	0.832	66.174	0.810	34.927	0.776	36.024
EF3	0.880	61.194	0.882	83.318	0.806	26.461	0.852	65.240
BP1	0.796	33.578	0.894	114.096	0.820	39.199	0.858	55.348
BP2	0.691	18.552	0.870	67.362	0.719	18.002	0.863	65.441
BP3	0.880	60.196	0.765	32.933	0.811	33.816	0.806	35.142
TN2	0.954	269.978	0.856	99.543	0.931	148.220	0.778	40.542
TN3	0.961	345.770	0.982	80.107	0.936	148.252	0.998	4.311
CP1	0.983	161.226	0.812	14.797	0.948	193.680	0.981	1.764
CP3	0.784	23.648	0.953	136.671	0.878	61.211	0.967	120.398
ERPU2	0.894	137.936	0.878	62.487	0.900	114.363	0.671	15.328
ERPU3	0.875	84.041	0.794	44.115	0.851	62.882	0.893	112.221
Construct	**CR**	**AVE**	**CR**	**AVE**	**CR**	**AVE**	**CR**	**AVE**
Compatibility	0.958	0.919	0.974	0.950	0.957	0.917	0.953	0.909
Complexity	0.925	0.860	0.874	0.702	0.861	0.757	0.889	0.728
Efficiency	0.847	0.649	0.903	0.756	0.854	0.661	0.868	0.688
Best Practices	0.834	0.628	0.871	0.692	0.827	0.616	0.857	0.667
Training	0.957	0.917	0.895	0.812	0.931	0.871	0.739	0.613
Comp. Pressure	0.882	0.791	0.913	0.839	0.910	0.835	0.814	0.693
ERP usage	0.878	0.782	0.835	0.718	0.868	0.767	0.886	0.796

Table 3 Path values of European SMEs

Hypothesis	Portugal		Denmark		Spain		Sweden	
	Path	t-stat*	Path	t-stat*	Path	t-stat*	Path	t-stat*
H1 compatibility	**0.386**	7.501	**−0.374**	14.776	0.068	1.939	**0.152**	4.297
H2 complexity	**−0.199**	8.034	**−0.109**	3.227	**0.150**	6.553	−0.010	0.377
H3 efficiency	**0.178**	7.543	**0.182**	9.101	0.055	1.670	**0.162**	5.299
H4 best-practices	**0.260**	9.856	**0.370**	11.186	**0.161**	4.547	**0.173**	5.299
H5 training	**0.146**	4.845	0.000	0.006	**0.212**	7.266	0.032	0.370
H6 competitive pressure	**0.123**	4.845	**0.152**	6.103	**0.288**	9.704	**0.370**	16.142
ERP usage (R^2)	52.9 %		33.3 %		52.0 %		42.4 %	

* t-statistics values greater than 1.982 are significant at $p < 0.05$, path value in bold is statistically significant

only H4, H5, and H6 are supported. That is, for Spanish firms, best-practices, training, and competitive pressure explain the variability of ERP usage in 52.0 %.

In the Swedish sample, four out of six DOI determinants are statistically significant; complexity and training are not significant. Thus, H1, H3, H4, and H6 are supported, while H2 and H5 are not supported. That is, our study finds that for Swedish SMEs the ERP usage variability was explained in 42.4 % through four variables of the model, more precisely; compatibility, efficiency, best-practices, and competitive pressure.

5 Discussion

Analysing the data from a different angle, it can be suggested that competitive pressure and best-practices are important factors for ERP usage for all countries. The underlying rationale for this would be that competition drives SMEs regardless of cultural differences or management practices. That is, in order to pursue a competitive advantage, SMEs use ERP "as is", with embedded best-practices. Contrarily to Bradford and Florin (2003), who claim that "the degree of reengineering to best practices of an ERP system will have a positive relationship with system usage", our study finds that among European SMEs the usage of ERP with best-practices (using standard protocols and few or no customisations) not only implies lower costs and risks, but also supports the belief that adopting built-in benchmarking workflows, such as management accounting and control, drives firms to use ERP as a platform to take them to the next level in terms of organizational enhancements (Buonanno et al. 2005; Quattrone and Hopper 2005). Furthermore, the urgency to level the playing field provides the focus and purpose to successfully overcome obstacles and resistance to innovation diffusion within the firm, that is, competitive pressure to adopt an ERP system "as is" (with best-practices) has a positive relationship with ERP usage.

Our study also finds that compatibility is an important factor for ERP usage in Portugal and Sweden. That is, these SMEs assess ERP compatibility with existing systems as an important determinant for ERP usage. The underlying rationale would be that certain software and hardware systems are retained and need to be integrated with the ERP system, such EDI, scanners, etc. The easier it is to integrate new IT with retained systems, the greater the chances of realising organizational benefits. Additionally, the more compatible the ERP is with remaining software and hardware, the more satisfied users will be, and consequently the more it will drive productivity (Ruivo et al. 2012a, b, c; Bradford and Florin 2003).

Moreover, our study finds that efficiency is an important factor for ERP usage in Portugal, Denmark, and Sweden. That is, these SMEs assess the ERP transactional efficiency as an important determinant for fast and real-time data, avoiding errors, higher inventories, lower profits, and non-value-added work, which has a direct impact on the decision making process and overall firm productivity (Gattiker and Goodhue 2005; Häkkinen and Hilmola 2008).

Furthermore, our study finds that complexity is an important factor for ERP usage among Portuguese, Danish and Spanish SMEs. That is, these SMEs assess system complexity as an important determinant for ERP usage, since characteristics such as familiarity with ERP reduce worries about manipulating the system in effective ways and obtaining worth from it. The underlining rationale would be that these SMEs perceive that adopting an ERP which is complicated to use will limit the capacity to realise its full benefits, and so its diffusion leads to resistance, which in turns leads to lower satisfaction and system performance (Bradford and Florin 2003).

In addition, our study finds that training is an important factor for ERP usage among Portuguese and Spanish SMEs. That is, these SMEs assess training as an important determinant of ERP usage. In connection with users trained through key-users and/or help-on-line tools, both are important drivers for ERP usage in both shakedown and post-implementation phases (Nicolaou 2004a, b; Nicolaou and Bhattacharya 2006). In line with Hakkinen and Hilmola (2008), poor helpdesk support and training (to reduce system complexity and create user skills), and customisations were the main barriers to best possible use of the ERP.

5.1 Academic and Managerial Implications

The results presented above have several important implications for the academic community. Through our empirical study we have demonstrated support for theoretical arguments claiming that DOI explains ERP usage among SMEs. Unlike the typical focus on ERP adoption reported in the literature, this study moves IS research beyond the dichotomous "adoption versus non-adoption". The framework presented could be used by other researchers for studying technology usage. Unlike earlier literature on SMEs, this is the first empirical study on differences and similarities in ERP usage among European SMEs.

The study shows that system compatibility is perceived as an important facilitator for ERP usage among Portuguese and Swedish SMEs, while it is an inhibitor for Danish firms. While system complexity is perceived as an important facilitator for Portuguese and Danish SMEs, it is an inhibitor for Spanish firms. It is also found that transactional efficiency is perceived as an important facilitator for Portuguese, Danish, and Swedish SMEs, and user training is perceived as an important facilitator only for Portuguese and Spanish firms. Moreover, best-practices and competitive pressure are perceived as important facilitators for ERP usage in all countries.

Our results have several important implications for management. They offer a useful framework for managers to assess both the organizational and technological conditions under which ERP is being adopted by Danish, Portuguese, Spanish, and Swedish SMEs. ERP vendors and providers of ERPs will gain a better understanding of what organizations experience about ERP usage. Those organizations that have not yet decided to adopt ERP will gain knowledge on the post-adoption of an ERP system.

5.2 Limitations and Future Work

The impact measures were subjective in the sense that they were based on Likert-scale responses provided by managers of SMEs. While we have taken care to assess potential biases inherently associated with such data, it would have been desirable to have more objective measures of impact. That is, although there probably is a relationship between firm size and both the countries and skill levels of users, the current use measures are only a proxy for ERP usage. Furthermore, our sample may represent advanced ERP firm users in each country rather than a representative sample. Therefore, a more complete test of the process model would require more comprehensive, longitudinal data or in depth case studies (Nicolaou and Bhattacharya 2006), and in this way reduce any misunderstandings of the questionnaire items method. Moreover, although our study reveals evidence that the importance for different determinants regarding usage varies across countries, we cannot speak empirically about the issue of whether the maturity stages play a role, nor on the effect of regions culture on ERP usage, in particular the negative path coefficient for compatibility in Denmark and complexity in Spain. An interesting alternative would be to study the maturity stages of ERP, as well as culture influences on ERP usage (Häkkinen and Hilmola 2008) among similar countries with very similar national cultures and similar ERP systems in use. Secondly, although data cover several industry types and ERP product systems, we cannot speak empirically on the issue of different industries or systems having different operating characteristics and environments, and the factors related to ERP usage may differ. Another interesting study would therefore be to compare industries and ERP products.

6 Conclusion

This chapter proposes a research model for evaluating determinants of enterprise resource planning (ERP) use among small and medium-sized enterprises (SMEs). We empirically test six determinants (compatibility, complexity, efficiency, best-practices, training and competitive pressure) based on the diffusion of innovation (DOI) literature to explain ERP usage among SMEs across four European countries. Through a structural equation modelling (SEM) on a dataset of 883 firms web-surveyed, we explore the differences and similarities in usage across Denmark, Portugal, Sweden, and Spain.

The cross-country analysis reveals that best-practices and competitive pressure are perceived as important facilitators in SMEs for ERP usage in all countries. While system compatibility is perceived as an important facilitator for Portuguese and Swedish SMEs, it is an inhibitor for Danish SMEs. System complexity is perceived as an important facilitator for Portuguese and Danish SMEs, but as an inhibitor for Spanish firms. The analysis also shows that transactional efficiency is perceived as an important facilitator for Portuguese, Danish, and Swedish SMEs, and user training is perceived as an important facilitator only for Portuguese and Spanish firms.

The fact that this research is based on a large scale survey among SMEs across European countries makes it important to understand the perceived ERP usage among SMEs, while also adding an international dimension to the diffusion of innovation literature.

The main finding is that Portuguese and Spanish SMEs show different results despite the fact that they seem to be so similar; the same result is also found between Danish and Swedish SMEs. Furthermore, an interesting finding from the study is the fact that among all four countries, SMEs, competitive pressure and best-practices are statistically significant determinants for ERP usage. From this it can be concluded that SMEs feel a need to implement ERP systems in order not to have a competitive disadvantage. It can also be concluded that they do see implementation of best-practices as potentially improving their business. This is an interesting finding that sheds some new lights into the debate whether ERP systems as such can create a competitive advantage, or if ERP systems are necessary to have in order to avoid competitive disadvantage by using ERP systems "as is", with embedded standard best-practices.

Appendix A. Items Measurements

Variable	Indicators	Literature support
Using a five-point scale, where 1 means 'low' and 5 'high', respondents were asked to rate their perception.		
Compatibility	Please rate the degree to which... CB1 ...is your ERP system compatible with others' software. CB2 ...is your ERP system compatible with others' hardware. CB3... is your ERP system compatible with others' networks*	(Bradford and Florin 2003; Elbertsen et al. 2006)
Complexity (reverse code)	According to users, please rate... CX1... how easy it is for them to learn the system* CX2 ...the intuitiveness of system CX3 ...how comfortable they feel using it	(Chang et al. 2011; Cooper and Zmud 1990; Kositanurit et al. 2006)
Efficiency	According to users, please rate the... EF1 ...effectiveness in executing repetitive tasks EF2 ...effectiveness of user interface EF3 ...speed and reliability of system	(Bendoly and Kaefer 2004; Rajagopal 2002; Gattiker and Goodhue 2005)

(continued)

(continued)

Variable	Indicators	Literature support
Best practice	According to standard ERP best practices, please rate the degree… BP1 … to which users setup the application BP2 … to which one can map workflows based on local requirements BP3 …of system adaptability to business needs	(Maguire et al. 2010; Chou and Chang 2008; Wenrich and Ahmad 2009)
Training	According to users programme training, please rate the degree of how … TN1 …was training on the system* TN2 …was their understanding of the content training material TN3 …worthy is navigating through the topics after training and applied in daily tasks	(Maguire et al. 2010; Bradford and Florin 2003; O'Leary 2000)
Competitive pressure	Please rate the degree to which … CP1 …has your firm experienced competitive pressure to use ERP? CP2 …would your firm have experienced competitive disadvantage if ERP had not been adopted?* CP3 …does the ERP usage in your firm's competitors affect your landscape market?	(Zhu and Kraemer 2005; Bradford and Florin 2003; Oliveira and Martins 2010)
ERP usage	According to ERP usage how… ERPU1 …many employees use the system daily? (#)* ERPU2 …much time per day do employees work with the system? (%) ERPU3 …many reports are generated per day? (%)	(Devaraj and Kohli 2003; Zhu and Kraemer 2005; Bradford and Florin 2003)

* CB3, CX1, TN1, CP2, and ERPU1 question-items were excluded after PLS model estimation due to low loadings

References

Bendoly, E., & Kaefer, F. (2004). Business technology complementarities: impacts of the presence and strategic timing of ERP on B2B e-commerce technology efficiencies. *Omega, 32*(5), 395–405.

Bradford, M., & Florin, J. (2003). Examining the role of innovation diffusion factors on the implementation success of enterprise resource planning systems. *International Journal of Accounting Information Systems, 4*(3), 205–225.

Buonanno, G., et al. (2005). Factors affecting ERP system adoption: A comparative analysis between SMEs and large companies. *Journal of Enterprise Information Management, 18*(1), 384–426.

Carvalho, R. A,. & Johansson, B. (2012). *Enterprise Resource Planning Systems for Small and Medium-sized Enterprises.*, in *Handbook of Research on Software Engineering and*

Productivity Technologies: Implications of Globalization. 2012, Engineering Science Reference. pp. 373–381.

Chang, H.-H., et al. (2011). *ERP Post-Implementation Learning, ERP Usage and Individual Performance Impact, in 15th Pacific Asia Conference on Information Systems*. Brisbane, Australia.

Chin, W. W., Marcolin, B. L., & Newsted, P. (2003). A partial least squares latent variable modeling approach for measuring interaction effects: Results from a Monte Carlo simulation study and an electronic-mail emotion/adoption study. *Information Systems Research, 14*(2), 189–217.

Chou, S. W., & Chang, Y. C. (2008). The implementation factors that influence the ERP (enterprise resource planning) benefits. *Decision Support Systems, 46*(1), 149–157.

Commission, E. (2011). *Annual Report on EU Small and Medium sized Enterprises 2010/2011*.

Cooper, R., & Zmud, R. (1990). Information Technology Implementation Research: A Technological Diffusion Approach. *Management Science, 3*(2), 123–139.

Davenport, T. H. (1998). Putting the enterprise into the enterprise system. *Harvard Business Review, 76*(4), 121–131.

Devaraj, S., & Kohli, R. (2003). Performance impacts of information technology: Is actual usage the missing link? *Management Science, 49*(3), 273–289.

Dillman, D. A. (2000). *Mail and internet surveys: The tailored design method* (2nd ed.). New York: Wiley.

Elbertsen, L., Benders, J., & Nijssen, E. (2006). ERP use: Exclusive or complemented? *Industrial Management and Data Systems, 106*(6), 811–824.

Gattiker, T. F., & Goodhue, D. L. (2005). What happens after ERP implementation on plant-level outcomes. *MIS Quarterly, 29*(3), 559–585.

Hair, J., et al. (1998). *Multivariate data analysis*. New Jersey: Prentice Hall.

Häkkinen, L., & Hilmola, O.-P. (2008). Life after ERP implementation: Long-term development of user perceptions of system success in an after-sales environment. *Journal of Enterprise Information Management, 21*(3), 285–310.

Klaus, H., Rosemann, M. & Guy, G. G. (2000). What is ERP? *Information Systems Frontiers, 2*, 141–162.

Kositanurit, B., Ngwenyama, O., & Osei-Bryson, K. (2006). An exploration of factors that impact individual performance in an ERP environment: An analysis using multiple analytical techniques. *European Journal of Information Systems, 15*, 556–568.

Light, B., & Papazafeiropoulou, A. (2004). *Reasons Behind ERP Package Adoption: A Diffusion of Innovations Perspective*, in *13th European Conference on Information Systems*. Turku, Filand, pp. 1062–1074.

Mabert, V., Soni, A., & Venkataramanan, M. A. (2003). The impact of organization size on enterprise resource planning (ERP) implementations in the US manufacturing sector. *Omega, 31*(1), 235–246.

Maguire, S., Ojiako, U., & Said, A. (2010). ERP implementation in Omantel: A case study. *Industrial Management and Data Systems, 110*(1), 78–92.

Nah, F., Tan, X., & The, S. H. (2004). An investigation on end-users acceptance of enterprise systems. *Information Resources Management Journal, 17*(3), 32–53.

Nicolaou, A. I. (2004a). Firm performance effects in relation to the implementation and use of enterprise resource planning systems. *Journal of Information Systems, 18*(2), 79–105.

Nicolaou, A. I. (2004b). Quality of post-implementation review for enterprise resource planning systems. *International Journal of Accounting Information Systems, 5*, 25–49.

Nicolaou, A. I., & Bhattacharya, S. (2006). Organizational performance effects of ERP systems usage: the impact of post-implementation changes. *International Journal of Accounting Information Systems, 7*(1), 18–35.

O'Leary, D. (2000). *Enterprise resource planning: Systems, life cycle, electronic commerce, and risk*. New York: Cambridge University Press.

Oliveira, T., & Martins, M. F. (2010). Understanding e-business adoption across industries in European countries. *Industrial Management and Data Systems, 110*(9), 1337–1354.

Oliveira, T., & Martins, M. F. (2011). Literature review of information technology adoption models at firm level. *The Electronic Journal Information Systems Evaluation, 14*(1), 110–121.
Quattrone, P., & Hopper, T. (2005). A 'time–space odyssey': Management control systems in two multinational organizations. *Accounting Organizations and Society, 30*(7), 735–764.
Rajagopal, P. (2002). An innovation-diffusion view of implementation of enterprise resource planning (ERP) systems and development of a research model. *Information and Management, 40*, 87–114.
Rogers, E. M. (1995). *Diffusion of innovations* (4th ed.). New York: The Free Press.
Ruivo, P., Oliveira, T., & Neto, M. (2012a). ERP Post-adoption: Use and Value–An Empirical Study on Portuguese SMEs. In *Knowledge and Technologies in Innovative Information Systems* (pp. 67–81). Berlin: Springer.
Ruivo, P., Oliveira, T., & Neto, M. (2012b). ERP use and value: Portuguese and Spanish SMEs. *Industrial Management and Data Systems, 112*(7), 1008–1025.
Ruivo, P., et al. (2012c). Determinants that influence ERP use and value: Cross-country evidence on Scandinavian and Iberian SMEs. *Procedia Technology, 5*, 354–362.
Shahin, D., & Ainin, S. (2011). The influence of organizational factors on successful ERP implementation. *Management Decision, 49*(6), 911–926.
Tornatzky, L. G., & Fleischer, M. (1990). The process of technology innovation. Lexington, MA.
Waarts, E., Van-Everdingen, Y., & Van-Hillegersberg, V. (2002). The dynamics of factors affecting the adoption of innovations. *Journal of Product Innovation Management, 19*, 412–423.
Wenrich, K., & Ahmad, N. (2009). Lessons learned during a decade of ERP experience: A case study. *International Journal of Enterprise Information Systems, 5*(1), 55–73.
Zhu, K., & Kraemer, K. L. (2005). Post-adoption variations in usage and value of e-business by organizations: Cross-country evidence from the retail industry. *Information Systems Research, 16*(1), 61–84.

ERP Implementation in an SME: A Failure Case

Eli Hustad and Dag H. Olsen

1 Introduction

This study focuses on a failed enterprise resource planning (ERP) implementation in an SME. ERP systems are integrated software solutions offered as off-the-shelf packages. ERP systems integrate information across the organization to manage organizational resources. There are several benefits of these systems: they encompass seamless information flow, provide access to real-time data, and enable process-orientation and improved communication across the enterprise (Akkermans and Van Helden 2002). When implementing an ERP system, legacy systems are normally phased out. ERP implementation projects have high organizational and technical complexity, and the human consequences and required changes in business processes are often underestimated (Volkoff et al. 2007). Implementation of ERP may require changes in the processes of a company and new routines and roles for the employees. Extensive training and preparation for these changes are often necessary to succeed. Many implementations have gone far over budget, have taken a longer time than estimated, and some have even failed (Markus and Tanis 2000).

Most large organizations have implemented an ERP system in one form or another, and a lot of ERP research has focused on complex ERP implementation processes in large organizations. In recent years, however, suppliers of ERP systems have started to pay attention to smaller businesses, and the ERP market has changed character (Van Everdingen et al. 2000). In line with this, there is a growing research interest on ERP implementation in SMEs (Haddara and Zach 2011), but there is still a paucity of research on this topic. To address this deficit, our study investigated an ERP in an SME that failed.

E. Hustad · D. H. Olsen (✉)
Department of Information Systems, University of Agder, Kristiansand, Norway
e-mail: dag.h.olsen@uia.no

E. Hustad
e-mail: eli.hustad@uia.no

J. Devos et al. (eds.), *Information Systems for Small and Medium-sized Enterprises*, Progress in IS, DOI: 10.1007/978-3-642-38244-4_11,

Small companies usually have tighter budgets for ERP implementation than large companies (Sun et al. 2005). They usually lack experience, knowledge, and skills related to implementation of ERP (Adam and O'Doherty 2000). Many SMEs have found that they obtained fewer benefits from their ERP systems than expected, something that may be due to a poor implementation phase. A failed or unexpectedly costly ERP implementation can be risky for an SME, which has limited resources. If the company chooses a system that is poorly fitted to the business's processes, this can have long-lasting consequences for the company's operations and growth (Teltumbde 2000).

Many studies have addressed the issue of critical success factors (CSFs) in ERP implementation (e.g., Somers and Nelson 2001; Finney and Corbett 2007; Moon 2007). However, there are still many unanswered questions. One important issue is how CSFs interact (Grabski and Leech 2007). We do not know how multiple CSFs interact (Grabski et al. 2011) or whether they interact in the same manner in various contexts or stages of the project.

We present an illustrative case to further our understanding of how CSFs interact. We have performed an in-depth study of an SME, which implemented an ERP that experienced severe problems. We argue that the dynamics of such factors is not well understood and need to be further researched (Grabski et al. 2011). A list of critical factors has a limited value if we do not have an appropriate understanding of how they interact and influence the implementation of the project. Providing illustrative cases helps us construct better models of the project dynamics of ERP. Such cases help us to comprehend how critical decisions and issues not appropriately dealt with may lead to ERP failure.

Our research question is:

How do CSFs in an ERP implementation project interact and lead to project failure?

We draw on the work and the propositions of CSFs in ERP implementation developed by Akkermans and Van Helden (2002) to explain our findings. Their work is presented in more detail in Sect. 2.

The paper is organized as follows. In Sect. 2, we briefly present the concepts of ERP and related research that are relevant for this study. Sect. 3 provides a description of the research site in which this research was conducted and presents our methodological approach. After that, we present our results in Sect. 4, and Sect. 5 analyses and discusses the findings. Finally, we present our conclusions and implications for further research in Sect. 6.

2 ERP and Related Research

We further elaborate on the ERP concept in this section and present relevant ERP literature. As the body of ERP research is huge, we concentrate mainly on ERP research related to CSFs identified and discussed in former research studies. We have also utilized review articles such as that of Moon (2007) who dealt with

313 articles from 79 journals in the period between January 2000 and May 2006 and looked at the ERP literature as a whole and that of Haddara and Zach (2011) who reviewed 77 articles, which focused on the ERP literature in relation to SMEs.

Klaus et al. (2000) defined an ERP system as a "comprehensive, packet-based software solution that attempts to integrate all the processes and functions within a company to create a complete overview of the enterprise from a single IT architecture". Moon (2007) defined an ERP system as an information system that is designed to integrate and optimize business processes and transactions in a company.

The objective of an ERP system is to enhance the performance of the company by integrating all business processes and data into one system, including integration of the supply chain, inventory management, management of customers' orders, accounting, and human resource management (Hong and Kim 2002; Kalling 2003). Implementing an ERP system, however, often leads to unexpected costs and problems, and may even lead to catastrophic consequences for the company. In a survey conducted in the United States, 70 % of companies believed their ERP implementation was a success. However, more than 55 % of those also admitted that the budget was exceeded during the implementation. If the budget overruns are counted as unsuccessful projects, the success rate was less than 50 % (Mabert et al. 2000).

In recent years, an increasing number of companies have acquired ERP systems. Having an ERP system no longer gives a competitive advantage. It is perceived as a necessity to remain competitive. What distinguishes the success of different companies is not really whether the company has an ERP system, but how well the ERP system suits the organizational structure and how well the organization is able to utilize the potential of the system (e.g., Teltumbde 2000).

The cost of an unsuccessful ERP implementation in an SME can be high (Sun et al. 2005). Normally, SMEs have limited financial resources and IT competencies compared to larger companies, and, therefore, ERP projects might be of higher risk (Fisher et al. 2004). SMEs may face problems with configuring ERP packages, and they often lack knowledge and experience about how to lead and organize enterprise-wide IT projects such as ERP projects. In fact, unsuccessful implementation projects in SMEs may threaten the existence of a company. Moreover, the lack of knowledge and experience with ERP systems make SMEs more dependent upon external consultants and support from vendors throughout the implementation process (Chen et al. 2008).

Several unsuccessful ERP implementations have been discussed in the literature (Ribbers and Schoo 2002; Soh et al. 2000; Willis and Willis-Brown 2002). This has led to an increasing focus on what is needed for the success of an ERP implementation. A number of CSFs have been identified to gain the abovementioned benefits (Finney and Corbett 2007; Somers and Nelson 2001, 2004). There are several obvious differences between large companies and SMEs. Therefore, it is debatable whether the same success factors are applicable to both types of firms. Loh and Koh (2004) examined the CSFs specific to SMEs. They conducted a thorough literature review and interviewed eight SMEs in the UK. They identified three critical elements—CSFs, critical people, and critical uncertainties—SMEs must consider for ERP implementation to be successful.

Markus and Tanis (2000) developed the "Enterprise System Experience Cycle," which consists of four phases: (1) the project chartering phase, which comprises investment decisions, definitions of the business case, and solution constraints; (2) the project itself, which involves configuration of the system, choosing the implementation and the rollout strategy and getting the system and end users up and running; (3) the shakedown phase, during which the system needs to be stabilized, bugs need to be eliminated, and the company must get back to normal operations as fast as possible, and (4) the onward and upward phase, which comprises maintenance of the system, user support, getting results, and upgrading decisions (Markus and Tanis 2000).

Related activities, challenges, and problems differ among these phases. Thus, it is important for a company to know what they should focus on during the different phases of the project. Problems that remain unsolved in one phase may magnify in a later phase. Somers and Nelson (2001, 2004) identified CSFs in ERP projects and also looked at the importance of different activities and players across different life cycle stages (Somers and Nelson 2004).

Building on this research, Akkermans and van Helden (2002) utilized the top ten CSFs provided by Somers and Nelson (2001) and found that several CSFs were interrelated (Akkermans and Van Helden 2002). For instance, if a project had poor top management support and weak project management, these were interrelated with other CSFs, and a vicious circle developed that created an unsuccessful outcome for the project. On the other hand, a virtuous circle of interrelated CSFs developed if commitment from top management was present and a good project team was established. These factors caused positive attitudes in the organization. Good communication and collaboration patterns among the employees developed, and, consequently, these improved the outcome of the implementation project. They developed some propositions based upon these findings, with one major proposition called P2. "These CSFs are causally linked in such a way that they reinforce each other in the same direction, hence leading to either vicious or virtuous cycles of ERP implementation performance" (ibid p. 44).

We utilize the propositions developed by Akkermans and van Helden (2002) as a point of departure to understand the dynamic of interrelated factors that played out in the ERP implementation context under study.

3 Research Methodology

In this section, we provide reasons for selecting this case study and introduce the research site. In addition, we provide a description of our methodological approach.

3.1 Research Site

We selected this organization (ABC—pseudonym) because we wanted to understand more about why ERP implementations in SMEs can go wrong. This company experienced many problems during its ERP project, and the implementation went far over budget. ABC had a difficult relationship with the consulting company, and there was great dissatisfaction among the employees during the course of the project. Our goal was to understand the pitfalls this company experienced. We came into the company in the stabilization phase, which turned out to be quite problematic. The employees were willing to give interviews, and they answered all questions in an open manner. Thus, they revealed quite sensitive data, which is not always easy for outsiders to collect (Walsham 1995). The case study provided opportunities to identify factors and yielded a better understanding of the dynamics of such complex ERP projects. In addition, we obtained insight into the roles of different employees and externals in the project team and how they experienced the process from different standpoints.

The company ABC is an SME with approximately 90 employees and revenues of approximately 300 million NOK (€40 million). It is located in southern Norway and sells various office supplies through stores and the web. It has sales offices in three different locations. ABC decided to replace its existing ERP system in 2008. It has outgrown the previous ERP system and needed to improve its logistics operations. A consulting company was involved in the project. In the middle of June 2009, the system was implemented.

3.2 Research Method

We wished to gain a deeper understanding of the source of ERP failure at ABC. We chose a case study approach to obtain a comprehensive in-depth understanding of the failed ERP implementation. A case study is valuable for revealing the uniqueness of one setting and for illuminating both the historical background and the internal contextual characteristics of the case (Yin 2003; Stake 2000). The single case study method also generates knowledge in the form of *thick* descriptions (Ryle 1949). A second reason for choosing the case study approach was that we felt the existing body of literature did not adequately describe the phenomenon under investigation (Eisenhardt 1989). Finally, the case study provides a more comprehensive in-depth analysis of one organization in which all the specificities that are unique to that organization are more carefully investigated. Finally, in interpretive IS research, it is important to understand the context of the information system and the interaction between the system and the context (Walsham 1993). This was the case in this study, where we wanted to understand the socio-technical dynamics and complexity of the ERP project.

The process of data collection and analysis proceeded in accordance with the interpretive research tradition (Walsham 2006). We conducted face-to-face interviews using a semi-structured interview guide with the employees and key personnel involved within the project, in addition to the top manager, the branch manager, and the external consultants. Table 1 lists the interviewees and their role in the organization and/or the project. The participants from accounting and logistics participated in group interviews (two interviews with the accountants and one interview with the employees from logistics).

The project team leader (not listed in the table) who was responsible for the project from the beginning left the firm in the summer of 2010. We contacted him, but he did not wish to participate in this investigation.

The top manager was interviewed several times. In addition, we attended a workshop for SMEs that focused on ERP implementation challenges. At this workshop, the top manager gave a talk about the situation and the problems in ABC. This talk created interesting discussions among the audience.

The interviews lasted approximately 1 h, were digitally recorded, and fully transcribed. The workshop lasted 2 h. This was also digitally recorded and is part of the data material. In addition, we used secondary material such as the project report developed from the preimplementation phase.

After transcription, the empirical material was further systemized and reduced (Miles and Huberman 1994). The meaning was then condensed by compressing long statements into briefer statements to obtain the main sense of the text. This also allowed us to create themes by interpreting the natural meaning units (Kvale and Brinkmann 2009). We combined existing theories and concepts from the

Table 1 The participants in this study and their roles in the project or organization

Participants and roles	Description
Top manager	Situated at the research site location, CEO of the whole company
Branch manager	Head manager at the main location—the research site
IS employee #1	Responsible for communication between the consultants and the users during the project, participant in the project team
IS employee #2	Logistics' manager, participant the project team, left the company in 2011
Employee #1 from the logistics' department	Employee working in the inventory department
Employee #2 from the logistics' department	Employee working in the inventory department, later logistics' manager taking over after IS employee 1 in 2011
Accountant #1	Working in the accounting department
Accountant #2	Working in the accounting department
Accountant #3	Working in the accounting department
Accountant #4	Working in the accounting department
Consultant #1	Responsible for the preimplementation of the project and the support function after the implementation, participant in the project team
Consultant #2	Consultant at the main location, responsible for the configuration and customization, participant in the project team

literature (e.g., ERP implementation literature, critical success factors and their interrelations) with empirical findings to obtain a broader understanding of critical issues during the ERP implementation in this SME and how CSFs were interrelated.

4 Results

This chapter describes the results of the interviews. We first describe the pre-implementation project and then the main findings.

The project commenced in the summer 2008 when ABC realized that it had out-grown its previous ERP system and decided to look for a new ERP system. The flow of goods had increased significantly, and ABC needed to become more efficient. The CEO noted that "We move ten times as much goods as we did for the same revenue 15 years ago". They evaluated four vendors and systems and selected the system and vendor by the end of 2008. It was a mid-market solution from a Scandinavian vendor.

ABC realized that it did not have enough competence internally to implement the system and looked for a consultancy company to lead the project. It decided to employ the skills of a large consultancy company, which was experienced in the chosen ERP system. The size of the consultancy company was deemed to be important to secure long-term access to the ERP competence. The consultancy company stated that it was very proficient on project management and would lead the process the whole way. ABC checked with previous customers and invited the consultancy company to tender for the job.

4.1 The Pre-implementation Project

The pre-implementation project was run in February 2009 by a group of consultants and department managers from ABC. They studied the business processes in ABC, and made a requirement analysis. One of the consultants was then assigned the main responsibility for the pre-implemention project and was located in ABC during the implementation project.

The CFO/COO was appointed the internal project leader and the spokesperson for the employees in the accounting department. The head of the logistics' department was also involved and represented the employees in the logistics' department. The CEO then withdrew from the process. He received the pre-implementation project report and found that it addressed the needs of the various departments appropriately. Shortly after the pre-implementation project, ABC advised the consultants to proceed with the project. ABC decided that the go-live date would be June 15, 2009, and it asserted that the system would be well under way by August when the busy season started.

The pre-implementation project was received positively by most managers. One of the regional managers commented that "the experience with the pre-implementation project was very positive. I felt that the employees we [recruited to the pre-implementation project] did a very thorough job, and we set aside enough time … to bring forward all elements and needs".

General employees were more critical. One criticism was that only managers were involved in the pre-implementation project group and that their voices were not heard in this process. Instead, department managers represented their departments and spoke on their behalf. One of the employees in the accounting department noted that the people in the project team were probably not aware of the extent of employees' work duties.

The go-live date was discussed thoroughly in the pre-implementation project. The issue was whether it should be before or after the summer. The CEO noted several benefits of going live before the summer, such as there being less activity during this period, and the CEO suggested that it would be easier to correct errors during this period. He further added that "implementing in August won't work".

Many of the respondents were more critical of the go-live date, especially end users. Several end users believed that the holiday would interfere with user training and had requested that the go-live date should be moved forward. Many employees went on holiday around the go-live date and were not proficient enough in using the ERP system when they returned from holiday. Consultant #1 commented that "what was unfortunate… was that some [employees] went right out on holiday. One [employee] went on holiday almost at the time we started. When she returned, the others were on holiday, and she was alone. It goes without saying that this will fail".

4.2 Project Management

Most of the respondents noted that the project management was poor and that this was a major reason for the problems that occurred in the project. Several aspects of project was poor. Firstly, the project leadership and planning was rather poor. ABC had given the consultancy company the responsibility for the project management. One of the IS employees (IS employee #1) noted that: "We wanted the consultancy company to come in and lead the project. That was [the service] that they sold". The branch manager commented that: "We buy a service, since this is not a topic [where we are competent]. As long as we [kept paying] more consultant hours, I feel that the responsibility lies fully with the consultancy company". He also recognized that they should have taken action sooner: "Of course we gave notice that we were not happy with things, but we should have painted it big and black on the wall".

Secondly, It was evident from the interviews that the project team lacked a strong leader during the process. Both the CEO and several of the employees noted that the CEO should have taken charge. Several of the respondents commented that the appointed internal project leader was not up to the task. IS employee #1 commented that "... if the CEO had [been the project leader], I believe that things would have been quite different. The CEO has been involved in such a transition earlier. I think that he [the CEO] would have taken action more firmly than the internal project leader. He [the internal project leader] was just too gentle".

The consultancy company admitted that their project management was not good enough, but it claimed that ABC was also to blame. It claimed that it recommended that ABC hire an external (third-party) project leader. The CEO dismissed this claim. One of the consultants (consultant #1) commented that: "We should have been firmer with [the CEO] and said that in such a large project one MUST have an external project leader (...) You will get this back eventually, because you have someone who looks after everything all the way".

Thirdly, communication and coordination was poor. Many of the employees commented that the communication with and between the consultants did not work properly. ABC addressed these problems several times and was promised that it would be better. According to the respondents, it did not improve. The branch manager noted that "Each consultant was perceived as competent on his part, but [the projects] lacked coordination and an active project leader who assured the quality along the way". IS employee #1 commented that "Several [consultants] worked [in parallel] and solved their tasks to finish fast, but they did not [communicate with each other] what this could imply. They killed each other's codes. We were set back all the way".

The consultancy company for its part felt that the customer's company had problems with its communication and project organization. One of the consultants noted that employees were supposed to route their requests for customization to IS employee #1, who would then forward it to Consultant #2. As noted above, the CEO had decided that there would be minimal customization. The assigned consultant still received many requests for customization of various parts of the ERP system.

Another problem was that many promises and messages were only given orally. This made it difficult to keep a record of what had been said and done. Both parties admitted that they should have documented things better.

4.3 Customization of the ERP System

Although the CEO had clearly stated that there would be as little customization as possible, the consultants made many adjustments to the system. Many of the adjustments were not necessary, for example, minor customizations of the screen images. It was noted that neither the consultant nor ABC was firm enough when employees requested adjustments. Consultant #1 felt that the CEO's requirement for minimum customization was not well understood by the employees: "It was not well enough grounded [among the employees] that we will change our work processes, instead of [having the system] adapt to us".

As we have noted above, IS employee #1 was supposed to route the requests for customization. This clearly did not work properly, and it led to disorder and many unnecessary adjustments. Moreover, no one had an overview of which adjustments had been done. IS employee #2 commented that: "Eventually, several [employees] had a dialogue directly with the consultant. At the end, I did not know what had been done and what had not been done".

4.4 Training and Use of the ERP System

The user training in itself was perceived as fairly good among employees and managers, but evidently there were some problems. One issue was that there were still done adjustments to the system on the day of the course. The two consultants were located in different places and did not communicate very well. This led to problems for several of the employees.

Another problem was the timing of the user training. It was right before most of the employees had their summer holiday.

> Things were in a hurry. Go-live was set to June 15, and then they pushed the training just before that. And then people were about to leave for holiday. Then the last adjustments needed to be done. Then people came back from holiday and were supposed to use a system in which they had just a few hours of training. (IS employee #2).

It was evident from the responses that the training was fairly basic, just enough to get a feel for the system. The CEO noted that this was not sufficient, and the company provided a new round of courses after the go-live. Some employees commented that the training had little focus on helping the users understand the system. They had little overview beyond their role, and, therefore, limited understanding of how their processes interacted with those of the other employees. The CEO commented that

> the people who process the receipts and do the accounting need to know why they do the things they do. They need to understand the connections between various parts of the system (…) they did not understand [anything]. One of the users, who has been our bedrock in accounting through all the years and who is very concerned about order and precision said that she had never had these explained to her, noting that she had asked and asked but got no explanation. This makes me genuinely sad.

Several of the respondents noted that there was not sufficient support during the training period. One consultant was assigned to this task, but he was fairly busy with other tasks. The users were, therefore, waiting for help and often resorted to workarounds. Several of the managers noted that the dissatisfaction and the resentment grew among users in this phase. One of the employees noted that "[that summer] was simply the worst I have ever experienced in a job". There were also plans for arranging super-user training for two of the managers, but that was never done.

As we have seen above, there were many problems with the system during and after the go-live period. These led to many of the users resorting to workarounds to get their work done. The employees found it difficult to follow the specified routines in the beginning, also taking into account that many employees were on holiday. One of the people in accounting stated that: "In logistics, things had to be done manually instead of in the system". She also noted that it was not taken into account that users needed to understand other parts of the system: "one was not supposed to think of what the others [users] were doing".

The respondents commented that this situation arose because it was difficult for the employees to perform their tasks when there was chaos in the data and the system. There was also a lot of frustration among the employees over the way the implementation process was handled. Many of the numbers in the ERP system were wrong, and this led to distrust in the system and the figures. One of the employees in accounting noted that: "Eventually we had to run things manually and drop the system from time to time, because it did not work. We felt fairly bad about it".

The internal project leader also used workarounds. Since the routines were not working properly, the accounting numbers did not match. There were errors up to 1.5 million NOK (€200,000). He resolved this by distributing the accounting errors manually among the departments.

4.5 Post-implementation Problem Resolution

The user support was very weak. As noted previously, the consultant in charge of the user support (Consultant #2) was very occupied with coding in the system. This led to long response times. The consultant was under a lot of stress. One of the employees expressed that: "I do not understand why any additional people from the consultancy company did not come".

The CFO/COO left ABC in June 2010, and the CEO took charge of responsibility for the ERP project. He soon discovered that there were serious problems with the accounting data. Work routines were also not performed correctly, which led to more errors in the transaction and accounting data. As a result, the annual statements for 2009 were incorrectly posted. The CEO fixed the accounting errors by distributing the missing amounts to the various departments.

The CEO and the consulting company then took control of the situation and brought in new and more competent consultants. The new consultants were able to fix the errors in a reasonable time. They also established a phone support service to alleviate the users' problems. These actions were enough to bring the situation under control.

5 Discussion

This ERP implementation project experienced severe problems. When we relate the results above to the corresponding CSFs in Finney and Corbett (2007), we find that most of these CSFs were involved. We will discuss the most prominent ones for this case below.

We conjecture from the results above that some of the CSFs were reasonably well handled, such as *selection of ERP*, *build a business case*, *legacy system consideration* and *IT infrastructure*. Two CSFs were well planned and handled from the start, but did not work out right during the implementation, *consultant selection and relationship* and *vanilla ERP*. We conjecture that the management did a good job in selecting consultants and establish a good relationship to the consulting company. However, it turned out that the consultants were not proficient enough, the relationship suffered and the ERP implementation did not become as "Vanilla" as it was supposed to be.

The results showed that a number of CSFs were improperly handled. Most significantly were *top management commitment and support*, *project champion*, *Implementation strategy and timeframe*, *project management* and *balanced team*. We argue that particularly three CSFs—*top management commitment and support, project management,* and *consultant selection and relationship*—had severe implications for how the implementation and the post-implementation unfolded, and thus interacted with other CSFs. We will discuss this in more detail.

The managers commended the pre-implementation project and asserted that it was fairly good. However, other employees were more critical of the pre-implementation project and asserted that it did not address the complexity of the work processes appropriately.

The problems started when the CEO decided not to lead or take part in the project team. This was in spite of the fact that he had experience with several IS implementation projects, one of them a recent CRM implementation project. Instead, he decided that the CFO/COO would be the project leader. He was given the responsibility of heading the project and being the spokesman for the employees in the accounting department. The CEO then withdrew from the project. This was the first major mistake in this project. The project leader was clearly not capable of leading the project. This is a very demanding role in such a project and would require significant understanding of IS and ERP implementation projects. Clearly, the project leader lacked these skills. In addition, we conjecture that he covered up the errors, and, thus, prevented appropriate actions being taken at an earlier stage. This is a case of "face-saving behavior" (Keil 1995). Thus, two CSFs were improperly handled from the start, *top management commitment and support and project management.*

The second major problem started when ABC hired a consultancy company to aid the implementation of the project. We conjectured that the company did a good job in hiring a proficient consultant company. However, the consultants who were assigned to the task were clearly not proficient. As the project progressed, this manifested itself in a number of problems. The consultants took charge of the projects, and the internal project leader played a secondary role. The skills of the project management and the project team were, thus, inferior from the start. The consultancy company claimed that it advised ABC to hire a third-party consultant to lead the project to ensure an experienced and professional leader. In contrast, the CEO of ABC claimed that this was never brought up. Thus, we conjecture that *consultant selection and relationship* were well handled from the start, but that they nevertheless performed poorly on this CSF when they failed to monitor the skills and the quality of the work of the assigned consultants.

The poor project team skills led to a chain of events and problems. First, there was poor communication between the project team and the employees, and the employees were, in general, not much involved in the process. Secondly, the communication and the coordination between the two consultants were not appropriate. They were also located in different places. Thirdly, there were many oral agreements and messages that were not documented and communicated to others. The communication and the coordination problems led to a lack of documentation on what had been said and done. The communication problem was raised, but according to the respondents, it did not improve. There was chaos in the dialogue between the employees and the consultants, with several employees having a direct dialogue, despite the fact that employees' requests were supposed to go through the internal IS employees. We therefore assess that the CSFs *change management, troubleshooting/ crisis management* and *communication plan* were not handled appropriately.

Fourthly, even though the CEO had decided that there would be minimal customization, the consultants did many customizations. This was based on requests from the users. Clearly this should have been avoided. Thus, the CSF *vanilla ERP* was properly handled by the CEO, but the consultants did not comply. Fifthly, it transpired that ground data had been improperly washed. Thus, the CSF *data conversion and integrity* were not handled properly.

Sixthly, the system was not fully configured at the time of the go-live. We conjecture that the consultants wasted a lot of time on poor communication and coordination and on unnecessary customization, time that might have been better spent on quality assuring the system configuration and washing the ground data. Thus, the CSF *system testing* was not appropriate.

Several factors contributed to poor-quality users' training. First, it was decided that the go-live date would be June 15. This was a quiet season, and it was asserted that the system would be running well and the users would be experienced when the busy season started in August. It transpired that this was not an optimal time because it was right before the holiday season, and some of the employees went on holiday immediately after the user training course. Many employees felt that this undermined the benefit of the training. Secondly, it was also evident from the interviews that the user training was not comprehensive enough. Thirdly, there was insufficient user support during the training period. Fourthly, the super-users never received the super-user training course. All these mistakes led to the users having a poor command and overview of the system. Thus, the CSFs *training and job redesign* and *empowered decision makers* were not properly addressed.

The poor user command of the system and the improper configuration and errors in the data had further implications, causing the users to apply manual workarounds to get their work done. This further compromised the data and led to errors in the accounts and the financial statements. However, it was not until the next year that the CEO discovered the extent of the problems.

We conjecture that in this case, the inappropriate handling of key success factors, in particular, *top management support, project management,* and *use of consultants*, led to a chain of adverse events and problems.

ABC was clearly not competent enough to run the implementation of the project and did not manage to assure the quality of the external consultants. The problems encountered and the extra resources needed for the consultants meant that the project ultimately cost three times the initial budget. The project was also very stressful for the organization and the employees. Key personnel in management and IS left ABC after the implementation. Therefore, it is fair to characterize this as a failed project, even if the system was eventually running well by the end of 2010.

6 Conclusions and Implications

This study illustrates how the inappropriate handling of key CSFs, in particular, *top management support, project management*, and *use of consultants*, had severe ramifications for the implementation project. This led to stress on the organization and a significant cost overrun.

This case study contributes to the literature on ERP implementation in SMEs. In particular, it contributes to our understanding of the dynamics of CSFs in ERP implementation projects. We also believe that it can be valuable in a teaching setting. Such teaching cases will help students assess the complexity and challenges of ERP implementations.

This was an exploratory study and was conducted in one organizational context only. Therefore, it has a number of limitations, which provide possibilities for future research. We should investigate more contexts to generate a more complete understanding of how CSFs interact and influence other parameters in an ERP implementation project. We see a need for further research into the dynamics and social mechanisms in ERP implementation projects, and their implications for the success of such projects.

Failed ERP cases are little documented in the IS research literature. Such cases can yield important insight into the complexity of ERP implementation projects and further our understanding of what may take place if CSFs are not handled properly. One reason for the scarcity of failed cases may be that the data may be quite sensitive, and, therefore, not easily available. Success stories will only tell the story about what worked, and not give us insights into the antecedents of failed projects. We conjecture that there should be more studies of failed ERP implementations. The findings from such case studies should then be addressed in quantitative studies to generate generalizable results.

It is also evident that in the case of the internal project leader, we have a case of face-saving behavior (Keil 1995). We believe that such behavior can be detrimental to ERP implementation projects. Further research, perhaps from a socio-technical perspective, should address to what extent this is a problem and how such behavior can be avoided.

In relation to the issue of consultant's competence, skills, and experience, we speculate that SMEs may be perceived by the consultancy companies as being less demanding and less important customers. Therefore, SMEs may receive less attention and be assigned less experienced consultants. Furthermore, it may be that SMEs are used as a training ground for junior consultants. Further research should investigate whether this is the case.

We believe that this case can serve as an illustrative example for other SMEs of how initial mismanagement of an ERP implementation project may have serious ramifications for many aspects of the project. It can serve to inform other SMEs of the pitfalls in such projects and highlight the importance of selecting proficient implementation consultants.

References

Adam, F., & O'Doherty, P. (2000). Lessons from enterprise resource planning implementations in Ireland—towards smaller and shorter ERP projects. *Journal of Information Technology, 15*(4), 305–316.

Akkermans, H., & Van Helden, K. (2002). Vicious and virtuous cycles in ERP implementation: A case study of interrelations between critical success factors. *European Journal of Information Systems, 11*(1), 35–46.

Chen, R. S., Sun, C. M., Helms, M. M., & Jih, W. J. (2008). Role negotiation and interaction: An exploratory case study of the impact of management consultants on ERP system implementation in SMEs in Taiwan. *Information Systems Management, 25*(2), 159–173.

Eisenhardt, K. M. (1989). Building theories from case study research. *The Academy of Management Review, 14*(4), 532–550.

Finney, S., & Corbett, M. (2007). ERP implementation: A compilation and analysis of critical success factors. *Business Process Management Journal, 13*(3), 329–347.

Fisher, D. M., Kiang, M. Y., Fisher, S. A., & Chi, R. T. (2004). Evaluating mid-level ERP software. *Journal of Computer Information Systems, 45*(1), 38–46.

Grabski, S. V., & Leech, S. A. (2007). Complementary controls and ERP implementation success. *International Journal of Accounting Information Systems, 8*(1), 17–39.

Grabski, S. V., Leech, S. A., & Schmidt, P. J. (2011). A review of ERP research: A future agenda for accounting information systems. *Journal of Information Systems, 25*(1), 37–78.

Haddara, M., & Zach, O. (2011). *ERP systems in SMEs: A literature review, Proceedings of the 44th Annual Hawaii International Conference on System Sciences* (*HICSS*), Hawaii, Jan 4–7, IEEE Computer Society, Los Alamitos, CA.

Hong, K. K., & Kim, Y. G. (2002). The critical success factors for ERP implementation: An organizational fit perspective. *Information and Management, 40*(1), 25–40.

Kalling, T. (2003). ERP systems and the strategic management processes that lead to competitive advantage. *Information Resources Management Journal, 16*(4), 46–67.

Keil, M. (1995). *Escalation of commitment in information systems development: A comparison of three theories. Proceedings of the Annual meeting of the Academy of Management* (Vol. 1995, pp. 348–352).
Klaus, H., Rosemann, M., & Gable, G. G. (2000). What is ERP? *Information Systems Frontiers, 2*(2), 141–162.
Kvale, S., & Brinkmann, S. (2009). *Interviews: Learning the craft of qualitative research interviewing*. Los Angeles: Sage.
Loh, T. C., & Koh, S. C. L. (2004). Critical elements for a successful enterprise resource planning implementation in small-and-medium-sized enterprises. *International Journal of Production Research, 42*(17), 3433–3455.
Mabert, V. A., Soni, A., & Venkataramanan, M. A. (2000). Enterprise resource planning survey of us manufacturing firms. *Production and Inventory Management Journal, 41*(2), 52–60.
Markus, M. L., & Tanis, C. (2000). The enterprise systems experience—from adoption to success. In R.W. Zmud (Ed.), *Framing the domains of it research: Projecting the future. Through the past.* (pp. 173–207). Cincinatti OH: Pinaflex Educational Resources.
Miles, M. B., & Huberman, A. M. (1994). *Qualitative data analysis: An expanded sourcebook.* Thousand Oaks, California: Sage.
Moon, Y. B. (2007). Enterprise resource planning (ERP): A review of the literature. *International Journal of Management and Enterprise Development, 4*(3), 235–264.
Ribbers, P. M. A., & Schoo, K. C. (2002). Program management and complexity of ERP implementations. *Engineering Management Journal, 14*(1), 45–52.
Ryle, G. (1949). *The concept of mind.* London: Penguin Books, Ltd.
Soh, C., Kien, S. S., & Tay-Yap, J. (2000). Enterprise resource planning: Cultural fits and misfits: Is ERP a universal solution? *Communications of ACM, 43*(4), 47–51.
Somers, T. M., & Nelson, K. G. (2001). *The impact of critical success factors across the stages of enterprise resource planning implementations. Proceedings of the 34th Hawaii International Conference on Systems Sciences (HICSS-3).* Maui: Hawaii.
Somers, T. M., & Nelson, K. G. (2004). A taxonomy of players and activities across the ERP project life cycle. *Information and Management, 41*(3), 257–278.
Stake, R. S. (2000). Case studies. In N. K. Denzin & Y. S. Lincoln (Eds.), *Handbook of qualitative research* (pp. 435-454), Thousand Oaks, California: Sage Publications, Inc.
Sun, A. Y. T., Yazdani, A., & Overend, J. D. (2005). Achievement assessment for enterprise resource planning (ERP) system implementations based on critical success factors (csfs). *International Journal of Production Economics, 98*(2), 189–203.
Teltumbde, A. (2000). A framework for evaluating ERP projects. *International Journal of Production Research, 38*(17), 4507–4520.
Van Everdingen, Y., Van Hillegersberg, J., & Waarts, E. (2000). ERP adoption by European mid-size companies. *Communications of ACM, 43*(4), 27–31.
Volkoff, O., Strong, D. M., & Elmes, M. B. (2007). Technological embeddedness and organizational change. *Organization Science, 18*(5), 832–848.
Walsham, G. (1993). *Interpreting information systems in organisations*. Chichester: Wiley.
Walsham, G. (1995). Interpretive case studies in is research: Nature and method. *European Journal of Information Systems, 4*(2), 74–81.
Walsham, G. (2006). Doing interpretive research. *European Journal of Information Systems, 15*(3), 320–330.
Willis, T. H., & Willis-Brown, A. H. (2002). Extending the value of ERP. *Industrial Management and Data Systems, 102*(1), 35–38.
Yin, R. K. (2003). *Case study research: Design and methods*. Thousand Oaks, CA: Sage Publications.

Understanding Marketing Information Systems from the Perspective of SMEs: Reviewing the Literature

Canan Eryigit

1 Introduction

Marketing is the activity, set of institutions, and processes for creating, communicating, delivering, and exchanging offerings that have value for customers, clients, partners, and society at large.[1] In order to create value for these parts a company has to match its marketing offerings with the marketing environment. Therefore, companies try to identify different market segments and develop appropriate marketing programs for their targeted segments. This requires systematic collection, analysis and use of information. In other words, companies need a system providing information that will help marketing managers to make better decisions about target marketing and planning, implementing and controlling of marketing mix elements (four Ps: product, pricing, placement, and promotion). Information systems and information technologies can help managers towards this direction through offering new methods and tools with computer technology for managing marketing information (Gounaris et al. 2007). Hence, marketing information systems (MKIS) has been used as a technique for applying data processing technologies to marketing specific decisions since 1960s (Hess and Rubin 2004). There has been increasing attention to the use of information systems to support marketing decisions by scholars as well.

Use of MKIS is particularly beneficial for SMEs. This is because marketing problems have been accepted as one of the most critical problems in SMEs and they can improve their marketing skills with appropriate information systems. Hence, providing theoretical and empirical knowledge on applications of IS in marketing for SMEs may be regarded as an essential topic. Although, it is generally accepted that the basic principles of marketing are applicable to both large

[1] Approved definition of marketing by the American Marketing Association Board of Directors.

C. Eryigit (✉)
Department of Business Administration, Hacettepe University, Ankara, Turkey
e-mail: canandemirsoy@yahoo.com; canand@hacettepe.edu.tr

J. Devos et al. (eds.), *Information Systems for Small and Medium-sized Enterprises*,
Progress in IS, DOI: 10.1007/978-3-642-38244-4_12,

and small businesses (Simpson et al. 2006) significant differences have been found between large and small businesses (Walsh and Lipinski 2009). Therefore, marketing for SMEs has been a significant research area for more than 20 years (Daša 2009). From this point, this study aims to examine current literature on marketing information systems in SMEs.

The rest of the study is organized as follows. At first, conceptualization of marketing information systems is provided. Then, application of information systems in various marketing related fields are examined from the point of view of large companies and SMEs. The last part reviews the literature on marketing information systems in SMEs for the last decade including methodology, results, research patterns and future research areas.

2 Marketing Information Systems

Marketing information system is "a structured, interacting complex of persons, machines and procedures designed to generate an orderly flow of pertinent information collected from both intra- and extra-firm sources, for use as the bases for decision-making in specified responsibility areas of marketing management" (Brien and Stafford 1968). In other words, it is "a set of procedures and methods for the regular, planned collection, analysis, and presentation of information for use in making marketing decisions" (Cox and Good 1967).

Marketing information systems includes assessing information needs, developing and distributing information. MKIS, at first, assess information needs of marketing managers. Then, based on the information needs, MKIS develop information from environment including target markets, marketing channels, competitors, publics, and macro-environmental factors. Subsequently, this information is distributed to marketing managers (Hess and Rubin 2004). Therefore, MKIS along with marketing communication may be regarded as a link between marketing managers and the market.

Marketing information systems can be classified into two subsystems as support systems and operating systems. Support systems generate and manipulate data whereas operating systems use the data to help planning and controlling marketing activities. Operating systems are divided into three subsystems as control, planning, and basic research. Control Systems provide monitoring of trends, problems, and marketing opportunities. Planning Systems simulate possible outcomes of alternate plans so that the manager can make a better decision. Basic Research Systems develop and test decision rules and cause-and-effect relations (Cox and Good 1967). Other information systems that are applicable to marketing is composed of operational transaction processing systems (TPS), management information systems (MIS), decision support systems (DSS), and expert systems (ES) (Talvinen 1995).

TPS or data-processing systems are "computerized information systems developed to process large amounts of data for routine business transactions"

(Kendall and Kendall 1992). Management information systems (MIS) provide reports to managers about the organization's current and past performance. Generally, MIS obtain the information from TPS, modify it as a routine summary or reports, and present it to management (Talvinen 1995). Marketing decision support systems (MDSS) is "a coordinated collection of data, systems, tools, and techniques with supporting software and hardware by which an organization gathers and interprets relevant information from business and environment and turns it into a basis for marketing action" (Little 1979). Expert systems (ES) assist in decision-making situations by solving problems that normally require human expertise (Talvinen 1995).

3 Applications of Marketing Information Systems

3.1 *Applications in Marketing Process and Competitive Advantage*

Marketing information systems are regarded as an essential tool for the entire marketing planning process (Talvinen 1995). Marketing planning process includes market analysis, segmentation, targeting, positioning, developing marketing mix, and controlling. Marketing information systems can be used throughout the process.

As the first step in the process, the purpose of market analysis is to identify problems, changes, and opportunities in marketing environment. The required data for this is the customers, competitors, and marketing environment. Support systems and operating systems including control and planning subsystems may be used to gather the required data. Also, TPS stores data gathered from customer base, competitors and other marketing environment (Talvinen 1995). MDSS may provide market status reports including sales, and market share (Little 1994). Use of geographic information systems which is s type of MDSS may also provide internal and external marketing intelligence (Hess and Rubin 2004). Next, operating systems including planning and basic research or MDSS can be used to segment markets and to record responses of customers, to select target markets and to position the product.

For the development of marketing mix elements planning and basic research subsystems, MDSS, and ES can be used. MDSS may provide market status reports price, promotion, and advertising. ES can support decisions on new product design, product launch, advertising and promotional planning, positioning, pricing and retail site selection. For example, a computer program may calculate profit of a retailer from promotion through drawing a baseline and determining the difference between the baseline and actual sales with the extensive use of ES ideas (Little 1994). Also, e-commerce information systems using web as a platform may be used to conduct business or for internationalization (Pather 2006). Internet based technologies may also be used for relationship management (Harrigan et al. 2011). Finally, control subsystem, and MDSS may be applied for the controlling of marketing planning process. MDSS may provide market response reports including price elasticity, promotional effectiveness, advertising impact on sales (Little 1994).

Besides these, successful management of information systems leads to higher customer value, which in turn, provides advantage to company against its competitors (Clarke 2005). Hence, the use marketing information systems facilitates gaining competitive advantage (Al-allak 2010). Information systems can be used to gain advantage against five forces of the competitive environment, which are competitors, suppliers, customers, new entries, and substitutes. With the use of IS a company can build loyalty among customers and suppliers through creating switching costs and customer value and raise barriers to entry (O'Brien 2005). Furthermore, information systems can be used to implement the generic competitive strategies as cost leadership, differentiation, and niche marketing. A company can reduce costs of business operations and customers or suppliers with use of IS. This may support cost leadership strategy of the company. A company that adopted differentiation strategy may develop new IS features to differentiate products and services. Developing unique new markets or market niches and focusing products and services at selected market niches can also be achieved with the help of IS (O'Brien 2005). However, it is not possible to gain sustainable competitive advantage from the implementation of IS. This is because competitors may have access to the same technology and systems. The advantage is derived from how they are used and whether the use is consistent with company objectives, company's position in the market and its competitive strategy (Clarke 2005).

3.2 Applications in Large Versus Small and Medium Sized Companies

In many large companies, use of marketing information systems has been growing and managers trust and rely more on these systems for decision-making (Duan and Kinman 2000). For example, an analysis of Fortune 500 companies revealed that marketing information systems, decision support systems, and expert systems are commonly used especially for sales forecast and market share estimation (Chern et al. 2002).

Based on some theoretical frameworks and empirical findings (Al-allak 2010; Bayraktutan et al. 2008; Li et al. 2001a, b; Xu 1999), a detailed list of fields where MKIS is used by large companies is provided in Table 1. As presented in Table 1, large companies use MKIS in a variety of marketing fields. For the whole marketing planning process, information systems are applied to related marketing fields.

Table 1 Fields of marketing information systems in large companies

Market analysis	Price
Market share	Determine price strategy
Market size	Cost analysis
Market structure	The level of demand
Environmental analysis (economic, technological, social, cultural, legal and political environment)	Price elasticity Trends in demand Placement
SWOT analysis	New distribution channels
The level of demand	E-commerce
Characteristics of demand	Logistics
Market position mapping	Retailer selection
Competition analysis	Promotion
Sales forecast	Direct marketing
Market segmentation	Sales force automation
Market targeting	Communication,
Product positioning	Managing sales and sales promotion
Product	Managing consumer relations
Product development	Advertising campaign
New product research and development	Media selection
New product evaluation	Control
Product launch	Monitoring effectiveness of marketing program

Also, managers of large companies regard information systems and information technology as assets which can contribute to the competitive advantage (Clarke 2005). For example, Dell Computer uses information technology for online build to order which makes the company lowest-cost producer. Federal Express used information technology for online package tracking and flight management that made the company market leader. AVNET Marshall used Customer/supplier of e-commerce and as a result, increases its market share. Citicorp used Global intranet that lead to growth in global market (O'Brien 2005).

Although marketing information systems are widely used in large companies, it is not always the case in small and medium sized enterprises. Studies conducted in 1990s showed that small business managers recognize that computers can support their decisions. Thus, they have positive attitudes to computer use and plan to increase their use of computer systems. However, they make little use of computer systems to support marketing decisions (Duan et al. 2002). On the other hand, recent studies show an increase in the awareness and use of information systems in small businesses (Street 2004). However, SMEs have applied IS mainly in the field of finance and accounting rather than marketing (Sharma and Bhagwat 2006).

For example, the study (Sharma and Bhagwat 2006) on 210 Indian SMEs showed that only 43 % of the sample use a formal IS in their organization. Majority of them implement IS to financial and accounting activities. Use of marketing information systems is relatively rare. Similar results occurred in another study (Duan and Kinman 2000) on SMEs operating in three countries, namely United Kingdom, Portugal and Poland. Nearly all SMEs in the sample used information technology mainly to support finance and accounting operations. Another study (Duncombe and Molla 2009) conducted on 90 African SMEs revealed that most of the SMEs use IS for accounting and financial purposes.

When we examine why and in which fields of marketing SMEs use MKIS, recent empirical findings revealed various practices and reasons with varying degrees of importance. Among 210 Indian companies, half of the sample apply IS in the field of sales and service, 18 % use for promotion campaigns, none of the SMEs use IS for forecasting and planning or product quality issues. For these SMEs communication with trading partners is the main reason for using information systems in marketing. Quick response to customer needs, improvement of overall efficiency, and dealing with short product life cycles also strongly motivate managers to implement MKIS (Sharma and Bhagwat 2006). In United Kingdom, information technology is also used to support marketing related functions like sales, customer sevice whereas it is moderately used in Poland and Portugal (Duan and Kinman 2000). Australian SMEs operating in the construction industry implemented MKIS to improve service quality and market share, support the strategic direction of the organization, and gain competitive advantage (Love and Irani 2004). Small health care companies in Turkey use marketing information systems to understand potential demand, patient satisfaction, image of the company, market shares, price levels and promotion strategies of competitors (Tanyeri et al. 2002). Another study (Yıldız 2008) on Turkish SMEs revealed that they use IS to enter into new markets and to create new products. A survey (Duan and Kinman 2000) on 133 small manufacturing companies in Bardfordshire, England revealed limited use of DSS in marketing related areas like sales/market analysis, long-range sales forecasting, research and development of new products.

Based on some theoretical frameworks and empirical findings mentioned above (Duan and Kinman 2000; Duncombe and Molla 2009; Levy and Powell 2000; Love and Irani 2004; Sharma and Bhagwat 2006; Tanyeri et al. 2002), a detailed list of fields where MKIS is used by small and medium sized companies is provided in Table 2.

As it can be seen from Tables 1 and 2, SMEs apply MKIS to relatively rare number of fields in marketing planning process. In other words, they make limited use of MKIS. It should be noted here that issues of highest importance for large companies get moderate or no attention by small and medium sized enterprises.

3.2.1 Barriers and Benefits of MKIS Applications in SMEs

One of the most common and strongest barrier for SMEs to implement marketing information systems is the lack of capital (Chern et al. 2002; Duan and Kinman 2000; Stockdale and Standing 2004) Small business managers are more concerned with cash flow than with return on investment. Consequently, the computer budget is often constrained. Besides, small businesses have limited staff, their managers must depend on personal experience rather than on information contained in staff

Table 2 Fields of marketing information systems in small and medium sized companies

Market analysis	Placement
Market share	Managing relations with channel members
SWOT analysis	
The level of demand	Entering new markets
Competition analysis	Promotion
Sales forecast	Managing sales and sales promotion
Product	Managing consumer relations
New product research and development	
After sales service	
Product quality	
Corporate image	

reports. Therefore, lack of people is another barrier to implement IS. Moreover, managers of SMEs lack information systems knowledge and trust in IS/IT industry. Because of this, they are less likely to plan a comprehensive electronic data processing operation (DeLone 1981). Furthermore; they resist changing traditional working styles and adopting innovations. Besides these, fear of supply chain breakdown and faith in supply chain linkages, poor infrastructural facilities, and disparity in trading partners' capabilities, inability to negotiate online creates barriers for implementing MKIS by SMEs. (Sharma and Bhagwat 2006).

However, it has been empirically proved that appropriate use of marketing information systems in SMEs results in improved performance, growth, and increased competitiveness, marketing skills and innovativeness (Aslan and Musa 2007; Duan et al. 2002; Street 2004). For example, the studies of Turkish SMEs (Aslan and Musa 2007; Gümüs and Ak 2005; Yildirim and Göksen 2005) indicated that use of information technology positively influence innovativeness, competitiveness and marketing skills of SMEs. The marketing information systems are also found to have a positive impact on price and product decisions of SMEs' managers (Raymond et al. 2001). Furthermore, it is revealed that information systems help SMEs to be more responsive (Sharma and Bhagwat 2006) which will facilitates better offerings to the market. Moreover, MKIS provide benefits like better quality, improved customer/supplier satisfaction, costs reduction, enhanced competitive advantage, improved market share, and improved forecasting and control.

Therefore, SMEs may improve their marketing skills with appropriate MKIS. As marketing problems have been accepted as one of the most critical problems in SMEs increasing the penetration of MKIS among SMEs is essential. Thus, there is a considerable interest in the use of marketing information systems in SMEs by practitioners and scholars. From this point, analyzing the existing research on MKIS in SMEs and providing and predicting future directions may contribute both to the theoretical and empirical knowledge. Accordingly, the next section represents a review of recent studies devoted to marketing information systems in SMEs.

4 MKIS Research in SMEs: A Review of Literature

4.1 Methodology

The scope of the review is restricted to empirically based research papers, journal articles, and to the period of 2002–2012. Initially, we searched Web of Science, Ebscohost (Business Source Complete and Academic Source Complete), and Science Direct databases using the keywords "information systems" or "information technology" and "small business" or "small and medium sized" in the title, abstract, or keywords. Then, articles were filtered according to two criteria as relevance to the topic of marketing and empirical research.

Afterwards, the leading journals covering information systems, business and marketing fields were closely examined. Based on the previous reviews (Besson and Rowe 2012; Hult et al. 1997; Nasir 2005; Piccoli and Ives 2005; Samiee and Walters 2003; Whitelock and Fastoso 2007) we choose the following journals Industrial Marketing Management, Information Systems Research, International Small Business Journal, Journal of Business Research, Journal of Management Information Systems, Journal of Marketing, Journal of Marketing Research, Journal of Strategic Information Systems, and MIS Quarterly.

4.2 Results

This method resulted in a set of 48 articles in the area of marketing information systems in SMEs that are published between 2002 and 2012 and in 33 different journals.[2]

4.2.1 Distribution by Journal

Fairly large numbers of articles were published in Journal of Strategic Information Systems (12.5 %) and International Small Business Journal (10.4 %). On the other hand, as shown in Table 3, most of the articles (52.1 %) were published in 25 different journals each publishing one article. Accordingly, we grouped 33 journals into four categories namely IS journals, business journals, marketing journals and others as shown in Table 4. The most common publication journals were IS and business journals (each publishing 37.5 %). The amount of articles published in marketing journals is relatively less (18.8 %). Therefore, it may be concluded that there is a strong interest in the topic in information systems and business journals rather than in marketing journals.

[2] For the list of the articles please contact with the author.

4.2.2 Research Areas Within the Analyzed Literature

Table 5 shows the distribution of the articles in terms of the research areas. There are six research areas covered by 48 articles. These are competitive strategy, e-marketing, performance outcomes, adoption, customer relationship management, and distribution strategy.

As shown in Table 5, majority of the studies (39.6 %) examined adoption of IS. This is followed by performance outcomes (18.8 %), competitive strategy (14.6 %), and e-marketing (10.4 %). Minority of the studies were devoted to distribution and customer relationship management (CRM) (8.3 % each).

"Adoption" area mostly covers adoption of information communication systems including e commerce/e-business/e-trade, and internet in general. The studies mostly applied theory of planned behavior, technology acceptance model, or theory of reasoned action to adoption of IS. The research area "performance outcomes" is related with the effects of information communication technology, virtual research and development, e-business, internet, and MKIS in general on performance. Performance measures include subjective and objective measures of variables like profitability, sales growth, loyalty, market share, return on investment, and innovativeness. The studies dedicated to competitive strategies investigated issues like resource based view, sustainability, and competitive position. "E-marketing" research area covers studies examining factors affecting success of e-marketing (e-trade, e-business, e-commerce) and user satisfaction. "Distribution

Table 3 Distribution of the articles by journals

Journal name	Number of articles	Percentage (%)
International small business journal	6	12.5
Journal of strategic information systems	5	10.4
Technovation	2	4.2
Information and management	2	4.2
Industrial marketing management	2	4.2
International journal of marketing studies	2	4.2
Industrial management and data systems	2	4.2
Journal of marketing management	2	4.2
Others[a]	25	52.1

[a] Other journals include Academia-Revista Latino Americano de Administracion, African Journal of Business Management, African Journal of Library, Archive and Information Science, Computers in Human Behavior, E&M Ekonomie A Management, European Journal of Information Systems, European Management Review, IEEE Transactions on Engineering Management, Information Development, International Journal of Electronic Commerce, International Journal of Information Management, International Journal of Production Research, Journal of Association For Information Systems, Journal of Business Economics and Management, Journal of Business and Industrial Marketing, Journal of Business Research, Journal Of Computer in Information Systems, Journal of Euromarketing, Journal of Global Information Management, Journal of Organizational Computing And Electronic Commerce, Marketing Intelligence and Planning Metalurgia International, MIS Quarterly, Service Industries Journal, Small Business Economics

Table 4 Distribution of the articles by scope of the journals

Journal name	Number of articles	Percentage (%)
Information systems journals	18	37.5
Business journals	18	37.5
Marketing journals	9	18.8
Others*	3	6.3

* Includes journals covering engineering and production

Table 5 Distribution of the articles by research area

Research area	Number of articles	Percentage (%)
Competitive strategy	7	14.6
E-marketing	5	10.4
Performance outcomes	9	18.8
Adoption	19	39.6
Customer relationship management	4	8.3
Distribution	4	8.3

strategy" research area covers issues related with the role of IS on logistics, outsourcing, direct sales, and multichannel distribution strategy. The studies focusing on customer relationship management investigated the role of internet technologies on CRM activities. One of the studies examined adoption of CRM by small hardware retailers. This study may be categorized in "adoption" area as well. Since, it is the only study devoted to CRM adoption and due to the rare number of CRM studies we prefer to cover it under "CRM" topic.

4.2.3 Distribution by Country of Analysis

Articles we have encountered in our literature review were conducted on 19 different countries. As shown in Table 6, majority of them were carried in United Kingdom, China and USA (16.7, 12.5, and 12.5 % respectively). The categorization of countries based on income level revealed that more than half of the studies (54.2 %) examined SMEs from high income countries. Moderate number of the studies (37.5 %) investigated SMEs operating in middle income countries. Studies conducted on SMEs in low income countries are relatively rare (8.3 %) (see Table 7).

4.2.4 Methodologies Used

We continued the analysis of the literature with research design of the articles. Table 8 revealed that most of the articles (81.3 %) used quantitative research design including survey method and mathematical models. Survey method is the

Table 6 Distribution of the articles by country

Countries	Number of articles	Percentage (%)
United Kingdom	8	16.7
China	6	12.5
USA	6	12.5
Spain, Ireland,	3	6.3
Canada, Chile, Iran, Malezia, Niger*	2	4.2
Romaine, Norway, Israel, Poland, Mexico, Vietnam, Sweden, Korea, Ghana**	1	2.1

* There exist two studies for each country
** There exists one study for each country

Table 7 Distribution of the articles by income level of country

Country classification*	Number of articles	Percentage (%)
High income country	26	54.2
Middle income country	18	37.5
Low income country	4	8.3

* Country classification is based on World Bank's classification theme

most common among these (90 %) whereas mathematical models using secondary data were occasionally used (10 %). Relatively fewer studies (20.8 %) used qualitative research design including interview and case studies.

4.2.5 Patterns in Past Research

Following the categorization of articles into research areas, countries and methodologies, we analyzed the patterns in past research. Initially, we analyzed the trends in articles based on publication year and topic. Figure 1 presents percentage of articles published in each year for the period of 2002–2012. Subsequently, Fig. 2 shows the distribution of the articles by research area and publication year. As it can be seen from the Fig. 1, the amount of articles on marketing information systems by SMEs has been growing since 2009. The highest increase in percentage of studies occurred in 2010 (from 10.4 to 16.7 %). The analysis of the distribution of articles by research area in each year revealed the following conclusions. Distribution strategy studies emerged in 2010. Thus, it may be regarded as a new

Table 8 Distribution of the articles by research design

Research design	Number of articles	Percentage (%)
Qualitative research design	10	20.8
Quantitative research design	39	81.3

Total number of articles exceeds 48 (100 %) as one study used both designs

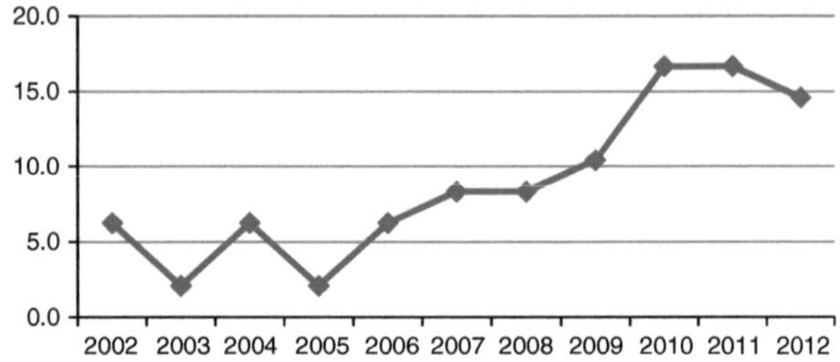

Fig. 1 Distribution of the articles by year

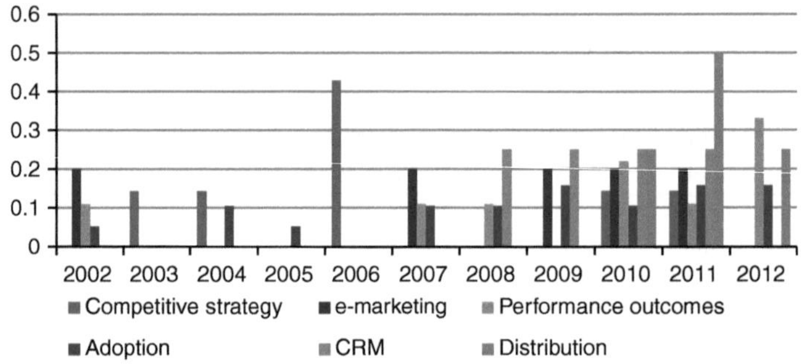

Fig. 2 Distribution of the articles by research area and year

topic in MKIS by SMEs. Studies examining performance outcomes of IS have been increasing while those examining competitive strategy have been decreasing over the past decade. The percentage of studies focusing on e-marketing and adoption may be regarded as stable over the past decade.

Furthermore, we tried to identify the patterns in past research with an emphasis on country and research area. Figure 3 presents distribution of articles by research area and country. As shown in Fig. 3, studies on competitive strategy, e-marketing, and distribution were concentrated on high and middle income countries. CRM was utterly examined for SMEs in high income countries. Studies on low income countries barely investigated adoption and performance outcomes of IS.

Additionally, we examined articles based on research area and design. Results shown in Table 9 indicated that quantitative research design is the most common absolutely for all topics. Adoption studies constitute the largest part of quantitative research design.

5 Areas for Future Research and Conclusion

As noted and concluded in the paper before, SMEs make little use of MKIS and issues of highest importance for large companies get moderate or no attention by practitioners and scholars spotlighting SMEs. This shows that use of information

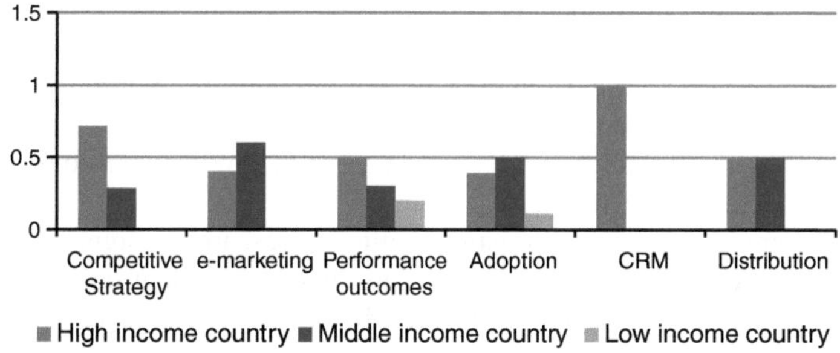

Fig. 3 Distribution of the articles by topic and country

Table 9 Distribution of the articles by research design

Topic	Qualitative research design (number of articles)	Quantitative research design (number of articles)
Competitive strategy	2	5
E-marketing	2	3
Performance outcomes	4	5
Adoption	4	15
Customer relationship management	–	4
Distribution strategy	–	4

systems in marketing in SMEs still takes a backseat. The transfer of systems developed for large organizations is unlikely to meet needs of SMEs. The differences between large and small businesses should be noticed in designing information systems. Although there are differences between managing small and large businesses (DeLone 1981) few studies have explored these differences in terms of the use of information systems, especially for marketing related activities. Thus, more research in this area may contribute to the current knowledge.

The analysis of the literature carried out in this review indicated that adoption of marketing information systems have been quite sufficiently examined as compared with other research areas. Besides, there is an increasing trend in the area of performance outcomes of MKIS. Therefore, more studies on this area showing effects of MKIS on performance may increase use of it by practitioners as well. Other areas of future research include issues like use of IS in CRM or distribution and factors affecting success of e-marketing. Future research may specifically focus on use of IS in CRM which is the least frequently examined research area in the literature though its importance in marketing communication. Consequently, more studies associated with technology mediated communication with channel partners, customers, B–B relations is needed.

The review showed that the literature mainly focused on high income countries whereas little attention is directed towards SMEs in middle and low income countries. Consequently, more studies in all research areas may be beneficial in those countries. Especially, there is a considerable scope to study IS in competitive strategy for SMEs in middle income and low income countries. In order to increase added value of SMEs to the economies of those countries, creation of more value in accordance with competitive advantage is required. In addition, there is a need to examine factors affecting e-marketing success in low income countries which has been neglected in the literature.

Finally, there is little research using qualitative research design. Future studies may prefer to use qualitative research design rather than quantitative one to get a more comprehensive understanding of the MKIS from the perspective of SMEs.

References

Al-allak, B. (2010). Evaluating the adoption and use of ınternet-based marketing ınformation systems to ımprove marketing ıntelligence (The case of tourism SMEs in Jordan). *International Journal of Marketing Studies, 2*(2), 87–101.

Aslan, S., & Musa, O. (2007). KOBI'lerde Bilgi Teknolojisi Kullanımının, Rekabet Gücü, Yenilikçilik, Girişimcilik Ve Pazarlama Kapasitesiyle İlişkileri: Otomotiv Sektöründe Bir Araştırma. *Ç.Ü. Sosyal Bilimler Enstitüsü Dergisi, 16*(2), 15–28.

Bayraktutan, Y., Arslan, I., Kaygısız, E. G., & Druıcăthe, E. (2008). Effects of ınformation technologies ın marketing. *Lex ET Scientia International Journal, XV*(2), 190–197.

Besson, P., & Rowe, F. (2012). Strategizing information systems-enabled organizational transformation: A transdisciplinary review and new directions. *Journal of Strategic Information Systems, 21*, 103–124.

Brien, R. H., & Stafford, J. E. (1968). Marketing information systems: A new dimension for marketing research. *Journal of Marketing, 32*(3), 19–23.

Chern, C., Chiang, D. M., & Ho, T. (2002). *Development of a DSS to estimate the sales for the retailing industry in Taiwan*. The 2nd International Conference on Electronic Business, Taipei, Taiwan.

Clarke, S. (2005). *Information systems strategic management: An ıntegrated approach*. London: Routledge.

Cox, D. F., & Good, R. E. (1967). How to build a marketing information system. *Harvard Business Review, 45*(3), 145–154.

Daša, D. (2009). Marketing activities of small businesses in Croatia: The case of Splitsko-Dalmatınska. *County Management, 14*(1), 39–58.

DeLone, W. H. (1981). Firm size and the characteristics of computer use. *MIS Quarterly, 5*(4), 65–77.

Duan, Y., & Kinman, R. (2000). Small manufacturing businesses: meeting decision support needs. *Journal of Small Business and Enterprise Development, 7*(3), 272–284.

Duan, Y., Mullins, R., Hamblin, D., Stanek, S., Sroka, H., Machado, V., et al. (2002). Addressing ICTs skill challenges in SMEs: İnsights from three country investigations. *Journal of European Industrial Training, 26*(9), 430–441.

Duncombe, R., & Molla, A. (2009). Formalisation of ınformation systems in sub-Saharan African small and medium enterprises: Case of Botswana. *The African Journal of Information Systems, 1*(2), 1–29.

Gounaris, S. P., Panigyrakis, G. G., & Chatzipanagiotou, K. C. (2007). Measuring the effectiveness of marketing information systems an empirically validated instrument. *Marketing Intelligence and Planning, 25*(6), 612–631.

Harrigan, P., Ramsey, E., & Ibbotson, P. (2011). Critical factors underpinning the e-CRM activities of SMEs. *Journal of Marketing Management, 27*(5–6), 503–529.

Hess, R. L., Rubin, R. S., & L. A. (2004). Geographic information systems as a marketing information system technology. *Decision Support Systems, 38*, 197–212.
Hult, G., Neese, W., & Bashaw, R. (1997). Faculty perceptions of marketing journals. *Journal of Marketing Education, 18*(1), 37–52.
Kendall, K. E., & Kendall, J. E. (1992). *System anaylsis and design*. USA: Prentice Hall.
Levy, M., & Powell, P. (2000). Information systems strategy for small and medium sized enterprises: An organisational perspective. *The Journal of Strategic Information Systems, 9*(1), 63–84.
Li, E. Y., McLeod, R., & Rogers, J. C. (2001a). Marketing information systems inFortune 500 companies: A longitudinal analysis of 1980, 1990, and 2000. *Information and Management, 38*, 307–322.
Li, E. Y., Chen, H. G., & Roan, J. S. (2001b). Marketing ınformation systems usage in Taiwan's top 1000 companies. *Journal of Computer Information Systems, 41*(2), 85–94.
Little, J. D. C. (1979). Decision support systems for marketing managers. *Journal of Marketing, 43*, 9–26.
Little, J. D. C. (1994). Information technology in marketing. In T. J. Allen & M. S. Morton (Eds.), *Information technology and the corporation of the 1990s*. New York: Oxford University Press.
Love, P. E. D., & Irani, Z. (2004). An exploratory study of information technology evaluation and benefits management practices of SMEs in the construction industry. *Information and Management, 42*, 227–242.
Nasir, S. (2005). The development, change, and transformation of management information systems (MIS): A content analysis of articles published in business and marketing journals. *International Journal of Information Management, 25*, 442–457.
O'Brien, J. A. (2005). *Introduction to ınformation systems*. New York City: McGrawHill.
Pather, S. (2006). E-commerce information systems (ECIS) Success: A South African study. Thesis, Cape Peninsula University of Technology.
Piccoli, G., & Ives, B. (2005). IT-dependent strategic initiatives and sustained competitive advantage: A review and synthesis of the literature. *MIS Quarterly, 29*(4), 747–776.
Raymond, L., Brisoux, J., & Azami, A. (2001). Marketing information systems practices in small manufacturing firms: Antecedents and consequences. *Journal of Computer Information Systems, 41*, 3.
Samiee, S., & Walters, P. G. (2003). Relationship marketing in an international context: a literature review. *International Business Review, 12*, 193–214.
Saydan, R. Gümüs, A. &, Ak, R. (2005). KOBI'lerde Bilisim Teknolojilerinin Kullanilmasi ve Rekabet Gücü Açisin dan Önemi (Van Ili Uygulamasi, 2. Kobiler ve Verimlilik Kongresi, Turkey.
Sharma, M. K., & Bhagwat, R. (2006). Practice of information systems: Evidence from select Indian SMEs. *Journal of Manufacturing Technology Management, 17*(2), 199–223.
Simpson, M., Padmore, J., Taylor, N., & Hughes, J. F. (2006). Marketing in small and medium sized enterprises. *International Journal of Entrepreneurial Behaviour and Research, 12*(6), 361–387.
Stockdale, R., & Standing, C. (2004). Benefits and barriers of electronic marketplace participation: An SME perspective. *Journal of Enterprise Information Management, 17*(4), 301–311.
Street, C. T. (2004). Small business growth and internal transparency: The role of information systems. *MIS Quarterly, 28*(3), 473–506.
Talvinen, J. M. (1995). Information systems in marketing: Identifying opportunities for new applications. *European Journal of Marketing, 29*(1), 8–26.
Tanyeri, M., Yesilada, F. A., & Yesilada, T. (2002). The use of marketing ınformation systems in small and medium size health care organizations. *Suleyman Demirel Universitesi Iktisadi Idari Bilimler Fakultesi Dergisi, 7*(2), 21–31.
Walsh, M. F., & Lipinski, J. (2009). The role of the marketing function in small and medium sized enterprises. *Journal of Small Business and Enterprise Development, 16*(4), 569–585.

Whitelock, J., & Fastoso, F. (2007). Understanding international branding: defining the domain and reviewing the literature. *International Marketing Review, 24*(3), 252–270.

Xu, X. M. (1999). The strategic orientation of marketing information systems: An empirical study. *Marketing Intelligence and Planning, 17*(6), 262–272.

Yildirim, F. K., & Göksen, Y. (2005). Bilgi Teknolojilerinin Türkiye'deki Kobilerin Rekabet Gücü Üzerindeki Rolünü Belirlemeye Yönelik Bir Saha Çalismasi. *2. Kobiler ve Verimlilik Kongresi*, Turkey.

Yıldız, M. S. (2008). Küçük ve orta ölçekli işletmelerde (KOBİ) bilgi teknolojilerinin kullanım düzeyi ve bilgi teknolojilerinin firmalar üzerindeki etkileri. *Electronic Journal of Social Sciences, 25*(7), 212–239.

Part IV
Capabilities and Knowledge

The Ability of SMEs to Use Trust in Managing Offshore Activities

Franz Josef Gellert and Hugo Velthuijsen

1 Introduction

Business models and business processes are undergoing tremendous changes because markets are changing, competition becomes stronger and consumer behavior is changing too (Miles et al. 2010). The chance for small and middle-sized enterprises (SMEs) to survive in rapidly growing dynamic market environments is a challenge (Business Week 2011; Willcocks and Craig 2010). Therefore, SMEs perceive a need to search for new business opportunities by thinking about networking and building alliances or outsourcing/offshoring of their business processes.

Outsourcing/offshoring is currently mostly related to IT processes that can be managed cheaper and more effectively outside the own company and the domestic market. SMEs are running a higher risk than bigger companies do when they outsource/offshore their business processes (Devos et al. 2009). Research and practice in the area of outsourcing/offshoring has been biased by experiences of large firms. But, as pointed out by Devos et al. (2009), a SME is not a scale model of a large firm and, therefore, generic research results and best practices do not necessarily offer the best advice to SMEs. Thus, it is relevant to look more specifically into how SMEs can manage the outsource and offshore activities properly to reduce costs, make processes more effective, retain market competitiveness and make use of expertise that is innovative although hard to get.

In our paper we concentrate on SMEs offshore activities because when leaving the home location and going abroad, the firm is faced with cultural differences of

F. J. Gellert (✉)
Hanze University of Applied Sciences, Groningen, International Business School, Zernikeplein 7, 9747 AS Groningen, The Netherlands
e-mail: f.j.gellert@pl.hanze.nl

H. Velthuijsen
Hanze University of Applied Sciences, Groningen, School of ICT and Business Development, Zernikeplein 11, 9747 AS Groningen, The Netherlands
e-mail: h.velthuijsen@pl.hanze.nl

J. Devos et al. (eds.), *Information Systems for Small and Medium-sized Enterprises*, Progress in IS, DOI: 10.1007/978-3-642-38244-4_13,

people involved. Therefore, we use the offshore definition of Contractor et al. (2010) who outlined that offshoring is restructuring the firm geographically away from the home location to a location abroad. Bearing this in mind we look at two theories: Cultural diversity theory and agency theory. From cultural diversity theory (Minkov and Hofstede 2011), we know that getting in contact with partners in foreign countries is a sensitive part that either fosters or hinders a good relationship. Therefore, the first contact with "others" is a crucial point for business partners in the offshoring process. Rottman (2008) found that a good relationship quality is important because almost 50 % of enterprises failed to offshore successfully due to weak relationship ties. Furthermore, we know that companies experienced contradicting results with regard to the relationship quality level between partners and formality of working methods when they offshore their processes (Rottman 2008; Devos et al. 2009).

Additionally, we know from agency theory that formal work is preferred by Anglo-Saxon companies in contrast to informal work approaches with a partner-based relationship practiced by Northern European companies (Adams et al. 2010; Mathrani et al. 2007). Also, SMEs appear to be more inclined towards informal working methods than large companies (Devos et al. 2009). Partner-based approaches are associated with relationships that are specifically defined by the trust level that is developed over time between human beings. The development of trust goes through different levels or stages of a process. As a starting point, trust can be built on positive experience, personal engagement, openness, honesty and integrity, sharing benefits and risks, commitment and patience (Stel 2011).

Although SMEs seem to be hesitant to offshore, they show increasing interest in networking, cooperation as well as sharing knowledge, resources and working tools. In this context, cooperation can be seen as a pre-step in the offshore process because, according to Stel (2011), cooperation requires the willingness to accept counterparts as they are and not as others perceive they should be. The initiative for cooperation lies in building a partnership. "A partnership works on the basis of trust and commitment or not at all" (Stel 2011). Starting a partnership opens the door for the development of offshore activities. Partnership in its origin is similar to cooperation, alliances or collaboration.

In this research we are particularly interested in how SMEs are at an advantage or disadvantage in managing trust in intercultural relationships/in being successful in offshoring compared to "regular companies". Therefore, our overarching aim in this paper is to position the current developments in SMEs whether they are willing to become effective players in offshore business while considering trust as an important relationship component.

Our paper is outlined as follows. Firstly, we start with reviewing appropriate literature on SMEs' outsourcing/offshoring activities and the factor trust. We continue with positioning offshore activities in relation to trust. The chapter is followed by the methodology and the results. We continue with the discussion and finalize the paper with our conclusions, theoretical and practical implications and future research.

2 Position of Outsourcing/Offshoring in SMEs

Research on outsourcing/offshoring has been quite extensively pursued over decades (Hätönen and Eriksson 2009; Contractor et al. 2010). The researchers highlighted that with regard to outsourcing/offshoring, a switch from purely cost reduction to optimizing resources, and thus from procurement to cooperation has taken place over years. This is also strongly related to a partner-based approach as outlined by Child et al. (2005). These researchers highlighted that trust is an essential part of cooperation since cooperation with a partner outside the company—and maybe in a foreign country—is expected to be challenging. Challenges lie in the development of a relationship among people from different cultural backgrounds because their thinking, beliefs and attitudes might be different and result in dimensions such as power distance, individualism or gender according to Minkov and Hofstede (2011). In this context, and taking into account the aforementioned dimensional aspects, the implementation of offshoring relationships becomes relevant. Dibbern et al. (2004) outlined that according to the stage model of IS outsourcing, the "how" question needs to be answered in the implementation phase. How to implement offshore activities refers to people involved (besides the technologies and methods to be used) and how their trustful relationship contributes to successful outcomes. We know from relationship theories that social and economic exchange is the root of successful interactions and that they lead to trust among partners (Dibbern et al. 2004). In this context Subherwal (1999) pointed out that two components appear when it comes to building and structuring relationships: (a) formal contract and (b) psychological contract. For us the psychological contract is even more important because individuals in a multi-cultural setting need to manage their differences in attitudes and behavior. According to Dibbern et al. (2004) "the belief of trustworthiness of a vendor might lead to the attitude of trust regarding the vendor". Therefore, trust may be defined as "the belief that others upon whom one depends, yet has little control over, will not take advantage of the situation by behaving in an opportunistic manner" (Devos et al. 2009). For an SME owner/manager, considered as an individual who represents his own business, it is vital at the beginning of a relationship to start working on the process that the counterpart trust him and that he can trust the other.

The relationship process might start with considering the competence of each other as outlined by Ibrahim and Ribbers (2009). The owner/manager is dependent on the first impressions of his partner in order to continue building a relationship (Dunning et al. 2011; Fetchenhauer and Dunning 2009). Additionally, following Duncan et al. (2009), the owner/manager's expertise, attitudes and behavior play a key role in defining the direction and condition of the SME.

The question might arise whether there is a difference in the way an SME goes about building a relationship as compared to the way a large company proceeds in this area. We know from studies (Perrini et al. 2007; Russo and Perrini 2009) that this must be not necessarily the case. The difference may lie in a company's needs, flexibility, purchasing power, financial and human resources (Perrini et al. 2007).

Additionally, as pointed out by Dibbern and Heinzl (2009), offshoring activities of SMEs might be selective and in SMEs the degree of offshore activities varies so that SMEs can be considered to be more individualistic than bigger companies. Furthermore, Dibbern et al. (2004) outlined that, referring to relationship theory, SMEs are more inclined to use trust as the basis for their relationship and therefore they are better at managing offshore activities. Thus, trust is a key for SMEs to successfully offshore and that "the establishment of a trustful relationship with foreign partners positively affects the success of participating companies" (Fink and Kraus 2007).

Bearing the aforementioned consideration in mind, we hypothesize the following:

- SMEs are intrinsically better qualified for building trustful relationships than large companies.
- SMEs are at an advantage to build multi-cultural relationships because of their informality.

The aforementioned hypotheses help us to structure our thinking and help us to point out what the crucial elements are when companies offshore. In this research, the trust levels between partners are divided into initial trust (pre-contract phase) and mutual trust (post-contract phase) as outlined in Fig. 1.

When establishing trust (pre-contract phase) and maintaining mutual trust (post-contract phase) among partners, an understanding of cultural differences develops over time. As shown in the graph the cornerstones (circles) are related (arrows) to each other and will be briefly described below.

Interpersonal relationships and interpersonal trust can be seen as a starting point for a trustful relationship which means that partners should be able to have a good level of communication with each other so that they also understand the essentials of cultural differences. Communication in this context means to observe others behavior, listen what others say and match the outcome with the own interest.

Additionally, being transparent helps to build a trustful relationship. Transparency in an offshore content means that the existing knowledge will be shared and that none of the partners hide things that are important for business.

With regard to HR involvement, the hiring process of staff is very sensitive and allows partners to test their trustful relationship. The partner abroad has to be involved in the recruitment process and which is even more important, needs to understand needs, wishes and desires of people hired. Additionally, the involved partner is more aware of requirements staff members have to fulfil and what the country specific rules and regulations are.

The fourth cornerstone is informal working methods. Informal working methods require a specific kind of mind set as well as an understanding of the cultural differences with the offshore partner. Business life can be easier when using informal methods but partners must mutually understand each other how informal is defined.

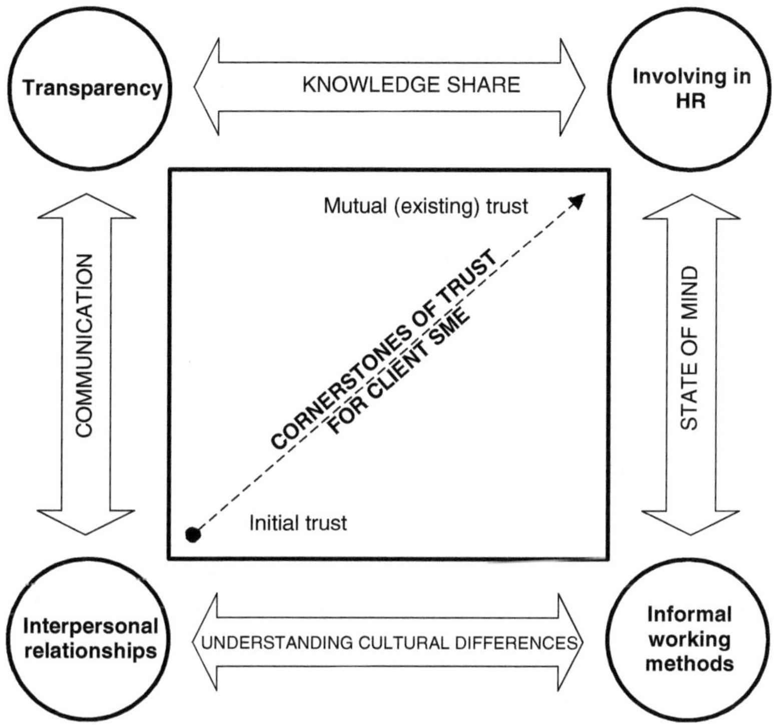

Fig. 1 Initial trust and mutual trust in an offshore development process

2.1 The Term "Trust"

Trust is something that we all need when we want to live and work together with other human beings. It does not appear on command. Trust develops over time and is a key in relationships, either in private life or in business. From a social science point of view, trust is something that is related to liking and disliking (Baumeister and Bushman 2010) and is also dependent on our first mutual impressions of each other (Fetchenhauer and Duning 2009). Stel (2011) laid out that trust can be defined as an emotional expression or as a rational consideration. However, we found various definitions and considerations of trust and based on this we take the variance as a starting point to bring the definitions down to initial trust and mutual trust.

Dividing trust in line with the contract life cycle (pre-contract and post-contract phase) clarifies the timeline of building trust from initial trust to mutual (existing) trust. The division into these two parts is drawn from the findings of an exploratory study of Bharadwa et al. (2010). With this particular division, the whole contract life cycle can be covered in a clear way. As Brown and Wilson (2009) state, "Offshoring can be viewed as a cycle, beginning with the decision-making process, followed by managing the contract, then evaluating the results and finally re-examining the offshoring contract".

2.2 Pre-contract Phase

During the pre-contract phase, organizations have to consider several important choices and decisions before starting actual offshoring relationship. These choices and decisions can include selecting the right supplier, agreeing on the content of the contract with the supplier, or defining the length of the contract of (Bharadwa et al. 2010). Moreover, SMEs have to look for smaller and therefore lesser known partners. This is a hard search since the process of finding acceptable partners is currently an underdeveloped issue. In the pre-contact phase one of the key factors involving these searches and decisions is the development, and at the end the existence, of the initial trust between the client and the supplier (Bharadwa et al. 2010).

2.3 Initial Trust

Lee and Huynh (2005) draw their findings from previous studies which show the beginning of inter-organizational relationships is the most critical time for building successful inter-organizational relationships. Initial trust plays a key role here: it creates the basis for the mutual, existing trust of the partners, and therefore highly affects the success of the partnership. The interview questions about initial trust were therefore formed from questions related to cognition-based initial trust and calculation-based initial trust (Lee et al. 2008).

The basis of cognition-based initial trust is cognitive reasoning (McAllister 1995). Cognition-based trust can be developed for example if the client is impressed and convinced by a supplier's experience and previous successful business relationships. It is reasonable to ask questions regarding cognition-based initial trust for gaining insights about the client's cognitive reasoning towards the service provider's earlier achievements.

2.4 Initial Distrust

When measuring initial trust in relationships between business partners, it is also important to take the effects of initial distrust into consideration. Lee et al. (2008) state that trust can be seen as confident positive expectations from one partner towards the other. Lewicki and Bunker (1995) define the meaning of distrust as the opposite of trust; it can be seen as confident negative expectations toward the other partner: "distrust evokes fear and actions to buffer oneself from the harmful conduct of the other party". Initial distrust can be divided further into psychology-based distrust and economic-based distrust. Lee et al. (2008) draw this division from the findings of McKnight et al. (1998). The interview questions about psychology-based distrust were built to get a client's initial view about how negative perceptions they had about the partner, regarding for example its honesty towards the client.

2.5 Post-contract Phase

In this paper, the post-contract phase covers the time period starting from the early stage of the business relationship when initial trust already exists, until the very end of the business relationship. The post-contract phase includes decisions such as should the contract be extended or not, or should a change of the supplier be taken into consideration. Also continuous performance monitoring of the supplier is done during the post-contract phase (Bharadwa et al. 2010). In this phase the level and existence of mutual trust is vital as is a good level of knowledge sharing.

2.6 Mutual (Existing) Trust

Mutual trust, or in other words the existing trust between the business partners, is an important factor in interactions between a customer and a service provider. According to Lee et al. (2008), these interactions can go beyond the rules, agreements and expectations specified in legal contracts because of the commitment and contributions of the partners in the relationship, and these commitments and contributions can go beyond what was defined in the contract.

Lee et al. (2008) state that projects involving new knowledge creation requires knowledge sharing. However, to have successful knowledge sharing, there must exist also a strong level of mutual trust between partners. Also, Inkpen and Tsang (2005) state that in regard to knowledge sharing, it is important to have sufficient trust so that the partners do not view each other as competitors. If the customer (client) identifies the existence of distinctive knowledge sharing factors, such as sharing business reports or sharing know-how, it indicates the existence of mutual trust.

2.7 Mutual Distrust

If both partners distrust each other, the relationship comes to an end. Distrust appears via negative experience, negative impressions or negative word-of-mouth promotion. Notwithstanding the trust level between two human beings, there is a neoclassical economics tendency to consider distrust in others–strangers–as something that should be avoided at all costs (Dunning et al. 2011). However, a relationship can still continue between partners because of business-related constraints.

3 Methodology

In our research we have chosen a qualitative inductive research strategy to get deeper into the elements of trustful relationship qualities and to ensure that we can develop practical recommendations for SMEs based on our findings. Therefore, we decided to conduct semi-structured interviews with owner/managers of SMEs in five selected European countries. According to Stel (2011), interview results need to be transformed, reduced and analyzed by identifying common patterns.

3.1 Sample

Our sample consists of 16 SMEs in five selected countries bearing in mind that one country (UK) is Anglo-Saxon oriented and four countries are Northern European countries (G, NL, D, SW). We followed the purposive sampling method (Yin 2011) by selecting the companies that have met the criteria: being international, a small or middle-sized company, have tried to offshore their business or are currently in an offshore relationship either in the IT business field or outside this field. The 16 selected companies, therefore represent an appropriate sample because the observed treatment effect in our study is causal (Judd and Kenny 2006).

With regard to a company's size, we followed the SME definition (turnover, employees, balance sheet total) of the European Commission (European Commission 2012). In Table 1, the 16 SMEs are listed with the type of business as well as with the number of employees.

3.2 Instrument

The semi-structured interviews consisted of questions drawn from the research of Lee et al. (2008) about trust between partners in offshore business. Those questions were associated with Bharadwaj et al. (2010)'s division of contract life cycle in outsourcing. Interviews were conducted with either a founder, director, or manager applying a semi-structure so that interviewees could express their feelings and emotions additionally. By following the framework of trust, the details of the interviews were structured by starting with a company overview and ending with an interview conclusion that illuminates the current company's thinking on offshoring and their related activities. The questions that were asked are listed at the end of the paper in Appendix 1.

Table 1 Summary of conducted interviews

Reference	Industry	Employees
Germany		
GC1	Telecommunication	75
GC2	Satellite-communication	35
GC3	Health supplements	2
GC4	Management Consulting	1
The Netherlands		
NC1	Foreign exchange (FOREX)	1
NC2	(Medical) care communication	1
NC3	Application development	15
NC4	Service desk, infrastructure management	800
NC5	Software development	65
NC6	Software development	<250
United Kingdom		
UC1	Software development	<250
Denmark		
DC1	Audio devices	25
DC2	Management consulting	<250
Sweden		
SC1	Biogas technology	<250
SC2	Communication	22
SC3	Management consulting	Up to 1500 employees placed all over the world

3.3 *Analysis*

Eleven interviews were recorded and notes were taken for five interviews. Afterwards, the content of the taped interviews was transcribed and results of the notes were inserted into an excel sheet with the purpose to find common patterns and to draw appropriate conclusions from that.

4 Results

In the following paragraph, we summarize the most interesting outcomes of the interviews in each selected country. Quotes from the original interview text were specifically marked. Finally we give an overview of results in Table 2 that reflects country specific outcome and themes they have in common.

Table 2 Overview of country-specific outcome and common themes

Country	Outcome	Common theme
Germany	Communication	Cultural knowledge
	Language	Trust
	Character of partners	
Netherlands	Trust	Cultural knowledge
	Quality of partners	Trust
United Kingdom	Work attitudes	Cultural knowledge
	Level of education	
Denmark	Cultural differences	Cultural knowledge
	Infrastructure	Trust
Sweden	Communication	Cultural knowledge
	Language	Trust

4.1 Germany

The interviewees state that they prefer to offshore/outsource to partners that have a close proximity. Also, geographically close partners have a better understanding of regulations important to the outsourcing/offshoring company.

All of the interviewed German companies have experienced the interaction with different cultures in their businesses. The companies stated that communication, and especially language, is one of their main concerns when interacting with different countries and cultures. Furthermore, characteristics and traits of partners of a different cultural background pose potential for misunderstandings that lead to difficulties.

To deal with difficulties, the interviewees argue that adequate and thorough preparation before starting a relationship is necessary and vital. It is important to understand the respective culture and adapting to it accordingly.

> Quotes:
>
> It is explained that a certain understanding of the partner's mentality is needed and that it must be known that different countries do have different work attitudes. It is especially important that partners find a common middle ground in order to avoid disappointments.
>
> Prior to actually engaging in new partnerships abroad, preparation time takes about one to one and a half years.

4.2 The Netherlands

The interviewees name cost factors and a lack of competences as the reason for offshoring.

The relationships of all Dutch companies are to some extent affected by cultural differences. Eastern states such as Belarus and Estonia, as well as Cyprus are mentioned as important business partners. The companies stated that trust and quality is important when engaging in offshoring/outsourcing partnerships. One must rely on the partner and his promises to deliver according to quality expectations. Improving the quality of communication was a key to bridge cultural differences complemented by knowledge sharing. The interviewees felt that interpersonal trust is a strong base for inter-organizational trust, and that especially from the SME's point of view, interpersonal trust is something very crucial for working with a partner outside the company. Furthermore, it was stated that a trustful relationship is easier to build with a smaller company than with a larger one, but that it is also easier to quit the relationship if necessary.

Quotes:

We think that the right way to build trust is by giving everybody the possibility to be trusted in the beginning. And to believe that we can trust each other until something else has been proven that it is not the case. (Relationship with Indian SME)

There is a honest relationship, but I don't think they tell us everything. I think they are honest if I ask, then they will tell everything. But again, it is more a cultural thing. If it is not asked, why should they say. (relationship with Eastern Europe SME)

4.3 United Kingdom

Flexibility, lower costs and the possibility to obtain higher quality are the main reasons to offshore/outsource for British SMEs.

Different expectations of work attitudes (e.g. with Russia) have led to misunderstandings and disappointments. A high educational level is perceived as important for mutual understanding. Business objectives should always be clearly understood, too, because this is a good point for trust development. Within the company cultural diversity exists and the knowledge how to handle cultural differences is apparent and can be brought into place when talking about outsourcing/offshoring activities.

Quotes:

It is important that offshore partners possess a high educational level as this allows them to think laterally. Further, the strategic business objective should be understood well.

A high educational level is important for mutual understanding and business objectives should always be understood.

4.4 Denmark

Main reasons to offshore/outsource for the interviewees were cost factors and tapping increased competences from offshoring/outsourcing partners. Given its size, Denmark and its companies do have global business ties. The interviewees referred to the offshoring/outsourcing activities to countries such as China or Ukraine. Also, outsourcing within Denmark happens frequently.

The expert had experienced that one of the main problems in outsourcing is the non-alignment of decisions with corporate strategy. Inadequate preparation and a certain naivety to do and expect the same abroad as from the home market is prevailing. Companies underestimate cultural differences because they think they can't affect them. Not only do they have self-imposed constraints but also limitations coming from the country's infrastructure.

Trust and preparation are important things to consider when deciding to offshore/outsource. Especially the latter implies the integration of corporate strategy with outsourcing/offshoring decisions.

Quotes:

The interviewee claims that along the chain from product invention to product launch, the Chinese production poses the biggest challenge.

Preparation and adequate integration of offshore decisions into corporate strategy is crucial for ensuring offshore success. Adaption to different cultures and the adjustment of own habits are similarly important.

4.5 Sweden

Reasons for offshoring were specified as the lack of own competences and an increased flexibility. Limited resources and budget constraints were mentioned as well. Further, outsourcing is used to address a lack of competences.

The main problems with offshoring are related to communication and language issues. Moreover, flexibility and cultural knowledge as well as mutual understanding are considered as important. Interviewees stated that an open mind is required too and that partners should act honestly and transparent. All in all a good preparation is required when getting in contact with partners from different cultural backgrounds.

Quotes:

Again, through mutual understanding, learning experiences, and the usage of a local partner network that has awareness about local norms, the company realized its success.

The representative considers language skills to be most important when interacting with different countries. It must be avoided that meanings are misinterpreted and therefore, parties involved should use the same level of language skills.

4.6 Summary of the Results

The aforementioned interviews revealed that the selected companies positively consider offshore activities when trust has been developed and when a good preparation in terms of taking into account cultural differences on an individual as well as on company level with other partners takes place. SMEs' offshore activities are aiming at closing the gap of lacking competences in the own company Language plays a significant role in this context.

Furthermore, the results suggest that trust building between parties involved in a relationship is of high importance. SMEs do not benefit from being very formal with partners. Informalities helps an SME to build and to maintain a trustful relationship with the other SME. In this context it becomes of importance to relate the own cultural background to the target culture of people involved as well as to take a company's history into account. Additionally, no opportunistic behavior was highlighted and could be found.

5 Discussion

Our intention was to find out whether SMEs can bridge cultural differences by using trust in their offshore activities. Our findings revealed that SMEs across the five selected countries consider trustful relationships as an important key for their offshore activities. Interesting that we could not find differences with regard to trust among SMEs with an Anglo-Saxon company culture or SMEs with a Northern-European company culture.

According to Child et al. (2005), trust is a complex phenomenon that can be examined through cost-benefit relationships, mutual understanding and development of friendship. Furthermore, trust can be perceived on three levels: calculative trust, understanding and personal identification. Calculative trust is trust on the level of expectations about costs and benefits whereas understanding is related to knowledge-based trust based on perceived similarities between partners. The personal identification is a social aspect that develops over time and is based on cultural affinity by people involved (Child et al. 2005). Fink and Kraus (2007) pointed out that mutual trustful relationships between SMEs can not only affect the outcome positively but also build up a starting point for sustainable—long term—business relations or trust-based cooperation. Thus our hypothesis that *SMEs are intrinsically better qualified for building trust than big companies* is confirmed.

Since offshoring decisions and experiences of SMEs in Germany, the Netherlands, United Kingdom, Denmark and Sweden are generally influenced by cultural differences, our research illuminated that a good preparation for a partnership influences offshoring activities too. A good preparation in this context means to be aware of different cultures and having the appropriate language skills. According to Devos et al. (2009), in a relationship between a vendor and a principal it might occur that three factors have additional influence on the relationship quality: goal differences, risk behavior differences and information asymmetry.

It was also found that misunderstandings and missing respect for cultural differences can lead to increased costs and disappointments. According to Winkler et al. (2008), cultural differences are a complex element to be managed and critically affect relationships when lacking a clear role definition, strong leadership and an active management of cultural differences. Devos et al. (2009) laid out that also knowledge retention and sustainable competitive advantage are not necessarily achieved when the relationship exists. Returns or promises (money, contract) that are not achieved can negatively influence a trustful relationship and are important criteria in the decision to offshore and for the selection process of potential partners. It is also important to take into account that trust can have different levels in different contexts as outlined by Janowicz and Noorderhaven (2006).

Beside the trust factor, flexibility was also mentioned as being important which is in-line with what Hätönen and Eriksson (2009) found. Thus, informality in working methods is a plus. Flexibility in the offshoring process allows for choosing the most suitable partners for a particular activity which seems to be easier for SMEs due to close connection to business and partners involved. According to Chell (2008), a SME owner/manager can more easily build up a good relationship with business partners than a manager of a large company when it comes to the relationship quality and its core element trust because of judgemental decisions he takes. Judgemental decisions are defined as "non-routine behavior by publishing private information and a subjective assessment of risks and investments" (Chell 2008). An owner/manager and his counterpart abroad start the relationship in a formal way but switch immediately to informal methods when both perceive that they can trust each other.

Taking into account that we have some snap shots based on 16 interviews, our hypothesis that *SMEs are at an advantage to build multi-cultural relationships because of their informality* is confirmed.

6 Conclusions

Although much research has been done on trust in offshoring activities, there has been little on specifics in the behavior of North West European SMEs with Anglo-Saxon SMEs when they start offshoring activities and in the resulting performance. With our study we extend the knowledge of trust in relationships among SMEs with different governance and cultural backgrounds. The development of trust and therefore the relationship quality level requires commitment of partners involved. The opportunity of offshoring activities for SMEs is a chance to stay competitive in the market and to sustain existing businesses. On the other hand, SMEs need to be aware of the risks (misunderstandings, disappointments, money, plagiarism) they take in the offshoring processes. Thus, a good preparation is a must in this context. Furthermore, we can conclude that, although SMEs under consideration might have different governance approaches, all SMEs highlighted the importance of trust in a relationship with regard to their offshoring activities.

There are some limitations associated with our research. First, the 16 interviews gave us only a snap shot about the complex phenomenon of trust in offshore activities and are not generalizable. One can argue whether the number of interviews is enough. However, according to Baker (2012) we found that using the purposive sampling method allows us to draw conclusions from the 16 interviews that can be considered as internally valid.

Additionally, the majority of selected companies was from the Northern European area. Another limitation was to find companies outside the IT world who are offshoring or who had done those activities and could refer to experience. Our study was a cross sectional study and therefore, a replication of the study is needed to see companies' development and to draw further conclusions from those findings.

7 Theoretical/Practical Implications/Future Research

With our research we extend the theory about offshore activities of SMEs and how much trust is involved in multi-cultural relationships. Furthermore we pointed out that SMEs with regard to relationship theory, are more individualistically driven by their owner/manager's beliefs, attitudes, and behavior than big companies are and therefore we contribute to know more about the influence factors.

In a broader sense we contributed to communication theory because ss part of bridging cultural differences in offshore activities, partners have to search for a common ground of communication. Partners should consider verbal and non-verbal communication, as well as the interpretation of meaning and adequacy of words. Partners with different native languages need to agree on a common language that fits for communication and understanding. If the chosen language is not the native language for at least one party, make an assessment (language test) if the language is sufficiently mastered and whether a translator might be a solution. The process begins before contracting the offshoring partner and continues during the relationship.

7.1 Practical Implications

Partners need to ensure that the risks of offshoring, including the quality of the offshoring partner and its activities, are under control. All potential internal and external risks of offshoring activities and their consequences such as increased costs, lower quality, and added time should be compared to the magnitude of the benefit the offshore company seeks.

SMEs should choose the offshoring partner that promises the most benefits while posing the least risks. That includes educational standards, laws and regulations, cost efficiency, production speed, quality and expertise. This must be done in the initial stage and facilitates the decision whether or not to offshore.

7.2 *Future Research*

This paper is a starting point for further research on the element of trust in relationships in which cultural differences need to be bridged. In this regard, the influence of culture can be subject to a more in-depth investigation with different countries. The countries under investigation can be analyzed separately and with a larger sample size.

The research explored the ideas, thoughts and experiences of companies' representatives and measured qualitative data. Therefore, future research may take an approach that takes more quantitative data into consideration to complement qualitative outcomes. Additionally, organizational culture may play an important role too in the relationship development when companies with an Anglo-Saxon and a Northern-European approach are under investigation. In the entire context of trust and relationships, one might think about how to measure trust. Of course one can ask people about trust or one can measure trust by a so-called trust game or investment game (Fetchenhauer and Dunning 2009). However, in business settings with different cultural backgrounds, it is even more interesting to measure trust at an objective level.

Finally, the study how relationships are managed best by either SMEs or large firms and if there are significant differences would require more data that includes comparative experience and insights gained by larger firms.

Acknowledgments We thank very much Ari Oksanen and Björn Ziemer for data collection and their contribution to this article.

Appendix 1

Pre-questions

- What is your position/role in the company?
- Could you describe briefly your organization, core businesses etc.?
- What kind of services/business functions are offshore outsourced in your company?
- In what extent have you done outsourcing?
  - When have you started offshore outsourcing?
  - How many contracts?
  - What have been the lengths of the contracts?
- What kind of service providers (vendors) you have had?
  - Size?
  - Location?

Pre-contract Phase

Cognition-based initial trust
Before working together with this service provider:

- We had a good impression of this service provider
- We heard of its good reputation
- We heard of its good ethical standard
- We knew that it treated its clients fairly

Calculative-based initial trust
Before working together with this service provider

- We heard that it usually acts in the interest of its clients
- We knew that it willingly provides assistance to its clients
- We heard that it usually tries to keep to its promises

Psychological initial distrust
Before working together with this service provider:

- We didn't think it is usually honest with its clients
- We didn't think it is usually benevolent to its clients
- We didn't think its employees are usually competent
- We didn't think its actions are usually predicable

Economical initial distrust
Before working together:

- We heard that it does not usually act in the interest of its clients
- We knew that it unwillingly provides assistance to its clients
- We heard that it does not always try to keep to its promises

Post-contract Phase

Customer's mutual trust
After working together with this service provider, we realize:

- It makes beneficial decisions to us under any circumstances
- It is willing to provide assistance to us without exception
- It reliably provides pre-specified support in a contract
- It is honest
- It cares about us
- It is sincere at all times

Explicit knowledge sharing
With this service provider, we share:

- Business proposals and reports
- Business manuals, models and methodologies
- Each other's success and failure stories
- Business knowledge obtained from newspapers, magazines, journals and television

Implicit knowledge sharing
With this service provider, we share:

- Know-how from work experience
- Each other's know-where and know-whom
- Expertise obtained from education and training

Outsourcing success

- We have been able to refocus on core business
- We have enhanced out IT competency
- We have increased access to skilled personnel
- We have enhanced economies of scale in human resources
- We have enhanced economies of scale in technological resources
- We have increased control of IS expenses
- We have reduced the risk of technological obsolescence
- We have increased access to key information technologies
- We are satisfied with our overall benefits from outsourcing

Additional open questions:

- Do you think that the central role of owner/manager of SME is crucial for creating trustful relationship with the service provider?
- Do you feel that you have experienced opportunistic behaviour from your service provider?
- If yes, how have you reacted to this opportunistic behaviour?
- How do you see the division of interorganizational trust and interpersonal trust from your organizations point of view?
- Do you think that the creation of interpersonal trust plays more important role than interorganizational trust in successful outsourcing relationship?
- Do you initially feel that building a trustful relationship is easier with a SME service provider than large service provider (or vice versa)?
- In which ways and with which tools you feel trust could be improved in your relationships with the service provider?

References

Adams, B. D., Flear, C., Taylor, T. E., Hall, C. D., & Karthaus, C. (2010). Review of Interorganizational Trust Models. *Human systems Incorporated,* DRDC Toronto CR 2010, p. 143.

Baker, S. E. (2012). *How many qualitative interviews is enough? Expert voices and early career reflections on sampling and cases in qualitative research.* National Center for Research Methods Review Paper, Middlesex University, UK.

Bharadwaj, S. S., Bhushan, K., Saxena, C., & Halemane, M. D. (2010). Building a successful relationship in business process outsourcing: an exploratory study. *European Journal of Information Systems, 19*, 168–180.

Baumeister, R. F., & Bushman, B. J. (2010). *Social psychology and human nature* (2nd ed.). Belmont: Wadsworth.

Brown, D., & Wilson, S. (2009). *The Black book of outsourcing: how to manage the changes, challenges, and opportunities.* New Jersey: Wiley.

Business Week Magazine. (2011). *The mortgage of the future.* http://www.businessweek.com/magazine/the-mortgage-of-the-future-11102011.html. Accessed: 15th November 2011.

Child, J., Faulkner, D., & Tallman, S. (2005). Trust in cooperative strategies. In J. Child, D. Faulkner, & S. Tallman (Eds.), *Cooperative strategy: Managing alliances, networks, and joint ventures* (2nd ed., pp. 50–70). New York: Oxford University Press.

Chell, E. (2008). *The entrepreneurial personality. A social construction* (2nd ed.). New York: Routledge.

Contractor, F. J., Kumar, V., Kundu, S. K., & Pedersen, T. (2010). Reconceptualizing the firm in a world of outsourcing and offshoring: The organizational and geographical relocation of high-value company functions. *Journal of Management Studies, 47*, 1417–1433.

Devos, J., Van Landeghem, H., & Deschoolmeester, D. (2009). IT governance in SMEs: Trust or control? *Information Systems, 301*, 135–149.

Dibbern, J., Goles, T., Hirschheim, R., & Jayatilaka, B. (2004). Information systems outsourcing: A survey and analysis of the literature. *The DATA BASE of Advances for Information Systems, 35*, 6–102.

Dibbern, J., & Heinzl, A. (2009). Outsourcing of information systems functions in small and medium sized enterprises: A test of a multi-theoretical model. *Business & Information Systems Engineering, 1*, 1–10.

Duncan, P., Wright, J., Duncan, D., & Wiggins, A. (2009). Strategic IS/IM in context. In K. Grant, R. Hackney, & D. Edgar (Eds.), *Strategic information systems management: priorities, procedures & policy.* London: Thomson/Cengage Learning.

Dunning, D., Fetchenhauer, D., & Schlösser, T. M. (2011). Trust as a social and emotional act: Noneconomic considerations in trust behavior. *Journal of Economic Psychology, 33*, 1–9.

European Commission. (2012). *Small and medium-sized enterprises (SMEs) What is an SME?* http://ec.europa.eu/enterprise/policies/sme/facts-figures-analysis/sme-definition/index_en.htm. Accessed July 12 2012.

Fetchenhauer, D., & Dunning, D. (2009). Do people trust too much or too little? *Journal of Economic Psychology, 30*, 263.

Fink, M., & Kraus, S. (2007). Mutual trust as a key to internationalization of SMEs. *Management Research News, 30*, 674–688.

Hätönen, J., & Eriksson, T. (2009). 30+ years of research and practice of outsourcing—Exploring the past and anticipating the future. *Journal of International Management, 15*, 142–155.

Ibrahim, M., & Ribbers, P. M. (2009). The impacts of competence trust and openness trust on interorganizations systems. *European Journal of Information Systems, 18*, 223–234.

Inkpen, A. C., & Tsang, E. W. K. (2005). Social capital, networks, and knowledge transfer. *Academy of Management Review, 30*, 146–165.

Janowicz, M., & Noorderhaven, N. (2006). Levels of inter-organizational trust: Conceptualization and measurement. In R. Bachmann & A. Zaheer (Eds.), *Handbook of trust research* (pp. 264–279). Cheltenham: Edward Elgar Publishing Limited.

Judd, C. M., & Kenny, D. A. (2006). Research design and research validity. In D. Vaus (Ed.), *Research design* (Vol. 1). UK: Sage Publications.

Lee, J., & Huynh, M. (2005). *An integrative model of trust on IT Outsourcing: From the service Receiver's Perspective: Proceedings of the 9th Pacific Asia conference*, pacis-net.org.

Lee, J., Huynh, M., & Hirschheim, R. (2008). An integrative model of trust on IT outsourcing: Examining a bilateral perspective. *Inf Syst Front, 10*, 145–163.

Lewicki, R. J., & Bunker, B. B. (1995). *Conflict, cooperation and justice*. Trust in relationships: A model of trust development and decline. Jossey-Bass, San Francisco.

Mathrani, A., Goel, G., & Parsons, D. (2007). *Building trust across virtual social spaces: The software vendors perspectives [online]*. Available at: http://aisel.aisnet.org/acis2007/17. Accessed: July 19 2012.

McAllister, D. J. (1995). Affect and cognition-based trust as foundations for interpersonal cooperation in organizations. *Academy of Management Journal, 38*, 24–59.

McKnight, D. H., Cummings, L. L., & Chervany, N. L. (1998). Initial trustformation in new organizational relationships. *Academy of Management Review, 23*, 473–490.

Miles, L. K., Nind, L. K., & Macrae, C. N. (2010). Moving through time. *Psychological Science, 21*, 222–223.

Minkov, M., & Hofstede, G. (2011). The evolution of Hofstede's doctrine. *Cross Cultural Management: An International Journal, 18*, 10–20.

Perrini, F., Russo, A., & Tencati, A. (2007). CSR strategies of SMEs and large firms. Evidence from Italy. *Journal of Business Ethics, 74*, 285–300.

Rottman, J. W. (2008). Successful knowledge transfer within offshore supplier networks: a case study exploring social capital in strategic alliances. *Journal of Information Technology, 23*, 31–43.

Russo, A., & Perrini, F. (2009). Investigating Stakeholder theory and social capital: CSR in large firms and SMEs. *Journal of Business Ethics, 91*, 207–221.

Sabherwal, R. (1999). The role of trust in outsourced IS development projects. *Communications of the ACM, 42*, 2.

Stel, F. (2011). *Improving the performance of co-innovation allicances*. Tilburg: Tilburg University.

Willcocks, L., & Craig, A. (2010). *The outsourcing enterprise outsourcing in difficult times: releasing cost but maintaining control*. www.logica.com. Accessed April 2011.

Winkler, J. K., Dibbern, J., & Heinzl, A. (2008). The impact of cultural differences in offshore outsourcing-Case study results from German–Indian application development projects. *Information System Frontier, 10*, 243–258.

Yin, R. K. (2011). *Qualitative research from start to finish*. New York: The Guilford Press.

Exploring Knowledge Capabilities in SMEs: Cases in Five Irish Software SMEs

Ciara Heavin and Frederic Adam

1 The Nature of Small to Medium Sized Organisations

Research provides a variety of definitions for SMEs (Lauder et al. 1994). The European Union has adopted a standardised definition of SMEs, classifying them as an enterprise satisfying a criterion for number of employees, micro fewer than 10, small fewer than 50, and medium fewer than 250 (European Commission 2003). To be classified as an SME, a firm's turnover should be less than €50 million, with a balance sheet of less than €43 million, while large company ownership should not exceed 25 % (European Commission 2003; Enterprise Ireland 2007). An SME must be autonomous i.e., less than 25 % owned by other enterprises and own less than 25 % of other enterprises (Enterprise Ireland 2007). If partnership with other organisations is greater than 25 % a proportion of the data of the partner organisations is included in the calculation to determine staff headcount and financial details (Enterprise Ireland 2007). These firms employ 50.4 % of the workforce and generate 39.9 % of the total value added (European Commission 2009). Ireland is a country where indigenous private sector economic activity is dominated by small businesses. Small and Medium-Sized Enterprises are often the unacknowledged backbone of the Irish economy significantly contributing to job creation in this country (Forfas 2006). In 2006 almost 63 % of all working people in Ireland were employed in small businesses with fewer than 50 employees (CSO 2007).

Still, SMEs are not like "little large businesses" (Wong 2005) or miniature editions of larger firms, they face different issues (Nissila et al. 2004; Pillania 2008). According to Penrose (1959), the differences between the administrative characteristic of very small and the very large firms are extensive making it

C. Heavin (✉) · F. Adam
Business Information Systems, University College, Cork, Ireland
e-mail: c.heavin@ucc.ie

F. Adam
e-mail: fadam@afis.ucc.ie

J. Devos et al. (eds.), *Information Systems for Small and Medium-sized Enterprises*, Progress in IS, DOI: 10.1007/978-3-642-38244-4_14,

difficult to draw similarities between the two, in other words a ‘caterpillar may not be defined as a butterfly’. In Audretsch et al. (1999) view, small organisations pursue a strategy independent of MNEs by focusing primarily on capturing small niche markets that enable them to define a profit margin separate to larger markets. They claim that this is achieved through an enhanced focus on customization and innovation (Audretsch et al. 1999). By pursuing product specialisation an SME can carve out a niche market, either by doing things better than an MNE in that area with longer term plans for growth, or by becoming an attractive proposition for takeover.

By their nature SMEs experience “resource poverty” (Welsh and White 1981, p. 18) such as lack of time, financial and human resources (Lee and Oakes 1995; OECD 2002; Welsh and White 1981). In support of this view, Kraaijenbrink (2006) contends that it is not the size of an SME that makes them different from large organisations; it is the lack of economies of scale. As a result, marginal changes in the organisation’s environment have a greater impact on smaller organisations in comparison to their larger counterparts (Welsh and White 1981). However, Teece (2000) contends that small organisations are structured so that decision-making and reactions to change are rapid. Additional extant research (Nissila et al. 2004; Vickery 1999) accredits the successes experienced by small business on their ability to adapt to new circumstances. Moreover, Duhan et al. (2001) identify the need for strategic planning enabling SMEs to respond to external environmental changes such as government policy. By building these capabilities, small companies may grow in spite of the external influences, such as customers, competitors and suppliers that surround them. Notwithstanding the issue of size, “knowing what you know” (Davenport and Prusak 1998; O’Dell and Grayson 1998) is imperative in the case of SMES, as Ghobadian and Gallear (1996) found in their study that employees are the key contributors to the success of an SME and should be treated as a company asset. The following section considers the significance of software SMEs operating in a knowledge intensive industry.

2 Software SMEs

The software industry is widely recognised as a knowledge rich industry sector. Hoch et al. (1999), p. 6 state that software is “nothing but pure knowledge in codified form—largely drives and enables today’s economy”. In support, Bernroider (2002, p. 562) comments that “the software industry…is a knowledge industry. Its major product is knowledge itself and its major output is research which translates into new products and services”. Essentially, software development may be characterised as knowledge work (Schönstrom and Carlsson 2003).

Considering software and KM, Sheremata (2002) contends that these areas are related because software development, like KM, is a human driven activity. Software projects are open to environmental changes and are innovative by nature, with the sole purpose of solving a specific problem (Sheremata 2002). In support, Schönstrom and Carlsson (2003), p. 1708 state that "the knowledge intensive nature of software development and its relation to a number of KM issues and challenges makes software development an interesting phenomenon to study from a KM perspective". Further considering this notion, the next section examines the significance of pursuing a KM approach in software SMEs.

3 The Importance of KM in SMEs

A significant portion of the KM literature concentrates on large multinational organisations. While researchers (Davenport and Prusak 1998; O'Dell and Grayson 1998) draw on KM studies carried out in large organisations, it must be acknowledged that the issues faced by SMEs may not be a scaled down version of large business experiences (Pillania 2008; Welsh and White 1981). Davenport and Prusak (1998), p. 17 make the assumption that small organisations, of two to three hundred employees, "have a reliable grasp of collective organizational knowledge".

From Hyland's (2000) perspective "smaller-sized companies were the forerunners of knowledge management". SMEs have been practising KM for centuries; this is exemplified in the relationship between a master craftsman and his student (Hansen et al. 1999). According to Chan and Chao (2008), p. 83 "in comparisons with large organizations SMEs could even be more nimble and flexible in adapting their systems and structures for KM purposes". This is claimed on the premise that SMEs have lower communication, implementation and replacement costs (Chan and Chao 2008) than their larger counterparts. In addition, Edvarsson (2006) claims that while only 24 % of Icelandic SMEs have a formal KM approach in place, empirical evidence indicates that employee skills, customer handling and decision making have all improved as a result of an official KM programme.

From an SME perspective knowledge is embedded in carefully cultivated social relationships (Hyland 2000). "Organizations are now hiring minds more than hands" (Wong 2005), p. 261. Considering this in relation to SME size and ability to acquire, codify, store, maintain, transfer and create knowledge, the effect of losing a staff members' tacit knowledge may be detrimental to an organisation where no formal knowledge system is deployed (Wickert and Herschel 2001; Wong and Radcliffe 2000). Judge (2007) purports that greater consideration given by SMEs to KM may mean a reduction of recurring solutions to the same problem, a reduction in redundancy of knowledge based activities and greater knowledge availability allowing more time for employee training and development. In the case of software SMEs, Baskerville and Pries-Heje (1999) support the view that software SMEs develop KM processes to substitute software engineering frameworks, such as CMM, that are too resource intensive for SMEs to consider. These processes are established with the objective of repeating success and avoiding past failures (Baskerville and Pries-Heje 1999). Hoch et al. (1999) purport that software companies with well-established structure and processes reduce low level software rework and facilitates software reuse. This leads to more enjoyable work for programmers as well as improved software product quality and time to market (Hoch et al. 1999).

4 Leveraging is to Support KM

KM seeks to break down information into a format that may be readily available throughout the organisation and stored and manipulated with other information when required. Technology used to manage knowledge allows smaller organisations to overcome this barrier. Increasingly, technology referred to as KMS are utilized by organisations to store the explicit and tacit knowledge of the employees, of the organisation as a whole as well as enabling improved access to customers, suppliers and collaborators (Wright and Etemad 2001). Standard KMS are typically implemented by large organisations to manage internal process and individual knowledge, however, they are considered too complex, time and resource consuming for smaller organisations (Bayer et al. 2005). Tsui (2004) goes a step further by arguing that the significant differences between large and small organisations "renders most if not all of the commercial KM software inappropriate for SMEs" (p. 16). Chan and Chao (2008) found that resource restrictions meant that SMEs were underinvested in KM-related technologies. While conflicting views surround the degree to which technology becomes an issue when implementing a KM approach, technology remains a component of the knowledge environment (Alavi and Leidner 2001), as knowledge intensive organizations implement and develop leading edge technology platforms to support the knowledge requirements of the organisation and its employees.

SMEs typically do not have the resources to invest in off the shelf KMS solutions and subsequently Internet technology plays a significant role in terms of enhancing an SME's technical capabilities; it proposes for instance, a more cost effective alternative to EDI (MacGregor and Bunker 2000). The uptake in Internet technologies has enabled SMEs access to a wider marketplace (Forfas 1999), essentially these technologies including social media technology and wikis have allowed the smallest of companies access to customers, suppliers and collaborators around the world (Asproth and Nyström 2008; Tetteh and Burn 2001; Wright and Etemad 2001). Internet technologies support knowledge activity, facilitating organisational knowledge acquisition about the market and competitors (Beckinsale and Levy 2004) as well as conveying a positive and progressive image (Chapman et al. 2000). The Internet also enables communication, collaboration and knowledge transfer (Banck and Nystrom 2005). These technologies offer advantages for organisations as a foundation for collaboration—both within the organisations as well as between organisations (Asproth and Nyström 2008). As a result of the Internet, email adoption has also been embraced by SMEs who actively utilise this technology as a means of internal and external communication

(Poon and Swatman 1999). Subsequently, effective use of the Internet may lead to new business opportunities for SMEs (Chapman et al. 2000). The following section considers the research approach used in this study.

5 Research Approach

This study pursued a qualitative analytical approach (Ägerfalk and Fitzgerald 2008) using multiple case studies, each case was selected using purposeful sampling (Patton 1990). The cases were selected based on their size and industry sector. The software industry "is a knowledge industry. Its major product is knowledge itself and its major output is research which translates into new products and services" (Bernroider 2002, p. 562) Software development may be characterised as knowledge work (Schönstrom and Carlsson 2003). Initially, eight small software organisations were selected for the purpose of this study; however, the number of cases was reduced to five. This choice is supported by Patton (1990), p. 186 who contends that "one may change the sample if information emerges that indicates the value of that change". Moreover, Eisenhardt (1989) raises the issue of 'reaching closure' and at what point a researcher should stop adding cases. After careful consideration, it was apparent that five cases provided the rich information necessary to fulfil the research objective outlined. Eisenhardt (1989) recommends that the researcher should stop adding cases when 'theoretical saturation' (p. 545) is reached; from the researcher's perspective the contribution of three further cases was marginal.

As the objective of this study was to explore the knowledge approach leveraged by small software development firms, the focus of the study was on the two core business processes of sales and software development. Based on a selection strategy, positional methods were used to uncover sales and technical managers while other respondents were selected based on reputation (Knoke 1994). Twenty eight individuals were interviewed; each interview was approximately one hour in duration. Interviews were taped and transcribed. The exploratory nature of the study coupled with the "thick transcripts" (p. 56) (Miles and Huberman 1994) meant that qualitative analysis could be conducted through the use of coding techniques (Miles and Huberman 1994). Table 1 presents the final set of categories utilised to code the interviews in all five cases.

The generation and use of categories facilitate theorizing, by enabling the construction and storing of "understandings, interpretations, models, ways of accessing complex data records and the relationships of categories to each other and to data" (Richards and Richards 1995, p. 80). The many classifications of knowledge activities (KAs) (not included as part of this study) have been assessed and evaluated to develop a complete classification of KAs for the purpose of data analysis in this study. Each KA was assigned a code and this code was utilised to classify the nature of KAs that occurred, these categories were then assigned chunks of data derived from the interview transcripts. The names of the KAs were

Table 1 Classification of knowledge activities with codes

Knowledge activity (KA)	Code	Definition
Acquire	A	Identify and capture knowledge from source to a company. Sources include written form, physical objects, people, courses, cooperation between source and recipient and outsourcing
Codify	CO	Assess the value of knowledge, distil, refine and assemble into comprehensive format
Store	S	Store knowledge in an artefact e.g., system, document
Maintain	M	Update on continuous basis, as a result of additional acquisition activities
Transfer	T	Identify receiver organize channel of communication and send
Create	C	New knowledge cultivated through knowledge transfer. Acquisition activities come into play as new knowledge is acquired

refined based on findings gathered from the first case study conducted at HelpRead Ltd. This case was selected as the initial case primarily due to the nature of innovative software products developed by the firm. This meant that this case displayed a wealth of KAs from the outset. In addition, the organisation's pioneering management style presented rich and interesting findings on initial investigation. This case was also leveraged to validate the interview protocol, as well as the data analysis and display techniques employed. The coding schema was confirmed and the data displays utilised were refined. The four subsequent cases were conducted in parallel.

Earl and Hopwood's (1980) Information Processing Mix matrix was adapted to explore the types of IS utilised to support KM in each case presented. Using the same concepts of routine, non-routine, official and unofficial, this study redefines Earl and Hopwood's Matrix to deal with knowledge processing (Fig. 1).

Figure 1 identifies routine knowledge processing as formalised systems that are leveraged to fulfil organisational tasks, defining routine information processing tasks as being either official or unofficial. Routine official activities include the utilisation of official organisational systems such as MIS, accounting systems, Intranet-based document management systems and digital/physical company

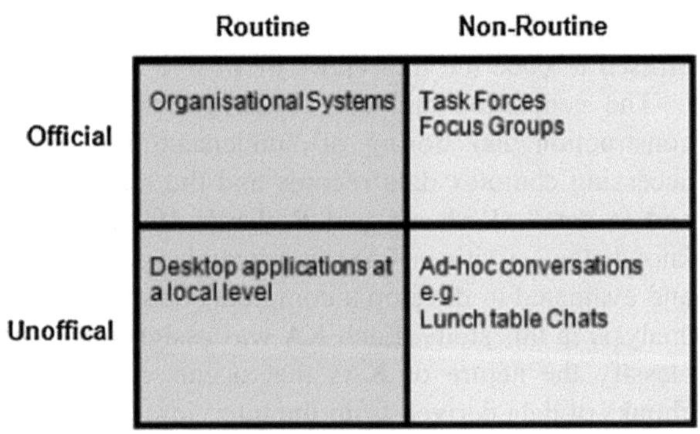

Fig. 1 Knowledge processing mix (after Earl and Hopwood 1980)

libraries. Routine unofficial activities involve the use of ad-hoc, local systems which include desktop application such as email and word processing applications at a local level. In their model Earl and Hopwood (1980), p. 6 define non-routine information processing as "investments in the capability to provide ad hoc information and mechanisms for furthering access to information" supporting the need for face-to-face interaction as a means of information/knowledge transfer (Kefalas 1973; Keegan 1974; Mintzberg 1975). Leveraging Earl and Hopwood's (1980) model, Fig. 1 seeks to capture those non-routine systems that enable the occurrence of KAs in each case. The occurrences of KAs were re-examined to establish the knowledge processing requirements needed to support the individual activities. Table 2 illustrates the tabular format used to present mode usage by KA.

The authors have synthesised the contents of these tables to provide a high level discussion of KAs per case. The completed tables are extensive and have not been included as part of this chapter.

6 Background to Cases

Case 1 HelpRead Ltd. produces assistive software to support learning disabilities. The complexity of the software product offering means that a deep understanding of customer requirements is essential to build a useful product. The complex customer requirements coupled with innovative management initiatives, such as brainstorming, provided rich insights from a KM perspective.

Case 2 TravelSoft Ltd. was established in the early 1990s. Their core offering at that time was to provide travel software to one main customer, who was also the company's main shareholder. In 2004, TravelSoft Ltd. took greater financial control of the organisation; while continuing to provide software to their former parent organisation. Change processes such as hiring new managers, pursuing product development and attracting 'third party customer' offered significant opportunities to study KM.

Case 3 Systems Solutions Ltd. develops software solutions in the client server market. Software consulting companies have been known to pursue formalised approaches to KM (Hansen et al. 1999), in Systems Solutions Ltd. this is not the case. While significant KA was required to support the divisions independently, as

Table 2 Sample tabular display of KM approach by company

Types of knowledge	Knowledge activity	Instance of knowledge activity	Routine modes		Non-routine modes	
			Official	Unofficial	Official	Unofficial

well as the transfer activity across divisions, much KA was informal and ad-hoc in nature, primarily driven by focused sales activity.

Case 4 FinSoft Ltd. is a Dublin based firm focused on developing investment fund management software. This strategic focus meant that formally managing knowledge did not featured high on the FinSoft agenda; however, the limited KM focus was primarily based on the need to meet compliance regulations in the financial investment sector.

Case 5 DocMan Ltd. is a small satellite operation for an edocument management software developer based in Givisiez, Switzerland. From a KM perspective, the size, location and functional specialization of the site presented unique characteristics for consideration.

Table 3 provides an overview of the five companies the in terms of size, type of software business and interesting features.

Two of the companies, HelpRead and TravelSoft concentrated on new product development. At the time, HelpRead had three learning disability products in the market while TravelSoft had moved away from their one core customer and were in the process of building a software product for the travel software sector. Two organisations selected for this study offered customised software solutions, Systems Solutions and FinSoft, FinSoft also offered financial data feeds as a product. DocMan (Ireland) operated as a software 'subsidiary' with seven employees working at the Irish site, with the headquarters located in Switzerland. All of the organisations had an Irish presence.

Table 3 Overview of cases

Company/ characteristic	HelpRead Ltd.	Traventec Ltd.	FinSoft Ltd.	Systems solutions Ltd.	Doc Man (Ireland) Ltd.
Core offering	Assistive technology	eTravel solutions	Investment and fund data solutions	Delivering eSolutions	Systems integrators for eDocuments
Head count	50	70	50	70	7 (Ireland) 250 Doc Man Ltd.
Analytical interest	Innovative product development	One core customer owning 10 % of organisation	Focused on high profile UK based financial institutions	Customer and sales focus	Remote subsidiary of swiss based firm

7 KM at HelpRead Ltd.

HelpRead focused on building a collective organisational memory that facilitated continued growth through the introduction of new hires and new products. This was particularly important in terms of acquiring external knowledge to inform new product development. Table 4 identifies *82 instance of KA* at HelpRead; the majority of activities presented themselves through knowledge acquisition, storage and transfer.

The study identified 82 KAs; 113 instances of knowledge types were uncovered. The difference in these figures can be explained by single KAs leveraging multiple knowledge types in some instances, thus increasing the instances of knowledge types identified in the analytic memos. It is also important to note that, at the time, HelpRead Ltd. was not in a new product development phase. Using Table 4, the difference in intensity between these types of activities is indicative of HelpRead's position as a growing organisation. Knowledge acquisition intensity at 21 % (n = 82) showed that 53 % of all knowledge acquisition activity was focused on gathering product knowledge supporting Groen's (2006), p. 124 view that in high-technology SMEs require knowledge from external sources to support new product development.

At 13 % (n = 82) codification activity was relatively low intensity, this was reflective of the uncertainty around what the company needs to know in the future. This is predominantly evident with the Technical FAQ, which lacked buy-in from the entire development team. The Development Manager admitted that as a team "they didn't know what they should know". Most codification activity was directly related to refining the discussions at group meetings into documents which are made available over the Intranet. Over 90 % (n = 11) of all codification activity identified in Table 4 was related to product development knowledge. Codification was largely not a sales related activity. The well-defined scope of the *Goldmine*^{TM} sales system meant that no KA was required to support the refinement

Table 4 Distribution of KAs at HelpRead Ltd

KA/Company	No. of KAs (%)/Knowledge focus by activity
Acquire	17 (21 %) 53 % product knowledge (9 of n = 17 activities)
Codify	1 (13 %) 90 % SW Dev, project and product knowledge (10 of n = 11 activities)
Store	24 (29 %) 71 % SW Dev, Product. Project knowledge (17 of n = 24 activities)
Maintain	8 % (10 %) 63 % project and SW Dev knowledge (5 of n = 8 activities)
Transfer	17 (21 %) 83 % product, project and SW Dev knowledge (14 of n = 17 activities)
Create	5 (6 %) 80 % product knowledge (4 of n = 5 activities)
Total	82

and distillation of sales related knowledge. In addition, the experience of the sales team meant they know what important customer and sales related knowledge should be stored for future use.

The high occurrence of storage activities at 29 % was indicative of the importance placed on storing knowledge in the new Intranet-based quality system—approx 74 % (17 of n = 24 storage activities) of storage activity involved the Intranet. These activities primarily included storing software project documents and employee skills documents, in line with the compliance requirements outlined by IS9001:2000. The codification intensity also included the level of customer information captured and stored by the sales team. This 29 % reflected the move to store the knowledge gathered from acquisition, codification and transfer activities. Maintenance activities at 10 % highlighted the company's focus on maintaining software and product development knowledge. Surprisingly, transfer activity was high intensity at 19 %—with closer inspection; the role of the Technical Director (TD) was integral to this. At 6 %, knowledge creation was very low. While Table 4 shows that 80 % of knowledge creation activity was focused on product knowledge, in line with company strategy, the lack of other types of knowledge creation may be explained by the pressures associated with the recent rapid growth in employee headcount and the increased product portfolio. The findings indicate that HelpRead embraced the need for a more formalised approach to managing knowledge however the overreliance on the TD may be identified as a weakness in this strategy. Without the TD as a pivotal player, these activities may not be as successful or may not even occur. In order to leverage the full potential of their approach; it is imperative that responsibility for KA is disseminated to all levels of the organisation.

8 KM at TravelSoft Ltd.

At the time of interview a new Application Solutions Manager had been in place at TravelSoft for approximately eight months. From a Telecoms background, he implemented a number of organisational strategies to develop embedded processes and most importantly to bring a new product to the travel software marketplace. It is primarily these management initiatives that contributed to the high number of KAs, *147 instances* presented in Table 5.

The KAs identified used more than one type of knowledge during a single KA, consequently providing the rationale for the 211 instances of knowledge types identified for TravelSoft. The knowledge focus at TravelSoft was quite consistent and reflected the company's strategic objectives. The emphasis on software development, project, process and product knowledge was marked. Knowledge of the travel industry made up a quarter of the knowledge acquisition activity.

At HelpRead Ltd. 82 instances of KAs were observed, KA at TravelSoft was considerably higher at 147 instances. This intensity may be explained by a number of factors. Knowledge acquisition activity at 11 % (16 of n = 147) was due to the

Table 5 KAs at TravelSoft Ltd

KA	No. of KAs (%)/Knowledge focus by activity
Acquire	16 (11 %) 44 % SW Dev knowledge (7 of n = 16 activities) 25 % travel industry knowledge (4 of n = 16 activities)
Codify	30 (20 %) 36 % SW Dev (11 of n = 31 activities) 32 % process/product knowledge (10 of n = 31 activities)
Store	31 (21 %) 41 % SW Dev and project knowledge (12 of n = 29 activities) 41 % process/product knowledge (12 of n = 29 activities)
Maintain	20 (14 %) 40 % SW Dev and project knowledge (8 of n = 20 activities) 40 % process/product knowledge (8 of n = 20 activities)
Transfer	41 (28 %) 68 % SW Dev and project knowledge (28 of m = 41 activities)
Create	9 (6 %) product knowledge (5 of n = 9 activities)
Total	147

acquisition of consultant knowledge on new product development, employee training, relevant books, journals and travel conferences. In terms of codification at 20 % activity, project related knowledge was refined and stored. At 21 % activity, storage activity was almost in line with the volume of codification activity. This shows that TravelSoft were good at following through on this type of activity. For example the steering committee refine and store the new Adept framework templates in the relevant artefacts. R&D acquisition, codification, storage and maintenance of knowledge contribute to the dense volumes of KA. Activities such as Internet research in the travel area added to the level of knowledge acquisition activities, while refining and storing this knowledge contributed to the volume of codification and storage activity. At 14 %, maintenance activity was lower than knowledge codification and storage activity. This could be owing to the fact that some of the knowledge stored did not require updating, for example conference and journal papers on the travel industry will not be changed although new papers may be added over time resulting in increased storage activity.

Knowledge transfer at 28 % (41 where n = 147) represented the highest volume of KA. Leveraging a variety of routine and non-routine modes (these are outlined in next section). This organisation encouraged knowledge transfer at all levels of the organisation. Knowledge creation was much lower at 9 instances (6 % where n = 147). These activities were all generated around new product and process development placing these initiatives at the core of all KAs of TravelSoft at that time. Table 5 shows a spread of 66 % of KA at TravelSoft across knowledge acquisition, codification, storage and maintenance activity, while transfer and creation activity account for 34 % of all KA. By comparison, the distribution at HelpRead for the same activities was 73 and 27 % respectively. This shows that through their change process, TravelSoft were good at leveraging the more 'valuable' types of KA.

9 KM at Systems Solutions Ltd.

KA at Systems Solutions was mostly characterised by its informal nature. The Managing Director admitted that when he is involved with requirements analysis for the business intelligence division the knowledge is documented and stored in an A4 pad. One Project Manager from the Application Division admitted that it was not uncommon to calculate a project price on the back of a piece of paper in the car park before attending a meeting with a prospective customer. Table 6 illustrates a total of *105 KAs* identified.

One hundred and thirty one instances of knowledge type were identified across the KAs; this indicated that some KAs leveraged multiple knowledge types. It is apparent that knowledge acquisition and maintenance were exceptions in terms of their knowledge focus. Knowledge acquisition was largely focused on product and customer knowledge, these knowledge types were mainly relevant to the Business Service Management and SAP Solutions divisions focused on software resale. Knowledge maintenance activity was focused on sales knowledge at 38 %; this emphasis on sales primarily reflected the knowledge requirements of these two divisions. From Table 6, it is evident that the other KAs were focused on software development and project knowledge serving the knowledge needs of the Business Intelligence (data warehousing) and Application Development divisions.

A considerable amount of Systems Solutions business was focused on the development of bespoke software for local pharmaceutical firms. Manifestly, this project related knowledge was codified, stored and maintained in order to meet the requirements of pharmaceutical customers in line with Food and Drugs Authority (FDA) regulations. From Table 6, it is evident that at 26 %, storage activity was higher than both codification and maintenance activity together at 21 %. This may mean that Systems Solutions store large volumes of documentation without

Table 6 KAs at systems solutions

KA	No. of KA (%)/Knowledge focus by activity
Acquire	16 (15 %) 44 % product knowledge (7 of n = 16 activities) 31 % customer knowledge (5 of n = 16 activities)
Codify	14 (13 %) 86 % Sw Dev and project knowledge (12 of n = 14 activities)
Store	27 (26 %) 67 % Sw Dev and project knowledge (18 of n = 27)
Maintain	13 (12 %) 35 sales knowledge (5 of n = 5 activities) 23 % project knowledge (3 of n = 3 activities)
Transfer	30 (29 %) 60 % Sw Dev and project knowledge (18 of n = 30 activities)
Create	5 (5 %) 80 % project knowledge (4 of n = 5 activities)
Total	105

refining and formatting it, and in the longer term, without updating it. As a result, it seemed that they hold these large volumes for the sole purpose of protecting themselves from external threats such as audits. At 15 %, knowledge acquisition appeared important, however, more than half of this activity was attributed to sales and customer interaction.

At 5 %, knowledge creation activity was very low. From the interviews, it was clear that the Managing Director was the main source of the knowledge creation activity at Systems Solutions. It seemed that the time pressures associated with meeting project deadlines meant that there was little time for knowledge creation activity amongst the divisions. In the case of Systems Solutions knowledge creation was not the responsibility of those at an operational level.

Knowledge acquisition, codification, storage and maintenance account for 66 % of all KAs while knowledge transfer and creation amount to 34 %. This was consistent with TravelSoft, though it differed in the case of HelpRead whose focus on knowledge storage activity through the new company Intranet tipped the balance of KA distribution towards the earlier activities such as acquisition and codification.

10 KM at FinSoft Ltd.

Largely driven by compliance in the financial services sector, we identified 111 instances of knowledge types across *78 KAs*. This indicated that the KAs identified leveraged more than one type of knowledge per KA.

Table 7 shows a consistent knowledge focus on software development and project knowledge across knowledge codification, storage, maintenance and transfer activity. At FinSoft knowledge acquisition activity focused on customer knowledge, while creation activity leveraged product knowledge. Knowledge acquisition activity was primarily related to the sales and customer knowledge. While 11 % (9 where n = 78) of KA was external knowledge acquisition, a large portion of this activity was impromptu in nature although it was driven by the Head of Sales and the Chief Technology Officer (CTO). Knowledge codification, storage and maintenance activity at 46 % (43 where n = 78) was predominantly related to project knowledge and software development activity. However, as FinSoft Ltd. is a supplier of investment fund data feeds and bespoke fund management software, this activity was conducted to protect the organisation from issues arising from regular internal audits.

Knowledge transfer at 29 % (23 where n = 78) intensity occurred amongst the teams, software developers, quality assurance (QA), data, sales and senior management. While it was admitted that knowledge transfer between the software development team and Quality Assurance was effective, the Head of the Data team acknowledged that knowledge transfer amongst the other division needed improvement. Table 7 illustrates that knowledge creation activity is extremely low at 3 instances (4 % where n = 78), management were typically involved in these activities focused around attracting new customers and creating potential new

Table 7 KAs at FinSoft Ltd

KA	No. of KA (%)/Knowledge focus by activity
Acquire	9 (11 %) 67 % customer knowledge (6 of n = 9 activities)
Codify	13 (17 %) 92 % SW Dev and project knowledge (12 of n = 13 activities)
Store	20 (26 %) 70 % SW Dev and project knowledge (14 of n = 20 activities)
Maintain	10 (13 %) 50 % SW Dev and project knowledge 5 of n = 10) 30 % customer knowledge (3 of n = 10)
Transfer	23 (29 %) 78 % SW Devand Project Knowledge (18 of n = 23 activities)
Create	3 (4 %) 67 % product knowledge (2 of n = 3 activities)
Total	78

product ideas. However, they did not seem to expend significant resources in creating new ideas in-house.

At FinSoft Ltd. the distribution of acquisition, codification, storage and maintenance activities to knowledge transfer and creation activities were at 66 and 34 % respectively. While at HelpRead this distribution was at 74 and 26 %, however, the focus there was on the development of the Intranet and collaborative wiki technologies, with knowledge storage activity accounting for a significant proportion of the 74 % (29 % storage activity). Both FinSofts' and Systems Solutions' overreliance on unofficial modes of knowledge processing is detrimental to their respective approaches to KM. Informal conversations and shared networks storing MS Office documents may serve their current needs adequately but these modes are limited and can lead to knowledge loss. In order to become more flexible and further develop knowledge creation capabilities it is important that these firms consider official modes of knowledge processing in the future.

11 KM at DocMan (Ireland) Ltd.

At DocMan (Ireland) the total volume of KA was low in comparison to the other cases considered. This may be endorsed by the nature of the well-defined work on software development components at the DocMan site in Ireland. The operations at the Irish site are part of a larger document management software component and the output from DocMan (Ireland) was integrated by the software integrator at the Swiss headquarters. As a result of this task specificity, there was a set of core KAs from which there was minimal diversification at the Irish site. The breakdown of KAs for DocMan (Ireland) Ltd. is presented in Table 8.

Table 8 KAs at DocMan (Ireland) Ltd

KA	No. of KA (%)/Knowledge focus by activity
Acquire	7 (12 %)
	57 % SW Dev knowledge (4 of n = 7 activities)
	43 % customer knowledge (3 of n = 7 activities)
Codify	11 (18 %)
	64 % SW Dev and project knowledge (7 of n = 11 activities)
Store	9 (15 %)
	67 % SW Dev and project knowledge (6 of n = 9 activities)
Maintain	7 (12 %)
	57 % SW Dev and project knowledge (4 of n = 7 activities)
Transfer	24 (40 %)
	79 % SW Dev and project knowledge (19 of n = 24 activities)
Create	2 (3 %)
	100 % SW Dev and project knowledge (2 of n = 2 activities)
Total	60

Table 8 illustrates a significant level of knowledge consistency across all of the KAs. Software development and project knowledge represented at least 57 % of the knowledge focus for all six KAs. This uniformity across activities also supports the task specialisation activity at the DocMan (Ireland) site.

DocMan (Ireland) leveraged some external knowledge resources at 12 % (7 where n = 60) knowledge acquisition, however the main source of knowledge is the headquarters in Switzerland and this was achieved through knowledge transfer activity which was very high at 40 % (24 where n = 60) of total activity. It is from here that the majority of customer requirements were received as well as any new product knowledge.

Knowledge creation activity was very low at 3 % (2 where n = 60). This may be the result of the location of this development team with most new ideas being generated at a higher level at company headquarters.

Although the total volume of KA was low, the split between the acquire, codify, store and maintain KA at 57 % and the knowledge transfer and creation activity at 43 % is more evenly balanced than that observed at HelpRead Ltd., at 73 to 27 % respectively. The geographic location, the task specialisation and the maturity of the parent organisation may be attributed to the knowledge transfer capabilities identified at DocMan Ireland. Unlike the other firms considered in this study, DocMan's (Ireland) KM capabilities are determined by their HQ. Perhaps this subsidiary should consider developing their own knowledge creation capabilities independent of HQ with the objective of feeding new ideas back. This strategy could further secure their position as a core component in the companywide strategy.

12 KM Approach Across Five Software SMEs

The previous sections presented and examined five software SMEs in terms of the instances of KAs identified. From this, a comparative analysis of the occurrences of KAs in all five cases considered in this study is presented in Table 9.

The cross-case analysis in Table 9 shows considerable disparities in levels of sophistication and formalisation in both the routine and non-routine official modes across the organisations. TravelSoft and HelpRead may be characterised as knowledge intensive organisations (Davenport and Prusak 1998; O'Dell and Grayson 1998). The considerable number of KAs identified at TravelSoft is the direct result of new product development and process formulation related activity. From a knowledge processing perspective, TravelSoft had established Intranet-based systems such as wiki and online discussion forums (Raman 2006) to support these companywide initiatives to capture, store and maintain important knowledge. TravelSoft also benefitted from management driven brainstorming sessions and formalised face-to-face interaction such as TIKES and IKXs to share and generate knowledge. HelpRead's customer oriented strategy resulted in significant knowledge activity. With a focus on new product development, HelpRead actively leveraged Intranet technology such as wikis to support collaborative knowledge activity and management driven brainstorming sessions to facilitate idea generation activity. Both TravelSoft and HelpRead relied heavily on external resources as a means of valuable knowledge acquisition. The emphasis on new product (Groen 2006) and in the case of TravelSoft new process development characterised the nature of the KM approach for these organisations. Essentially, HelpRead and TravelSoft utilised KAs to support their product development activity (Kraaijenbrink et al. 2006). However, this is done in different ways, depending on the current needs of the company. For example in the case of TravelSoft, who did not have a software product but were working towards achieving that goal, the total number of KA was significant. Their focus on software development knowledge, but also on travel industry and process knowledge was substantial and they had implemented collaborative web technology and face-to-face workshops (Daft and Lengel 1984) (e.g., Internal Knowledge Exchange sessions (IKXs)) to support this goal. In essence, their KM approach met the immediate needs of the goals set by the company. The 'balanced' mix of knowledge processing modes pursued by TravelSoft shows innovativeness and forward thinking on their part; however, it is important that the influence of the Telecoms background of key players in the firm does not 'over formalise' their approach to managing knowledge. It is essential that TravelSoft continue to pursue a balanced outlook with the aim of further developing their knowledge creation activities.

It was observed that HelpRead, although not working through new product development at the time, also leverage their KM approach to achieve the goals set out by the organisation. It would be expected that periods of new product activity would intensify their knowledge focus on customer driven product development. Supporting the view of Davenport and Prusak (1998), p. 178 who state that

Table 9 Synthesis of KM approach in five software SMEs

Company	Knowledge activities	Modes of knowledge processing
HelpRead Ltd Knowledge focus on customer driven new software feature and product development	• 82 knowledge activities • Significant management involvement in KA • Highest volume: 30 % store • Lowest volume: 6 % create	Distribution of mode usage • Routine 69 % • Non-routine 31 % • Official 64 % • Unofficial 37 % Examples: Intranet and wiki technology
TravelSoft Ltd. Knowledge focus on facilitating organisational change e.g., new process and product development	• 147 knowledge activities • Significant management involvement in KA • Highest volume: 28 % transfer • Lowest volume: 6 % create	Distribution of mode usage • Routine 70 % • Non-routine 30 % • Official 69 % • Unofficial 31 % Examples: Intranet and wiki technology
Systems Solutions Ltd. Knowledge activity informal driven by sales opportunity and compliance requirements	• 105 knowledge activities • Limited management involvement in KA • Highest volume: 29 % transfer • Lowest volume: 5 % create	Distribution of mode usage • Routine 56 % • Non-routine 44 % • Official 59 % • Unofficial 41 % Examples: Shared networks, Tempas™ and desktop applications
FinSoft Ltd. Knowledge activity ad-hoc in nature with sales opportunity and compliance focus	• 78 knowledge activities • Limited management involvement in KA • Highest volume: 29 % transfer • Lowest volume: 4 % create	Distribution of mode usage • Routine 63 % • Non-routine 27 % • Official 62 % • Unofficial 38 % Examples: shared networks and desktop applications
DocMan (Ireland) Ltd. Knowledge activity driven by knowledge transfer activity with parent organisation	• 60 knowledge activities • Limited management involvement in KA • Highest volume: 40 % transfer • Lowest volume: 3 % create	Distribution of mode usage • Routine 73 % • Non-routine 27 % • Official 66 % • Unofficial 34 % Examples: Jira™, Atlas™ and Intranet technology

"knowledge and learning should always serve the broader aims of the organisation", depending on their activities and goals HelpRead leveraged KM to fit their needs.

Systems Solutions had no formalised approach to managing knowledge; however, as a **1** high-technology software consulting organisation KAs typically occurred organically, although some activity was driven by industry regulation. From the analysis, it was evident that Systems Solutions did not focus on niche industry knowledge. In addition, the company relied on readily available company technology such as desktop applications and shared folders to support all KAs. In the same way, FinSoft did not have a formalised approach or sophisticated information systems in place, relying on desktop applications such as MS Office and shared servers to support KAs. However, they too were driven by industry regulation to maintain accurate and up to date documentation. They were extensively dependent on non-routine modes such as meetings and informal conversations to support KAs. While Systems Solutions and FinSoft leveraged knowledge for reasons different to those of HelpRead and TravelSoft, they too pursued KAs that meet the needs of the organisation. For both of these organisations, compliance was a key driver of KA. In addition, senior management sales strategy in both companies created a focus on customer and sales knowledge and supporting activities. With the external compliance pressures and an emphasis on generating sales opportunities, KAs were used to support the needs of these organisations.

As a small satellite office to Swiss headquarters, DocMan's (Ireland) KAs were largely determined by head office. As a result, the nature of their work was highly bound to software component development, while the volume of KA in general was quite low, significant knowledge transfer occurs between the Irish and Swiss office. The disparate geographic locations meant that DocMan (Ireland) was largely reliant on routine modes of knowledge processing. As a 'large' and established SME, DocMan leveraged sophisticated technologies such as JIRA^{TM} (see Table 9) for knowledge processing and did not heavily engage non-routine modes, as they were not necessary to support their needs. Essentially, DocMan (Ireland) operated as a specialist function, producing and transferring software components to Switzerland for further integration. The company's extensive reliance on knowledge transfer activity reflected the nature of these business objectives, where a KM approach that serves the goals of the Irish based subsidiary is pursued.

13 Conclusions

Surprisingly, knowledge creation activity was observed as being relatively low across the five SMEs. This may be because it is a more difficult phenomenon to observe retrospectively compared to the other five KAs. However, another reason for the low count of knowledge creation activities could be attributed to the nature of SMEs where it is typical for the manager to be the "driving force" behind the organisation (Nunes et al. 2005) and where the founder has the initial idea and continues to have significant hands on involvement in the running of the organisation (Schein 1993). In other words, knowledge creation may be the responsibility of a few people in a SME, namely the founder and senior management. Chan and Chao (2008) contend that knowledge generation in SMEs can be improved if management provide more opportunities to software developers in terms of providing opinions and ideas based on their expertise.

There remains a paucity of empirical work in the area of KM for software SMEs. The empirical evidence gathered from this study provides a solid foundation for future research in terms of considering the complex but important issue of KM in SMEs. The main finding of this research presents an actionable mechanism for supporting software SMEs to understand and improve their KM approach, based on their mode usage and the instances of KA generated by the organisation. In an area where tangible measurements are difficult and complex to produce, this provides a basis for consideration in terms of facilitating an evaluation of a SMEs' approach to managing and developing important knowledge capabilities to better serve the needs of the organisation in the future.

References

Ägerfalk, P., & Fitzgerald, B. (2008). Outsourcing to an unknown workforce: Exploring open sourcing as a global sourcing strategy. *MIS Quarterly, 32*(2), 385–409.

Alavi, M., & Leidner, D. E. (2001). Knowledge management and knowledge management systems: conceptual foundations and research issues. *MIS Quarterly, 25*(1), 107–136.

Asproth, V., & Nyström, C. A. (2008). Communication and information exchange among SMEs and their local environment. *Journal of Organisational Transformation and Social Change, 5*(2), 175–189.

Audretsch, D. B., Prince, Y. M., & Thurik, R. A. (1999). Do small firms compete with large firms? *Atlantic Economic Journal, 27*(2), 201–209.

Banck, B. & Nystrom, C. A. (2005). Intranet use—a study of five swedish organisations. *Journal of Organisational Transformation and Social Change,2*(2), 153–180.

Baskerville, R., & Pries-Heje, J. (1999). Managing knowledge capability and maturity. *Databases for Advances in Information Systems, 20*(2), 26–43.

Bayer, F., Enparantza, R., Maier, R., Obermair, F., & Schmeidinger, B. (2005). Know-com: Decentralised knowledge management systems for cooperating die and mold making SMEs. In M. E Jennex (Ed.), *Case studies in knowledge management* (pp. 186–210). Hershey: Idea Group Publishing.

Beckinsale, M., & Levy, M. (2004). SMEs and internet adoption strategy: Who do SMEs listen to? *Proceedings of the 12th European Conference on Information Systems, Turku, Finland* (pp. 177–188).

Bernroider, E. (2002). Factors in SWOT analysis applied to micro, small-to-medium, and large software enterprises: an austrian study. *European Management Journal, 20*(5), 562–573.

Central Statistics Office (CSO) (2007). *Small business in Ireland* http://www.cso.ie/releasespublications/documents/other_releases/smallbusiness.pdf. Last Accessed June 16, 2009.

Chan, I., & Chao, C. K. (2008). Knowledge management in small and medium sized enterprises. *Communications of the ACM, 51*(4), 83–88.

Chapman, P., James-Moore, M., Szczygiel, M., & Thompson, D. (2000). Building internet capabilities in SMEs. *Journal Logistics Information Management, 13*(6), 353–360.

Daft, R. L., & Lengel, R. H. (1984). Information richness: A new approach to managerial behaviour and organisation design. *Research in Organisational Behaviour, 6*, 191–233.

Davenport, T. H., & Prusak, L. (1998). *Working knowledge. How organizations manage what they know*. Boston, Mass: Harvard Business School Press.

Duhan, S., Levy, M., & Powell, P. (2001). Information systems strategies in knowledge-based SMEs: the role of core competencies. *European Journal of Information Systems, 10*(1), 25–40.

Earl, M. J., & Hopwood, A. G. (1980). From management information to information management. In H. Lucas, F. Land, T. Lincoln, & K. Supper (Eds.), *The information systems environment*. Amsterdam: North Holland Publishing Company.

Edvardsson, I. (2006). Knowledge management in SMEs: The case of Icelandic firms. *Knowledge Management Research and Practice, 4*, 275–282.

Eisenhardt, K. (1989). Building theories from case study research. *Academy of Management Review, 14*(4), 532–550.

Enterprise Ireland (2007). http://www.enterprise-ireland.com/CommonPages/SME.htm. Last Accessed March 3, 2009.

European Commission (2003). *Facts and figures—SMEs in Europe* http://ec.europa.eu/enterprise/entrepreneurship/facts_figures.htm. Last Accessed March 3, 2009.

European Commission (2009). *SBA fact sheet, United Kingdom, report by European Commission Enterprise and Industry*. Brussels: European Commission.

Forfas (1999). *Ireland could become world centre for distribution of software* http://www.forfas.ie/media/forfas990729_ecommerce_press_release.pdf. Last Accessed June 14, 2009.

Forfas (2006). *Annual Report 2006*, [online], available: http://www.forfas.ie/publications/forfas_annrpt06/forfas-annual-report-2006-english.pdf, February 2, 2008.

Ghobadian, A., & Gallear, D. N. (1996). Total quality management in SMEs. *International Journal of Management Science, 24*(1), 83–106.

Groen, A. (2006). Assessment—making sense of it all. In A. Jetter, J. Kraaijenbrink, F. Wijnhoven (Eds.), *Knowledge integration: The practice of knowledge management in small and medium sized enterprises*. Germany: Springer, (pp. 115–126).

Hansen, M., Nohria, N., & Tierney, T. (1999). What's your strategy for managing knowledge? *Harvard Business Review, 77*(2), 106–116.

Hoch, D., Rodeing, J., Purkert, C., & Lindner, S. K. (1999). *Secrets of software success: Management insights from 100 software firms around the world*. Boston, MA: Harvard Business School Press.

Hyland, A. (2000). Small companies also need knowledge management http://www.eknowledgecenter.com/articles/1005/1005.htm. Last Accessed March 3, 2009.

Judge, R. (2007). The influence of information linkage on user acceptance of knowledge management systems in small to mid-sized enterprises (SME). In *Proceedings of the 4th Hawaii International Conference on System Sciences*.

Keegan, W. J. (1974). Multinational scanning: A study of the information sources utilized by executives in multinational companies. *Administrative Science Quarterly, 19*(7), 680–689.

Kefalas, A. (1973). Scanning the business environment—some empirical results. *Decision Science, 4*(1), 63–74.

Knoke, D. (1994). Networks of elite structure and decision making. In S. Wasserman & J. Galaskiewicz (Eds.), *Advances in network analysis: Research in the social and behavioural sciences*. Thousand Oaks, CA: Sage.

Kraaijenbrink, J., Faran, D., & Hauptman, A. (2006). Knowledge integration by SMEs—framework. In A. Jetter, J. Kraaijenbrink, H. Schroder, & F. Wijnhoven (Eds.), *Knowledge integration: The practice of knowledge management in small to medium sized enterprises* (pp. 17–28). Germany: Springer.

Lauder, D., Boocock, G., & Presley, J. (1994). The system support for SMEs in the UK and Germany. *European Business Review, 94*(1), 9–16.
Lee, G. L., & Oakes, I. (1995). The 'pros' and 'cons' of total quality management for smaller firms in manufacturing: Some experiences down the supply chain. *Total Quality Management, 6*(4), 413–426.
MacGregor, D. J., & Bunker, R. C. (2000). EDI and small/medium enterprises. In S. M. Rahman & M. S. Raisinghani (Eds.), *Electronic commerce opportunities and challenges* (pp. 142–151). Hershey: Idea Group Publishing.
Miles, M. B., & Huberman, A. M. (1994). *Qualitative data analysis: An expanded Sourcebook.* Thousand Oaks, CA: Sage.
Mintzberg, H. (1975). The Manager's job: Folklore and fact. *Harvard Business Review, 53*(4), 29–61.
Nissila, J., Lauri, A. T., Suoimmi, R., & Puhakainen, J. (2004). The house that jack built: eBusiness models for SMEs, *17th Bled eCommerce Conference eGlobal.* Slovenia: Bled, June 21–23.
Nunes, M. B., Ananasingh, F., Eaglestone, B., & Wakefield, R. (2005). Managers' perceptions of the value of knowledge management in small and medium sized knowledge-intensive enterprise (SMEs). *Journal of Knowledge Management Practice*, December 2005.
O'Dell, C., & Grayson, C. J. J. (1998). *If only we knew what we know: The transfer of internal knowledge and best practice.* New York: The Free Press.
OECD (2002). OECD information technology outlook 2002 www.sourceoecd.org. Last Accessed March 3, 2009.
Patton, M. (1990). *Qualitative evaluation and research methods.* Newbury Park, CA: Sage Publications.
Penrose, E. (1959). *The Theory of the Growth of the Firm.* Oxford: Oxford University Press.
Pillania, R. (2008). Strategic issues in knowledge management in small and medium enterprises. *Knowledge Management Research and Practice, 6*, 334–338.
Poon, A., & Swatman, P. M. C. (1999). An exploratory study of small business internet commerce issues. *Information and Management, 35*(1), 9–18.
Raman, M. (2006). Wiki technology as a "Free" collaborative tool within an organizational setting. *Information Systems Management*, pp. 59–66.
Richards, T., & Richards, L. (1995). Using hierarchical categories in qualitative data analysis. In U. Kelle (Ed.), *Computer-aided qualitative data analysis* (pp. 80–95). London: Sage.
Schein, E. H. (1993). On dialogue, culture, and organizational learning. *Organizational Dynamics, Fall, 22*(2), 40–51.
Schönstrom, M., & Carlsson, S. A. (2003). Methods as knowledge enablers in software development organizations. In *Proceedings of the Eleventh European Conference on Information Systems* (pp. 1707–1718).
Sheremata, W. A. (2002). Finding and solving problems in software new product development. *The Journal of Product Innovation Management, 19*, 144–158.
Teece, D. (2000). *Managing intellectual capital: organizational, strategic, and policy dimensions.* New York: Oxford University Press.
Tetteh, E., & Burn, J. (2001). Global strategies for SME-business: Applying the SMALL framework. *Logistics Information Management, 14*(1), 171–180.
Tsui, E. (2004) Tracking the role and evolution of commercial knowledge management software. In C. W. Holsapple (Eds.), *Handbook on knowledge management* (Vol. 2, pp. 5–28). Berlin: Verlanger.
Vickery, G. (1999). Business and industry policies for knowledge based economies. *OECD Observer, A*(215), 9.
Welsh, J., & White, J. (1981). A small business is not a little big business. *Harvard Business Review, 59*(4) 18–32.
Wickert, A., & Herschel, R. (2001). Knowledge management issues for smaller businesses. *Journal of Knowledge Management, 5*(4), 329–337.

Wong, K. Y. (2005). Critical success factors for implementing knowledge management in small and medium enterprises. *Industrial Management and Data Systems, 105*(3), 261–279.
Wong, K. Y., & Radcliffe, D. F. (2000). The tacit nature of design knowledge. *Technology Analysis and Strategic Management, 12*(4), 493–512.
Wright, R. W., & Etemad, H. (2001). SMEs and the global economy. *Journal of Information Management, 7*, 151–154.

Business Agility and Flexibility in Enterprise Service-Based Information Systems: Application to PLM Systems

Safa Hachani, Hervé Verjus and Lilia Gzara

1 Introduction

In a constantly changing environment, industrial companies face an increasingly challenging customer and competitor base. To remain competitive, a company must develop the business agility to enable it to meet customer demands that are increasingly immediate, as well as broader changes in its market environment and its own functioning. To do so, it must adopt diverse approaches to facilitate collaborations and improve product development. Among these approaches, Product Lifecycle Management (PLM) plays an essential role by managing product data in all phases of its lifecycle (design, industrialization, manufacturing, delivery, recycling, etc.) and especially during product design phase (Saaksvuori and Immonen 2005). Thus, the PLM system supports the management of product information by storing and managing it according to many business tools (for example, project management tools, CAD, CAM, etc.). It also allows the management of product design processes (PDPs) (functional analysis, configuration management, change management, etc.) associated with the product, along its entire lifecycle. These PDPs organize the creation, exchange, use and evolution of product information. Most PLM systems adopt workflow management approaches and propose basic workflow design and workflow engine to cope with PDPs. These approaches do not usually handle dynamic behaviors, such as dynamic changes on running workflows instances (Bowers et al. 1995). However, PDPs are emergent and non deterministic because of the creativity aspect in manufacturing product design projects. Furthermore, various unpredictable situations may occur during PDPs due to external constraints (e.g. evolving customer requirements, changing

S. Hachani (✉) · L. Gzara
Grenoble Institute of Technology, G-SCOP Laboratory,
46, Avenue Félix Viallet, Grenoble 38031, France
e-mail: safa.hachani@grenoble-inp.fr

H. Verjus
LISTIC Laboratory, University of Savoie, BP 80439, Annecy-le-Vieux 74944, France

J. Devos et al. (eds.), *Information Systems for Small and Medium-sized Enterprises*,
Progress in IS, DOI: 10.1007/978-3-642-38244-4_15,

standards, sub-contractor or supplier constraints, etc.) and/or internal constraints (e.g. changes in business priorities and opportunities, delays, technical feasibility problems, staff/resource availability, etc.). PDPs are thus constantly changing. Reflecting these changes on time is critical and represents an ongoing challenge. The automated support of business operations is necessary to reflect such changes. Given these two findings (1) instability of design process and (2) rigidity of workflow technology used in PLM systems we identify a critical need to deal with PDPs flexibility in the PLM system. So, what might be an alternative approach for flexible design processes and how might we allow dynamic change of PDPs in PLM systems?

The aim of the work presented in this chapter is to propose an alternative approach that allows PDPs flexibility in PLM systems. The objective is to specify, design and implement the PDPs in a very flexible way so they can rapidly adapt to changing conditions. In our proposal, Service-Oriented Architecture (SOA) and service orientation is a means for addressing this issue by facilitating enterprise solution flexibility, and therefore business agility. We can therefore say that a service-oriented approach, based on the concept of service, known as a repeatable business unit, can promote a support of flexible PDPs by considering a PDP as a series of generic services which can be linked together like re-usable building blocks.

Small and medium sized enterprises (SMEs) will remain competitive as they will be able to be agile and responsive to the business environment. Unfortunately, most SMEs are governed by rigid processes (due to IS rigidity, organization rigidity, etc.) and they cannot anticipate changes, market variations and business opportunities. Service-based information system architectures appear to be considered a solution to improve enterprise agility (Verjus et al. 2011a). The approach presented in this chapter can be implemented and therefore have a positive impact on SMEs. The use of such a proposal may increase the responsiveness (time to market) of the enterprise, facilitate new strategies and reduce process failures. We also think that our approach reduces the gap between the business domain and the IT solution.

This chapter is structured as follows. Section 2 illustrates how dynamic process change happens in PLM systems with a motivation example. Section 3 provides an overview of existing approaches in the area of process flexibility. We then present our approach for flexible process support in PLM systems (Sect. 4). Subsequently, we provide the first elements for the service identification approach we propose (Sect. 5). Section 6 details our service identification approach and catalogs. Section 7 presents the testing and feasibility of the proposed approach. The chapter closes with some concluding remarks and ideas for future work.

2 Motivation Example

In this section, we introduce a process frequently managed in PLM systems to illustrate the implementation and dynamicity issues of product design processes in these systems. This example describes an industrial setting based on a field study

(a)

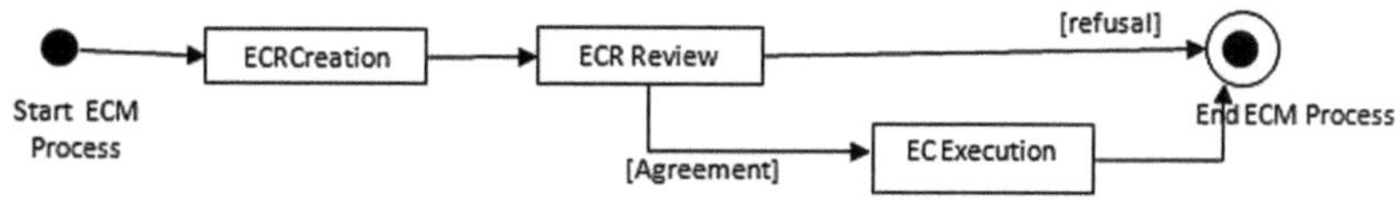

Fig. 1 Engineering change management (*ECM*) process

which aimed to map an Engineering Change Management (ECM) process within a manufacturer. This ECM process is related to a breakage problem which occurs during the drilling along an axis. The process shown in Fig. 1a describes the activities related to the creation of the Engineering Change Request (ECR) which asks for a modification of the drilling diameter, the review of this ECR and the execution of the ECR.

In order to be managed in PLM system, this process should be automated. The first step consists of creating all the functionalities necessary for fulfillment of the process (for instance, request review function) and storing them on the PLM database. Once the functionalities are stored, the workflow template should be defined. Finally, the workflow can be initiated from the template and executed until its completion. As this PDP is executed several times, the process model may change due to practical situations. Changes are driven by many factors, such as technology shift, internal organizational changes or external changes (for example, customers' requirements, products' standards and environmental laws). Changes cannot be anticipated when modeling the product design process. Some of these factors, for example, external changes (in order to satisfy suppliers, partners or customers needs), may only cause temporary changes in a PDP. Some other factors, such as regulation changes, may cause permanent changes. For example, the reviewer of the ECR may conclude that the breakage problem is not due to the value of the diameter but rather to the material type of the axis. So, it is preferable to request information relating to the origin of the breakage problem before making any change in order to save time. To deal with this constraint, the ongoing process will evolve to the one shown in Fig. 2.

Once process changes occur, new workflow templates are defined and workflow instances are initiated accordingly (cf. Fig. 3). Defining new workflow templates requires creating and storing the new functionalities in the PLM database. Thus, the deployment of new functionalities requires time and effort. In addition, it is necessary to handle the previous workflow instances, which are initiated from old workflow templates.

(b)

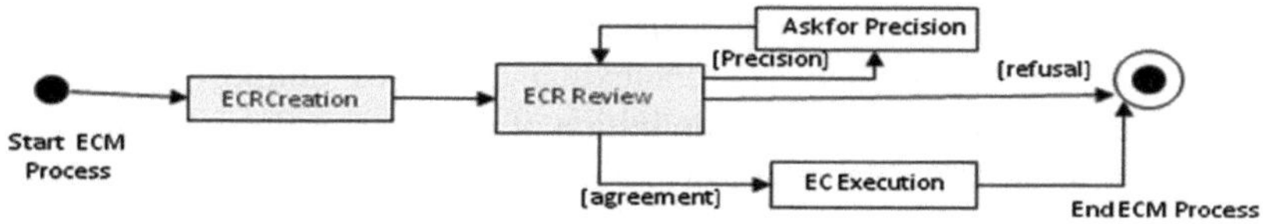

Fig. 2 Changes in engineering change management (*ECM*) process

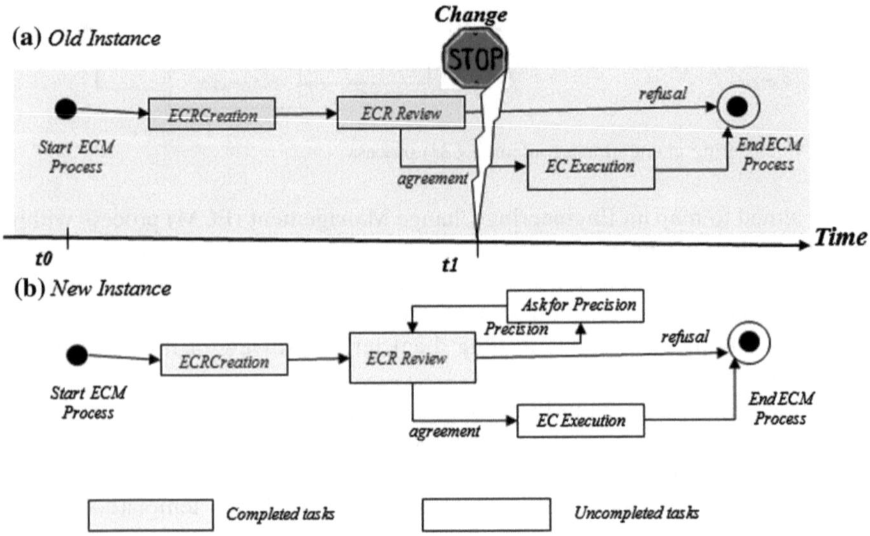

Fig. 3 Changes in workflow definition

Most workflow systems used in PLM consider two steps: (1) before applying the new workflow template, the old instance has to be stopped and (2) a new one is started according to the new workflow template from the beginning. Indeed, after restarting the workflow instance, some completed tasks must be repeated, whereas they have been already achieved. Operating in such environments is becoming increasingly difficult. Indeed, enterprises require the agility to be able to operate under such pressures and thus ensure the survival of their PDPs.

3 Related Works

Currently, there are numerous process modeling approaches, which aim to manage flexibility. Bessai et al. (2008) propose a context aware-based approach. The concept of context is used to describe the state of manipulated objects in the environment. The context is also used to characterize an activity (designed to operate in a particular state of the world). In this work, the role of the process is to precisely define the order and the context of activities to be performed. The one that should be executed is chosen according to the object's state. This approach allows flexible modeling of the business process (BP) by using conditions which allow one to choose between contextual activities aiming to meet business objectives. In contrast, advanced definition of the flow results in the decrease of the flexibility of the BP. Zhao and Liu (2007) propose a version-based approach. This work proposes to model versions of BP schemas using graphs: nodes of a graph correspond to activities of a process, while arcs between nodes represent the patterns used to link activities. Moreover, this work presents a set of operations enabling real time graph updates; it also defines two strategies required to extract versions of BP schemas from these graphs. Nevertheless, all versions should have been anticipated in advance, which is not possible in practice. Lezoche's et al. (2008) work proposes a rule-based approach. This approach assumes that activities are components reacting to events. Here, the result of one activity represents an initiating event for other ones according to a given set of rules. So, an instance of a process model corresponds to one of planned paths. The advantage of this approach is that the activities binding can be made later by using a triggering event to choose between activities. However, this assumes that all activities are anticipated. Boukadi et al. (2008) resort to SOA. They focus on building flexible BP based on service composition and service adaptability. This work defines a BP as a sequence of activities. The creation of the BP is essentially based on selecting one or more goal-templates and specifying the flows connecting those goals. The goals-templates correspond to the tasks to be completed. The composition of the different goals-templates leads to an abstract BP model. Based on the goals-templates, services will be selected to replace them and the executable BP will be generated. The services offered are adaptable and have different behaviors depending on the context of their uses. This allows some flexibility in how to meet the objective. Moreover, by fixing the goals-templates in advance, the flexibility of the process structure decreases.

In summary, on the one hand, the proposed approaches allow a BP to be modeled whilst maintaining some flexibility in how the business objectives are met. This can be done by using conditions and/or triggering event to choose between activities versions. The disadvantage of these modeling approaches is that they imply anticipation of all scenarios. These approaches are well adapted to representation of a process with a limited degree of complexity. However, they are more difficult to use to design a process with an emerging structure, in which the execution of each process depends on the availability of certain resources and the effective participation of each actor. On the other hand, Boukadi's work allows one to model reusable activities unlike other works (rule, context-aware and version-based approaches), which make it possible to design decoupled activity that can be used by different BPs. Moreover, by defining the flows and fixing the goals-templates in advance, the flexibility of the BP is decreased. The author's vision of flexibility is limited to the capability of changing the manner in which the activities can meet the objectives, rather than focusing on the flexibility of the process structure.

Based on the findings outlined above, we conclude that flexible PDPs require specific methods for their design and implementation. Thus, the expected approach is one in which not only the behavior of activities are not defined *a priori* but also the relationships between them.

4 Our Service-Based Approach

We resort to a SOA in order to map PDPs to a service-oriented solution. The idea is to propose reusable activities as services and evolvable PDPs as service composition. Thus, the concept of service defined as providers of reusable functions can be reused and composed to quickly respond to PDP changes. That assumes that once changes occur we can add, delete or replace one service by another one. Indeed, the generalization of SOA to information systems (and thus, the design and requirements analysis layers) would allow the definition of PDPs and their implementation by reusing existing and generic services.

The main characteristic of our service-based approach is that it provides a flexible and dynamic process structure (i.e. new nodes can be added to/replaced on/removed from the process), which provides the necessary agility to face changing conditions. To reach this objective, we must (a) define the concept of services at the business level, (b) propose a catalog of generic business services for PDP, (c) propose a new modeling approach, which allows PDPs to be built from the set of business services, (d) provide a dynamic orchestration of the designed process and (e) ensure alignment between the business and technical levels (cf. Fig. 4).

If we therefore revisit the ECM process introduced in the motivation example section, we can use and orchestrate a set of IT support system services (presented by solid arrows in Fig. 4) in order to automate the process. These IT services could be Web services that expose software functionalities and wrap specific software applications (i.e. PLM system, CAD tools, etc.). We can first use a PLM system service in order to create the ECR and to send it to the approver (cf. arrow (1) in Fig. 4) and then use a PLM system service to consult the ECR and a CAD tool service to consult the 3D assembly related to the broken axis (cf. arrows (2) in Fig. 4), in order to evaluate the change. When the approver accepts the change, Project Management tool services are used to plan the activities related to the EC realization (cf. arrows (3) in Fig. 4). Once a change occurs in ECM process, the appropriate services needed to automate the new activities (those presented by dotted arrows in Fig. 4) should be chosen and dynamically added to the orchestration. Thus, new service invocations should be dynamically added between the second and third arrows (cf. arrows (2.1) and (2.2) in Fig. 4).

5 Product Design Process as a Service Orchestration

The aim of a PDP model is to depict interactions between business partners and model their corresponding activities. In the last few decades, these processes could operate in relatively predictable environments but current, more active market dynamics pose a heightened threat to PDP stability; process flexibility in relation to the ease of PDP model modification and development of new business activities

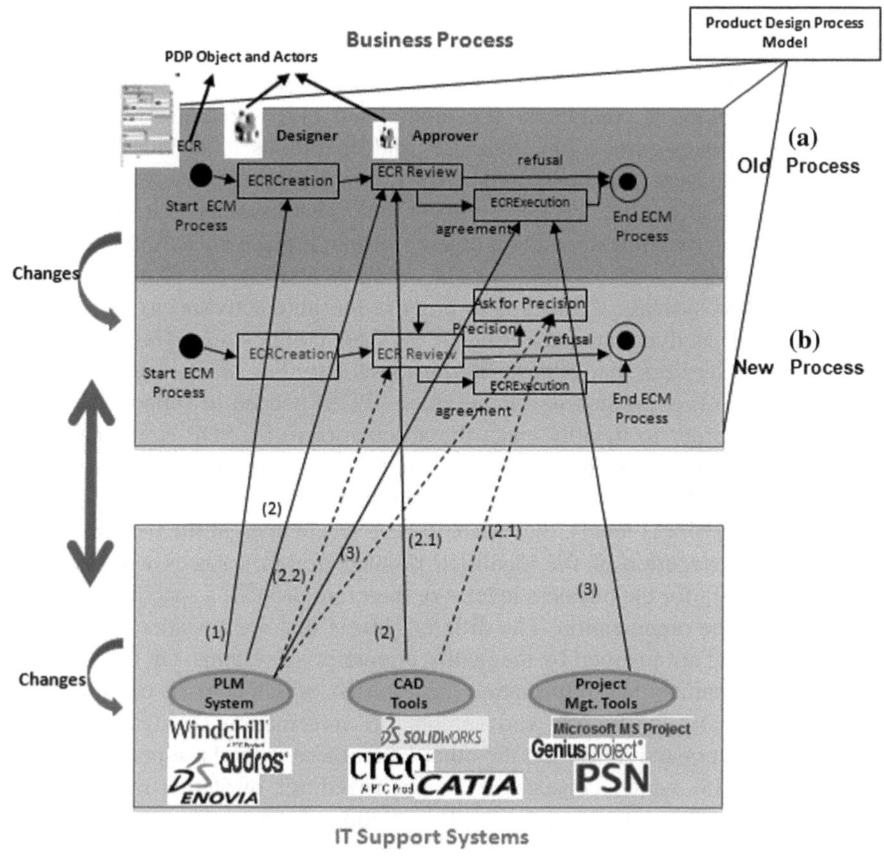

Fig. 4 Diagram demonstrating the need for alignment between business and technical levels

is imperative. This perception of process flexibility arises from the requirement for a method, which allows evolvable PDP models to be composed. In other words, flexibility requires processes made of elements of functionalities that can work together and that can be quickly reconfigured. The challenge here is to address the mechanisms needed for solid implementation of dynamic PDP change on a real PLM system.

To fulfill these expectations, we propose an enrichment of the formalization of PDP models and open the way for process modeling, by dynamic service composition. In fact, we propose the use of service as a means for describing the business functionalities needed to support the PDPs. Services are defined as providers of reusable business functions in an implementation-independent function that is loosely coupled to other business functions (Credle et al. 2008). These loosely coupled services may then be organized and composed according to needs and expectations in order to enact the articulations of business in a flexible manner. This process is called services composition (Manouvrier and Ménard 2007).

Dynamic services composition stands for assembling and re-assembling services while the process is executing. Thus, the concept of service can be composed and reused to rapidly respond to PDP change and to achieve the new model without needing to replace it completely (i.e. completed tasks need not be repeated). Further, as services expose functionalities and operations independently of their real enactment, they can be reused even if the enactment is changing (some changes do not affect the services composition). This assumes that once change happens, we can dynamically add to, delete from, or replace an activity (service or composite service) with another one. In order to address the problem of PDP rigidity in PLM systems, the idea is to propose reusable activities as services and evolvable PDP as dynamic and evolvable services composition. Thus, we should have a set of services that expose the business activities of the industrial engineering domain (i.e. product design services—PDS) needed to support the PDPs. Thereafter, in order to flexibly enact the articulations of a PDP, we dynamically compose the necessary identified PDSs. This PDP can then be materialized by an orchestration of PDSs. Moreover, in order to deal with alignment issues between technical and business levels, there should be a mechanism at the technical level, which allows execution of the identified product design services with the same technique chosen for the business level. We therefore propose a specific service for each level of the organization. The different levels that we consider necessary to achieve our goal are justified by the reality of enterprise systems. On the one hand, we find the organizational Information System (IS), which consists of information (business objects) and actors who act on this information through their work methods (business activities). On the other hand, there is the IT support system or computerized IS, which consists of an organized set of items, machines and software applications. It allows the implementation of the working methods of the company and the organization of their information. Moreover, the actors of the organizational IS use the computerized IS through the interfaces provided by its tools. Thus, there are three levels in the enterprise IS (Verjus and Pourraz 2011): the business level associated with organizational IS, the technical level associated with computerized IS and the functional level associated with the interfaces of the computerized IS. We propose three levels of services in relation to this classification.

Firstly, we propose a catalog of Product Design Services (PDS). A PDS is a collection of PDS operations reflecting solutions to the business needs of a product design domain. The proposed PDS operations are generic relevant business functionalities (i.e. in the PDP domain). In the proposed approach, each PDS operation partly reflects a business activity typically presented in PDPs. These PDS operations will be used and composed by PDP designers to build PDPs. Secondly, we propose a catalog of Functional PLM Services, which (1) ensures alignment between business and technical levels (cf. Fig. 4) and (2) aims to be independent of any PLM system. A Functional PLM service is a collection of Functional PLM service operations. Functional PLM service operations represent all functions of the PLM as seen by PLM users independently of any existing PLM tool. A set of functional PLM service operations support a business need defined in

PDS operation. They will be used by process performers (PLM system users) and composed to achieve the PDS. In other words, once a new business activity is needed to perform a change at the business level (in a PDP), a PDS operation is invoked and added to the orchestration and thus operations of functional PLM services can be solicited from the repository to execute the new business activity. Finally, we propose a set of technical PLM services that allow the real implementation of functional PLM services and thus the automation of product design services. These Technical PLM services cover all technical operations carried out in a PLM system, and they are dynamically orchestrated during the enactment of PDPs. They are intended to PLM editors.

This distinction between functional and technical PLM services allow the reuse of process models, defined only in terms of business and functional PLM services, on different PLM systems. Indeed, once a process is deployed on a new PLM system, we have to make correspondence between functional PLM services and technical PLM services.

In order to achieve the proposed approach, we must initially propose the services catalogs, then propose a means for allowing PDPs to be expressed as service orchestration and finally we should propose alignment techniques that allow movement from a business to technical level. These techniques should ensure a continuum of transformation from specification to implementation of PDPs. In the rest of this chapter we concentrate on the first two steps of our approach (services identification and PDP definition as service orchestration) as other efforts in this area are mainly empirical and not reproducible (not generic enough).

6 Service Identification Approaches

As discussed above, we aim to offer three services catalogs: (1) PDS catalog expressing business needs related to PDPs, (2) functional PLM services catalog enabling the execution of PDS through a functional PLM services orchestration, and (3) technical PLM services catalog enabling the implementation (as IT services) of functional PLM services. To define the services catalogs, we should first define an identification approach. The proposed identification approach might use existing techniques and procedures that can serve as a foundation for the identification method we propose. Thus, we conducted an initial pass of service identification technique.

6.1 Service Identification Techniques

Several approaches relate to the development of SOA (Emig et al. 2006; Papazoglou and Heuvel 2006; Chang and Kim 2007), all of which are based on Service-Oriented Modeling Architecture (SOMA), which focuses on techniques for the identification, specification and realization of services (Arsanjani and Allam 2006). Previous studies define the activities that should be carried out to develop an SOA and how each activity should be conducted. We focused specifically on services identification activity and studied the proposed services identification techniques. We identified a set of complementary techniques used to identify candidate services: domain decomposition, asset analysis and Goal Service Modeling (GSM) techniques (Arsanjani and Allam 2006).

- Domain decomposition uses an analysis technique that focuses on business domain and uses case modeling to identify candidate services. This method provides structural portioning of the business domain into distinct areas. This provides a natural means of identifying services. Moreover, by analyzing the use case of the system, it is advisable to have a clear understanding of interactions between the various identified services.
- The asset analysis technique involves taking the enterprise level application portfolio analysis and other assets that may be used to identify good candidates for services exposure. In general, the target of this technique is typically the basis service, such as, information life-cycle service for each of the key entities.
- In GSM, the two first techniques are combined. On the one hand, a generalized statement of the goal relevant to the scope of the enterprise or the project is decomposed into sub-goals that must be met. This hierarchical decomposition then leads to a set of actionable goals, which lead to identification of the services that will help in fulfilling the sub-goals. On the other hand, it analyses the application level in order to identify services and then combines them with the first identified set of services.

6.2 Requirement for the Service Identification Approach

Based on the analysis of existing identification approaches, the following requirements are derived for the services identification approach. A top–down method for the derivation of product design services is mandatory (i.e. by adhering to domain decomposition techniques, e.g. proposing process decomposition method or functional domain analysis of product design domain, etc.). None of the analyzed approaches provides any insight about the possible ways of defining business services in a bottom–up manner. For the derivation of functional PLM services, a bottom-up method is suitable, since most organizations will have existing application systems in place that cannot be easily substituted. Here, we can utilize asset analysis technique as a foundation for our identification approach. We note that the identification approach cannot be the same for high (business) and low-level (IT) services. Since they don't have the same service consumer and encompass different types of information (business needs vs. application functionalities), different identification criteria, which reflect the service orientation and the perspective of service consumer, should be fixed.

7 The Service Identification Approach

The aim of this section is to present the techniques and steps required to achieve the services identification stage and propose the three service catalogues.

7.1 Product Design Services Identification Approach and Catalog

A PDS is a collection of operations achieved during PDP by design actors. Hence, each operation of PDS consists of one product design step, which operates on one or more business objects (i.e. product design object). A product design object is a concept or abstraction that makes sense to the actors of the product design domain and corresponds to the entities manipulated by actors during design (e.g. drawing, bill of material, CAD model, etc.). The product design object is used to describe the entities manipulated by the actors within the description of the job (i.e. product design action). A product design action is an act that can be done by an actor in order to achieve a specific outcome (e.g. To Create). The top-down method proposed for the identification of PDS consists of four steps: (1) identifying product design objects, (2) identifying product design actions, (3) crossing product design actions with product design objects to obtain candidate product design operations and (4) grouping the identified product design operations in product design services. Following the proposed identification method we initially started by the identification of product design objects and then by product design actions.

To conduct the first step (identifying product design objects), two kinds of research was conducted. The outputs of interviews done within four French companies in the PD domain were analyzed. Although, meeting with researchers from G-SCOP laboratory working on product engineering design, were organized in order to determine the shared vocabulary among product design actors. Thereafter, to analyze DP models, a literature review was carried out in order to determine the different steps and their corresponding outcome (Tollenaere 1998; Scaravetti et al. 2005; Pahl and Beitz 2007). An outcome marks the transition between two stages. It is often associated with a deliverable to validate this transition. As a result, the following list of product design objects was identified such as Delay, Quotation, Quantity, Market Analysis Sheet, Drawing Assembly, 3D Assembly, Prototype, Validation Report, Design Solution, Bill of Materials, Drawing Part, etc. (Table 1). These objects represent an abstraction or representation of the desired product (e.g. Design solution, 3D Assembly, 3D part, Drawing Assembly, Drawing Part, Prototype, etc.). They also constitute a vector of cooperation between design actors (e.g. Specification sheet, Functional Specification Sheet, Validation Report, etc.).

The second step is the identification of product design actions. The product design objects identified cannot be seen outside the unusual situation. In the

Table 1 An excerpt from product design object list

FMECA document	Describes a document which lists the failure modes, with a relatively high probability and severity of consequences, allowing remedial effort to be directed where it will produce the failure
Delays	Specifies the estimated delay in which the desired quantity can be delivered
Quotation	Estimates the total cost of production
Quantity	Specifies the number of units to produce
Market analysis sheet	Represents a document which aims to specify market situation, needs and opportunities
3D Assembly	Represents a numerical model of the entire product
3D Part	Represents a numerical modeling of one part of the product
Prototype	Represents a small scale model or rough draft of an unfinished product. It is used to visualize and test shapes and ideas without incurring the cost and effort of producing a full scale product
Customer plan	Represents a drawing which contains the first graphical representation of the product as it is desired by the customer
Pieuve	Represents a diagram, which shows the relationship between the product and its surrounding environments. It contains the functions for which the product is created and those which restrict freedom of the designer
Bill of materials	Defines the type, number, quantity, and relationships of parts and assemblies that define a product
Materials	Describes raw materials that define one part or the entire product
Functional specification sheet	Describes a document, which aims to specify product functions and detail the product including causes and effects and any constraints that may limit the solution

creation and usage, we talk about the concept of action. Actually, in designing a new product many actions such as intellectual activity, decisional activity, creation activity, etc. need to be performed. To identify the total list of product design actions, two different information sources were used. First, two examples of industrial PDP models were analyzed in order to identify recurrent actions. We dissected the process into its most granular process steps. Each process step can be regarded as a potential product design action. Many candidate product design actions were listed. However, we noted that there are many actions (i.e. process steps), which don't have the same designation and not operate on the same product design object but they have the same logic. Then, in order to see how the DP can be broken down, literature in the domain of DP models was analyzed (Micaelli 2002; Robin and Barandiaran 2004; Scaravetti et al. 2005). Some works break down the DP into phases (Pahl and Beitz 2007), while others break down the DP into activities (Micaelli 2002). While the concept of phase describes the stages of the DP clearly, staked temporally, the notion of activity reflects the different tasks of the actors. These tasks are closer to our list of actions previously identified by process decomposition. They represent a generalization of our identified actions. Thus, the identified list of actions was reviewed according to the proposed ones. As a result, a list of product design actions was fixed: produce information, produce solution, produce organization, produce evaluation, produce decision/agreement, request information, request solution, request organization, request evaluation, request decision/agreement. Outfitted with this list of product design actions, the PDP can be described as a network of product design actions operating on product design objects and iterating continuously to produce a result. The next step of our identification approach consists of crossing the product design objects with the product design actions to get candidate product design operations (e.g. produce evaluation of design solution, produce solution for drawing part) (Hachani et al. 2012). However, some crossed objects and product design actions lead to operations that have no meaning in product design domain (for instance, produce organization for specification sheet or produce solution of customer plan, etc.). These operations have to be excluded from the product design operations list. Moreover, meaningful names for the identified list of PDS operations were defined (e.g. Elaborate Test Plan, Create Prototype, etc.).

The last step of the identification approach consists of grouping the identified operations in product design services. To do so, the principle of service cohesion plays an important role as operations should be grouped together that are functionally related. However, the operations are grouped based on other criteria such as business rules and sequence logic. In fact, during the analysis of design process model we identified recurring cycle between product design actions. For example, *ElaborateTestPlan*, *TestPlanEvaluationRequest*, and *EvaluateTestPlan* are usually used together. This is justified by the fact that there is a cycle between the formulation of the problem and its resolution. In addition, the production of some product design objects need information about other objects. For example, to produce prototype solution, a designer must request information about 3D Assembly. These operations must be grouped together into a single service. As a result, fifteen PDSs were proposed. Figure 5 shows an excerpt of this catalog.

7.2 *Functional PLM Services Identification Approach and Catalog*

A functional PLM service is a collection of PLM operations which reflect functions expected by PLM system users. Each operation implements the concept of an automated business task and displays a function of PLM that can be reused and

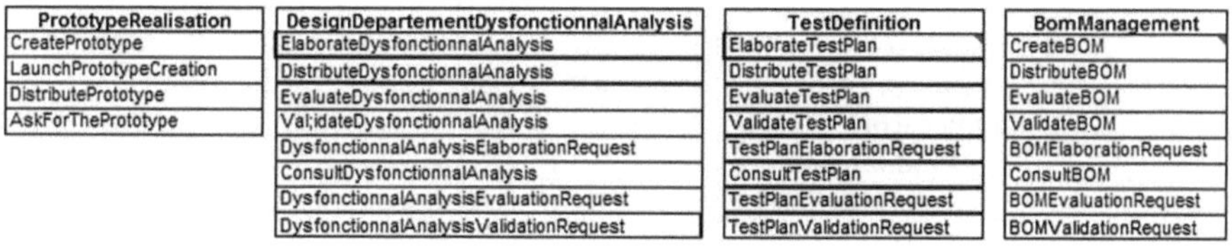

Fig. 5 An excerpt from product design service catalog

composed based on business needs. We propose a bottom–up method for functional PLM services identification in which existing PLM systems should be analyzed in order to identify low-level services. This identification method consists of three steps: (1) identifying PLM data categories, (2) identifying operations on each data category and (3) grouping identified operations in functional PLM services. Therefore, some criteria are needed to decide which operations can be grouped together. We identify two kinds of criteria: those related to functional dependencies and those related to process dependencies. Below are the details of this identification approach: the first step consists of the identification of PLM data categories and the second consists of the identification of functional PLM operations. Two kinds of information sources were used to conduct these two first steps. At first, two off-the-shelf PLM software products were examined to identify the product data categories and their related operations (one mainly used in small and medium enterprises and one mainly used in big groups). Thus, three major categories were identified: product management, product process management and organization. Each category was then broken down into sub-categories and for each sub-category a first set of operations offered in PLM systems were identified (for instance, *Display product structure* and *Compare BOMs* for the product configuration sub-category). Meetings with experienced PLM users were then organized to validate and enrich the list of identified operations. The results of these two first steps are shown in Fig. 6.

The last step of the identification method is to classify the identified operations in functional PLM services. The classification is carried out using a dependency matrix in which column headers are the same as the corresponding row headers and they correspond to the identified operations. The aim is to test functional dependencies and process dependencies between the identified operations. Functional dependencies are those between operations, which have a common global purpose. In this case, the matrix element (a_{ij}) records the relationship between $\text{OperationPurpose}_i$ and $\text{OperationPurpose}_j$ in binary values, which have either the same (1) or not the same (0) purpose. Process dependencies are those between

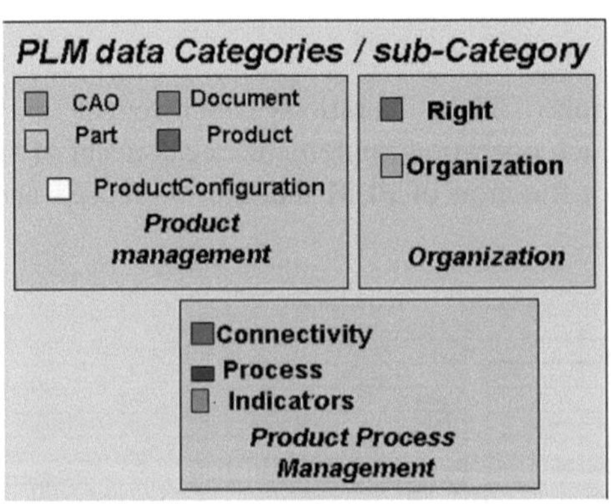

ProductConfiguration

LinkComponentToProduct	BrowsingUpDocument
LinkDocumentToProduct	MoveComponentFromProduct
LinkDocumentToComponent	MoveComponentFromComponent
UpdateLinkCPQuantity	MoveDocumentFromProduct
UpdateLinkDPQuantity	MoveDocumentFromComponent
UpdateLinkDCQuantity	CompareProductsStructure
DisplayComponentStructure	CompareComponentsStructure
DisplayProductStructure	CompareProductStructure
LinkProductToProject	CompareComponentStructure
BrowsingUpComponent	CopyProductStructure
GetComponentTopParent	CopyComponentstructure

Fig. 6 Cartography of PLM data categories and an excerpt from functional PLM operations list

BOM Management	Compenent Management	Product Management	Document Management
LinkComponentToProduct	DefineComponent	DefineNewProduct	NewDocument (type)
LinkDocumentToProduct	DefineComponentData	DefinePartData	DefineDocumentData
LinkDocumentToComponent	CreateFromComponent	CreateFromProduct	AddDocumentAttachment
UpdateLinkCPQuantity	UpdateComponentData	UpdateProductData	NewDocumentFromModel
UpdateLinkDPQuantity	NewComponentVersion	NewProductVersion	EditDocumentAttachement
UpdateLinkDCQuantity	NewComponentRevision	ChangeProductStatus	CompleteDocumentData
BrowsingUpDocument	DisplayComponentEditor	DisplayProductAtachment	ExportDocumentToModel
CompareProductStructure	DisplayComponentHistoric	DisplayProductEditor	SearchDocument
CompareComponentStructure	DeleteComponent	DisplayProductHistoric	PrintAttachment
CopyProductStructure	GetComponentVersion	DeleteProduct	PrintAttachmentToPDF
CopyComponentstructure	LockComponent	GetProductVersion	ExportDocumentToModel
GetComponentTopParent	UnlockComponent	LockProduct	DisplayDocumentEditor
		UnlockProduct	DeleteDocument
			GetDocumentVersion

Fig. 7 An excerpt from Functional PLM service catalog

operations that are choreographed together to make a high-level goal. In this case, each matrix entry (a_{ij}) corresponds to the relationship between OperationHighLevelGoal$_i$ and OperationHighLevelGoal$_j$ in binary values. So, the first stage consists of identifying the purpose and the high-level goal for each identified operation. The second stage of the classification step consists of building two dependency matrices in order to identify the coupled operations. The dependency matrices are filled according to the operation purpose and high-level goals. Thus, if an entry, excluding the diagonals has the same couple's element (binary value equal to 1) it means that there is a dependency between its corresponding row and column operations and so they are coupled (see (Hachani et al. 2011) for more detail).

To group identified operations, the final decision is elaborated by superposition (i.e. Union) of the identified dependency matrix (functional and process). As a result, nine functional PLM services were obtained. Figure 7 shows an excerpt of the catalog.

7.3 *Technical PLM Services Identification Approach and Catalog*

A technical PLM service displays a set of technical operations of a PLM system, which can be consumed separately by several entities.

With regards to PLM systems, recent attention has been directed towards the use of SOA in this field (Bergsjo et al. 2008; Gunpinar and Han 2008; Kim and Weissmann 2006). Some standardization organizations have been involved in the development of standards for PLM with SOA. There are currently two initiatives in terms of PLM services: OMG PLM Services is an OMG standard specification (Lammer and Bugow 2007; Object Management Group 2008), which was developed to implement, operate, and support online access and batch operation using several international standards. It is based on PDTnet standard (Credle et al. 2008), which defines mechanisms to query, and traverse instances of the data schema defined for the PLM services specification. This standard proposes a set of services to launch the execution of PDTnet queries, which provide the necessary computational functionalities to create, read, update and delete instances of data. The second standard, OASIS PLCS PLM Web Services (ISO10303-239 2005) is an ISO STEP standard and is an information exchange standard that provides a number of functional modules. Each functional module targets a specific area of PLM information. These modules provide services such as searching for PLM objects or loading information objects. The analysis of these two standards enables us to conclude that they propose a low level PLM services which provide the necessary PLM computational functionalities. These services may represent a first track of services we target to use.

Indeed, for the technical level, we propose that a set of technical PLM services be selected and defined from the two standards (OMG PLM Services and PLCS Web Services) that cover all technical operations carried out in a PLM system. Several PLM systems are already based on these two PLM standards which will facilitate the deployment of designed process model, defined in terms of the identified product design services and functional PLM services, on many PLM systems. Two categories of services for the technical PLM service catalog were identified. First, a set of necessary PLM computational functionalities, characterized by a service boundary encompassing one or more PLM related entities, was identified such as searching for PLM entities (e.g. document, part, etc.) or loading information objects (e.g. owner, properties, etc.). This first category of technical PLM services allows the effective implementation of the functional PLM services operations. Secondly, a set of services, which provide cross-cutting functionalities related to processing data within legacy application, was identified such as authentication service, mail connection service, CAO tool access services, etc. This second category of technical PLM services allows the support of the execution of the functional PLM service operation in PLM systems.

8 Testing and Feasibility of the Proposed Approach

This section describes the feasibility of the proposed approach. To do so, we consider the ECM process presented previously (Version A in Fig. 1). We start by modeling the ECM process using the Product design service catalog. This step aims to test if the ECM process can be defined using the identified list of product design services operations, enabling the demonstration that they allow all PDPs to be defined.

Figure 8a presents a part of the industrial setting modeled using our business service-based model (not mentioned in this chapter). A designer initiates an engineering change request elaboration (*ElaborateEngineeringChangeRequest* operation) and then distributes it for validation (*DistributeEngineeringChange-Request* operation). On receiving the Engineering Change Request from a designer, the application engineer evaluates it for validation (*ValidateEngineeringChangeRequest* operation). One of the concurrent sequences paths (Agree/Not Agree) will be initiated depending on the result of ECR validation step.

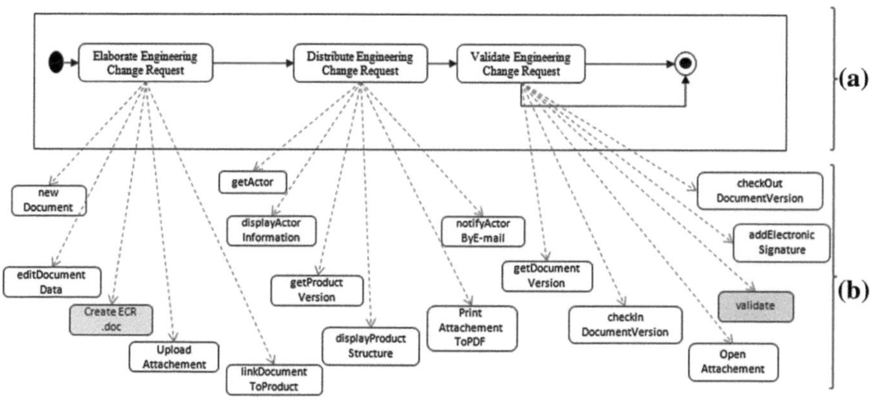

Fig. 8 **a** engineering change management process modeled using PDS operation list. **b** Mapping of PDS operations to Functional PLM services operations

The ECR process modeled using PDS operations should then be mapped with functional and technical services in order to test the articulation between the different service levels. Each PDS operation corresponds to a set of functional PLM services operations that can be executed in turn by invocation of technical PLM services operations. Dotted arrows represent the articulation from one service level to another (cf. Fig. 8b).

This testing illustrates how PDPs can be expressed in terms of the identified PDS catalog. Many other PDPs have been considered to test the suitability of the identified PDS catalog. This helped us to refine the PDS catalog (we detected that some business operations were omitted) and to ensure that the functional PLM services operations can meet all PDS operations.

In Fig. 8 we illustrate the approach on the new ECM process instance (version B in Fig. 1). This new instance integrates the change needed to ask for precision about the origin of the breakage problem produced during the drilling of an axis. To do so, new PDS operations (*Askfor3DAssembly, DistributeValidationReport* and *ModifyECR*) are added to the ECM process definition (cf. Fig. 9a). The corresponding functional PLM services operations (represented using grey dotted arrows) are added to the services orchestration (cf. Fig. 9b).

This change can be integrated and processed so that the main flows of the Engineering Change Management Process is not interrupted. This can be made by using an evolving orchestration language such as Yaml (van der Aalst and ter Hofstede 2005), π-Diapason (Pourraz and Verjus 2008) and PXL (*Process eXtensible Language*) (Verjus et al. 2011a). These two latter orchestration languages allow a service orchestration to be dynamically changed while running and substituting the new orchestration with the old one. Finally, to make the transition from one level to another, a conceptual architecture (cf. Figure 10), based on a model driven-engineering approach (Schmidt 2006) is proposed; the correspondences/

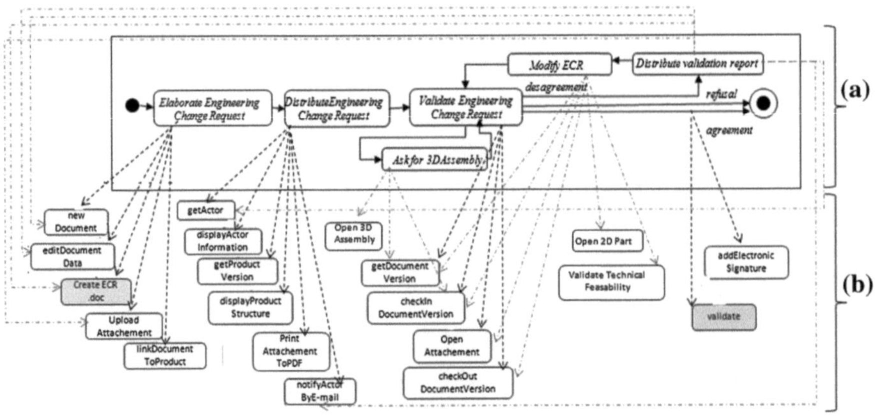

Fig. 9 Change in the engineering change management process

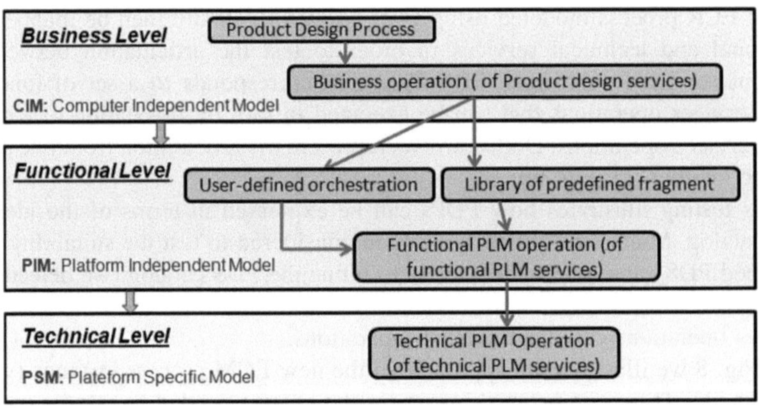

Fig. 10 Conceptual architecture of the proposed approach

mappings rules, which are outside the scope of this chapter, are still under development. In fact, once the PDP model in terms of PDS operations has been established, the next step consists of executing the correspondences/mappings rules from the PDP model to the execution model. An eclipse-based engineering environment for supporting and enacting our approach (Business Services Orchestration modeling, correspondences/mappings between levels—i.e. between services from one level to another) will be proposed, and is now under development.

9 Conclusion and Future Work

In this chapter, we discussed the problem of PDPs flexibility in PLM system: PDPs are emergent and product design actors cannot deal with existing technical solutions. Existing modeling approaches and perspectives dealing with process flexibility will be discussed and analyzed. The assumption made is that flexible PDPs require specific methods for their design. Our contributions respond to the limitations and problems described above by providing a methodological approach that aims to provide PDP flexibility by adhering to service orientation. To allow dynamic PDP change in PLM system, an approach based on service technology is introduced. This approach proposes to deal with PDP model as a product design services composition. The challenge here is to react quickly to changes either by replacing some services or by adding new services to the composition. In order to deal with alignment issues between the technical and business levels, we first propose a service type for each level. We then aim to propose an orchestration model at each level (business, functional and technical) and a means that allows the transformation of the business orchestration model to a functional orchestration model by adhering to MDE (Model Driven Engineering) techniques (Verjus et al. 2011a). Finally, according to the PLM system used, a mapping between the functional services of the functional orchestration model and the technical services of the PLM system should be carried out using the same deployment techniques. Whilst our approach was illustrated by focusing on the PLM system, it could be extended to other IS components and sub-domains (CAD, CAM, etc.). The same approach as the one proposed in this chapter may be employed to identify the business services, and the same modeling technique may be used to orchestrate and manage alignment between levels. This modeling approach has also been validated in a Manufacturing Executing System scenario that illustrates its generic nature and application for architecting a service-based IS (Verjus et al. 2011a); implementation techniques has also been proposed to cope with services definition and supporting business processes services orchestrations design, execution and runtime evolution.

In this chapter, our non-empirical method only concentrated on the identification stage and presented the identification approaches for each service catalog and for each level. The proposal allows one to consider and design an information system as a set of services at different levels that are orchestrated according to support business processes. Quality of services, quality of service orchestrations and evolution strategies are still ongoing work streams. Providing support for selecting relevant services according to business needs and/or objectives, business rules and/or constraints is an open challenge that is now receiving significant interest.

Acknowledgments The authors would like to thank the Region Rhône-Alpes for their financial support in this research.

References

Arsanjani, A., & Allam, A. (2006, 18–22 Sept). Service oriented modeling and architecture for realization of an SOA. In: *On The Proceedings of IEEE International Conference on Service Computing* (SCC'06). IEEE, (p. 521) Chicago, IL.

Bergsjo, D., Catic, A., & Malmqvist, J. (2008). Implementing a service-oriented PLM architecture focusing on support for engineering change management. *International Journal of PLM, 3*, 335–355.

Bessai, K., Claudepierre, B., Saidani, O. & Nurcan, S. (2008, 16–20 June). Context aware business process evaluation and redesign. In: *International Workshop on Business Process Management, Design and Support, at International Conference on Advanced Information Systems*, (pp. 407–414). Montpellier, France.

Boukadi, K., Ghedira, C., Chaari, S., Vincent, L. & Bataineh, E. (2008, 23–27 June). *CWSC4EC: how to employ context, web service, and community in enterprise collaboration*. In: *The 8th International Conference on New Technologies of Distributed Systems*, 23-27 June, Lyon, France.

Bowers, J., Button, G., & Sharrock, W. (1995, 11–15 Sept). Workflow from within and without: technology and cooperative work on the print industry shop floor. In: *Proceedings of the 4th European Conference on CSCW* (pp 51–66), Stockholm, Sweden: Kluwer Academic Publishers.

Chang, S. H. & Kim, S. D. (2007, 7–11 July). A service-oriented analysis and design approach to developing adaptable services. In: *The IEEE International Conference on Services Computing* (SCC 2007), (pp 204–211). Hawaii, USA.

Credle, R., Bader, M., Brikler, K., Harris, M., Holt, M., & Hayakuna, Y. (2008). *SOA approach to entreprise integration for product life cycle management*, (pp 66–80). IBM International Technical Support Organization, October.

Emig, C., Weisser, J., & Abeck, S. (2006, 19–25 Feb). Development of SOA-based software systems—an evolutionary programming approach. In: The Advanced International Conference on Telecommunications and International Conference on Internet and Web Applications and Services (AICT/ICIW 2006), (pp 182–187), Guadaloupe, French Caribbean. IEEE Computer Society.

Gunpinar, E., & Han, S. (2008). Interfacing heterogeneous PDM systems using the PLM services. *Advanced Engineering Informatics, 22*, 307–316.

Hachani, S., Gzara, L., & Verjus, H. (2011). support of business processes flexibility in PLM systems using a services-based approach. *Proceedings of the International Conference on Industrial Engineering and Systems Management* (IESM'2011), (pp 547–555), International Institute for Innovation, Industrial Engineering and Entrepreneurship.

Hachani, S., Gzara, L., & Verjus, H. (2012). A service-oriented approach for flexible process support within enterprises: application on PLM systems, Enterprise Information Systems, 2012, doi:10.1080/17517575.2012.688221.

ISO10303-239:2005. Industrial automation systems and integration—product data representation and exchange—part 239: application protocol: product life cycle support. Geneva, Switzerland: International Organization for Standardization.

Kim, S. R., & Weissmann, D. (2006). Middleware-based integration of multiple CAD and PDM systems into virtual reality environment. *Computer-Aided Design & Applications, 3*, 547–556.

Lammer, L. & Bugow, R. (2007). PLM services in practice. In: *The Future of Product Development, Proceedings of the 17th CIRP Design Conference*, (pp 503–512). Berlin, Heidelberg: Springer.

Lezoche, M., Missikof, M., & Tinini, L. (2008, 16–20 June). Business process evolution: a rule-based approach. In: *International Workshop on Business Process Management, Design and Support, at international conference on advanced information systems*, (pp 407–414) Montpelier, France.

Manouvrier, B. & Ménard, L. (2007). Intégration applicative EAI, B2B, BPM et SOA. Hermès Science—Lavoisier.

Micaelli, J. -P. (2002). Institutionnalisme, évolutionnisme : le défi de la conception. Actes desJournées d'étude Institutionnalismes et Evolutionnismes-Confrontations autour de perspectives empiriques. Lyon.

Object Management Group. (2008). *PLM Services* 2.0[Online]. Available from: http://www.omg.org/spec/PLM/2.0/ [Accessed May 11, 2012].

Pahl, G., & Beitz, W. (2007). *Engineering design—a systematic approach.* London: Springer.

Papazoglou, M. P. & Heuvel, W.-J. (2006). Service-oriented design and development methodology. International Journal of Web Engineering and Technology (IJWET), *2*, 412–442.

Pourraz, F. & Verjus, H. (2008). Managing service-based EAI architectures evolution using a formal architecture-centric approach, volume 3 of Lecture Notes in Business Information Processing, (pp 269–280). Berlin, Heidelberg: Springer.

Robin, V., Girard, Ph., & Barandiaran, D. (2004, 5–7 April). A model of design environments to support collaborative design management. In: *5th International Conference on Integrated Design and Manufacturing in Mechanical Engineering*, IDMME, Bath.

Saaksvuori, A., & Immonen, A. (2005). *Product lifecycle management.* Berlin: Springer.

Scaravetti, D., Nadeau, J.-P., Pailhes, J., & Sebastian, P. (2005, April). Structuring of embodiment design problem based on the product life cycle. International Journal of Product Development, Special Issue on Product Life cycle Management. *2*(1/2), 47–70.

Schmidt, D. C. (2006). Guest editor's introduction: model-driven engineering. Computer Journal, *39*(2), 25–31.

Tollenaere, M. (1998). *Conception de produits mécaniques: méthodes, modèleset outils.* Paris: Hermès Science.

van der Aalst, W. & ter Hofstede, A. (2005). YAWL: Yet another workflow language. Information Systems *30*(4), 245–275.

Verjus, H. & Pourraz, F. (2011). Une Architecture pour l'Ingénierie des Systèmes d'Information à base de Services. Information—Interaction—Intelligence Journal *10*, 37–66.

Verjus, H., Pourraz, F., & Fakhfakh, N. (2011a). Cadre conceptuel pour la modélisation et la supervision d'architectures à base de services. Une approche pour l'ingénierie des SI à base de services. Développement des SI à base de modèles : exigences, traçabilité et co-conception—Ingénierie des Systèmes d'Information—Revue des sciences et technologies de l'information, *16*(5), 43–72.

Zhao, X. & Liu, C. (2007, 24–29 Sept). Version management in the business change context. In: International Conference on Business Process Management, (pp. 198–213). Brisbane, Australia.

Part V
Innovation

Open Innovation in SMEs: Prospects and Challenges

Hakikur Rahman and Isabel Ramos

1 Introduction

Innovation refers to transformation of products, processes, services or organizational management (White 2006; Chason 2008; Rahman 2010) for value addition (Beacham 2006; Vaitheeswaran 2007; Barker 2008) leading to benefits of the community (Cox 2008). However, the real importance of innovation activities has been linked with several simultaneously affecting societal phenomena, such as having easier familiarization with the globalization, obtaining benefits from deregulation and liberalization of markets, utilizing benefits from the ICT revolution, and adopting the dynamic changes in the market demand patterns (Schienstock and Hämäläinen 2001). Along the roadmap of innovation, inclusion of open contexts is becoming popular day by day. Success stories such as those of Open Source, Google, Skype or Microsoft (though they are not particularly, SMEs) teach us at least one lesson—no one could ever know where the next big idea will be coming from! (Oxford Business School 2008).

Innovation has various effects on SMEs within various schools of thoughts in terms of economics. It leads them to evolutionary economics, institutional economics, new regional economics, the economics of learning and the economics of innovation (Lundvall 1999). But, successful innovation is crucial for business success and SMEs growth that underpins any region's long term economic achievement (Roper and Hewitt-Dundas 2004). In general, innovation in SMEs may lead to product innovation, as well as process innovation including providing impact in employment. However, this proxy is relatively challenging, since the importance of innovations is not only due to the impact they have on employment, but also depend on other variables, such as turn-over, economic growth, sustainability, etc. (Nählinder 2005).

H. Rahman (✉) · I. Ramos
University of Minho, Braga, Portugal
e-mail: email@hakik.org

J. Devos et al. (eds.), *Information Systems for Small and Medium-sized Enterprises*, Progress in IS, DOI: 10.1007/978-3-642-38244-4_16,

Table 1 Search counts with citation rates and selected literatures

Search engine	Search string	Hit counts	Citation counts	Observations
Google scholar	'open innovation' + smes + prospects	161	10 selected with citation counts above 20	Articles included books, book chapters, journal papers, conference proceedings
Google scholar	'open innovation' + smes + challenges	450	15 selected with citation counts above 20	

In recent years, the contribution of SMEs to economic growth, job creation, innovation and promotion of enterprise has been widely recognized. While SMEs are important in terms of their overall share of GDP, but is also believed that many smaller firms lack both managerial and technical skills, which inhibit their effectiveness. Therefore, improving the competitive advantage of SMEs is important to individual firms and to the national economy as a whole (Tilley and Tonge 2003). This study remains confined within the context of prospects and challenges of innovation for SMEs to growth effectively for providing better products, processes or services. The study is an outcome of a progressive research on the influence of open innovation in entrepreneurship development. As a longitudinal literature review[1] (see Hsu and Lin 2006; Weerakkody et al. 2009), the study searched literatures through search engines like; Google scholar, Scopus, ScienceDirect and the university digital library using specific search strings ('open innovation'.AND.'SMEs'.AND.'prospects'), and ('open innovation'.AND. 'SMEs'.AND.'challenges'), and selected literatures with higher citation rates (Google Scholar) and relevance ratios (generic search engines, like Google and Bing) as the search criteria or methodology.

The search criterion for citation index is listed in Table 1 below:

The second search was conducted on ScienceDirect with the university's integrated digital library service. The hit counts and selection criteria is listed in Table 2.

Further to these, after a thorough review of classical concept papers, research articles, including contemporary literatures on open innovation and SMEs development, the themes were chosen among the prospects and challenges by looking into an iterative count from those selected literatures. Citation index, literature review and search criteria were adopted from Kitchenham 2004; Cochrane Collaboration 2004, 2006, 2008; and Cowan and Daim 2011.

The chapter has been segmented into six parts. After providing the introduction and background literature review in the first two, it has tried to provide synthesized arguments on issues of prospects and challenges of open innovation in entrepreneurships, emphasizing SMEs, in the third and fourth parts. The last two segments comprise of research recommendations and conclusion. However, as an important

[1] http://www.experiment-resources.com/longitudinal-study.html

Table 2 Literature review from ScienceDirect and Digital Library

Search engine	Search string	Hit counts	Limited to 2006–2013	Limited to topics
ScienceDirect + b-on + digital library	'open innovation' AND smes AND prospects for all sources and all fields since 1993	739	116	20 articles selected[a]
	'open innovation' AND smes AND challenges for all sources and all fields since 1993	1,826	1,283	30 articles selected[b]

[a] Sorted by relevance and topics, such as absorptive capacity, firm, innovation, high-tech, intellectual property, international relationship, product innovation, public research, outward FDI, and patent, with hit count over 20 from the journal list shown in Table 3

[b] Sorted by relevance and topics, such as firm, innovation, innovation system, product development, business model, and open innovation, with hit count over 20 from the journal list shown in Table 4

Table 3 List of journals with hit counts over 20

Journals	Hit counts
Research policy	62
Technovation	39
Technological forecasting and social change	30
Journal of business venturing	22

Table 4 List of journals with hit counts over 20

Journals	Hit counts
Technovation	158
Research policy	135
Technological forecasting and social change	58
Industrial marketing management	50
European management journal	49
International business review	48
Journal of business venturing	43
International journal of production economics	38
International journal of information management	31
Journal of world business	29
Journal of business research	26
World patent information	25

element, this study develops an innovation opportunity framework for researchers, academics and practitioners.

2 Background

The term innovation refers to incremental, radical, and revolutionary changes in thinking, products, processes, services or organizations for a novelty.[2] Innovation then could be defined as the creation, improvement and implementation of a new product, process, service, or organizational change aiming to increase efficiency, effectiveness or competitive advantage (Chesbrough 2003b, 2006; EIRMA 2004). Innovation links to the creativity and the creation of unique ideas, and involves processes for taking those innovative ideas and turning them into reality through invention, research and new product development.[3] Furthermore, innovation can be seen as the process that translates knowledge into economic growth and social well-being. It encompasses a series of scientific, technological, organizational, economic and commercial activities. Researches in the context of innovation are targeted towards one of these activities and may be carried out at different phases of the process[4] (Chesbrough et al. 2006).

Innovation tends to be a major source of economic performance and social welfare of a country (Hamalainen and Heiskala 2007; Ghili and Tavana 2011; Abreu et al. 2011). It directly affects productivity, efficiency and job creation in firms; citizens' welfare in society and assists to address global challenges such as the economic crisis, health, education and environment (OECD 2009). Furthermore, innovation no longer depends solely on how firms, universities, and research institutes perform independently, but, progressively more and more, on how they collaborate (OECD 1999).

On the other hand, open innovation (OI),[5] a term recently supplemented to the industries and organizations to promote open ended ideas, thoughts, processes, and researches to improve product development, provide better services, increase efficiency and enhance value-addition. In terms of process dynamics, it incorporates accumulation of ideas, knowledge, licenses, intellectual properties, patents, copy rights and inventions (through licensing, joint ventures, spin-offs, and start-ups); and in terms of concept dynamics, it incorporates user innovation, market innovation, cumulative innovation, collaborative innovation and distributed innovation. Further, open innovation emerges on issues like, the widely distributed

---

2 http://www.merriam-webster.com/dictionary/innovation; http://dictionary.reference.com/browse/innovation; http://en.wikipedia.org/wiki/Innovation

3 http://www.digitalstrategy.govt.nz/Resources/Glossary-of-Key-Terms/

4 http://www.arc.gov.au/general/glossary.htm

5 a term promoted by Henry Chesbrough, a professor and executive director at the Center for Open Innovation at Berkeley.

knowledge that are available in the diverse world of the Internet, which solitary enterprises cannot afford (economically and organizationally) and rely entirely on their own research and resources, but may instead collaborate, buy, lease-out or license processes or inventions (patents, intellectual properties) from other companies, organizations or institutions (Chesbrough 2003a, 2006; Chesbrough et al. 2006). Currently, many companies are promoting open innovation and among them IBM, IdeaConnetion, InnoCentive, InnovationXchange, Nerac, NineSigma, Nokia, Procter and Gamble, and Yet2.com[6] are widely recognized. These names actually do not represent the SMEs community, but they are the forerunners in utilizing open innovation strategies since many years, and this research observes that these emerging concepts are yet to be matured among SMEs. This research argues further; learning from these forerunners would provide in-depth knowledge about various stages of open innovation, from which the SMEs community can piggy-back, their learning curves.

It has been observed that companies recognize open innovation as a strategic tool to explore new growth opportunities and at the same time to lower risks. However, the most important benefit they see that it provides an extended base of ideas and technologies. Companies look at open innovation as a close collaboration with external partners, such as customers, consumers, suppliers, competitors, researchers or other individuals that may have an input to the future development of their company. The main motives for joining forces is to seize new business opportunities, share risks, pool complementary resources and realize synergies (OECD 2008; Sousa 2008). Referring to the importance of innovation in SMEs, Davenport (2006: 3) stated that, "Innovation is important for SMEs—a massive 60 % of innovations come from the small and medium enterprise sector, and it is crucial that this total must not diminish against competing pressures in the modern market". This research, however, limits the literature review to prospects and challenges related to SMEs context in establishing an open innovation opportunities framework, and looks into possible discourse of enhanced inclusion of SMEs within the innovation process. Various prospects and challenges of open innovation in SMEs are being discussed next.

3 Prospects of Open Innovation in SMES

In spite of their diversified characteristics, SMEs have been found to be more adaptable to open innovation with a significant contribution on targeting issues and perspectives in relation to their development, such as product, process and service innovation (OECD 2000a; De Jong and von Hippel 2005, 2009; IBM 2007; Hass and Hochrinner 2008; Maes 2009; Van de Vrande et al. 2009) leading to increased

[6] http://en.wikipedia.org/wiki/Open_Innovation

competition, demanding customers, knowledge acquisition, and better positioning in the market (De Jong 2006; NOUS 2007; Lemola and Lievonen 2008).

It has been observed that open innovation has created various prospects or opportunities for SMEs in terms of their development. SMEs play an important role in the open innovation world. They can explore smaller markets that are of less importance to large firms, provide specialized technological support to others including large companies, easily enter into a growing market with innovative business model, partner with other dominant businesses and platforms of large companies, and remain in a niche where large firms have lesser interest (Chesbrough 2010).

Thus, ranging from benefits like gaining knowledge from external sources, or adopting OI strategies for internal development, or creating new business opportunities, or improving access to markets, business skills and information SMEs can take the advantage from being exposed to open innovation. However, varying in terms of acceptability or satisfactoriness, there are arguments on specific parameters of open innovation processes, whether they are beneficial or challenging to SMEs.

As mentioned in the methodology, this research has selected the following prospects (shown in Table 5) and challenges (shown in Table 6), and then some important aspects from them (both prospects and challenges) are being discussed using exploratory literature review. Later on a framework on innovation prospects has been devised for the benefit of the SMEs communities and at the same time to instigate a background for further research.

3.1 Earlier Adapter of New Products, Platforms and Markets

Stiglitz (1998) argued that SMEs are not able to produce radical innovations due to their limited size and thus fail to create innovative market, but Parrilli (2006) mentioned that, due to their small size and taking it as an advantage, they may rather benefit from being part of an innovation system. Cooke (1996) and Cooke and Wills (1999) supported the idea of incorporating SMEs in an innovation system comprising public and private institutions and other firms to promote innovation via collective effort. Design Council's (2005) survey found the evidence of this fact that, SMEs could be easily adapted to new products due to their rather flexible nature. Chesbrough (2010) supported the idea of SMEs being in advantageous position to easily adapt new platform or market as explorer, specialist, or forerunner in unexplored areas of less importance to large firms.

3.2 Easier Adoption of Open Innovation Strategies and Policies

With certain technological capacities at hand in order to imitate the innovation, SMEs are in a better position to adopt technological new products, though the imitator's major task is to overcome the barriers (Schewe 2001). Furthermore, in the open innovation paradigm, in addition to in-house resources, firms' external relations are performed as assets, which contribute to their overall performance (Zaheer and Bell 2005; Smed et al. 2012). Firms cannot rely solely on the in-house resources, but also need to explore, adopt and tag pool of external resources as an integral element in the development of unique products for the market (Smed et al. 2012).

The diffusion of open innovation strategies has been largely acknowledged within SMEs (Lazzarotti et al. 2008) through collaborative and open business model (Sautter and Clar 2008). SMEs are more adaptable to embrace open innovation strategies, such as inward and outward licensing, cross-regional R&D collaboration, regional innovation and joint ventures (Asheim 2003; Asheim et al. 2003; Scherngell and Barber 2009) due to their flexibility in accelerating innovation, especially in terms of radical innovation and manage themselves within the innovation process and influence others (Edwards et al. 2005). Furthermore, Van

Table 5 Prospects associated to open innovation affecting SMEs development

Prospects	**Sources**
Ability to adopt quickly with new products, platforms and markets	Cooke 1996; Stiglitz 1998; Cooke and Wills 1999; Design Council 2005; Parrilli 2006; Avlonitis and Salavou 2007; García-Moralesa et al. 2007; Chesbrough 2010
Easily adopt open innovation strategies such as inward and outward licensing, R&D collaboration and joint ventures, and policies	Schewe 2001; Havas 2002; Bougrain and Haudeville 2002; Asheim et al. 2003; Edwards et al. 2005; Lazzarotti et al. 2008; Sautter and Clar 2008; Batterlink 2009; Cervantes 2009; Van de Vrande et al. 2009; Scherngell and Barber 2009; Smed et al. 2012
Adaptability to technological, product, process or service innovation	Evangelista 2000; OECD 2000a; Bougrain and Haudeville 2002; Tilley and Tonge 2003; Asheim et al. 2003; Gassmann and Enkel 2004; Toivonen 2004; Cosh et al. 2005; Nählinder 2005; Salavou 2006; Avlonitis and Salavou 2007; Dargan and Shucksmith 2008; Lichtenthaler 2007, 2010; Maes 2009; Van de Vrande et al. 2009; Commonwealth of Australia 2009
Enabler of employment generation	Smallbone et al. Smallbone et al. 2003; European Commission 1997, 2000
Adoptive to the abundance of knowledge, opportunities and interactions as knowledge acquisition enabler	European Commission 2003a; 2003b; Cosh et al. 2005; Lemola and Lievonen 2008

Table 6 Challenges associated to Open Innovation affecting SMEs development

Challenges	Sources
Lack of managerial and technical skills, lack of scarce resources (finance, government policy)	Hadjimanolis 1999; Van Hemel and Cramer, 2002; Nauwelaers and Wintjes 2002; Tilley and Tonge 2003; Del Brío and Junquera 2003; Hayton 2004; McAdam and Gibson 2004; García-Moralesa et al. 2007; Van de Vrande et al. 2008; Massa and Testa 2008; Rahman and Ramos 2010; Hotho and Champion 2011; Woerter 2012
Inconsistency in turn-over, pattern of economic growth, relationship among partners, development patterns (product, process, service, managerial aspect)	O'Sullivan 2000; European Commission 2002; Havas 2002; Nählinder 2005; Edwards et al. 2005; NOUS 2007; OECD 2007; Government of UK 2008; Herstad et al. 2008; Woerter 2012
Multiple innovation channels are counterproductive	Carlsson and Eliasson 2002; Chesbrough 2003b; Interact 2004; Nählinder 2005; Parrilli 2006; Lazonick 2007; De Jong et al 2008
Differences in organization and culture between the individual partners	Wei and Morgan 2004; Callegati and Grandi 2005; De Jong 2006; Lichtenthaler and Ernst 2006; Barba-Sánchez et al. 2007; Government of UK 2008; TIEKE 2009; Van de Vrande et al. 2009; Herzog and Leker 2010; Chesbrough 2010
Incompetency in handling knowledge issues	OECD 2008; Vanhaverbeke 2010; Ann and Minshall 2012
Increased globalization	Nauwelaers and Wintjes 2000; Spanos et al. 2001; Dhungana 2003

de Vrande et al. (2009) argued that, even with the lack of financial resources, scant opportunities to recruit specialized personnel and small innovation portfolio, open innovation practices are increasingly adopted in SMEs due to their other inherited natures, such as flexible to transformations or changes, receptive to open calls, and adaptive to new environment. Batterlink (2009) supported the same through a study of the decade 1994–2004 and mentions that SMEs are catching up in recent years in adopting open innovation strategies.

This study has find that local and national policies play important role in the early stage of the adoption process among SMEs for appropriate market placement (Havas 2002; Bougrain and Haudeville 2002; Dargan and Shucksmith 2008).

3.3 *Adoptive to Technological, Product, Process or Service Innovation*

Technological changes play important role in service sectors, particularly. In this aspect, process innovation among other innovation investments, including acquisition and internal development represent the most effective channels for service innovation (Evangelista 2000). Along this route, SMEs are found to be more flexible in adapting to new customers' requirements by making necessary work force changes and adapting to new equipment and techniques (OECD 2000a). Moreover, their dynamic capabilities enable them to address rapidly changing environments for the development through integration and reconfiguration of external and internal competencies (Maes 2009). One of the major advantages of SMEs is their ability to respond more rapidly to changing signals from the market. Thus, concentrating on a range of incremental innovations based on ideas adopted from clients, competitors and suppliers to improve both products and processes is likely to be more effective way of improving their overall competitiveness (Tilley and Tonge 2003).

A report of Telemetica Institute (2008) mentions that technological innovations trigger new services, better care for clients, new ways of working, and new means of exchange of ideas. This study argues that technological innovation acknowledging product, process, service and organizational management creates opportunities or scopes of improvements to firms belonging to the small and medium business sector. If entrepreneurs can genuinely be developed through skilled human resources, or at least be developed, at university or research house, they will ultimately act as starters of a market economy, including social enterprises (Mueller and Goic 2003). Hence, understanding technological trends allows one to anticipate better on near-future possibilities for tangible problems for consumers and organizations through exploitation of technologies (Avlonitis and Salavou 2007), and in this aspect SMEs act as a catalyst of innovation promotion (Telemetica Institute 2008; Hagen 2008; Brouwers et al. 2009).

3.4 Enabler of Employment Generation

Since the publication of the Bolton Report in 1971, the contribution of SMEs to economic growth, job creation, innovation and promotion of enterprises has been largely recognized (Tilley and Tonge 2003). Innovations generate economic growth, but also induce employment generation. However, in terms of employment generation, the impact of product innovation seems to be more catalytic than the impact of process innovation (Nählinder 2005).

In the 1970s the World saw the reversal trend towards increasing size of enterprises and business establishments, and the share of small enterprises started to grow, especially in terms of employment generation (Sengenberger et al. 1990). During the 1980s, at a time when corporate enterprises were cutting down their labor, the apparent ability of small firms to create jobs attracted the attention of policy-makers in many countries (Smallbone et al. 2003).

3.5 Adoptive to the Abundance of Knowledge, Opportunities and Interactions as Knowledge Acquisition Enabler

Innovation involves generating, disseminating and applying of knowledge. It is not a linear process, and involves an originator at one end and a receiver at the other. There are many players involved, and they interact and influence each other in multifaceted ways. Ideas can come from anywhere and may lead to unexpected directions (Commonwealth of Australia 2009). In this aspect, external linkages, both public (including higher education institutions and research houses) and private (intermediaries and knowledge brokers), benefit SMEs innovations. These linkages can be important sources of knowledge that directly strengthen the technological competences of the SMEs and their competitive advantage. Furthermore, collaboration with customers, suppliers, higher education institutions, even competitors, allows entrepreneurs to expand their range of expertise, develop specialist products, and achieve various other corporate objectives (Cosh et al. 2005).

External knowledge utilization refers to commercializing knowledge exclusively or in addition to its application in a firm's own products and services (for example, out-licensing or out-sourcing) (Lichtenthaler 2007). Firms' transfer of knowledge to recipients outside their organization has recently become wider, and they may gain access to new markets or establish their own technologies as industry standards (Lichtenthaler 2010). Furthermore, opening up the internal innovation process by integrating suppliers and/or customers is not new. Supplier involvement can provide buying firms with substantial benefits that range from more "operational" benefits, such as the earlier identification of technical problems, fewer re-engineering issues, or readymade availability of prototypes, to more "strategic" benefits, such as enhanced utilization of internal resources, access to new or supplementary product and process technologies, reduced technical and financial risks, improved product features, or relatively shorter time-to-market for new products. The benefits of outsourcing includes gaining access to new areas of knowledge (complementary knowledge), managing capacity problems (more flexibility), concentration of core competencies, speed (reducing time-to-market), and the sharing of costs (Toivonen 2004; Gassmann and Enkel 2004).

4 Challenges of Open Innovation in SMES

Abulrub and Lee (2011) referred to the contemporary studies that have investigated differences in the degree of open innovation depending on four environmental factors, such as the industry type (manufacturing industry, or service industry), the company size (large company, or SMEs), the technology intensity (high-tech industry, or low-tech industry), and the market type (foreign markets, or domestic markets). However, when one searches about specific challenges associated to SMEs development utilizing open innovation, investigations are rare and lead to scarce human resources, misaligned consistency in the information about open innovation strategies, unawareness among SMEs about the actual benefit of open innovation, and foremost, incompetency in handling intricate knowledge resources that are being treated as open innovation tools in the current information era. Furthermore, working with new technologies, radical innovation is considered to involve greater interdependence and information interexchange and thereby a greater need for control and more costs that can be a problem for SMEs because of resource scarcity (Tijsterman 2010). Also, as a new concept, open innovation in SMEs are yet to be treated in the experimental or observational state, and thus may lead to be a costly and risky process (Rahman and Ramos 2010).

Antti Peltomäki, the Deputy Director General of European Commission (European Communities 2008) mentions that, innovation is a costly process. He reiterated further, that only one out of 3000 product ideas makes it on the market, which means that there are hundreds of unsuccessful products beyond every success. Moreover, even successful products may be far from being user friendly. Surveys show that 75 % of all users find their tools more stressing than relaxing. In such a context, user-centric validation can play an important role in speeding up effectively the innovation process through addressing the actual users' needs. OECD (2000b) finds that, most of the obstacles to growth and innovation in services are the same as in manufacturing. Insufficient access to finance and risk capital, lack of internal capacity to innovate, insufficient expertise in applying appropriate knowledge and high risk are characteristically the main barriers to innovation in all sectors.

Hence, it is relevant that, as a newly emerged field of research, open innovation for SME development deserves a prolonged and strategically developed qualitative and quantitative synthesis on literature review, including other forms of validation. However, during the early process of this research, this manuscript likes to carry out qualitative discussion based on a few challenge parameters (as depicted in Table 2). It is expected that as the research grows, it will be able to provide some more in-depth parameters related to challenges associated to open innovation affecting SMEs development.

4.1 Lack of Human Skills, Scarce Resources and Policy Constraints

While SMEs are important in terms of their overall contribution to GDP, it is also believed that smaller firms lack both managerial and technical skills that inhibit their growth (Tilley and Tonge 2003, Hayton 2004). There are typical management challenges for SME managers (mostly, owner-managers), which are quite different than those of managers of large firms that want to expedite the organic growth engine in their company, and this is an interesting uncharted area for future research (Chesbrough et al. 2006; Van de Vrande et al. 2008; Rahman and Ramos 2010; Hotho and Champion 2011).

In an earlier study, Hadjimanolis (1999) found that in addition to other barriers (external and internal) in the open innovation process, the lack of skilled labor is an important one, which is also common among developed and developing nations. He emphasized that perception of top managers on innovation may seem as a barrier and that extends further due to lack of motivation. In another study, Van Hemel and Cramer (2002) observe that lack of appropriate knowledge is a barrier to specific fields of innovation, while Gerstenfield and Roberts (2000) added that those could be due to lack of training and awareness. Moreover, many smaller firms lack both managerial and technical skills (focused training or short-term orientation) that inhibit their effectiveness in innovation (Del Brío and Junquera 2003; Tilley and Tonge 2003; García-Moralesa et al. 2007).

Nauwelaers and Wintjes (2000, 2002) argue that with limited resource base, SMEs need external orientation to understand and proactively adapt to the new environment, so that they engage in innovation on an informal mode. The main role for innovation policy, which aims to increase the capabilities of its SMEs to innovate, and the overall capacity of a region, should be to foster interactive learning within the companies and within the region. They further argue that this calls for an interactive mode of policy intervention, which is a challenge to the SMEs. Massa and Testa (2008) adds to this that the ability of regional human resources to realize innovation objectives and to contribute to the growth of the targeted regions face challenges due to proper knowledge. Furthermore, inconsistency in the development process model, and weak relationship among stakeholders, like weak supplier relation can present significant challenges for SMEs when attempting to integrate and operate supplier dependent development process models (Edwards et al. 2005).

4.2 Inconsistency in Turn-Over, Pattern of Economic Growth, and Collaboration

Innovation is explicitly characterized as a process that is cumulative, collective, and uncertain. Along this route, apart from resource allocations, organizational restructuring, or strategic positioning, it may have effects on other variables as well, such as inconsistency in turn-over, pattern of economic growth, collaboration and cooperation, etc. Though they be seen as minor from outside or for the time being, but these parameters affect innovation channels in the longer run (O'Sullivan 2000; Havas 2002; Nählinder 2005). Turn over data effects critical benchmarking indices of SMEs (European Commission 2002), that reflects input on development contexts, such as human development (NOUS 2007; OECD 2007), and thus excessive external turn-over of personnel seems to be a challenge at the end (Herstad et al.

2008). Furthermore, Woerter (2012) mentions that collaboration potential or knowledge and technology transfer potential between the private and the public research sector face challenges due to many factors, such as technology proximity, lack of information, lack of transfer ability, secrecy, and technology oriented policy initiatives.

4.3 Multiple Innovation Channels

The Open Innovation model entails that enterprises can use internal and external ideas, technologies and knowledge to advance their innovation processes, and internal ideas can be taken to the market through external channels (for example, spin-offs, external licensing of intellectual property, etc.) to generate additional value (Nählinder 2005). This new paradigm inspires enterprises to find the most appropriate business model to commercialize new products or services, regardless of any model that exists within the enterprise or must be sought externally (Chesbrough 2003b; De Jong et al. 2008). In this context, utilization of new innovation channels for business cooperation are imperative (Interact 2004), and in doing so, smaller equity companies experimenting with alternative technologies create multiple channels of innovation (Carlsson and Eliasson 2002). Often, it eliminates the need for commitment to specific technologies or R&D projects. However, problems may arise at the point of acquisition, specifically, it is critical for the acquiring firm that it gains control over not just for a specific issue but the competencies embedded in the acquired organization and its personnel (Parrilli 2006; Lazonick 2007). In this aspect, multiple innovation channels in SMEs are found to be counterproductive[7] (Interact 2004).

4.4 Organizational and Cultural Differences

SMEs face structural disadvantages when it comes to open innovation. They often lack many of the capabilities necessary to ascertain, convey and realize external ideas and technologies effectively from outside into their firms (Chesbrough 2010). Furthermore, forcing of technology is one of the main reasons behind the failure of attempts of the SMEs to simply use technologies effectively. Also, there are organizational and cultural differences showing NIH (not-invented-here) syndrome, not accepting risk-taking initiatives and being non-responsive in managerial support where desired (Lichtenthaler and Ernst 2006; Herzog and Leker 2010).

---

[7] Firms may also have made more than one innovation channel, where the innovation-induced employment changes are counteractive, thus resulting in little visible employment change.

In addition, the introduction of new technologies in SMEs can bring a real modification in the way of their working environment, hence the introduction of technology-based processes should take into account the specific culture of the company, especially the background of the entrepreneur and/or the managers, as well as their openness to innovation orientation (Wei and Morgan 2004; Barba-Sánchez et al. 2007; Van de Vrande et al. 2009).

4.5 Incompetency in Handling Knowledge Issues

Studies find that open innovation offers several benefits for SMEs in low-tech industries. Even so, it also creates new challenges. One of these challenges is how to deal with the delicate and intricate intellectual property (IP) issues arising from co-created technologies (Vanhaverbeke 2010). Similar studies have revealed that the characteristics of internal members in an organization can affect the patterns of knowledge capability building (Ann and Minshall 2012). Furthermore, SMEs are usually confronted with increased risks in collaborating with larger companies due to their smaller resources and limited expertise in intellectual property rights (IPR) issues (OECD 2008). Even under certain circumstances, where SMEs operate in environments with strong IP protection, they have sufficient differentiation and negotiation leverage to access external ideas and technologies. Also in majority of the SMEs, the ability to profit from intellectual property is limited because of lack of enforcement power and their economic dependence on larger firms (Chesbrough 2010).

5 Increased Globalization

With the increased globalization, abundant resources, low labor rates and even large target markets are no longer indispensable factors for development, nor sufficient attractions for investors. To combat the situation, one needs to improve the essential infrastructure, enhanced skills, technological capability and improved management practices as major key elements of competitiveness in the emerging pattern of global competition and industrialization. While business remains the principal engine for economic growth and overall prosperity, but at the same time, due to the liberalized process, increased globalization of industry and extraordinary and rapid pace of technological innovations and adaptation, new (sometimes, unknown) challenges are being created for the industrialization (Nauwelaers and Wintjes 2000; Dhungana 2003).

Along this perspective, European firms, and especially SMEs are facing the double challenge of confronting both the global competition and factors related to the integration in the European Union (Spanos et al. 2001). Spanos et al. (2001) argue that in spite of many opportunities, SMEs are facing increased challenges within the European economic environment. Innovation, flexibility, cost control, and organizational changes constitute as the main managerial imperatives for organizations competing in the Economic Monitoring Union (EMU) area.

6 A Framework

Based on the discussion of scopes, arguments, prospects, and challenges pertinent to the SMEs, this research has constructed an innovation opportunities framework leading to create new dimension of business opportunities through the establishment of improved business environment, by focusing improved access to market, increased access to finance, and creation of new business (see Fig. 1). The study recommends that by improving the access to markets, knowledge about business skills and knowledge of the emerging market, as well as increasing access to finance and scarce resources the overall business environment can be improved and new opportunities can be created.

7 Research Recommendations

Innovation has been treated as a key factor of economic achievement in many countries and subsequently as a prerequisite for sustainable development. Following the trend, in recent years open innovation models have become an integral part of the entrepreneurship strategies and business models. In this aspect, academics, researchers, practitioners, agencies, intermediaries, and the governments are playing active role by providing more attention to the contribution of science and innovation to economic growth and have introduced a variety of new initiatives and transformations. Several countries, including Australia, Canada, Hungary, Ireland, South Korea and Spain have introduced comprehensive policy frameworks to guide developments in science, technology and innovation.

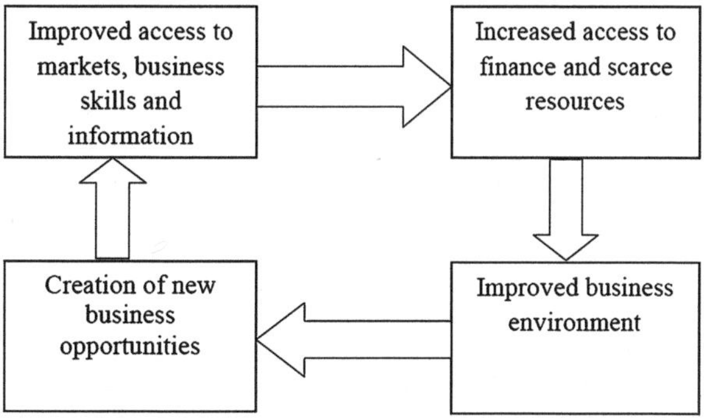

Fig. 1 Innovation opportunities framework

Similarly, in a number of countries, government institutions and development agencies have been restructured to improve the governance of innovation systems, and at the same time policy evaluation has become more widespread. In addition to these, public research systems are being reformed to better contribute to economic and social needs by creating innovative opportunities for researches and practitioners (OECD 2002). However, it has been observed that for successful adoption of open innovation in SMEs, extensive collaborative practices need to be encouraged, especially at the grass roots level of the entrepreneurships.

Moreover, the 'SME pact' (the main objective is to strengthen relations between innovative SMEs and large companies and/or organizations, through commercial contracts or R&D collaboration[8]) foresees the positive mobilization of larger entrepreneurs or organizations (private or public) to promote innovative ways of SME's development. Within this pact, programmes foster R&D-collaboration between innovative SMEs and large enterprises. If large enterprises are interested by SME's innovative products or services while still needing further development, these programmes support R&D projects that facilitate the testing and adaptation of the products and services to the specific needs of the large enterprise (OECD 2007, 2008; Cervantes 2009). Thus, SMEs could find their places among and within the open innovation business chains and value addition processes, which need thorough investigation of the nature and characteristics of the partnership, and demand to be properly focused through in-depth studies.

Finally, as the outcome of this study it recommends that to reinforce the innovative SMEs action research need to be carried out, especially at the outer peripheries of the entrepreneurships where these firms actually interface with their customers. Apart from strengthening through the innovation opportunity framework, the action need to be taken under locally developed collaborative networks before bringing to the global market.

8 Conclusions

Evidently, innovation has become a potential factor for economic success in many countries; and in a complex and highly competitive global market, entrepreneurs have to innovate and develop commercially viable products and services faster than ever, not only for their economic growth, but most of the time just only to survive. To meet these new challenges, companies are increasingly adopting new approaches to their innovation strategies and processes (OECD 2008). In a world of transformation and competition, innovating is not a luxury anymore, it is essential. All businesses need to innovate, though it may take any number of forms

---

[8] http://erawatch.jrc.ec.europa.eu/erawatch/opencms/information/country_pages/fr/supportmeasure/support_mig_0031?searchType=simple&sort=&action=search&matchesPerPage=5&orden=LastUpdate&query=&displayPages=10&reverse=true&country=fr&searchPage=5&index=Erawatch+Online+EN&tab=template

(or reforms), from the steady refinement of established products to the leap in the unknown when an untried idea is launched and exposed to the outside world. For every business, whether by introducing new technology, getting people to work in new ways, or creating new products, process, or service, or management reform one must innovate to survive (ACCA 2008), which implies to SMEs equally (De Jong 2006).

Open innovation is an emerging paradigm that assumes that enterprises can and should use both external and internal ideas and paths to the market, to discover and realize innovative opportunities thus embracing the challenges and risks. The open paradigm assumes that internal ideas can also be taken to markets through external channels, outside the current businesses of the enterprise, to generate value addition. Furthermore, future of businesses utilizing innovative ICTs that include business practice like electronic business or e-business is rising. In this aspect, e-businesses using open innovation methods will enhance value addition to the entire life cycles of businesses. Additionally, as open innovation involves open ended participation of stakeholders from all social stratus, thus forming a comprehensive format of social networks, it is assumed that inclusion of these techniques will add a newer dimension of entrepreneurship with vibrant contribution in the arena of social media (The Business Link 2010).

However, a key observation is that, the open innovation model should not completely upset traditional policymaking to legitimize policy interventions, including spillovers, system failures and market failures, which still apply equally to SMEs (De Jong et al. 2008). This research has emphasized on the adoption of knowledge acquisition processes, acting as catalyst and being earlier adapter of open innovation. However, there are challenges at the peripheries, such as organizational and cultural differences, including lack of knowledge and skills. This research concludes that by learning about the scopes, prospects and challenges in ahead, SMEs and their groups or associations will be benefited and other researchers in this field will also be able to develop a better framework for enhancing the business value following the one that has been developed here.

References

Abreu, M., Grinevich, V., Kitson, M., & Savon, M. (2011). *The changing face of innovation policy: implications for the northern ireland economy, (Programme on regional innovation.* UK: University of Cambridge.

Abulrub, A. G., & Lee, J. (2011). Open innovation management: challenges and prospects, A paper from the *International Conference on Leadership, Technology, and Innovation Management (ICLTIM)*, December 2–4, 2011, Istanbul, Turkey.

ACCA. (2008). *Director's Briefing: Strategy*. UK: BHP Information Solutions Ltd.

Ann, J., & Minshall, T. (2012). The influence of the characteristics of CEO on open innovation in SMEs. Paper presented at the DRUID Academy 2012. University of Cambridge/The Moeller Centre, January 19–21.

Asheim, B. (2003). *Regional Innovation Policy for Small + Medium Enterprises*. Cheltenham: Edward Elgar Publishing.

Asheim, B. T., Coenen, L., Svensson-Henning, M. (2003). Nordic SMEs and Regional Innovation Systems, Final Report, Department of Social and Economic Geography, Lund University, Sweden.

Avlonitis, G. J., & Salavou, H. E. (2007). Entrepreneurial orientation of SMEs, product innovativeness, and performance. *Journal of Business Research, 60*, 566–575.

Barba-Sánchez, V., Martínez-Ruiz, M. P., & Jiménez-Zarco, A. I. (2007). Drivers, benefits and challenges of ICT adoption by small and medium sized enterprises (SMEs): a literature review. *Problems and Perspectives in Management, 5*(1), 103–114.

Barker, J. E. (2008). The foundations of innovation, Transformation and Change, a WiKi book from the AussieInvention dot com.

Batterlink, M. (2009). Profiting from external knowledge: how firms use different knowledge acquisition strategies to improve their innovation performance. PhD Thesis, Wageningen University, Netherlands.

Beacham, J. (2006). 60 minute guide to innovation: turning ideas into profit, succeeding through innovation. Department of Trade and Industry, Published by TSO, UK.

White, B. (2006). *Leading technical professionals 2006 Report*. NJ: Inc Princeton.

Bougrain, F., & Haudeville, B. (2002). Innovation, collaboration and SMEs internal research capacities. *Research Policy, 31*(2002), 735–747.

Brouwers, J., Van Duivenboden, H., Thaens, M. (2009). The Triple Helix triangle: stimulating ICT-driven innovation at regional level. A Paper from the 2009 Annual Conference of EGPA, Malta, Sep 2009.

Callegati, E., & Grandi, S. (2005). Cluster dynamics and innovation in SMEs: the role of culture. Working paper No. 03/2005, International Centre for Research on the Economics of Culture, Institutions, and Creativity (EBLA), Università di Torino, Turin, Italy.

Carlsson, B., & Eliasson, G. (2002). Industrial dynamics and endogenous growth. *Industry and innovation, 10*(4), 435–455.

Cervantes, M. (2009). Open Innovation in Global Networks: Recent OECD work, Policy issues and Open questions. A paper from Trade and Development Board Investment, Enterprise and Development Commission Multi-year expert meeting on enterprise development policies and capacity-building in science, technology and innovation, Geneva, 20–22 Jan 2009.

Chason, M. (2008). *The Innovator*, 1(1), IXL Center, MA, USA.

Chesbrough, H. (2003a). *Open Innovation: the new imperative for creating and profiting from technology*. Boston: Harvard Business School Press.

Chesbrough, H. W. (2003b). The era of open innovation. *MIT Sloan Management Review, 44*(3), 35–41.

Chesbrough, H. W. (2006). *Open business models: How to thrive in a new innovation landscape*. Boston: Harvard Business School Press.

Chesbrough, H. W. (2010). Open innovation: A key to achieving socioeconomic evolution- how smaller companies can benefit from open innovation, Cover story. *Economy, Culture & History* Japan Spotlight Bimonthly, JAPECO, Japan Economic Foundation.

Chesbrough, H. W., Vanhaverbeke, W., & West, J. (Eds.). (2006). *Open innovation: researching a new paradigm*. London: Oxford University Press.

Cochrane Collaboration (2004). Cochrane Handbook for Systematic reviews of Interventions 4.2.2, Updated March 2004.

Cochrane Collaboration (2006). Cochrane Handbook for Systematic reviews of Interventions 4.2.6, Updated September 2006.

Cochrane Collaboration (2008). Method Group June 2008, MG Newsletter, The Cochrane Collaboration.

Commonwealth of Australia (2009). *Powering Ideas: An Innovation Agenda for the 21st Century*, Commonwealth of Australia 2009.

Cooke, P. (1996). Building a twenty-first century regional economy in Emilia-Romagna. *European Planning Studies*, *4*(1), Carfax Publishing.

Cooke, P., & Wills, D. (1999). Small firms, social capital and the enhancement of business performance through innovation programs. *Small Business Economics*, *13*, Kluwer publisher.

Cosh, A., Fu, X., Hughes, A. (2005). *Management Characteristics, Collaboration and Innovative Efficiency: Evidence from UK Survey Data,* Working Paper no. 311 (Cambridge: Centre for Business Research, 2005), p. 8.

Cowan, K. R., & Daim, T. U. (2011). Review of technology acquisition and adoption research in the industry sector. *Technology in Society, 33*, 183–199.

Cox, G. (2008). Defining innovation: what counts in the University of Cape Town landscape? *A proceedings of ASCILITE Melbourne*, Melbourne.

Davenport, C. (2006). In: A Quotation. In:Beacham, J (Eds.), *60 minute guide to innovation: turning ideas into profit, succeeding through innovation* (p. 3), Department of Trade and Industry. TSO: UK.

Dargan, L., & Shucksmith, M. (2008). LEADER and innovation, european society for rural sociology. *Sociologia Ruralis, 48*(3), 274–291.

De Jong, J. P. J. (2006). Open innovation: practice, trends, motives and bottlenecks in the SMEs *(Meer Open Innovatie: Praktijk, Ontwikkelingen, Motieven en Knelpunten in het MKB)*, EIM, Zoetermeer.

De Jong, J. P. J., Vanhaverbeke, W., Kalvet, T., Chesbrough, H. (2008). Policies for open innovation: theory, framework and cases. Research project funded by VISION Era-Net, Helsinki: Finland.

De Jong, J. P. J., & von Hippel, E. (2005). User innovation in SMEs: incidence and transfer to producers, SCALES-initiative (Scientific AnaLysis of Entrepreneurship and SMEs), the Netherlands Ministry of Economic Affairs.

De Jong, J. P. J., & von Hippel, E. (2009). Transfers of user process innovations to process equipment producers: A study of Dutch high-tech firms, *MIT Sloan School of Management Research Paper No. 4724-09,* March, 2009.

Del Brío, J. Á., & Junquera, B. (2003). A review of the literature on environmental innovation management in SMEs: implications for public policies. *Technovation 23*(12), 939–948.

Council, Design. (2005). *National survey of firms*. London: Design Council.

Dhungana, B. P. (2003) Strengthening the competitiveness of Small and Medium Enterprises in the globalization process: prospects and challenges. In: *Investment Promotion and Enterprise Development Bulletin for Asia and the Pacific,1*: 1–32. (ESCAP). New York: United Nations Publications.

Edwards, T., Delbridge, J., & Munday, M. (2005). Understanding innovation in small and medium-sized enterprises: a process manifest. *Technovation, 25*, 1119–1127.

EIRMA (2004). Technology Access for open innovation. Working Group Report WG63, Eirma: Paris.

European Commission (1997). The European Observatory for SMEs, Fifth Annual Report, Report submitted to the Enterprise Directorate-General of the Commission of the European Communities, European Network for SME Research, European Commission.

European Commission (2000). The European Observatory for SMEs, Fifth Annual Report, Report submitted to the Enterprise Directorate-General of the Commission of the European Communities, European Network for SME Research, European Commission.

European Commission (2002). Observatory of European SMEs 2002/No 2, SMEs in Europe, including a first glance at EU candidate countries, Report submitted to the Enterprise Directorate-General of the European Commission by: KPMG Special Services and EIM Business & Policy Research in the Netherlands in co-operation with: European Network for SME Research (ENSR), and Intomart.

European Commission (2003a). Innovation policy in seven candidate countries: the challenges. *Final Report* Vol 1, March, Brussels.

European Commission (2003b). Innovation policy in seven candidate countries: the challenges, Vol 2.7, *Innovation Policy Profile: Turkey,* Brussels.

European Communities (2008). Antti Peltomäki In Foreword of *Living Labs for user-driven open innovation: An overview of the Living Labs Methodology, Activities and Achievements*, Directorate-General for the Information Society and Media, Unit F4 New Infrastucture Paradigms and Experimental Facilities, European Commission Information Society and

Media, January 2009, Luxembourg: Office for Official Publications of the European Communities, 2008.

Evangelista, R. (2000). Sectoral patterns of technological change in services. *Economics of Innovation and New Technology, 9*, 183–221.

García-Moralesa, V. J., Lloréns-Montesa, F. J., & Verdú-Jover, A. J. (2007). Influence of personal mastery on organizational performance through organizational learning and innovation in large firms and SMEs. *Technovation, 27*, 547–568.

Gassmann, O., & Enkel, E. (2004). Towards a theory of open innovation: Three Core Process Archetypes, In: *Proceedings of the R&D Management Conference (RADMA)*, Sessimbra.

Gerstenfield, A., & Roberts, H. (2000). Size matters Barriers and prospects for environmental management in small and Medium- sized enterprises. In R. Hillary (Ed.), *(2000), Small and medium-sized enterprises and the environment, business imperatives*. Sheffield: Greenleaf Publishing.

Ghili, S., & Tavana, M. (2011). Innovation or imitation: some economic performance and social welfare policy perspectives. *International Journal of Information System and Social Change, 2*(3), 48–66.

Government of UK. (2008). Accelerating the SME economic engine: through transparent, simple and strategic procurement, Government of UK., Crown copyright 2008.

Hadjimanolis, A. (1999). Barriers to innovation for SMEs in a small less developed country (Cyprus). *Technovation, 19*(9), 561–570.

Hagen, S. (2008). From tech transfer to knowledge exchange: European universities in the marketplace. In: L. Engwall, D. Weaire (Eds.) Wenner-Gren International Series. *The University in the Market* (pp. 103–117), Vol 84, London: Portland Press.

Hamalainen, T. J., & Heiskala, R. (Eds.). (2007). *Social innovations, institutional change and economic performance: making sense of structrual adjustment processes in industrial sectors, Regions and Societies*. Northampton: Edward Elgar Pub.

Hass, J., & Hochrinner, H. (2008). Enhancing product- and process innovation in SMEs through cooperative education, ASET Annual Conference 2008. The placement and employability professionals' conference, 2–4 September 2008, Robbins Conference Centre, Plymouth, UK.

Havas, A. (2002). Does innovation policy matter in a transition country? The case of hungary. *Journal of International Relations and Development,* 5(4), 380–402.

Hayton, J. C. (2004). Strategic Human Capital management in SMEs: An empirical study of entrepreneurial performance, Human Resource Management. *Winter, 42*(4), 375–391.

Herstad, S. J., Bloch, C., Ebersberger, B., van de Velde, E. (2008). Open innovation and globalisation: Theory, evidence and implications, Eurostat.

Herzog, P., & Leker, J. (2010). Open and closed innovation- different innovation cultures for different strategies, *International Journal of Technology Management (IJTM), 52*(¾).

Hotho, S., & Champion, K. (2011). Small businesses in the new creative industries: innovation as a people management challenge. *Management Decision, 49*(1), 29–54.

Hsu, Li-Ling, & Lin, Tsong-Ming. (2006). The longitudinal literature review on the interaction between manufacturing and marketing: a multidimensional content analysis. *International Journal of Management and Enterprise Development, 3*(1/2), 114–146.

IBM. (2007). *Service Science: The next frontier in service innovation*. IBM Singapore Pte Ltd: IBM Corporation.

Interact (2004). Project "Embrace" Preparation and Implementation: lessons learnt and recommendations to Potential Applicants, INNOSTART National Business and Innovation Centre, a project paper submitted to European Regional Development Fund, European Union and presented at Translational INTERREG IIIB CADSES Seminar, Katowice, Poland.

Kitchenham, B. (2004). Procedures for Performing Systematic Reviews, Joint Technical Report, NICTA Technical Report 0040001lT.1, July 2004.

Lazzarotti, V., Manzini, R., & Pizzurno, E. (2008). *Managing innovation networks of SMEs: a case study, a proceeding of the International Engineering Management Conference: managing engineering, technology and innovation for growth (IEMC Europe 2008)* (pp. 521–525). Portugal: Estoril.

Lazonick, W. (2007). The stock market and innovative enterprise. *Industrial and Corporate Change, 16*(6), 983–1035.
Lemola, T., & Lievonen, J. (2008). The role of innovation policy in fostering open innovation activities among Companies, a report from Vision Era.net, Finland.
Lichtenthaler, U., & Ernst, H. (2006). Attitudes to externally organizing knowledge management tasks: a review, reconsideration and extension of the NIH syndrome. *R&D Management, 36*(4), 367–386.
Lichtenthaler, U. (2007). The drivers of technology licensing: an industry comparison. *California Management Review, 49*, 67–89.
Lichtenthaler, U. (2010). Outward knowledge transfer: the impact of project-based organization on performance. *Industrial and Corporate Change, 19*(6), 1705–1739.
Lundvall, B-Å. (1999). Innovation Policy and Economic Theory. In G. Schienstock, O. Kuusi (Eds.): *Transformation Towards a Learning Economy. The Finnish National Fund for Research and Development—Sitra*. Report no. 213. Helsinki.
Maes, J. (2009). SMEs' Radical Product Innovation: the Role of the Internal and External Absorptive Capacity Spheres, *Job Market Paper July 2009,* Katholieke Universiteit Leuven, Faculty of Business and Economics, Belgium.
Massa, S., & Testa, S. (2008). Innovation and SMEs: Misaligned perspectives and goals among entrepreneurs, academics, and policy makers. *Technovation, 28*(2008), 393–407.
McAdam, R. S., & Gibson, D. A. (2004). Innovation and Organisational size in Irish SMEs: an empirical study. *International Journal of Innovation Management, 8*(2) 147–165.
Mueller, S. L., & Goic, S. (2003). East-west differences in entrepreneurial self-efficacy: implications for entrepreneurship education in transition economies. *International Journal of Entrepreneurship Education, 1*, 613–632.
Nählinder, J. (2005). *Innovation and Employment in Services: The case of Knowledge Intensive Business Services in Sweden*, PhD Thesis, Department of Technology and Social Change, Linköping University, Sweden, Unitryck Linköping.
Nauwelaers, C., & Wintjes, R. (2000). *SME Policy and regional dimension of Innovation: Towards a new paradigm for innovation policy?* (pp. 00–023). Maastricht: MERIT Research Memoranda.
Nauwelaers, C., & Wintjes, R. (2002). Innovating SMEs and regions: the need for policy intelligence and interactive policies. *Technology Analysis & Strategic Management, 14*(2), 201–215.
NOUS (2007). Today's knowledge intensive SME: where, why and how? Discussion Paper, Department of Innovation, Industry and Regional Development, The Nous Group, Australia.
OECD (1999). *Benchmarking Knowledge-based Economies,* OECD Science, Technology and Industry Scoreboard, OECD, Paris.
OECD (2000a). Enhancing the Competitiveness of SMEs in the Global Economy: Strategies and Policies Enhancing the Competitiveness of SMEs through Innovation, Conference for Ministers responsible for SMEs and Industry Ministers, Bologna, Italy, 14-15 June 2000.
OECD (2000b). OECD Science Technology and Industry Outlook 2000, OECD, France
OECD (2002). OECD Science Technology and Industry Outlook 2002, OECD, France.
OECD (2007). SME Policy Index 2007, Report on the Implementation of the European Charter for Small Enterprises in the Western Balkans, OECD.
OECD (2008), Open Innovation in Global Networks, OECD Policy Brief, November 2008, Paris.
OECD. (2009). *OECD Science, Technology and Industry Scoreboard- 2009 Edition.* Paris: OECD.
O'Sullivan, M. (2000), *Contests for corporate control.* Oxford University Press.
Oxford Business School (2008). Introducing the Oxford Centre for Entrepreneurship and Innovation, Retail Policy Issues, The Retail Digest, Oxford SAID Business School, pp. 30–31.
Parrilli, M. D. (2006). A Tripartite Innovation Framework for Small Firms in Developing Regions: Key Issues for Analysis and Policy, Paper Number 2007-01, *Institute for Economic Development Policy Discussion Paper Series,* University of Birmingham, UK.

Rahman, H. (2010) Open innovation: opportunities and challenges for SMEs. In: M. M. Cruz-Cunha, J. Varajão (Eds.) *E-Business Issues, Challenges and Opportunities for SMEs: Driving Competitiveness*, IGI Global, pp. 87–100.

Rahman, H., & Ramos, I. (2010), Open Innovation in SMEs: From closed boundaries to networked paradigm. In *Proceedings of the Issues in Informing Science and Information Technology Education Conference*, Cassino, Italy June 19–24, pp. 471–487.

Roper, S. & Hewitt-Dundas, N. (2004). *Innovation, Networks and The Diffusion of Manufacturing Best Practice: A Comparison of Northern Ireland and the Republic of Ireland*, A report from Northern Ireland Economic Research Centre Queen's University of Belfast, UK.

Salavou, H.E. (2006). Exploring Product Innovativeness Determinants in SMEs, PhD Thesis, Athens University of Economics & Business, 2006.

Sautter, B., & Clar, G. (2008). Strategic Capacity Building in Clusters to Enhance Future-oriented Open Innovation Processes, Foresight Brief No. 150, The European Foresight Monitoring Network, www.efmn.info.

Schewe, G. (2001). Imitation- A strategic option of technology management. In T. M. Khalil, L. A. Lefebvre, & R. M. Mason (Eds.), *Management of technology: the key to prosperity in the third millennium*. Kidlington: Elsevier.

Schienstock, G., & Hämäläinen, T. (2001). Transformation of the Finnish innovation system. A network approach. The Finnish National Fund for Research and Development—Sitra. Report series No. 7. Helsinki.

Scherngell, T., & Barber, M. J. (2009). Spatial interaction modelling of cross-region R&D collaborations: empirical evidence from the 5th EU framework programme, Papers in Regional Science, Vol 88 No 3 Aug 2009, 531–546.

Sengenberger, W., Loveman, G., & Piore, M. J. (Eds.). (1990). *The Re-emergence of Small Enterprises: Industrial restructuring in industrialized countries*. Geneva: International Institute of Labour Studies.

Smallbone, D., North, D., & Vickers, I. (2003). The role and characteristics of SMEs in innovation. In B. T. Asheim, A. Isaksen, C. Nauwelaers, & F. Todtling (Eds.), *Regional innovation policy for small-medium enterprises* (pp. 3–20). Northampton: Edward Elgar Publishing.

Smed, M., Salomo, S., Schultz, C., Getz, K. A. (2012). Users ability to share knowledge when integrated in new product development- evidence from pharmaceutical industries, A paper presented at the DRUID Academy 2012 (Jan 19–21).

Sousa, M. (2008). Open innovation models and the role of knowledge brokers, Inside Knowledge magazine, Mar 2008: 18–22.

Spanos, Y., Prastacos, G., & Papadakis, V. (2001). Greek Firms and EMU: contrasting SMEs and large-sized enterprises. *European Management Journal, 19*(6), 638–648.

Stiglitz, J. (1998). *Towards a new paradigm for development, 9th Raul Prebisch Lecture*. Geneva: UNCTAD.

Telemetica Institute (2008). Service innovation and ICT: Vision and ambition, Telemetica Institute, The Netherlands.

The Business Link. (2010). *E-Business Marketing, The Business Link*. Canada: Alberta's Business Information Service.

TIEKE. (2009). *ICT Cluster Finland Review 2009*. Finland: TIEKE Finnish Information Society Development Centre.

Tijsterman, M. N. F. (2010). *Requirements on conditions for SMEs to collaborate in an Open Innovation Environment : Do they do it? Why do they do it? With whom do they do it? How do they do it—the (im)possibilities of SMEs in open innovation*. Essay (Master), University of Twente, Netherlands.

Tilley, F., & Tonge, J. (2003). Introduction. In O. Jones & F. Tilley (Eds.), *Competitive Advantage in SME's: Organising for Innovation and Change*. New York: Wiley.

Toivonen, M. (2004). Expertise as Business: Long-term development and future prospects of knowledge-intensive business services (KIBS), Laboratory of Industrial Management, Helsinki University of Technology, Doctoral dissertation series 2004/2.

Vaitheeswaran, V. (2007) Special report: innovation. *The Economist*. http://www.economist.com/specialreports/displaystory.cfm?story_id=9934754.

Van Hemel, C., & Cramer, J. (2002). Barriers and stimuli for ecodesign in SMEs. *Journal of Cleaner Production*, 10(5), 439–453.

Van de Vrande, V., de Jong, J. P. J., Vanhaverbeke, W., & de Rochemont, M. (2008) Open innovation in SMEs: Trends, motives and management challenges. A report published under the SCALES-initiative, as part of the 'SMEs and Entrepreneurship programme' financed by the Netherlands Ministry of Economic Affairs.

Van de Vrande, V., de Jong, J. P. J., Vanhaverbeke, W., & de Rochemont, M. (2009). Open innovation in SMEs: trends, motives and management challenges. *Technovation, 29*(6–7), 423–437.

Vanhaverbeke, W. (2010). The benefits of open innovation in low tech SMEs: the quilts of Denmark story. In P. Silberzahn, W. Van Dyck (Eds.) *The balancing act of innovation* (pp. 195–214), Lannoo Campus.

Weerakkody, V., Dwivedi, Y. K., & Irani, Z. (2009). The diffusion and use of institutional theory: a cross-disciplinary longitudinal literature survey. *Journal of Information Technology, 24*, 354–368.

Wei, Y., & Morgan, N. (2004). The supportiveness of organizational climate, market orientation, and new product performance in Chinese firms. *Journal of Product Innovation Management, 21*, 375–388.

Woerter, M. (2012). Technology proximity between firms and universities and technology transfer. *Journal of Technology Transfer, 37*:828–866.

Zaheer, A., & Bell, G. G. (2005). Benefiting from network position: firm capabilities, structural holes and performance. *Strategic Management Journals, 26*, 809–825.

Government Support to Information Systems Innovation in Small and Medium Enterprises

Vega Arturo and Chiasson Mike

1 Introduction

In the last decades, governments and economic blocs have been backing small and medium enterprise (SMEs) with a vast range of public programmes in order to support their business initiatives, including information systems (IS) adoption (e.g., European Commission 2010; Economic Commission for Latin America and the Caribbean 2008; United Nations Conference on Trade and Development 2011). In the case of the United Kingdom, the policy focus on SMEs has been modified numerous times according to the view of governments regarding the global economic environment and the outcome of previous policies. For example, in the 1990s the government realised that the country was at a competitive disadvantage in comparison with other members of the Organisation for Economic Co-operation and Development. There was also a clear need to open, privatise and deregulate markets. All of this added to a concern about the high rate of enterprise failures. Within these circumstances, the government redirected its efforts to support existing SMEs more than the creation of new enterprises (Greene et al. 2008).

The amount of assistance to existing and new enterprises was balanced in the years since 2000 as part of a policy focus on local growth and high-value sectors, and with the so-called third mission of universities as suppliers of public services to businesses (Lambert 2003). In the 2010s, the United Kingdom government has been trying to refine the mechanisms used in the past in order to give more autonomy to local levels and as a consequence of the international financial crisis.

V. Arturo (✉)
Department of Business and Management, Canterbury Christ Church University, Canterbury, United Kingdom
e-mail: arturo.vega@canterbury.ac.uk

C. Mike
Department of Management Science, Lancaster University Management School, Lancaster, United Kingdom
e-mail: m.chiasson@lancaster.ac.uk

J. Devos et al. (eds.), *Information Systems for Small and Medium-sized Enterprises*, Progress in IS, DOI: 10.1007/978-3-642-38244-4_17,

Whilst there has been a reduction in the number of support schemes for SMEs, the new schemes have a national scope while being adaptable to local needs. In addition, the schemes focus on strategic initiatives such as the adoption of IS, access to international markets, and the generation of consumer demand (Department for Business Innovation and Skills 2010).

The focus of the chapter is on the programmes that support IS initiatives of SMEs (e.g., Berkeley et al. 1996; Cuadrado and Garcia 2004; Gengatharen et al. 2005; Lebre 1996; Martin and Matlay 2001; Simpson and Docherty 2004; Wiggins 2010). For example, an SME has to pass through a series of stages to adopt an IS in order to match the system to the strategic objectives of the company, to conduct a financial analysis of the adoption, to select product and service suppliers, to design, manage and carry out an implementation project, to modify internal processes and external relationships, to train and raise the employees' awareness of the system, to put the system into operation, to establish a maintenance and contingency plan, and to evaluate the benefits of the adoption. In attempting to do so, many SMEs need external support given knowledge, infrastructure and financial limitations.

The entry point for this study is the discretion exercised at policy implementation. There is extensive research that has demonstrated that the personnel in charge of delivering public services tend to exert a great deal of discretion (e.g., Ellis et al. 1999; Maynard-Moody and Musheno 2003). This situation eventually changes their role to the one of policy-makers. Given the potential and considerable freedom of implementers to modify, ignore or extend policies, it is important to understand the contexts that drive the decisions and actions of these providers. The results of past research strongly indicate that the policy contexts can be problematic, which directly impacts the behaviour of public workers (e.g., Lipsky 1980, 2010). The occurrence of both considerable discretion and problematic delivery contexts has been confirmed in many countries in public service areas such as agriculture, education, health, justice, policing and welfare (e.g., Hertogh 2009; Juma and Clarke 1995; Lewis and Glennerster 1996; Lispky 2010; Maynard-Moody and Musheno 2003; Pitts 2007; Winter 2000), but not in IS policy and programme delivery.

The aim of the chapter is to adapt and apply these frameworks to better understand the public programmes which support IS in SMEs in order to improve their performance. To do so, the research was based on eight case studies of programme support to IS initiatives in English SMEs. The delivery of the services was done by two programme organisations, which were in charge of several public programmes. We paid special attention to the existence and extent of discretion, the outcome of the IS initiatives, and the contributions of the programmes to these outcomes. Complementing this was an analysis of the extended policy contexts in order to understand the underlying causes that foster discretion and programme worker behaviour, as well as to make broader generalisations of the findings to other programme contexts. Although the empirical work was done in England, we believe the results of the research are relevant for other countries and public administrations.

The chapter is structured as follows. It begins by presenting the evidence and causes of considerable discretion in the implementation of SME policies. Then, we explain the reasons that make the programme contexts problematic and widespread. In these two sections we mix theory, case data and contextual information in order to support our conclusions, as suggested by Yin (2009). Finally, in the last section there is a summary of the findings and a presentation of some considerations for the improvement of IS programme contexts.

2 Discretion of Programme Workers

To determine the existence and extent of discretion, it is necessary to understand which programme activities should be carried out when programmes interact with SMEs. The concept of the scope of action of the programmes is used for this objective. We then consider the reasons that make possible programme delivery discretion based on a deep analysis of the policy system. Pivotal for this analysis are the definitions of formal and informal discretion.

2.1 Scope of Action of the Programmes[1]

It is important to note that programme workers must exert a certain level of discretion to carry out a job that is often difficult, subjective and variable from case to case. For example, a programme that focuses on the design and development of business applications requires programme workers to have the necessary discretion to analyse the specific needs of each SME and to deliver potentially diverse services such as process and database design, software selection, software installation, systems development, systems integration and so on. However, it is necessary to provide a broader definition of programme activities in order to know with more precision what the programmes are supposed to do and to provide a more accurate and relevant analysis of discretion. This concept is called the scope of action of the programmes (Vega et al. 2013).

To begin, there are three basic groups of policies that programme organisations must meet when they implement programmes. These policies are contractually agreed with the policy administrators, on behalf of the funding bodies, when they award public funds. Certainly, these contracts encapsulate the programmes' scopes of action. The first group are the statements of the economic policy frameworks, such as the Single Programming Documents of the Directorate General for Regional Policy (DGRP) of the European Union, the policies of the Department for Business, Innovation and Skills (DBIS) of England, and the Regional

[1] Reproduced from Sect. 3 of Vega et al. (2013).

Economic Strategies of the English regions. For example, the Regional Economic Strategies normally contemplate priority sectors (e.g., creative industries or nanotechnology), functional areas (e.g., information systems or marketing) and cross-cutting themes (e.g., ethnic minorities or the environment).

The second group are the application criteria of the funds that are awarded, such as the European Regional Development Fund of the DGRP, the Higher Education Innovation Fund of the DBIS, and the Regional Development Agency Fund for the English regions. For example, the European Regional Development Fund is oriented to investments that foster production in geographical areas with structural difficulties. Finally, the programme organisations themselves differentiate aspects of their proposals in order to increase their chances of obtaining public funds. For instance, the type of service (e.g., consultancy or project management), delivery method (e.g., face-to-face or call centre), and service providers (e.g., programme workers or external consultants).

2.2 Existence and Extent of Discretion

Having a clear definition of the scope of action of the programmes as well as the evidence of the eight case studies, we found that programme workers exerted considerable discretion to the point of making policy in almost each interaction with the SMEs. Discretion is the variation of programme activities from the scope of action of the programmes. For instance, a programme was originally aimed at delivering high level knowledge transfer from the academics of the computing department to information technology SMEs. However, the programme mostly delivered traditional information systems services using third-party providers to SMEs from different industrial sectors. Another programme was designed to train individual SMEs using electronic and face-to-face methods. Nevertheless, the programme delivered web design services and marketing consultancy. Finally, another programme delivered information systems services instead of marketing services.

2.3 Reasons for Discretion

There are numerous reasons which permit considerable discretion (Vega and Brown 2011; Vega et al. 2013), as shown in Fig. 1.[2] Firstly, in the ambit of public services there is a constant political imperative to deliver a very high quantity of services while being extremely efficient in the use of resources (e.g., Lewis and Glennerster 1996; MacDonald 1990; Talbot 2005). This was strongly confirmed by

---

[2] © IFIP International Federation for Information Processing, 2011.

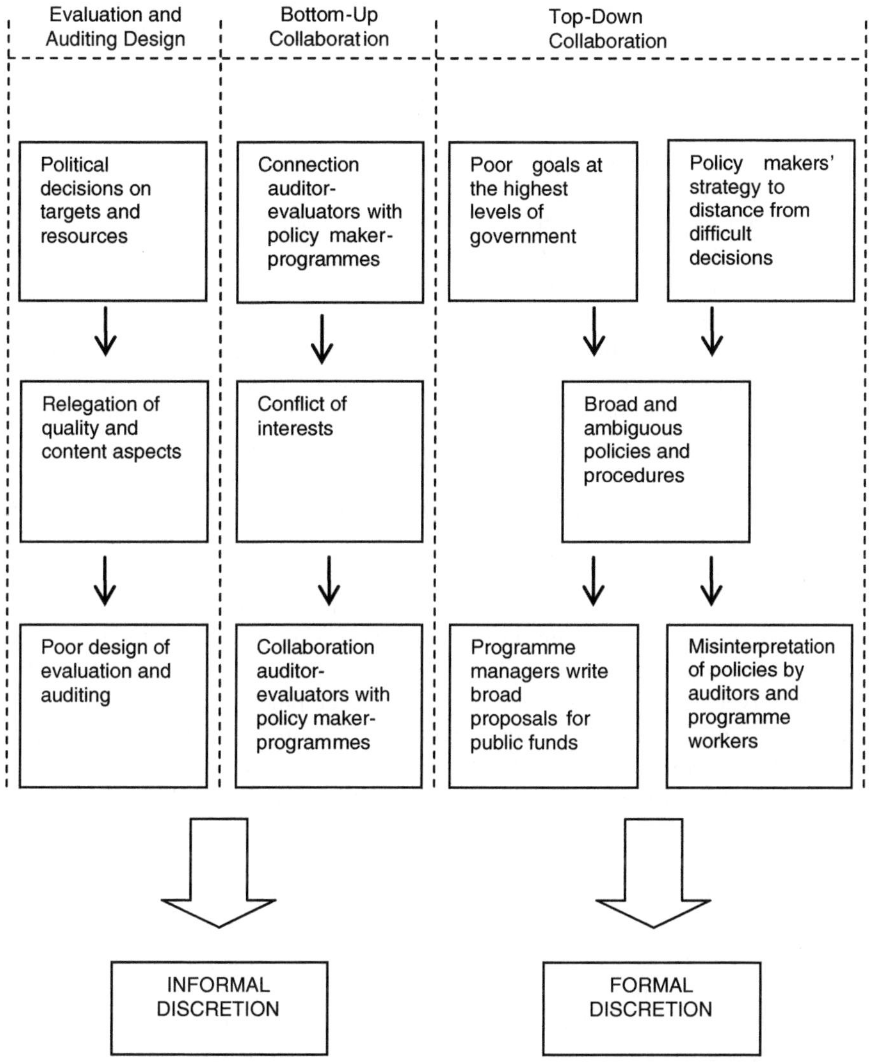

Fig. 1 Factors affecting discretion in programmes (reproduced from Vega and Brown 2011)

the programme managers of the cases. This imperative often implies that the evaluations and auditing focus on politically relevant indicators, i.e. outputs and expenditures, but not necessarily on content and quality aspects (Lipsky 1980, 2010).

In effect, the information reveals that the funding bodies tend to design coarse-grained evaluation and auditing mechanisms. Apart from strict financial controls, the core indicators used by the European Regional Development Fund and the Regional Development Agency Fund are the number of companies assisted, as well as increases in and safeguarding of jobs and sales. In measuring the latter, the

SME personnel have to only fill in a form with speculative answers to these questions. The Higher Education Innovation Fund only verifies the number of companies assisted. Additionally, the Regional Development Agency Fund and the Higher Education Innovation Fund require a simple conformity letter from the SMEs in order to account for the services. These numerical indicators do not tell much about the outcome of the IS initiatives, the impact of the programme support, or even much about the content of the services. As a result, the evaluative information is largely inaccurate and unfocused, favouring the possibility and non-detection of discretion. As the activities and delivery choices of programme workers are not recorded, this type of behaviour is called informal discretion (Vega et al. 2013).

Another factor affecting discretion appears to be the bottom-up collaboration of the policy administrators when they performed the auditing and evaluation of programmes. Programme personnel often expressed that the policy administrators only verify the documentary evidence of the finances and evaluation forms, but they do not analyse the content of the services. An important reason for this could be the commission of fund administration to entities that are connected to the policy-making teams or the programme organisations (e.g., Curran et al. 1999; Matlay and Addis 2003; Storey 2006). For example, the Northwest Universities Association was the administrator of the knowledge transfer initiatives of the Single Programming Document in the north-west of England. But the programme organisations that implemented these policies are members of this association, namely universities. Similarly, the Regional Development Agencies have administered the implementation of the Regional Economic Strategies. Nevertheless, these agencies have been the leaders of the development of the strategies. This potential collaboration would increase the possibility of informal discretion because policy administrators would not scrutinize the choices of programme workers.

Public policies can also be broad and ambiguous, which could be another factor which allows discretion. This is called top-down collaboration. As a difference with the previous cases of informal discretion, this modality is definitely formal because the all-inclusive and confusing policies themselves give programme workers considerable freedom to define the scope of action for each SME and thus legalize and legitimise discretion (Vega et al. 2013). This was also known and used by the programme personnel in all the cases. These types of policies appear to be a consequence of the formulation of poor goals at the highest levels of government (e.g., Bannock and Peacock 1989; Bovens et al. 2006; Dahler-Larsen 2005). They can also be caused by policy-makers interested in distancing themselves from the complex decisions to balance demand and public resources (e.g., Ellis et al. 1999; Harrison 1998; Hill 2009).

Many policies addressed by programmes are effectively broad and ambiguous. For instance, there was a policy in a Single Programming Document with the core statements about sophisticated innovations and inter-organisational networks, accompanied by indicative actions such as websites, SME links with universities and development of advanced e-commerce solutions. Clearly, the development of a website is too easy a task to meet the highly ambitious core statements. Accordingly, the programme managers wrote broad proposals to access public funds in order to take advantage of these all-embracing policies and to formalise discretion. A further issue is that auditors and programme workers often misinterpret these policies (e.g., Evans and Harris 2004; Lewis and Glennerster 1996; Scott 1990). This potential problem was found in most of the case studies. For example, a programme organisation based in a university delivered a short report about the basics of improving the information technology platforms for an SME. This simple service was unrelated to sophisticated innovations or inter-organisational networks but the auditors and programme workers appear to have interpreted this as meeting the requirements of developing SME links with universities.

3 Programme Contexts

Knowing the degree of discretion and the causes which allow it during the implementation of information systems policies for SMEs, it is important to understand the contexts that drive the behaviour of programme workers. That is to say, we need to understand why programme workers decide to opt for discretion by altering the scope of action of their programmes. We start by explaining how a group of important contextual components could interact and affect programme worker decisions and actions. The section concludes with an analysis of the case and policy system information in order to confirm the existence of these contexts and to make broader generalisations of the findings.

3.1 Effects of Contexts

According to the street-level bureaucracy theory (Lipsky 1980, 2010), public services are normally surrounded by problematic contexts, which are composed of evaluation mechanisms, power between public organisations and the recipients of the services, access to resources, demand for public services and the alienation of public workers. These problematic contexts drive the decisions and actions of programme workers towards programme goals instead of social or recipient goals, primarily to the accomplishment of numerical targets. The scheme is presented in Fig. 2.

To begin, the results of the evaluations tend to be too generous with the public organisations. This is because of the inappropriate or vague evaluation mechanisms, as explained before, and given the potential existence of power of the public organisations over the beneficiaries of the services. Therefore, the evaluation results not only affect discretion but also represent an inaccurate measurement of quantity and quality. This could signify an undesired license for public workers to determine different aspects of the service level provision. Certainly, the context

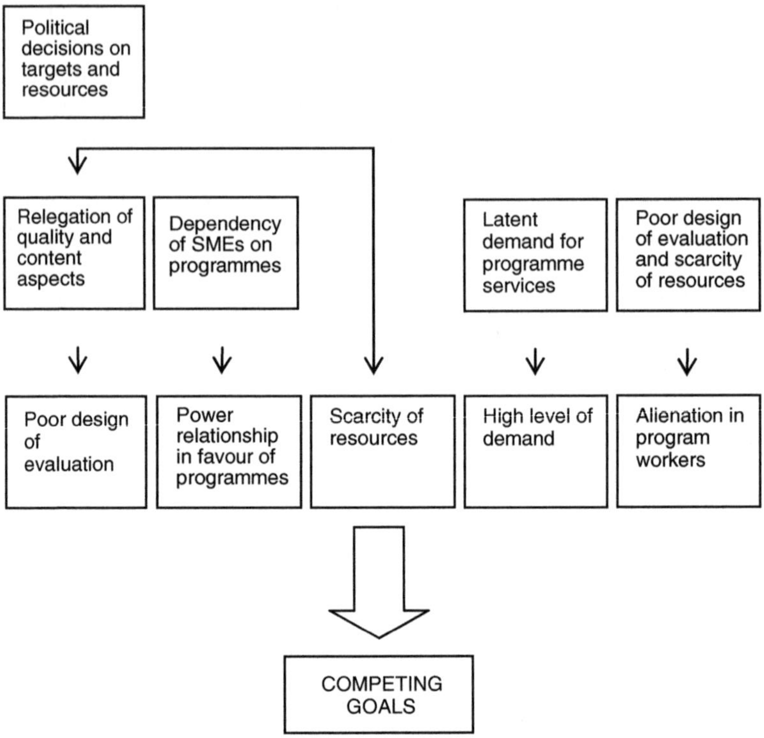

Fig. 2 Context components affecting programmes

would be very problematic if a public organisation had operational problems that put it at risk. This would be the case if there was limited access to resources, if the demand for the public services was too high or if there was public worker alienation.

The combination of misleading evaluation results and operational problems might direct the behaviour of programme workers towards programme goals instead of client needs, which would be negative. Regrettably, in practically all the cases both the IS initiatives and the programme delivery were unsatisfactory. For instance, a web-based portal for job seekers and employers had a poor response time, the session manager software randomly collapsed and the operating costs were very high. Another example is an intranet to manage the interaction with language service providers and clients. This application had numerous bugs and the migration of data from the legacy system was never completed. In the two cases the systems were not used by the SMEs. As one might expect, the SME personnel reported to us a series of issues regarding the programmes' deliverables, for example that they were unaccepted, reversed, inappropriate, incomplete and unnecessary.

3.2 Evidence of Problematic Contexts

There is a high possibility of problematic contexts in the general ambit of the public programmes that support SME business initiatives (Vega et al. 2008). The ill-designed evaluation mechanisms of the cases, which were based on outputs, were discussed in the previous section. A critical missing component in the cases is the evaluation of the IS itself, i.e. the outcome of the SMEs' initiative. According to Lenihan et al. (2007) and Storey (2006), similar flawed mechanisms are present in most of the public programmes that support SMEs in England. Moreover, Talbot (2005) has commented that the United Kingdom government constantly focus on outputs, and not outcomes, in practically all public sector areas.

With regard to the power imbalance in favour of programmes over SMEs, it is fostered by the dependency of the beneficiaries of the services on the public organisations (Lipsky 1980, 2010). In fact, many SME owner-managers anticipated several future business initiatives, which would depend on further free or low-cost assistance from programme organisations. Furthermore, this dependency could be a trend given the distinctive lack of knowledge, infrastructure and financial resources in the SME sector.

There is also evidence that many programmes could have problems with resources and low demand, not only the ones in the cases. This is generated, again, due to the propensity of policy-makers to source programmes with tiny resources while setting too ambitious targets that are inconsistent with the potential demand for the services (e.g., Lewis and Glennerster 1996; MacDonald 1990; Talbot 2005). In effect, the programmes in our cases tended to present problems of resources in terms of time, knowledge, information and budget. For example, an SME that launched an e-marketplace for the building supplies sector asked a programme for a very complex service, namely to increase the web traffic and the conversion and retention rates of clients based on modifications to the web presence. However, the total time employed by the programme was 5 man-days, including the selection of the SME, definition of requirements and services, proposal to the SME, consultancy, customer report, presentation, administrative tasks and trips.

In addition, many programmes had delayed starts given the slow contractual procedures of the policy administrators, which affected their ability to find SMEs in order to reach delivery targets. The demand could become even more challenging if the services are oriented towards IS innovations and, by definition, innovations are very difficult to diffuse (Vega et al. 2011). Clearly, these findings contradict those stipulated by the street-level bureaucracy on high levels of latent demand for public services, which is triggered as soon as more services are available (Lipsky 1980, 2010). Nevertheless, the case findings are still problematic in a different way.

Finally, programme worker alienation is a constant risk too. This can be caused by the reduced participation of the programme workers in the initiatives of the receivers of the services or because of a disconnection with the rest of these initiatives (Lipsky 1980, 2010). These issues can make programme workers believe that their role is irrelevant to the SMEs. Reduced participation and disconnection can be caused initially by a lack of resources given to the programmes and limited evaluation mechanisms that do not assess the success of the entire initiatives of the beneficiaries, respectively. In the case studies, programme workers showed alienation when they ignored and did not care about the use of their deliverables by the SMEs or the final outcome of the IS initiatives.

4 Conclusions

The aim of the chapter is to understand the public programmes that support IS in SMEs in terms of the existence of discretion and the contexts that influence the decisions and actions of programme workers. The evidence reveals that programme workers exerted considerable discretion which changed their role from policy-implementers to policy-makers. Although programme workers should apply some discretion to judge complex, subjective and varied situations, the cases illustrate that they considerably modified, ignored, extended, and interpreted policies. The reasons for this are diverse. To begin, policy-makers tend to set high targets but provide few resources to programmes. This appears to influence funding bodies to focus the auditing and evaluative designs on politically relevant metrics instead of content and quality aspects of the programme services and IS initiatives.

In addition, the auditing organisations were connected to the policy-making teams or the programme organisations, which could have allowed discretion. Finally, policy-makers also formulate broad and ambiguous policies. This could be because of a previous design of poor policy goals and the probable aim of disconnecting themselves from the difficult decisions to balance demand and public resources. Broad and ambiguous policies further exacerbate discretion when programme managers design broad programmes in order to formalise discretion. It can also cause the misinterpretation of auditors and programme workers when they compare the policies with the programme services actually delivered.

Given the great deal of discretion in programmes, it became relevant to study the contexts that influence the behaviour of programme workers in order to understand why they opt for discretion. The contexts that we found were indeed problematic, including poor evaluation mechanisms, power of the programme organisations over SMEs, restricted resources, low demand for programme services and the alienation of programme workers from the work. The main reasons for this are that most of the funding bodies employ inappropriate evaluation mechanisms, SMEs tend to depend on external support to accomplish their business initiatives, policy-makers normally set excessively high targets but provide limited resources, as well as the slow contractual procedures which affect the time of programmes to reach targets. Alienation is a consequence of poor evaluations and low resources.

Some additional implications can be inferred from the analysis of discretion and programme contexts. To begin, we believe that the reform needed to IS policy is very difficult and impracticable, as it has been the case in other public service areas to date. A plausible option could be to improve and focus on a critical part of the system and get a major total effect. For example, a proper configuration of programme contexts would ensure an appropriate delivery capacity in order to reach targets, which at the same time would help to mitigate the main reason of programme workers to opt for discretion. However, a direct attempt at curtailing discretion without improving programme contexts would fail. In this scenario, programmes would have to strictly operate within tight scopes of action but surrounded by negative context components such as imbalance of power, low access to resources and low demand for services. Pragmatically, programmes would have difficulties to reach targets, which would affect the survival of the programme organisations in the middle term. The former option would be better than the latter.

It is important to emphasize that programme organisations are not responsible for the improvement of the context in which they work. In fact, most of the public service organisations of different areas have to survive within problematic contexts and appear to deliver relevant services in efficient ways (Lipsky 1980, 2010). The actors in charge of the improvement of programme contexts are located at diverse parts of the system (Vega et al. 2012). For instance, the redesign of the evaluation mechanisms is in charge of the funding bodies at European and national levels. The evaluators would also have to be independent, probably a non-departmental public body. The inherent power of programmes over SMEs could be addressed in diverse ways, for example by improving the participation of the SME associations in the policy process or creating a more competitive environment for IS programmes at local and regional levels.

Similarly, the resources allocated to programmes are mostly determined by the European and national entities in charge of IS or SME policies. Programmes could improve their resources using other options, for example employing specialised consultants accredited by professional bodies or public-private partnerships. The general low demand for programme services could be addressed by the regional entities in charge of IS policies in various ways, for instance with awareness campaigns. The funding bodies could also reengineer their contractual procedures in order to give more time to programmes to reach targets. Finally, as implied above, improvements in evaluation and resources would positively affect alienation.

Noticeably, many of the examples of the initiatives to improve programme contexts are political in nature. In addition, this complex network of actors, their particular interests, and their relative power make the work of reforming the provision of programme services to SMEs an especially difficult undertaking. This situation is even more compelling if it is taken into account that the presence of the SME sector in the political landscape has been generally irrelevant (e.g., Bennett 2011; Coen 1998; Dannreuther 1999; Moran 2009; Storey 1994). SME associations must act by themselves given the long-lasting failure of the political forces to effectively empower them in the policy process. More strategic, better integrated, and well-informed SME associations are crucial to counterbalance the priorities of the different participants in the policy process with the technical view of the beneficiaries of the services (Vega et al. 2012).

References

Bannock, G., & Peacock, A. (1989). *Government and small business*. London: Paul Chapman.

Bennett, R. (2011). *Local business voice: The history of chambers of commerce in Britain, Ireland, and Revolutionary America 1760–2011*. Oxford: Oxford University Press.

Berkeley, N., Clark, D., & Ilbery, B. (1996). Regional variation in business use of information and communication technologies and implications for policy: Case study evidence from rural England. *Geoforum, 27*(1), 75–86.

Bovens, M., Hart, P., & Kuipers, S. (2006). The politics of policy evaluation. In M. Moran, M. Rein, & R. Goodin (Eds.), *The Oxford handbook of public policy* (pp. 319–335). Oxford: Oxford University Press.

Coen, C. (1998). The European interest and the nation state: Large-firm lobbying in the European Union and member states. *Journal of Public Policy, 18*(1), 75–100.

Cuadrado, J., & Garcia, A. (2004). ICT policies for SMEs and regional disparities: The Spanish case. *Entrepreneurship and Enterprise Development, 16*(1), 55–75.

Curran, J., Berney, R., & Kuusisto, J. (1999). *A critical evaluation of industry SME support policies in the United Kingdom and the Republic of Ireland—Stage one report: Introduction to SME policies and their evaluation*. Helsinski: Ministry of Trade and Industry of Finland.

Dahler-Larsen, P. (2005). Evaluation and public management. In E. Ferlie, L. Lynn Jr, & C. Pollitt (Eds.), *The Oxford handbook of public management* (pp. 615–639). Oxford: Oxford University Press.

Dannreuther, C. (1999). Discrete dialogues and the legitimation of EU SME policy. *Journal of European Public Policy, 6*(3), 436–455.

Department for Business, Innovation and Skills (2010). Backing small business. British Government. http://www.bis.gov.uk/assets/biscore/enterprise/docs/b/10-1243-backing-small-business.pdf. Accessed 5 February 2011.

Ellis, K., Davis, A., & Rummery, K. (1999). Needs, assessment, street-level bureaucracy and the new community care. *Social Policy and Administration, 33*(3), 262–280.

Evans, T., & Harris, J. (2004). Street-level bureaucracy, social work and the (exaggerated) death of discretion. *British Journal of Social Work, 34*(6), 871–895.

Economic Commission for Latin America and the Caribbean. (2008). San Salvador Commitment: Plan of action eLAC 2010. United Nations. http://www.eclac.cl/socinfo/noticias/noticias/3/32363/2008-2-TICs-San_Salvador_Commitment.pdf. Accessed 18 June 2012.

European Commission. (2010). ICT and e-business for an innovative and sustainable economy. DG Enterprise and Industry. http://www.empirica.com/themen/ebusiness/documents/EBR09-10.pdf. Accessed 10 June 2012.

Gengatharen, D., Standing, C., & Burn, J. (2005). Government supported community portal: Regional e-marketplaces for SMEs—evidence to Support a staged approach. *Electronic Markets, 15*(4), 405–417.

Greene, J., Mole, K., & Storey, D. (2008). *Three decades of enterprise culture: Entrepreneurship, economic regeneration and public policy*. Basingstoke and New York: Palgrave Macmillan.

Harrison, S. (1998). Clinical autonomy and health policy: Past and future. In M. Exworthy & S. Halford (Eds.), *Professionals and the new managerialism in the public sector* (pp. 50–64). Buckingham: Open University Press.

Hertogh, M. (2009). Through the eyes of bureaucrats: How front-line officials understand administrative justice. In M. Adler (Ed.), *Administrative justice in context* (pp. 203–225). Oxford: Hart Publishing.

Hill, M. (2009). *The public policy process* (5th ed.). Essex: Pearson.

Juma, C., & Clarke, N. (1995). Policy research in sub-Saharan Africa: An exploration. *Public Administration and Development, 15*(2), 121–137.

Lambert, R. (2003). Lambert review of business-university collaboration. Her Majesty's Treasury. http://www.hm-treasury.gov.uk/d/lambert_review_final_450.pdf. Accessed 25 February 2011.

Lebre, R. (1996). IT diffusion in small and medium-sized enterprises: Elements for policy definition. *Information Technology for Development, 7*(4), 169–180.

Lenihan, H., Hart, M., & Roper, S. (2007). Industrial policy evaluation: Theoretical foundations and empirical innovations: New wine in new bottles. *International Review of Applied Economics, 21*(3), 313–319.

Lewis, J., & Glennerster, H. (1996). *Implementing the new community care*. Buckingham: Open University Press.

Lipsky, M. (1980). *Street-level bureaucracy: The dilemmas of individuals in public services*. New York: Russell Sage Foundation.

Lipsky, M. (2010). *Street-level bureaucracy: The dilemmas of individuals in public services* (2nd ed.). New York: Russell Sage Foundation.

MacDonald, G. (1990). Allocating blame in social work. *British Journal of Social Work, 20*(6), 525–546.

Martin, L., & Matlay, H. (2001). Blanket approaches to promoting ICT in small firms: Some lessons from the DTI ladder adoption model in the UK. *Internet Research, 11*(5), 339–410.

Matlay, H., & Addis, M. (2003). Adoption of ICT and e-commerce in small business: An HEI-Based consultancy perspective. *Journal of Small Business and Enterprise Development, 10*(3), 321–335.

Maynard-Moody, S., & Musheno, M. (2003). *Cops, teachers, counsellors: Stories from the front lines of public service*. Ann Arbor: University of Michigan Press.

Moran, M. (2009). *Business, politics and society*. Oxford: Oxford University Press.

Pitts, D. (2007). Representative bureaucracy, ethnicity and public schools: Examining the link between representation and performance. *Administration and Society, 39*(4), 497–526.

Scott, J. (1990). *A matter of record: Documentary sources in social research*. Cambridge: Polity Press.

Simpson, M., & Docherty, A. (2004). E-commerce adoption support and advice for UK SMEs. *Journal of Small Business and Enterprise Development, 11*(3), 315–328.

Storey, D. (1994). *Understanding the small business sector*. Andover: Thomson Learning.

Storey, D. (2006). Evaluating SME policies and programmes: Technical and political dimensions. In M. Casson, B. Yeung, A. Basu, & N. Waldeson (Eds.), *The Oxford handbook of entrepreneurship* (pp. 248–278). Oxford: Oxford University Press.

Talbot, C. (2005). Performance management. In E. Ferlie, L. Lynn Jr, & C. Pollitt (Eds.), *The Oxford handbook of public management* (pp. 491–517). Oxford: Oxford University Press.

United Nations Conference on Trade and Development (2011). Information economy report—ICTs as an enabler for private sector development. United Nations. http://unctad.org/en/PublicationsLibrary/ier2011_en.pdf. Accessed 15 June 2012.

Vega, A., & Brown, D. (2011). Systems of innovation, multidisciplinarity and methodological pluralism: A realist approach to guide the future of information systems research and practice. In M. Chiasson, O. Hendridsson, H. Karsten, & J. DeGross (Eds.), *Researching the future of information systems* (pp. 249–1268). New York: Springer.

Vega, A., Brown, D., & Chiasson, M. (2012). Open innovation and SMEs: Exploring policy and scope for improvements in university based public programmes through a multidisciplinary Lens. *International Journal of Entrepreneurial Behaviour and Research, 18*(4), 457–476.

Vega, A., Chiasson, M., & Brown, D. (2007). Extending the research agenda on diffusion of innovations: The role of public programs in the diffusion of e-business innovations. In T. McMaster, D. Wastell, E. Ferneley, & J. DeGross (Eds.), *Organisational dynamics of technology-based innovation: Diversifying the research agenda* (pp. 379–392). New York: Springer.

Vega, A., Chiasson, M., Brown, D. (2011). *Adoption and programme contexts effect in the support to the informatisation of SMEs*. Paper presented at the 34th Institute for Small Business and Entrepreneurship (ISBE) Conference: Sustainable Futures: Enterprising Landscapes and Communities, Sheffield, 9–10 November.

Vega, A., Chiasson, M., Brown, D. (2013). Understanding the causes of informal and formal discretion in the delivery of enterprise policies: A multiple case study. *Environment and Planning C: Government and Policy*, *31*(1), 102–118

Wiggins, A. (2010). *Worlds apart: SMEs, e-business and policy initiatives*. Saarbrucken: LAP LAMBERT Academic Publishing.

Winter, S. (2000). *Information Asymmetry and Political Control of Street-Level Bureaucrats: Danish Agro-Environmental Regulation*. Paper presented at the 22nd Annual Research Meeting of the Association for Public Policy Analysis and Management (APPAM), Seattle, 2–4 November.

Yin, R. (2009). *Case study research: Design and method* (4th ed.). London: Sage Publications.

Part VI
Internet and Internet-Related Technologies

Forums and Blogs and Wikis, Oh My!—An Analysis of On-Line Sources of Support for End-User Development

Henri Korvela

1 Introduction

There are approximately 23 million small and medium-sized enterprises (SMEs) in the EU which represents 99 % of all businesses, and according to the European Commission[1]: "are a key driver for economic growth, innovation, employment and social integration" and that "[it] aims to promote successful entrepreneurship and improve the business environment for SMEs, to allow them to realize their full potential in today's global economy". A big part of this will undoubtedly be the use of information systems (IS) and information and communication technology (ICT) to enable improvements in current work methods and introduce new possibilities. However, SMEs often lack the resources to acquire and maintain large IS, especially among the smallest section, the so-called micro enterprises. For many SME organisations state of the art is still represented by basic software solutions, many of which they have developed themselves. Working with and planning ICT projects involving micro enterprises, we found most of them were still mainly using basic office applications and using these to create simple IS, e.g. a billing form with some database functions in Microsoft Excel. While rudimentary in function these could still represent a major improvement in functionality and/or efficiency over manual processes. The problem for the people doing this basic software development was often the lack of adequate support sources to assist them if they had difficulties. They had the ideas, but lacked in ability to execute them. End-user development (EUD) is common in many organisations, but often not adequately supported. Lack of development support seems common regardless of the size of the organisation, though likely more pronounced in smaller organisations where resources are scarcer. The focus of this research has

[1] http://ec.europa.eu/enterprise/policies/sme/index_en.htm

H. Korvela (✉)
Department of Information Technologies, Åbo Akademi University, Turku, Finland
e-mail: Henri.Korvela@abo.fi

J. Devos et al. (eds.), *Information Systems for Small and Medium-sized Enterprises*, Progress in IS, DOI: 10.1007/978-3-642-38244-4_18,

been on the developers we have met with in practice who have been mainly characterised by being less skilled and working in small organisations. We see going on-line as one way to solve the equation of providing support for this particular need, but also in a wider context.

The definition of an end-user developer varies, but is usually a variation on the theme that the developer is not formally trained to do so. Lieberman et al. (2006) introduces the following definition: "EUD can be defined as a set of methods, techniques, and tools that allow users of software systems, who are acting as non-professional software developers, at some point to create, modify, or extend a software artifact". Furthermore, EUD seems primarily intended to support other work or activities and does not form the main focal point for the effort (Ko and Myers 2005; Nardi 1993; Sutcliffe et al. 2003). End-user development is a tool, not a means.

EUD is a very common practice found in most organisations, whether small companies or large multinational corporations. Perhaps the most common instance is spreadsheet and database applications (Scaffidi et al. 2005). Extrapolating the estimate for computer usage in (Scaffidi et al. 2005) would suggest that there are around 55 million, potential and actual, end-user developers in the United States alone. This would mean that the population of end-user programmers and developers outnumber professional programmers many times over. In addition to the more traditional areas of EUD, such as spreadsheets and databases, web design, web mash-ups and related activities are relatively new areas where many more end-user developers can be found. End-users are also an important part of the so called "Web 2.0" world (Fischer 2009). Though not always actual software development, it will likely be an area were more and more SMEs will be applying EUD. Increasingly, regular software allows for extensive customisation that is pushing the envelope towards being out-right EUD, e.g. through the introduction of macros and scripting. In addition, cloud computing grows as an area where we can expect SMEs to perform development activities, e.g. by selecting and combining services and/or software from a cloud computing platform. In this and other ways, users are gradually taking on the role of developers and consequently facing a growing need to support these new tasks. However, it seems there is a bad fit between traditional sources and the needs of end-user developers. The Internet provides access to most old and a few new sources that could help alleviate some of the lack of support end-users face.

EUD is a knowledge-intensive process combining user-domain knowledge and computer knowledge. For the developer this process of information seeking and problem solving has the goal of achieving actionable knowledge (Cross and Sproull 2004), which in this case is represented by an application to solve a problem or task. Accessing support further complicates the process as this is an additional process of knowledge seeking in the domain the developer is often weaker in, i.e. computers. The constructivist perspective (Cross and Sproull 2004) fits well the domain of end-user developers where a more holistic approach to development with strong focus on context (Repenning and Ioannidou 2006) and iterative development (Repenning and Ioannidou 2006; Brandt et al. 2008) makes the developer very much like Clarke's "opportunistic developer" (Clarke 2007) who:

- Writes code in an exploratory fashion.
- Develops a sufficient understanding of a technology to understand how it can solve a business problem.
- Prides themselves on solving business problems.

Previous research has focused on the use of computer support in general, often within one organisation, e.g. (Carr 2006; Constant et al. 1996; Govindarajulu et al. 2000; Govindarajulu 2002, 2003; Nilsen and Sein 2004; Seeley and Targett 1997; Shaw et al. 2002). Studies on support sources often focus on the characteristics of one type of source in a general setting [e.g. (Phang et al. 2009; Purchase and Worrill 2002)] or on a certain tool [e.g. (Stylos and Myers 2006)] or in a different setting [e.g. (Lakhani and Von Hippel 2003)].

The aim of this paper is twofold. Firstly, to create a framework based on an extensive literature review for the most important factors that are relevant for end-user development support. We will model characteristics of knowledge seeker, source and relationship simultaneously. Secondly, to use the framework to analyse and compare the effectiveness of several existing support sources for end-user developers, namely: personal contacts, help desks, trial and error, several different knowledge repositories, virtual communities and Internet searches.

The paper is structured as follows. Section 2 introduces the concept of support for EUD and available sources. Section 3 introduces the framework of four EUD factors that can determine the choice of what source is used. Section 4 analyses on-line support with regards to the EUD factors. Section 5 compares the suitability of the different sources for EUD support. The paper concludes with some implications of the results.

2 Previous Research in End-User (Development) Support

2.1 End-User Support

When investigating EUD support it is natural to begin with general end-user support. EUD can be seen as extending end-user computing, and as such general end-user support forms the basis for understanding development support. Previous studies have investigated what support users prefer. In (Govindarajulu 2003) user groups ranked friends the most preferred support method. Furthermore, friends and local IT support were preferred over helpdesks in (Govindarajulu 2002), while executives mentioned contacting colleagues for assistance in most cases in (Seeley and Targett 1997). However, in (Govindarajulu 2000) middle level managers preferred local IS/IT staff and information centres over other support. In (Cross and Sproull 2004) most managers mentioned people as important sources of

Table 1 Reported support use from two studies in small organisations

	Study 2 (Korvela and Packalén 2010)				Study 1 (Korvela and Packalén 2009)			
	Work problems (n = 60)		*Computer problems (n = 60) (%)*		*Work problems (n = 19)*		*Computer problems (n = 19)*	
Support source used								
Personal contacts	47	78 %	51	85	15	79 %	15	79 %
Trial and error	18	30 %	28	47	5	26 %	9	47 %
Internet searches	41	68 %	21	35	11	58 %	4	21 %
Internet forums	8	13 %	6	10	3	16 %	3	16 %
Application help function	–	N/A[a]	16	27	–	N/A[a]	5	26 %
Help desk	–	N/A[a]	6	10	–	–[b]	–	–[b]
Books	19	32 %	1	2	2	11 %	3	16 %

[a] Not applicable to work-related problems
[b] Was not included in study 1

information instead of the computerized knowledge repositories that were promoted in the organisation examined. In two empirical studies previously conducted by the author on support use in small organisations developers favoured personal contacts (see Table 1). These studies divided the problems the persons had into work problems and computer problems, in lieu of asking about "development problems" as the participants were not expected to recognize their development efforts as such. Table 1 presents how support was used in those studies in small organisations (Korvela and Packalén 2009, 2010). The main findings were a strong support for personal contacts (between 78–85 % reported using them), followed by Internet searches (used by 21–68 %) and Trial and error (used by 26–47 %). Interestingly there is a switch in usage between Internet searches and Trial and Error in the two types of problems. We would posit this is due to a knowledge gap in skills and/or self-efficacy for computer problems compared to work problems. This is supported by a further study which suggested skill was the most influential attribute of a developer to impact on support source use (Korvela and Back 2012). The work domain is familiar to the respondents and they can make meaningful use of information searches, whereas the unfamiliar computer domain leads to not using information searches and attempting to solve a problem with whatever information the developer has. Other sources are hardly used. It seems we are facing a situation where the developers do not know enough to make use of the sources available to them.

2.2 On-line End-User Support

As mentioned earlier, end-users may have problems with finding and/or using support, and this seems to be even more pronounced for end-user developers.

Table 2 On-line and corresponding off-line support sources

Off-line source	On-line source
Magazine and other articles	Articles (copy), blogs and "tips and tricks" web-pages(substitute)
Manuals, books	Manuals, books (copy), knowledge bases, wikis (substitute)
Application help function	Knowledge bases, wikis (copy/substitute)
Software libraries/APIs	Software libraries/APIs (copy)
Personal contacts, advice from social network	Virtual communities (substitute)
Helpdesk/information centre	Helpdesk (copy)
–	Internet search
Trial and error	–

Indeed, in many cases the end-user developer has nowhere to turn to for support. The helpdesk and other IT support may provide only limited development support (Govindarajulu 2002) or none at all (Govindarajulu et al. 2000). Small organisations may not have the resources for a formal support structure, such as a helpdesk. Many end-users are not part of any organisation at all. As a result many developers are left with limited support options, mainly from their social network. These sources may not always able to provide adequate and reliable advice. It is likely that the user's social network is on par with the user in terms of knowledge (Constant et al. 1996). Compared to earlier decades today's developers have a virtual (figurative and literal) treasure trove of information in the form of the Internet. Using the Internet as a channel allows an end-user developer to access support sources that could overcome many of the obstacles that often make traditional sources inadequate for end-users.

Most sources are available both off- and on-line, in one form or another, either directly as a copy (same source, but a different medium) or as a substitute (similar content/function, but a different source). Examining sources based on typical content and the way information is provided Table 2 shows the corresponding off-/on-line versions of sources. E.g. magazine articles can be found on-line (as copies), but they also share a similarity in content to blogs (substitute). Both typically describe a feature the author thought interesting and wanted to share to a wider public. Many organisations have an on-line version of their helpdesk where you can post questions or access other available support resources; the online source is a copy of the off-line version. A virtual community works as a substitute for contacting colleagues, friends and family through various methods such as e-mail, chats and forums, both sources have the same core function. On-line sources are generally speaking the same as off-line sources. What makes the on-line sources special is usually that they can use features brought in by the medium that enhance their function (Purchase and Worrill 2002).

2.3 Factors Impacting Choice of Support for End-User Development

User attitudes toward a source will influence their choice more than subjective norms (Govindarajulu 2000). Informal support like a developer's social network often seems the default source, probably because it is easily accessible. Other sources may need to show a benefit to be considered by users. Since we cannot normatively change support use we must tackle the attitude towards it instead. But how are these attitudes formed?

The preference and usage of support sources will vary according to the end-user's characteristics and expectations, as well as the properties of the support sources themselves. End-user developers are a very heterogeneous group (Klann et al. 2006) so the impact will likely be considerable. There is unfortunately no "one size fits all" solution. This is important when considering different types of sources as different users can and will prefer to use different sources. Some characteristics are prevalent for all types of information seeking such as gender, job type and relation to the source (Cross and Sproull 2004). Also, characteristics such as age, computer self-efficacy and computer skills form the basic contextual frame of reference for the end-user and will influence the choice of support source.

Skill is related to usage, higher computer skills increases confidence in using computers (Liaw 2002). Gender and computer self efficacy is likely to influence the choices of support source (Nilsen and Sein 2004). Males are more comfortable with computers and the web (Liaw 2002) and gender impact areas of end-user development such as debugging (Beckwith et al. 2006) and self-efficacy in end-user developers (Beckwith et al. 2007). To be able to use Internet sources people would need to be comfortable with computers and using the Internet and search engines (Liaw 2002). People who have grown up with technology are more familiar and comfortable with its use (Brown 2002). Proximity (both mentally and physically) to the user can also be an important factor (Govindarajulu et al. 2000; Nilsen and Sein 2004). All these factors will impact on the choice of support.

3 Framework

Like Cross and Sproull (2004) we attempt to model characteristics of knowledge seeker, source and relationship simultaneously. Likewise the sources have very different characteristics and concepts such as "ease of use" and "ease of access" have widely different meanings for an electronic version of a paper manual versus a virtual community and are thus not easily used to compare sources. With the great many factors potentially impacting choice of source we asked: are there any factors unique to or particularly interesting with regards to the end-user developer? We have reviewed the literature by searching with Google Scholar and other research and science journal databases such as ACM Portal, IEEE Explorer, etc. for

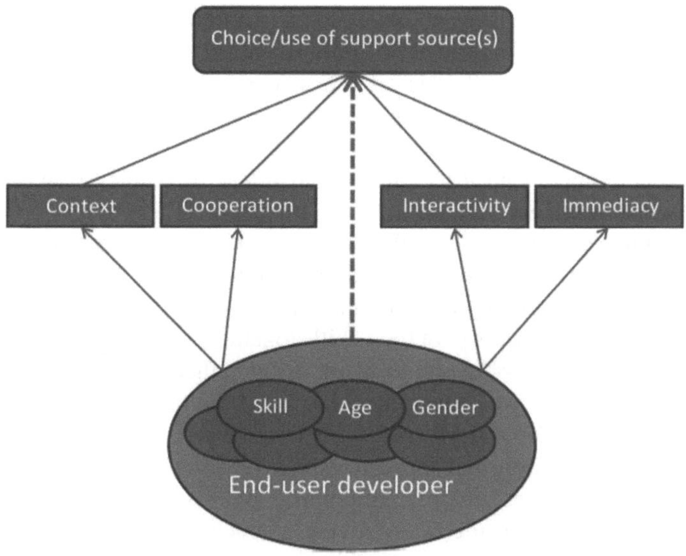

Fig. 1 Research framework

keywords such as, end-user computing/development, on-line support and end-user support. Additionally we have followed the main outlets in the field. It would seem that there are indeed certain characteristics or common themes particularly relevant for the end-user developer's pursuit of actionable knowledge. Following is an attempt to summarize these themes into the four factors of **context**, **cooperation**, **interaction** and **immediacy**. In creating these factors, we also draw inspiration from experiences of real-world end-users (Korvela and Packalén 2009, 2010) as well as finding support in the literature on end-user and development support.

Figure 1 illustrates how it is proposed the factors relate to the choice and use of support sources. Choosing or using a support source will depend on the combined skills and characteristics of the end-user developer. These have a direct relationship to the source, indicated by the dashed line, mainly in the form of an impact of the developer's computer skill (Korvela and Back 2012). We also propose that these collective abilities of a developer will be mediated through the four end-user developer factors.

Context represents the domain the developer works within, the language by which the developer understands his or her field and the motivation to make the development effort. Age, gender, job, skill and organisational context (Ko and Myers 2005; Cross and Sproull 2004; Nilsen and Sein 2004; Liaw 2002; Beckwith et al. 2006, 2007; Brown 2002; Ko et al. 2011) form part of the context in which the end-user developer works. Syntonicity (Papert and Harel 1993), being able to put oneself into the context, is important in end-user development (Repenning and Ioannidou 2006). The dialect a domain experts use in their work and the tacit knowledge they can apply is important for context (Costabile et al. 2006).

A developer will need to be able to recognize a future benefit so as to motivate the development effort (Sutcliffe et al. 2003; Blackwell 2002; Blackwell and Green 1999) as the development effort is often a secondary activity to the end-user and attention is not focused on the implementation used in the environment (Ko and Myers 2005; Nardi 1993; Sutcliffe et al. 2003; Segal 2007). It should also be noted that context here implies information easily available or visible to the user. A large database, while containing the information sought, will not support context if the end-user is unable to find it or sift it from all the other information. This also relates to immediacy as the speed at which information can be digested could be considered part of providing a timely answer.

Cooperation means users pool their skills together. Nardi notes how developing spreadsheets often is a collaborative work effort rather than an individual effort (Nardi 1993). Furthermore, cooperation was important for successful development in EUD (Nardi 1993). Ko and Myers (2005) describe programmers contacting more expert users forming "informal apprenticeships" and in (Repenning and Ioannidou 2006) it is suggested that building community tools is beneficial to EUD. Cooperation could also be considered involving a touch of human interaction. Help involving other people may be preferable simply because it involves interaction with other humans (Costabile et al. 2008). Moreover, as mentioned earlier there certainly seems a strong bias towards using people as sources.

Interactivity in end-user development means that the developer can more or less directly see the cause and effect between code and action performed. Several authors indicate a close relationship with development and execution (Ko and Myers 2005; Nardi 1993; Segal 2007) and using short edit-debug cycles (Brandt et al. 2008). End-user development tools should support incremental development and allow for immersion (Repenning and Ioannidou 2006). The end user's somewhat tenuous grasp of the development environment means they are not apt at predicting behaviour of code.

Immediacy is the ability to act, exactly when the developer wants to. Repenning and Ioannidou (2006) suggest the developer experiences a flow (Csikszentmihalyi 1990) state of mind. Immediacy would represent the need to get back into the flow. The end-user seems to be very much "in the moment" when developing. The importance of the ability to act (Arias et al. 2000) and the users' wish to act or react to the situation at hand (Ko and Myers 2005) are both indications of a need for immediacy. As mentioned above about context immediacy is also being able to make use of the information. If the user is overloaded with information then the feel of being able to act rapidly will diminish, you will fall out of the flow experience. People also solicit multiple sources simultaneously to increase the audience and hence likelihood of getting a timely reply.

While we argue these four factors are especially important for end-user developers, this in no way implies that other factors are less or not at all important. When using information systems usability is an important factor, e.g. when using a virtual community (Phang et al. 2009). Similarly ease of use and system reliability (Phang et al. 2009) and the system and information quality (DeLone and McLean 2002) (if the source is an information system) provided by the source are important. Nevertheless, this is equally true for all types of sources and all types of users.

4 Analysis of the Different Support Sources

To aid analysis we have categorised sources based on their primary function: sources that act as knowledge repositories and sources that facilitate communication between people. Some sources combine both functions or do not easily fall into either category.

4.1 Knowledge Repositories

The knowledge repositories' main function is that they provide information for other users, though some of these have a communicative function as well. They contain a wealth of information of various levels, ranging from quick answers to simple questions to advanced technical information and source code. Knowledge repositories provide developers with information on development, as well as "how-to" and code examples. To some degree they all share two fundamental problems, (1) *how to find information* and (2) *how to apply the information* once found.

There is a general problem of finding information in large information systems (Belkin 2000). In addition to the so called vocabulary problem (Furnas et al. 1987) potential issues with syntax exist (Mili et al. 1998). These two problems are often interconnected as you need to know the exact terms used (vocabulary problem) and in what order to use them (syntax problem). Modern search engine technologies and other enhancements such as tagging (Heymann et al. 2008), and tools, such as Mica (Stylos and Myers 2006), can alleviate some of the issues, but fundamentally the problem remains that searchers need to some degree know what they are looking for.

The other problem is that the solution needs to be fitted into the developer's work. The developers face the problem of adapting information or code found in the knowledge repository to their needs. Ko and Meyers (2005) mention how end-users had difficulties understanding what and how code worked, even code they themselves had previously written. Furthermore, end-users will tend to learn just enough of programming to do what they want instead of a whole process (Ko and Myers 2005).

4.1.1 Software Libraries and Application Programming Interfaces

Microsoft Excel's functions can be extended with the help of the Visual Basic for Applications programming language.[2] As with many other programming languages there are thousands of built-in or externally produced objects, classes or functions. These built-in functions and extensions can be utilized by a developer in their own applications. For this purpose programmers can use (on-line) software libraries (SL)/application programming interfaces (API), a structured repository of information containing code (usually in modules). The main difference to a knowledge base or wiki is that the SL/API predominantly contains code, though the two forms are similar and may be combined. A SL/API will have a wide range of solutions (i.e. different code modules) available and can thus provide extensive developer support solving a wide range of problems.

A developer using a SL/API may suffer from the problem of finding the right code to use. Despite considerable effort problems associated with finding code in the library remain (Mili et al. 1998). Users of the SL/API cannot formulate queries correctly if they do not know the correct syntax used. The correct syntax is dependent on what kind of structure the software library has (Mili et al. 1998). Better searching tools in general or specific ones, such as Mica (Stylos and Myers 2006), help to some degree. However, a developer would usually need to know or be able to guess what a function is called in the development environment to be able to find it in a SL/API. Also the code would likely need to be adopted for the developer's specific problem, something end-users often struggle with (Ko and Myers 2005). Ko et al. (2011) suggest SL/APIs need to be designed to support EUD activities.

A SL/API can be a valuable tool for those able to make use of them. However, context is weakly supported as the developer is faced with a significant attention investment. Similarly, immediacy is weakly supported as syntax and vocabulary needs to be understood and searching strategies developed based on them disengaging the user further from the development process. A SL/API supports cooperation and interactivity only weakly if at all.

4.1.2 Books, Manuals and Application Help Function

Books and manuals was one of the main ways to provide support for software before widespread use of application help functions. The purpose and content is similar to that of the help function that has largely replaced them, except that it can easily contain more information and can take advantage of the computer's information processing capabilities. Microsoft Excel has a built-in help function that contains information on most aspects of use, e.g. tutorials and examples, as well as technical information about the application.

---

[2] Available at: http://msdn.microsoft.com/en-us/library/bb726434(v=office.12)

Context is weakly supported. The information content is as general and broad as possible to appeal to the largest audience which reduces context for the end-user developer. Thus, interactivity and immediacy are weakly to moderately supported. The help function can be shown side by side to the application and the user can copy and paste a solution or example from the help to the application strengthening interactivity and immediacy. Books and manuals have weak immediacy and no interactivity. However, there is a risk for information overload due to the large amount of information provided. If the search is too general it may provide too many or inappropriate answers which detaches the user from the development process. Also a complex problem may require significant effort of finding and applying the answer found in the sources.

4.1.3 Knowledge Bases/On-line Manuals and Wikis

It is common that vendors provide on-line manuals for products in electronic form, e.g. a pdf version of the paper manual. In this basic form there is little difference to a paper version, except for the ability to keep it updated with corrections and other modifications more easily. A living (hypertext) document or wiki is a form of manual that uses the capabilities of the medium more directly, by using hypertext capabilities to link different parts together. It can also be seamlessly updated with new information. Lists of frequently asked questions (FAQs) along with answers are also commonly found on-line. A knowledge base is a database that has information on known problems and workarounds or answers to question users may have, in essence an advanced FAQ system. You can do text searches in the knowledge base to try and find solutions to problems. Some software programs can link directly to knowledge bases based on an error code or use the code as a search parameter. Most of these sources are official support from the software provider, but a wiki can easily be semi or completely unofficial. Using these on-line sources makes it easy to distribute information and to keep it current for all potential users to benefit. Whereas distributed help (manuals, application help function) is current to the situation when it was written. It is also possible to use the medium to further expand the available support by linking to other forms of help, e.g. on-line tutorials. There is an extensive knowledge base for Microsoft Excel.[3]

Context, cooperation, interactivity and immediacy are all weakly supported. Context is not focused on the end-user developer's specific interest, but instead general and as broad as possible to appeal to the largest audience. Manuals and knowledge bases are not inherently cooperative, though wikis are. However, this cooperation in wikis may not exist in way that supports the end-user developer, particularly if it is an official wiki, which likely limits the editing permissions. While these sources have some interactivity and can be changed and expanded easily they do not change in response to a developer's specific problem. The large

[3] Available at: http://support.microsoft.com/

amount of information contained and the associated issues with finding the right information means immediacy is usually weakly supported.

4.1.4 Blogs and "Tips and Tricks" Web-Pages

A "tips and tricks" site contains a number of solutions that people are likely to be interested in. Similarly a blog can contain pieces of code or ideas the author thought was interesting. Often these will consist of simple but clever tricks, e.g. HTML and/or Java Script tricks, such as how to create different effects when the cursor is scrolled over a link or an image. These are often simple to create if you know the correct syntax. These sites can also contain more exotic code that is not extensively covered in manuals or the application help function or have interesting workarounds that the author has discovered. Jon's Excel Charts and Tutorials is a good example of very advanced Excel charting tricks.[4]

In essence these are akin to software libraries, containing code to copy and use, except that they are not as extensive and likely not organised as rigorously. This has two implications, one is that the potential exists for vocabulary issues (Furnas et al. 1987), on the other hand it is more likely that colloquial terms are used which would help those not knowledgeable in the terms used in a specific programming language. The code will generally work with little modification and is usually self-encompassing and straightforward to use, literally a question of copy and paste. This reduces the need to understand the code and the issues associated with this (Ko and Myers 2005; Ko et al. 2011). In most cases the user only needs to replace the "your text here" part. In many ways the software libraries and "tips and tricks" sites are opposites of each other, one is broad in scope, structured and formal, the other narrower and unstructured, but less formal and perhaps easier to use.

As knowledge repositories the EUD factors are mostly weakly supported. It is possible to consider context moderately supported as the information is presented more easily and will have some contextual meaning. The narrower scope also moderately supports immediacy as any answers should be easier to find. Interactivity and cooperation is possible as these sites can support commenting and discussion. However, the nature of these sites lends itself more to discussion of the information already posted rather than new topics. As such we can conclude that, though technically possible, for our purposes interaction and cooperation are not adequately supported.

4.2 Communicative Sources

Communicative support sources primarily function by enabling communication, but they can also have some informative function when the record of the

---

[4] Available at: http://peltiertech.com/Excel/Charts/ChartIndex.html

communications are stored and made available. These sources facilitate communication between people allowing them to engage in support activities.

4.2.1 Personal Contacts and Helpdesk

Personal contacts are very popular as a source (see Table 1) and as such may be the first port of call for a developer with a problem. It entails contacting colleagues, friends or other persons for advice on solving a problem. The helpdesk is an ICT support function found in many organisations. Both cases are similar as the developer is contacting people with whom they have a formal or informal relationship.

All four factors are strongly supported. The developer can focus on their specific problem context. They can work in cooperation with the contact. This work can be interactive, while response would likely be relatively rapid. The main problem with contacts lies in availability and knowledge content. Helpdesks provide none (Govindarajulu et al. 2000) or only limited development support (Govindarajulu 2002) while it is likely that the user's social network is on par with the user in terms of knowledge (Constant et al. 1996). Not everyone has their own spreadsheet guru at hand, unfortunately.

4.2.2 Virtual Communities

Internet forums are places where people can post messages creating a platform for asynchronous communication and discussion. A forum is a collection of topics that members can read and post a reply, which can then in turn be commented upon by others, creating a chain of discussion. Email discussion lists are similar to forums and provide essentially the same function. The main difference is the separate channel (email client versus web browser) it is accessed by and that emails are pushed to the user while the user has to pull information from the forum. A social network works similarly to a forum, but usually includes an assortment of other facilities that allow people to connect, share information and interact in different ways. All of these can be considered as different types of virtual communities. In addition to allowing communication between members a virtual community normally saves the messages that have been posted. Old messages and discussions can be read or even revived with new replies. In this way they will also function as knowledge repositories, though due to their communicative focus this function is often less effective compared to regular knowledge repositories. This ad-hoc knowledge repository will share the burden of vetting and maintaining it over many individuals, though at a potential cost to accuracy (Ko et al. 2011). A very good example of a community for Excel help is the Mr Excel forums.[5]

---

[5] Available at: http://www.mrexcel.com/forum/forum.php

As a communicative source a virtual community allows interaction between the end-user developer seeking support and the information providers. This allows a negotiated or mediated approach, which forms a natural "informal apprenticeship" (Ko and Myers 2005). This interaction and cooperation means that during the process both parties have the ability to interpret what the other is saying and if required ask for clarifications. Neither is bound to a frame of reference fixed at some previous point and can adapt, e.g. negotiating a common vocabulary if one did not previously exist. When a problem has been posted the members of the community can then either correct the code, provide information on how to solve the problem or where to find the information to do so or even provide alternate solutions leading to a cooperative development effort similar to those described in (Nardi 1993).

A virtual community strongly supports context, collaboration and interactivity. The developer can go through several iterations to solve the problem or refine the solution as well as explaining the exact circumstances with real data if needed supporting an iterative development process. In this way context is very much present. It also makes the supporting activity collaborative and interactive. The helpers can explain a difficult concept to the developer or correct code that would have had a different behaviour from what was expected. Immediacy can be anything from weakly to strongly supported as the timeliness of any answers will depend on the activity of other users.

4.3 Other Sources

Several additional support sources are found on-line. In many cases, they are not unique for the medium though again their usefulness is greater as an on-line form as they can more easily be updated and linked together with other sources. Some examples include, but are not limited to on-line training, tutorials, video/animated demonstrations. Often these are found as a part of another knowledge repository or communicative source.

4.3.1 Internet Searches

In some senses the search engine could be considered a support source. For the end-user "searching the Internet" is a perfectly valid source, even though the search engine merely reflects other sources. In this capacity it will be a knowledge repository with dynamic content reflecting the keywords/search term used. Similarly to other knowledge repositories context, interactivity and cooperation is weakly supported while immediacy will be weak to moderate. While responses will essentially be immediate the large amount of information likely provided by the search engine will require considerable effort to sift through. This will be compounded by the impact of the used terms, i.e. the vocabulary used. However, unlike a formal knowledge repository the user can provide their own keywords (which do not need to correspond to the formal terms used) and still likely get some relevant responses due to the wider range of sources accessed by the search engine. The search engine will likely form the initial contact point for most information seekers providing a way to find the other support sources. It is in fact unlikely that the end-user can find any other source without the search engine (unless directed to them somehow, e.g. a colleague or some other referral). For most intents and purposes the search engine equals the information sources it can find even though it is technically speaking a tool and not a source.

4.3.2 Trial and Error

Trial and error simply means the developer experimenting with different solutions to find what works, testing different approaches and variables. It is not a support source as such, but more of an iterative development process that may or may not include referring to other sources. It is, however, a common way of solving development problems, in many ways for end-user developers the whole development process is one of trial and error [i.e. iterative development (Repenning and Ioannidou 2006; Brandt et al. 2008)].

Context, interactivity and immediacy are all strongly supported as the process is naturally anchored in what the developer is trying to do and results will be immediately visible as each change is made. Cooperation may be a part of the process, but in that case, we may find that it is a question of accessing personal contacts.

4.4 Hybrid and Mixed Sources

While the different types of sources are presented here as separate entities it is common to find several sources combined, or co-existing, together in the same place i.e. a website. Modern web technologies makes it fairly easy, one could even say encourage, the integration of the different functions into a complete package. As we have noted earlier some of the knowledge repositories can have communicative functions, for example a feature for posting comments enabling discussion. Likewise a communicative source that archives the communications will form a basic knowledge repository. In this way most on-line sources will probably combine features and provide both communicative and information resources as well as including several different sources on the same site. It is perhaps not a question of what type of support one picks but more which site one uses. We can also see how the lines between types and support sources start to blur in many cases. E.g. in the Excel help we find that the application help function can work in an on-line mode connecting to the Excel knowledge base as well as providing a communication channel for a community. In addition links to other third party sources, such as the Mr Excel forums mentioned earlier, are provided. This combines distributed help, extended dynamic on-line content and community aspects. Such a package will likely create a sum total value higher than its constituent parts.

5 Comparison of EUD Support Sources

As we noted earlier end-user developers are a very diverse group (Klann et al. 2006) and are likely to pick those sources that seem to fit their personal preferences and abilities. If we can understand those preferences better it is possible to provide better support for people, or at least steer them the right way. The second aim of this paper, analysing and comparing the effectiveness of support for end-user developers essentially asks the question: "how well does each source work for a developer?" Table 3 provides this answer by summarizing the properties of on-line sources. The sources have been given a rating of *weak*, *moderate* or *strong* as discussed in the analysis in Sect. 4 based on how well the sources map to the requirements of the four factors as described in the framework in Sect. 3. Special regard was given to the abilities and considerations we found in actual and potential end-user developers in the real world (Korvela and Packalén 2009, 2010; Korvela and Back 2012). It also allows us to some degree to explain why some methods of support are not used very much by users in real life. By comparing Tables 1 and 3 we see the sources with many *strong* ratings are also those mainly used, with one exception: virtual communities. The main challenge seems to be that sources with high information content rate poorly for most of the EUD factors as they require more skill from the developer to apply any information found.

Software libraries/APIs seem the least appropriate for the end-user developer, especially a novice one. Not only does it require understanding of the development language it also requires knowledge about the library itself. This requires a much larger investment of attention than the average end-user developer may feel is justified. There is also the issue with adapting generic code to the specific problem at hand. On the plus side, a software library/API has solutions for a wide range of issues, but the developer has to find them and be able to adapt them for their own problem.

Knowledge bases, wikis, books, manuals and the **application help function** similarly contain a wide range of solutions, but suffer from the same issues with formalism as software libraries/APIs. They are geared toward as many people as possible and will therefore provide less contextually relevant support. To benefit fully from these sources the developer needs a larger degree of skill to find and apply the information they require.

Blogs and **"tips and tricks" sites** have less extensive information content, but the information they contain would mostly be easier to absorb for the end-user developer. The skill needed to apply them is less as examples tend to be presented in context. Further, the facility for communication allows for some interaction and

Table 3 Degree of support for end-user development factors in sources

Support sources	EUD factors			
	Context	Cooperation	Interactivity	Immediacy
Knowledge repositories				
Software libraries/ APIs	Weak	–	–	Weak
Knowledge bases, wikis	Weak	Weak	Weak	Weak
Books, manuals, application help function	Weak	–	Weak → Moderate	Weak → Moderate
Blogs and "tips and tricks" web-pages	Moderate	Weak	Weak	Moderate
Other sources				
Internet search	Weak → Strong	–	–	Weak → Moderate
Trial and error	Strong	–	Strong	Strong
Communicative sources				
Personal contacts, helpdesk	Strong	Strong	Strong	Strong
Virtual communities	Strong	Strong	Strong	Weak → Strong

thus an option for even more specifically contextual support. This source has some benefits for the less experienced user. The content may be geared more towards them and have stronger contextual support, but the main issue is a lack of breadth of information.

Internet searches reflects the information content of knowledge repositories featured in the results and as such its suitability for end-user developers is large the same. The main issue lies in begin able to makes sense of and applying the results received.

The **trial and error** process relies on the developer having a good knowledge of the software and problem to make informed decisions. If the developers is less knowledgeable then it effectiveness must be questioned. The strong support for the factors helps explain why it is so popular even though it may be ineffective for those lacking knowledge.

Personal contacts and **helpdesks** as communication sources provide strong support for the EUD factors, but can often lack in information content. As mentioned earlier a developer's social network may not contain the requisite knowledge and the helpdesk most likely cannot provide this type of support.

A **virtual community** seems to solve both the problem of finding information and how to apply it by allowing its members to interact and discuss a problem. Developers can post their problem in their own words and provide sample data or troubleshoot their existing code by posting it. The information to solve even the most complex problems can usually be found. Furthermore, even a very novice user can make use of the answers as through interaction the solution can be explained to them. In an extreme case the end-user need not even understand the solution as it can be served to them ready to use based on the data they provided.

As such a virtual community not only has a wide range of solutions, but it allows any type of user to benefit from it. Much of the interesting features of a virtual community come from the interaction of its members of differing abilities and knowledge. This interaction with novice and other advanced users is part of the pay-off for participating in a virtual community. Participating in a community rewards all participants, not only as one would surmise the people being helped. As we can see from Table 3 virtual communities rate strongly in all factors and should therefore be acceptable to most developers. E.g. for a spreadsheet developer this is as close to having one's own personal spreadsheet guru by one's side as most people are going to get.

6 Conclusions and Future Research

In this paper, we have presented and analysed/compared several support sources for end-user developers. The analysis/comparison was based on four factors that it is argued would be important for users in determining the suitability and/or effectiveness of each source. The four sources, context, cooperation, interactivity and immediacy, were derived from an extensive literature search. As noted earlier virtual communities seem to be a very suitable support source for end-user developers, as they strongly support the four factors. With properties similar to the very popular personal contacts there is some hope that users can be steered to virtual communities and thus benefit from a much broader range of expertise than is normally available from a user's social network.

Research indicates that users in many cases are disappointed by traditional sources and as such do not utilise them extensively. Sometimes the sources are completely absent. Understanding the properties of sources and users and why users use a source is important to furthering our understanding of the relationship between users and the sources they use. This means we can design support to fit the users better as suggested by Ko et al. (2011). If the users are novice developers then a massive manual or application help-system might not be helpful. Alternatively, we can endorse and steer the user to certain types of support. E.g. local IT support may not possess the knowledge to support development in a particular application, but could refer the user to a good virtual community instead. In this way on-line sources can supplement the off-line sources and can also take advantage of the medium to leverage the supporting function to better help the users.

The four factors presented in this paper were identified mainly in existing literature so future work would include verifying them with actual end-user developers. Furthermore, the framework may need expanding, there is no consideration whether the relative importance of the factors is the same, and there may be other factors not readily identified in literature. This research has not primarily considered information quality of different sources, but it would naturally vary between sources. E.g. it may be possible that other considerations are rated above information content. We have seen some indications of this with regards to use especially of personal contacts.

A further important issue is how the use of a virtual community could be promoted to those users it would most likely be beneficial to. Teaching the use of office suits tends to be limited to features and functions and not more general development skills.

References

Arias, E., Eden, H., Fischer, G., Gorman, A., & Scharff, E. (2000). Transcending the individual human mind—creating shared understanding through collaborative design. *Transactions on Computer Human Interactions, 7*, 84–113.

Beckwith, L., Kissinger, C., Burnett, M., Wiedenbeck, S., Lawrance, J., Blackwell, A., Cook, C. (2006). Tinkering and gender in end-user programmers' debugging. *Proceedings of the 2006 SIGCHI Conference on Human Factors in Computing Systems* (pp. 231–240).

Beckwith, L., Inman, D., Rector, K., Burnett, M. (2007). On to the real world: Gender and self-efficacy in excel. *IEEE 2007 Symposium on Visual Languages and Human-Centric Computing* (pp. 119–126).

Belkin, N. (2000). Helping people find what they don't know. *Communications of the ACM, 43*, 58–61.

Blackwell, A. F. (2002). First steps in programming: A rationale for attention investment models. *IEEE 2002 Symposium on Human Centric Computing Languages and Environments* (pp. 2–10).

Blackwell, A. F., Green, T. (1999). Investment of attention as an analytic approach to cognitive dimensions. *Collected Papers of the 11th Annual Workshop of the Psychology of Programming Interest Group* (pp. 24–35).

Brandt, J., Guo, P., Lewenstein, J., Klemmer, S. (2008). Opportunistic programming: How rapid ideation and prototyping occur in practice. *Proceedings of the 4th Int Workshop on End-User Software Engineering* (pp. 1–5).

Brown, J. S. (2002). Growing up digital how the web changes work, education, and the ways people learn. USDLA Journal, 16.

Carr, C. (2006). Reciprocity: The golden rule of IS-user service relationship quality and cooperation. *Communications of the ACM, 49*, 77–83.

Clarke, S. (2007). What is an end user software engineer? In: M. H. Burnett., G. Engels., B. A. Myers., G. Rothermel (Eds.), *End-User Software Engineering. Internationales Begegnungs- und Forschungszentrum für Informatik (IBFI)*. Schloss Dagstuhl: Germany.

Constant, D., Sproull, L., & Kiesler, S. (1996). The kindness of strangers: The usefulness of electronic weak ties for technical advice. *Organization Science, 7*, 119–135.

Costabile, M., Fogli, D., Mussio, P., & Piccinno, A. (2006). End-user development: The software shaping workshop approach. In H. Lieberman, F. Paternò, M. Klann, & V. Wulf (Eds.), *End user development*. Netherlands: Springer.

Costabile, M., Mussio, P., Provenza, L., Piccinno, A. (2008). End users as unwitting software developers. *Proceedings of the 4th International Workshop on End-User Software Engineering* (pp. 6–10).

Cross, R., & Sproull, L. (2004). More than an answer: Information relationships for actionable knowledge. *Organization Science, 15*, 446–462.

Csikszentmihalyi, M. (1990). *Flow: The psychology of optimal experience*. New York: Harper Collins.
DeLone, W. H., McLean, E. R. (2002). Information systems success revisited. *HICSS 2002 Proceedingsof the 35th Annual Hawaii International Conference on System Sciences* (pp. 2966–2976).
Fischer, G. (2009). End-user development and meta-design: Foundations for cultures of participation. In V. Pipek, M. Rosson, B. de Ruyter, & V. Wulf (Eds.), *End-user development*. Berlin: Springer.
Furnas, G. W., Landauer, T. K., Gomez, L. M., & Dumais, S. T. (1987). The vocabulary problem in human-system communication. *Communications of the ACM, 30*, 964–971.
Govindarajulu, C. (2000). End-user types and end-user support: A study. *Proceedings of the 2000 Information Resources Management Association International Conference on Challenges of Information Technology Management in the 21st century* (pp. 1190–1191).
Govindarajulu, C. (2002). The status of helpdesk support. *Communications of the ACM, 45*, 97–100.
Govindarajulu, C. (2003). End users: Who are they? *Communications of the ACM, 46*, 152–159.
Govindarajulu, C., Reithel, B., & Sethi, V. (2000). A model of end user attitudes and intentions toward alternative sources of support. *Information and Management, 37*, 77–86.
Heymann, P., Koutrika, G., Garcia-Molina, H. (2008). Can social bookmarking improve web search? *Proceedings of the International Conference on Web Search and Web Data Mining* (pp. 195–206).
Klann, M., Paternò, F., & Wulf, V. (2006). Future perspectives in end-user development. In H. Lieberman, F. Paternò, M. Klann, & V. Wulf (Eds.), *End user development*. Netherlands: Springer.
Ko, A., Myers, B. (2005). Human factors affecting dependability in end-user programming. *Proceedings of the First Workshop on End-user Software Engineering* (pp. 1–4).
Ko, A., Abraham, R., Beckwith, L., Blackwell, A., Burnett, M., Erwig, M., Scaffidi, C., Lawrance, J., Lieberman, H., Myers, B., Rosson, M., Rothermel, G., Shaw, M., Wiedenbeck, S. (2011). The state of the art in end-user software engineering. ACM Computing Surveys, 43.
Korvela, H., Back, B. (2012). The impact of skills and demographics on end-user developers' use of support. *AMCIS 2012 Proceedings*. http://aisel.aisnet.org/amcis2012/proceedings/EndUserIS/14.
Korvela, H., Packalén, K. (2009). On-line support-a virtual treasure trove for end-user developers in small organisations? *AMCIS 2009 Proceedings*. Paper 630. http://aisel.aisnet.org/amcis2009/630.
Korvela, H., Packalén, K. (2010). Looking beyond the veil–what makes the micro organisation end-user developers tick? *AMCIS 2010 Proceedings*. http://aisel.aisnet.org/amcis2010/360.
Lakhani, K. R., & Von Hippel, E. (2003). How open source software works: "Free" user-to-user assistance. *Research Policy, 32*, 923–943.
Liaw, S. (2002). An Internet survey for perceptions of computers and the World Wide Web: Relationship, prediction, and difference. *Computers in Human Behavior, 18*, 17–35.
Lieberman, H., Paternò, F., Klann, M., & Wulf, V. (2006). End-user development: An emerging paradigm. In H. Lieberman, F. Paternò, M. Klann, & V. Wulf (Eds.), *End user development*. Netherlands: Springer.
Mili, A., Mili, R., & Mittermeir, R. (1998). A survey of software reuse libraries. *Annals of Software Engineering, 5*, 349–414.
Nardi, B. (1993). *A small matter of programming: Perspectives on end user computing*. Cambridge: MIT Press.
Nilsen, H., Sein, M. K. (2004). What is really important in supporting end-users? *Proceedings of the 2004 SIGMIS Conference on Computer Personnel Research* (pp. 48–54).
Papert, S., & Harel, I. (1993). *Constructionism*. Norwood: Ablex Publishing Corporation.
Phang, C., Kankanhalli, A., & Sabherwal, R. (2009). Usability and sociability in online communities: A comparative study of knowledge seeking and contribution. *Journal of the Association for Information Systems, 10*, 721–747.

Purchase, H. C., & Worrill, J. (2002). An empirical study of on-line help design: Features and principles. *International Journal of Human-Computer Studies, 56*, 539–567. doi:10.1006/ijhc.1009.

Repenning, A., & Ioannidou, A. (2006). What makes end-user development tick? 13 design guidelines. In H. Lieberman, F. Paternò, M. Klann, & V. Wulf (Eds.), *End user development*. Netherlands: Springer.

Scaffidi, C., Shaw, M., Myers, B. (2005). Estimating the numbers of end users and end user programmers. *Proceedings the 2005 IEEE Symposium on Visual Languages and Human-Centric Computing* (pp. 207–214).

Seeley, M. E., & Targett, D. (1997). A senior executive end-user framework. *Information Systems Journal, 7*, 289–308. doi:10.1046/j.1365-2575.1997.00019.x.

Segal, J. (2007). Some problems of professional end user developers. *IEEE 2007 Symposium on Visual Languages and Human-Centric Computing* (pp. 111–118).

Shaw, N., DeLone, W., & Niederman, F. (2002). Sources of dissatisfaction in end-user support: An empirical study. *SIGMIS Database, 33*, 41–56.

Stylos, J., Myers, B. A. (2006). Mica: A web-search tool for finding API components and examples. *IEEE 206 Symposium on Visual Languages—Human Centric Computing* (pp. 195–202).

Sutcliffe, A., Lee, D., Mehandjiev, N. (2003). Contributions, costs and prospects for end-user development. HCI International 2003. Lawrence Erlbaum: Mahwah.

Internet Technologies to Support SMEs' Growth in New Markets

Cerquitelli Tania, Chianese Stefano, Ferrero Merlino Chiara, Raimondi Francesca, Scapeccia Giuseppe, Spagnuolo Michele and Zolotukhina Irina

1 Introduction

The number of Internet users is growing rapidly every year, thus changing the nature of interaction and the sourcing of information. Furthermore, this unsurprisingly leads to the presence of companies with their products and services in the World Wide Web, while traditional channels of distribution are progressively being replaced by online ones giving new opportunities and creating a global market. Internet technologies are therefore becoming strong tools to support SMEs in their market expansion and internationalization decisions. Traditional institutions still continue to exist, but their value and ability to satisfy companies' needs is turning out to be weaker. As a consequence, there are a great number of agencies, banks and government bodies, which aim to help SMEs not only to go

C. Tania (✉)
Politecnico di Torino, Dipartimento di Automatica e Informatica,
Corso Duca degli Abruzzi 24, 10129 Torino, Italy
e-mail: tania.cerquitelli@polito.it

C. Stefano · F. M. Chiara
Alta Scuola Politecnica—Politecnico di Milano, Politecnico di Torino, Torino, Italy
e-mail: stefano.chianese@asp-poli.it

F. M. Chiara
e-mail: chiara.merlino@asp-poli.it

R. Francesca · S. Giuseppe · S. Michele · Z. Irina
Alta Scuola Politecnica—Politecnico di Milano, Politecnico di Torino, Milano, Italy
e-mail: francesca.raimondi@asp-poli.it

S. Giuseppe
e-mail: giuseppe.scapeccia@asp-poli.it

S. Michele
e-mail: michele.spagnuolo@asp-poli.it

Z. Irina
e-mail: irina.zolotukhina@asp-poli.it

J. Devos et al. (eds.), *Information Systems for Small and Medium-sized Enterprises*, Progress in IS, DOI: 10.1007/978-3-642-38244-4_19,

online, but also to enlarge the scope of their support activities and variety of provided services.

The aim of this chapter is to analyze in what ways the existing Internet technologies can support SMEs in their internationalization decisions, with special emphasis on the Internet portals, platforms, and services they provide to help these companies grow internationally.

A section is devoted to presenting the scenario of Italian SMEs, how they are distributed in the Italian regions, and which their role is in the internationalization market.

We propose two classifications to analyze the available portals and websites: the first one is based on the nature of the provider activity (public institutions, banks and consulting agencies, private institutions); while the second is focused on the type of services offered by these numerous entities. The latter classification potentially includes: access to databases, financial banking and consultancy, automatic matching with potential partners, and cultural mediation.

Furthermore, a section is dedicated to studying the portals and services available in two important countries and developing markets, France and Russia, in order to determine whether is it possible to identify some useful practices.

Finally, after the analysis of the state of the art of Internet services for the internationalization of small and medium enterprises, we have evaluated other portals like LinkedIn,[1] Kickstarter[2] and Tripadvisor.[3] Clearly these websites are not directly dedicated to the support of SMEs. Nevertheless, it can be effective to analyze their functional paradigm, e.g., the way LinkedIn provides automatic matching between professional partners, and how Kickstarter helps potential entrepreneurs to share their project, raise funds and launch their business.

2 The Italian Scenario

SMEs play an important role in the economic and industrial context of Italy. There are about five million SMEs in Italy, 95% of which have fewer than nine employees and 60% are self-employed entrepreneurs. SMEs are not evenly distributed: 43% of them are mainly concentrated in four of the 20 Italian regions. According to ISTAT[4] (the Italian National Institute of Statistics) the data in the Lazio region shows that big companies dominate the scene, while in Tuscany micro-industry is predominant. Small businesses (10–49 employees) are common in Marche and Umbria. In southern Italy, micro-companies are present in the territories of Campania, Calabria and Sicily; the secondary sector is primarily present in Apulia, Basilicata, Abruzzo, Molise and Sardinia.

[1] Linkedin https://www.linkedin.com/.

[2] Kickstarter http://www.kickstarter.com/.

[3] Tripadvisor http://www.tripadvisor.com/.

[4] ISTAT—Italian National Institute of Statistics http://www.istat.it/en/.

It is estimated that Italian small enterprises account for 54% of the national Gross Domestic product. It is nevertheless true that in recent years these companies realized a much lower performance in comparison with bigger enterprises. This fact has been mainly caused by an important decrease in demand since the beginning of the economic crisis in 2008. Internal private demand is suffering from the crisis, along with negative demographic trends and unequal earning distribution. On the other hand, the internal public demand is constrained by the need to combine general infrastructure modernization with public debt rehabilitation.

A good chance for small companies to overcome the crisis and to ensure their future growth and development could be to concentrate their efforts and resources on expanding their business abroad.

Despite its dimensional constraints, Italy is already a country with a foreign vocation, with a 3.2% share of world exports. Moreover, import/export trends show that since the beginning of the crisis export flows have been growing significantly (+18% according to ICE (Italian Trade Promotion Agency)[5] and Eurostat[6] sources).

The import and export operations of Italian SMEs are mainly carried out within European market. Other European countries take 40.1% of this flow, but new trends occur and indicate interesting new directions of development: between 2009 and 2010 the Italian goods exchange increased by 28.6% with China, by 24.2% with Turkey, by 21.3% with India and by 19.1% with the US.

In order to achieve good results in their export activities SMEs have to penetrate foreign markets rapidly, at a low cost and maintaining control over core technologies and products. At the same time they are forced to adapt product features to the requirements and preferences of the local customers. In this way it is possible to identify several obstacles that companies have to face before affirming their position abroad. Entrepreneurs have to find and evaluate potential partners, and overcome differences in business cultures which may include language limitations and a lack of knowledge about foreign accounting rules in terms of tax laws, banking legislation and so on.

3 Literature Review

In last few decades' multinational enterprises have been growing up and their investments for production and exports abroad have increased. Nowadays big firms are not the only ones aiming to invest their money in international business. This is also the case for Italian companies which are described later in this book.

The main phases of the internationalization of value-added activities by a firm have been identified (Dunning 1993), namely:

---

[5] ICE—Italian Trade Promotion Agency http://www.italtrade.com/.

[6] Eurostat—European statistics http://epp.eurostat.ec.europa.eu/portal/page/portal/eurostat/home/.

1. Export
2. Direct sales and marketing
3. New foreign production
4. Regional or global integration.

In the case of small and medium enterprises, the internationalization process is mainly related to the first two steps, since the dimensions and the gross capital of these companies are limited and they cannot usually afford multiple foreign production lines. For this reason, we are now dealing with the issue of their entry into the new markets, in order to understand why SMEs should try to expand into a new market and how third-party companies and online services might help in this process.

The firm's reasons for entering a foreign market may influence the way in which it does so.

For example, many firms try to avoid investing their money simply on sales or purchasing: exporting their product into a new market can be very risky due to their ignorance of local demand and other uncertainties. In particular, small enterprises usually prefer to buy third-party services provided by local sales agents or by Internet providers when they choose to enter a foreign market.

Another way of entering a new market and starting to invest abroad may be to create a product dedicated to that specific market in order to adapt it to the requirements of the buyers. This may be advantageous because it can meet consumer needs but it requires much higher R&D investments and a very good knowledge of the new market.

Finally, a large number of Italian SMEs apparently conduct both their national and international business by establishing a direct contact with the final consumer (which might be another company, B2B, or a final consumer, B2C). In this case the production is very often idiosyncratic or irregularly traded, and for this reason many firms may use the services provided by a broker or an internet service in order to search for, or negotiate with, suppliers and customers.

Internet has become a very powerful tool for all small and medium enterprises aiming to create opportunities to broaden their market and scale their business to global reality (Mehrtens et al. 2001). In his work "Organizational innovation: a meta-analysis of effects of determinants and moderators" Damanpour et al. (1991) states that an innovation is something that is "new to the adopting organization". In the case of SMEs, the adoption of IT by the CEOs of small companies is a great step forward for publicity, advertising, online selling, communication and collaboration. Several case studies can be presented to support the idea that IT industries can benefit from the web in order to become multinational. However, in the reality of the Italian SMEs' world where, according to ISTAT, there are millions of micro-enterprises (with fewer than 9 employees), the adoption of this kind of innovation might be very difficult due to their general lack of IT knowledge.

The idea of our research is to look for all those Internet portals that work as brokers which would enable SMEs to become more international and to benefit from the Internet.

4 Research Methodology

This section of the chapter briefly presents the research methodology adopted in order to collect the data.

Since the aim of the analysis was to study the way the existing Internet technologies can support SMEs in their internationalization decisions, the research was conducted entirely on the Internet, between April and May 2012.

In order to identify the online portals, platforms and services that internet brokers provide to help companies grow internationally, the first step was to determine a set of keywords to be used to perform the research via the common web-search engines like Google.

The keywords were translated into different languages: English, Italian, French and Russian. This made it possible to increase the results of the online research and to analyze portals from different countries.

The keywords were chosen according to different criteria. Some of the keywords were expected to narrow the research to specific services for small and medium enterprises. In other cases the research focused on the support within the internationalization process. Other keywords aimed to find specific services such as automatic matching between potential counterparts, business social networking or financial banking. The following are examples of the keywords used: "Small and medium enterprises", "Internationalization of small and medium enterprises", "Business internationalization", "Business online services", "Business for small and medium enterprises, "Social networking for business", Small business matching algorithm", "Network companies", "Small companies export", "Business to business social networking", "Internationalization strategy", "Internationalization support", "online banking".

Each portal found during the online survey was then accurately analyzed in order to obtain a comprehensive list of all the services provided.

Other aspects like the accessibility level or the available languages have been taken into consideration as well.

All these elements made it possible to establish criteria to analyze and classify the portals and platforms. The criteria for classification will be further presented in next sections of the chapter.

5 Criteria to Analyze Websites Promoting SMEs Internationalization

Small and medium enterprises can rely on several Internet portals and websites, either to start a new internationalization process or to promote their business abroad. The analysis of the currently available web services that help SMEs to extend their market abroad was performed considering two different kinds of subdivisions: one is based on the providers' main activity, while the other considers the typology of services offered to clients. Moreover, a further classification was used to distinguish between Italy-related websites and foreign ones.

The first classification is based on the nature of the institution which manages the portal: Public Institutions, Banks and Consulting, Private Entities."Public Institutions" means Chambers of Commerce, National Organizations like Governmental Institutions (Ministries, Departments, Offices, etc.) or Supranational ones, such as European entities. In the group "Banks and Consulting" there are all the Credit or Consultancy Institutions which back SMEs aiming at growing international. Websites run by private individuals or managed by companies which do not belong to the previous classes have been categorized with the label "Private Entities".

The second classification was conducted according to the services offered by the websites. We identified four classes, each of which groups different service sets.

Figure 1 shows a visual summary of the proposed classification. Each class was named with representative names, specifically coined for this study: (1) contact-raising, (2) hard-skilling the client, (3) soft-skilling the client and (4) distribution.

Contact-raising involves the practice of network-building. The label "Hard-skilling the client" is used to describe services that support an enterprise financially, legally and analytically. When "Soft-skilling the client", websites give their users a way to improve an already-existing commercial partnership. The Distribution is made up of marketing and logistics. A fifth class, based on general criteria, was also presented.

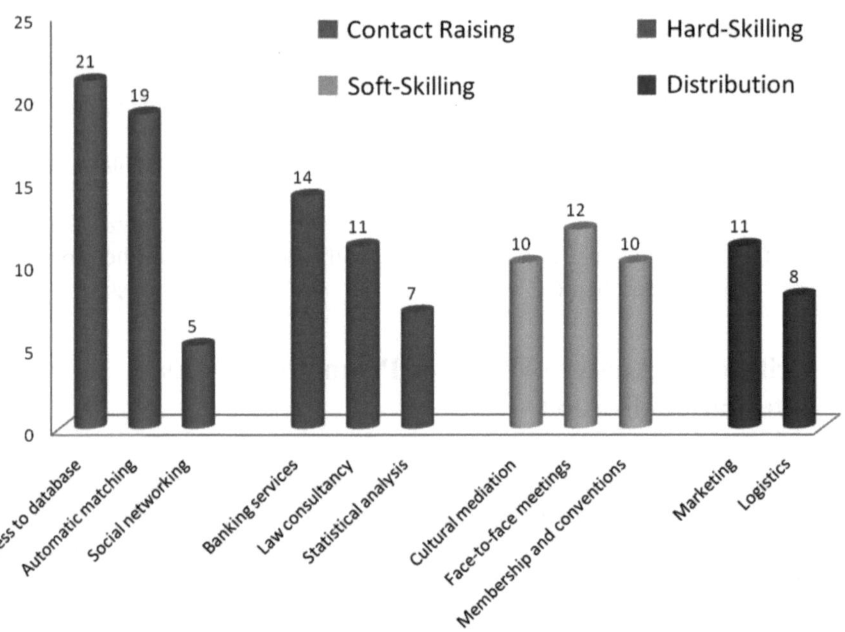

Fig. 1 Number of websites per offered service

Table 1 Overview of our classification

Contact-raising	Hard-skilling the client	Soft-skilling the client	Distribution	Further classification
Overview of the classification				
Access to database	Banking services	Cultural mediation	Marketing	Geographical domain
Automatic matching with potential partners	Law consultancy	Face-to-face meeting	Logistics	Commercial paradigm
Social networking	Statistical analysis	Membership and conventions		

Each class will be explained in more detail in the following pages (Table 1).

5.1 Contact-Raising

The term "Contact-raising" recalls the "fund-raising" practice. In fact, just like in fund-raising, websites belonging to this macro-group provide their clients with the means to raise contacts and create an online network with potential commercial partners. All websites offer either services of database consultancy or services of automatic matching between economically-compatible enterprises.

5.1.1 Access to Databases

The website offers free online consultation of databases to registered members of the community. It is therefore possible to gain access to the list of all the other members or even to confidential pieces of information. Databases usually collect profiles of manufacturers, importers, wholesalers, traders, agents, representatives and, more in general, potential suppliers and buyers. In some cases, databases containing "good practice" are also made public, where existing projects sustaining SMEs are sponsored.

5.1.2 Automatic Matching with Potential Partners

The website provides its registered members with an automatic matching system which displays the possible commercial partners available. In other words, the single user does not have access to the whole database, but he is given the chance to question the website whether members of the online community are willing to set up commercial relationships with him. This kind of service can be divided into two sub-classes, depending on the type of matching algorithm.

- The website shows **results on a generic basis**. It is not possible to set parameters to filter possible commercial partners. The user requires to be matched to another entrepreneur and all the available buyers or suppliers of the community are simply made visible.
- The website makes it possible to match enterprises by **filtering** them **according to sensitive parameters**. The user is able to ask for a collaborator by specifying, for example, the sector of competence, geographical area, and language spoken.

5.1.3 Social Networking

The website itself is a platform of social networking for enterprises or it links back to the most famous social networks. The website might also be providing methods to increase enterprises' visibility on existing social networks.

The possibility to post articles, reports and notes, the creation of blogs and forums and the chance to upload CVs, resumes, and public brief descriptions of the enterprises are also included in this classification

5.2 Hard-Skilling the Client

Hard skills are specific and teachable activities that can be quantified and measured. In the category "hard-skilling the client" we collected all those services of economic backing as well as financial, legal and statistical consultancy that a newcomer enterprise would presumably need in order to start its business. They are the rough and ready instruments that an enterprise would take into account when considering to expand its business abroad. This does not mean, however, that such services may not be required from advanced and internationally-grown entities as well.

We identified the following main service sets.

5.2.1 Banking Services

A wide range of banking services can be offered to an SME willing to widen its market. The most significant ones are:

- **Financial backing and loans**. The disbursement of money is mostly made after the entrepreneur has made personal contact with bank representatives. The first steps of this procedure, however, can be provided online.
- **Financial consultancy**. Specialized finance teams help the entrepreneur settle strategic positioning analysis, investment analysis and any evaluation of his investments' profitability.
- **Insurance**. Defense against commercial bank insolvency or other economic downturns is provided.

5.2.2 Law Consultancy

The website offers specialist assistance in the law sector. This service can be provided either at the upstream phase in which a SME decides whether to expand abroad or not, or even in the downstream phase, in case the enterprise were under trial or were facing controversies against international partners.

- **Initial phases**. The website provides legal interpretations and explanations about corporate and commercial laws in the foreign country, about labor unions' organizations, tax systems and about accessibility to the foreign market.
- **Resolution of controversies**. The website backs its community's members in the resolution of legal disputes.

5.2.3 Statistical Analysis

Statistical analyses are often provided online to model import/export goods flows in a foreign country, commercial trends or market dynamics.

5.3 *Soft-Skilling the Client*

In contrast to the hard skills, the term "soft-skilling itself" means the process that an enterprise undergoes in order to better and improve an already existing commercial partnership. The member of the website is offered the means to improve his personal and individual approach towards foreign cultures. The website can improve an enterprise's soft skills by enhancing both communication and cultural exchange thanks to services of cultural mediation or cultural compatibility through face-to-face meetings. The Internet portals belonging to this macro section might be also offering conventions and discounts in certain facilities abroad, in order to let its clients travel more easily to their commercial partners.

5.3.1 Cultural Mediation

The websites offer different services to foster intercultural exchange between potential commercial partners, particularly if they come from different cultures. We have identified two different categories of this service.

- **Translation**. The entrepreneur has the opportunity to hire expert translators to mediate with the commercial counterpart. Online dictionaries may be also provided.

- **Courses**. The entrepreneur is given the opportunity to follow language courses in the country of origin or abroad. There may also be courses in the fields of economics, management or human resources.

5.3.2 Face-to-Face Meetings

The websites not only put the possible clients in contact, but they also provide face-to-face meetings on request. This is more likely to happen if the two members willing to meet operate in distant geographical areas and if the website represents a physical institution which can provide physical locations such as offices or meeting rooms. Extra services might be also offered on payment, such as secretary service, cultural mediation, and a translator.

5.3.3 Membership and Conventions

Users from the internet community are given membership cards which make them eligible for special prices and discounts in certain facilities, typically hotels, bars and restaurants in the foreign countries where members of the community operate. By doing so, face-to-face meetings between commercial partners are encouraged. Conventions may also concern useful products for an entrepreneur to open up a new operational base abroad, for example convenient foreign phone tariffs or conventions to buy office furniture.

5.4 Distribution

This definition entails the entire chain of the physical distribution of the goods. The Internet portal offers its clients means to provide transport and warehousing (and more in general, logistics) as well as to promote their goods in the foreign country through marketing campaigns. This class collects services offered by the Internet portal to foster a client direct and concrete commercial action both in the national and foreign market.

5.4.1 Marketing

Promotional activities are organized to increase an enterprise's visibility in the market. This includes running advertisement campaigns and participating at Fairs and Exhibitions (or even organizing them).

5.4.2 Logistics

The websites provide the enterprise with management instruments to control the flow of goods between the point of origin and the destination point or puts the client in contact with specialized firms operating in the sector. The services offered are those of information, transportation, inventory, warehousing, material handling, packaging and often security.

5.5 Further Classification

We also propose an additional classification to analyze each website based on (1) the geographical area in which the website operates and (2) the commercial paradigm adopted.

5.5.1 Geographical Domain

The website connects firms and enterprises from a specific, limited geographical area.

5.5.2 Commercial Paradigm

According to the distribution paradigm, the website might be focusing on B2B (Business-to-Business) transactions, B2C (Business to Consumer) or both of them.

6 Analysis of the Services Offered Online to Promote SMEs Internationalization

The research focused on 28 different websites and Internet portals. The majority of them are operating inside the European Union (18). Six Russian Internet portals were also analyzed, together with three North-American portals and a Chinese one. Moreover, the Chambers of Commerce of each of these countries were also included in the study. Websites mainly adopt a B2B business paradigm, therefore offering services to put enterprises and companies in contact with each other. On the other hand, 10 websites mediate between business entities and customers (B2C) and 3 out of the 28 follow an agency economic paradigm, that is to say they also have institutions as a counterpart of the mediation.

A large number of the websites studied (15 out of 28) were founded and are now managed by *Public Institutions*, mostly Chambers of Commerce and

Ministries. Three websites are run by Banks or Consulting Companies, while eleven belong to the classification *Private Entities*, being managed by dedicated companies.[7]

6.1 Public Institutions

We considered the following public institutions:

Italy-related websites: *Camera di Commercio Italo-Slovacca/Talianko-Slovensk Obchodn Komora*;[8] *Enterprise Europe Network*;[9] *Solvit*.[10]

Non-Italian websites: *Handwerk International Baden-Wuerttemberg*;[11] *Chamber Trade*;[12] *Enterprise Ireland*;[13] *PACTE PME*;[14] *OSEO*;[15] *UBIFRANCE*;[16] *UCCIFE*;[17] *Ministère de l'économie, des finances et de l'industrie/Ministere du budget des comptes publiques et de la reforme de l'Etat*;[18] *Enterprise Europe Network—The Russian Euro Info Centre*;[19] *Informational Portal on Export Support and Fund Raising*;[20] *Russian Agency for Small and Medium Business Support*;[21] *Ministry of Economic Development of the Russian Federation*.[22]

With the only exception of *Solvit*, whose aim is to solve legal proceedings problems caused by the misapplication of Internal Market laws by European public authorities, all the websites analyzed offer *contact-raising* services such as the querying of commercial partners' databases or social networking services.

---

[7] One of the websites ("PACTE PME") is managed both by a public Ministry and Banks and is therefore catalogued in both groups.

[8] Camera di Commercio Italo-Slovacca/Talianko-SlovenskObchodnKomora http://www.camitslovakia.sk/camera-di-commercio-italo-slovacca.tab.it.aspx.

[9] Enterprise Europe Network http://www.enterprise-europe-network.ec.europa.eu/index_en.htm.

[10] Solvit http://ec.europa.eu/solvit/site/about/index_en.htm.

[11] Handwerk International Baden-Wuerttemberg http://www.handwerk-international.de/Handwerk-International.aspx.

[12] Chamber Trade http://www.chambertrade.com/.

[13] Enterprise Ireland http://www.enterprise-ireland.com/.

[14] PACTE PME http://www.pactepme.org/international.

[15] OSEO http://www.oseo.fr.

[16] UBIFRANCE http://www.ubifrance.fr.

[17] UCCIFE http://www.uccife.org/en.html.

[18] Ministere de l'economie, desfinances et de l'industrie http://import-export.gouv.fr/.

[19] Enterprise Europe Network—The Russian Euro Info Centre http://www.euroinfocenter.ru/en/.

[20] Informational portal on export support and fund raising http://moscow-export.com/about/.

[21] Russian Agency for small and medium business support http://www.siora.ru.

[22] Ministry of economic development of the Russian Federation http://www.ved.gov.ru/rus_export.

Thirteen out of 15 are also able to back SMEs financially or offer them legal assistance as well as statistical studies. In other words, almost all the websites have the capacity to *hard skill their clients*.

Twelve portals provide services aimed at *soft-skilling the client*, mostly related to cultural mediation, with translation services being the most common.

Only 8 out of the 15 websites can sustain their clients through marketing and logistics (distribution category).

Governmental websites, Chambers of Commerce and Institutional websites are not only the most common and numerous, but they are probably some of the most complete. Indeed many of them (11/15) offer a wide range of services, covering at least three of the four macro-sections of possible services. The explanation for such a distribution of services is the great availability of cash and funds that public Institutions usually have.

The weakest point is the *distribution*, as little more than half of the websites cover such a service. It is no coincidence that marketing and logistics are usually the domain of specialized and private sectorial companies.

6.2 Banks and Consulting

In this study we focused on:

Non-Italian websites: *Business Development Bank of Canada*;[23] *PACTE PME*; *Socièté Gènèrale*.[24]

All the three Bank websites offer services of *contact-raising*, *hard-skilling* and *soft-skilling for the client*. Among the functionalities of the "contact-raising", however, none of the websites offer either a link to social networks or to its own social networking platform. In the "hard-skills" sphere, all three websites offer financial backing and analytical analysis, but law consultancy and legal assistance are not present in any of the websites. The Canadian Bank is the most complete in relation to the *soft-skilling* features, offering all the services available in that segment. In addition to this, the *Business Development Bank of Canada* is the only one to be active in the distribution segment as well (logistics).

6.3 Private Entities

Among the wide range of private entities, we considered:

Italy-related websites: *Italoblog*;[25] *B2B.it*;[26] *Eureka*.[27]

---

[23] Business Development Bank of Canada http://www.bcd.ca.

[24] Socièté Gènèrale https://entreprises.societegenerale.fr/dossiers/international/export.html.

[25] Italoblog http://www.italoblog.it/tag/pmi.

[26] B2B.IT http://www.b2b.it.

[27] Eureka http://www.eurekanetwork.org.

Non-Italian websites: *CARDOMAT;*[28] *Alibaba;*[29] *MAGNAT;*[30] *Straker TRANSLATIONS;*[31] *LTC;*[32] *Enterprise Marketing and Communications;*[33] *INTERNET MARKETING, INC;*[34] *WERNER Enterprises.*[35]

Six of the websites analyzed offer services of *contact-raising*, that is to say the consultation of databases of potential commercial partners. What is peculiar about them is that the portals' structure is that of a social network, with the sole exception of *Alibaba. Eureka* is the only one to also offer *hard-skilling* services, along with *distribution*. Not surprisingly, it is the only one which can rely on public financing, as it works in close contact with European Institutions, though remaining a private website. The research also took into account five specific and sectorial websites operating solely in the fields of marketing, distribution and cultural mediation, catalogued within the families *distribution* and *soft-skilling the client*. Moreover, *Eureka* and *Alibaba* are the only multi-sectorial websites also offering *soft-skilling* services.

7 Services Distribution Through Internet Portals

This section presents and discusses services distribution through Internet Portals.

The results of our research highlight that many websites all around the world are offering a wide range of economic and financial services, therefore covering the great majority of the economic requirements that this work has taken into account. The best practice in the economic field is then provided by several websites. However, the weak point is the visual interface, which is seldom clear and user-friendly. Links and menus are often hard to find and no online social interaction between registered members is available. Moreover, no mobile versions of the websites are available: portals are consultable only through a personal computer.

On the other hand, social networks for managers and entrepreneurs are numerous. However, they are detached and not connected to those websites offering concrete and material services.

Among the websites surveyed it appears clear that social online services and financial or economic services are not to be found together: no platform is offering both of them. Also simplified platforms for mobile devices are not yet widespread.

[28] CARDOMAT http://cardomat.ru/.

[29] Alibaba http://www.alibaba.com.

[30] MAGNAT http://magnat.su/.

[31] Straker TRANSLATIONS https://www.strakertranslations.com/.

[32] LTC http://www.langtech.co.uk/.

[33] Enterprise Marketing and Communications http://www.enterprisemarketing1.com/.

[34] INTERNET MARKETING, INC. http://www.internetmarketinginc.com/.

[35] WERNER Enterprises http://www.werner.com/.

Figure 1 shows the number of websites per service offered. The services offered are clustered according to the classification proposed in the previous section.

Among the analyzed websites, 21 out of 28 offer access to databases collecting data from SMEs and, generally, from potential suppliers and buyers (manufacturers, importers, wholesalers, traders, agents and representatives). Nineteen websites also provide their clients with an automatized service to match them with potential partners on a geographical basis. Among these 19 sites, 16 are able to filter such results through specific parameters.

Websites which permit members to consult databases often allow their registered members to meet face-to-face. Twelve portals give managers from SMEs the opportunity to get to know their potential commercial partners personally. As such a service requires the availability of physical places in which managers may organize meetings, this possibility is only offered by state institutions or by websites that are affiliated to those banks and credit institutes that have detached departments abroad.

Half of the websites offer banking services: 14 out of 28 have financial consultancy services and 12 can back enterprises financially. Insurance, instead, is offered only by 9 websites, demonstrating that such a banking service is not as common as the previous two.

Few portals deliver legal services: 11 sites offer law consultancy aim at helping SMEs in their initial phases of expansion abroad, whereas only seven of them continue to follow SMEs legally, by backing them during legal disputes. Statistical analysis is also a service offered by few websites: seven portals are able to create charts or provide numerical studies upon commercial trends or market dynamics.

Promotional activities and marketing campaigns are run by 11 of the websites analyzed. However, this activity is not uniform: apart from two companies, whose only core business is marketing, only bank-related websites are able to follow their clients actively through marketing and advertising campaigns. On the other hand, almost all portals offer participation and enrolment for fairs and exhibitions, which are run and organized by third parties. Just like marketing and advertising services, logistics is provided either by specific companies operating just in that field, or mostly by websites affiliated to banks or credit institutes. In fact, only eight websites are able to follow the flow of goods exported by the enterprise or to provide it with information, transportation, inventory, warehousing, material handling, packaging or security services.

One of the services which are least offered is cultural mediation: only five websites out of the 28 listed run courses for SMEs' managers willing to learn a foreign language or to acquire notions in economics, management or human resources. Ten websites offer their members means to communicate with foreign partners, such as expert translators or more simply online dictionaries. Among these 10, two websites manage specifically cultural mediation as their core business.

Social networking by means of direct communication between managers is offered only by five portals out of the 28.

Finally, 10 websites are able to offer their online-registered users membership cards and conventions in order to make them eligible for special prices and discounts in certain facilities, typically hotels, bars and restaurants in foreign countries.

As shown in Fig. 2, the services provided by each Internet website are different and correctly fulfill the classification we made in the previous section. However, some of them can be classified in more than a single class, depending on the variety of possible fields in which they are employed.

It is now possible to cluster the services offered and analyze them by means of a percentage over the total group, ordering such services from the most to the least widespread.

Most of the websites offer classical services relating to economic analysis and consultancy, as well as access to members' databases. Indeed an average of 57.1% of the websites analyzed provide SMEs with a collection of banking, law and database services. Purely banking services are available on 50% of the websites studied.

In relation with the consultation of potential partners through online databases, Internet portals also run face-to-face meetings between members of the community. Approximately 43% of the Internet portals studied offer such a service, therefore demonstrating the availability of offices and free rooms throughout different nations. Governments, state institutions and banks are the entities that mostly back this service, as they are those that possess detached departments all over the world. In order to facilitate face-to-face meetings, 36% of the websites analyzed also provide the irregistered members with affiliation or membership

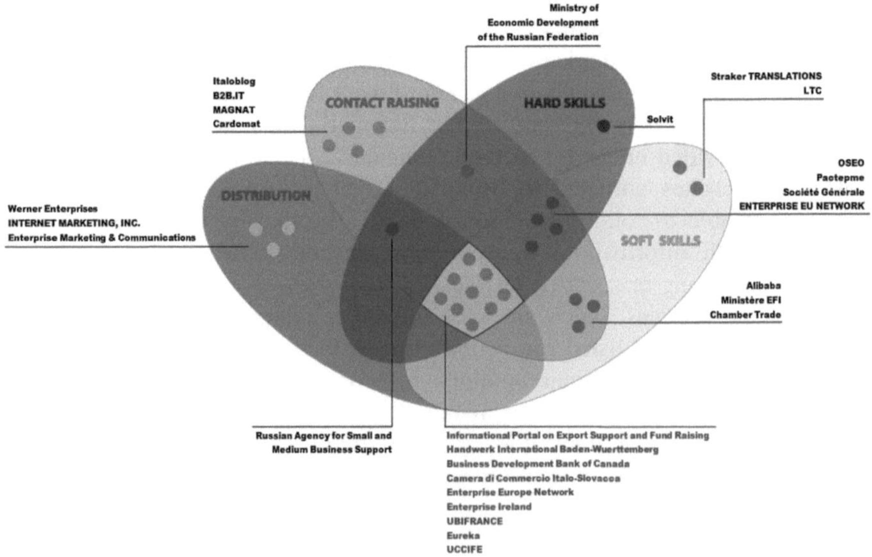

Fig. 2 Graphical representation of websites and internet portals by service class division

cards, loyalty programmes and conventions which ensure special prices in restaurants, bars and hotels in foreign countries.

Other sectors which can be closely related to the most classical economic ones are law consultancy and statistical analysis. 43% of the websites are able to perform law and legal consultancy services of any kind. Statistical and numerical analysis is offered by 25% of the websites analyzed. Again, these services are mostly provided by those websites relying on partnerships with banks and credit institutions.

Marketing and logistics are respectively offered by 39 and 29% of the Internet portals analyzed. Such services are usually outsourced and put in charge of third parties, with the exception of three websites whose only activities were exclusively within the *distribution* area.

Cultural mediation in the form of courses and translation services is offered by 36% of the websites analyzed. In both cases such functions are outsourced and provided by third parties, such as cultural mediation Institutions and language schools, with the only exception of two websites whose sole business is to provide professional translation for companies aiming to expand abroad.

Soft services such as social networking are offered only by 18% of the websites studied.

Tables 2 and 3 list the complete set of services offered online to SMEs willing to extend their business abroad for all the websites and Internet portals analyzed in this study.

8 A Window on France and Russia

8.1 France

The kinds of services offered by French Internet portals are various. International synergies have been constituted to help SMEs thanks to the affiliation of their members, which are major big enterprises in France and the main associations such as Chambers of Commerce (e.g., *PACTE PME*).

Some other institutions offer a basis for a SMEs' projects, market analysis, implementation and easier access to financing (e.g. *OSEO*, *Sociètè Gènèrale*, *UBIFRANCE*).

UBIFRANCE also deals with the organization of trade fairs, exhibitions and seminars; sales contacts; advice for export projects; management of international volunteers ("VIE programme") for temporary assignments abroad, from a diagnosis to the complete execution of projects in foreign markets. On the other hand, *Eureka* and *Eurostar Program* support SMEs launching pan-European projects to develop innovative products, processes and services, and dealings with financial, technical and commercial partners. Finally, *UCCIFE* consists of an association of

Table 2 Summarizing table of the services provided by the websites studied

	Contact-raising				Hard-skilling the client					
	Automatic matching w/potential partners				Banking services			Law consultancy		
	Database	Results on a generic basis	Filtering w/ parameters	Social networking	Financial banking	Consultancy	Insurance	Initial phases	Controversy resolution	Statistical analysis
Camera di Commercio Italo-Slovacca	X	X	X		X	X	X	X	X	X
Italoblog—Social platform for Italian and Slovak enterprises				X						
Business development bank of Canada	X	X	X		X	X				
Alibaba	X	X	X							
B2B.it	X	X		X						
Enterprise Europe network	X	X	X	X		X		X		
Handwerk international Baden—Wurtemberg	X	X	X					X		
Solvit									X	
Chamber trade	X	X	X							
Enterprise Ireland	X	X			X	X		X		
PactePME	X	X			X	X	X			
Oseo	X	X	X		X	X	X			
UBI France	X	X	X		X	X	X	X	X	X
Eureka	X	X	X		X	X	X	X	X	X
UCCIFE	X	X	X		X	X	X	X	X	X
Societe Generale	X	X	X		X	X	X			
Ministère de l'économie, des finances et de l'industrie	X									

(continued)

Table 2 (continued)

	Contact-raising				Hard-skilling the client					
	Automatic matching w/potential partners				Banking services			Law consultancy		
	Database	Results on a generic basis	Filtering w/ parameters	Social networking	Financial banking	Consultancy	Insurance	Initial phases	Controversy resolution	Statistical analysis
Enterprise Europe network Russia	X	X	X			X	X	X	X	
Informational portal on export support and fund raising	X	X	X			X		X		X
Russian agency for small and medium business support					X	X	X	X		X
Ministry of economic development of the Russian federation	X	X	X		X	X		X	X	X
CARDOMAT	X	X	X	X						
MAGNAT—system for searching partners	X	X	X	X						
Straker TRANSLATIONS										
LTC										
Enterprise marketing and communications										
INTERNET MARKETING, INC.										
WERNER enterprises										

Table 3 Summarizing table of the services provided by the websites studied

	Soft-skilling the client				Distribution		Further classification	
	Cultural mediation		Face-to-face meeting	Membership and conventions	Marketing	Logistics	Commercial paradigm	Geographical domains
	Translation	Courses						
Camera di Commercio Italo-Slovacca	X	X	X	X	X	X	B2B	Italy, Slovakia
Italoblog—Social platform for Italian and Slovak enterprises							B2B	Italy, Slovakia
Business Development Bank of Canada	X	X	X	X		X	Agency	Canada, rest of the world
Alibaba				X			B2B	China
B2B.it							B2B	Italy
Enterprise Europe Network	X		X				B2B	Europe
Handwerk International Baden—Wurtemberg			X		X		B2B	Germany (Stuttgart region), rest of the world
Solvit							Business and private	Europe
Chamber trade			X				B2B	Companies from all over the world
Enterprise Ireland			X		X	X	B2B	Ireland, rest of the world
PactePME			X	X			B2B, BTC, BTS	France toward foreigner countries
Oseo				X			B2B, B2C	France
UBI France	X	X	X	X	X	X	B2B, B2C	France
Eureka	X	X	X	X	X	X	B2B	Europe
UCCIFE	X	X	X	X	X	X	B2B, B2C	France
Societe Generale				X			B2B, Agency	France

(continued)

Table 3 (continued)

	Soft-skilling the client				Distribution		Further classification	
	Cultural mediation		Face-to-face meeting	Membership and conventions	Marketing	Logistics	Commercial paradigm	Geographical domains
	Translation	Courses						
Ministère de l'économie, des finances et de l'industrie				X			Agency	France
Enterprise Europe network Russia	X		X		X	X	B2B	All world Russia
Informational portal on export support and fund raising	X		X		X		B2B	Moscow region
Russian agency for small and medium business support					X		Agency	All world Russia
Ministry of economic development of the Russian federation							B2B, B2C	All world Russia
CARDOMAT							B2B, B2C	All world
MAGNAT—system for searching partners							B2B, B2C	All world
Straker TRANSLATIONS	X						B2B, B2C	USA, EU, Australia
LTC	X						B2B, B2C, Agency	UK, USA
Enterprise marketing and communications					X		B2B	USA
INTERNET MARKETING, INC.					X		B2B	USA
WERNER enterprises						X	B2B	USA, rest of the world

107 French Chambers of Commerce and Industry Overseas, which together represent the largest private network of French companies in the world.

8.2 Russia

Russian Internet space has a large variety of web pages which provide companies with services in their internationalization decisions through supporting activities and research for foreign business partners.

Portals have different formats and can be divided into two main groups—governmental and market places.

The majority of the web-pages are well established, have been developed by state bodies or in cooperation with them and share numerous similarities: high interaction with companies, precise matching engines, broad databases and a good variety of services along with their high quality.

Market places, on the other hand, have simple and less specified engines but they give companies an opportunity to present themselves by creating a profile and get access to the database of potential partners without the provision of any additional services.

Websites are orientated on markets all over the world—this means that companies are not limited by geographical locations. One more feature is that, along with Russian companies, the target audience covers international companies which want to enter the Russian market, collect data on legislation, statistics, the business environment, etc. This demonstrates that such websites are good and appreciated tools not only for Russian companies willing to export, but also for foreign ones interested in operating in the Russian market.

9 Some Potential Internet Services for SMEs Internationalization

After analyzing the state of the art of some specific Internet services available to support the internationalization process of SMEs, we then included some other web-based services that are not directly dedicated to that purpose in the analysis. However, their paradigm may be usefully exploited to provide new Internet technologies to help SMEs grow internationally.

Two main portals were identified: LinkedIn and Kickstarter. It was also considered useful to study the success of a totally different platform: Tripadvisor.

LinkedIn is a social network dedicated to simplifying matching between professionals based on a hierarchical organization: it considers as first connections the people in one's network and scales to second or third degree whenever the research points to people that are in the network of "friends". Moreover, queries are performed also considering the geographical distribution of contacts and their belonging to some groups—like Alumni groups—or fields of interests.

Kickstarter, on the other hand, is a showcase for all the projects which need some kind of grant to be realized. They are shown as possible investments for all users which want to contribute and become part of something that could potentially become famous. It helps people in starting their own business just by sharing their goals and the amount of money they need to build their business with the community. Everybody can contribute by donating any amount of money and therefore become a backer (depending on the money spent on the project the backers will then have some benefits).

It can also be really interesting to study a very popular internet phenomenon like Tripadvisor, which is used to help users find information regarding places to visit, as well as in order to be informed by the community about services offered by flight companies or hotels. Tripadvisor allows users to become part of the content, adding impressions and ranking the companies or the places they have been to, and this can be used also for business matching—sharing the experience of the users as the basis for a ranking between enterprises.

10 Conclusions and Further Developments

This chapter summarized the study performed on the existing Internet technologies that can support SMEs in their internationalization process. Two classifications are presented to categorize Internet portals and websites based on the services provided.

Web 2.0 opens new perspectives for the expansion strategies of SMEs. Social networks created for different purposes can stimulate the development of such portals and become valuable sources of expertise. They would transfer knowledge from other industries and make it possible to develop new ideas to foster the success of a web portal dedicated to SMEs internationalization.

The first fundamental issue is to allow SMEs to look easily for stakeholders, counterparts or financial investors when they want to broaden their market.

For this reason it may be useful to have a tool based on the idea of a professional social network, such as LinkedIn, where every registered member (companies) can create its own profile and describe its results and on-going activities and build up a network with other "friend-businesses". This new kind of web platform should be mainly committed to B2B interaction, with the possibility to join professional groups organized on the basis of interests, preferences or geographical locations, with maps monitoring the on-going internationalization projects or the willing-to-go ones.

Another main issue for a SME that plans an expansion abroad is to finance its growth and find stakeholders: for this reason we chose to study an emergent Internet web site like Kickstarter. The simplicity of the system is the main feature that could be interesting to transfer from the world of start-ups to that of SMEs. A portal that supports the internationalization of companies should have a section where each entrepreneur has the possibility to indicate the projects he is interested to develop, thereby giving investors or potential business partners an opportunity to detect him and consider the idea to give him financial or infrastructural support.

The aim of this study was to gather a list of current services offered online to ease SMEs' internationalization. Using this information, the next step is to develop the design for an efficient and original tool to promote such a managerial process. The research work was conducted online, analyzing websites from Public Institutions, Banks and Consulting Agencies and Private Entities. Clearly, the sources for such a work are numerous and abundant, as websites operating in the field have been developed all over the world, at least wherever governmental Institutions have gained access to the Internet. A complete, universal analysis of all of these portals, however, would have exceeded the time constraints imposed on this work and would be unlikely to radically enhance the results of the research radically. There might well be online services that are different from those catalogued by this study. However, the 28 portals taken into account fitted the suggested classification well and did not highlight any further offer of additional aid-means for enterprises.

The theoretical and "bibliographical" approach adopted by this work shows the need for further validation and confirmation. This can only be gained through a direct consultation with the protagonists of this research: the small and medium enterprises. In the following phase of this research-project, the authors' aim will therefore be to talk first-hand with such entrepreneurs. Interviews will be conducted with them on the consistency of the classification proposed in order to set a scale of importance for each of the suggested service and identify SMEs' priority needs when opening in a new market.

References

Damanpour, F., et al. (1991). Organizational innovation: A meta-analysis of effects of determinants and moderators. *Academy of Management Journal, 34*(3), 555–590.

Dunning, J. H. (1993). *Multinational enterprises and the global economy*. Wokingham: Addison-Wesley.

Mehrtens, J., Cragg, P. B., Mills, A. M., et al. (2001). A model of internet adoption by SMEs. *Information & Management Journal, 39*(3), 165–176.

Appendix 1
A Pragmatic Set of Management Practices to Govern it in SME'S

J. Devos et al. (eds.), *Information Systems for Small and Medium-sized Enterprises*, Progress in IS, DOI: 10.1007/978-3-642-38244-4,

Plan process	Practice	Measure
1. Define and communicate what is expected from IT *(EDM02, APO02, APO11)*	1.1. Communicate the goals of the enterprise and state what you expect from IT in support of that. Be clear on the balance needed between cost, speed, quality and risk	• Percent of joint presentations of solutions • Clarity of solutions
	1.2. Require that IT and business people always resolve that together. Ensure they always think in terms of value for the enterprise	• Number of major deviations in IT solutions and services
	1.3. Consider the current state of the infrastructure and the potential of new but proven technology	• Number of critical business processes supported by obsolete (or soon-to-be obsolete) infrastructure
2. Set up an enterprise data model *(APO03)*	2.1. Obtain an efficient data model for the enterprise with rules for its syntax and for who can access and modify the data	• Frequency of updates to the data enterprise model
	2.2. Identify one person preferably from the business who is the owner of the data model	• Number of problems with deficient data due to syntax or access rules
3. Establish a flexible and responsive IT organisation *(APO01)*	3.1. Assign clearly and regularly review IT-related roles and responsibilities, with proper authority and reasonable expectations. Pay particular attention to responsibilities in the area of security and quality. Communicate these responsibilities to all	• Number of issues with conflicting or unresolved responsibilities • Number of resourcing conflicts
	3.2. Assess that people have the resources to exercise these responsibilities and be aware that concentrated roles and responsibilities can be misused. In absence of resources, define where outside contracting and/or outsourcing can be applied and agree up front how they will be controlled	

(continued)

(continued)

Plan process	Practice	Measure
4. Secure optimal value from investments in IT-enabled business projects *(APO05, APO06)*	4.1. Show leadership in investment management by applying appropriate level of analysis of potential investments, especially the value/risk balance. To this end require full business cases covering cost, benefits and schedule throughout their full economic life-cycle 4.2. Accept uncertainty but manage it by requiring that assumptions in the business case are at appropriate times re-evaluated. Ensure benefits will be received and if that is in doubt do not hesitate to stop a project 4.3. Plan and manage IT expenditures within an annual budget, in line with what is expected from IT and reflecting the enterprise's priorities. Track expenditures against expected benefits	• Up-to-date budget with link to strategy • Percent of projects with benefits defined up front • Percent of post-project review of benefits

(continued)

(continued)

Plan process	Practice	Measure
5. Define and disseminate management aims and directions with respect to IT *(APO01, EDM03)*	5.1. When making decisions relative to IT communicate consistently to key personnel from IT and the business together, generally in an informal manner and make sure they cascade the messages down into the organisation	• Frequency of joint meetings • Degree of understanding at lower levels • Number of violations of do's and don'ts
	5.2. Discuss rules of use as well as acceptable and reasonable behaviour, while encouraging responsiveness relative to risks and external requirements (e.g., intellectual property, privacy etc). Establish some simple do's and don'ts	• Degree obsolescence/usefulness of documents
	5.3. Document In hard copy only for important and frequently used information that needs to be at hand (reference cards, bulleting board, checklists, customer/product data); where possible leverage an intranet	
6. Hire, train and maintain qualified personnel *(APO01, APO07)*	6.1. Consider educational experience and past responsibilities to obtain the IT skills needed to support the IT infrastructure and enterprise goals when hiring IT staff. Assign roles that correspond with skills. Verify reference checks	• Personnel satisfaction • Percent of IT staff members with career path • Number of year-end job reviews
	6.2. Motivate regularly with clear career paths and verify annually whether skills and qualifications are up-to-date and act accordingly	
	6.3. Ensure that essential IT tasks do not depend on one person	

(continued)

(continued)

Plan process	Practice	Measure
7. Identify, prioritise, contain or accept relevant IT related risks *(EDM03, APO12)*	7.1. At appropriate times, discuss with key staff what can go wrong with IT that would impact the business objectives significantly. Especially consider data that are critical for the success of the business. State the level of risk the enterprise is willing to take	• Frequency and effectiveness of the IT risk assessment process • Number of significant incidents caused by risks that were **not identified** by the risk assessment process
	7.2. Establish staff understanding of the need for responsiveness in risky situations	• Number of significant incidents caused by risks that were **identified** by the risk assessment process
	7.3. Consider cost-effective means to manage the risks identified through insurance coverage and protection practices (e.g., effective backup, basic access control, virus protection, firewalls)	

Build process	Practice	Measure
1. Establish project management that enables stakeholder participation and monitors project risks and progress *(BAI01)*	1.1. Ensure the correct prioritisation and co-ordination of all projects, by clearly defining what needs to be achieved, by whom, when, at what cost and with which benefits	• Degree of stakeholders involvement in projects • Completeness of project documents
	1.2. Require that all projects explicitly state their scope, the final acceptance criteria of deliverables, and how they will monitor deliverables, cost, schedule and risks on an ongoing basis	• Quality of the change plans
	1.3. Support the business changes linked to the project with a proper training plan for those involved in the change	
2. Define technically feasible and cost-effective solutions *(BAI02)*	2.1. Be clear on how the solution will change and benefit the business. Ensure that the solution's functional and operational requirements are measurably specified, including maintainability, performance, reliability, security and compatibility with current systems. Review requirements with key personnel	• Quality of the business change plan • Ease of turning requirements into test plans •Time between identification of needs and definition of solutions
	2.2. Consider whether to buy or build, and whether to upgrade, do nothing or apply a manual solution. If there is no clear idea about how to improve business processes, do not inject technology	

(continued)

(continued)

Build process	Practice	Measure
3. Manage suppliers to procure IT resources in an efficient but risk-averse manner *(APO10)*	3.1. Define the approach to supplier selection by obtaining a reference checklist to ensure that contractual arrangements cover legal, financial, organisational, security and performance requirements. Invite more than one vendor to bid and once selected, develop an open and fair relationship	• Clear agreement on deliverables with mutual satisfaction of in- and outsourcer • Number of changes to the agreement after signing the contract
	3.2. Agree on pricing considering cost of ownership, maintenance cost, license fees and delivery bonuses/penalties	• Number of disputes related to procurement contracts
4. Acquire and maintain application software, infrastructure and IT resources *(BAI03)*	4.1. Ensure with the supplier/developer that the needs are clearly understood: i.e., the functional requirements but also everything required to deploy, operate, maintain, support and secure solutions, or skills, capabilities and past experiences for insourced staff. Obtain commitment on benefits expected. Consider impact on existing systems	• Number of changes to the design during development and testing • Percent of users satisfied with the functionality delivered
	4.2. Obtain processing descriptions and user documentation for new solutions and ensure they are in line with the enterprise data model	• Quality of staff provided
5. Provide user and operational training and documentation *(BAI08)*	5.1. Require that knowledge and skills for effective and efficient operation and use of new and current systems are easily available and up-to-date. To this end, consider early involvement of key operational and business personnel in the design, development and testing of solutions	• Comfort of operators and business users with new solution • Accuracy and completeness of documentation (to be verified during testing)

(continued)

(continued)

Build process	Practice	Measure
6. Manage the planning and impact of changes *(BAI06)*	6.1. Ensure changes are categorised, assessed for impact, prioritised, authorised with appropriate test material and implementation guidance, with the objective to minimise errors	• Percent of total changes that are emergency fixes • Number of backlogged change requests
	6.2. Set up a process to initiate changes and track the progress, risks and benefits; consider the impact of all changes on existing documentation and training	• Number of disruptions or data errors caused by inaccurate specifications or incomplete impact assessment
	6.3. Allow for an emergency change process (including criteria to invoke it, procedures, etc.) and ensure that every emergency change is recorded and authorised	
7. Install and accredit solutions and changes *(BAI07)*	7.1. Consider that implementation may entail data conversion and if so, analyse impact and plan for it. Also consider the impact on other applications and processes and the degree of verification required to ensure they still operate correctly	• Quality of the testing plan • User comfort with implementation plan • Number of significant errors in tests
	7.2. Test the new solution or change in a representative environment against all requirements, incl. operational and user documentation, so that it is fit for purpose and free of significant errors. Do not test on the live production system. Involve future users and operators	• Number of errors on other systems caused by changes or new solutions
	7.3. Perform final acceptance by evaluating all test results, involving key staff who will use, run and maintain the system. Evaluate against original acceptance criteria and original expected benefits	

Run process	Practice	Measure
1. Define and monitor internal and external service levels *(APO09, APO10)*	1.1. Identify services delivered by IT. Define, agree upon and regularly review service level agreements. They cover service support requirements, related costs, roles and responsibilities, etc., and should be expressed in business terms	• Percentage of services meeting service levels defined in the SLAs • Number of services that are not covered by an SLA
	1.2. Consider the dependence on third-party suppliers and mitigate continuity, confidentiality and intellectual property risk by, e.g., escrow, legal liabilities, penalties and rewards	• Number of identified and documented issues • Number of SLA revisions after problems
	1.3. Assess the professional capability of third parties and ensure they provide a clearly identified contact person who has the authority to act upon enterprise requirements and concerns	• Time lost in service disputes due to unclear roles and responsibilities
2. Manage and monitor performance and capacity of IT resources *(BAI04)*	2.1. Based on business needs and the current and future workloads, define the minimum availability, performance and capacity requirements of IT services and systems. Monitor accordingly and act proactively where possible	• Frequency of capacity and performance adjustments • Number of incidents due to insufficient performance or capacity

(continued)

(continued)

Run process	Practice	Measure
3. Build the capabilities to carry out the day-to-day automated business activities with minimal, acceptable interruption. *(DSS01, DSS04, DSS05)*	3.1. Identify critical business functions and information, and those applications, third-party services, supplies, data-files, etc., that are critical to support them. Minimise key dependencies where possible	• Percentage of critical business functions with clearly defined mitigation arrangements
	3.2. Establish basic principles for safeguarding and reconstructing IT services, including alternative processing procedures, how to obtain supplies and services in an emergency, how to go back to normal processing after the major event and how to communicate with customers and suppliers	• Percent of successful use of alternative processing and back up procedures • Frequency of testing of the back-up and recovery procedure
	3.3. Together with key employees define what needs to be backed up and stored offsite to support recovery of the business—e.g., critical data files, documentation and other IT resources—and secure it appropriately. At regular intervals, ensure the backup resources are usable and complete and that data cannot be retrieved at disposal	• Number of hours of unplanned outage • Frequency of service interruption of critical systems
	3.4. Ensure that data are properly stored, archived and disposed by defining retention periods, archival requirements and storage terms for documents, data and programs. Ensure that they comply with user and legal requirements	• Number of times critical business information was not properly recovered

(continued)

(continued)

Run process	Practice	Measure
4. Establish IT security practices to monitor, detect and resolve security vulnerabilities and incidents. *(APO13, DSS02, DSS05)*	4.1. Implement procedures to control access based on the individual's need to view, add, change or delete data. Especially consider access rights by service providers, suppliers and customers	• Time it takes to grant, change and remove access rights
	4.2. Make sure one person is responsible for managing all user accounts and security tokens (passwords, cards, devices, etc.) and that appropriate emergency procedures are defined. Periodically review/confirm his/her actions and authority	• Number of access violations • Number of accounts everyone can use
	4.3. Log important security violations (system and network, access, virus, misuse, illegal software). Ensure they are reported immediately and acted upon in a timely manner	• Time since last security patch • Number of incidents due to unauthorized access
	45. Ensure that all users (internal, external and temporary) and their activity on IT systems are uniquely identifiable	• Frequency of review of the security log
	4.4. Implement virus protection, update security patches, and enforce use of legal software. Put preventive, detective and corrective measures in place to protect from malware. Install and configure firewalls to control network access and information flow	

(continued)

(continued)

Run process	Practice	Measure
5. Implement a service desk/support function to respond and resolve problems and user queries. *(DSS02, DSS03)*	5.1. Set up a service desk/support function to monitor incidents and user calls. Ensure quick response, clear escalation and expedient resolution of IT related problems	• Percentage of unresolved incidents • User satisfaction with first line support
	5.2. Follow up problems, significant incidents and recurring user queries. Investigate the root cause of all problems, identify and initiate sustainable solutions addressing the root cause in a timely manner	• Number of unjustified escalations • Percent of problems for which the root cause was analysed • Average time between logging and analysis of problems • Number of recurrent problems
6. Review configuration of all IT assets and licenses. *(DSS02, BAI10)*	6.1. Build and regularly update an inventory of IT hardware and software configuration. Review it on a regular basis to ensure all installed software is authorised and licensed properly	• Time since last update of the configuration inventory • Number of unauthorised software installations • Time lost due to incorrect inventory data
7. Operate the IT services in a sufficiently secure environment and in line with agreed-upon service levels *(DSS01, DSS05)*	7.1. Physically secure the IT operational assets and consider a no-break system. Be aware of other environmental factors such as heat, natural hazards, dust and humidity and, if applicable, obtain expert advice. Pay special attention to the security of mobile or portable IT assets	• Number of physical security incidents • Downtime due to physical security incidents
	7.2. Document and review basic, standard IT operations on a regular basis to ensure that processing occurs as planned (timing, sequence, quality, etc.). Check operation logs to ensure correctness and completeness of processing	• Frequency of review of the operations log • Time since last update of operations documentation • Number of delays due to operations failure

Evaluate process	Practice	Measure
1. Continuously monitor current IT performance, future requirements and related industry trends *(MEA01, MEA03)*	1.1. Identify together with key IT staff and key users a limited number of relevant and measurable results and performance indicators of IT to be tracked on an ongoing basis. Act upon results with improvement initiatives	• Number of improvement actions driven by monitoring activities
	1.2. At appropriate times, identify if anything needs to be done to comply with safety, health, ergonomic, privacy, legal, regulatory and intellectual property requirements, electronic commerce agreements and insurance contracts	• Number of recurring performance issues • Number of non-compliance issues
	1.3. Consider, but with caution, how comparable enterprises address IT issues and major IT decisions	• Cost of fixing non-compliance and performance issues

Appendix 2
Sourcing Guidelines for SME'S

J. Devos et al. (eds.), *Information Systems for Small and Medium-sized Enterprises*, Progress in IS, DOI: 10.1007/978-3-642-38244-4,

S	Selection guidelines: making a request for proposal (RFP)
S1	The RFP should be driven by a strategy document with "real tangible objectives", such as lower cost, improved core business performance, shorter product lifecycles, higher security, higher availability, outsource build functions etc
S2	The RFP should not be open ended, with vague references. The issuer's business needs to be clearly identified (prepare an information package about your company for the vendors). The expectations need to be specific which will save much iteration
S3	The RFP must have a clear purpose and scope, a validity period, and a clear process description for the submission, selection and awarding of the contract
S4	Issuer must focus and be clear on what he will maintain and run coupled with the reasons why—what he will manage and how, coupled with reasons why—what will be expected from the supplier coupled with reasons why
S5	Determine a high level classification of requirements prior to developing detailed requirements, distinguishing between 'must' and 'want' features. Targeted technical requirements (has to run on this platform), the minimum necessary requirements, support for the installation and ongoing support would be *mandatory* high level requirements. *Valued* high level requirements would be that the product/service has most of the functionality and that the vendor is financially stable. *Nice-to-have* criteria could be that the product and vendor are forward looking in nature and support the future technical and functional direction of the enterprise
S6	The scope of the RFP should cover the product, deployment services (e.g., system and product installations) to bring the product to operational readiness, and support services such as build tools, automated test tools, documentation and training modules for: administrative personnel; software maintenance personnel; and end users
S7	Response should include both for the Bidder and sub-contractors: • Corporate profile, including identity of shareholders, directors and managers, company size, growth rate, business divisions, historical perspective; • Financial situation (at least the last two annual reports shall be attached, preferably the last five)
S8	The RFP should request details on the following subjects: • Project and program management; • Risk assessment/management; • Compliance with product/service requirements; • Migration planning/execution; • Service handover/acceptance; • Knowledge transfer and documentation; • Service management and support organisation; • Total cost of ownership; • Approach to help desk, provisioning and configuration management; • Implementation plan outline demonstrating the overall timescale necessary to meet service objectives defined; • The technology solution (software, hardware, middleware, networking etc) and how to gear up in the future; • Future budget costing per year; • Maintenance and enhancements process, compensation and schedules

(continued)

(continued)

S	Selection guidelines: making a request for proposal (RFP)
S9	Responders should be asked to state the degree of compliance with the requirements: • **Complies**—The proposed solution meets the requirements exactly as stated; • **Does not comply**—The proposed solution does not meet the requirements; • **Alternate comply**—Bidder proposes alternate solution; • **Will comply**—The requirements will be met at a future specified date
S10	The RFP should provide clear agreements on defect definition, severity classification and response requirements. Response to problems should be specified in function of this classification, both for acknowledgement of the problem and for fixing the problem. The following table illustrates severity and response time classification
S11	The RFP should require that responders provide a quality plan covering: ● Software development lifecycle, its development stages and supporting activities; ● Reviews that will be carried out with objective, scope and how quality faults will be classified; ● Documentation of project files and summary of all technical documentation; ● Quality targets and metrics; ● Tools, techniques and methodologies concerning: project, change, integration, configuration and development management
S12	Vendor should submit for approval, the résumés of all human resources he intends to employ on the project and makes all reasonable endeavours to ensure that such human resources remain on the project for the scheduled duration
S13	Agree on a clear timetable linked to the deliverables and the quality plan and include a process to make changes to the different plans. Also agree on a change procedure to add/ delete functionality from the original specification
S14	Any development should be defined by: activities; timing of activities; milestones and deliverables; schedule for project steering meetings
S15	Define an acceptance process based on pre-agreed test scenarios and acceptance criteria and augmented with a process to report and handle those functions that failed to meet the tests. The RFP issuer may consider producing all acceptance test documentation, including test data
S16	Reference should be made to all documentation already exchanged prior to the RFP and all RFP documents need to be covered by confidentiality agreements
S17	RFP response scoring methods, incl. the weights of the different response elements, need to be worked out in advance and top management's buy-in needs to be obtained for method and scoring before the selection starts

E	Selection guidelines: evaluating the responses to the RFP
E1	Response Assessment should include: • Ability to demonstrate an understanding of the requestor's business and experience in providing the same or equivalent services into other similar organisations; • Perceived alignment of the solution with the requestor's business requirements, both current and future; • A scorecard taking into account; security, reliability, quality, ease of migration, costs (capital as well as operational expenditure) and requestor's staff satisfaction; • Ability to change as business requirements change and to migrate easily to future technologies; • Ability to demonstrate effective project management experience on similar scale projects; • Appropriateness of the management proposed to plan, implement, test and commission the solution, and generally to manage the requirements and account; • Access to vendor's research and development material; • Degree of understanding the issuer's requirements
E2	Ascertain that evaluation gives the right focus and value on the (fewer) high level requirements (see R5) and is not skewed towards the (more abundant) detailed requirements. Begin with matching the "Mandatory" requirements to the proposed product's strengths
E3	Functionality provided could be evaluated in function of the degree to which it • automates the business processes, • supports the integration across business functions and • provides fast and flexible end-user access to information
E4	The solution should fit with the enterprise's existing technical environment and should cover development tools for future maintenance
E5	The technical solution proposed by the supplier must be evaluated both in terms of appropriateness for the product and with regard to the supplier's capability with this technology
E6	The functions to be delivered in the form of a product must be accounted for in infinite detail
E7	The contractor must provide historic information in regards to the company's financial record for the recent past as well as its current financial stability
E8	In order to gain an understanding of the soundness of a contractor the past experiences and company practices of the contractor should be reviewed
E9	In order to do business with any contractor, it is imperative to understand the contractor's business, size of operation, production and delivery processes
E10	Past experiences with the contractor should be given due consideration and references must be checked, e.g., site visits to existing customers and calling of a number of company references with a prepared questionnaire. Questionnaires should have—in addition to specific questions—open-ended questions allowing respondents to mention problems. Third party implementers are also a good source to find out about implementation issues
E11	Ascertain the vendor adequately applies software configuration management, change management functions as well as software quality functions
E12	It is important that the project management roles are clearly defined and that the vendor assigns a project/program manager to cooperate with the issuer's project manager
E13	The milestones, responsibilities, deliverables and configuration management of the deliverables must be clearly stated

(continued)

(continued)

E	Selection guidelines: evaluating the responses to the RFP
E14	The project plan will be used as a controlling document for managing the project and will allow issuer to track against progress and costs
E15	During the development of the product it is essential that the supplier convey appropriate status and reporting information to management
E16	The responders should demonstrate adequate quality management to be applied to the project
E17	Suppliers must provide visibility of the quality aspects of their defined software development processes
E18	Acceptance tests shall demonstrate to issuer's satisfaction that each and every requirement within the agreement is met as specified. Each requirement expressed in the product/ service specifications is subject to acceptance testing
E19	The supplier should be able to provide guidance to the issuer in the planning and execution of acceptance testing by making recommendations and suggestions. During the acceptance of the product, acceptance criteria must be specified
E20	A process of provisional acceptance should be set up that will verify that the product meets all the requirements stated in this RFP; that the product meets all the performance criteria; that the documentation provided is complete and accurate; and that the package can be built from its sources and off-the-shelf components
E21	The supplier must be able to provide staff with appropriate skill to successfully complete the project
E22	If a contractor is going to be able to develop, deliver and maintain a quality product, the company must provide a stable environment for its employees. Employee turnover is critical in determining the working environment. A yearly turnover rate of greater than 5 % should be construed as an indication of potential risk
E23	As changes to the product desired are inevitable, adequate change management practices must be in place to accommodate them
E24	The contractor must be prepared to respond efficiently to correction requests
E25	A clearly defined cost for maintenance work must be stated
E26	The contractor's responsibilities in supporting the software once it has been accepted and placed into operation must be clearly identified. This support includes both technical support and the management thereof
E27	Contingencies should be pre-defined
E28	Don't overly rely on consultants for the implementation because cost will go up and knowledge will be lost, and certainly let them not be influencing the selection decision

c	Contract guidelines: making a contract following the selection
C1	Don't accept vendor's standard terms and conditions but always strive to apply—and be heard to apply—fair contract terms
C2	Insist on user based rather than CPU based pricing for licences and drop initial maintenance rate by 3–4 %. If no drop in maintenance % then insist on service increases. Negotiate a 2–5% drop for being a reference
C3	Suppliers to break out each cost component, then negotiate each one piece at a time
C4	Pay in escrow, release upon delivery
C5	Always keep a second supplier for leveraging
C6	Agreed standard terms and conditions should address the areas of: • nondisclosure rules • billing • payments • arbitration rules • responsible individuals from issuer and the contractor • length of contract
C7	It should be clear the requestor is not obligated to award the contract and if so, it will be subject to duly agreed terms and conditions between the parties
C8	RFP shall not be binding on issuer, i.e., an RFP is not a promise to acquire the product or services
C9	Agree on clear terms of agreement for termination
C10	Consider service level agreements for support after delivery including compensation and reporting of non-compliance
C11	Consider incentives and recognition for quality service provided and for exceeding service level agreements (SLA's)
C12	Consider to appoint an independent auditor to review and conclude that the strategy can be met and objectives not compromised. Too often vendors don't live up to their promises
C13	Consider establishing audit rights or SAS70-like exercises
C14	Provide protection against the chosen vendors outsourcing or being taken over
C15	Provide for confidentiality agreement identifying what is confidential and how it needs to be handled
C16	RFP documents to be covered under confidentiality agreements and unsuccessful Bidders when advised in writing, to destroy all RFP documents with confirmation in writing that they have done so
C17	The responder has to warrant correctness of facts and opinions and to not omit relevant information; also to be ready to provide additional information if requested which then becomes integral part of RFP
C18	Make it clear that a feature response to the RFP will become part of the software delivery contract
C19	Exclude material or fiscal responsibility for costs, etc. that may be incurred by any vendor in the preparation of their RFP response.
C20	Bidder to provide a list, description and other relevant information of all Intellectual Property involved, used for, useful for, or relevant to the proposal : • Intellectual property owned by bidder; • Intellectual property rights licensed or sub-licensed to the bidder; • Patents and pending patents; • Trade secrets; • Copyrights; • Trademarks; • Claims and litigation relevant to the above list; • Internal policies in relation to ownership of inventions, copyrights etc

(continued)

(continued)

c	Contract guidelines: making a contract following the selection
C21	Vendor to grant to issuer a license or transfer ownership, that is non-exclusive, worldwide, irrevocable, perpetual and royalty-free, with unrestricted right to sub-license for use, of all Intellectual Property used for, useful for, or relevant to the product/service or any other deliverable
C22	Make escrow agreements, i.e., vendor to deposit with e.g. a notary, all source codes, designs and documentation such that the product/service can be independently reconstructed in case of need. Define what the conditions are for access to escrow objects. All costs related to the escrow shall possibly (to be negotiated) be borne by the vendor. Causes for access to the escrowed objects could be • default, receivership, bankruptcy or insolvency by the vendor; • issuer becoming aware of any viruses, time bombs, worms or other programming devices or features not identified to issuer; • written permission from the vendor
C23	Vendor to adhere to the internal control and security policies of the issuer
C24	Provide coverage for hidden defects and fundamental and inherent system faults (including software design faults) relating to the product/service
C25	Define development, maintenance and implementation location and consider requiring access to the vendor location by issuer's auditors
C26	Define clearly all logistics involved in the project: travel, office support, communications etc
C27	The warranty period is a safeguard to issuer in the case of a faulty product
C2!	The warranty must clearly state what is covered and how corrective action will be performed. It must specify the conditions under which the warranty is invalidated. Issuer should verify whether the warranty is acceptable for the type of product/service under evaluation
C29	The warranty period should specify the duration and any items that are specifically excluded. It should include software, hardware, support services and free of charge correction of defects in line with the priority/urgency
C30	Insist on a set of traditional warranties with associated indemnities, liabilities and insurance: • vendor has all rights, titles, licenses, permissions and approvals necessary to perform its obligations and grants to issuer the necessary rights ; • the rights granted by the vendor do not conflict with the rights of a third party with whom the vendor already has an agreement; • all the rights to support the development, use and onward sale by issuer of the product/service have been transferred by the vendor; • the product/service will, when delivered, be in good working order and free from defects, and will operate in conformity with the functional specifications defined; • the support services will be provided in a professional and timely manner and for the term stipulated
C31	The contractual considerations of any project legally obligate issuer and the contractor and therefore should be thoroughly reviewed by the appropriate legal parties. The objective is to ascertain that all parties will be able to agree and perform to a suitable contract

(continued)

(continued)

c	Contract guidelines: making a contract following the selection
C32	Some projects may be sensitive to certain parameters and these items should be detailed and penalties established for non-compliance in order to avoid costly litigation. To be considered are: • penalty for late delivery (one time or increasing with each day, week or month late); • measurable quality level guaranteed with a penalty for not meeting this goal; • penalty for partial delivery of the product; • penalty for the contractor breaching any non-disclosure agreement; • penalty for failure of the contractor to meet the warranty obligations
C33	The contractor should provide liability coverage in cases where excessive down-time was incurred due to the unresponsiveness of contractor support

MIX
Papier aus verantwortungsvollen Quellen
Paper from responsible sources
FSC® C105338

If you have any concerns about our products,
you can contact us on
ProductSafety@springernature.com

In case Publisher is established outside the EU,
the EU authorized representative is:
Springer Nature Customer Service Center GmbH
Europaplatz 3, 69115 Heidelberg, Germany

Printed by Libri Plureos GmbH
in Hamburg, Germany